THE PROCESS OF INTERNATIONAL LEGAL REPRODUCTION

That all states are free and equal under international law is axiomatic to the discipline. Yet even a brief look at the dynamics of the international order calls that axiom into question. Mobilising fresh archival research and drawing on a tradition of unorthodox Marxist and anti-colonial scholarship, Rose Parfitt develops a new 'modular' legal historiography to make sense of the paradoxical relationship between sovereign equality and inequality. Juxtaposing a series of seemingly unrelated histories against one another, including a radical re-examination of the canonical story of Fascist Italy's invasion of Ethiopia, Parfitt exposes the conditional nature of the process through which international law creates and disciplines new states and their subjects. The result is a powerful critique of international law's role in establishing and perpetuating inequalities of wealth, power and pleasure, accompanied by a call to attend more closely to the strategies of resistance that are generated in that process.

ROSE PARFITT is a Lecturer in Law at Kent Law School, a Senior Fellow at Melbourne Law School, where she holds a Discovery (DECRA) Award from the Australian Research Council, and teaches regularly at Harvard Law School's Institute for Global Law and Policy (IGLP) Workshops.

AF722144

CAMBRIDGE STUDIES IN INTERNATIONAL AND COMPARATIVE LAW: 137

Established in 1946, this series produces high quality, reflective and innovative scholarship in the field of public international law. It publishes works on international law that are of a theoretical, historical, cross-disciplinary or doctrinal nature. The series also welcomes books providing insights from private international law, comparative law and transnational studies which inform international legal thought and practice more generally.

The series seeks to publish views from diverse legal traditions and perspectives, and of any geographical origin. In this respect it invites studies offering regional perspectives on core *problématiques* of international law, and in the same vein, it appreciates contrasts and debates between diverging approaches. Accordingly, books offering new or less orthodox perspectives are very much welcome. Works of a generalist character are greatly valued and the series is also open to studies on specific areas, institutions or problems. Translations of the most outstanding works published in other languages are also considered.

After seventy years, Cambridge Studies in International and Comparative Law sets the standard for international legal scholarship and will continue to define the discipline as it evolves in the years to come.

Series Editors
Larissa van den Herik
Professor of Public International Law, Grotius Centre for International Legal Studies, Leiden University
Jean d'Aspremont
Professor of International Law, University of Manchester and Sciences Po Law School

A list of books in the series can be found at the end of this volume.

THE PROCESS OF INTERNATIONAL LEGAL REPRODUCTION

Inequality, Historiography, Resistance

ROSE PARFITT

Kent Law School, University of Kent and
Melbourne Law School, University of Melbourne

CAMBRIDGE
UNIVERSITY PRESS

CAMBRIDGE
UNIVERSITY PRESS

University Printing House, Cambridge CB2 8BS, United Kingdom

One Liberty Plaza, 20th Floor, New York, NY 10006, USA

477 Williamstown Road, Port Melbourne, VIC 3207, Australia

314-321, 3rd Floor, Plot 3, Splendor Forum, Jasola District Centre, New Delhi - 110025, India

79 Anson Road, #06-04/06, Singapore 079906

Cambridge University Press is part of the University of Cambridge.

It furthers the University's mission by disseminating knowledge in the pursuit of education, learning and research at the highest international levels of excellence.

www.cambridge.org
Information on this title: www.cambridge.org/9781108468466
DOI: 10.1017/9781108655118

© Rose Parfitt 2019

This publication is in copyright. Subject to statutory exception and to the provisions of relevant collective licensing agreements, no reproduction of any part may take place without the written permission of Cambridge University Press.

First published 2019
First paperback edition 2020

A catalogue record for this publication is available from the British Library

ISBN 978-1-316-51519-8 Hardback
ISBN 978-1-108-46846-6 Paperback

Cambridge University Press has no responsibility for the persistence or accuracy of URLs for external or third-party internet websites referred to in this publication, and does not guarantee that any content on such websites is, or will remain, accurate or appropriate.

Benjamin felt a nose nuzzling at his shoulder. He looked round. It was Clover. Her old eyes looked dimmer than ever. Without saying anything, she tugged gently at his mane and led him round to the end of the big barn, where the Seven Commandments were written. For a minute or two they stood gazing at the tarred wall with its white lettering.

'My sight is failing,' she said finally. 'Even when I was young I could not have read what was written there. But it appears to me that the wall looks different. Are the Seven Commandments the same as they used to be, Benjamin?'

For once Benjamin consented to break his rule, and he read out to her what was written on the wall. There was nothing there except a single Commandment. It ran:

> ALL ANIMALS ARE EQUAL
> BUT SOME ANIMALS ARE MORE EQUAL THAN OTHERS.

George Orwell, *Animal Farm* (1945).

CONTENTS

FIGURES

MAPS

ACKNOWLEDGEMENTS

I am, as I am writing this, in my office at Melbourne Law School, where most of this book has been written. The Law School stands on land which belongs to, and has never been ceded by, the Wurundjeri people of the Kulin Nations, and it is therefore to them that this book owes its greatest debt of gratitude. I would like to acknowledge the Wurundjeri people as the traditional owners and custodians of this land, and pay my respects to the Elders of the Kulin Nations, past, present and future.

* * *

In late 2015, I was lucky enough to be awarded a Discovery Early Career Research Award (DECRA) by the Australian Research Council to undertake a three-year project on the historical relationship between fascism and international law. Not long afterwards, I found myself in the archives of the Italian Ministry of Foreign Affairs in Rome, sifting my way through a mountain of documents from the 1920s and 30s with the help of Alice Riccardi, my entirely brilliant research assistant and friend. The hunch I was working with was that 'fascism' in the 1920s and 30s (insofar as a stable meaning can be attached to that term) was actually far closer to its purported nemesis, 'international law', than scholars of international law have so far tended to assume. As I read through report after telegram after letter after speech, I had what many historians will recognise as a very typical archival experience. Some of the things I discovered were extremely exciting. Other things, however, told me about nothing in particular beyond the minutiae of the day-to-day diplomatic grind for those of Mussolini's ministers, ambassadors, government lawyers and secretaries whose initials I was learning to recognise. In short, sometimes these officials did indeed employ a recognisably 'fascist' discourse and logic in their work. At other times, however, they used a much more familiar rationale, grounded firmly in the accepted liberal doctrine of international law.

As I worked, one episode that came up again and again was an episode I already knew something about: the gigantic diplomatic crisis that accompanied Mussolini's infamously unlawful (and yet successful) annexation, in 1936, of its fellow League of Nations member, the Ethiopian Empire. As I untied the disintegrating ribbon on bundles and yet more bundles of documents, finding more and more fragments relating to that crisis, it struck me that what was so interesting and strange about this episode, from an international legal perspective, was not only the way in which Ethiopia's rights and duties as a sovereign state were being narrated as malleable by Italian officials and lawyers when attempting to justify Italy's use of force against Ethiopia using an overtly fascist discourse and logic. Also and equally curious was the way in which Ethiopia's rights and duties were being narrated as malleable during much more routine diplomatic exchanges with the officials and lawyers of other states and of the League of Nations itself. These included some of international law's most famous figures from this period, from Eric Drummond (Secretary-General of the League of Nations from 1920 to 1933 and later British Ambassador to Rome) to Nikolaos Politis (Greek representative at the League during the crisis itself and later President of the Institute of International Law). In short, whether allied to fascist or to non-fascist states and organisations, the international legal rationale employed by many of the diplomats, lawyers and statesmen (they were all men) during the so-called 'Abyssinia Crisis' was deeply schizophrenic. In the same breath, they described the Ethiopian Empire as a sovereign state *and* as a less-than-sovereign territory whose right to territorial integrity, for instance, was uncertain.

Meanwhile, outside of the Ministero degli Affari Esteri archives in which Alice and I were working, the 'international community' was, in the face of the fall-out from its intervention in Libya in 2011, debating what it might mean to insist that Syria and North Korea had a 'responsibility to protect' their populations (as though these communities, territories and their problems had never before been touched by the hand of 'the international'). And as I tuned in and out of those debates, shuffling them together with the inter-war debates I was then trying to disentangle, I couldn't get the question out of my mind: if the Ethiopian Empire could be simultaneously sovereign *and* less-than-sovereign in the 1930s – if its transformation into an Italian controlled territory could be justified on the basis of the advancement of individual 'freedom' and 'equality' by fascists *and* non-fascists alike – what about all the other states, from the Chinese Empire c. 1842 to Iraq in 2003, which have suddenly found their armour of rights to be made of plastic rather than titanium? How could one even begin to investigate this weirdly hybrid, both-sovereign-and-not-sovereign quality to 'international personality' from within a discipline (international law) whose central assumption it is that all states, due to 'the simple fact of [their] existence', are 'juridically equal, enjoy the same rights, and have equal capacity in their exercise' (to quote the 1933 Montevideo Convention, Article 4)? I realised during those months in Rome, in other words, as I stared at the fragile documents on the table in front of me, that if I wanted to ask about the relationship between fascism and international law, I needed to start, not with fascism, but with international law. And I needed, most of all, to find a new way of tackling international legal history. At that moment, my project split in two, and this book is the product of the first half of it – a half which brings together elements of the work I have been engaged in over a number of years, with the help of numerous friends, colleagues and institutions, without whom none of this would have been possible. Before I begin, let me stress that all the mistakes (and the translations, unless otherwise stated) are my own.

The first person I must thank is Luis Eslava for discussing the ideas in this book at every stage of their existence, for coming up with some of the best ones and for miscellaneous rescue operations of every kind. From the bottom of my heart, I also thank Jenifer Evans for her incredibly kind and precise editing; Genevieve Painter, Kate Grady and Charlie Peevers for their amazingly generous comments on parts of or earlier versions of the text; Ariana Callejas Capra for her beautiful maps; Tsegaye Ararssa for his immense knowledge and research assistance, on the Ethiopia side of things in particular; Mia Tamarin for her prolonged attack on the monster bibliography; Alice Riccardi for her excellent company and expertise in the Archivio; Eric Loefflad for his help with the images; Archie Moore for very kindly allowing me to include a reproduction of his extremely powerful work, *Blood Fraction* (2015); and and my fantastic editor, Finola O'Sullivan, together with Tahnee Wager, Sarah Payne, Deborah Hey and other members of the team at Cambridge University Press, for their faith in this project and for their immense patience with its idiosyncrasies. Many thanks also to the editors of the Cambridge Studies in International and Comparative Law series, Larissa van den Herik and Jean d'Aspremont, for their vote of confidence.

A special thank you is also due to the many librarians and archivists who helped me turn my hunch into an argument at the Melbourne Law Library (especially Robin Gardner and Fiona MacDowall for their titling expertise and Joseph Huntley and Stephen Polesel for their help with the footnotes); the English and Amharic libraries at the Institute of Ethiopian

Studies, Addis Ababa University; the Historical Documents Archive at the Italian Ministry of Foreign Affairs in Rome; the Library of the Italian Chamber of Deputies and Senate in Rome; the League of Nations Archives and its photo library in Geneva; the SOAS Library, Archives and Special Collections in London; the British Library photo archive in London; the Smithsonian American Art Museum's Research and Scholars Center in Washington DC; the World Bank and United Nations photo libraries in Washington and New York City; the National Gallery of Australia; the Commercial Gallery in Sydney; the British Museum in London; and to Christian Curle, who very generously invited me to look at the papers of her father, Sandy Curle, which are kept in a fridge in her former organic cheese factory at the bottom of her beautiful garden at her house in the Scottish Borders.

The Australian Research Council and Melbourne Law School (MLS) are the institutions which have really made it possible for this research to come to fruition. I am especially grateful to Carolyn Evans, MLS's Dean for most of my time here, to Mas Generis at the Research Office, and to everyone at the Institute for International Law and the Humanities (IILAH) which has been my institutional home since I arrived in Australia in 2013 as McKenzie Fellow. IILAH's directors (sequentially) Anne Orford, Di Otto and Sundhya Pahuja, have been unstinting in their encouragement, as have its administrators, in particular the fabulous Vesna Stafanovski. The same is true of many other friends and colleagues at, in or once in Melbourne and elsewhere in Australia, including Tom Andrews, Luis Bogliolo, Sam Balaton-Chrimes, Olivia Barr, Jeremy Baskin, Jenny Beard, Meli Benavides, Kathleen Birrell, Melanie Chaves, Maddy Chiam, Michael Cichocki, Martin Clark, Karen Crawley, Julia Dehm, Sara Dehm, Bianca Dillon, Debolina Dutta, Maria Elander, Katherine Fallah, Belinda Fehlberg, Ben Golder, Ann Genovese, Jake Goldenfein, Kirsty Gover, Kathryn Greenman, Xan and Jo Hamilton, Matthew Harding, Vannessa Hearman, Kevin Heller, Alex Howard, John Howe, Fleur Johns, Richard Joyce, Adil Khan, Melissa Martin, Mark McMillan, Shaun McVeigh, Jacquie Mowbray, Zim Nwokora, Georgio Palamo, James Parker, Sophie Rigney, Anthony Rodriguez, Anna Saunders, Gerry Simpson, Oishik Sircar, Cait Storr, Ntina Tzouvala, Fabia Verçoso, Lulu Weis, and of course Lucy Best (and Liam and Jude), among others, without whose unlimited willingness to be simultaneously brilliant and ridiculous I would not have made it.

I am also enormously grateful to Kent Law School – and in particular to two Heads of School, Didi Herman and Toni Williams – for the huge amount of support they have given me, thanks to which I was able to take up the DECRA; and to many other colleagues at (or until recently at) Kent, including Donatella Alessandrini, Valery Alzaga, Kate Bedford, Ruth Cain, Helen Carr, Donal Casey, Emilie Cloatre, Mairead Enright, Hayley Gibson, Emily Grabham, Emily Haslam, Hyo Yoon Kang, Sara Kendall, Connal Parsley, Nick Piska, Sinéad Ring, Sharon Rouse, Gavin Sullivan, Dermot Walsh and Thanos Zartaloudis, among many others.

This work has also benefited very greatly from the support of the Institute for Global Law and Policy (IGLP), Harvard Law School. To David Kennedy and to the indefatigable Kristen Verdeaux, I could not be more grateful, as I am to all those who, over the years, have become my friends and collaborators thanks to IGLP, thanks to the Law and Society Association 'International Law and Politics' Collaborative Research Network, and/or whom I have encountered in this lovely, ever-expanding transnational family. These include Aziza Ahmed, Amaya Alvez, Matilda Arvidsson, Tony Anghie, Eliana Augusti, Grietje Baars, Amar Bhatia, Lina Buchely, Ruth Buchanan, Lina Buchely, Irina Ceric, B. S. Chimni, Paul Clark, Dan Danielson, Dennis Davis, Karen Engle, Michael Fakhri, Chris Gevers, Markus Gunneflo, Priya Gupta, Vanja Hamzić, Mark Harris, John Haskell, Jeffery Hewitt, Jason Jackson, Sheila Jasanoff, Ioannis Kalpouzos, Ratna Kapur, Martti Koskenniemi, Tor Krever, Vidya Kumar, Boris Mamlyuk, Anne-Charlotte Martineau, Mark Mazower, Roger Merino, Zina Miller, Claire Mummé, Usha Natarajan, Vasuki Nesiah, Luigi Nuzzo, Liliana Obregón, Zoran Oklopcic, Umut Özsu, Genevieve Painter, Reut Paz, Kerry Rittich, Nahed Samour, Hani Sayed, Mohammed Shahabuddin, Thomas Skouteris, Immi Talgren, Chantal Thomas, Illan Wall, Robert Wei, Nathasha Wheatley, Sujith Xavier and Peer Zumbansen, to name only a few of them.

This project would, quite clearly, never have materialised had it not been for those at SOAS who saw me through my early doctoral work on the Ethiopian Empire – in particular the Arts and Humanities Research Council which funded it, my fantastic supervisors Catriona Drew and Matthew Craven, and my very generous examiners, Susan Marks and Nathaniel Berman, to whose thinking this thesis is greatly indebted. I would also like to thank Abebew Yigzaw, Nesrine Badawi, Cedric Barnes, Jason Beckett, Piyel Haldar, John Haskell, Gina Heathcote, Florian Hoffmann, Rob Knox, Andrew Lang, Marica Moscati, Scott Newton, Matthew Nicholson, Yoriko Otomo, Charlie Peevers, Akbar Razulov, Rupa Reddy whose recent death has been a terrible blow for us all, Alain Tamagnone, Lynn Welchman, Ralph Wilde and all the others who were in or around the University of London at that time, or whom I met during these years.

I must also extend a huge thank you to everyone who helped me in Addis Ababa during the months I spent there as a visiting fellow at the Institute of Ethiopian Studies (IES), in particular Dee-Dee and the late and sorely missed Michael Dobell, in whose house at Bole Matemia (full of whisky roses, sunshine and maps) I lived, as well as Dr Ibrahim and Tedesse. More than anyone else, it was the marvellous Tilaye Gebre-Medhin whose knowledge, patience, understanding, boundless generosity, enormous network of contacts and large collection of elegant hats inspired the ideas in the second half of the book at every point. Without those many mornings spent upstairs in the Amharic section of the IES Library, next to the poor, motheaten stuffed lion, with Tilaye quizzing first me and then the librarians, collecting an armful of Amharic texts, and then sitting down to translate chunks of them for me on the spot, there would be no argument about Ethiopia and the League, and (since the whole argument stems from Ethiopia and the League) there would be no book. It was the late, great Richard Pankhurst who, together with Rita Pankhurst, who first invited me to tea at their house and put me in touch with Tilaye, and it is entirely thanks to them, to Tilaye, to the IES librarians, and to the IES's Assistant Director, Yonas Admassu, that I was able to make some sense of the sources I had access to, and to meet all the amazing scholars and writers whose ideas influenced me so greatly. These include Gabremeskel Alemu, Eyerusalem Getaneh, Lemma Tolessa, Mamo Haile, Asfaw Damté, Ian Campbell, Peter Garretson, Izabella Orlowska, Shiferaw Bekele, Demeke Berhane, and, at the French Centre for Ethiopian Studies, the late Berhanu Abebe, as well as the chief librarian there, whose name I was too shy to ask and now am unable to find out, and the late Dr-*Dejazmatch* Zewde Gabre-Sellasie. A big thank you also to my friend Jo Dunlop.

Finally, a very special thank you is reserved for my friends and for my family – for all my aunties and uncles, cousins, for my grandad-no-longer, Sidney Parfitt, and especially for my wonderful Great Uncle Jas; for my fantastic parents-in-law, Esther Julia, Carlos and Martha, and my aunt-/uncles-in-law (especially John and Miriam); and for my many honorary family members, including my late, great faux-grandmothers, Cressida Ridley and Eileen Richmond, as well as the still-very-much-in-the-prime-of-life Jonas Eiring, Sophie Dinning, Alfred and Catherine Stockham, Caroline Stone, the late and greatly missed Paul Lunde and Alex and James. Finally, of course, a huge thank you to my London, Edinburgh,

Cairo and Canterbury friends, especially Amy, Susan and Joe(l); to everyone at the French House (especially Lesley, Annabel, Hilary, Duane and Gavin); to my buddies Charlie, Polly, Peter, Melissa, Tom, Gemma, Sam, Lizzie, Nick, Lel, Nicki, Eric, Dan, Lucy, Tom, Liberty, Jules, Julie, Ned, Katia, Hania, Pip, Emma, Nina, Charles, Anna, Andeel, Eduardo, Carla, William, Eva, James, Noriko; to all the kids(!); and to Pete Buckenham (On the Corner) and Dom Servini and Adam Scrimshire (Wah Wah 45s) for all the music and all the nights out that kept me on the straight and narrow. Above all, however, I must thank the five people who hold the five corners of my heart in their hands for all the encouragement and all the sacrifices they have made to allow this book to get itself written. These are, of course, Sara Paton and David Parfitt, my bezzies (and my parents); my lovely step-kids, Martin and Tomas; and again Lufe, my favourite creature on the planet.

ABBREVIATIONS AND TITLES

List of abbreviations:

AJIL	*American Journal of International Law*
CUP	Cambridge University Press
EC	Ethiopian Calendar
EJIL	*European Journal of International Law*
FO	UK Foreign Office
HIJL	*Harvard International Journal of Law*
JHIL	*Journal of the History of International Law*
LNOJ	*League of Nations Official Journal*
LONA	League of Nations Archives
MAE	Ministero degli Affari Esteri (Italian Ministry of Foreign Affairs)
OUP	Oxford University Press
UKNA	UK National Archives

List of titles in the Ethiopian Empire[1]

Abba	'Father'; the title of a priest
Bäjerond	'Treasurer'
Balabbat	A local official who mediated between the people and the government; meaning 'one who has a father'

[1] The definitions of Ethiopian titles are based on the glossary in Harold G. Marcus, *Haile Selassie I: The Formative Years, 1892–1936* (2nd edn Lawrenceville, NJ: Red Sea Press, 1995), xv–xvi.

Blatte	A title given to learned men and councillors
Dejazmatch	'Commander of the Gate'; equivalent to the European title of 'Count'
Echege	Bishop of the monastery of Debre Libanos and administrative head of the Ethiopian Church
Kenyazmach	'Commander of the Right'; equivalent to the European title of 'Baron'
Lijj	'Boy'
Negus	'King'; a title granted only to a very few provincial lords who governed directly under the authority of the Emperor
Negusa Nagast	'King of Kings'; the title of the Emperor
Ras	'Head'; often translated as 'king' but in fact equivalent to the European title of 'Duke'
Shum	Governor (of a particular district)

Stand

Conditionality and Sovereign Inequality

On 3 October 1935, Mussolini's troops crossed the Mareb River separating the Italian colony of Eritrea from the Empire of Ethiopia, starting a war of legendary brutality. Barely equipped Ethiopian troops, defenceless villagers and livestock were attacked using flame-throwers, aerial bombardment and banned poison gas. This was an unvarnished deployment of fascist hyper-modernity against what the Italian government portrayed as a bizarre, backwards relic of African feudalism.[1] Like the Ethiopian Empire itself, at the time of the invasion Italy was a member of the League of Nations and a signatory to the Covenant, the League's founding treaty. As such, both states were understood axiomatically to be sovereign equals, meaning both were bound to 'respect and preserve as against external aggression the territorial integrity and existing political independence of all Members of the League', as the Covenant put it at Article 10.[2] Under the League's innovative collective security provisions, any violation of that obligation was to be regarded as 'an act of war against all other Members of the League' entailing collective economic, financial and ultimately military sanctions.[3]

However, by the time Ethiopia's Emperor Haile Selassie I had fled, and King Emanuele III of Italy had been proclaimed *Imperatore d'Etiopia* in his stead on 9 May 1936,[4] Italy was not the only League member to have

[1] See generally Anthony Mockler, *Haile Selassie's War* (New York: Olive Branch Press, 2003); George W. Baer, *Test Case: Italy, Ethiopia, and the League of Nations* (Stanford, CA: Hoover Institution Press, 1976), 12–13.

[2] *Covenant of the League of Nations*, annexed to *Treaty of Peace between the British Empire, France, Italy, Japan and the United States (the Principal Allied and Associated Powers), and Belgium, Bolivia, Brazil, China, Cuba, Czechoslovakia, Ecuador, Greece, Guatemala, Haiti, the Hedjaz, Honduras, Liberia, Nicaragua, Panama, Peru, Poland, Portugal, Roumania, the Serb-Croat-Slovene State, Siam, and Uruguay, and Germany*, Versailles, 28 June 1919, Art. 10 ('Covenant').

[3] Covenant, Art. 16.

[4] Italian Government, 'Royal Decree placing Abyssinia under Italian Sovereignty, 9 May 1936', in Stephen Heald (ed.), *Documents on International Affairs 1935*, Vol. II (Oxford University Press, 1937), 472–3.

violated its obligations under the Covenant. Although the Italian invasion of Ethiopia was condemned as illegal by the League's Council (precursor to the United Nations (UN) Security Council),[5] the economic sanctions that were eventually imposed on Italy excluded oil and other essential war materials, and were halted within a year. Military sanctions were avoided altogether. Over the next five years, Italy's sovereignty over Ethiopia was recognised by all but five of the world's existing states.[6] The Ethiopian Empire was abandoned to its fate as a fascist colony until its 'liberation' became of strategic significance after the outbreak of the Second World War.[7]

This rendition of the so-called 'Abyssinia Crisis', as it is still known today, in spite of the fraught ethnic connotations of the term 'Abyssinia',[8] is one of the most infamous episodes of twentieth-century history – a staple of undergraduate international relations and international law textbooks, and a regular feature on school history curricula. The reason for its notoriety concerns not so much an interest in Ethiopia's history or welfare, but rather the role of the Crisis as a trigger for the Second World War. Ethiopia's annexation, as historian A. J. P. Taylor once put it, was 'the deathblow to the League as well as to Abyssinia'.[9] In the field of international law, the verdict is very similar. Peter Malanczuk, editor of the seventh edition of *Akehurst's International Law*, asserts, for example, that '[t]he League system failed for a variety of institutional and political reasons', the most important of which was 'inherent contradiction in the concept itself of collective security in the form of a mere association of self-interested and sovereign states'.[10] According to Malanczuk, it was for this reason that the League 'remained incapable of dealing with the Japanese aggression against China in 1932 [*sic*] when it occupied Manchuria, and with the Italian aggression against Abyssinia in 1935–6'.[11] The Abyssinia Crisis is, in other words, generally understood as the first episode in a long and tragic

5 'Report of the League of Nations Council Committee' ('Committee of Six'), 7 October 1935, in 30 *AJIL*, Sp. Supp. (1936): 37–40 at 40.

6 These were the US, Mexico, the USSR and China, as well as the British dominion of New Zealand.

7 See Bahru Zewde, *A History of Modern Ethiopia, 1855–1991* (2nd edn Oxford, Athens OH, Addis Ababa: James Currey, Ohio University Press, Addis Ababa University Press, 2002), 166–77; David Shirreff, *Bare Feet and Bandoliers: Wingate, Sandford, the Patriots and the Part they Played in the Liberation of Ethiopia* (London, New York: Radcliffe Press, 1995).

8 See below, Item 4. I will stop using scare quotes from this point, but the term Abyssinia Crisis should continue to be understood as problematic.

9 A. J. P. Taylor, *The Origins of the Second World War* (London: Hamish Hamilton, 1961), 95.

10 Peter Malanczuk, *Akehurst's Modern Introduction to International Law* (7th edn London, New York: Routledge, 1997), 25.

11 Ibid., 25.

series of attempts at fascism's 'appeasement' which culminated ultimately in the notorious Munich Agreement of September 1938.[12]

The lesson offered in this account by the Abyssinia Crisis, and by the 'failure' of the League more generally,[13] is clear: international law had not yet, in the League era, been codified and institutionalised sufficiently strongly, such that its core principles (in particular that of sovereign equality) were overwhelmed by the toxic power politics of the 1930s. In this way, the failure to enforce international law during the Crisis is framed as an instructive example of precisely how the international order ought not (or ought no longer) to operate – one that, indeed, is still brought out regularly by global leaders today whenever a diplomatic crisis requiring collective action is at hand. During the run-up to the 2003 Iraq War, for example, a group of the world's most powerful world leaders met in Munich to discuss the rationale for invasion. As then-US Defense Secretary Donald Rumsfeld asserted in his address to the conference:

> To understand what is at stake, it is worth reminding ourselves of the history of the UN's predecessor, the League of Nations. When the League failed to act after the invasion of Abyssinia, it was discredited as an instrument of peace ... The lesson of that experience was best summed up at the time by Canadian Prime Minister Mackenzie King, who declared: 'Collective bluffing cannot bring about collective security'. That lesson is as true today, at the start of the 21st century, as it was in the 20th century. The question before us is – have we learned it?[14]

This standard mobilisation of the Abyssinia Crisis encourages us to understand international law as a discipline, and as a set of institutional practices, which re-emerged from the debacle of the Second World War all the stronger for the lessons 'we' (the 'international community') learned from

[12] *Agreement for the Cession by Czechoslovakia to Germany of Sudeten German Territory, with Declarations*, Munich, 29 September 1938 ('Munich Agreement'). For a brilliant critical comparison of the two crises, see Nathaniel Berman, 'Beyond Colonialism and Nationalism? Ethiopia, Czechoslovakia, and "Peaceful Change"', in Berman, *Passion and Ambivalence: Colonialism, Nationalism and International Law* (Leiden: Martinus Nijhoff, 2012), 319–83.

[13] For a brilliant contestation of the assumption that the League of Nations was a failure, see Usha Natarajan, 'Creating and Recreating Iraq: Legacies of the Mandate System in Contemporary Understandings of Third World Sovereignty', 24 *Leiden Journal of International Law* (2011): 799–822.

[14] Earlier on the same day, Senator John McCain had expressed his anxiety to the conference that 'Iraq could be to NATO what Abyssinia was to the League of Nations'. Speeches presented on 8 February 2003, 39th Munich Conference on Security Policy, Munich, 7–9 February 2003, at www.acronym.org.uk/old/archive/docs/0302/doc12.htm#07 (accessed 25 February 2017).

it. For example, the Covenant's failure to prohibit war outright is assumed to have been addressed, in 1945, by the prohibition against the unilateral use of force under Article 2(4) of the UN Charter.

This assumption – bolstered by the standard account of the Abyssinia Crisis – that international law has progressed away from the dark days of the 1930s, has been given a new twist over the last couple of decades by the emergence of the narratives of 'failed' statehood, 'earned' sovereignty and the 'responsibility to protect' (R2P). Advocates of these ideas, such as the historian of international legal personality, Janne Nijman, claim that:

> If a state functions well and its citizens are represented properly by the government, the ILP [international legal personality] which the state derives from its citizens remains with the state. The state is then the legitimate representative of its citizens at the international level with the authority to pursue their interests. However, if the state fails, collapses or falls victim to civil war or the oppression of minorities, the ILP of that state is withdrawn or returned to the people it was supposed to represent. In situations such as these, humanity, by way of its international community, has to open up its institutions and law, even if only temporarily, to include these human beings and by this international recognition to reaffirm their 'personality' ... The well-functioning state has full ILP, but only derived from its citizens.[15]

From this perspective – shared, at least in principle, by the UN[16] – the rights and duties possessed by states as 'subjects' or 'persons' of international law,[17] should be, and increasingly are being, treated as *conditional* on their willingness to 'protect' a core set of rights belonging to the individuals within their jurisdiction. It is the responsibility of 'humanity', in the guise of the 'international community', to police the adherence of states to this standard, and to take on that 'responsibility' if they 'fail'.

This framing of state sovereignty as conditional has an important consequence. It allows manifestations of sovereign *in*equality – for example, when certain states are subject to military interventions, non-consensual occupations, onerous 'conditionalities' limiting domestic social policy in return for 'development' loans, externally authorised 'statebuilding' missions and so on – to be characterised as legitimate responses, on the part

[15] Janne Elisabeth Nijman, *The Concept of International Legal Personality: An Inquiry into the History and Theory of International Law* (The Hague: TMC Asser Press, 2004), 468.

[16] See especially '2005 World Summit Outcome', GA Res. 60/1, 24 October 2005, paras. 138–9.

[17] The terms 'sovereignty', 'international legal subjectivity' and 'international personality' under international law will be used interchangeably in this book to refer to the set of rights and duties possessed by states (in the 'full' sense), and (to a lesser extent) by certain other entities under international law.

of the international community, to the 'failure' of certain states to uphold a set of supposedly universal individual rights. The case of Libya, for example, subjected in 2011 to the first full-scale military intervention to be justified explicitly under the rubric of the 'responsibility to protect', offers a useful illustration of international personality's 'logic' or 'dynamic' (as we might call it) of conditionality.[18] See, for example, the language used by then-US Secretary of State Hillary Clinton before the UN Human Rights Council as she made the case for the use of force to 'protect' Libyan civilians from forces loyal to the government of Muammar Qadhafi:

> Colonel Qadhafi and those around him must be held accountable for [their] acts, which violate international legal obligations and common decency. Through their actions, they have lost the legitimacy to govern ...
>
> The international community is speaking with one voice and our message is unmistakable. These violations of universal rights are unacceptable and will not be tolerated ...
>
> Ultimately, the people of Libya themselves will be the ones to chart their own destiny and shape their own new government. They are now braving the dictator's bullets and putting their lives on the line to enjoy the freedoms that are the birthright of every man, woman, and child on earth ...
>
> [S]upporting these transitions [in Libya and elsewhere in the Arab world] is not simply a matter of ideals. It is also a strategic imperative. Without meaningful steps toward representative, accountable, and transparent governance and open economies, the gap between people and their leaders will only grow, and instability will deepen ...
>
> So the process of transition must be protected from anti-democratic influences from wherever they come. Political participation must be open to all people across the spectrum who reject violence, uphold equality, and agree to play by the rules of democracy. Those who refuse should not be allowed to subvert the aspirations of the people ...
>
> These are not Western principles or American ideals. They are truly universal, lessons learned by people all over the world who have made the difficult transition to sustainable democracy ...[19]

[18] I borrow these images from B. S. Chimni and Antony Anghie, to whose thinking this book is profoundly indebted. See B. S. Chimni, *International Law and World Order: A Critique of Contemporary Approaches* (2nd edn Cambridge University Press, 2017), 30–5; Antony Anghie, *Imperialism, Sovereignty and the Making of International Law* (Cambridge University Press, 2004), 4.

[19] Hillary Clinton, Address to the UN Human Rights Council, New York, 3 March 2011, at https://geneva.usmission.gov/2011/02/28/sec-clinton-hrc-geneva-2011/ (accessed 6 Apr 2018). A fortnight later, the UN Security Council authorised a NATO-led force to use 'all necessary measures' short of 'foreign occupation' to 'protect civilians and civilian populated areas' (SC Res. 1973, 26 February 2011, para. 4 and Preamble).

Figure 1 Workers weigh spaghetti in a factory established with assistance from the World Bank, Sarris, Ethiopia, January 1959. Photograph by Terence Spencer/Black Star for the World Bank. Country Photographs/Ethiopia/Loan 32/Ref. 32-ET-20. Courtesy of World Bank Group Archives.

For Clinton, only states which display 'representative, accountable, and transparent governance and open economies' can be assured that their actions will be 'tolerated' by the 'international community'.

Radically progressive as it might have sounded, however, Clinton's assertion was, in fact, far from new. On the contrary, and as I demonstrate in this book, drawing on a long and complex history dating back to the early sixteenth century, 'sovereignty' has always been conditional in precisely this way – since the dawn of the very ideas of the state and of international law. As the following pages will demonstrate, using a very wide variety of case studies and illustrations, the process of becoming a state, and in doing so becoming eligible for the full set of international rights and duties, has historically been a costly one. Only those entities deemed to be in possession of a particular set of legal and institutional arrangements – arrangements dedicated to offering the individuals within that jurisdiction a very specific and very narrow set of rights and duties – have, under international law, been able to pass as states. The name given to this legal and institutional apparatus is, of course, 'government'. Thus, to put it more schematically, my argument here is that international legal subjectivity has always been conditioned, in practice, in the reproduction of individual legal subjectivity. As the case studies examined in this book reveal, the rights associated individual legal subjectivity in this context – that is to say, the individual rights which aspiring sovereigns have been asked to protect in order to obtain rights and duties under international law – have, historically, been restricted to a very specific, narrow, and indeed (from a Western political theory perspective) classic set, comprising the rights of the individual to 'property, that is, ... life, liberty, and estate' (as the philosopher John Locke articulated them in 1689),[20] or to 'life, liberty and the pursuit of happiness' (in the interpretation of the American Declaration of Independence of 1776).[21] As we shall see, in the practice of creating new states (and other subjects of international law), this set of rights has consistently included individual rights to personal security, private property, freedom of travel, trade and contract, equality before the law, freedom of worship and (for the full set of sovereign rights, as we shall see) also political participation. These are, of course, the basic individual rights associated with the 'rule of law' – a term (though used in many ways) which at its core refers to a set of 'formally neutral and objectively ascertainable rules, created in a process of popular legislation', whose purpose it is to 'reconcile' individual freedom with social order.[22] These are the rights, in other words, whose purpose it is to establish and maintain a 'level playing field' within the state, upon which questions of distribution among individuals can (and should) be worked out privately. Consistently excluded from the set of individual rights upon whose protection the acquisition of international personality has, historically, been conditioned, meanwhile, are rights whose purpose it is to bring about greater material equality. This goes for material equality among humans and human groups (for instance, rights to food, water, housing, education, healthcare, rest, childcare and so on) and between the human and the non-human world (as we might characterise animal welfare and environmental protection laws). In short, as I will explain further below, the type of domestic legal system upon which 'sovereignty' is conditioned amounts, no more and no less, to the set of individual rights and duties which capitalist relations of production and exchange require to thrive and expand.

[20] John Locke [1689], 'Of Civil Government', in Ian Shapiro (ed.), *John Locke: Two Treatises of Government and a Letter Concerning Toleration* (New Haven, CT, and London: Yale University Press, 2003), 247–484 at 327–8.

[21] *American Declaration of Independence*, Philadelphia, 4 July 1776, Preamble.

[22] Martti Koskenniemi, *From Apology to Utopia: The Structure of International Legal Argument* (Cambridge University Press, 2005), 71.

If this argument is correct, the implications are twofold. Firstly, far from being a neutral discipline dedicated to facilitating the capacity of states to make their own 'sovereign' decisions about how to organise their internal affairs, international law has, in fact, been engaged, over the course of some five centuries of emergence and consolidation, in reproducing a very particular mode of human self-organisation, which is based on a historically and geographically extremely specific understanding and organising the relationship between individual human beings, human communities and the non-human world. Secondly, this apparatus, the self-governing state, whose reach has now become virtually universal, is itself dedicated, at a fundamental level, to the widening and deepening of capitalist relations of production and exchange, and to the systematic upwards redistribution of wealth, power and pleasure which those relations imply.

In making this argument, this book builds on a longstanding and extremely rich body of critical international legal scholarship. Contributors to this body of work have been pointing out for some decades now that the tendency of international legal practitioners and mainstream scholars of international law to understand the history of their discipline as a teleological story of evolution from violence and barbarism to 'international legal obligations and common decency' (as Clinton put it) is deeply problematic. Gerry Simpson, for example, argues that the 'juridical sovereignty' of states (their rights and duties as subjects of international law) has historically been 'marked' not only by the language of sovereign equality, but also by two other languages: those of 'Great Power prerogative' and 'outlawry (or anti-pluralism)'.[23] On the one hand, the principle of sovereign equality interacts, in practice, with regimes of 'legalised hegemony: the realisation through legal forms of Great Power prerogatives'. On the other hand, however, Simpson points out that international law is also involved in 'the constitution and regulation of outlaw states' – states which are 'mad', 'bad' (being 'serial violators of the dominant mores of the international legal order') and/or 'dangerous' (presenting 'a threat to the international legal order because of some internal malfunction or propensity to disorder').[24] Sovereignty in international law should therefore be understood as irrepressibly 'protean and flexible'.[25] Sara Kendall, too, has noted that, in the era of the 'war on terror' in particular, inter-

[23] Gerry Simpson, *Great Powers and Outlaw States: Unequal Sovereigns in the International Legal Order* (Cambridge University Press, 2004).

[24] Ibid., x–xi.

[25] Ibid., ix–x.

national law is increasingly coming to be divided between 'states that can adequately handle threats of force and those who cannot, either due to a lack of will or capacity'. For the latter, sovereignty becomes 'contingent'.[26]

Moreover, and as many contributors to this body of critical work point out, those states that are deemed to have 'failed' are usually located in the Global South. Post-colonial states are historically much more likely to be subjected to what Anne Orford calls 'military and monetary interventions' than the wealthy and powerful states of the Global North.[27] Moreover, the afterlife of the European colonial project (from the long-term effects of racist social categorisation to the 'path dependency' experienced by territorial entities that have been groomed to become exporters of primary products) is connected directly to the vulnerability of post-colonial states to international interference of various kinds. Third World states have, in other words, been destined, if not designed, to 'fail'.[28] One scholar who has made this point forcefully is Anthony Anghie. Anghie's work flips international law's progress narrative on its head with the argument that it was, in fact, in and through the process of denying international legal subjectivity to the 'natives' found, inconveniently, to be inhabiting desirable tracts of land in the Americas, Africa, Asia and the Pacific, that the very idea of sovereignty was forged. As a result, 'Third World sovereignty is ... rendered uniquely vulnerable and dependent by international law'.[29] For Anghie, indeed, 'no adequate account of sovereignty can be given without analysing the constitutive effect of colonialism on sovereignty'.[30] Anne Orford has made an equally powerful argument in relation to the contemporary international order. International law, she notes, 'has always operated to constitute as its subjects those who resemble the idealized self-image of European sovereign peoples'.[31] Today, as she argues, 'only one "choice" is being made available to the new subjects of international law',[32] namely 'to

[26] Sara Kendall, 'Cartographies of the Present: "Contingent Sovereignty" and Territorial Integrity', in Martin Kuijer and Wouter Werner (eds.), 47 *Netherlands Yearbook of International Law* (2016): 83–105 at 100.

[27] I borrow this phrase from Anne Orford, 'Locating the International: Military and Monetary Interventions after the Cold War', 38 *HIJL* (1997): 443–85.

[28] See e.g. Makau wa Mutua, 'Why Redraw the Map of Africa? A Moral and Legal Inquiry', 16 *Michigan Journal of International Law* (1995): 1113–76.

[29] Anghie, *Imperialism, Sovereignty*, 6.

[30] Ibid., 37.

[31] Anne Orford, *Reading Humanitarian Intervention: Human Rights and the Use of Force in International Law* (Cambridge University Press, 2003), 27.

[32] See e.g. Orford, 'Locating the International'; Orford, 'Muscular Humanitarianism: Reading the Narratives of the New Interventionism', 10 *EJIL* (1999): 679–711.

be governed by economically rational governments under the tutelage of the international economic institutions who follow the military as representatives of the international community'.[33]

Feminist literature on the concepts of statehood and personality, meanwhile, has also connected the inequality of non-European subjectivity under international law to the unequal subjectivity of women under domestic law. Hilary Charlesworth and Christine Chinkin point out, for example, that '[l]ike the heterosexual male body, the state has no "natural" points of entry, and its boundedness makes forced entry the clearest possible breach of international law'. This applies only to sovereign equals, however; whereas '[e]ntities that cannot assert control over a coherent unified territory, or that straddle borders, such as many indigenous minority peoples' are 'seen as having permeable, negotiable, penetrable, vulnerable boundaries in the same way that women's bodies have been constructed in criminal law'.[34] Similarly, a number of queer theorists of international law have highlighted the way in which colonial patterns of independence and domination continue to be narrated in heteronormative terms. Teemu Ruskola, for instance, has analysed 'the injury of colonialism as a kind of homoerotic violation of non-Western states' (would-be) sovereignty', pointing to 'the normative masculinity that is attributed to sovereign states' to argue that 'non-Western states' variously deviant masculinities, together with their civilizational and racial attributes, rendered them rapable' during the heyday of the European colonial project.[35]

In different ways, all these arguments converge on the same fundamental point: that, whether deliberately or accidentally, the 'progressive' bias of international law's autobiography eclipses the discipline's colonial history, and hence its ongoing implication in precisely the problems it purports to resolve. The first aspect of the argument that I make in this book, concerning international law's instrumentalisation of Ethiopia's annexation by Italy, dovetails straightforwardly with this post-colonial critique. As we shall see, the Ethiopian Empire was not, at the time, formally 'equal' to Italy, Britain or France in any straightforward sense. This makes it difficult

[33] Orford, *Reading Humanitarian Intervention*, 27.

[34] Hilary Charlesworth and Christine Chinkin, *The Boundaries of International Law: A Feminist Analysis* (Manchester University Press, 2000), 129–30. See also Gina Heathcote, *The Law on the Use of Force: A Feminist Analysis* (London: Routledge Cavendish, 2011); Karen Knop, 'Re/Statements: Feminism and State Sovereignty in International Law', 3 *Transnational Law and Contemporary Problems* (1993): 293–344.

[35] Teemu Ruskola, 'Raping Like a State', 57 *UCLA Law Review* (2009–10): 1477–536 at 1477. See generally Dianne Otto (ed.), *Queering International Law: Possibilities, Alliances, Complicities, Risks* (New York: Routledge, 2017).

to cast Italy's invasion as having been straightforwardly unlawful under the (deeply racist) international law of the time. The standard account of the 'Abyssinia Crisis' is, quite simply, incorrect. This is not, however, the end of the story.

As I have just suggested, responses to the question of why certain states appear to be more vulnerable to external intervention than others tend to fall into two categories. Either they assume that such intervention is necessary for the purpose of law enforcement (the response of much mainstream thinking in international law), or (in the case of more critical commentators) they argue that this kind of intervention reflects the persistence of colonial patterns of power and resource distribution. A significant number of anomalies remain, however, which are difficult to explain solely by reference to the history and ongoing effects of racism and colonialism, central as these indisputably were and are to the structure of the contemporary international order. For example, two of the most intrusive multilateral programmes of military and institutional intervention to have taken place in the last quarter-century – in Bosnia and Herzegovina and in Serbia, the latter resulting in the secession and 'reconstruction' of Kosovo as a purportedly new international person – had European states as their target. Similarly, Russia and the other states of the former Soviet bloc more generally possess an idiosyncratic history and an ongoing experience of interventionism that do not fit neatly into a dynamic centred on European colonialism and its aftermath.[36] Equally, the programme of 'shock therapy' imposed, during the 1990s, on several post-Soviet states by the International Monetary Fund (IMF) bears more than a passing resemblance to the programmes of 'structural adjustment' that states in the Global South had been experiencing from the 1970s onwards. In the aftermath of the 2008 financial crisis, meanwhile, Spain, Greece, Cyprus, Portugal and Ireland, in particular, have been forced to undergo very similar programmes of painful, internationally mandated and supervised 'austerity' in order to tackle their high levels of public debt.

The situation is equally blurred within the (formally) non-European world. For example, unlike the settler states of North America and Australasia, states in Latin America have endured a long history of external financial and military interventionism and possess a powerful Third

[36] See e.g. Lauri Mälksoo, *Russian Approaches to International Law* (Oxford University Press, 2015).

World identity,[37] even though from the perspective of Indigenous peoples their record of oppression is no less horrifying than that of Australia or Canada, for example.[38] China, meanwhile, fell victim to European imperialism in the nineteenth century without ever becoming an outright colony; its Security Council veto, its long history of regional interventionism, its powerful economy and its new territorial interests in sub-Saharan Africa all bear out its paradoxical geopolitical position.[39] At the same time, the question of the legal personality of Indigenous peoples all over the world, from the Amazon to Scandinavia, and from Taiwan to the Torres Strait, continues to confound not only the metropole/colony dichotomy but the very distinction between 'international' and 'domestic'.[40]

As this suggests, the comfortable idea that we inhabit a planet divided neatly into (approximately) 193 'sovereign equals' is becoming harder and harder to maintain, but so is its most familiar critique: the image of a world of that can be sorted into a 'West' and a 'rest'. The actions of Third World actors are exerting an increasing influence on the global order. Meanwhile, the states of the Global North are in some cases beginning themselves to 'fail' on precisely the same indicators ('representative, accountable, and transparent governance and open economies', to use Clinton's formulation) that have typically been used to describe Third World state 'failure'. In this context, the task of making sense of the relationship between sovereign equality and inequality – and of doing so in a way that can open up possibilities for arresting, and perhaps even reversing, the escalating situation of distributional inequality and violence with which that world is faced – is becoming an increasingly urgent one.

It is this puzzle that I address here through an examination of a process that I call 'international legal reproduction'. This term refers to the process through which new subjects of international law are brought into being and later disciplined by more 'successful' members of the so-called international community. In the following pages I examine the operation and consequences of the process of international legal reproduction in numerous very different contexts, from the transformation of the Chinese Empire

[37] See e.g. Liliana Obregón, 'Between Civilization and Barbarism: Creole Interventions in International Law', 27 *Third World Quarterly* (2006): 815–32.

[38] See e.g. Silvia Rivera Cusicanqui, *'Oprimidos pero no vencidos': Luchas del Campesino Aymara y Qhechwa, 1900–1980* (La Paz: La Mirada Salvaje, 1984).

[39] See Ruskola, 'Raping Like a State'.

[40] See e.g. Glen Coulthard, *Red Skins, White Masks* (Minneapolis: University of Minnesota Press, 2014); Julie Evans et al., *Sovereignty: Frontiers of Possibility* (Honolulu: University of Hawai'i Press, 2013); Brenna Bhandar, 'Plasticity and Post-Colonial Recognition: "Owning, Knowing and Being"', 22 *Law and Critique* (2011): 227–47.

into a 'sovereign state' (Item 2) to the Indigenous struggle for self-determination on Indigenous terms in Canada, Australia and elsewhere ('Lid'). However, the book's primary case study concerns the Ethiopian Empire (Items 1, 4, 5 and 6), whose annexation by Italy it explains by placing Ethiopia's metamorphosis into a sovereign state against a 'long' historical background, which it builds up layer by layer. On the one hand, this re-examination of the significance of the Abyssinia Crisis for international law does call attention to the way in which the discipline was, and remains, deeply implicated in the project of European colonialism and its aftermath. On the other hand, by examining this extended case study against a background composed of a whole series of other examples of the process of international legal reproduction in action (Items 2 and 3), the experience of the Ethiopian Empire also reveals another much more ubiquitous pattern, germane to the process according to which subjectivity under international law is created and regulated in general. Together, I suggest, this pattern and this process can help us make sense of some of the North/South shifts, anomalies and malleabilities that I have just described.

As we shall see, viewing statehood and international personality from the perspective of the process of international legal reproduction casts doubt on the idea that 'sovereign statehood' should be understood as the apotheosis of collective emancipation for all human communities everywhere, as international law encourages us to assume. International personality will emerge, from the history I lay out here, not as a complete, once-and-for-all set of rights and duties, but rather as a changeable and hybrid status – a 'plastic' form of subjectivity, to draw on the work of Brenna Bhandar.[41] Having been constituted on a conditional basis, the rights and duties of international law's subjects *remain* conditional, leaving them vulnerable to being disciplined at a later date if, and to the extent that, they renege on their conditions of constitution. With the possible exception of those (very few, exclusively Western European) states which international law considers to have been members of the so-called family of nations 'since time immemorial',[42] states and other subjects of international law should therefore be considered to be both sovereign *and* less-than-sovereign simultaneously, with a set of rights and duties which wax and wane depending on their 'success' in meeting these conditions. These conditions, I will suggest, are none other than the criteria

41 Bhandar, 'Plasticity and Post-Colonial Recognition'.

42 Thomas J. Lawrence, *The Principles of International Law* (London, New York: MacMillan, 1895), 84.

for statehood themselves: defined territory, fixed population, government, and diplomatic independence. As we shall see, moreover, the most important component of this 'standard of statehood' (as we might call it) is *government* – a term which, as I suggested above, has been used to refer precisely to the apparatus whose role it is to protect the rights associated with individual legal subjectivity, conceived in its narrowest sense. Nonetheless, while this pervasive hybridity is clearly an Achilles' Heel in the armour of sovereignty which casts the remaining 'otherness' of certain sovereigns as a pathology requiring an external cure, this book will also suggest – in keeping with what Bhandar calls the 'double-edged' idea of plasticity as a political concept – that the hybrid quality of international personality can sometimes be mobilised as a weapon of resistance.[43]

The argument I present here, then, is both general and particular. In a general sense, it points to a new understanding of sovereignty, which, if it is correct, explains something new about international law and how it operates. On the other hand, however, this understanding is anchored in a detailed examination of a single, and perhaps unexpected case study, namely the international legal history of the Ethiopian Empire. The argument I present in this book therefore also has certain methodological implications. According to international law's core doctrine of 'sources', ideas and practices acquire normative force and become 'legal' in and through the playing-out of a particular type of history. This history is the history of states – or, more specifically, this history is composed of the accumulation of the 'official' actions and words of states (found, for example, in treaties and in the utterances of state representatives, officials and judges) and, to a lesser extent, the 'teachings' of certain 'highly qualified' scholars.[44] International law, according to sources doctrine, moves forward through time, growing and changing, in and through the accretion of official words and actions over time. As I have argued elsewhere,[45] this means that international law possesses what is, in effect, an inbuilt self-validating historiography, which silences all but a few non-state actors while imbuing the words and actions of states with exclusive legitimacy. This means, quite simply, that those who wish to look critically at international law and its material effects cannot do so without reaching

[43] Bhandar, 'Plasticity and Post-Colonial Recognition', 245. Bhandar here is drawing on the work of Catherine Malabou. See in particular Catherine Malabou, *Plasticity at the Dusk of Writing: Dialectic, Destruction, Deconstruction* (trans: Carolyn Shread) (New York: Columbia University Press, 2010).

[44] *Statute of the International Court of Justice*, Art. 38(1).

[45] Rose Parfitt, 'The Spectre of Sources', 25 *EJIL* (2014): 297–306.

beyond sources doctrine, which in turn puts at risk their claim that what they are 'doing' is indeed 'international law'.

This book adopts a combined approach in an effort to overcome the problems created by this inbuilt, self-legitimating historiography. In the first place, the history it offers is – as the doctrine of sources insists it should be – grounded in the examination of treaties, custom, state practice and the teachings of 'highly qualified publicists' (a grounding which is also reflected in the title and organisation of the book's bibliography). In addition, however, and in the tradition of 'critical legal history',[46] I contextualise these sources with the aim of disrupting the teleological progress narrative which encourages us to view the emergence and expansion of the sovereign state as a necessary, inevitable and natural process. Most importantly, however, the book also attempts to go beyond this, in order to avoid what Susan Marks has called the trap of 'false contingency'.[47] In order to take this third step, I develop what I call a 'modular' approach to the history of international law. The various chapters in this book are offered up, not as links in a single chain, but instead as separate but related historical 'items' placed within a theoretical 'frame'. While the book format unfortunately makes it difficult to get away from linearity completely, readers are encouraged (as I explain further in the Frame) to imagine this book as a shadow-box (see Figures 3 and 11), which they are free to walk around and view from different angles, and whose contents they are invited to move around and add to, using their own histories, their own knowledge and their own ways of making sense of the world. Above all, readers should not feel obliged to engage with the various Items in the shadow-box in any particular order. Instead, they should feel at liberty to put them together in any combination they might find interesting or productive. My hope is that this modular approach to the history of international law will allow new affinities and patterns to jump out – patterns which, as in a kaleidoscope, reconfirm the underlying structure, but in an unlimited number of different ways.

[46] See e.g. Robert W. Gordon, 'Critical Legal Histories,' 36 *Stanford Law Review* (1984): 57–125.

[47] Susan Marks, 'False Contingency', 62 *Current Legal Problems* (2009): 1–21, discussed further in the Frame, Section 1.1.

Frame

Modular History and the Process of International Legal Reproduction

As suggested in the Stand, this first chapter operates as a frame for the shadow-box, into which the six historical items which follow will then be stacked. The materials from which this frame is constructed are drawn, above all, from the work of a group of three renegade Marxist theorists: Bernard Edelman, Walter Benjamin and Mikhail Bakhtin. Though very different in many ways in terms of their methods and concerns, these theorists are united by a profoundly unorthodox approach to the philosophy of Marxism and, in particular, by a committed materialism combined with a rejection (whether explicit or implicit) of the economic determinism which, from the era of Joseph Stalin onwards, came to characterise the official ideology of the Soviet Union and its apologists. In different ways, their thinking, together with that of other fellow-travellers examined here, points to an understanding of historical materialism that is redemptive without being teleological; that is structuralist while insisting on the ever-present possibilities for resistance; and that has the potential to throw new light on the material dimensions and impact of international law on the world we inhabit, and on the distribution of wealth, power and pleasure within it.

This chapter, then, draws on their thinking to lay out the theoretical underpinnings of the process of international legal reproduction. The task of Items 1–6 is then to fill this theoretical framework with historical content. As we shall see, the work of Benjamin (Section 1) underpins the book's historiographical approach, and that of Edelman (Section 2) grounds its theory of the relationship between 'micro' (individual) and 'macro' (international) legal subjectivity. The insights of Bakhtin and his colleagues (Section 3), as applied in the post-colonial context by Homi Bhabha, will then be discussed in relation to the question of resistance.

1 Towards a Materialist History of International Law

Since the end of the 1990s the question of historiography in the legal and international legal academy has undergone protracted debate, giving rise to an important body of methodological critique and scholarly innovation. Roughly speaking, one side of the debate is occupied by the sub-field of 'critical legal history' – now a well-established approach, with its roots in the United States' critical legal studies (CLS) movement of the 1980s and 90s. Scholars on this side of the debate share a willingness to reach into the toolbox of mainstream history for a range of critical methodological devices. Perhaps the most important of these is the idea that events must be understood in their context – that is, on the basis of the actual personalities, ideas and institutions from which they arose, and not on the basis of today's equivalents. These devices, when employed as a way of making sense of the *legal* past, offer an external and highly effective way of criticising mainstream international law's own teleological biases. Pushing back against this, however, a second group of scholars has begun to challenge what for 'critical legal historians' constitutes a series of methodological red lines.

1.1 Historicism and Critical Legal History

I am using the term 'mainstream' history here to refer, in a very general sense, to history produced using the approach of historicism – a method of writing history that emerged in Western Europe in the early nineteenth century and which remains the standard approach today.[1] Historicism's most famous exponent, perhaps, was the German historian Leopold von Ranke (1795–1886), for whom the historian's task was, quite simply, to 'show, essentially, how things happened'.[2]

[1] The term 'historicism' is sometimes used in very different ways. Robert Young, for example, following Louis Althusser, defines historicism teleologically as 'an abstract philosophical scheme that imposes an overall process of transformation upon historical events'. See Robert J. C. Young, *White Mythologies: Writing History and the West* (2nd edn London, New York: Routledge, 2004), 89. See the discussion, revisited below, in Christopher Tomlins and John Comaroff, 'Afterword, "Law As ...": Theory and Practice in Legal History', 1 *UC Irvine Law Review* (2011): 1039–79 at 1043.

[2] Leopold von Ranke [1824], 'Preface to the First Edition', in George Iggers (ed.), *Histories of the Latin and German Nations*, trans. Wilma Iggers (Indianapolis, IN: Bobbs-Merill, 1973), 136, 138. See also Wilhelm von Humboldt [1822], 'On the Historian's Task' (trans. Louis O. Mink), 6 *History and Theory* (1967): 57–71, 57.

Given how squarely this method continues to occupy the centre ground in the discipline of history today, notwithstanding many challenges,[3] it is worth remembering that it was developed as a critique and continues to have immense critical power. Specifically, Ranke and his followers took issue with the then-dominant, explicitly teleological 'idealist' historiography of Georg Hegel (1770–1831) and others, the assumptions of which were then being brought into question by the social trauma inflicted by the industrial revolution.[4] The subject of history for historicism is 'mankind as it is, explicable or inexplicable'.[5] Debunking the idealist assumption that 'progress resides in the higher potentiality of each age in the life of man',[6] Ranke insisted that 'before God all generations of mankind possess equal rights' and that 'the historian must view things accordingly'.[7] To understand time as imbued with an inevitably progressive impulse was, in other words, both incorrect and dangerously utopian, capable of legitimating all kinds of horrors in the name of 'human' advancement. Instead, time should be understood as what it was: a neutral medium within which the past's events had played out according to their own logic.

Today, many legal historians, and historians more generally, feel a very similar duty towards the individuals who populate our past – a duty 'to use the ordinary techniques of historical enquiry to grasp their concepts, to follow their distinctions, to appreciate their beliefs and, so far as possible, to see things their way', as the intellectual historian Quentin Skinner put it in 2002.[8] By contrast, 'teleological forms of explanation' – from Hegel to the international legal progress narrative – make the fundamental mistake of assuming that the past 'has to await the future to learn its meaning'.[9] It is still essential, therefore, that historical events, objects, texts, speeches

[3] I refer to the immense contribution of Marxist historians, from Braudel to C. L. R. James to Hobsbawm, against which the post-Cold War reinvigoration of historicism sets itself decisively (my thanks to Robert Knox on this); to those, like Hayden White, for whom 'the term "history" is the signifier of a concept rather than a reference to a thing or domain of being having material presence', and many others. Hayden White, *The Practical Past* (Evanston, IL: Northwestern University Press, 2014), x.

[4] HD Kittsteiner, Jonathan Monroe and Irving Wohlfarth, 'Walter Benjamin's Historicism', 39 *New German Critique* (1986): 179–215 at 182.

[5] Ranke, 'Preface to the First Edition', 136, 138.

[6] Leopold von Ranke, *Über die Epochen der neueren Geschichte* (Darmstadt: Wissenschaftliche Buchgesellschaft 1965), 7, cited in Kittsteiner, Monroe and Wohlfarth, 'Walter Benjamin's Historicism', 180–1.

[7] Ibid., 181.

[8] Quentin Skinner, *Visions of Politics, Vol. I: Regarding Method* (Cambridge University Press, 2002), viii.

[9] Ibid., 74.

and so on be understood in context. 'Any statement is inescapably the embodiment of a particular intention on a particular occasion, addressed to the solution of a particular problem, and is thus specific to its context in a way that it can only be naive to try to transcend', meaning that the task is to understand what the author 'intended or meant'.[10] This approach contains a 'final moral': that 'agency deserves after all to be privileged over structure in social explanation'. We may, Skinner concludes, 'be freer than we sometimes suppose'.[11]

As we have seen, historicism's destabilising, profoundly anti-teleological potential has been embraced by critical legal historians as a singularly effective critical device.[12] Robert W. Gordon, for instance, argued in the 1990s that '[l]awyers are overtly presentist. They want to bring past practices into the present to serve present purposes, whereas historians regard naked presentism as a sin'.[13] For this reason, '[v]irtually all history as practiced by modern historians turns out to be critical to some degree if introduced into legal discourse'.[14] The conclusions of critical legal history thus dovetail neatly with one of the central tenets of the CLS movement, from which it was an offshoot: the so-called 'indeterminacy thesis', articulated most famously in the international law context by David Kennedy[15] and Martti Koskenniemi[16] in the 1980s. In brief, both argued that international law has, throughout history, found itself trapped in an eternal see-saw between 'concrete' and 'normative' modes of justification, tending towards apologism and utopianism/totalitarianism respectively. International law therefore cannot provide 'a coherent, convincing justification for solving a normative problem' because things could always have gone – and will go – the other way.[17]

[10] Ibid., 88.

[11] Ibid., 88.

[12] On the methodological and political limitations of 'critical legal history' as defined by Gordon, see Christopher Tomlins, 'After Critical Legal History: Scope, Scale, Structure', 8 *Annual Review of Law and Social Science* (2012): 31–68 at 31. In the international law context, see Anne Orford, 'On International Legal Method', 1 *London Review of International Law* (2013): 166–97 at 175.

[13] Robert W. Gordon, 'Forward: The Arrival of Critical Historicism', 49 *Stanford Law Review* (1997): 1023–9 at 1024–5.

[14] Ibid., 1024.

[15] David W. Kennedy, 'Theses About International Law Discourse', 23 *German Yearbook of International Law* (1980): 353–91;

[16] Martti Koskenniemi [1989], *From Apology to Utopia: The Structure of International Legal Argument* (Cambridge University Press, 2005).

[17] Ibid., 67.

It was interesting, while working on this book, to discover how few international legal historians attempting to understand 'what really happened' during the run-up to the Abyssinia Crisis of 1935–36, for example, had been motivated to move beyond the sources (treaties, state practice, *opinio juris*) laid down as 'law-creating' by Article 38(1) of the 1945 *Statute of the International Court of Justice* (see Item 1). As Items 4–5 demonstrate, 'contextualising' the Abyssinia Crisis in the classically historicist sense *did* have the effect predicted by Gordon. For instance, the archival research that I conducted showed immediately how misleading is the assumption that the Ethiopian was a 'sovereign equal' in any straightforward sense at the time of Italy's invasion. Yet these discoveries also underscored some of historicism's limitations. The materials I uncovered did not leave me with a sense that the events leading up to the Crisis were *entirely* contingent when it came to the functioning of the Ethiopian Empire's international personality. After all, the fact remains, as noted in the Stand, that, even if the League of Nations did condemn the invasion as illegal, Ethiopia's annexation was subsequently recognised *de jure* by almost the entire international community. Was this simply a matter of chance; something that might have gone the other way if, say, Emperor Haile Selassie had delivered his June 1936 speech to the League of Nations Assembly in French rather than in Amharic? Or must we consider the possibility that the annexation, by a fascist European 'power', of the last remaining autochthonous African polity, and later its recognition by the international community of the time, might have been connected to certain structural factors built into the legal framework itself?

1.2 Histories of the Present

The attempt to respond to these questions by pushing against some of historicism's methodological red lines places this book in conversation with the work of a group of 'situated' critical scholars of international legal history (as we might call them, following Donna Haraway).[18] We saw in the Stand that Third World Approaches to International Law (TWAIL), feminist, queer and other writers such as Antony Anghie, Gina Heathcote, Teemu Ruskola and others have been concerned to attend to the *pattern* of distributional inequality across time and space.[19] If 'agency'

[18] See Donna Haraway, 'Situated Knowledges: The Science Question in Feminism and the Privilege of Partial Perspective,' 14 *Feminist Studies* (1988): 575–99.

[19] See Stand, notes 28–36.

really 'deserves ... to be privileged over structure' as Skinner suggests – if international law really *is* normatively indeterminate – then how is it that certain communities always draw the short straw when it comes to the allocation and exercise of power and resources? How can we account, in other words, for what Koskenniemi, in a later modification of his work on indeterminacy, calls 'structural bias'?[20] In responding to questions such as these, one might say – following Michel Foucault – that the aim of such 'situated' histories is one of writing 'histories of the present' – histories written not merely 'in terms of the present',[21] but rather with the aim of rendering the present 'intelligible and, therefore, criticizable'.[22]

For example, both Anne Orford and Christopher Tomlins have pointed out, in different ways, that legal and international legal history lends itself to this kind of 'presentist' analysis. Discussing a number of virulent attacks by historians on the supposedly 'deplorable' anachronism embraced by this group of critical international legal historians,[23] for example, Anne Orford makes the point that historians 'who seek to stamp out anachronism in international legal scholarship' by thinking about 'ideas in context' seem to be oblivious of 'the criticisms to and challenges of [this] method that have since developed in [their] own field'.[24] Orford goes on to point out that international law is 'necessarily anachronic, because the operation of modern law is not governed solely by a chronological sense of time in which events and texts are confined to their proper place in a historical and linear progression from then to now'. The past, therefore, 'far from being gone, is constantly being retrieved as a source or rationalisation of present obligation'.[25]

As Tomlins points out, meanwhile, the consequence of the kind of radical historicism which insists on the value of contingency and agency over determinacy and structure is to create a situation in which 'whatever

[20] Koskenniemi, *From Apology to Utopia*, 562–617.

[21] Michel Foucault [1975], *Discipline and Punish: The Birth of the Prison*, trans. Alan Sheridan (New York: Vintage Books, 1997), 30–31.

[22] Michel Foucault [1978], 'On Power' in Lawrence Kritzman (ed.), *Michel Foucault: Politics, Philosophy, Culture: Interviews and Other Writings, 1977–1984* (New York: Routledge, 1988), 101.

[23] Orford, 'On International Legal Method', 173. Orford quotes here from Randall Lesaffer, 'International Law and its History: The Story of an Unrequited Love', in Matthew Craven, Malgosia Fitzmaurice and Maria Vogiatzi (eds.), *Time, History and International Law* (The Hague: Martinus Nijhoff, 2007), 27–41 at 34–5: 'This kind of historiography sins against the most basic rules of historical methodology, and the results are deplorable.'

[24] Orford, 'On International Legal Method', 173.

[25] Ibid., 175.

the realm of action in relation to which law is situated, the outcome is the same: indeterminacy marked by contingency, alternative possibilities, paths not taken'.[26] The risk is that a narrative produced solely on the basis of this approach will be 'marked by an abandonment of authoritative causal explanation',[27] and divested of political commitment. As Tomlins points out, writing with anthropologist John Comaroff, the 'watchword' of what they call 'scientific history' is 'context – from which follows a rigid distinction between then and now, a cæsura that underscores the absolute difference of the past'.[28] However, 'the phenomena studied by the scientific historian are recurrent – for example, human behavior' and are 'not so easily sequestered in the past', but rather 'lure the historian toward "presentism"'.[29] Accepting this lure, and drawing inspiration from Walter Benjamin, Tomlins and Comaroff set out to discover 'the conditions of possibility for a critical knowledge of the here-and-now', making it possible to retrieve the past in order 'to confront the present'.[30]

With this debate in mind, let me turn to examine these two radical responses to historicism more closely: firstly, the Nietzschean/Foucaultian 'genealogical' attempt to generate a form of historical 'knowledge' that is made for 'cutting' rather than for 'understanding';[31] and secondly, Benjamin's own more revolutionary call for 'a historical materialism which has annihilated within itself the idea of progress'.[32]

1.2.1 'Genealogy' and Contingency

The metaphor of genealogy was first introduced as a historiographical approach in the late nineteenth century by Friedrich Nietzsche,[33] but it was developed most famously in the 1970s by Michel Foucault.[34] Foucault accused what he called 'traditional history' of an 'apocalyptical objectivity' – of a hubris that was itself teleological in its assumption that the

[26] Tomlins, 'After Critical Legal History', 31.

[27] Ibid., 31.

[28] Tomlins and Comaroff, 'Afterword', 1042–3.

[29] Ibid., 1042.

[30] Ibid., 1044.

[31] Michel Foucault, 'Nietzsche, Genealogy, History', in Paul Rainbow (ed.), *The Foucault Reader* (New York: Pantheon, 1984), 76–100 at 88.

[32] Walter Benjamin, *The Arcades Project*, ed. Rolf Tiedemann, trans. Howard Eiland and Kevin McLaughlin (Cambridge, MA: Harvard University Press, 1999), 460.

[33] See e.g. Friedrich Nietzsche, *On the Genealogy of Morality*, ed. Keith Ansell-Pearson, trans. Carol Diethe (Cambridge University Press, 2006).

[34] Foucault, 'Nietzsche, Genealogy, History'. See also Michel Foucault, *The Archaeology of Knowledge*, trans. Alan Sheridan Smith (London, New York: Routledge, 2002).

past could, indeed, be retrieved as a complete whole.[35] Instead, the task of the genealogist was to 'record the singularity of events outside of any monstrous finality'.[36] There is, for this approach, no unity, no 'essential meaning': even the concept of self – the presumed 'unity of man's being through which it was thought that he could extend his sovereignty to the events of his past' – is an 'empty synthesis' which it is the purpose of genealogy to 'shatter'.[37] Genealogy, therefore, does not 'pretend to go back in time to restore an unbroken continuity that operates beyond the dispersal of forgotten things'; nor does it see it as its duty 'to demonstrate that the past ... continues secretly to animate the present'.[38] Instead, 'to follow the complex course of descent' is 'to identify the accidents, the minute deviations – or conversely, the complete reversals – the errors, the false appraisals, and the faulty calculations that gave birth to those things that continue to exist and have value for us; it is to discover that truth or being does not lie at the root of what we know and what we are, but the exteriority of accidents'.[39]

This approach was taken up in international law perhaps most famously by Nathaniel Berman, who in 1999 laid out an imaginary dialogue between two disciplinary archetypes: the 'Restater-Renewer' and the 'Genealogist'.[40] For the former, the crucial moment in international law's biography is the Peace of Westphalia: '*1648*: the break between empire and law'.[41] Westphalia's 'legacy' is 'the duty to cleanse international law of any residual elements of imperial or patriarchal injustice'.[42] As the Genealogist proceeds to demonstrate, however, the idea of a historical-conceptual Westphalian 'break' with exclusivity and hierarchy is an ideological device that allows the Restater-Renewer to structure his/her biography of international law in a way that automatically validates its claim to 'truth'. For example, in its desire to be normatively relevant, the project of disciplinary 'renewal' risks overlooking the way in which 'specific, current problems' are 'fram[ed] within general schemas bequeathed by history' such as the hubris of the powerful in assuming their norms to

35 Ibid., 86–7.
36 Ibid., 76.
37 Ibid., 85, 87.
38 Ibid., 81.
39 Ibid., 81.
40 Nathanial Berman, 'In the Wake of Empire', 14 *American University International Law Review* (1998–99): 1521–54.
41 Ibid., 1523. Emphasis in the original.
42 Ibid., 1523.

be universal.[43] Equally, however, the project of disciplinary 'restatement' is essentially one of '[p]rojecting certain parts of international law ... into some non-legal sphere called "empire"', thereby giving international law 'an alibi, a claim it was not present at those events the discipline now condemns'.[44] Berman, in this way, offers genealogy as a critical alternative to the mainstream oscillation between 'restatement' and 'renewal' on the grounds that

> ... genealogy sees international law – its doctrines as well as its participants – as normatively impure, culturally heterogeneous and historically contingent. This approach enables it both to mourn legal history's horrors and to believe in law's ever-present emancipatory potential. For genealogy, it is precisely international law's lack of coherence, the instability of its transitory configurations of rules and players, that makes it a hopeful enterprise.[45]

Unlike 'traditional history', then, genealogy emphasises the capacity of power and violence not just to introduce contingency, but actually to distort, reverse or even destroy previous meanings and systems of value.[46] It is not the case, as Nietzsche had insisted, that history is characterised by 'absolute randomness' or by a 'mechanistic senselessness of all events', however comforting that would be to believe.[47] On the contrary, a '*power-will* is acted out in all that happens', such that 'everything that occurs in the organic world consists of *overpowering*, *dominating*, and in their turn, overpowering and dominating consist of re-interpretation, adjustment, in the process of which their former "meaning" [*Sinn*] and "purpose" must necessarily be obscured or completely obliterated'.[48] Or as Foucault explains, history is 'effective' 'to the degree that it introduces discontinuity into our very being', thereby uprooting even *its own* 'traditional foundations' and disrupting even *its own* 'pretended continuity'.[49] 'Effective history' is thus 'without constants', implying that '[n]othing in man – not even his body – is sufficiently stable to serve as the basis for self-recognition or for understanding other men'.[50] It is in this sense that Foucault was

[43] Ibid., 1538.

[44] Ibid., 1537.

[45] Ibid., 1523–4.

[46] See e.g. Melissa Lane, 'Doing our Own Thinking for Ourselves: On Quentin Skinner's Genealogical Turn', 73 *Journal of the History of Ideas* (2012): 71–82. As Lane points out at p. 81, although Skinner has taken up the theme of genealogy in his recent work on the state, this emphasis is 'misleading'.

[47] Nietzsche, *On the Genealogy of Morality*, 52.

[48] Ibid., 51–2. Emphasis in the original.

[49] Foucault, 'Nietzsche, Genealogy, History', 88.

[50] Ibid., 88.

able to claim that 'knowledge is not made for understanding; it is made for cutting'.[51] Genealogical knowledge *is* effective history; the 'rancorous will to knowledge' is no less 'malicious' than the 'will to power'.[52] Indeed, the two are, for him, identical. Also unlike 'traditional history', genealogy emphasises the continuity between the history of ideas and the history of things. The physical body, for example, 'manifests the stigmata of past experience',[53] according to Foucault, because of the way in which '[t]he domination of certain men over others leads to the differentiation of values' – the manner in which power and violence are solidified and reproduced in the formation of new values, or in the investing of existing values with new meanings.[54] For Foucault, it is the task of genealogy 'to expose a body totally imprinted by history and the processes of history's destruction of the body'.[55]

As we shall see, the history of the Ethiopian Empire's encounter with international law, for instance, can be told as an 'endlessly repeated play of dominations'.[56] Not only did the 'Abyssinia Crisis' display the European 'will to power' in some of its most aggressively imperialist, racist, fascist and extractionist manifestations but, at the same time, the Ethiopian Empire was engaged in its *own* 'internal' project of imperial domination – a project whose wounds continue to fester today.[57] However, notwithstanding its attentiveness to power and violence, and its recognition that history is never 'the spectacle of a struggle among equals',[58] genealogy remains committed to the task of exposing the essential 'contingency of the present' – a contingency which is not borne out by the 'long' history of the Abyssinia Crisis that I present in Items 4, 5 and 6.[59] Interestingly, this

51 Ibid., 88.
52 Ibid., 95.
53 Ibid., 83.
54 Ibid., 85.
55 Ibid., 83.
56 Ibid., 85.
57 See e.g. 'Dozens Killed in Ethnic Clashes in Ethiopia's Oromia,' *Al Jazeera News*, 19 December 2017, at www.aljazeera.com/news/2017/12/dozens-killed-clashes-ethiopia-oromia-region-171218140529256.html (accessed 25 January 2018).
58 Foucault, 'Nietzsche, Genealogy, History', 84.
59 Colin Koopman, *Genealogy as Critique: Foucault and the Problems of Modernity* (Bloomington and Indianapolis, IN: Indiana University Press, 2013), 140. Koopman argues that genealogy is a method of 'critical historiography' designed to 'reveal, but also to shake up, the present'. This is, he argues, 'a vision of critique as an inquiry into those historical conditions of possibility that constrain us not with the iron fist of necessity but with the gentle yet persuasive arm of contingency … Genealogy focuses on our constitutive constraints as temporal-historical processes of universalization that are contingent and complex all the way down. In this way genealogy ably inflects the practice of critique as

commitment comes through most clearly in Foucault's treatment of law. 'Humanity', Foucault observes, does not 'gradually progress from combat to combat until it arrives at a universal reciprocity, where the rule of law finally replaces warfare.'[60] Instead, 'humanity instils each of its violences in a system of rules and thus proceeds from domination to domination.'[61] This would seem to imply that power is inscribed into the very 'rules' themselves. Yet Foucault insists that these rules are in fact '*empty* in themselves'; that the 'successes of history belong to those who are capable of seizing the rules', 'invert[ing] their meaning and redirect[ing] them against those who had initially imposed them.'[62]

But what if the history in question were to be written by one of the perennial negatives of the 'free' and 'equal' legal subject – non-white, non-rich, non-European, non-heterosexual, perhaps even non-human? Could the past really be expected to appear – to *Bäjerond* Täklä-Hawaryat Täklä-Maryam, for example, head of the Ethiopian Delegation to the League of Nations in the 1930s, when the prejudices of his colleagues at Geneva brought him to tears of rage[63] – as a collection of 'accidents', accumulated at certain places in certain formations due to ultimately impermanent manifestations of one 'will to power' or another? Or as another critic of international law, Susan Marks, has put it:

> There is a great deal of talk about how things that are contingent are made to seem as if they were necessary, in virtue of being natural, universal, rational, eternal, etc., but much less discussion of voluntarist mystifications. Terry Eagleton brings out something of the significance of this omission when, writing about literary history, he asks: 'For whom exactly does experience seem like a swirl of vivid odds and ends? It might have seemed this way to Virginia Woolf, but it is unlikely that it did so to the servants who rose not long after dawn to lay her fires and polish her fenders.' To those at the less comfortable end of social relations, Eagleton implies, the patterning of privilege and deprivation will be quite plain, or at any rate of interest and worth investigation.[64]

---

an inquiry into conditions of possibility with a historicist rather than a transcendentalist sensibility.' Ibid., 19

60 Foucault, 'Nietzsche, Genealogy, History', 86.

61 Ibid., 86.

62 Ibid., 86. My emphasis.

63 Bahru Zewde, *Pioneers of Change in Ethiopia: The Reformist Intellectuals of the Early Twentieth Century* (Oxford, Athens, OH, Addis Ababa: James Currey, Ohio University Press, Addis Ababa University Press, 2002), 63.

64 Susan Marks, 'False Contingency', 62 *Current Legal Problems* (2009): 1–21, 14, quoting Terry Eagleton, *The English Novel* (Oxford: Blackwell, 2005), 311.

As Marks suggests, the danger of insisting on the inherent contingency of the order we inhabit is that 'the injustices of the present order are made to appear as though they were random, accidental and arbitrary'.[65] In such a situation, the 'prospects of changing them' come to seem 'every bit as remote' as they do when the same injustices are understood as somehow fated or structurally pre-determined by God, relations of production (as in the 'vulgar Marxist' account of historical materialism) or anything else (the 'monstrous finality' opposed by Foucault).[66] From a more sophisticated Marxist (or 'anti-anti-Marxist'[67]) point of view, by contrast, the distribution of privilege and deprivation is neither wholly contingent nor wholly pre-determined, but rather 'patterned' in a particular way, such that certain groups consistently find themselves 'at the less comfortable end of social relations'.[68] In place of a search for 'determinism', therefore, Marks directs us towards the activity of 'determination' – the desire to 'investigate in particular circumstances what individual and collective action can achieve, what relation is established between structure and agency, how the world works as an organic totality'.[69]

It is towards this task of 'determination' that this book's attempt to draw attention to international legal reproduction *as* a historical process is directed. In contrast both to genealogists like Berman and 'anti-anti-Marxists' like Marks, however, I make the slightly more apprehensive argument here that we are not at liberty merely to expose the 'stigmata of past experience' in the hope that revealing the true extent of history's wounds *might* open up possibilities for change. It seems to me that there is no longer any question of the existence, or historical nature, of such wounds. The past does not, in my view, offer us the option of acting, but rather *demands* that we take action to transfigure it. As Walter Benjamin wrote in 1940, in Paris, on the eve of the Nazi occupation, '*even the dead* will not be safe from the enemy if he is victorious. And this enemy has never ceased to be victorious.'[70]

65 Marks, 'False Contingency', 2.
66 Ibid., 20.
67 Ibid., 21.
68 Ibid., 14.
69 Ibid., 9.
70 Walter Benjamin, 'On the Concept of History' [1940], in *Walter Benjamin: Selected Writings*, Vol. 4: 1938–1940, eds. Howard Eiland and Michael W. Jennings, trans. Harry John (Cambridge, MA: Harvard University Press, 2003), 389–400 at 391. Emphasis in the original.

1.2.2 The Constellation and the Shadow-Box

Above all, Benjamin's philosophy of history is underpinned by a critique of the assumption that historical time was linear in nature. For time, as Benjamin wrote just a few months before he chose suicide over the death camps, is not a 'homogeneous, empty' void into which a 'mass of data', culled from the archives by industrious historians, could simply be piled up and filed away in chronological order. Nor was it legitimate to link 'the sequence of events' together by specious threads of linear causality, as though the past could be strung together in a single line 'like the beads of a rosary'.[71] In its assumption that '[t]he truth will not run away from us',[72] Benjamin contended, historicism's attempt to construct a single 'universal history' propagated a complacency about the relationship between past, present and future that systematically defused time's political charge. Historicism is for this reason no less dangerous – no less complicit in shoring up the status quo – than the idealism which 'modern' historicism ostensibly set out to challenge.[73] As Michael Löwy explains, 'the alleged[ly] neutral historian, who has access directly to the "real" facts, in reality only reinforces the view of the victors – the kings, popes and emperors (the preferred object of Ranke's historiography) of all ages'.[74] It was to the regal, papal, imperial records that fill the official archives that Ranke and his successors directed their students – not to the 'rags and refuse' left to rot in the gutter by generations of oppressed and voiceless workers.[75]

However, if historicism was to be accused of rendering time 'homogeneous' and 'empty' through its systematic silencing of the history of the downtrodden, Benjamin pointed out that the same was equally true of mainstream ('social democratic') Marxism. Indeed, Benjamin was just as scathing of mainstream Marxism's 'vulgar' historical materialism as he was of historicism's teleological bias. As he recognised, the complacency generated by both sides of the dominant debates of the 1930s – mainstream historicism, with its quasi-accidental habit of 'empathizing with the victor' in a way that 'invariably benefits current rulers' on the one hand;[76] mainstream 'social democracy' on the other, with its 'dogmatic' faith in the inevitability of

71 Ibid., 396–7.
72 Ibid., 390.
73 Ibid., 391.
74 Michael Löwy, *Fire Alarm: Reading Walter Benjamin's 'On the Concept of History'*, trans. Chris Turner (London: Verso, 2005), 42.
75 Benjamin, *The Arcades Project*, 460; Benjamin, 'On the Concept of History', 394.
76 Benjamin, 'On the Concept of History', 391.

'the progress of humankind itself'[77] – should be held responsible for having created the conditions under which fascism had not only arisen but stood potentially to triumph. Indeed, for Benjamin the distinction between these two theories of history, deemed so fundamental by both sides, was immaterial. For in fact '[t]he concept of mankind's historical progress cannot be sundered from the concept of its progression through a homogeneous, empty time. A critique of the concept of such a progression must underlie any criticism of the concept of progress itself.'[78] Indeed, 'nothing', according to Benjamin, 'ha[d] so corrupted the German working class as the notion that it was moving with the current.'[79] With this 'stubborn faith in progress', he continued, social democratic politicians cemented 'their servile integration in an uncontrollable apparatus' – the apparatus of capitalism. The damage wrought by this mythology to the prospects for genuine revolution, in his view, was disastrous. In 'cast[ing] the working class in the role of a redeemer of *future* generations', social democracy had cut 'the sinews of its greatest strength'. This strength consisted in 'its hatred and its spirit of sacrifice', better 'nourished', Benjamin argued, 'by the image of enslaved ancestors rather than by the ideal of liberated grandchildren.'[80]

Benjamin's response was to turn back to those parts of Marx's work in which he saw a truer reading of the idea of historical materialism, which he summed up in the injunction to 'brush history against the grain.'[81] To historicism's past-oriented complicity with 'the triumphal procession in which current rulers step over those who are lying prostrate',[82] and to orthodox Marxism's future-oriented complacency in the face of the ongoing immiseration of the disadvantaged, Benjamin answered with a form of methodological dynamite – a deeply unorthodox, revolutionary messianism, steeped in Jewish mysticism, and focused above all on a critical importance of now-time, the *jetztzeit*. This term, in Benjamin's work, refers not just to the present but to a revolutionary, situated 'now' that has been actively 'blasted out of the continuum of history', drawn into a 'constellation' with the 'what-has been', and, in this way, momentarily 'arrested' to form a 'historical image', representing 'dialects at a standstill'.[83]

[77] Ibid., 394.
[78] Ibid., 394–5.
[79] Ibid., 393.
[80] Ibid., 394. Emphasis in the original.
[81] Ibid., 392.
[82] Ibid., 391.
[83] Benjamin, *The Arcades Project*, 462.

Whereas the historian works slowly and steadily through the official archive, convinced that in it lies the 'truth', solid and unable to 'run away', and where the social democrat concentrates her efforts on distracting her constituents with optimistic predictions, the historical materialist's task is a more dangerous one. She must explode the 'continuum of historical succession';[84] 'recognise' and 'appropriat[e] a memory as it flashes up in a moment of danger';[85] and in this way 'crystallise' the 'constellation into which [her] own era has entered, along with a very specific earlier one'.[86] Thus, 'while the relation of the present to the past is purely a temporal, continuous one, the relation of the what-has-been to the now [*jetztzeit*] is dialectical'.[87] The past, therefore, is not historical automatically and of its own accord. *Only* through the intervention of 'the historical materialist', she who recognises that '[t]he subject of historical knowledge is the struggling, oppressed class itself'[88] (and not, as Ranke argued, 'mankind as it is, explicable or inexplicable'[89]) can the past be *made* historical, by 'carry[ing] over the principle of montage into history' in this way.[90]

It is important to note that Benjamin meant something very specific with this invocation of montage (a technique favoured by Benjamin's Surrealist contemporaries) as a historiographical method. In the first place, like the constellation, montage hovers somewhere between the two- and the three-dimensional, suggesting that context need not imply proximity. Secondly, the crucial gesture of 'making' the past historical by 'carry[ing] over the principle of montage into history' is, Benjamin explained, not necessarily that of reproducing the scrapbook-like structure of his own *Arcades Project*. It is, instead, a question of scale – or, in the terms of this book, a question of the relationship between the micro and the macro. Montage as a historical method involves 'assembl[ing] large-scale constructions out of the smallest and most precisely cut components', with the aim of 'discover[ing] in the analysis of the small individual moment the crystal of the total event'.[91] Only in this way, according to Benjamin, can the nexus between past and present become 'a revolutionary chance in the fight for the oppressed past', such that the present comes to be 'shot

[84] Ibid., 475.
[85] Benjamin, 'On the Concept of History', 391.
[86] Ibid., 397, 390.
[87] Ibid., 396.
[88] Ibid., 397, 394.
[89] Leopold von Ranke, 'Preface to the First Edition', 136, 138.
[90] Benjamin, *The Arcades Project*, 461.
[91] Ibid., 461.

through with splinters of messianic time'.[92] It is, in other words, ludicrous to imagine the revolution as something that 'progress' would eventually deliver automatically; for progress *is itself* the catastrophe which only revolution can 'arrest'.[93]

Equally important, here, is the significance of Benjamin's redemptive language. As Löwy points out, Benjamin's messianic take on Marxism sprang, not from a reactionary nostalgia, but instead from a connection he had forged between Jewish mysticism and classical Romanticism's 'cultural critique of modern (capitalist) civilisation in the name of pre-modern (pre-capitalist) values'.[94] What Benjamin, as a German Jew writing in 1940, sought from the revolutionary romanticist tradition was 'not a *return* to the past, but a *detour* through the past', in order to bring about the 're-enchantment' of a world which modernity had degraded, and threatened to destroy completely.[95] In this spirit, the ideas of the 'critical constellation' and of the *jetztzeit* drew sustenance from Benjamin's materialist reading of Charles Baudelaire's themes of '*la vie antérieure*' and of '*les correspondances*'.[96] *Correspondances* – sudden memories sparked off by a melody, for instance, or (famously, in Proust) by a taste – constituted for Benjamin 'the data of remembrance – not historical data, but data of prehistory'.[97] A *correspondance*, often forged by reference to rituals such as festival days and ancient rites, was a flash-back of a certain, potentially highly political kind, which generated a material 'encounter with an earlier life'.[98] As such, *correspondances* are that which make it possible to 'fathom the full meaning of the breakdown' which capitalist modernity had unleashed.[99] But, as we have seen, 'fathoming' was not enough, for according to Benjamin,

> The past carries with it a secret index with which it is referred to redemption. Doesn't the breath of air that pervaded earlier days caress us as well?

[92] Benjamin, 'On the Concept of History', 396–7.

[93] Thus, as Löwy notes, '[c]ontrary to vulgar evolutionary Marxism Benjamin does not conceive revolution as the "natural" or "inevitable" outcome of economic and technical progress (or of the "contradiction between the forces and relations of production"), but as the interruption of a process of historical evolution leading to catastrophe'. Löwy, *Fire Alarm*, 9.

[94] Ibid., 23.

[95] Ibid., 23.

[96] Charles Baudelaire [1857], 'Correspondances', in *Les Fleurs du Mal* (Boston, MA: David R. Godine, 1982), 193, 199.

[97] Walter Benjamin, 'On Some Motifs in Baudelaire', in Howard Eiland and Michael W. Jennings (eds.), *Walter Benjamin: Selected Writings*, Vol. 4: 1938–1940 (Cambridge, MA: Belknap Press, 2006), 313–55 at 333–4.

[98] Ibid., 334.

[99] Ibid., 333.

> ... If so, then there is a secret agreement between past generations and the present one. Then our coming has been expected on earth. Then, like every generation that precedes us, we have been endowed with a weak messianic power, a power on which the past has a claim. Such a claim cannot be settled cheaply. The historical materialist is aware of this.[100]

These ideas of the critical constellation, of history-as-montage and of the *correspondance* form the foundation of the historical approach I develop in this book, which takes the Abyssinia Crisis as its 'crystal' and the process of international legal reproduction as its 'total event'. The question of how to embrace this 'weak messianic power', however, is a much more difficult one. The challenge – like the catastrophe – seems much too big for any scholar to take up. As a starting point, however, it seems that one place a *legal* scholar might begin is with Benjamin's juridical image of the 'secret agreement' (*geheime Verabredung*) between past and present generations. This secret agreement suggests a connection between his critique of history and his earlier critique of law.[101] In 1921, Benjamin had pointed out that while violence might be hidden by the 'demonically ambiguous' equality of rights ('for both parties to the treaty, it is the same line that may not be crossed'), it is also violence which gives law its potency.[102] So why, then, use a quasi-legal image to characterise what was, for him, the most powerful of all historical relationships – namely the trans-generational link which figures the 'last enslaved class' as 'the avenger', charged with 'the task of liberation in the name of generations of the downtrodden'?[103]

It is at this point that Benjamin's idea of law as a violence 'crowned by fate' becomes important. As he wrote: 'if violence, violence crowned by fate, is the origin of law, then it may be readily supposed that where the highest violence, that over life and death, occurs in the legal system, the origins of law jut manifestly and fearsomely into existence'.[104] This applies not only to ('law-preserving') punishments like the death penalty, but also to ('law-creating') moments like the victory of one army over another. For law's legitimacy, grounded in an insistence on a formal equality between

[100] Benjamin, 'On the Concept of History', 390.

[101] Walter Benjamin, 'Critique of Violence' [1921], in *Walter Benjamin: Selected Writings*, Vol. 1: 1913–1926, eds. Marcus Bullock and Michael W. Jennings, trans. Edmund Jephcott (Cambridge, MA: Harvard University Press, 2003), 236–52.

[102] Ibid., 249. Many thanks to John Goode, Christine Schwöbel-Patel, Sinja Graf, Daniela Andersen and Reut Paz for their translation advice here.

[103] Benjamin, 'On the Concept of History', 394.

[104] Benjamin, 'Critique of Violence', 242.

contracting parties, is, as Benjamin points out, always and inevitably planted on a battlefield strewn with corpses:

> Where frontiers are decided, the adversary is not simply annihilated; indeed, he is accorded rights even when the victor's superiority in power is complete. And these are, in a demonically ambiguous way, 'equal' rights: for both parties to the treaty, it is the same line that may not be crossed. Here appears, in a terribly primitive form, the mythic ambiguity of laws that may not be 'infringed' – the same ambiguity to which Anatole France refers satirically when he says, 'Poor and rich are equally forbidden to spend the night under the bridges'.[105]

To illustrate the point, we might turn to the material implications of one central assumption of international law which lies at the centre of my argument. This is the idea that states, in order to be recognised as such, must possess an 'effective' and territorially 'exclusive' government, which exercises its 'responsibility' to its population by constructing for them a national 'level playing field' upon which they can exercise their individual 'equality of opportunity'. Excellent as this may sound in principle, what it means in practice is that both 'government' and 'statehood' (today the only legitimate form of collective 'emancipation' available) are predicated on the successful, and inevitably violent, suppression of all alternative claims to the land ('territory') upon which the state is founded, and on the exclusion of all alternative understandings of what it means to belong to a community beyond that of relating to one's fellow human beings as formal equals. In other words, despite its pretention to neutrality,[106] the idea of 'government' as a criterion of statehood is in fact saturated both with normative content and with violence, both material and epistemic. It might be argued, then, that the relationship between legal subjectivity and history-as-progress implicates law not only in the tendency to *narrate* history in progressive terms, but also in the unfolding of history *itself* along a set of lines laid down by that materially catastrophic form of progress that is associated with the seemingly inexorable expansion of capitalist relations of production and exchange. The 'secret agreement' between past and present generations can thus be understood as containing within it the violence of 'progress', endowed with material form by law. The question of *how* law materialises 'progress' in this way, ensuring that capitalist relations of production and exchange continue to widen and deepen, and that the world's wealth, power and pleasure continue to

[105] Ibid., 249.

[106] See Item 2, Section 1.2.

be diverted away from 'struggling, oppressed' peoples towards the 'ruling classes',[107] is the question to which this book is addressed.

The materialist critique of progress must, in other words, include a critique of law's relationship with progress, pointing to a fundamental connection between the critiques of history, capitalism and law. With this in mind, the next section brings Benjamin's 'most peculiar' version of historical materialism[108] into conversation with two other equally unorthodox Marxist thinkers: the legal scholar Bernard Edelman and the scholar of language Mikhail Bakhtin. Viewed in the light of Benjamin's critique of historicism and historical idealism, I will suggest that their work offers an alternative perspective not only on the question of the legal underpinnings of the capitalist mode of production but also, and for that reason, on the question of history itself.[109]

2 Towards a Materialist Theory of Legal Subjectivity

Bernard Edelman's *Le droit saisi par la photographie. Éléments pour une théorie marxiste du droit* came out in 1973.[110] In this cryptic and at points very ironical work, Edelman set out to knit together two crucially important interventions into Marxist legal theory: Evgeny Pashukanis's commodity-form theory of law, devised in the 1920s, and Louis Althusser's theory of ideology, first published in the 1970 article 'Idéologie et appareils idéologiques d'État'.[111] Reading Pashukanis and Althusser together, Edelman placed law at the centre of the reproduction of capitalist relations

107 Benjamin, 'On the Concept of History', 392.

108 Hannah Arendt, *Men in Dark Times* (New York: Harcourt, Brace & World, 1968), 163.

109 For a number of productive attempts to apply Benjamin's theory of history to the field of law, see numerous works by Christopher Tomlins (e.g. those cited above); in the field of international law see Richard Joyce (e.g. Richard Joyce, 'International Law and the Cold War – Reflections on the Concept of History', in Matthew Craven, Sundhya Pahuja and Gerry Simpson, *International Law and the Cold War* (Cambridge University Press, forthcoming) and Matthew Nicholson (e.g. Matthew Nicholson, 'Walter Benjamin and the Re-Imageination of International Law', 27 *Law and Critique* (2016): 103–29); and in the context of abolition and the evolution of international finance capital, see Ian Baucom, *Specters of the Atlantic: Finance Capital, Slavery, and the Philosophy of History* (Durham, NC: Duke University Press, 2005).

110 Bernard Edelman, *Le droit saisi par la photographie. Éléments pour une théorie marxiste du droit* (Paris: Éditions François Maspero, 1973). English translation: Bernard Edelman, *Ownership of the Image: Elements of Marxist Theory of Law*, trans. Elizabeth Kingdom (London: Routledge and Kegan Paul, 1979).

111 Louis Althusser, 'Idéologie et appareils idéologiques d'État (Notes pour une recherche)', 151 *La Pensée* (June 1970). English translation: Louis Althusser, 'Ideology and Ideological State Apparatus (Notes towards an Investigation)', trans. Ben Brewster, in Louis Althusser,

of production.[112] In doing so, however, one might also say that Edelman also placed law at the centre of the unfolding of history itself, in the sense that his purpose was to force us to understand the determining influence that law has had on the way in which the past has, at least since the collapse of feudalism, unfolded along a very specific, self-reinforcing set of lines. Thus, where Benjamin challenged his readers to reconsider mainstream (historicist or idealist) history as the autobiography of capitalism's unfolding catastrophe, Edelman's purpose was to insist on the role of law in creating the material conditions for that unfolding.

2.1 *Pashukanis's Theory of the Legal Subject*

Edelman's approach is closely aligned with Pashukanis's influential argument that 'the philosophy of law based on the category of the subject with his capacity for self-determination ... is actually, basically, the philosophy of an economy based on the commodity, which specifies the most universal abstract conditions under which both exchange can take place according to the law of value, and exploitation can occur in the form of the "free contract"'.[113] While most of his colleagues in the Soviet legal academy agreed that law could very easily be co-opted by the 'ruling classes' to suit its own ends, Pashukanis's critique of law went much further. Law, or rather the legal form, was an inherent part of capitalism's ideological apparatus, arising in and through the practice of exchanging commodities, including labour, for profit. From this it followed, for Pashukanis, that there could be no such thing as a 'proletarian law', just as there could be no such thing as a 'proletarian commodity'. Come the revolution, law would 'wither away' along with the state, and along with the very attributes of legal subjectivity themselves. In communist society, Pashukanis suggested, human beings would no longer understand themselves as 'isolated monads' – as separate individuals defined by their formal liberty (which freed them only to sell their labour-power on the market) and by their relation of negative equality (which described no more than their formal capacity to own and exchange private property). However, as the Stalinist state consolidated its juridical apparatus over the course of the

Essays on Ideology (London: Verso, 1984), 1–60. See Laurent de Sutter (ed.), *Althusser and Law* (Abingdon: Routledge, 2013).

[112] Althusser, 'Ideology and Ideological State Apparatus', 1.

[113] Evgeny Pashukanis, 'Preface to the Second Russian Edition', in Evgeny Pashukanis [1924], *The General Theory of Law and Marxism*, trans. Barbara Einhorn (New Brunswick, London: Transaction Publishers, 2002), 37–45 at 39.

1930s, extending the post-1917 'transition' period and hence the Soviet state's 'withering away' indefinitely, this view singled Pashukanis out as a source of dangerous dissent and, having been denounced as a 'trotskyite saboteur', he was liquidated in September 1937.[114]

Pashukanis's central argument remains one of the most devastating analyses of both law (in the Western 'rule of law' sense) and international law in existence. To summarise very briefly, building on the work of Robert Knox,[115] China Miéville[116] and others, for Pashukanis a more accurate name for 'formal democracy', as he put it, would be the 'republic of the market'; for at its heart representative democracy was nothing but an institutional and ideological arrangement that, in assuming and enforcing law's formal understanding of equality between all its subjects, including both employers and employees, 'masks' the 'despotism of the factory' extremely effectively.[117] It was Pashukanis's argument, therefore, that '[l]egal fetishism complements commodity fetishism'.[118]

Marx had already argued that 'in and through the production and exchange of commodities', qualitative, material, social relationships (between different things and different individuals) were transformed into quantitive, abstract relationships mediated by money as the 'universal equivalent'.[119] Commodities, he pointed out, 'cannot themselves go to market and perform exchanges in their own right'. In order for inanimate objects to 'enter into relation with one another as commodities', it was necessary that their (human) 'guardians', conceiving themselves as owners of private property, should 'place themselves in relation to one another as persons whose will resides in those objects', and should 'behave in such a way that each does not appropriate the commodity of the other, and alienate his own, except through an act to which both parties consent'.[120] This relation, created by the mutual recognition of two individuals as equal in

[114] Piers Beirne and Robert Sharlet, 'Editors' Introduction', in Beirne and Sharlet (eds.), *Pashukanis: Selected Writings on Marxism and Law*, trans. Peter B. Maggs (London: Academic Press, 1980), 1–36 at 26–7.

[115] See e.g. Robert Knox, 'Marxism, International Law and Political Strategies', 22 *Leiden Journal of International Law* (2009): 413–36.

[116] China Miéville, *Between Equal Rights: A Marxist Theory of International Law* (Leiden, Boston, MA: Brill, 2005), 9–37.

[117] Pashukanis, 'Preface to the Second Russian Edition', 39.

[118] Pashukanis, *General Theory*, 117.

[119] Dragan Milovanovic, 'Introduction to the Third Edition', in Pashukanis, *General Theory*, i–xxvi at xii.

[120] Karl Marx, *Capital: A Critique of Political Economy*, Vol. 1, trans. Ben Fowkes (Harmondsworth: Penguin, 1978), 178.

terms of their rights to own and exchange their goods and labour power, and free in the negative sense to do so (however hungry one might be in relation to the other), was the essence of the 'juridical relation', which in turn 'mirror[ed] the economic relation'.[121]

It was on this aspect of Marx's writings that Pashukanis focused his attention. Three elements of his focus in this regard are central to Edelman's argument, and will be equally central to the elaboration of the process of 'international legal reproduction' made in this book. Firstly, Pashukanis argued, the 'free' and 'equal' legal subject is not a creation which emerges vertically from the command of the sovereign, but rather horizontally, through the practice of exchanging commodities. As China Miéville has emphasised, this argument solves international law's classical conundrum (as to the origins of legal obligation in the absence of an international sovereign) instantly.[122] Indeed, for Pashukanis, early international law arose precisely through practices of exchange between 'tribes' and other non-state communities.[123] Secondly, the fact that law should be understood as part of the 'ideology' of capitalism did not mean, Pashukanis claimed, that law had 'an *exclusively* psychological significance'.[124] On the contrary, the relationship between the material (practices of commodity production and exchange and their results) and the ideological (individuals' self-understanding as formally free, negatively equal subjects of law) was, in his view, a dialogical one (to borrow a term from Pashukanis's contemporary, Mikhail Bakhtin).[125] To focus on the coercive aspect of law's character exclusively, as though it were 'the central, fundamental, and only characteristic trait of legal phenomena', was to ignore the equally important question of 'the fundamental characteristics of the legal superstructure as an objective phenomenon'. Most importantly, it was to ignore the question of the 'free' and 'equal' legal subject,[126] the 'atom of legal theory' – embodying a status which, far from being the natural 'birthright of every man, woman and child' (to recall Hillary Clinton's words), follows 'with absolute inevitability from the conditions of the economy based on the commodity and money'.[127] But how does this actually happen; does

121 Marx, *Capital*, Vol. 1, 178.

122 Miéville, *Between Equal Rights*, 9–37.

123 Pashukanis, *General Theory*, 95.

124 Ibid., 74. Emphasis in the original.

125 Ibid., 76.

126 Ibid., 39–41.

127 Pashukanis, *General Theory*, 109. According to Miéville, Pashukanis missed the point that 'violence and coercion are immanent in the commodity relationship itself' (Miéville, *Between Equal Rights*, 133). On my reading, this correction does not seem necessary, for

it mean that all individuals within any capitalist society have been transformed into automatons, unable to conceptualise any alternative; and what does any of this have to tell us about the relationship between equality and inequality in the sphere of the international?

2.2 *Interpellation, from Althusser to Edelman*

In order to respond to the first part of this question, Edelman turned to Althusser's elaboration of the process through which the individual citizens of capitalist states come to recognise themselves as 'always already subjects' of that very particular form of society.[128] Althusser, like Pashukanis, argued that the answer involved both coercion and consent. This was a question both of what Althusser called the 'repressive' apparatus of the state (the government, army, police, courts and so on), and of the state's 'ideological' apparatus (operating through the various institutions of everyday life, including the church, the school, the family, the media and the law).[129] Ideology, according to Althusser, drawing on the work of both Antonio Gramsci and Sigmund Freud, was thus 'a "representation" of the imaginary relationship of individuals to their real conditions of existence'.[130]

Also like Pashukanis, Althusser argued that 'the decisive central term on which everything else depends' is 'the notion of the subject', whose constitution is the purpose of ideology, and whose purpose is, in turn, to reproduce that ideology.[131] The crucial term in this process of mutual constitution and reproduction is 'interpellation' – the call ('*Hey, you there!*') which 'hails' the individual as a subject of a particular kind, belonging to a particular society, and hence not just as an answering but also as a 'hailing' subject themselves.[132] But what is the origin of this circular process? According to Althusser, the interpellation of individuals as subjects presupposes 'the "existence" of a Unique and central Other Subject' – that is, God – 'in whose Name the religious ideology interpel-

the coercive element of law is Pashukanis's point of departure, just as it is Benjamin's. Moreover, and as Robert Knox has pointed out, there are two dangers that stem from overemphasising the coercive character of law: first, that of downplaying other non-material (economic and ideological) forms of force; second, that of underestimating the space for resistance (Knox, 'Marxism, International Law and Political Strategies', at 423–6).

128 Althusser, 'Ideology and Ideological State Apparatuses', 46.

129 Ibid., 16–17.

130 Ibid., 36.

131 Ibid., 44–5.

132 Ibid., 47–51.

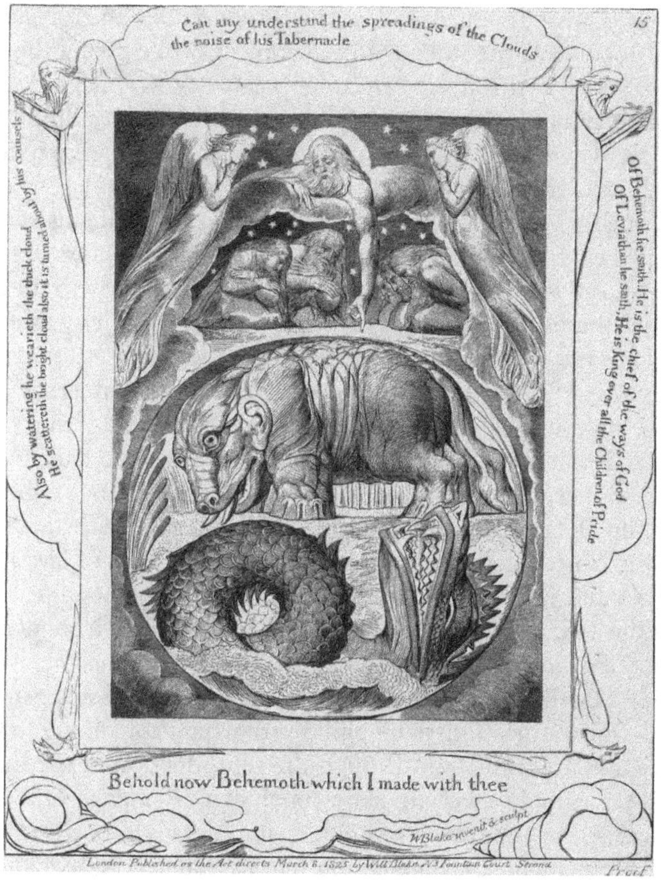

Figure 2 William Blake, 'Behemoth and Leviathan' (plate 15, fragment), from *Illustrations of the Book of Job* (London, 1825), engraving © The British Library Board, K.T.C.7.b.4, p. 15; asset: 076210, by kind permission.

lates all individuals as subjects'.[133] In Althusser's words: 'the structure of all ideology, interpellating individuals as subjects in the name of a Unique and Absolute subject is *specular*, i.e. a mirror-structure, and *doubly* specular: this mirror duplication is constitutive of ideology and ensures its functioning'.[134] In this way, 'the Absolute Subject ... interpellates around

[133] Ibid., 53.
[134] Ibid., 54. Emphasis in the original.

it the infinity of individuals into subjects in a double mirror-connexion such that it subjects the *subjects* to the Subject, while giving them in the Subject in which each subject can contemplate its own image … the absolute guarantee that everything really is so, and that on condition that the subjects recognize what they are and behave accordingly, everything will be all right: Amen – '*So be it*'.[135]

Yet Althusser's response leaves one very big question unanswered: who or what is the Absolute Subject and how does s/he or it come into being? Althusser is only really able to respond to this question with the analogy of a single (that is, monotheistic) God, a cultural specificity that is compounded by his hypothetical society's unabashedly Western European characteristics.[136] This helps us little when it comes to understanding the role of the state, and of law, in spreading capitalist relations of production and exchange out over the world as a whole. But Edelman has a more convincing response. The 'great subject', for him, is not God but rather *capital itself*. Capital, he suggests, is precisely what is reproduced when the individual, thinking of herself as a 'free' and 'equal' subject of law, identifies her powers and products as private property and sets about exchanging them on the 'free' market.[137] Again, this process is as much about coercion as it is about interpellation. But while its coercive dimensions have been theorised,[138] Edelman's contribution is to offer a materialist explanation of the forces of mystification, habit and desire which contribute to the process of capital accumulation through the reproduction of the individual legal subject. Simply by going about one's daily existence in a capitalist state, governed by the rule of law, Edelman points out, one is interpellating, whether palpably or imperceptibly, as capital, through one's identification as a legal subject who is formally 'free' and 'equal' in the way this form of subjectivity implies. Above all, this conditioning takes place in the 'sphere of circulation' or exchange – that is, when we clock in at work in the morning, buy food for our children, stay awake at night worrying about the price of fertiliser or, indeed, deny a pay rise to the workers in our chain of shops – a sphere that Edelman identifies with that of 'civil society' itself.[139] '*Homo oeconomicus*', he writes, 'is the producer of

[135] Ibid., 54–5. Emphasis in the original.

[136] On Althusser's efforts to escape Marxism's Eurocentrism see Young, *White Mythologies*, 83–114.

[137] Edelman, *Ownership of the Image*, 97.

[138] See, for example, Robert Hale, 'Coercion and Distribution in a Supposedly Non-Coercive State', 38 *Political Science Quarterly* (1923): 470–94 at 472–3.

[139] Edelman, *Ownership of the Image*, 94.

commodities, and he alone is the active member of civil society'.[140] It is law that 'fixes' civil society/the sphere of circulation as separate from the 'sphere of production', with profoundly ideological consequences.[141] For in concretising this separation, the law 'promulgat[es] the decrees of the rights of man and of the citizen' and puts 'the marks of property, freedom, and equality on the face of exchange value'.[142] But in convincing us that 'real life', as it were, takes place within civil society/the sphere of circulation, the law encourages us to forget that in the 'sphere of production', that 'secret "other place"', as he calls it, 'these marks are read as exploitation, slavery, inequality and sacred egoism'.[143] To put it in simpler terms, Edelman's argument is that the practice of existing, in the material world, while thinking of oneself as a legal subject, has the effect of collapsing production into circulation, as though production were just another aspect of circulation, in which it is natural and proper that labour-power should be bought and sold like any other commodity. But this, Edelman underscores, is an illusion, for the only thing that is visibly produced (or rather reproduced) in the sphere of circulation is legal subjectivity itself.[144]

Interestingly, this reading allows Edelman to reinterpret the idealist histories of the transformations of seventeenth-century Europe written by two of the great critical philosophers of the Enlightenment as having laid the normative ground from which capitalist relations could be celebrated as the apotheosis of individual emancipation. Both Kant and Hegel, Edelman argues, interpret the collapse of feudalism, and the gradual metamorphosis of serf into citizen, as a revolutionary process of universal emancipation in which an individual could no longer be treated as the property of another. As Edelman points out, however, drawing on Engels,[145] these changes altered little about the material conditions of daily existence for serfs-turned-free-labourers. Indeed (and as we shall see further in Item 2), by framing their labour as having been freely given to an individual of equal status in exchange for wages, that transformation endowed their conditions with a new legitimacy, facilitating ever-greater levels of exploitation.[146] Indeed, as Edelman points out, since legal

[140] Ibid., 166.
[141] Ibid., 92.
[142] Ibid., 94.
[143] Ibid., 94.
[144] Ibid., 97.
[145] See especially Frederick Engels [1877], 'Anti-Dühring. Herr Eugen Dühring's Revolution in Science', trans. Emile Burns, in *Marx and Engels: Collected Works*, Vol. 25 (Lawrence & Wishart Electronic Book, 2010), 5–311 at 88–98.
[146] Edelman, *Ownership of the Image*, 159.

subjectivity is 'defined through the juridico-political framework ... in virtue of its being opposed to slavery, it is slavery that constitutes [legal] personality'; thus, 'only the suppression of slavery will permit [legal] personality to achieve universalisation.'[147] This leads us to 'the amazing revelation that the juridical production of freedom is the *production of oneself as slave*.'[148] This capitalist form of slavery – wage labour, in short – is arguably no less diabolical, since it is enacted by the self upon the self. The capitalist subject, *qua* 'subject in law,' is thus 'alienated' even 'from his own freedom.'[149]

2.3 Government and the Micro/Macro Legal Subject

Yet there is still a large piece missing from this puzzle. Notwithstanding the central role played by the state in both Althusser and Edelman, neither offers any explanation as to how the state *itself* – the *international* legal subject – is reproduced. Meanwhile, Pashukanis, while he does tackle this question, offers little more than a critical take on the 'domestic analogy'. There might be lesser subjects of international law, such as colonies or protectorates, just as there are lesser subjects of domestic law, such as children or animals; yet the epitome of international legal subjectivity, the sovereign state, continues to be characterised, following Vattel, as the individual subject of domestic law 'writ large.'[150] Just as capitalists are permitted by law to dominate the dispossessed, Pashukanis argued, so capitalist states are permitted to dominate weaker polities, and less powerful 'sovereign equals'. This leads him to his famous conclusion that 'modern international law is the legal form of the struggle of the capitalist states among themselves for domination over the rest of the world.'[151] As Miéville has emphasised in particular, this suggests that in the international legal context (as Marx noted in the context of domestic labour law) '[b]etween equal rights, force decides.'[152]

147 Ibid., 183.
148 Ibid., 73. Emphasis in the original.
149 Ibid., 73. Emphasis in the original.
150 As Thomas Holland put it, 'The Law of Nations is but private law "writ large". It is an application to political communities of those legal ideas which were originally applied to relations between individuals.' Quoted in Thomas Erskine Holland, *Studies in International Law and Diplomacy* (Oxford: Clarendon Press, 1898), 152. See further Item 2, Section 2.1, below.
151 Pashukanis, 'International Law' [1925], in *Selected Writings*, 168–83 at 169. Emphasis removed.
152 Marx, *Capital*, Vol. 1, 344.

However, if this is the *only* conclusion we can come to about international law, it leaves many questions unanswered. Why (to return to some of the issues highlighted in the Stand) have certain communities, repeatedly crushed by the operation of international law, continued to fight so consistently for the right to become sovereign states themselves? How can we explain the success of some of them in doing so if international law is determined exclusively by those states with the greatest access to coercive power? How is it possible, conversely, that immensely powerful empires have now been reduced to marginal players, struggling under a mountain of international debt? As we are about to see once we move in from the Frame to the contents of this shadow-box, one way of responding to these questions is by discarding the assumption that the relationship between micro (individual) and macro (international) legal subjectivity is simply analogous, and considering, instead, the possibility that there might be a material connection between the two. As the following chapters will show, the process of interpellation can be understood as applying at the level of international legal subjectivity no less forcefully than it does at the domestic level. Moreover, this interpellative process does more than just mirror its equivalent at the domestic level. On the contrary, Items 2 and 3 will demonstrate that the process of international legal reproduction, as I have called it, *supports* the process of individual legal reproduction under domestic law in a particular way. The mechanism through which it does this is the apparently innocuous concept of 'government', which, far from operating as a neutral 'criterion' of statehood, has in the context of reproducing new international persons historically referred to a legal and institutional apparatus that is dedicated to reproducing human beings as individual legal subjects in the sense described by both Pashukanis and Edelman. Again, as I will demonstrate, this process operates both though coercion and through desire. On the one hand, the non-European world has gradually been forced to reconstitute its myriad alternative normative orders and practices of self-organisation in this way or face the consequences – consequences which have ranged from outright colonisation to more recent forms of armed intervention designed, for example, to 'protect' communities from their supposedly inadequate 'governments'. On the other hand, having been denied the rights associated with legal subjectivity on the grounds of alleged barbarity and backwardness, dominated individuals and communities across the world have responded with counter-assertions of civilisation and advancement, accompanied by the demand to be treated as 'free' and 'equal'. Meanwhile, this conditional relationship between international and individual legal subjectivity has, historically, allowed those international personalities which have proved themselves most efficient at protecting and reproducing the rights and duties associated with legal subjectivity to police and discipline those who have not, justifying their actions on the basis of the claim that the latter's rights, for example, to non-intervention and territorial integrity have been forfeited.

As the Ethiopian Empire's experience underscores, however, no less than the present-day struggle for Indigenous self-determination on Indigenous terms, not every consciousness has been successfully 'interpellated', nor has every body (whether individual or collective) been fully coerced. Important as the process of international legal reproduction is in helping to explain how our world has come to look and feel the way it does, we should not fall into the trap of 'false necessity'[153] by overestimating the extent to which that process determines, in an absolute sense, the subjectivity of individuals and communities across the world. Even when communities *have* made the decision to identify as states in the hope of being treated as formally equal sovereigns under international law, they often continue, in sometimes very subtle ways, to insist that this 'sameness' must not be understood as extinguishing their right to be treated equally on their own terms. It is for this reason that international personality is presented, in this book, as an essentially hybrid status. Having been constituted, in all but a tiny handful of 'prototypical' Western European states, on the basis of an external template, almost all subjects of international law retain something along the lines of what the philosopher Emmanuel Lévinas called the 'trace of the other'.[154] As the next section will demonstrate, examining the work of Mikhail Bakhtin, as taken up by Homi Bhabha, while hybridity may be a curse in many respects, it can also be deployed, under certain circumstances, in self-defence.

3 Towards a Materialist Theory of Hybridity and Resistance

The concept of hybridity has been taken up recently by a number of historians of international law, and in particular by a group of Latin American international legal scholars. Pioneering in this body of work is Liliana Obregón's 'Between Civilization and Barbarism: Creole Interventions in

[153] Marks, 'False Contingency', 2–5.

[154] See Emmanuel Lévinas, 'La Trace de L'Autre', 25 *Tijdschrift voor Filosophie* (1963): 603–23; English translation: 'The Trace of the Other', trans. Alphonso Lingis, in Mark Taylor (ed.), *Deconstruction in Context* (University of Chicago Press, 1986), 345–59.

International Law', which came out in 2006.[155] In this article, Obregón draws our attention to the development of a particular '*Criollo* legal consciousness' in Latin America up to the mid twentieth century, corresponding to the paradoxical position of Creole elites in the region as European in heritage and yet also non-European – and hence beyond the pale of 'civilised' international law – by birth. A few years later, in 2014, Arnulf Becker Lorca took up the theme, putting forward the idea of a 'mestizo' understanding of international law. According to Becker, 'during the second half of the nineteenth century, non-Western jurists appropriated classical international law, transforming European international law into a universal regime'.[156]

Like Obregón and Becker, I treat hybridity in this book as a metaphorical device through which to think about international law's mixed origins and impact. I also understand hybridity in two other ways as well, however. Firstly, hybridity is approached here as a material condition relating to the legal make-up and distributive effects of international personality. Secondly, I also engage with what Bakhtin terms the process of hybridisation, understood here as a tactic of discursive resistance. The following subsections will unpack these two understandings of hybridity one by one.

3.1 Substantive Hybridity and International Personality

The term hybridity, referring to the product of two different species of animal or plant, was rarely used in relation to human beings before the mid nineteenth century, when the Enlightenment's 'humanitarian ideas of universality, sameness and equality' began to give way.[157] In Spanish and Portuguese America, for instance, so-called *métissage* ('miscegenation') between colonials and Native Americans was commonplace until the late eighteenth century.[158] However, by about 1850, as the post-colonial theorist Robert Young points out, the so-called polygenesis ('many species') argument, to the effect that 'the White and the Negro are two distinct

[155] Liliana Obregón, 'Between Civilization and Barbarism: Creole Interventions in International Law', 27 *Third World Quarterly* (2006): 815–32.

[156] Arnulf Becker Lorca, *Mestizo International Law: A Global Intellectual History, 1842–1933* (Cambridge University Press, 2014), 15.

[157] Robert J. C. Young, *Colonial Desire: Hybridity in Theory, Culture and Race* (New York, London: Routledge, 1985), 8.

[158] Jane Samson, *Race and Empire* (Harlow: Pearson Education, 2005), 63.

species',[159] had risen to the position of reigning orthodoxy within the nascent social sciences. The starting point of the debate over 'human hybridity' was the biological axiom that animal hybrids are infertile (hence the term *mulatto*, from the Old Spanish word, *mulo*, for the offspring of a donkey and horse).[160] The debate therefore hinged on the rather startling question of the fertility or infertility of mixed-race individuals.[161]

One of the most common theories as to the consequences of miscegenation included the hypothesis that 'inferior' racial characteristics could be 'bred out' through 'amalgamation'. Another was its negative, the supposition that 'miscegenation produces a mongrel group ... a corruption of the originals, degenerate and degraded, threatening to subvert the vigour and virtue of the pure races with which they come into contact'.[162] On the one hand, Charles Darwin himself had argued that '[w]hen civilised nations come into contact with barbarians the struggle is short', indicating that the white race had little to fear from racial 'contamination'.[163] Yet the terror of such 'contamination' remained a powerful driver of colonial policy. According to majority opinion in the United States during the early twentieth century, there was 'great hazard in the mongrelising of distinctly unrelated races no matter how superior the original strains may be'.[164] From the complex *sistema de castas* used from the seventeenth century onwards throughout the Spanish Empire to designate the proportion of Spanish, Indigenous and African (and hence slave or former-slave) 'blood' in any given individual, to the long-lived British, French, Dutch and other European empires, terms such as *cholo* (the child of Indigenous American and *Mestizo*, i.e. Indigenous/white, parents), *zambo* (born to Indigenous American and African parents) and 'quadroon' (with one parent of European descent, the other 'half-caste', of mixed European and African or, in the Australian context, Aboriginal descent) were invented to designate the rank and social status of mixed-race individuals (see Figure 10).[165] Many, however, still

[159] Edward Long [1774], *The History of Jamaica: Reflections on its Situation, Settlements, Inhabitants, Climate, Products, Commerce, Laws and Government* (Montreal: McGill-Queen's University Press, 2003).

[160] Douglas Harper, 'Mulatto', *Online Etymology Dictionary*, 2014, available at www.etymonline.com/index.php?term=mulatto (accessed 10 August 2017).

[161] Young, *Colonial Desire*, 16–17.

[162] Young, *Colonial Desire*, 7.

[163] Charles Darwin, quoted in Young, *Colonial Desire*, 13.

[164] Michel Guyer quoted in Daniel J. Kevles, *In the Name of Eugenics: Genetics and the Uses of Human Heredity* (Cambridge, MA, London: Harvard University Press, 1995), 75.

[165] Sampson, *Race and Empire*, 36.

argued that mixed marriages ought to be encouraged on the grounds that the white race was naturally dominant.[166] In Australia, for example, some 100,000 Aboriginal and, in particular, part-Aboriginal children were taken from their homes with the aim of 'absorbing' them into white society. The purpose of this policy of 'absorption' – which went on, in various forms, until the 1970s – was, according to one Australian official, 'to breed out the colour by elevating female half-castes to white standard with a view to their absorption by mating into the white population'.[167]

By the first decades of the twentieth century, then, so-called 'human hybridity' had come to be understood as an objective process that could be controlled and even harnessed via the application of scientific and technological developments. This approach reached its apogee in the eugenics movement of the 1920s and 30s[168] – a movement founded on the idea that 'the physical, mental, and behavioural qualities of the human race could be improved by suitable management and manipulation of its hereditary essence'.[169] On the one hand, 'positive' eugenics aimed to 'foster more prolific breeding among the socially meritorious', while 'negative eugenics' intended to 'encourage the socially disadvantaged to breed less – or, better yet, not at all'.[170] Between 1907 and 1917, sixteen Southern states in the US had enacted compulsory sterilisation laws targeting 'habitual or confirmed criminals, or persons guilty of some particular offence, like rape', as well as the mentally ill.[171] But the most infamous eugenics programme of all remains that of Nazi Germany, where the 1933 *Law for the Prevention*

[166] See e.g. F. James Davis, *Who is Black? One Nation's Definition* (University Park, PA: Pennsylvania State University Press, 1991). Black and Native Americans were treated differently under US law, with Southern states tending to use the 'one-drop rule' in the African-American context, and the so-called 'blood quantum' rule, according to which only those with more than one-sixteenth Native American blood were considered 'Indian', in the Native American context.

[167] Quoted in Sampson, *Race and Empire*, 78. For example, Cecil Cook, chief medical officer and chief protector of Aborigines in North Australia (today the Northern Territory), 1927–39, argued that '[t]he problem of our half-castes will be quickly eliminated by the complete disappearance of the black race, and the swift submersion of their progeny in the white'. Ibid., 137. Cook was 'proud to report in 1934' that '[p]ractically all half-caste children of both sexes, formerly left to live with aboriginals in compounds and bush camps' had been 'removed to half-caste institutions under Government control'. Tim Rowse, 'Cook, Cecil Evelyn Aufrere (Mick) (1897–1985)', *Australian Dictionary of Biography*, Vol. 17 (Melbourne University Press, 2007),

[168] Kevles, *In the Name of Eugenics*, 57–61.

[169] Ibid., ix.

[170] Ibid., 85.

[171] Ibid., 100.

of Genetically Diseased Offspring mandated the compulsory sterilisation of all German citizens who suffered from diseases deemed 'hereditary' in order to avoid 'poisoning the entire bloodstream of the [German] race'.[172] Anyone with '1. Congenital feeble-mindedness, 2. Schizophrenia, 3. Manic-depression, 4. Hereditary epilepsy, 5. Hereditary St Vitus dance (Huntington's Chorea), 6. Hereditary blindness, 7. Hereditary deafness, 8. Serious hereditary physical deformity', or 'chronic alcoholism' was destined for the *Hitlerschnitt* ('Hitler cut').[173] Simultaneously, positive eugenics strategies designed to create an Aryan elite were rolled out, with generous loans provided to 'biologically sound couples whose fecundity would likely be a credit to the *Volk* ['nation']'.[174] In 1935, the Nazi eugenics and racial programmes were merged when the 'Nuremberg laws' prohibited all unions between the two sides of a new dichotomy: 'Germans' and 'Jews'. And in 1939 'the Third Reich moved beyond sterilisation to inaugurate euthanasia upon certain classes of the [supposedly] mentally diseased or disabled in German asylums', including homosexuals, as well as Jews, Roma, Poles, Slavs and other 'enemies of the state'.[175]

Importantly, however, whether 'positive' or 'negative', the eugenics movement consistently referred back to a template based on an idealised image of the rational individual. The role of race, in this context, was to operate as a marker of rationality. Whether race was viewed as something that could be 'bred out', overwritten via socialisation, or would render an individual permanently 'retarded', human beings were assumed to be less-than-rational to the extent that they were less-than-white. Crucially, as we shall see further in Item 2, the rationality considered germane to 'Caucasian' individuals was closely linked to the profit-maximising rationality of the *homo oeconomicus*, as Jennifer Beard has pointed out, drawing on Étienne Balibar's history of the emergence of '*Man as* (a, the) *subject*'.[176] Balibar's central point here is that the notion of the subject that

[172] Ibid., 116–17.

[173] *Law for the Prevention of Genetically Diseased Offspring*, 14 July 1933, reprinted in US Chief Counsel for the Prosecution of Axis Criminality, Nazi Conspiracy and Aggression. Vol. 5 (Washington, DC: United States Government Printing Office, 1946), Document 3067-PS, 880–83 (English translation by the staff of the Nuremberg Court); Robert N. Proctor, *Racial Hygiene: Medicine under the Nazis* (Cambridge, MA: Harvard University Press, 1990), 105–7.

[174] Kevles, *In the Name of Eugenics*, 117.

[175] See generally Henry Friedlander, *The Origins of Nazi Genocide: From Euthanasia to the Final Solution* (Chapel Hill, NC: University of North Carolina Press, 1995).

[176] Étienne Balibar, 'Subjection and Subjectivation', in Joan Copjec (ed.), *Supposing the Subject* (London: Verso, 1994), 1–16 at 4. Emphasis in the original.

emerged in the Christian Western European context 'is basically a *responsible*, or an *accountable*, subject'. This means, Balibar argues, 'he has to ... give an account (*rationem reddere*) of himself, i.e. of his actions and intentions, before another person, who righteously interpellates him. Not a Big Brother, but a Big Other – as Lacan would say'. Whereas in the political 'field' the subject 'is subjected *to* the sovereign, the lord, ultimately Lord God', in the metaphysical 'field' that subject 'necessarily *subjects himself to himself* or, if you like, performs his own subjection' independently of any external authority.[177] Rationality, as Beard points out, is precisely this 'interiorized voice' – no more and no less than that which Adam Smith called the 'invisible hand'.[178] As we shall see, for example in the following chapter's discussion of the work of Francisco de Vitoria, moreover, just as individual irrationality (often assumed on the basis of race) was used to justify the denial of individual rights (to reproduce, for example, or sit down in the bus) at the domestic law level, so international law has used a collective understanding of (ir)rationality to legitimise varying degrees of external control, including full-scale colonisation. This collective manifestation of rationality (of which race has also been used as a marker) is more commonly known as 'government', or more specifically, as I will argue, as 'self-government'.

3.2 Discursive Hybridisation as a Strategy of Resistance

We have just seen how, thanks to the association between hybridity and impurity, to be designated 'mixed' in any substantive sense has often enabled and legitimated practices of oppression. However, if we move into the sphere of language, mixed-up-ness has far more positive connotations, as semioticians and post-colonial theorists have argued. Hugely influential in this regard has been a group of materialist theorists of language and

177 Ibid., 9–10. Emphasis in the original.

178 Jennifer Beard, *The Political Economy of Desire: International Law, Development and the Nation State* (Abingdon, New York: Routledge-Cavendish, 2007), 6. For a related point in the human rights context, see Balakrishnan Rajagopal's argument that 'the "human" in human rights is the *Homo oeconomicus*, the modern market being who is possessed of full rationality, and whose attempts to realize his or her full potentialities are confined within the moral possibilities of the state and the material conditions of the global market' – one reason, he suggests, why 'international law has remained oblivious to the violence of the development encounter'. Balakrishnan Rajagopal, 'International Law and the Development Encounter: Violence and Resistance at the Margins', 93 *American Society of International Law Proceedings* (1999): 16–27 at 23.

literature active in Russia during the first decades after the Soviet revolution, the most famous of whom is Mikhail Bakhtin.[179]

In a direct challenge to the then-dominant linguistic structuralism of Ferdinand de Saussure, these theorists argued that the relationship between any two concepts should be assessed on the basis, not of a series of rigid binaries, but instead on the basis of a scale grounded in the material relations of social life, running from the oppositional or 'dialectical' to what they called the 'dialogical'. Concepts, words, phrases – 'utterances' in general – were, they argued, always and inevitably mixed. As Bakhtin put it: '[t]he living utterance, having taken meaning and shape at a particular historical moment in a socially specific environment, cannot fail to brush up against thousands of living dialogic threads, woven by socio-ideological consciousness around the given object of an utterance; it cannot fail to become an active participant in social dialogue'.[180] Individual 'utterances' (or *paroles*, to use Saussure's term) did not simply reflect the overall linguistic system (*langue*) but were affected themselves both by that system/code *and* by extra-systemic, socio-economic forces and structures. As Bakhtin's colleague Valentin Vološinov put it in *Marxism and the Philosophy of Language*, 'the word is a *two-sided act* ... determined equally by *whose* word it is and *for whom* it is meant'.[181]

Utterances, then, were not just passive reflections of an external linguistic structure, but rather bore within them the traces of different constellations of power and resources, and were themselves oriented towards affecting such constellations. Bakhtin therefore pointed to a continuum between two forms of 'discourse' – that of the status quo, on the one hand, and that of those who might have reason to challenge it, on the other. 'Authoritative' discourse, contained in the utterances of states, fathers, managers and so on, he said, was concerned to close off, petrify and 'finalise' the meaning of words; to shut down channels by which official meaning, given to them from 'on high', as it were, might be contested.[182] For 'authoritative discourse' is 'indissolubly fused with ... political power, an institution, a person'; it 'demands that we acknowledge it, that we make it

[179] Among the other semioticians active in the 'Bakhtin Circle' were Matvei Isaevich Kagan, Pavel Nikolaevich Medvedev, Lev Vasilievich Pumpianskii and Valentin Vološinov.

[180] Mikhail Bakhtin, 'Discourse in the Novel', in Michael Holquist (ed.), *The Dialogic Imagination: Four Essays by M. M. Bakhtin*, trans. Caryl Emerson and Michael Holquist (Austin, TX: University of Texas Press, 1981), 259–422, at 276.

[181] Valentin Nikolaevich Vološinov, *Marxism and the Philosophy of Language*, trans. Ladislav Matejka and I. R. Titunik (Cambridge, MA: Harvard University Press, 1986), 86. Emphasis in the original.

[182] Graham Allen, *Intertextuality* (London: Routledge, 2000), 22.

our own' and 'binds us, quite independently of any power it might have to persuade us internally' so that 'we encounter it ... with its authority already fused to it'.[183] This kind of language should therefore be understood as 'monologic' and as acting as a 'centripetal force' on social meaning.[184] By contrast, the kind of language that flourishes when authoritarian conditions are challenged is 'dialogic', in Bakhtin's terminology – open, free, egalitarian, 'internally-persuasive' (as opposed to 'authoritative') and 'unfinalisable' – its meaning continually subject to contestation and innovation.[185] Under conditions of social liberty and material equality, Bakhtin argued that language tends towards the dialogical, and therefore acts upon existing linguistic systems as a 'centrifugal force', pulling meaning outwards in all directions. Otherness becomes, under such conditions, not an element to be pacified and incorporated but, instead, the key to 'creative' understanding.[186] In a truly 'dialogic encounter', therefore, the differences between 'self' and 'other' become multiple and flexible, rather than singular and oppositional.[187] In societies not stifled by authoritarian structures of power and hugely unequal distributions of resources, in other words, the self, like the dialogised word, becomes 'unfinalisable',[188] and the attempt to finalise it can only be an act of violence.

However, the conditions we are experiencing in the world today are not those of social liberty and material equality. On the contrary, the 'self-governing' state is now the only possible vehicle for collective emancipation, with the result (according to the argument presented here) that the human and material world has become a dangerously unequal place. To put this process in Bakhtinian terms, we can say that this incredibly specific form of 'self' or subject has become 'finalised', as attempts to articulate alternatives continue to be violently suppressed. If we were to

[183] Bakhtin, 'Discourse in the Novel', 342–3.

[184] Mikhail Bakhtin, 'Towards a Methodology for the Human Sciences', in *Speech Genres and Other Late Essays*, trans. Vern W. McGee (Austin, TX: University of Texas Press, 1986), 162.

[185] By contrast, 'internally-persuasive' discourse – the language used in dialogue between equals – is 'affirmed through assimilation', and is, therefore, hybrid by nature, being always 'half-ours and half-someone else's' – part that of the speaker, part that of those to whom she has listened, and part that of her interlocutor's anticipated response. Bakhtin, 'Discourse in the Novel', 345 (n. 5).

[186] Bakhtin, 'Towards a Methodology for the Human Sciences', 162.

[187] Mikhail Bakhtin, 'Response to a Question from the *Novy Mir* Editorial Staff', in *Speech Genres and Other Late Essays*, trans. Vern W. McGee (Austin, TX: University of Texas Press, 1986), 7.

[188] Mikhail Bakhtin, *Problems of Dostoevsky's Poetics*, ed. and trans. Caryl Emerson (Minneapolis, MN: University of Minnesota Press, 1984), 68.

bring Edelman's materialist theory of the reproduction of the legal subject together with Bakhtin's materialist linguistics, it becomes possible to characterise the language in which capital, the Absolute Subject, 'hails' the legal subject as the 'authoritative' and hence 'monologic' language of international law. International law is, after all, constructed primarily out of words of a particular type – namely the 'official' words uttered by states and their representatives. Not only do these words issue by definition from an authority that is backed up (as Benjamin and Pashukanis pointed out) by the threat of force. These words actually constitute and reconstitute that authority by positioning themselves as the 'source' of that authority. And if Benjamin is correct to argue that law's violence is a violence 'crowned by fate' – if the authority of states rests, by definition, on the bloody victory of one normative order and the suppression of all others – then the language of international law re-enacts this originary act of violence continually. Having lost the initial war (or refused to engage in it), non-state communities are, in effect, perpetually re-vanquished in the confrontation between their own normatively defanged words and the always-already violent discourse of international law.[189]

Nonetheless, Bakhtin's insistence on the irrepressibly dialogical quality of all language draws our attention to the fact that the potential for resistance must always exist somewhere. This brings us to his concept of 'hybridisation', referring to the 'mixture of two social languages within the limits of a single utterance, between two different linguistic consciousnesses, separated from one another by an epoch, by social differentiation or by some other factor'.[190] Hybridisation, Bakhtin argues, can take two different forms. The first is 'unconscious' and refers to the process through which different 'social languages' or 'socio-linguistic ... world views' mingle together 'organically' over time.[191] The second type of hybridisation is 'conscious' and refers to the practice by which a speaker or author intentially juxtaposes two discourses against one another in order to highlight a normative hierarchy between the two, and in particular the hypocrisy of one when contrasted against another.[192] 'Intentional' hybridisation, Bakhtin argues, is thus 'an act of authorial unmasking'.[193] The complete 'utterance', its splicing together of two 'social languages',

[189] See Rose Parfitt, 'The Spectre of Sources', 25 *EJIL* (2014): 297–306.
[190] Bakhtin, 'Discourse in the Novel', 358.
[191] Ibid., 360.
[192] Ibid., 307.
[193] Ibid., 304.

becomes 'double-voiced'.[194] Indeed, Bakhtin continues, sometimes 'one and the same word will belong simultaneously to two languages, two belief systems that intersect in a hybrid construction – and, consequently, the word has two contradictory meanings, two accents ...'[195]

The political potential contained in this idea has been explored, among others, by the post-colonial theorist Homi Bhabha in his figure of the colonial subject as 'mimic man'.[196] As Bhabha points out, colonial subjects are hybrid subjects by definition – at once 'self' to the extent that they either elect or are forced to mimic the pseudo-universal characteristics of the 'civilised' coloniser, and 'other' to the extent that the particular elements of their own existence remain – most visibly, of course, skin-colour. But as Bhabha notes, hybridity as a property of subjectivity is *itself* hybrid, at once oppressive, as we have seen, but also emancipatory to the extent that it can be instrumentalised by the colonial subject. The 'mimic man' is thus he (perhaps also she) whose very residual otherness plays out, for the coloniser, as mimicry, ridicule, or even as a menacing duality – at once familiar and disturbingly unfamiliar. From this perspective, the gap between 'original' (colonist) and 'copy' (colonial subject) can be used to '[unsettle] the mimetic or narcissistic demands of colonial power' while 'reimplicat[ing] its identifications in strategies of subversion that turn the gaze of the discriminated back on the eye of power.'[197]

As this and the previous subsection have indicated, then, these two (substantive and discursive) forms of hybridity are closely related. Hybridisation as a strategy is available only to those subjects who are, in a substantive sense, hybrids themselves. But we should also take care to read Bakhtin's contrasting modes of hybridisation critically and to attend to the relationship between them. It may be that in some contexts 'organic' hybridisation takes place peacefully. However, in the material world of unequally distributed power and other resources, this notion has clearly assimilationist implications, pointing to a risk that powerful 'social languages' might well 'organically' assimilate their less powerful ('internally-persuasive') partners, allowing for the quiet obliteration of entire 'world views', together with the communities they correspond to.

[194] Ibid., 360.

[195] Ibid., 304–5.

[196] Homi K. Bhabha, 'Of Mimicry and Man: The Ambivalence of Colonial Discourse', in Homi K. Bhabha, *The Location of Culture* (London, New York: Routledge, 1994), 121–31.

[197] Ibid., 142.

Figure 3 *Left*: Joseph Cornell, *Untitled: Mond-Oberflache (verso)* (1955), assemblage, mixed media, 15 5/8 x 17 3/16 x 2 3/8 in. *Right*: Joseph Cornell, *Pavilion (recto)*, (1953), assemblage, mixed media, 18 15/16 x 11 3/4 x 6 9/16 in © The Joseph and Robert Cornell Memorial Foundation. VAGA/Licenced by Viscopy, 2018. Photographed by Peter A. Juley & Son © Peter A. Juley & Son Collection, courtesy of the Smithsonian American Art Museum.

4 Conclusion

In building this Frame, I have responded to some of the methodological questions that were generated by the question posed at the very start of this book. In short, to paraphrase George Orwell, why are some sovereigns more equal than others? The task of bringing together the materialist historiography of Walter Benjamin, the materialist jurisprudence of Bernard Edelman and the materialist linguistics of Mikhail Bakhtin has been aimed at putting together a strong methodological framework for what follows – a modular history of international legal reproduction. I have given this modular history the form of a shadow-box. This assemblage technique was developed by the Surrealist movement – most famously by the American artist Joseph Cornell (see Figures 3 and 11) – as a method for assembling collections of found objects and images. With its capacity to act as a hinge between surface and depth, the shadow-box pushes the technique of montage another step away from the two-dimensional towards the three-dimensional, allowing different components to be layered on top of and juxtaposed against one another. When these elements are viewed together from different angles – angles which are both opened up and constrained by the shape of the box – a series of resonances (or *correspondances*, we might say, again recalling Benjamin) click into place – resonances that are at once spatial and temporal; at once dictated by the form of the box and introduced by the spectator.

This Frame, then, is designed to order and hold the contents of the box together in a particular manner, while also regulating the way in which the light falls into it, figuratively speaking, and orientating the gaze of the viewer in certain ways. Into that Frame, I will now place a series of six historical 'items'. Each is designed to tell a story of its own. However, when inserted into the box, both on top of and next to its other components, seen within the context of the Frame, each new historical item is designed to alter our perception of the whole, bringing certain elements into relief while rendering others less visible. Thus, Item 1 lays out the debate over the significance, for international law, of the Abyssinia Crisis. Item 2 adds a new dimension to the existing critical history of international law's origins. Through an examination of the emergence of a diverse set of international persons and non-persons, from the Island of Palmas to the 'Indians' of the 'new world' to the Chinese Empire to the Principality of Bulgaria, its aim is to draw attention to the way in which the nascent idea of international personality was tied, from the very beginning, to a particular understanding of the individual legal subject. In contrast to this 'long' history, Item 3 offers a more succinct (hi)story of international legal reproduction under the League of Nations. Similarly, this chapter contributes a new element to ongoing debate about international law and the League by linking together the experience of 'mandated territories', 'national states', 'enemy states' and other League entities as parts of a single story: the story of international legal reproduction.

Items 4, 5 and 6 then jump from a general history of the emergence of new international persons to a very specific history of the transformation of the Ethiopian Empire into a subject of international law. This part of the book, in particular, draws on research conducted at the Institute for Ethiopian Studies and the Centre français des études éthiopiennes in Addis Ababa, the League of Nations archives in Geneva, the archives of the Italian Ministero deli Affari Esteri in Rome and the UK National Archives in London. Item 4 outlines three historiographies of Ethiopia, beginning in the third century CE. Items 5 and 6 then juxtapose the 'view from Geneva' against the 'view from Addis Ababa' in their retelling, first of the story Ethiopia's entry into the League and then of the Crisis itself. In and through this process, the Abyssinia Crisis is shown to be both a unique episode, belonging to a particular time and place, *and* a paradigmatic example of the process of international legal reproduction, of its role in sustaining and expanding the material inequalities which pervade our global order, and of the cracks in that order which might be exploited for emancipatory ends.

Rather than offering a conclusion (something that would be out of place at the end of an argument whose objective it is to open up rather than to close down), the final component of the shadow-box operates as its lid. Taking another leap across a gap of more than eighty years, this chapter sets out to bring the process of international legal reproduction up to date. It does so firstly by pointing out some familiar qualities in the language of 'governance', 'responsibility' and 'prevention' that is currently being deployed by international institutions like the World Bank, the United Nations, the European Union and NATO. Secondly, it draws attention to what is undoubtedly the most resilient movement of resistance against the oppressive forms of international and individual subjectivity associated with international legal reproduction. This is, of course, the struggle of Indigenous peoples all over the world for self-determination on Indigenous terms – a struggle that is as old as the very earliest incarnations of the sovereign state.

Item No. 1

The 'Abyssinia Crisis' and International Law

This first Item in the shadow-box operates as the backdrop against which the other five Items can be viewed more clearly. The following pages explain why the Abyssinia Crisis is so important to the stability of international law's progress narrative. As we saw in the Stand, the story of the Abyssinia Crisis is constantly retold in almost exactly the same way. It is a regular feature on pedagogical programmes for international law, international history and international relations students. It is wheeled out just as regularly by state officials and diplomats in public speeches, particularly when questions of collective security arise. But what ideological work does this standard account perform to help prop up the manifestly unequal global status quo we inhabit today? And does the critique usually made of this account fare any better?

These are the questions to which I respond in this chapter. I first unpack the standard account and its imbrication with international law's teleological autobiography. I then examine two critiques that have been made of this standard account. The first argues that the League of Nations imposed a Eurocentric 'standard of civilisation' on Ethiopia. Yet, as we shall see, this account ends up reinforcing the very 'progress narrative' it sets out to attack. The second critique emerges from a 'genealogical' reading of the Crisis which blows any sense of international law's inherent progressivism to smithereens. However, like other genealogies, it leaves us with a conclusion that is normatively, and therefore politically, indeterminate. Finally, I return to the suggestion that only a more radically materialist legal history of the Abyssinia Crisis is capable of bringing to light precisely how closely its unfolding was implicated in a much wider process aimed at reconstructing the world in the image of a particular kind of 'free' and 'equal' or 'sovereign' legal subject.

1 Ethiopia and the League of Nations: The Standard Account and its Pathologies

In the field of diplomatic history, in particular, the significance of the Abyssinia Crisis is seen as lying in its capacity to illustrate the terminal shortcomings of the League system, underpinned by a well-meaning but toothless system of international law. Frank Hardie's account, written in the 1970s, remains typical:

> In the three years and six weeks between the end of the Abyssinian crisis and the start of the European War a whole world was shattered by the hammer blows of Franco, Hitler, Mussolini and Tojo; only in Spain and China were Fascism and foreign aggression stoutly resisted, as they had been in Abyssinia. Irresolute pressure on Mussolini had the effect, anticipated by many, of driving him into Hitler's camp ... The pace of the ... descent into Hell was appalling. The world of 1936–9 was in no sense unified by a League of Nations; much of it was divided into two armed and hostile camps; powerful States acted with no respect whatsoever for their pledged word. This indeed was 'international anarchy'.[1]

For Hardie, as this suggests, the Abyssinia Crisis should be understood as a tragic story of the world's 'descent into Hell' (anarchy) as the commitment of the League's member states to their 'pledged word' (international law) crumbled in the face of the fascist (political) threat.

One indication that Hardie's account, though published in 1974, is still fully in line with today's popular understanding of the significance of the Crisis can be found if we turn to the materials used by the 2016 London International Model United Nations (LIMUN) conference. Through the simulation of diplomatic crisis through role-play, LIMUN aims to 'equip youth with mediation, analytical and leadership skills, while stressing the interdependence of the modern world' in the hope that the 'next generation of global leaders will face issues of common concern with the spirit of international cooperation'.[2]

After the Abyssinia Crisis was chosen as the topic for competitive re-enactment in 2016, the conference organisers distributed a set of materials to participants containing background information about the episode. Participants were informed that:

> The Abyssinian Crisis of 1934–6 is seen as one of the key moments in the League's history, not only as a major international event in the inter-war

[1] Frank Hardie, *The Abyssinian Crisis* (London: Batsford, 1974), 226–7.

[2] See *London International Model United Nations* (LIMUN), at https://limun.org.uk (accessed 20 July 2017).

> period but as a monumental moment of failure for the League of Nations. The League's failure to act decisively in the conflict exposed it as powerless [and] contributed to the total loss of respect borne for it.[3]

In this very familiar interpretation, the substance of the Crisis was a situation in which 'Abyssinia' (a 'small state', in the League's vernacular) came to be caught between fascist Italy's legally nihilistic aggression and the cowardice of the leading League states (Britain and France in particular), whose fear of 'pushing Mussolini into Hitler's arms' led them to sacrifice Ethiopia's sovereignty in a desperate attempt to save their own. 'Abyssinia' (as Ethiopia is referred to throughout, even though, as their authors note, this is 'the European name for the Ethiopian Empire'[4]) is represented here as a straightforward victim of Depression-era international politics – a politics rendered so toxic by the rise of fascism that it was able to destroy international law's nascent commitment to collective security. The 'failure' of the League to prevent Ethiopia's annexation is thus bundled in with appeasement. As is well known, that ill-fated policy neither prevented fascist Italy's dreaded alliance with Nazi Germany, nor stalled the fascist bid for world domination; on the contrary, it ushered in precisely the second global conflagration that it had been the League's *raison d'être* to prevent. Appeasement, according to this standard account, began in Ethiopia.

The point of re-enacting the Abyssinia Crisis, from the point of view of LIMUN organisers, is evidently not to discover whether this interpretation has stood the test of time. The point, instead, is to extract a lesson which the 'next generation of global leaders' can utilise in their future careers. Most important among these is the lesson that the use of force in international relations will not be discouraged, and the rights both of sovereign equals and of 'free' and 'equal' individuals will not be protected, unless the legal system in place has 'teeth'. Having extracted this lesson from the 'failures' of the 1930s, international law can then be understood as having emerged all the stronger having learned, as it were, the hard way.

A very similar assessment of the meaning of the Abyssinia Crisis is to be found in histories of the discipline of international law. Arthur Nussbaum, for example, argued in 1950 that '[t]he fatal blow to the prestige of the League was its retreat before fascist Italy after Mussolini's

[3] 'League of Nations', *LIMUN* 17th Session, 2016, 4 at http://limun.org.uk/FCKfiles/File/2016_LoN_Guides.pdf (accessed 18 June 2016) (LIMUN 2016 Materials).

[4] LIMUN 2016 Materials, 4.

invasion and conquest of Abyssinia'.[5] Likewise, present-day undergraduate textbooks on international law invariably devote a sentence or two to the Abyssinia Crisis in their introductory chapters, deploying it as an illustration of the weakness and/or immaturity of the League of Nations system when compared with its successor. Antonio Cassese, for example, a former President of the International Criminal Tribunal for Yugoslavia, argues in the second edition of his well-known textbook that the 'naive hope' that the Covenant's failure to outlaw war completely in favour of a mandatory 'cool[ing] off' period 'proved illusory, as is shown by the case of the Italian aggression against Abyssinia, in 1935–6'.[6]

Underlying the lesson of the Crisis, then, is the bedrock assumption of international law: that all states, whatever their material strength and geopolitical position, possess a formally equal set of rights and duties. Italy, a materially strong state, is understood to have acted illegally by annexing Ethiopia, a materially weak state, because in doing so it violated a long-standing principle of customary international law, that of the sovereign equality of states – a principle which had also been codified in Article 10 of the Covenant, to which both states were signatories. From this position, the roles of the various protagonists in the standard account of the Abyssinia Crisis fall easily into place: fascist Italy is the determined aggressor, utterly contemptuous of international law; Ethiopia is the innocent victim of power politics, whose recognised rights the League states selfishly failed to vindicate. The inter-war system is thereby constructed as having failed for institutional and political reasons, rather than for legal reasons.

Nor is this rendition of the story of the Abyssinia Crisis confined to the schoolroom and the lecture hall. On the contrary, it is re-told again and again by the most important 'representatives' of the 'international community'. Lord Owen, a former co-chairman of the European Union Conference for the Former Yugoslavia, for example, wrote of his time in Geneva during the early 1990s, that 'sometimes, as I wandered at night through the deserted art deco halls, I felt haunted by the 1930s and wondered whether Yugoslavia would do to the UN what Abyssinia did to the League of

[5] Arthur Nussbaum, *A Concise History of the Law of Nations* (New York: Macmillan Company, 1950), 249–50.

[6] Antonio Cassese, *International Law* (2nd edn Oxford University Press, 2005), 37. For other similar examples in international law textbooks see e.g. Malcolm N. Shaw, *International Law* (7th edn Cambridge University Press, 2014), 884; Wade Mansell and Karen Openshaw, *International Law: A Critical Introduction* (Oxford and Portland, OR: Hart, 2013), 110–11; Marco Gerardo Monroy Cabra, *Derecho Internacional Público* (6th edn Bogotá: Temis, 2011), 469; Jan Klabbers, *International Law* (2nd edn Cambridge University Press, 2017), 171.

Nations'.[7] Similarly, the Security Council's alleged paralysis was lambasted in 2003, during the fraught run-up to the invasion of Iraq, by US President George W. Bush on the grounds that '[w]e created the United Nations Security Council, so that, unlike the League of Nations, our deliberations would be more than talk, our resolutions would be more than wishes'.[8] Yet if we step back from the events of 1935 to view them in the context of the mid 1930s, it becomes apparent very quickly that the core assumption which underpins this standard account – that Ethiopia and Italy were sovereign equals at the time of the invasion – is implausible. Most importantly, there were, at the time of the Crisis, only three Black independent states in existence, each facing profound status problems of their own – Haiti and Liberia being the other two. The rest of Africa, the Caribbean and the Pacific, and a great deal of Asia, had been subjected, whether directly or indirectly, to the European *mission civilisatrice*. The Covenant itself spelled out that 'certain' groups were considered, by international law, 'not yet able to stand by themselves under the strenuous conditions of the modern world'.[9] That the representatives and interventions of the Ethiopian Empire could have been both regarded and treated as 'equal' to the representatives and interventions of, say, France or Britain in the context of an international legal order grounded in such social Darwinist assumptions is therefore highly unlikely and indeed turns out to be incorrect, as we shall see.[10]

That said, it is certainly the case that many throughout the world of the mid 1930s were horrified by what they saw as Ethiopia's betrayal by those charged with the enforcement of the Covenant. Ethiopia's betrayal, denounced by the Black community in the United States and Europe and by colonised peoples throughout the world, had a crucial galvanising

[7] David Owen, *Balkan Odyssey* (San Diego: Harvest Books, 1995), 41, quoted in Berman, 'Beyond Colonialism and Nationalism?', 319.

[8] Cited in Alexandru Grigorescu, 'Mapping the UN-League of Nations Analogy: Are There Still Lessons to be Learned from the League?' 11 *Global Governance* (2005), 25–42, 25. Bush used this analogy more than forty times in the two months which followed that speech (26).

[9] Covenant, Art. 22.

[10] This assumption is rarely questioned, whether on the political right or left of the spectrum of international law scholarship. Compare Carl Schmitt, 'Die siebente Wandlung des Genfer Völkerbundes,' in Carl Schmitt, *Positionen und Begriffe in Kampf mit Weimar-Genf-Versailles 1923–39* (2nd edn Berlin: Duncker & Humblot, 1988), 2010–13, on the one hand, with China Miéville, *Between Equal Rights : A Marxist Theory of International Law* (Leiden, Boston, MA: Brill, 2005), 260, 243, and Martti Koskenniemi, *From Apology to Utopia: The Structure of International Legal Argument* (Cambridge University Press, 2005), 592. See also Carl Schmitt [1950], *The Nomos of the Earth* (New York: Telos Press, 2003), 242. My thanks to Reut Paz for the translation.

effect on civil rights and decolonisation movements globally.[11] In Britain, Sylvia Pankhurst, daughter of Emmeline Pankhurst, dedicated herself to pressuring the British government to come to Ethiopia's aid, organising dozens of demonstrations and publishing a regular campaign newspaper, *The New Times and Ethiopia News*.[12] And in Europe more broadly, the public outcry which met the December 1935 leaking of the 'Hoare-Laval Pact' – a secret plan hatched by Britain, France and Italy which proposed to resolve the Crisis, essentially, by partitioning the Ethiopian Empire – was so violent that both of the foreign ministers from which the pact took its name were forced to resign.[13]

It is not my intention to dispute this outrage. Nor do I want to suggest that the League's official determination as to the war's illegality, together with its decision to place sanctions on Italy (though limited and highly ineffective), in accordance with Article 16 of the Covenant, should be taken lightly. My contention is, instead, that to move straight from this to the conclusion that the Ethiopian Empire was *therefore* Italy's sovereign equal, entitled as such to all the rights associated with full international

[11] Regretfully I do not have space, here, to examine in detail the reaction among Africans and the African diaspora to the news of the annexation. However, this story, which touches, among other things, on Marcus Garvey's Universal Negro Improvement Association and the rise of the Rastafari movement, has been told in many wonderful histories. See e.g. Joseph E. Harris, *African-American Reactions to War in Ethiopia, 1936–1941* (Baton Rouge, LA: Louisiana State University Press, 1994); William R. Scott, *The Sons of Sheba's Race: African-Americans and the Italo-Ethiopian War 1935–41* (Bloomington, IN: Indiana University Press, 1993); Robbie Shilliam, 'Intervention and Colonial-Modernity: Decolonising the Italy/Ethiopia Conflict Through Psalms 68:31', 39 *Review of International Studies* (2013): 1131–47; Shilliam, 'What about Marcus Garvey? Race and the Transformation of Sovereignty Debate', 32 *Review of International Studies* (2006): 379–400; and E. David Cronon, *Black Moses* (Madison, WI: University of Wisconsin Press, 1955), 19. Some of the most important interventions stemming directly from the annexation include G. G. Maragh (Leonard P. Howell) [1935], *The Promised Key* (Kingston, Jamaica: Headstart Printing and Publishing, 2003); W. E. B. Du Bois, 'Inter-Racial Implications of the Ethiopian Crisis: A Negro View', *Foreign Affairs* (October 1932): 82–92; C. L. R. James, 'I.L.P. Abyssinian Policy', *Controversy* (October 1935); James, 'Intervening in Abyssinia', *The New Leader*, 4 October 1935; George Padmore, 'Ethiopia Thrown to the Wolves', *The Crisis* (July 1935): 48; Padmore, 'Abyssinia Betrayed by the League of Nations', *The Crisis* (June 1937): 166–8; Charles H. Wesley, 'The Significance of the Italo-Abyssinian Question', *Opportunity*, May 1935: 148–51; J. M. Kenyatta, 'Hands off Abyssinia', *Labour Monthly*, September 1935: 532–45.

[12] Sylvia Pankhurst was knighted by Haile Selassie and moved to Addis Ababa with her son in 1956, where she is buried in state in Kidist Selassie [Holy Trinity] Cathedral. See Richard Pankhurst and Estelle Sylvia Pankhurst, *Sylvia Pankhurst, Artist and Crusader: An Intimate Portrait* (London: Paddington Press, 1979).

[13] See Item 6, Section 1.4.

personality, as reinforced by the rights in the League Covenant, is to move too quickly, short-circuiting a long and complex history of international legal ambivalence concerning the extent and resilience of Ethiopia's sovereignty.

Items 4, 5 and 6 unpack this ambivalence, as manifested in state practice and treaty-making, in some detail. Its most obvious manifestation, however, can be seen almost instantly. When the Ethiopian Empire applied for membership of the League of Nations in September 1923, the League's Sixth Committee (Political Questions),[14] whose job it was to examine the application, expressed doubts as to Ethiopia's capacity to meet the conditions set out in Article 2, paragraph 1 of the Covenant – most importantly, the condition that League membership was only open to 'self-governing' entities. Of particular concern to the Committee was the ongoing and widespread practice of slavery in the Ethiopian Empire at that time. In consequence, the Sixth Committee elected to make Ethiopia's accession to the Covenant conditional on its fulfilment of three conditions, or 'special obligations', as they were called. The Ethiopian Delegation was asked to accede, via a Special Declaration, firstly to Article 11 of the *Convention Revising the General Act of Berlin* (1919),[15] and secondly to Article 6 of the *Convention for the Control of the Trade in Arms and Ammunition* (1919).[16] Thirdly, Ethiopia agreed to the supervision of Ethiopia's performance of these undertakings by the League Council. The implications of the 'special obligations' emerged perhaps most glaringly 12 years later, during Italy's efforts to justify its impending invasion and annexation of the country (justifications which, as we shall see, were acceptable to many leading members of the League). As Italy argued in a lengthy memorandum, presented to the League Council on 4 September 1935:

> The Covenant has set up among the Members of the League a system of obligations and rights which are interdependent. No Member of the League can invoke rights derived from the Covenant unless it has ... failed to fulfil the general and special undertakings incumbent upon it in view of its membership. On the other hand, it would be contrary to all the principles of right and justice to expect that the members of the League should be called upon to observe the provisions of the Covenant in their relations

[14] 'Abyssinia's Request for Admission', Fifth Meeting, 20 September 1923, Records of the Fourth Assembly, Meetings of the Committees, Minutes of the Sixth Committee (Political Questions), in *LNOJ*, Special Supplement no. 19 (1923): 17–21.

[15] *Convention revising the General Act of Berlin, February 26, 1885, and the General Act and Declaration of Brussels, July 2, 1890*, Saint-Germain-en-Laye, 10 September 1919, Art. 11(1).

[16] *Convention for the Control of the Trade in Arms and Ammunition, and Protocol*, 10 September 1919, Saint-Germain-en-Laye, Art. 6.

> with a Member State which has placed itself outside the Covenant by violating the obligations undertaken.[17]
>
> The admission of Ethiopia to the League was a political act based on the belief that, through participation in the system of international co-operation represented by the League, Ethiopia could be led to make by herself the efforts necessary to approach, even though only gradually, the level of civilisation of the other peoples belonging to the international community ... Ethiopia has shown that she does not possess the qualifications necessary to enable her to obtain, through participation in the League, the impulse required to raise herself by voluntary efforts to the level of the other civilised nations ...
>
> Ethiopia has openly placed herself outside the Covenant of the League and has rendered herself unworthy of the trust placed in her when she was admitted to membership. Italy is rising up against such an intolerable situation, is defending her security, her rights and her dignity. She is also defending the prestige and good name of the League of Nations.[18]

Italy's argument was, quite simply, that the Ethiopian Empire had not met the conditions attached to its membership of the League and therefore was no longer entitled to the protections either of the Covenant or of international law more generally.

2 The Standard Critique of the Standard Account

This Section examines the most important arguments that have so far been launched against the standard account of the Abyssinia Crisis. The first point to note about these critiques is that most of them put forward more or less the same argument: namely that the Crisis should be understood as a classic illustration of the way in which international law, at least prior to 1945, was characterised by a Eurocentric 'standard of civilisation' which made it possible for the European powers to sacrifice Ethiopia's sovereignty much more easily than they would have been able to had Ethiopia been a European state. All three of the scholars examined in this Section suggest, in other words, that the League of Nations had clearly failed to fully throw off the social Darwinist assumptions of the nineteenth century.

Up to this point, there is much to be said for this argument. As soon as one looks carefully at the way each of them articulates it, however, a number of contradictions appear. Together, these contradictions underscore

[17] 'Situation in Ethiopia: Memorandum by the Italian Government, and Documents Relating Thereto', 4 September 1935, in *LNOJ* (November 1935): 1355–1417, 1416 ('Italian Memorandum').

[18] Italian Memorandum, 1416.

one of the key theoretical points made in the Frame, namely that international law's progressivist or teleological bias is impossible to exorcise on its own terms.

2.1 The 'Special Obligations' as a Standard of Civilisation

The international relations scholar Gerrit Gong, author of *The Standard of 'Civilization' in International Society*, is one of the most famous historians of the 'standard of civilisation' concept. Gong offers up 'Abyssinia' as a 'particularly pertinent' illustration of how the unabashedly Eurocentric 'standard of "civilization" was applied and received in Africa'.[19] Perhaps surprisingly, however, Gong's appraisal is positive overall. In his view, this originally European 'standard' was one of the most important of the 'catalysts for change' which eventually transformed the world, in the nineteenth and early twentieth centuries, into a 'society of states' defined by 'certain fundamental commonalities: common interests and values, commonly binding rules, and common institutions'.[20] That this standard had come to be universally accepted as a rule of customary international law by 1905 'at the latest' is his point of departure.

As Gong correctly points out, the question of the Ethiopian Empire's level of 'civilisation', and in particular the problem of slavery, were central to the debate which took place over Ethiopia's application for League membership. The Sixth Committee's rationale for admitting Ethiopia into the League was (as the Italian memo of 1935 noted) that this would 'help Abyssinia raise herself on the scale of civilisation, which it was possible she might do more effectively if she became a Member of the League'.[21] In other words, and as Gong suggests, the decision to welcome Ethiopia into the League on condition of its abolition of slavery confirms that it was judged to have failed to meet the conditions laid out in the questionnaire. In admitting Ethiopia as a member, the League saw itself as having taken on the duty of helping Ethiopia to meet these benchmarks or standards *in the future*, via their formalisation as a pair of 'special obligations' and the oversight of the League Council.

[19] Gerrit W. Gong, *The Standard of 'Civilization' in International Society* (Oxford: Clarendon Press, 1984), 119.

[20] Ibid., 3–4.

[21] Comments of Joseph Cook, Australian Delegate to the Sixth Committee, in 'Minutes of the Sixth Committee, Meetings of the Committees', Records of the Fourth Assembly, *LNOJ, Special Supplement* (Geneva, 1923), 13–15.

The international legal historian Jean Allain makes a similar argument.[22] As Allain puts it, Italy invoked Ethiopia's alleged non-fulfilment of the conditions in 1935 in order 'to de-legitimise Ethiopia as a less-than-equal State, as unworthy of membership in the League of Nations'.[23] On the one hand, Allain anchors his argument in the idea that '[t]he standard of civilisation which was applied in the Ethiopian context, upon which its admission to the League of Nations was predicated and later used to justify Italian aggression, was the abolition of slavery and the slave trade on its territory'.[24] On the other hand, however, Allain also argues, from the fact that compulsory economic sanctions *were* imposed on Italy by the League under Article 16, that Italy's arguments regarding Ethiopian 'barbarity' ultimately 'failed to carry the day' at Geneva.[25] The first part of his argument suggests that Ethiopia's annexation was provided for under international law; that the invasion was 'legal'. The second, however, suggests that Ethiopia was indeed an 'equal state' in relation to Italy after all, and that when Italy invaded Ethiopia it violated international law.[26] Allain concludes that '[d]espite having labelled Italy the aggressor, the European Powers abandoned Ethiopia to its fate, as the geo-politics of Europe meant that the "civilised nations" concentrated on positioning themselves for the barbary [*sic*] of what would come to be termed: the Second World War'.[27] This suggests, again, that Ethiopia was indeed an 'equal state' and that (as in the standard account) if only the Covenant had been properly enforced (if only the 'civilised nations' had not reneged on their responsibilities to protect Ethiopia's sovereign rights) the annexation would not have happened.

There is, in other words, an ambiguity in the ostensibly critical arguments offered by Gong and Allain on the basis of the standard of civilisation. Both authors imply, at certain points, that the 'special obligations' did provide a solid legal rationale for Ethiopia's annexation. However, both scholars also suggest that *Italy* is to be blamed for having instrumentalised those conditions illegitimately, implying that Ethiopia *was*, in fact, Italy's sovereign equal, notwithstanding the 'special obligations'. The former approach involves placing the blame with international law itself; the

[22] Jean Allain, 'Slavery and the League of Nations: Ethiopia as a Civilised Nation', 8 *JHIL* (2006): 213–44.
[23] Ibid., 238.
[24] Ibid., 213.
[25] Ibid., 238.
[26] Ibid., 238.
[27] Ibid., 244.

latter approach involves blaming the unsavoury politics associated with the rise of fascism, leaving international law itself unscathed.

A further difficulty concerns the substance of the standard of civilisation that Gong and Allain see as embodied by the 'special obligations' which, as we have just seen, were largely focused on the abolition of slavery in Ethiopia. Allain, an expert on slavery and international law, takes note of the gigantic controversy that arose over this question in 1922 and 1923.[28] As he notes, this controversy led not only to the decision to impose the 'special obligations', but also to 'the drafting of what is often considered the first international human rights instrument, the 1926 Convention to Suppress the Slave Trade and Slavery', something which Allain naturally commends.[29] In a structural sense, however, this of course causes problems for his core suggestion that the 'special obligations' constituted an illegitimate and racist standard of civilisation imposed illegitimately on Ethiopia by a Eurocentric international law.

Gong, for his part, resolves this contradiction straightforwardly by commending the 'standard of civilisation' as having been, ultimately, a good thing for Ethiopia. Indeed, Gong even goes so far as to cast Italy's central question – that of 'whether or not Ethiopia conformed to "civilised" standards' – as itself a legitimate one, the inherent reasonableness of which was obscured by the bombastic language of fascism. As he puts it: '[s]lavery, the wild conditions on the [Ethiopian] frontier, the barbaric mutilations which were still the punishment for crime, the cruelty of many native customs, the lack of imperial control over outlying provinces, the primitive state of legal development – whatever impact these claims against Abyssinia might have had was effectively neutralised by Italy's extremist efforts at self-justification'.[30] For Gong, then – more explicitly than for Allain – the true 'irony' of the 1935 Crisis lies in the way in which Italy, having condemned Ethiopia's 'barbarism', was soon to embrace a different kind of (fascist) barbarity itself. 'With Hitler on the rise,' Gong concludes (in line with the standard account), 'the allies were in 1935 eager to appease Mussolini in the hope of preserving the League and saving peace'.[31] 'It was ironic,' he adds, 'that Italy's appeal against Abyssinian barbarism was a harbinger of the Nazi and Fascist barbarisms that were to follow.'[32] Gong seems reluctant to appreciate, here, not only

[28] See Item 5, Section 1.1.
[29] Allain, 'Slavery and the League', 243.
[30] Gong, *The Standard of Civilization*, 128.
[31] Ibid., 128–9.
[32] Ibid., 128–9.

that fascist 'barbarisms' were already well under way, but also that so-called non-European 'barbarity' had consistently been surpassed by the brutalities of European colonialism, from Tenochtitlan to Herero.

Ultimately, then, both scholars succumb to the lure of the progress narrative and sacrifice their critique of the Abyssinia Crisis as an example of international law's complicity with the European 'civilising mission' in the process. Let me underline at this point that it is certainly not my intention, in pointing this out, to celebrate the practice of slavery either in the Ethiopian Empire or elsewhere. It is, instead, to reveal the contradictions in these accounts, and to underscore precisely how difficult it is, when faced with such a practice of systematic discrimination and horrifying violence, to get away from international law's teleological narration of its own history.

This difficulty can also be seen in the on-the-face-of-it critical account of the Crisis offered by the historian Ian Spears.[33] Spears makes no mention of the 'special obligations'. However, in contrast to the standard account, Spears argues that the failure to enforce the provisions of the Covenant in relation to Ethiopia's rights stemmed from the racist attitudes of the League's member states, rather than from their self-centred anxieties about the rise of fascism in Europe. Ethiopia was, Spears argues, the victim of a 'double standard that Europe applied to non-European states' which allowed the European states to sacrifice Ethiopia's sovereignty in a way they would not have done, had Ethiopia been European itself.[34] Like Gong and Allain, however, Spears goes on to undermine the force of this argument by sympathising with the reasons *behind* this 'double standard'. This sympathy, it appears, stems from Spears' endorsement of the 'juridical states' thesis, put forward by Robert Jackson and Carl Rosberg in the early 1980s.[35] Summing up this thesis, Spears argues that it is regrettable that, in the 1950s and 1960s, post-colonial 'African states did not earn their sovereignty but were granted it on the basis of having been former colonies'.[36] African states today 'continue to survive in whole or in part on the basis of their legal existence', even though 'what remain[s] consistent into the independence era [is] the condition of internal weakness manifested by

[33] Ian S. Spears, 'The Ethiopian Crisis and the Emergence of Ethiopia in a Changing State System', in G. Bruce Strange (ed.), *Collision of Empires: Italy's Invasion of Ethiopia and its International Impact* (Farnham: Ashgate, 2013), 34–51.

[34] Ibid., 33.

[35] Robert H. Jackson and Carl G. Rosberg, 'Why Africa's Weak States Persist: The Empirical and the Juridical in Statehood', 35 *World Politics* (1982): 1–24. See also Robert H. Jackson, Quasi-states: Sovereignty, International Relations and the Third World (Cambridge University Press, 1990).

[36] Spears, 'The Ethiopian Crisis', 49.

political instability, limited authority, and political disorder stemming from ethnic divisions'.[37] Returning to the 'Ethiopian crisis', Spears then proceeds to hold it up not as a failure to enforce international law (as in the standard account), or as an illustration of international law's inherent pro-European biases, but instead as a *success* on the part of a justifiably Eurocentric international law. This Crisis was, he argues, 'the last example where an African state' was 'punished for being anarchic', and Spears regrets that 'today the international community goes to great lengths to overlook weakness and keep [such] states solvent and intact'.[38] Even more explicitly than Gong's, then, Spears's argument suggests that Italy's attempts to justify its invasion and impending annexation of Ethiopia were both lawful and legitimate.

Even more surprisingly, Spears goes on to assert that Ethiopia's Emperor, Haile Selassie, must *himself* have shared that view at the time. Referencing the Emperor's autobiography, Spears commends Haile Selassie's 'efforts to bring [his] country the benefits of civilization' during the 1920s and 30s,[39] and suggests that, were he still alive today, the Emperor would deplore 'the contemporary situation [of African states] where the juridical nature of states is respected regardless of the degree of corruption, the ineptitude of the leadership, or the arbitrariness of the governments'.[40] For, he argues, Haile Selassie 'quite rightly believed that Ethiopia had a right to exist and embraced many of the trappings and attributes of contemporary statehood which, he maintained, would improve the wellbeing of his people and *secure Ethiopia's future as a sovereign country*'.[41] According to Spears, in other words, Haile Selassie realised that Ethiopia's sovereignty, in 1935, still lay in the 'future', and would only be secured if and when Ethiopia 'embraced ... the trappings and attributes of contemporary statehood'.[42] This can only suggest that the Emperor *himself* aligned himself with the Italian case, according to which his country's lack of 'civilisation' rendered it less-than-fully sovereign. Spears concludes from this historical example that present-day African states should accept that their poor human rights records give the international community a right to intervene in order to 'protect' their citizens. This argument – a version of the 'failed states' and 'responsibility to protect' arguments discussed in the Stand – is one that

37 Ibid., 49–50.
38 Ibid., 50.
39 Haile Selassie, Speech before the League of Nations Assembly, June 1936, quoted in Spears, 'The Ethiopian Crisis', 47.
40 Spears, 'The Ethiopian Crisis', 51.
41 Ibid., 51. Emphasis added.
42 Ibid., 51.

many Ethiopians and many Africans more generally would, I think, find difficult to accept. What are the 'trappings' of statehood to which Spears refers? He does not provide us with an answer, but presumably he regards them as the opposite of those negative characteristics which he uses to describe African states in general: 'internal weakness manifested by political instability, limited authority, and political disorder stemming from ethnic divisions'.[43] To put this more succinctly, where Ethiopia 'failed' in 1935, thereby forfeiting its sovereign rights according to Spears, was in its failure to have put in place a 'government' worthy of the name.

3 A Crisis among Crises: Modernism, Nationalism and 'Self-Government'

All three of the scholars examined in the previous section return to at least some of the official documentation surrounding the Abyssinia Crisis in an attempt to contextualise, and hence offer a different reading of the Abyssinia Crisis from that presented in the standard account. Yet none succeeds in challenging international law's central tropes, most importantly those of state sovereignty and universal human rights, both of which they accept as radiating out, in a normative sense, from Western Europe. All three take the efficacy of such tropes for granted, with the result that each of these narratives remains resolutely teleological. At best, these accounts suggest that the Ethiopian Empire's failure, well into the twentieth century, to have emancipated its slave population, had indeed rendered its claim to possess an equal set of rights and duties to other states under international law questionable at best. This was (as we saw in the Frame and as we shall see further in Items 5 and 6) precisely the argument made by fascist Italy. The cause of abolitionism, this version of the progress narrative suggests, though initially sullied by its association with European colonialism and fascism, has since been cleansed in and through its gradual acceptance, by all nations of the world, as a universal principle of international law.

Before tying the three 'critical' accounts in with this book's wider argument concerning the process of international legal reproduction, let me first turn to one last, and very different, critical history of the Crisis. This account comes from Nathaniel Berman, whose elaboration of the genealogical method in the context of international legal history I examined in the Frame. In contrast to Gong, Allain and Spears, Berman does not shy away from subjecting international law's tropes to a radical process

43 Ibid., 49–50.

of historicisation.[44] The result is, in effect, to shatter any semblance of a progressive linearity to the history of international law. Berman's interest is not in the Abyssinia Crisis per se, but rather in the question of what it can tell us about the pervasive contradictions and ambivalences of international law. He approaches this question through a comparison of the Abyssinia Crisis with the 'Sudetenland Crisis' of February 1938, in which Nazi Germany's annexation of a large region of south-western Czechoslovakia was 'appeased', without Czechoslovakia's consent, in a conference of Great Powers gathered at Munich.

Berman's conclusion is that this comparison shows us that 'African nationalists' at the time, who charged the international community with racism when it failed to uphold Ethiopia's rights under the Covenant, were 'mistaken to think that Ethiopia was treated worse than a "caucasoid" country would have been treated',[45] for both debacles were symptoms of the same malaise: the gradual collapse of the experiments initiated at the Paris Peace Conference, many of them inspired (as his work has long suggested) by an internationalist effort to harness the 'primitive' and yet powerful promise of nationalism. This conclusion connects with Berman's wider thesis that a 'new international law' had been under construction since 1919 by certain 'modernist' officials and jurists. 'Modernist' international law was founded on 'a paradoxical "alliance" of the "experimental" and the "primitive" against the construct that formerly constituted international law's foundation: the state'.[46] This 'asymmetrical alliance', Berman's work shows, involved the 'juxtaposition of the new status for nations and a new autonomy for the international community' in the form of the League of Nations.[47] Its aim was to allow international law to bypass the state by means of a 'double' movement of re-authorisation 'up' to the level of the international and 'down' to that of the national.[48] In this way, 'heterogeneous elements – reflecting such disparate sources of authority as the state, the nation, the individual, and the various organs of the international community'– would be able to 'coexist in international legal discourse, doctrines, and institutions'.[49]

44 Nathaniel Berman, '"But the Alternative is Despair": European Nationalism and the Modernist Renewal of International Law', in Berman, *Passion and Ambivalence: Colonialism, Nationalism and International Law* (Leiden: Martinus Nijhoff Publishers, 2012), 422.

45 Berman, 'Beyond Colonialism and Nationalism?', 455.

46 Berman, 'But the Alternative', 1806, quoting Jean Lucien-Brun, *Le Problème des minorités devant le droit international* (Lyon: Imprimerie Express, 1923), 47.

47 Berman, 'But the Alternative', 1806, quoting Lucien-Brun.

48 Berman, 'But the Alternative', 1803.

49 Ibid., 1820.

For Berman, the crises in Ethiopia and Czechoslovakia stemmed above all from a discursive strategy adopted by entities discontented with the Versailles settlement, not least Nazi Germany and Fascist Italy. This strategy involved usurping and instrumentalising the League's three 'cardinal principles' – 'sovereign equality, national self-determination, and the West's "civilising mission"'[50] (including the abolition of slavery) – in order to turn them back on and undermine the juridical system whose legitimacy rested on their inter-relationship. Thus 'automised', these three principles could then be, and were, 'parodied' in an internal 'realist' attack on the League system. For example, in relation to the Ethiopian Empire, Italy parodied the sovereignty principle by alleging that Ethiopia did not 'possess the degree of governmental organisation which is essential to the membership of the community of civilized nations'; it parodied the self-determination principle by arguing that Ethiopia was 'composed of an Abyssinian nucleus living on other conquered African peoples'; and it parodied the 'civilising mission' principle with the claim that 'the mission of colonisation should only be entrusted to progressive states' like Italy and not to oppressive states like the Ethiopian Empire itself, which it accused of oppressing its subordinate populations.[51]

This 'parodic realist' attack, Berman argues, exposed the inherent indeterminacy of these principles, which could be deployed just as well against the Versailles system as on that system's behalf. The 'great power conclaves' meeting in Paris[52] and Munich also undermined the League's claim to be the only international authority lawfully empowered to balance these principles against one another. In consequence, the League 'came to acquire the parasitical taint of its revisionist double'.[53] The result, Berman contends, was that international authority itself came to be transformed, taking on a new capacity not only to move entities (like 'mandated territories', for instance[54]) 'up' the 'civilisation' scale, but also to downgrade even recognised states like Ethiopia and Czechoslovakia to the level of entities whose consent, even to their own partition, was not required.[55] '[O]nly a transformed and culturally specific international authority', Berman argues, 'could arrogate to itself the power... not merely to "override normal rights" but actually to transform the legal status of the "parties con-

[50] Berman, 'Beyond Colonialism and Nationalism?', 321.
[51] Italian Memorandum, 76–9; Berman 'Beyond Colonialism and Nationalism?', 348.
[52] See Item 6, Section 1.2.
[53] Berman, 'Beyond Colonialism and Nationalism?', 371.
[54] See Item 3, Section 4.
[55] Ibid., 368.

cerned" on the basis of a substantive cultural evaluation'.[56] Yet this attack only exposed the fact that the 'Versailles System' was brought into being in 1919 'always already fractured'.[57] 'Parody', Berman concludes, 'teaches the impurity of the "original", its complicity in its own perversion'.[58]

4 Conclusion

The history into which Berman weaves the Abyssinia and Sudetenland Crises is, one might argue, a genealogy of the idea of the international and its deeply unstable relationship with nationalism. Unlike those of Gong, Allain and Spears, his is not a story of international law's journey from barbarity to civilisation, but rather one of the relentless, inescapable 'oscillation', as he puts it,[59] between internationalism and nationalism. Attempts to realise the internationalist 'dream' of a normatively homogeneous 'international society' were met with counter-claims concerning sovereign 'realities' or desired realities, then responded to with scaled-down 'revisionist' compromises, so much so that 'the distinction between legitimate, formally valid [international] authority and illegitimate power-politics' became 'destabilized and unpredictable'.[60]

Such a carefully contextualised account adds hugely to our understanding not only of the Abyssinia Crisis itself, but also of the contradictory, indeterminate nature of the inter-war international order. It also has important implications for the relationship between international law's past and its present, as discussed in the Frame. Berman is explicit about the present-day implications of his work. He argues, for instance, that the 'parodic' invocation of international law's core principles and the 'maddeningly difficult' task of demonstrating the 'falseness' of the 'realist' position in the 1930s had a deeply 'unsettling familiarity' in the late 1990s, when this chapter was first published as an article. This was the moment, he points out, in which 'peace plans for Bosnia ... combined calls for "realistic" adaption to the hard facts with barely argued, taken-for-granted, and yet ironic, pronouncements about "rights to live with one's kin" and "implacable nationalist passions"'.[61] One might make a similar connection to today, when far-right groups like Pegida (*Patriotische Europäer gegen die Islamisierung*

[56] Ibid., 365.
[57] Ibid., 371.
[58] Ibid., 378.
[59] Ibid., 378.
[60] Ibid., 383.
[61] Ibid., 383, 326.

des Abendlandes, or 'Patriotic Europeans Against the Islamisation of the West') cast their explicitly Islamophobic agenda as a call for the protection of the 'human rights' of women, Jews and sexual minorities.[62] Berman's is, then, a 'history of the present' in the Foucaultian sense. It draws our attention to a 'process of universalizability' while insisting on the inherent contingency of the 'conditions of possibility' that gave rise to it.[63]

Far from finding fault with such an approach, the methodological step I want to take here is to suggest that we can – and, if Benjamin is correct, we must – push the analysis one step further. Berman's genealogy of the Abyssinia Crisis is incredibly valuable in revealing *both* the contingency of the very particular set of circumstances that caused the Crisis to unfold in the way it did, *and* the 'universality' of the way in which those contradictions continue to manifest themselves in the present. But what would happen if, rather than restricting our study to the comparison of a limited series of relatively similar situations (in Berman's case, by comparing the Abyssinia Crisis with the contemporary Sudetenland Crisis and the 'Balkan Crisis' of the early 1990s), we were to take a more radical approach to the question of what constitutes an appropriate 'context' or 'background' against which to assess an episode's significance? What would happen, for example, if we were to zoom out in such a way as to make it possible to compare Italy's invasion of Ethiopia in the mid-1930s with the establishment of Spanish sovereignty over a vast area of 'America' in the sixteenth century *and* with the second 'Opium War' between the British and Chinese Empires in the late nineteenth century *and* with the attempts, culminating in the 'Roadmap for Peace', to make 'peace in the Middle East' at the turn of the twenty-first century *and* with the ongoing struggle over the ontology of Indigenous 'self-determination' in Canada, Australia and elsewhere? All of these situations involve contestations over the question of what it means to be a subject of international law, who is eligible for such subjectivity, how much of it they might be eligible for, and how that subjectivity fares in the long term. However, gaps of centuries and distances of many thousands of miles tend, even from a genealogical

[62] See e.g. Sebastian Murphy-Bates, 'Anne Marie Waters of Sharia Watch UK and Pegida UK to address Barking and Dagenham Ukip', *Barking and Dagenham Post*, 17 March 2017, available at www.barkinganddagenhampost.co.uk/home/anne-marie-waters-of-sharia-watch-uk-and-pegida-uk-to-address-barking-and-dagenham-ukip-1-4936838 (accessed 31 July 2017).

[63] Colin Koopman, *Genealogy as Critique: Foucault and the Problems of Modernity* (Bloomington, Indianapolis, IN: Indiana University Press, 2013), 119.

perspective, to preclude historians from considering a collection of such disparate 'events' as comparable, let alone as part of the same 'process'. It is this book's suggestion, however, that if we were to do precisely that – if we were to place all these (and other such) historically and geographically very disparate episodes into the same box – a pattern would emerge with such clarity that it seems worthy, at least, of remark.

To illustrate the point, let me conclude this chapter by returning to one of Berman's arguments concerning the Versailles system's 'contradictory' elements. According to Berman, Ethiopia and Czechoslovakia were (mis)treated by the international order of the 1930s even though 'projections of intra-European cultural difference and Europe/non-Europe civilizational difference were treated quite disparately [under the League] and never fully integrated'.[64] Zooming out in the way I have suggested causes this inconsistency ('culture' versus 'civilisation') to pale, and instead 'brings out' a consistency between Czechoslovakia and Ethiopia that would not, otherwise, be visible. For both states had obtained their rights and duties under international law only after they had been assessed as having a 'government', or, more specifically, as being 'self-governing'. This commitment, as we shall see, tied them, like other states, into the system of global capitalism and rendered their sovereign rights conditional and, therefore, capable of becoming (being treated as) stronger or weaker, depending on the degree of their adherence to the conditions in question. This is not, of course, to deny that international law was (and remains) deeply contradictory, or to downplay any of the legal 'lumpiness' (as Lauren Benton has put it) by which the extension of international law's jurisdiction has, from the beginning, been characterised.[65] It is, however, to draw attention to the fact that, in the long-term, international law's normative contradictions and jurisdictional unevenness tend to play out in a *particular* way – in a way that undermines and threatens *specific* communities and species. It is also to suggest that shifting our focus from states and international personality themselves to the relationship between them, and above all to the *process* in and through which they have, historically, been reproduced, can help us understand how that bias operates, and whose interests it serves. Returning to the standard account of the Abyssinia Crisis, for example, this shift in focus suggests that if the violence of conditionality

[64] Berman, 'Beyond Colonialism and Nationalism?', 337.

[65] Lauren Benton, *A Search for Sovereignty: Law and Geography in European Empires, 1400–1900* (Cambridge University Press, 2010), xii.

is a routine element of the process through which international law's subjects are constituted and disciplined, then the League's authority did not need to be 'transformed' in order 'to arrogate to itself the power' necessary to 'transform the legal status' of Ethiopia, Czechoslovakia or any other inter-war entities, as Berman suggests. For international law already possessed – and has always possessed – that power.

Item No. 2

State, Colony, Individual: The *Longue Durée* of International Legal Reproduction

The axiom that 'Sovereign States exclusively are International Persons – i.e. subjects of International Law' in the 'perfect' or 'full' sense, is international law's foundational assumption.[1] Since Lassa Oppenheim made that statement in 1905, however, a good deal about the nature of 'international society' has changed.

At the turn of the nineteenth century, the international community was still an extremely diverse and hierarchical place, populated not only by 'sovereign states' (primarily the states of Western Europe and parts of the Americas) but also by what Oppenheim called 'not-full' subjects of law. These ranged from less-than-fully sovereign states (such as the Principality of Serbia, for instance, a 'vassal state' of the Ottoman Empire; the 'Native States' of India, subordinated to Britain; 'semi-sovereign' states such as the Chinese and Siamese Empires; 'international protectorates' such as Morocco, constituted in the 1906 Act of Algeciras; and 'protected states', such as Tonga in relation to the United Kingdom) to non-state entities – most importantly, colonies of various types.[2]

Today, by contrast, both the diversity and the hierarchies of the international community have, in a formal sense, been much reduced as a result of two changes. The first is the 1945 UN Charter's insistence on the 'sovereign equality of all its Members'.[3] The second is the emergence, through the process of decolonisation in the 1950s and 1960s, of the customary 'right of all peoples to self-determination', based on the principles that '[i]nadequacy of political, economic, social or educational preparedness should never serve as a pretext for delaying independence', and that 'all powers' should immediately be transferred to colonised peoples 'without any conditions or reservations, in accordance with their freely expressed will and

[1] Lassa Oppenheim, *International Law: A Treatise*, Vol. I (London, New York, Bombay: Longman, Green and Co., 1905), 99.

[2] See generally James Crawford, *The Creation of States in International Law* (2nd edn) (Oxford University Press, 2007), 282–328.

[3] *Charter of the United Nations*, San Francisco, 26 June 1945, Art. 2(1) ('UN Charter').

desire, without any distinction as to race, creed or colour, in order to enable them to enjoy complete independence and freedom'.[4] Today, with the exception of a few cases (notably Palestine and Western Sahara) in which this right continues to be violated, and a number of remaining 'dependent territories' (such as Puerto Rico) whose 'freely expressed will and desire' to remain such has, in theory, been ascertained, the international community is populated exclusively by 'sovereign states', each of which possesses the full set of rights and duties under international law. These include the rights to territorial integrity, self-defence, equality before the law, political independence and law-making capacity, and the duties of non-intervention and lawful conduct, among others.[5]

Notwithstanding this complex and shifting hierarchy of different forms of subjectivity under international law, however, the 'sovereign state' has always been the pinnacle – the most complete conjoinment of the 'objective' characteristics of states (territory, population, government and independence) and the 'subjective' legal status (the rights and duties) which stem from them. Or, as Gerry Simpson has recently reminded us, channelling Tomas Baty, international law has always had 'something to do with States'.[6] No wonder, then, that the question of when, where and how the idea of the sovereign state first arose has been such an important one for historians of international law. Indeed, one of the most striking interventions made recently by critical historians of international law has been to challenge the tendency of mainstream international law to identify the 1648 Peace of Westphalia as the point of origin for the sovereign state and hence also for the discipline.[7] As we saw in the Frame, Nathaniel Berman is one such scholar. Another is Antony Anghie, who traces the emergence of international law in and through the 'colonial encounter', beginning in the late 1400s.[8] For Berman, like Anghie, 'the legal notion of sovereignty' must be understood as having been 'forged not only in such

[4] *Declaration on the Granting of Independence to Colonial Countries and Peoples*, GA Res. 1514 (XV), 14 December 1960, paras. 3 and 5 ('Colonial Declaration').

[5] The precise content of 'international personality' in terms of rights and duties remains controversial. For a (failed) attempt to construct a definitive list, see *Draft Declaration on Rights and Duties of States*, annexed to GA Res. 375 (IV), 6 December 1949.

[6] Gerry Simpson, 'Something to do with States', in Florian Hoffmann and Anne Orford (eds.), *Oxford Handbook of the Theory of International Law*, 564–83; Thomas Baty, *The Canons of International Law* (London: Murray, 1930), 1.

[7] See e.g. Nathanial Berman, 'In the Wake of Empire', 14 *American University International Law Review* (1999): 1521–69.

[8] Antony Anghie, *Imperialism, Sovereignty and the Making of International Law* (Cambridge University Press, 2004), 13–31.

Figure 4 Tiny workers pass the scaffolded Inner Tiananmen Gate, Peking (Beijing), c. 1907. The Gate's pillars had been damaged by cannon-fire from the forces of the Eight-Nation Alliance (Austria-Hungary, Britain, France, Germany, Italy, Japan, Russia and the United States), which intervened to protect foreign citizens during the 'Boxer Rebellion' in 1900. On 25 December 1911, the imperial edict announcing the abdication of the last Qing emperor, Puyi, was issued by the Empress Dowager Longyu from the top of the Gate. On 1 January 1912, China declared itself to be a republic. Photographer unknown. Courtesy of the Library of Congress Prints and Photographs Division, Ref. LC-USZ62-54321.

intra-European crucibles as the Thirty Years War, but also in the fires of colonial conquest, such as the Spanish expansion in the Americas – predating Westphalia by more than a century'.[9] The crucial move made by

[9] Berman, 'In the Wake of Empire', 1523–4. See also e.g. Jennifer Beard, *The Political Economy of Desire: International Law, Development and the Nation State* (Abingdon, New York:

critical scholars writing in this vein is to challenge the idea that international law derives from the encounter 'between two sovereign states', as in the classical 'positivist' model, and to insist, instead, on the constitutive character of the encounter 'between a sovereign European state and a non-European society that was deemed by jurists to be lacking in sovereignty – or else, at best only partially sovereign'.[10]

The aim of this chapter is to build on and contribute to this line of analysis by focusing on two questions: one concerning the emergence and consolidation of the state as a concept and practice; the other concerned with the peculiar character of subjectivity under international law. How did the state – understood not just as a set of characteristics implying a particular set of rights and duties, but also as a material, lived reality – come to spread itself out across the world? How can we make sense of the fact that sovereignty seems to vary, both over time and between 'sovereigns' of various kinds, including (but not limited to) states?

In order to respond to these questions, this chapter adds a second 'item' into the shadow-box, which is designed to be viewed in relation to Item 1, and to the Frame and Stand, but also to alter our perspective on their suggestions. For instance, in the book's earlier discussion of materialist jurisprudence,[11] I outlined a theoretical position closely aligned with Pashukanis's argument that '[t]he spread and development of international law occurred on the basis of the spread and development of the capitalist mode of production'.[12] However, I also challenged the rootedness of his theory in the idea of the 'domestic analogy' on the grounds that this analogical approach cannot account for the conditional, and therefore material, relationship between individual and international legal subjectivity. Engaging Edelman's ideas about the interpellation of the legal subject in the image of capital, I argued that the reproduction of international personality was anchored in a simultaneously interpellative and coercive process. Then, in Item 1, I introduced international law's implicit

Routledge, 2007); Karl-Heinz Ziegler, 'Die Bedeutung des Westfälischen Friedens von 1648 für das europäische Völkerrecht', 37 *Archiv des Völkerrechts* (1999): 129–51; Richard Joyce, 'Westphalia: Event, Memory, Myth', in Fleur Johns, Richard Joyce and Sundhya Pahuja (eds.), *Events: The Force of International Law* (Abingdon: Routledge, 2011), 55–68; Meinhard Schröder, 'Der Westfälische Friede – eine Epochengrenze in der Völkerrechtsentwicklung?', in Meinhard Schröder (ed.), 350 *Jahre Westfälischer Friede: Verfassungsgeschichte Staatskirchenrecht, Völkerrechtsgeschichte* (Berlin: Duncker and Humblot, 1999), 119–37.

10 Anghie, *Imperialism, Sovereignty*, 5.

11 Frame, Section 2.

12 Evgeny Pashukanis [1925], 'International Law,' in Piers Beirne and Robert Sharlet (eds.), *Pashukanis: Selected Writings on Marxism and Law*, trans. Peter B. Maggs (London: Academic Press, 1980), 168–83, at 171–2.

obsession with the Abyssinia Crisis as a prism through which to view this process more critically. I drew attention to the way in which several supposedly critical histories of the Crisis ended up condemning the Ethiopian Empire for its 'uncivilised' practices, in particular that of slavery, while commending the 'international community' (and in some cases even the aggressor, Italy) for having stepped in to discipline Ethiopia accordingly. Viewed together, the Frame and Item 1 both indicate, in different ways, that the history of international law may be a story not only of the interaction among different communities, both European and non-European, but also of the co-constitution of the macro and micro dimensions of legal subjectivity through the mechanism of conditionality. This suggests, in turn, that international law, far from being the solution to the problems of distribution, violence and environmental degradation that have been thrown up by the intensification of capitalist processes throughout the world, may in fact be closely implicated in their reproduction. This suggestion is borne out by the history that I present in this chapter. Among other things, attending to the conditional nature of the process according to which international law's subjects are created and disciplined tells us that 'sovereignty' is not, as David Kennedy has put it, 'an on/off affair', something that communities, upon becoming states, obtain in full, once and for all.[13] Instead, as we shall see, and as we saw Simpson point out above,[14] 'sovereignty' or subjectivity under international law is better understood as a status that is both hybrid and inherently malleable in nature, both 'self' and 'other' simultaneously; constantly in the process of waxing and waning.

1 Recognition and International Personality: From the Standard of Civilisation to the Standard of Statehood

Mainstream doctrinal thinking about statehood and international personality or 'sovereignty' is (as every student of international law has had drilled into their brains) grounded in the 'great debate' between advocates of the 'constitutive' and 'declaratory' theories of state recognition.[15] I have

[13] David Kennedy, 'International Law and the Nineteenth Century: History of an Illusion', 65 *Nordic Journal of International Law* (1996): 385–420, at 407.

[14] Gerry Simpson, *Great Powers and Outlaw States: Unequal Sovereigns in the International Legal Order* (Cambridge University Press, 2004), ix–x. See Stand, above.

[15] Crawford dedicates the book's opening chapter to a discussion of this debate. James Crawford, *The Creation of States in International Law* (2nd edn Oxford University Press, 2007), 1–36.

discussed the well-known contours of this debate elsewhere,[16] so let me return to them here only very briefly.

1.1 State Recognition: The 'Great Debate'

The theory and practice of 'constitutive' recognition became dominant during the late nineteenth century, and was particularly popular among an influential group of British and North American international lawyers such as Henry Wheaton, John Westlake, James Lorimer and, of course, Oppenheim. According to advocates of this now largely discredited constitutive view, communities and territories deemed 'uncivilised' could be, should be, and indeed were, consistently denied some or all of the rights and duties associated with international personality through the simple means of their non-recognition, or only partial recognition, as persons of international law, regardless of whether they met or did not meet the formal criteria for statehood. The effect was to render the annexation of territory inhabited by such communities entirely lawful, or, in the case of so-called 'semi-civilised' entities like the Ottoman and Chinese Empires, to make it possible to constitute their international rights and duties only to a limited extent. Thanks to the implicit racism ingrained in this process of using an ostensibly universal but inherently Eurocentric 'standard of civilisation' to deny rights and duties to non-European polities, this approach has, in the post-decolonisation era, been condemned right across the spectrum of international legal scholarship as one of the most obvious ways through which international law came to undergird and extend the European colonial project.[17]

By contrast, the 'declaratory theory' of recognition, which (nominally) returned to customary status during the inter-war period, is celebrated for having dispensed with the 'standard of civilisation' in favour of an exclusive focus on the four supposedly 'factual' or 'objective' customary criteria for statehood (territory, population, government and formal independence). When these criteria were later codified, in the 1933 *Inter-American Convention on the Rights and Duties of States* (more commonly

[16] See generally Rose Parfitt, 'Theorizing Recognition and International Personality', in Florian Hoffmann and Anne Orford (eds.), *The Oxford Handbook of the Theory of International Law* (Oxford University Press, 2016), 583–99; Matthew Craven and Rose Parfitt, 'Statehood, Self-Determination and Recognition', in Malcolm D. Evans (ed.), *International Law* (5th edn Oxford University Press, 2018), 177–226.

[17] Compare e.g. Antonio Cassese *International Law* (2nd edn Oxford, New York: Oxford University Press, 2005), 74; Crawford, *The Creation of States*, 19–22; Hersch Lauterpacht, *Recognition in International Law* (Cambridge University Press, 1947), 31; and Anghie, *Imperialism, Sovereignty*, 75–8.

known as the Montevideo Convention), they had been in use for several decades.[18] Occasionally it is argued that 'extra' conditions, relating, for instance, to the 'rule of law' or to adherence to 'universal human rights' standards, have been *added on* to the Montevideo criteria in the form of a new 'standard of civilisation'.[19] However, while the concept of the state has been criticised,[20] the possibility that the four formal criteria for statehood might *themselves* be considered a 'standard of civilisation' has been taken up by few, if any, scholars of recognition and personality.

To give one recent example, Arnulf Becker Lorca argues in an important new work of international legal history that '[t]he novelty of Montevideo rests ... on how it combined statehood and recognition as formal statehood and declaratory recognition in order to decouple sovereignty from civilization.'[21] The Montevideo Convention, he argues, 'excludes both the criterion of independence, replacing it with "government", and the constitutive doctrine, replacing it with a declaratory doctrine of recognition'.[22] For Becker, therefore, the 'formal conception of statehood' that was finally consolidated in 1933 'marked the dissolution of the standard of civilization', because this purely formal conception of statehood 'excluded any substantive criterion within the definition of statehood', together with 'all substantive qualifiers that had previously been considered relevant to attribute sovereignty', including 'reference to the race, religion or culture of the population, to the size of the territory, to the nature of the government, or to the type of relations – equal or unequal – that non-Western states had established with Western states'.[23]

[18] Inter-American Convention on the Rights and Duties of States, Montevideo, 26 December 1933 ('Montevideo Convention'), Art. 1. See Crawford, *The Creation of States*, 130–1 and Cassese, *International Law*, 75. Both describe the criteria as 'factual'. See also Colin Warbrick, 'States and Recognition in International Law', in Malcolm D. Evans, *International Law* (2nd edn Oxford University Press, 2006), 217–75 at 265. For a useful critical history of the Montevideo criteria, see Thomas D. Grant, 'Defining Statehood: The Montevideo Convention and its Discontents', 37 *Columbia Journal of Transnational Law* (1998): 403–57.

[19] See e.g. Catriona Drew, 'The Meaning of Self-Determination: "The Stealing of the Sahara" Redux?', in Karin Arts and Pedro Pinto Leite (eds.), *International Law and the Question of Western Sahara* (Leiden: International Platform of Jurists for East Timor (IPJET), 2007), 87–105, at 95–100; Jack Donnelly, 'Human Rights: A New Standard of Civilization?', 74 *International Affairs* (1998): 1–23.

[20] Many scholars have made this argument. For one powerful example, see Makau wa Mutua, 'Why Redraw the Map of Africa: A Moral and Legal Inquiry', 16 *Michigan Journal of International Law* (1994–5): 1113–76.

[21] Arnulf Becker Lorca, *Mestizo International Law: A Global Intellectual History 1842–1933* (Cambridge University Press, 2014), 308.

[22] Ibid., 308.

[23] Ibid., 307–10.

I share Becker's view of the crucial importance of the periphery and semi-periphery to the development of the discipline of international law wholeheartedly. However, with respect to the question of statehood, the conclusions I reach in this chapter are different. For the criteria for statehood, though 'formal', are hardly objective. On the contrary, as Martti Koskenniemi has pointed out, these criteria 'form the normative code which regulates the attainment of statehood'.[24] They are, in other words, 'constitutive' themselves. This point becomes especially clear when one takes into account their very specific genesis in medieval Western Europe. There seems to be no reason why the criteria for statehood should be experienced by communities existing in different spaces and times as any less subjective (or any less Eurocentric) than the criterion of 'civilisation' which the Convention's passage into customary international law supposedly rendered obsolete. And indeed, as this chapter will show, these criteria have been experienced as external, subjective and hence totalitarian 'standards' by many entities, including the Ethiopian Empire. It is these criteria, in other words, which supply the external template to which other entities must conform if they want to obtain rights and duties under international law. It is this 'standard of statehood', as we might call it, just as much if not more than the notorious 'standard of civilisation', which describes the 'self' of international law – a 'self' which no 'other' can ever fully become. To regard 'civilisation' as something separate from 'statehood', therefore, is something of a red herring – a distraction from the main problem.

Moreover, and as we are about to see, the concept of 'civilisation' and the 'criterion' of 'government' have consistently been treated as indistinguishable both in theory and practice. If my interpretation of the history described in this chapter is correct, this suggests that, rather than being 'dissolved' by the arrival of the declaratory approach to recognition, the clearly subjective and deeply Eurocentric standard of civilisation with which Becker, Anghie and many other post-colonial critics of international law rightly take issue was – and arguably still is – *embedded in* the apparently objective and neutral 'criteria' for (or standard of) statehood. In doctrinal terms, one implication is that the constitutive and declaratory theories of recognition in fact have very little to distinguish them. More importantly, it also points us toward an explanation as to why the emancipatory promise of the sovereign state system and the core individual rights associated with citizenship, near-universalised over the past half-century, have proved to be

[24] Martti Koskenniemi, *From Apology to Utopia: The Structure of International Legal Argument* (Cambridge University Press, 2005), 274.

such a bitter illusion.[25] In short, I argue, with Ntina Tzouvala in her indispensable new history of 'capitalism as civilisation', that 'compliance with the "standard of civilisation" essentially meant transformation into a capitalist state' – something that implicates international 'profoundly' in the 'global spread of the CMP [capitalist mode of production]'.[26] Or indeed, one might even go so far as to say that historically 'civilisation' and 'statehood' have been impossible to separate, making the idea of a 'capitalist state' almost a tautology for international law. As I show below, states have only been regarded as possessing rights and duties to the extent that they have been regarded as 'self-governing' and, thus, capitalist.

1.2 The 'Criteria' for Statehood

Still, at the end of the sixteenth century, the proportion of the world's numerous, highly organised human polities which could plausibly be called 'states', in the sense that the drafters of the Montevideo Convention later had in mind, remained extremely small. All were to be found in Western Europe, moreover, and even there only in a minority. France, Sweden and Britain provide some of the most well-known examples, but it is much more difficult to classify the medieval city-states like Venice, for example, in the same way. Very few of the most important political entities of this period – from the Holy Roman Empire (a huge, loosely elected polity composed of many hundreds of sub-units including 'free imperial cities', principalities and duchies) to the Chinese Empire (an equally complex and hierarchical entity organised on the basis of Confucian principles whose boundaries could only very loosely be called 'territorial') – were states in this sense.

By the end of the nineteenth century, however, a long series of revolutions and wars of independence, from Latin America to Haiti to Southern Europe, together with Italian and Germany unification and the territorial fall-out from the 1877–78 Russo-Turkish War, had increased the total number of states enormously. That it was at this moment that the discipline of international law first emerged *as* a discipline is no coincidence.[27] As Koskenniemi

[25] I share this suspicion of the state with many other critical scholars of international law. See Anghie, *Imperialism, Sovereignty*; Eslava, *Local Space, Global Life*; B. S. Chimni, *International Law and World Order: A Critique of Contemporary Approaches* (Cambridge University Press, 2017); Sundhya Pahuja, *Decolonising International Law: Development, Economic Growth and the Politics of Universality* (Cambridge University Press, 2011); Beard, *The Political Economy of Desire.*

[26] Konstantina Tzouvala, 'Letters of Blood and Fire: A Socio-Economic History of International Law' (PhD thesis, Durham University, 2016), 26, 29.

[27] Martti Koskenniemi, *The Gentle Civilizer of Nations: The Rise and Fall of International Law 1870–1960* (Cambridge University Press, 2001).

has shown, by 1873, when the *Institut de Droit International* was founded in Ghent, and certainly by 1896, the year in which the American Society of International Law was established, the state was already well-settled on the pedestal that had been constructed for it by a series of towering European intellectuals – most famously, perhaps, Georg Hegel. By the turn of the century, most Europeans and their descendants overseas could take it for granted that the state was, quite simply, the ultimate (or penultimate, from some contemporary Marxist perspectives) form of collective self-organisation, towards which societies everywhere must be tending. This conviction was only reinforced, over the course of the twentieth century, by the disintegration of the German, Ottoman and Austro-Hungarian Empires into a series of 'national states' and 'mandated territories' (both formations that reinforced the idea that the nation-state was the only bearer of 'full' subjectivity under international law);[28] then by the process of decolonisation in the 1950s and 1960s, in which the vast majority of former European colonies in Asia, Africa and the Pacific opted for statehood in the process of creating and claiming the emergent 'right of peoples to self-determination';[29] and then, again, in the 1990s with the collapse of the Soviet Union and Yugoslavia into yet another new collection of states.[30]

Witnessing what must have been the astonishing spectacle of the unfolding of this apparently universal system of collective self-organisation, one of the initial tasks the first generation of 'professional' international lawyers in the late nineteenth century[31] set themselves was to boil the state's characteristics down to a set of four abstract 'criteria'. To quote Oppenheim's formulation, for a state to be considered such:

> There must, first, be a *people*. A people is an aggregate of individuals of both sexes who live together as a community in spite of the fact that they may belong to different races or creeds, or be of different colour ...
>
> There must, secondly, be a *country* in which the people has settled ...
>
> There must, thirdly, be a *Government* – that is, one or more persons who are the representatives of the people and rule according to the law of the land. An anarchistic community is not a State.
>
> There must, fourthly and lastly, be a *Sovereign* Government. Sovereignty is supreme authority, an authority which is independent of any other earthly authority. Sovereignty in the strict and narrowest sense of the term

28 See below, Item 3.

29 See e.g. Jörg Fisch, *The Right of Self-Determination of Peoples* (Cambridge University Press, 2015).

30 See Lid, below.

31 See Koskenniemi, *The Gentle Civilizer*.

> includes, therefore, independence all round, within and without the borders of the country.[32]

The four criteria later articulated in the 1933 Montevideo Convention are almost identical: 'The state as a person of international law should possess the following qualifications: (a) a permanent population; (b) a defined territory; (c) government; and (d) capacity to enter into relations with the other states'.[33]

According to Crawford (currently a judge at the International Court of Justice and author of the magisterial volume *The Creation of States in International Law*), of these four still-customary criteria, it is 'government' which constitutes 'the most important single criterion of statehood, since all the others depend upon it'.[34] If an authority is to be considered a 'government' for the purposes of statehood, Crawford explains, its control must be both 'exclusive' and 'effective'. '[T]o be a State, an entity must possess a government or a system of government in general control of its territory, to the exclusion of other entities not claiming through or under it.'[35] Crawford insists, however, that 'international law lays down no specific requirements as to the nature and extent of this control, except that it include some degree of maintenance of law and order and the establishment of basic institutions'.[36] Plausible and neutral as it may sound, however, Crawford's definition begs the question in a number of ways. In the first place, defining a government on the grounds of its exclusivity and effectiveness offers us no assistance in the task of distinguishing a government from some other thing – say, a chair (to borrow Crawford's own external standard of comparison).[37] Equally, if governments are things that maintain 'law and order' and establish 'basic institutions', one might ask what type of control counts as 'law and order', and what type of arrangements meet the benchmark of 'basic institutions'? In attempting to respond to these questions, I will begin with the *Island of Palmas Case*,

[32] Lassa Oppenheim, *International Law: A Treatise*, Vol. 1 (London, New York and Bombay: Longmans, Green and Co., 1905), 99–101. Emphasis in the original. For some related articulations, see e.g. Georg Jellinek, *Allgemeine Staatslehere* (3rd edn Berlin: Verlag von O. Häring, 1914), 396; Hans Kelsen, 'The Pure Theory of Law and Analytical Jurisprudence', 55 *Harvard Law Review* (1941–42): 44–70 at 70; Pasquale Fiore, *International Law Codified and Its Legal Sanction or the Legal Organization of the Society of States* (New York: Baker, Voorhis and Company, 1918), 106.

[33] Montevideo Convention, Art. 1.

[34] Crawford, *The Creation of States*, 56.

[35] Ibid., 56.

[36] Ibid., 56.

[37] Ibid., 5.

decided by the Permanent Court of Arbitration in 1928 – a case widely used in the analysis of international legal doctrine as the starting point when it comes to determining the parameters of territorial sovereignty.[38]

1.3 *The Principle of Effectiveness*

According to the famous maxim of the Swiss jurist Max Huber, Arbiter in the *Island of Palmas Case*, '[s]overeignty in the relations between States signifies independence. Independence in regard to a portion of the globe is the right to exercise therein, to the exclusion of any other State, the functions of a State.'[39] Interestingly, however, it is worth recalling that the question Huber was called upon to examine in this case was not whether the Island of Palmas was or was not a state, but, instead, which of two existing states – the United States and the Netherlands – had the better claim to sovereignty over the island. There is also another side to Huber's judgment which seldom forms the focus of inquiry. For the figures of the 'state' (the United States, the Netherlands) and of the 'colony' (the Island of Palmas) were not, in fact, the only types of legal personality whose rights and duties Huber took into account. If we look hard, we also find the figure of the *individual* legal subject lurking in the margins of his judgment.

In order to determine which of the two states was, in fact, exercising sovereignty over the Island of Palmas, Huber argued, it was necessary to determine which of them was exercising 'the functions of a State' upon its territory. For territorial sovereignty, Huber argued, 'involves the exclusive right to display the activities of a State':

> This right [he continued] has a corollary duty: the obligation to protect within the territory the rights of other States, in particular their right to integrity and inviolability in peace and in war, *together with the rights which each State may claim for its nationals in foreign territory*... Territorial sovereignty cannot limit itself to its negative side, i.e. to excluding the activities of other States; for it serves to divide between nations the space upon which *human* activities are employed, in order to *assure them at all points the minimum protection of which international law is the guardian.*[40]

If we view this statement in conjunction with Crawford's description of 'effectiveness', above, an important indicator as to what 'law and order'

[38] *Island of Palmas Case* (*Netherlands* v. *USA*), 4 April 1928, Reports of International Arbitral Awards, Vol. II, 829–71.

[39] Ibid., 836.

[40] Ibid., 838–9. Emphasis added.

and 'basic institutions' might mean comes to light. Crucially, Huber's definition demonstrates that what 'effectiveness', or exercising 'the functions of a state', actually involves in international law is a willingness and capacity to protect the existing rights of those entities (international and individual legal subjects) which *already have* rights under international law. Clearly, this refers to the rights of other states. Yet Huber also refers to the *citizens* of other states, were they to arrive on the island, probably as traders, missionaries, explorers, or for any other reason.

In the process of his attempts to work out whether the US or the Netherlands was exercising 'the functions of a state' upon the Island, moreover, it did not occur to Huber to consider that this 'small and distant island, inhabited only by natives' (as he put it) might *itself* possess rights and duties under international law, or whether the 'natives' might collectively possess some kind of sovereignty.[41] On the contrary, Huber took it as self-evident that the institutions of collective self-organisation belonging to the 'natives', if they existed at all, did not, and could not, perform those functions – i.e. those of protecting the rights of other states and their citizens. In other words, it went without saying, for Huber, that the 'natives' did not possess a 'government'; they were not 'self-governing'. The 'standard' which would determine whether the US or the Netherlands could successfully claim title over this territory was accordingly much lower, according to Huber's reasoning, than it would have been if the question confronting him had been whether or not the Island of Palmas was itself a state. Thus, he argued, the 'manifestations of sovereignty' in question were not required to be 'frequent' or to 'go back to a very far distant period' for sovereignty to have been established.[42]

In addition to being 'effective' in the sense of being capable of protecting the pre-existing rights of visiting 'foreigners' (i.e. citizens of foreign states), Huber also considered it necessary that the exercise of control should have been largely 'peaceful'. Again, perhaps counter-intuitively for those not familiar with the doctrine of international law, the term 'peaceful' here was not intended to indicate that the 'natives' should have *consented* to Dutch or American control. Rather, 'peaceful' in this context meant that the territorial control of one state had not been contested, in a legal sense, by any other state.[43] The Island's natives, being no more citizens than their polity was a state, therefore possessed neither individual nor collective

[41] Ibid., 867.
[42] Ibid., 867.
[43] Ibid., 867.

legal subjectivity of their own accord.[44] There was therefore no question, for Huber, that the US or the Netherlands should be required to attend to the rights of the natives in making their claim, for the natives had no rights. In order that its governing institutions over the Island should be considered 'effective', it was enough that the Netherlands (which eventually won the arbitration) should have attended to the rights of its *own* citizens (*qua* legal subjects), and likewise to the sovereign rights of other states and of their citizens.

What is significant about Huber's assessment, I suggest, is therefore not only the extent to which it underscores the dialectical relationship or 'dynamic of difference' that existed, during the colonial period, between the state (the European 'self' of international law) and the colony (the discipline's non-European 'other') in the establishment of sovereignty, as Anghie, following Edward Said, has argued so elegantly.[45] Huber's judgment certainly does testify to the casual racism that was still explicit in international law's language and logic in 1928. However, the judgment also does something else in laying bare the role played by the *individual* subject of law in the process of bestowing or denying territorial sovereignty. The task of the rest of this chapter is to lay out some fragments of the history of this largely unexplored connection, and to examine their interrelationship. Drawing a circle all the way back from the early twentieth century to the mid sixteenth century, it will argue that each of these fragments illustrates what is, in essence, the same process, though one that has played out in very different ways in different contexts. This process of international legal reproduction refers to the co-*re*production of international and individual legal personality, connected by a mechanism of conditionality and mediated through the 'criterion' of government.

2 'Government': A Triangular Story

As we have just seen, Judge Huber in 1928 determined the extent of 'territorial sovereignty' on the basis of the degree to which a state claiming to exercise such sovereignty proved both willing and able to protect the rights of foreign states and of their citizens. This section sets out to elaborate on

[44] As Hannah Arendt would point out 23 years later, it is only by virtue of belonging to a state as one of its citizens that the individual human being acquires 'the right to have rights' in any practical sense. Hannah Arendt, *The Origins of Totalitarianism* (New York: Harcourt Books, 1994), 292.

[45] Anghie, *Imperialism, Sovereignty*, 9. See Edward Said [1978], *Orientalism* (London: Penguin, 2003).

the emergence and consolidation of this conditional relationship by means of a 'modular' version of the structuralist, *longue durée* history envisaged by Ferdinand Braudel,[46] Eric Hobsbawm[47] and, more recently, Jo Guldi and David Armitage, among others.[48] It proceeds in three sections, which track the relationship between three legal figures, representing three forms of legal subjectivity: the state, the colony and the individual. The state and the colony can be conceived of as opposites – one being the only holder, potentially at least, of 'full' subjectivity under international law, and the other representing the paradigmatic object of international law, lacking international rights and duties. As I argue, however, the assumption of legal subjectivity on the part of the state, and the denial of legal subjectivity to the colony, were processes mediated through another figure – that of the individual. Or, to be more specific, the process of international legal reproduction both depended on and, in the process, constituted or reproduced three different types of individual: citizens ('free' and 'equal' legal subjects); slaves (legal objects, over whom legal subjects could exercise property rights); and natives (colonial subjects, possessed, usually, of the right not to be enslaved and to own and exchange property, but of few other rights).

In order to track this complex relationship between macro and micro legal subjectivity, this Section therefore takes a triangular form. In the first subsection, I examine how the state and the individual developed, in parallel, in the thinking and practice of European colonialism from the late sixteenth century onwards. In the second subsection, I look at the way in which the relationship between colonial rule and individual rights was articulated in debates over the state's extension of its territorial sovereignty. In the third subsection, I complete the triangle by revisiting some familiar aspects of the theory and practice of international law in the nineteenth century in order to examine the relationship between the colony and the state. It is the concept and practice of 'government', as we shall see, which holds the three sides of this triangle together.

2.1 State/Individual

The sovereign state and the individual citizen or legal subject have always been paired together in the doctrine of international law. As we saw in the

[46] See, most famously, Fernand Braudel, 'Histoire et Sciences sociales. La longue durée', 13 *Annales. Histoire, Sciences sociales* (1958): 725–53.

[47] See e.g., among many others, Eric Hobsbawm, *On History* (London: Hachette, 2011).

[48] Jo Guldi and David Armitage, *The History Manifesto* (Cambridge University Press, 2014).

Frame, however, this relationship has usually been understood in analogical terms. Sovereign states are viewed, according to the 'domestic analogy', as 'collective persons' which 'have rights and are under obligations', and who 'are in the same relation as that in which individuals stand to each other who are subject to the law'.[49] Sovereign states, in the famous phrase, are to be understood as individual citizens 'writ large' – formally equal to one another, and 'negatively' free to do everything that does not impinge on the liberty of other sovereign states.[50] Yet this analogical tradition of thinking about the relationship between states and individuals is ahistorical to say the least. For instance as historians of human rights and 'humanitarian intervention' have argued, international law has frequently sanctioned interventions aimed at protecting the rights of religious minorities in particular,[51] suggesting that individual and collective (sovereign) rights have always had some kind of material relationship. Indeed, once we start examining the history of international law through the lens of international legal reproduction, we can find evidence of this conditional relationship even in the discipline's most foundational moments.

2.1.1 Westphalia and the Individual Legal Subject

Take, for example, the Peace of Westphalia.[52] The emphasis placed throughout this complex settlement on 'the Liberty of the Exercise of Religion'

[49] Hall, *A Treatise on International Law*, 18, 44. For an excellent critique of the 'domestic analogy', see Chiara Bottici, *Uomini e Stati: Percorsi di un'analogia* (Pisa: ETS, 2004), published in English as *Men and States: Rethinking the Domestic Analogy in a Global Age*, trans. Karen Whittle (Basingstoke: Palgrave Macmillan, 2009).

[50] For a history of the idea of 'negative' liberty going back to Machiavelli, see Quentin Skinner, 'The Idea of Negative Liberty: Machiavellian and Modern Perspectives', in Quentin Skinner, *Visions of Politics, Vol. II: Renaissance Virtues* (Cambridge University Press, 2004), 186–212. As Skinner shows, '[i]t would be no exaggeration to say that this assumption – that the only coherent idea of liberty is the negative one of being unimpeded – has underpinned the entire development of modern contractarian political thought from Thomas Hobbes onwards' (187).

[51] See e.g. Carole Fink, *Defending the Rights of Others: The Great Powers, the Jews, and International Minority Protection, 1878–1938* (Cambridge University Press, 2004).

[52] The two treaties of Osnabrück and Münster which made up this settlement – between the 'Holy Roman Empire of the German Nation' and Sweden on the one hand, and between the Empire and France on the other – were signed on 24 October 1648, bringing an end to the 'Thirty Years War' (1618–48). This immensely complicated war took place among Catholic and Protestant elements within the Holy Roman Empire allied with various 'great powers', the most important being the Catholic Hapsburg Empire on the one hand, and Catholic France together with Protestant Sweden, Denmark and the Dutch Republic on the other. Entangled with this settlement was a second, agreed only a few months earlier, on 30 January 1648, between the Dutch Republic and the Kingdom of Spain. See generally Derek Croxton, 'The Peace of Westphalia of 1648 and the Origins of Sovereignty', 21

within the jurisdictions of 'the Sacred Roman Empire, [and] the other Princes and States' is, as we saw in the Frame, frequently taken as the origin of the idea that international law has developed in such a way as to recognise all states as being, by right, free to choose their own mode of internal self-organisation within a stable set of borders, and hence as equal in rights to one another.[53] This is the meaning of the term 'Westphalian sovereignty', a term popular in international law and international relations scholarship.[54] However, in their understanding of legal subjectivity, the treaties which made up the settlement were in some ways far more limited, and in other ways far more complex, than this mainstream reading suggests.[55]

Firstly, far from reconfiguring the 'international' structure of Europe on the basis of a new principle of sovereign equality, the settlement of 1648 represented, in effect, a compromise between two different tendencies. While there was at work something that might be seen as the early stirrings of sovereign statehood – for example, in the recognition of the independence of the United Provinces and of Switzerland[56] – much of the text was devoted to reasserting elements of the extremely complex, pre-existing feudal order, in which what we might call (if anachronistically) 'international' and 'domestic' elements were inextricably intertwined. The question of status was not the least complex of these elements. On the 'international' side, among the 109 delegations which attended the negotiations, only a few (France and Sweden, for instance) were states. Others, notably the Holy Roman Empire and the Spanish Empire, were territorial empires.[57] Meanwhile, from the free imperial cities to the

The International History Review (1999): 569–91; Benno Teschke, *The Myth of 1648: Class, Geopolitics, and the Making of Modern International Relations* (London, New York: Verso, 2003).

53 *Treaty between the Holy Roman Empire of the German Nation and Sweden and their Respective Allies*, Münster, 24 October 1648 ('Treaty of Münster), Art. 49, Preamble.

54 As a rough indicator, a search for this term on Google Scholar returns 3,760 results. See https://scholar.google.com.au/scholar?hl=en&aas_sdt=0%2C5&q=%22westphalian+sovereignty%22&btnG= (accessed 26 January 2018).

55 See e.g. Croxton, 'The Peace of Westphalia', 573; Heinz Duchhardt, 'Das "Westfälische System": Realität und Mythos', in Hillard von Thiessen and Christian Windler (eds.), *Akteure der Aussenbeziehungen: Netzwerke und Interkulturalität im historischen Wandel* (Cologne: Böhlau Verlag, 2010), 393–401.

56 Although as Derek Croxton points out, elements of formal legal subordination to the Empire, in the Dutch case via the Spanish Empire, remained in both cases. Croxton, 'The Peace of Westphalia', 576.

57 Stuart Elden, *The Birth of Territory* (Chicago, IL, London: University of Chicago Press, 2013), 314. The Holy Roman and Spanish Empire had been ruled at one point, 130 years earlier, by the same king, Charles V – one reminder of the dynastic rather than territorial character of intra-European relationships during this period.

Swiss Confederacy to the Republic of Venice and beyond, the conference at Westphalia hosted an enormous array of different kinds of political-territorial entities, all engaged in different relations of subordination and independence in relation to these empires, as well as to the Papacy itself – a territorial power at this point. On the 'domestic' side, however, the diversity of the social hierarchies that were in some cases altered and in other cases re-asserted by the settlement defies any attempt retrospectively to separate the 'domestic' from the 'international' in this context. The Treaty of Münster, for example, articulates its signatories' intention to restore those rights possessed prior to the war *both* to 'all and every one of the Electors of the sacred Roman Empire, the Princes and States (therein comprehending the Nobility, which depend immediately on the Empire)', *and* to all 'their Vassals, Subjects, Citizens, [and] Inhabitants', bearing out the sheer complexity of the mixture of interlocking individual and collective, human and territorial forms of status.[58]

A second way in which the reality of the 1648 settlement confounds the cliché of 'Westphalian sovereignty' concerns the question of formal equality. This idea enters the Peace of Westphalia not only at the 'international' level but also at the 'individual' level. See, for instance, the injunction that to:

> all and each of the Officers, as well Military Men as Counsellors and Gownmen, and Ecclesiasticks ... from the highest to the lowest, without any distinction or exception, with their Wives, Children, Heirs, Successors, Servants, as well concerning their Lives and Estates, shall be restor'd by all Partys in the State of Life, Honour, Renown, Liberty of Conscience, Rights and Privileges, which they enjoy'd before the abovesaid Disorders.[59]

As this fragment makes clear, even military and religious officials were understood, by the negotiators, as occupying different positions in a hierarchy that ran 'from the highest to the lowest'. Nonetheless, it is also clear that, in contrast to their 'Wives, Children, Heirs, Successors, [and] Servants', the 'Officers', 'Military Men', 'Counsellors', 'Gownmen' and 'Ecclesiasticks' were the *only* individuals considered to have possessed something approximating a mutual status of formal equality among themselves. According to the text, these men had possessed, prior to the war, a set of rights that included 'Liberty of Conscience, Rights and Privileges' – a status the settlement set out explicitly to restore through the mechanism of what we would now call a multilateral agreement.

[58] Treaty of Münster, Art. 6.
[59] Ibid., Art. 43.

Even at this relatively early moment in the unfurling of the concept and practice of sovereign statehood, then, it is clear that the collective legal status of the entities concerned was closely tied to the question of the protection of the rights and duties of certain individuals. The Treaty of Münster laid down, for example, that 'Contracts, Exchanges, Transactions, Obligations, Treatys, made by Constraint or Threats, and extorted illegally from *States or Subjects* ... shall be ... annull'd and abolish'd'.[60] In doing so, it treated the property rights of a particular class of (Christian, male, propertied) individual subject conterminously with the territorial rights of the various collectivities which signed the treaty, from 'empires' to 'republics' to 'confederations' and beyond. The collective and individual dimensions of the issue of religious freedom – the burning issue of the day – are also impossible to disentangle. On the one hand, the Peace of Westphalia confirmed (as opposed to creating, as is commonly assumed) the principle of *cuius regi, eius religio* ('whose realm, his religion').[61] Meanwhile, *new* rights guaranteeing freedom of conscience were allocated to religious minorities within the signatory entities via the constitution, in the two treaties of 1648, of a new 'international' duty to this effect. In practice, however, at the collective level this meant the liberty to choose, exclusively, among three types of Christianity: Catholicism, Lutheranism and now also Calvinism.[62] The conclusion we should draw from this is not that these rights to religious freedom were granted in bad faith; the point is that scope of the idea of 'religion' itself was restricted to (three forms of) Christianity.

In other words, while the rights and duties restored to or bestowed on the signatories at the conference did include a limited right to religious freedom, this cannot be taken as indicating – as it does in the standard account of Westphalia – that each signatory was therefore free ('sovereign'), from that point onwards, to organise its internal affairs as it pleased. On the contrary, the 'international' principles of the settlement were integrated with a common set of assumptions about how signatories' internal

[60] Ibid., Art. 38 (Emphasis added).

[61] This had been granted to territorial rulers within the Holy Roman Empire nearly a century earlier, in the 1555 Treaty of Augsburg. Croxton, 'The Peace of Westphalia', 575.

[62] And even though, at the individual level, the text of the treaties did allow practices to emerge, especially in the Dutch Republic, which permitted a limited freedom of worship for Jews, the 'freedom' to practise other religions remained out of the question for a settlement dedicated 'to the Glory of God, and the Benefit of the Christian World' (Treaty of Münster, Preamble). See Gordon A. Christenson, 'Liberty of the Exercise of Religion in the Peace of Westphalia', 21 *Transnational Law and Contemporary Problems* (2013): 721–61 at 741–2; Miriam Bodian, '"Liberty of Conscience" and the Jews in the Dutch Republic', 6 *Studies in Christian-Jewish Relations* (2011): 1–9.

affairs should be organised. As Derek Croxton notes, 'far from making religion an aspect of internal politics, the Peace of Westphalia made religious liberty a matter of international responsibility'.[63] Rather than originating and guaranteeing the idea of state sovereignty, 'the endorsement of individual rights at Westphalia' actually 'limited state sovereignty' by making it conditional on respect for a particular, extremely narrow, set of individual rights. This remained the case however limited those rights might have been in practice, and however restricted the category of 'individual' for the purpose of rights protected at the level of international law.[64]

2.1.2 Early Theories of the State and the Individual Legal Subject

The micro/macro juridical relationship that I have just described is also evident in much of the political theory which emerged during this period. The key figures in this long debate about how best to organise a political community are well known. They include early republican theorists like Niccolò di Bernardo dei Machiavelli (1469–1527); contractarian theorists like Thomas Hobbes (1588–1679); natural law theorists like Francisco de Vitoria (1492–1546), Francisco Suárez (1548–1617) and Hugo Grotius (1583–1645); and later republicans like John Locke (1632–1704) and Jeremy Bentham (1748–1832). While the differences between these writers are just as important as the many victories and defeats by which this debate was characterised, the similarities which cut across it over a period of nearly three centuries are also suggestive. These similarities concern, as this section will elaborate, the connection between the concepts of 'state' and 'government' (or 'civil government'), the legitimacy of which was grounded in the supposedly 'natural' freedom and equality of 'all men'.

Though sometimes overlooked by international lawyers as relevant only to the fields of constitutional law and political theory, a recognisably 'modern' theory of the state had already reached an important stage of trans-regional consensus by 1648, even if there were still only a few states in existence at this time. In English, the very term 'state' is derived from the idea of the 'civill estate', put forward in the late sixteenth century as the

[63] Croxton, 'The Peace of Westphalia', 583.

[64] Indeed, according to Croxton, 'France and Sweden insisted throughout the Thirty Years War that their intervention had always been justified on this basis. Rather than fighting *against* the [Holy Roman] Empire, France claimed to be fighting *for* it by defending the German estates from an assault on their [pre-existing] constitutionally defined privileges and immunities.' It had defended its earlier interventions in Catalonia and Portugal 'on the same legal grounds: that of protecting the constitution of the Spanish monarchy against illegitimate attempts to impose absolutism'. Croxton, 'The Peace of Westphalia', 575, 583.

ideal model for collective human self-organisation.[65] This norm spread so rapidly that by the mid eighteenth century it had become the dominant understanding of political power in continental Europe.[66] Developed by the early contractarians such as Bodin and Hobbes, it leaned heavily (if dialectically) on the approaches they rejected. Above all, their intellectual rivals were the originators of the republican tradition that came to be consolidated during the high renaissance period in the Italian city-states such as Venice and Florence. Republican scholars such as Gasparo Contarini and, perhaps most famously, Machiavelli[67] had equated monarchy straightforwardly with tyranny, building their case on the classical philosophy of Aristotle and Cicero.

The republican starting point was the assumption that the only way to avoid the corrosive influence of power upon the ruler of any polity was to allow the community to govern itself. This implied that the community's magistrates should be held strictly responsible to the community, so that its welfare and self-authored laws would remain paramount and that the community would be able to remain independent, free from external interference.[68] These republican theorists were 'the earliest group of political writers [to] speak with full self-consciousness of a categorical distinction between states and governments', according to Quentin Skinner, and the first to 'express this distinction as a claim about the independent structures of *stati*, *états* and states'.[69] Nonetheless, Machiavelli and his colleagues sought explicitly to identify the powers of the state with those of the community itself, rather than to separate the two.[70]

65 Thomas Hobbes [1651], *Leviathan, or, the Matter, Forme and Power of a Common-Wealth Ecclesiastical and Civil* (London: J. M. Dent & Sons, 1914), 71.

66 Skinner, 'From the State of Princes to the Person of the State', in Skinner, *Visions of Politics*, Vol. 2, 408.

67 See Gasparo Contarini [1543], *Casparis De republica Venetorum libri quinque* (Lugd. Batavorum: Ex officina Elseviriana, 1628); Niccolò Machiavelli, *I discorsi di Nicolo Machiavelli*, Bk II (Palermo: Antonielli; London: J. Wolfe, 1584).

68 In the form of the church and of the Holy Roman Empire for British and French republicans of the early sixteenth century, for example. Skinner, 'From the State of Princes', 382.

69 Skinner, 'From the State of Princes', 386.

70 The refusal, on the part of these republican theorists, to distinguish the powers of the state from the powers of the community was shared by a second group of scholars attacked by Hobbes, Bodin and their fellow contractarians – the so-called 'monarchomachs' ('those who fight against kings'). These theorists challenged the orthodoxy of their day, grounded as it was in absolutist ideas about monarchical power, by advocating what was essentially a form of constitutional monarchy as the ideal form of polity. Insisting upon the natural freedom of all men, the monarchomachs deduced from this starting point that the individuals of whom every political community was comprised must, at some point, have consented to their subjection to the government under which

By contrast, the political inclinations of Hobbes and Bodin were straightforwardly absolutist, grounded in the 'descending' reasoning of natural law theory, rather than in the 'ascending' logic of republicanism (to adopt Koskenniemi's formulation).[71] Hobbes shared the republicans' assumptions concerning the equal natural freedom of all men. He also agreed that, once bound together under a single ruler and a single body of law, the population of the state (the *civitas* or *universitas*) should be regarded as a single *persona*, with a single, consolidated will.[72] However, he rejected the idea that the social contract or 'covenant' had the effect of imposing any restrictions whatsoever on the exercise of governing power. In the first place, Hobbes argued, only the 'awe' inspired by absolute power was enough to prevent individuals from lapsing into a barbaric, pre-political 'state of nature', meaning that any opposition to absolute power should be understood as irrational and therefore contrary to the 'laws of nature'.[73] In the second place, it was only in and through the act of submitting to the authority of the state that the individuals in question came to be joined together *as* a single political community.[74] The covenant, in his view, existed *not* between king and citizens (as for the republicans), but among the citizens themselves. Each and every citizen-to-be, he argued, had been transformed, by the act of covenanting, into an individual subject of the civil state or 'commonwealth', subject to its laws and for that reason to the authority which held the commonwealth together in the form of the king. Any right of rebellion was therefore ruled out.[75]

---

they lived. By the same token, they reasoned, these individuals must have imposed conditions on the exercise of public power, including – and this was their most controversial thesis – a right to resist tyrannical rulers. Skinner, 'From the State of Princes', 388–9.

71 Martti Koskenniemi, *From Apology to Utopia: The Structure of International Legal Argument* (Cambridge University Press, 2005), esp. 74–89.

72 Skinner, 'From the State of Princes', 389–92.

73 'Covenants without the sword, are but Words, and of no strength to secure a man at all', as Hobbes argued; for man's natural freedom, leaving him at liberty to 'use his own power for the preservation of his own Nature', ensured that 'there can be no security to any man' unless all agree to 'be contented with so much liberty against other men, as he would allow other men against himself'. Hobbes, *Leviathan*, 66–7, 87.

74 As Jean Bodin argued, it was only subjection to the 'soveraintie of power which unitieth in one body all the members and families' of a *république* or *civitas*. Jean Bodin, quoted in Skinner, 'From the State of Princes', 398.

75 As Hobbes put it, 'Because the Right of bearing the Person of them all, is given to him they make Soveraigne, by Covenant onely of one to another, and not of him to any of them; there can happen no breach of Covenant on the part of the Soveraigne; and consequently

Nonetheless, it remained the case that the foundation of the sovereign's power was the social contract itself, according to Hobbes, which he understood as the rational outcome – indeed, the *only* rational outcome – of the natural and equal liberty of all men.[76] In handing over part of this natural freedom in exchange for security in the form of law and order, the members of the 'multitude' or 'civitas' not only brought sovereign power into existence; they also authorised the sovereign 'to act in the name of the state'. Crucially, as Skinner notes, this meant that the multitude 'remain[ed] the authors of all the actions of the sovereign, and hence (by attribution) of all the actions of the state'.[77] With this conclusion, Hobbes gave birth to the concept of the unified legal 'personality' of the state. '[T]he Multitude,' he asserted, 'so united in one Person, is called a COMMON-WEALTH, in latine CIVITAS. This is the Generation of that great LEVIATHAN, or rather (to speak more reverently) of that *Mortall God*, to which wee owe under the *Immortall God*, our peace and defence' (see Figure 2).[78]

As even this very brief foray into the debate over the foundation of state authority indicates, the state was always, from the moment of its birth, a 'civill' state. It was, from the beginning, a political construction whose purpose and legitimacy were expressed in its formal connection to the individuals within its jurisdiction, however coercive or bloodthirsty its exercise of authority towards them might be, in theory or practice. It was to this relationship between the legal capacities of the state and the rights of the individuals within the state that the concept of 'government' or 'civil government' referred, whether tyrannical or quasi-democratic in nature.

To reiterate, this is not to suggest that statehood has ever been identified with one *type* of government only; still less that 'government' for the purposes of statehood was, or should be, understood as synonymous with 'popular' or 'democratic' government. On the contrary, the first iteration of the 'modern' theory of the state *as* 'state', with its powers carefully distinguished both from those of its individual ruler *and* from those of its population, came from *opponents* of the thesis of popular

none of his Subjects, by any pretence of forfeiture, can be freed from his Subjection'. Hobbes, *Leviathan*, 91.

[76] In Dudley Digges's articulation, 'Freedome is the birth-right of mankinde, and equally common to every one, as the Ayre we breath in, or the Sun which sheds his beames and lustre, as comfortably upon Beggars, as upon the Kings of the earth'. Dudley Digges [1648], *The Unlawfulness of Subjects Taking up Arms Against their Soveraigne* (London: Peter Parker, 1679), 2.

[77] Skinner, 'From the State of Princes', 404.

[78] Hobbes, *Leviathan*, 89 (Emphasis in the original).

sovereignty. This was the case, as Skinner notes, whether this opposition came 'in its republican guise as a claim about "free states" or in its legal and neo-scholastic form as a claim about the inalienable rights of communities'.[79] The crucial distinction for all these early scholars was thus between 'arbitrary government' and 'civil government' – between an authority which ruled at will and hence on behalf of itself, and one whose power was limited by the law of (and authored by) the community. It was primarily a formal distinction. Tyranny existed when the legal limitations which constituted the foundation of state power had been transgressed – not when the violence of political power reared its head. Moreover, this was a distinction that held whether the law in question was understood to derive from a once-and-for-all relinquishment of natural individual liberty (as in Hobbes's *Leviathan*), or whether it continued to be subject to the will of the people in an ongoing expression of that liberty (as in Locke's later republican argument for the 'freedom of men under government').[80]

As we have just seen, these early accounts are focused almost exclusively on the state's internal legitimacy; much less so on its external legitimacy in the eyes of other collective entities. Yet the 'outside' can seldom have been far from the minds of the sixteenth- and seventeenth-century theorists whose work we have just examined. These men were, after all, witnesses to one of the most dramatic shifts in perspective ever to have taken place in human history, as the world opened up literally before their eyes via the mechanisms of intercontinental trade, exploration and expansionist war. As several recent histories have emphasised, the different ways of being, thinking and organising collective life which the Europeans encountered during the 'Age of Discovery' had an enormous impact on the political theory of this period of so-called 'enlightenment', frequently serving as a foil against which European ideas and practices could be (favourably) contrasted.

Hobbes's hypothetical 'state of nature', for example, drew its inspiration directly from contemporary (and fundamentally misguided) assumptions about the 'savage' inhabitants of 'divers places in America'.[81] In the state of nature, Hobbes wrote, there was:

79 Skinner, 'From the State of Princes', 395.

80 Hobbes, *Leviathan*, 87–90; John Locke [1689], 'Of Civil Government', in Ian Shapiro (ed.), *John Locke: Two Treatises of Government and a Letter Concerning Toleration* (New Haven, CT, London: Yale University Press, 2003), 247–484, at 268.

81 Thomas Hobbes [1640], *The Elements of Law, Natural and Politic*, ed. J. C. A. Gaskin (Oxford University Press, 2008). See Pat Maloney, 'Hobbes, Savagery, and International

> no place for Industry; because the fruit thereof is uncertain: and consequently no Culture of the Earth; no Navigation, nor use of the commodities that may be imported by Sea; no commodious Building; no Instruments of moving; and removing such things as require much force; no Knowledge of the face of the Earth; no account of Time; no Arts; no Letters; no Society; and which is worst of all, continuall feare, and danger of violent death.

For his part, Hugo Grotius began his 1625 *De jure belli ac pacis* – routinely celebrated as international law's most important foundational text[82] – by contrasting 'civil Societies' with 'the *Aborigines*, the first Inhabitants of *Italy*, and of several People in *Africa*'.[83] Grotius described all of these peoples as 'savage' or 'uncivilized' societies because they lived, he said, 'without Laws or Government'.[84] Very similar references can be found in the works of Samuel von Pufendorf, Emer de Vattel, Locke, Jean-Jacques Rousseau, Montesquieu and many other of international law's 'founding fathers' of the Early Modern and Enlightenment periods.[85]

As many post-colonial theorists have shown, Europeans developed a dishonourable and apparently endless series of tropes to deploy as evidence of the supposed cultural, moral, aesthetic, psychological and physical inferiority of non-European peoples. In a *political* sense, it was, crucially, the supposed absence of 'Laws or Government' which caused these men to describe the peoples they encountered in the 'new world' as 'uncivilised savages' undeserving of the rights associated with the nascent concept of sovereignty. It was not, of course, unheard of for 'earlier' European peoples – such as 'the first inhabitants of Italy' or the Huns, Gauls and Goths – to fall into this category. The difference was that non-European and especially non-Caucasian peoples *could be assumed a priori* to fall into it – an assumption that strengthened with time, as

Anarchy', 105 *American Political Science Review* (February 2011), 189–204; John F. Moffitt and Sebastían Santiago, *'O Brave New People': The European Invention of the American Indian* (Albuquerque, NM: University of New Mexico Press, 1996), 284–5.

82 Both the American Society of International Law and the British Institute of International and Comparative Law (formerly known as the Grotius Society) run an annual 'Grotius Lecture', delivered by leading international lawyers and scholars of international law. These remain two of the most prestigious lecture series for the discipline worldwide.

83 Hugo Grotius [1738], 'The Rights of War and Peace', in *Three Books. Wherein are Explained, the Law of Nature and Nations, and the Principal Points Relating to Government* (Indianapolis, IN: Liberty Fund, 2005), Book 1, Ch. 1, 1 (n. 2).

84 Grotius, 'The Rights of War and Peace', 1 (n. 2).

85 See generally Kaius Tuori, *Lawyers and Savages: Ancient History and Legal Realism in the Making of Legal Anthropology* (Hoboken, NJ: Taylor & Francis, 2014); Ronald L. Meek, *Social Science and the Ignoble Savage* (Cambridge University Press, 1976).

colonialism and in particular the African slave trade grew to immense proportions by the mid seventeenth century, and later with the rise of social Darwinism. After all, the Greek word βάρβαρος (*barbaros*), 'barbarian', originally operated as an antonym for πολίτης (*politēs*), meaning 'citizen', the citizen of a πόλις (*polis* or city-state). The adjective 'civil', meanwhile, as in 'civill estate' or 'civil government',[86] is defined in the Oxford English Dictionary as:

> 'Of or relating to citizens or people who live together in a community; relating or belonging to members of a body politic'; 'Having or demonstrating proper public or social order; well-governed; orderly'; 'Legal; in the eyes of the law and the community; in terms of legal rights or status. Opposed to *natural*'.[87]

When used in the context of political theory and practice, in other words, the term 'civil', 'civility' or 'civilised' referred, at this time, to the presence of the particular legal order, founded on the social contract, whose objective it was to render concrete the 'natural' (God-given) freedom and equality of all 'men'. The increasingly common name for this order was 'civil state', or, to avoid tautology, simply 'state' – one among many forms (if an increasingly popular one) of political community in existence at this point in Europe.

What is important about this etymology is the way it helps us make sense of the fact that European communities were held to the *same standard* as non-European communities in the early doctrine and practice of what would eventually become international law. This standard, of course, played out in very different ways, as we shall see further below. Non-European communities, typically organised, as one might expect, in different ways from European communities, were assumed on that basis to

[86] Skinner, 'From the State of Princes', 405. John Locke, for example, describes his second 'treatise' as 'an essay concerning the true original, extent, and end, of civil government'. John Locke [1689], 'Of Civil Government', in Ian Shapiro (ed.), *John Locke: Two Treatises of Government and a Letter Concerning Toleration* (New Haven, CT, London: Yale University Press, 2003), title page.

[87] 'Civil, adj., n. and v.', *Oxford English Dictionary* (Oxford University Press, 2016). As the OED points out, moreover, the word 'civil' was also in common use as a verb during the second half of the sixteenth century. The editors give a line from the collection of tales *Pan his Syrinx* by William Warner (c. 1558–1609), also an attorney in the Court of Common Pleas in London, to illustrate its meaning in this context: 'Whosoeuer had extirped Tyraunts, ciuiled Nations, confounded Monsters ... was magnified for more than a man'. See 'Civil, v.', *Oxford English Dictionary*; 'Warner, William (c. 1558–1609)', in Arthur F. Kinney and David W. Swain, *The Routledge Encyclopedia of Tudor England* (New York, London: Garland Publishing, 2001), 743.

be 'uncivil/ised'. At the same time, however, the very fact and operation of this standard meant that the sovereignty even of European states was never considered immutable. Grotius, for example, agreed with Hobbes that individual citizens did not have the right to take up arms against their own sovereign; yet they insisted nonetheless that sovereigns *could* intervene in other jurisdictions to assist the unfortunate citizens of tyrannical states. Thus, discussing 'Whether we have a just Cause for War with another Prince, in order to relieve his Subjects from their Oppression under him', for example, Grotius wrote:

> True it is, that since the Institution of Civil Societies, the Governors of every State have acquired some peculiar Right over their respective Subjects ... But if the Injustice be visible, as if a Busiris, a Phalaris, or a Thracian Diomedes exercise such Tyrannies over Subjects, as no good Man living can approve of, the Right of human Society shall not be therefore excluded. Thus Constantine made War against Maxentius and Licinius; and other Roman Emperors against the Persians, or threatened them with it at least, unless they left off persecuting Christians on the account of their Religion only.[88]

The standard of 'civil' government, regarded as an attribute of statehood, was, in other words, treated as an ongoing test to which states would continue to be held if their sovereign rights were to persist in full. From the several interventions launched by Elizabeth I of England (r. 1558–1603) into France and the Netherlands, to the multiple interventions of the European powers into the Ottoman Empire under the legal rubric of the 'capitulations' regime from the sixteenth century to the mid nineteenth century and beyond,[89] the protection of oppressed individuals, and in particular the members of religious minorities, was deployed again and again to justify what would otherwise have been an illegitimate violation of the rights of a sovereign equal.[90] My point here is not just that 'humanitarian' intervention has a long history. We can, in addition, say something much more precise:

[88] Hugo Grotius, *The Rights of War and Peace*, Bk 2, Ch. 24, 1159–62.

[89] See Umut Özsu, 'The Ottoman Empire, the Origins of Extraterritoriality, and International Legal Theory', in Hoffmann and Orford (eds.), *The Oxford Handbook of the Theory of International Law*, 123–37; Davide Rodogno, 'European Legal Doctrines on Intervention and the Status of the Ottoman Empire within the "Family of Nations" Throughout the Nineteenth Century', 18 *JHIL* (2016): 5–41; Basile Homsy, *Les capitulations & la protection des chrétiens au Proche-Orient aux XVIe, XVIIe et XVIIIe siècles* (Harissa: L'Imprimerie Saint Paul, 1956); Maurits H. van den Boogert, *The Capitulations and the Ottoman Legal System: Qadis, Consuls, and Beraths in the 18th Century* (Leiden, Boston, MA: Brill, 2005).

[90] See generally Brendan Simms and D. J. B. Trim (eds.), *Humanitarian Intervention: A History* (Cambridge University Press, 2011).

that the violation of a narrow set of individual rights associated with formal equality and negative freedom has constituted the rationale for intervention since the very earliest incarnations of the state system. This limited set of 'civil' rights is identical to the limited set later associated, by Pashukanis, Edelman and others, with the rights of the individual legal subject.

2.1.3 International Trade and the Individual Legal Subject

That the sovereign state possessed, in practice, and was conceptualised as possessing, a central and specific set of responsibilities towards the rational and hence 'naturally' free and equal individual is also evident if we examine the influence of the expansion of international trade on the development of the theory and practice of the state. As Koskenniemi has argued recently, the essential theoretical point which links the private law regime of trade together with the unfolding of the state as a subject of public international law concerns a *subjective* conception of right and a *commutative* conception of justice. These were the conceptions of right developed by some of the most influential theorists in this area – Grotius, Vitoria, Suàrez, Pufendorf and others, whose treatises were frequently acted on directly in the form of legal advice to states including the Spanish Empire, the United Provinces and Sweden.[91]

As Koskenniemi explains, 'subjective' rights, understood as possessed by all 'men' at all times and in all places, were of two kinds. 'Perfect' rights, or what Grotius called 'faculties', constituted 'strict, enforceable law'. The most important of these were rights of *dominium* – including 'the power that one has over oneself (that is to say, one's personal liberty) and those under one's tutelage (wife, children or slaves) as well as over one's property'.[92] As Koskenniemi notes, the 'network of relations between *facultates*' was therefore 'covered by expletive (commutative) justice, the horizontal

[91] Martti Koskenniemi, 'International Law and the Emergence of Mercantile Capitalism: Grotius to Smith', in Pierre-Marie Dupuy and Vincent Chetail (eds.), *The Roots of International Law/Les fondements du droit international* (Leiden: Brill, 2013), 1–37; Koskenniemi, 'Empire and International Law: The Real Spanish Contribution'.

[92] The question of private property posed some difficulties here, for it was agreed that this institution of private property deviated from man's natural state, at creation, of enjoying *dominium* in common. Nonetheless, as Vitoria and others argued, man also enjoyed *dominium* over his own actions, meaning that this deviation need not be regarded as a violation of natural law. Instead, although it stemmed from man's natural freedom, and hence from his *dominium* over his own actions, the right to private property – like the associated rights to freedom of trade and of travel – was not itself part of natural law, but was, instead, part of the *jus gentium* – the law that had arisen in the practice of all (rational) human beings to the extent that their actions were in accordance with natural law principles. Koskenniemi, 'The Emergence of Mercantile Capitalism', 5, 13–15.

system of inter-individual relations characterised by the exercise of such subjective rights on the one hand, and everyone's duty to respect them on the other'.[93] By contrast, 'imperfect' rights or 'aptitudes' were derived *not* from the natural order created by God, or from the *jus gentium* which reflected that order in human practice, but instead from the real-life communities to which every individual inevitably belonged. Imperfect rights were thus specific, rather than general, having been allocated by the rulers of those particular, living communities to different classes of person on the basis of principles like merit or charity. Imperfect rights were therefore treated as belonging to a different normative order, one based on the earthly principle of distributive or 'allocative' justice. They were not, therefore, regarded as 'hard' natural law, and such rights were certainly not enforceable against any (universal) rights of *dominium* with which they might conflict.[94]

This distinction between perfect and imperfect subjective rights is crucial for our understanding of the simultaneous emergence of international law, mercantile capitalism and the colonial project. For as Koskenniemi points out, the conviction that 'perfect' rights must always trump 'imperfect' rights meant in practice that '[t]he task of the State was not to distribute property according to some allocative principle but to give effect to the relations of *dominium* as they existed in the network of relations of commutative justice that governed the relationships of subjective right holders to each other'.[95] At the same time, the theory of subjective rights also meant that the violation of rights of *dominium* could and should be punished either by the state or even – if the punishment occurred beyond the state's jurisdiction (on the high seas, for example, or in territories only recently 'discovered') – by the individual right-holder. On the one hand, then, rulers were prohibited from intervening for the purpose of redistribution and they could only tax their subjects 'for the good of the community' as a whole.[96] On the other, meanwhile, 'just' war could therefore be waged against those, including individuals and companies, who violated the 'system' of international commerce then being consolidated.[97] It was with this scholastic

[93] Ibid., 5.

[94] Ibid., 5.

[95] Ibid., 4–5.

[96] Ibid., 4–5.

[97] As Francisco Suàrez reasoned, it had been 'established by the *ius gentium* that commercial intercourse shall be free, and it would be a violation of that system of law if such intercourse were prohibited without reasonable course'. Francisco Suàrez, 'On Laws and God

tradition in mind that Grotius developed his famous apology for the belligerent activities of the Dutch East India Company on the basis of the principle of self-preservation, which he (like Vitoria before him and Locke after him) saw as the most fundamental of all individual rights, stemming from the natural (and equal) liberty of all men.[98]

As republican theorists like Locke and Rousseau later pointed out, natural law theories of sovereignty like those of Hobbes and Grotius harboured unabashedly absolutist tendencies.[99] Nonetheless, Koskenniemi notes, the fact that '[Grotius's] *De jure belli ac pacis* contained both a theory of an authoritarian state and of almost unlimited private rights' did not involve any contradiction. For while it was certainly true that 'the foundational of civil community lay in nature, natural rights had no real role to play inside it' after the social contract had been concluded.[100] Subjective rights, on the other hand, were crucial. Indeed, for Grotius, Suàrez and others it was precisely the function of governments to protect individual subjective rights – not because they believed such rights to be exercisable *against* the state (as the republicans insisted), but, on the contrary, because their enforcement was in the best interests of the community, and hence also of the 'system' created by the *jus gentium*, as a whole.

2.1.4 The Individual Legal Subject and the Transition from the Absolutist to the Republican State

For all that they disagreed with the absolutist tendencies of natural rights theorists like Hobbes, Grotius and others,[101] later republican theorists like Locke and Rousseau charged the governments which *they* held to be legitimate with a very similar task: that of protecting the liberty and equality of all (rational) human beings ('men'), expressed in a narrow set

the Lawgiver', in *Selections from Three Works, Vol. 2*, trans. G. Williams (Oxford University Press, 1965), 3–754, 347, cited in Koskenniemi, 'International Law and the Emergence of Mercantile Capitalism', 17. The classic text on the history of the 'commercial revolution' is Roberto Sabatino Lopez, *The Commercial Revolution of the Middle Ages* (Cambridge, New York: Cambridge University Press, 1976).

98 On the co-constitution of the state and the corporation during this period, see e.g. Sundhya Pahuja, 'Public Debt, The Peace of Utrecht, and the Rivalry between Company and State,' in Alfred Soons (ed.), *The 1713 Peace of Utrecht and its Enduring Effects* (Leiden: Brill, forthcoming); Grietje Baars, *Law, Capital and the Corporation* (Leiden: Brill, forthcoming, 2018); Koen Stapelbroek, 'Trade, Chartered Companies, and Mercantile Associations', in Bardo Fassbender and Anne Peters (eds.), *The Oxford Handbook of International Legal History* (Oxford University Press, 2012), 338–58 at 347.

99 Jean-Jacques Rousseau [1762], *The Social Contract* (Harmondsworth: Penguin, 1968), 51.

100 Koskenniemi, 'International Law and the Emergence of Mercantile Capitalism', 23.

101 See e.g. Rousseau, *The Social Contract*, 51.

of rights concerning the protection of their 'lives, liberties and estates'.[102] The republican rationale for this was, however, very different. Simply put, from the natural law perspective, as we have just seen, governments were duty-bound to enforce rights of *dominium* which pre-existed their own authority. These rights, like sovereign power itself, were derived from the *jus gentium*, and the *jus gentium* was itself a human outgrowth of the universal normative structure founded upon God's will. From the republican perspective, by contrast, governments were duty-bound to respect individual rights because these rights were the condition upon which their holders had consented to, constituted and rendered conditional the brute fact of sovereign power.[103] It was in this sense that republicans began to use the term 'responsible' to describe a government which derived its powers from the consent of the governed (who therefore possessed a right of rebellion – a right which Hobbes and his colleagues rejected categorically). In short, to return to Koskenniemi's earlier formulation, one argument was 'descending' in its approach to reconciling 'individual freedom' with 'social order', while the other was 'ascending'.[104] Neither, however, questioned the idea that the fundamental problem of politics and law was that of how best to realise 'individual freedom'. From whichever direction these rights were derived, moreover, their substance remained in its essence the same – as did the commutative (as opposed to distributive) notion of justice that underpinned it.[105] Both groups of scholars, natural

[102] Quentin Skinner, *Liberty before Liberalism* (Cambridge University Press, 1998), 21, discussing the work of Needham, Algernon Sidney, Henry Neville, Marchamont Nedham and John Locke. As Skinner points out: 'It is no part of the purposes of these writers to list these natural rights [which they saw it as the function of government to protect] in any detail. But they generally take them to include freedom of speech, freedom of movement and contract, and they often summarise them in the form of the claim that all citizens have an equal right to the lawful enjoyment of their lives, liberties and estates' (20). With the important exception of the right of freedom of speech, the overlap between the natural rights assumed by their 'absolutist' opponents is striking.

[103] Koskenniemi, *From Apology to Utopia*, 74–89.

[104] Ibid., 71.

[105] It is true that Hobbes suggests that his conception of justice is distributive as opposed to commutative (Hobbes, *Leviathan*, 77–80). However, his definition of distributive justice as equity is an idiosyncratic one, which relies on a rejection of the very distinction between commutative and distributive justice. Hobbes insists that it is a 'precept of the Law of Nature' that in order to 'judge between man and man', judges and arbitrators must 'deale Equally between them' in 'acknowledgement of [their] naturall equalitie' (80), pointing to a procedural rather than a substantive conception of justice. At the same time, distributive justice or equity in Hobbes's formulation 'is due by grace alone'; as a subject, '[y]ou deserve what the sovereign gives you: there is no desert prior to and independent of his allocation of rights' meaning that 'distributive justice does not track but create merit'. Contrary to

law theorists and republicans, relied on the same assumption to ground the legitimacy of their arguments: that the good of the community would follow automatically from the enforcement of this narrow set of individual rights (and, thus, from this vindication of commutative or 'expletive' justice) as if led (in Smith's famous formulation) 'by an invisible hand'.[106]

It was in the gradual rejection of the state's originally absolutist tendencies, however, with the republican revolutions of the eighteenth and nineteenth centuries, that the relationship between individual and international legal subjectivity came to be spelled out definitively, together with the striking capacity of these supposedly universal categories to exclude four-fifths of humanity or more without endangering their legitimising logic in the least. For example, one of the first acts of the French Revolutionary National Constituent Assembly in the wake of the French Revolution of 1789 was to '[abolish] the feudal system entirely' by revoking all rights concerning 'personal servitude' without compensation.[107] Three weeks later, the Assembly published the *Déclaration des droits de l'homme et du citoyen*, which announced that '*Les hommes naissent et demeurent libres et égaux en droits*' and that '*Le but de toute association politique est la conservation des droits naturels et imprescriptibles de l'Homme … la*

---

the orthodox understanding of distributive justice, therefore, in Hobbes's theory of the state, 'citizens cannot invoke equity to claim a fair share of the goods distributed'. Johan Olsthoorn, 'Hobbes's Account of Distributive Justice as Equity', 21 *British Journal for the History of Philosophy* (2013): 13–33, at 13. See also Dennis Klimchuk, 'Hobbes on Equity', in David Dyzenhaus and Thomas Poole (eds.), *Hobbes and the Law* (Cambridge University Press, 2012), 165–85. It is also the case that Bodin argues for a combination of distributive and commutative justice into the principle of 'harmonic justice', to which a 'legitimate monarchy, whether elective, hereditary, or founded in a conquest voluntarily submitted to', is best suited, since 'the king's relations to his subjects is that of a father to his children, for he does justice among them'. Jean Bodin [1576], *Six Books of the Commonwealth*, abridged and trans. M. J. Tooley (Oxford: Blackwell, 1955), available at www.constitution.org/bodin/bodin.txt (accessed 1 November 2015). However, Bodin's attention here is turned inwards to the question of the hierarchy of individual subjects common at that time to feudal Europe. His wish is to avoid a situation in which (using marriage as his example) either 'princes should only marry princesses, wealthy men rich wives, poor men poor ones, and slaves slaves' (pure commutative justice) or in which 'marriages were arranged by casting lots, a slave might marry a king' (pure distributive justice), for 'these two principles of government both involve many disadvantages, for by the one the poor are oppressed, and by the other the nobles slighted'.

[106] Adam Smith [1776], *An Inquiry into the Nature and Causes of the Wealth of Nations* (London, J. M. Dent & Son; New York: E. P. Dutton & Co., 1910), Book IV, Ch. 2, available at www.gutenberg.org/files/3300/3300-h/3300-h.htm (accessed 25 June 2016).

[107] Decree of 4 August 1789, in John Hall Stewart (ed.), *A Documentary Survey of the French Revolution* (New York: Macmillan, 1951), 107.

liberté, la propriété, la sûreté, et la résistance à l'oppression'.[108] Similarly, the American Declaration of Independence of 4 July 1776 proclaimed:

> We hold these truths to be self-evident, that all men are created equal, that they are endowed by their Creator with certain unalienable Rights, that among these are Life, Liberty and the pursuit of Happiness. – That to secure these rights, Governments are instituted among Men, deriving their just powers from the consent of the governed, – That whenever any Form of Government becomes destructive of these ends, it is the Right of the People to alter or to abolish it, and to institute new Government ...[109]

The content of these rights was, in other words, not dissimilar to the content of the 'subjective' right of *dominium*, with two exceptions: the derivation of the 'just powers' of government from 'the consent of the governed'; and, stemming from that, the right to resistance against oppression.

Viewed in the light of the previous discussion, the French and American Declarations offer two very useful articulations of the structure and content of legal subjectivity. 'All men' may have been 'born' free and 'equal in rights'; yet it was only as 'citizens' of the French state that these natural rights acquired material force. Equally, the question remained as to who should count as a 'man' in the first place. Women, for one, certainly did not and Olympe de Gouges, author of the 1791 *Déclaration des droits de la femme et de la citoyenne*, was executed precisely for asking why women's 'right to mount the scaffold' was not matched by any such right 'to mount the speaker's rostrum'.[110] Nor, indeed, for the revolutionaries did certain male individuals count as 'men'. This applied, notably, to men of African descent. Thus, in one of the most dramatic illustrations of the interpellative 'pull' of the conjoined ideas of sovereign statehood and legal personality,[111] between 1791 and 1804 the slave population of the French colony of Saint-Domingue successfully overthrew French rule and established Haiti as an independent republic, alluding explicitly to the proclaimed universality of French Revolutionary principles as their inspiration.[112] Even within France (as in

[108] *La Déclaration des droits de l'Homme et du citoyen*, Assemblée nationale constituante, 26 August 1789, Arts. 1–4.

[109] *American Declaration of Independence*, Philadelphia, 4 July 1776, Preamble.

[110] *Déclaration des droits de la femme et de la citoyenne* (1791), Art. 10. See Jacques Rancière, 'Who Is the Subject of the Rights of Man?', 103 *South Atlantic Quarterly* (2004): 297–310 at 303–4.

[111] See Frame, Section 2.

[112] Susan Buck-Morss, for example, has pointed to the almost incredible contradiction between the philosophy of the Enlightenment, founded on the axiom of the 'natural' freedom of 'all men', and the legal relations and material reality of the increasingly globalised economy in which that philosophy developed, founded on slave labour and the slave trade. Susan Buck-Morss, 'Hegel and Haiti', 26 *Critical Inquiry* (2000): 821–65, at 821. It could

the settlement of 1648, and as in many other states well into the twentieth century), only propertied adult males who (in this case) paid 'a direct tax equal at least to the value of three days' labor' were considered 'men' with eligibility for 'active' citizenship, including the power to vote.[113] For its part, the American Declaration was followed, 11 years later, by a Constitution which, among other things, enshrined the distinction between 'free Persons' and slaves, and excluded all women from the vote.[114]

These contradictions did not stem from error or bad faith. For the 'natural' condition of freedom and equality pertaining to 'all men' was, from the beginning, derived from something that all these jurists, philosophers and practitioners considered a fact: the distinctive rationality of 'mankind'. This did not mean, however, that all human beings were to be considered *equally* rational. It was this question of different levels of (ir)rationality which thus held out the possibility of different degrees of legal subjectivity. Hobbes, for example, took care to distinguish the 'civil' life of the political community from the merely instinctive life of the beehive or ant colony.[115] It did not occur to him, however, to justify the exclusion of women, 'savage peoples', serfs or slaves from the 'multitude' of 'men' whom he theorised as having covenanted collectively in order to constitute the civil state. On the contrary, that such individuals were akin to 'Children, Fooles, and Madmen that have no use of reason' was something that he took for granted.[116] Notwithstanding the shift that took place in the meantime from contractarianism to republicanism, or from natural law to positivist thinking, an almost identical logic underpinned the decision of the authors of the first

be argued, however, that her argument in some ways misses the point: that, as Orlando Patterson puts it, 'slavery and freedom' have always been 'intimately connected' both in theory and in practice. Orlando Patterson, *Slavery and Social Death: A Comparative Study* (Cambridge, MA: Harvard University Press, 1985), ix.

113 *Constitution of the French National Assembly*, 3 September 1791, Ch. I, Sec. II, para. 2. On the logic of the property qualification, see John Adams (1735–1826), second President of the United States, who argued in 1776 that 'men ... in every society, who are wholly destitute of property, are also too little acquainted with public affairs to form a right judgment, and too dependent upon other men to have a will of their own' and will therefore 'talk and vote as they are directed by some man of property, who has attached their minds to his interest'. John Adams to James Sullivan, 26 May 1776, in Philip B. Kurland and Ralph Lerner (eds.), *The Founders' Constitution*, Vol. 1 (University of Chicago Press, 1987), Ch. 13, Doc. 10, available at http://press-pubs.uchicago.edu/founders/documents/v1ch13s10.html (accessed 3 September 2017).

114 Constitution of the United States of America, 17 September 1787.

115 Hobbes, *Leviathan*, 88–9.

116 Ibid., 85.

American Constitution of 1787 to count a slave as being worth three-fifths of a free individual for the purposes of taxation.[117]

Or, for a theoretical illustration of the way in which assumptions about rationality and its nature made it possible to claim the 'natural rights' of 'all men' to 'life, liberty and property' as a universal principle, and thus 'civil' government as the ultimate form of collective self-organisation, whilst simultaneously subjugating the majority of the world's human beings to patriarchal and/or colonial forms of individual and collective unfreedom, including straightforward enslavement, we need only look to perhaps the most famous republican theorist of all, John Locke (1632–1704). Locke's is perhaps the paradigmatic understanding of the 'ends of political society and government'. As he argued:

> If man in the state of nature be so free as has been said; if he be absolute lord of his own person and possessions, equal to the greatest, and subject to nobody, why will he part with his freedom, why will he give up this empire, and subject himself to the dominion and control of any other power? To which it is obvious to answer, that though in the state of nature he hath such a right, yet the enjoyment of it is very uncertain, and constantly exposed to the invasion of others ... [I]t is [therefore] not without reason that he seeks out, and is willing to join in society with others ... for the mutual preservation of their lives, liberties, and estates, which I call by the general name property.[118]

Since the 'chief end' of 'men's uniting into commonwealths, and putting themselves under government, is the preservation of their property', and since men 'enter into society' and 'give up the equality, liberty, and executive power they had in the state of nature' only for this reason – 'for no rational creature can be supposed to change his condition with an intention to be worse' – 'the power of the society ... can never be supposed to extend farther than the common good; but is obliged to secure every one's property'.[119] At the same time, even as he began his *Two Treatises of Government* by condemning slavery as a 'vile and miserable' institution,[120] Locke had no objection to the inclusion of African

[117] *Constitution of the United States of America*, 17 September 1787, Art. 1, Sec. 2(3). Slavery was partially outlawed by Amendment XIII, 13 January 1865, 'except as a punishment for crime whereof the party shall have been duly convicted'.

[118] John Locke, 'Of Civil Government', in Ian Shapiro (ed.), *John Locke: Two Treatises of Government and a Letter Concerning Toleration* (New Haven, CT, London: Yale University Press, 2003), 247–484 at 365–6, paras. 123–4.

[119] Locke, 'Of Civil Government', 366, 370.

[120] Ibid., 40.

human beings within the sphere of property.[121] As Buck-Morss points out, 'Locke's outrage … was not a protest against the enslavement of black Africans on New World plantations … Rather, slavery was a metaphor for legal tyranny, as it was used generally in British parliamentary debates on constitutional theory.'[122] And while Locke did not discuss the institution of material, as opposed to metaphorical, slavery, he was clear that the right to freedom existed only insofar as an individual's rationality had developed. As he wrote: the 'freedom … of man, and liberty of acting according to his own will, is grounded on his having reason … To turn him loose to an unrestrained liberty, before he has reason to guide him, is … to thrust him out amongst brutes, and abandon him to a state as wretched.'[123] Locke was, here, describing the relationship between fathers and children, but, as we are about to see, a long tradition was already in existence by this time to suggest that a similar standard could be applied to communities which were judged, on the basis of their institutions of collective self-organisation, to be less than fully rational.

What effect did this 'logic of contradiction', as the sociologist Orlando Patterson has called it,[124] have on those individuals who were excluded from the supposedly universal human category of 'all men'? If they were not 'full' legal subjects, then what *were* these individuals, in legal terms, and what did they desire to be? How did the denial of international legal subjectivity to collectivities deemed not to be 'self-governing' affect the rights of the individuals within them? How did territories deemed not to be states articulate their demands to be treated properly? In order to answer these questions, the next subsection will turn to the second side of the triangle.

2.2 *Individual/Colony*

One of the earliest and most famous accounts of the legal implications of the encounter between the European states and the communities of the 'new

[121] Locke was heavily involved in the development of colonial policies in the Americas, and especially in Carolina. It was he who authored Carolina's *Fundamental Constitutions* of 1 March 1669, which stated at Art. 110 that 'Every freeman of Carolina shall have absolute power and authority over his negro slaves, of what opinion or religion soever'. David Brion Davis, *The Problem of Slavery in Western Culture* (New York: Cornell University Press, 1966), 118.

[122] Buck-Morss, 'Hegel and Haiti', at 826.

[123] Locke, 'Of Civil Government', 305.

[124] See generally Patterson, *Slavery and Social Death.*

world' upon whom they would wreak such havoc is Vitoria's *De Indis et de Iure Belli*, first published in 1532. His purpose in making this analysis was a dual one. He sought not only to work through the question of whether the Spaniards had appropriated the so-called Indians' land legitimately, thereby substituting Spanish for Indigenous sovereignty, but also – in fact, primarily – to work out whether the Spaniards were justified in enslaving individual members of those Indigenous communities and transforming them into human property. Crucially for the relationship examined in this chapter, the device which he used to connect the two elements of his argument together was the notion of 'self-government'.

2.2.1 'Natural' Slavery, Colonisation and Self-Government in the 'New World'

In his reasoning, Vitoria positioned himself between two of the debate's best-known prosecutors: Bartolomé de las Casas and Juan Ginés de Sepúlveda. Where Las Casas argued that the Indigenous peoples encountered by the Spanish were fully rational and therefore possessed of rights which could not legitimately be violated, and where Sepúlveda insisted that the 'Indians' were no more rational than wild beasts and could therefore be conquered and enslaved legitimately, Vitoria concluded that the Indians were not entirely 'of unsound mind' and had 'according to their kind, the use of reason'.[125] Vitoria reached this opinion as to the level of the Indians' rationality through an examination of systems they had developed for organising their lives collectively. He based his opinion, in particular, on reports coming from the 'new world' which indicated that local Indigenous communities possessed a working conception of property. For him this was crucial, in that it meant that 'the aborigines undoubtedly had true dominium in both public and private matters, just like Christians', and hence that 'neither their princes nor private persons could be despoiled of their property on the ground of their not being true owners'.[126]

As Anghie points out, however, the humanitarian reputation Vitoria obtained as a result of this insistence on the rationality and humanity of the 'Indians' appears in a different light as soon as the 'natural duties', as well as the 'natural rights', associated with inclusion in the *jus gentium* are taken into account. For Vitoria argued that these 'natural rights' meant

[125] Francisco de Vitoria [1532], *De Indis et de Iure Belli Reflectiones*, trans. John Pawley Bate (Washington, DC: Carnegie Institution of Washington, 1917), 127.

[126] Ibid., 128.

that Spanish individuals had 'a right to travel to the lands of the Indians and to sojourn there so long as they do no harm, and they [could] not be prevented by the Indians'; that they might 'carry on trade among the Indian aborigines, so long as they do no harm to their own country, by importing the goods which the aborigines lack, etc., and taking away gold and silver and other articles in which the Indians abound'; and that 'the princes of the Indians [could] not prevent their subjects from trading with the Spaniards, etc' or 'prevent the Spaniards from a communication and participation in those things which they treat as common alike to natives and to strangers'.[127] As Anghie points out, Vitoria's incorporation of the Indians into a legal system they had never heard of wove them into an 'inescapable system of norms which are inevitably violated by the Indians',[128] who could then rightfully be punished – waged war upon or even enslaved – for their violation ('when the Indians deny the Spaniards their rights under the law of nations they do them a wrong. Therefore, if it be necessary, in order to preserve their right, that they should go to war, they may lawfully do so').[129]

However, if it was clear to Vitoria that the Indians, like the Spanish, possessed individual rights of *dominium* under the *jus gentium*, and therefore could not be enslaved unless this was deemed necessary to enforce the rights of *dominion* carried by Spanish individuals into their territories, he was less certain as to the question of the Indians' collective right of *dominium* over their territory, to the exclusion of the Spanish. There was, he felt, 'a certain method in their affairs, for they have polities which are orderly arranged and they have definite marriage and magistrates, overlords, laws, and workshops, and a system of exchange, all of which call for the use of reason'.[130] Yet he also acknowledged that there was a contrary view then in circulation, according to which the Indians were 'not wholly unintelligent, yet they are little short of that condition, and so are unfit to found or administer a lawful State up to the standard required by human and civil claims'.[131] According to this view, the Indians had 'no proper laws nor magistrates, and are not even capable of controlling their family affairs; they are without any literature or arts, not only the liberal arts, but the mechanical arts also; they have no careful agriculture and no artisans;

[127] Ibid., 150.

[128] Antony Anghie, *Imperialism, Sovereignty and the Making of International Law* (Cambridge University Press, 2005), 21.

[129] Vitoria, *De Indis*, 154.

[130] Ibid., 127.

[131] Ibid., 160–1.

and they lack many other conveniences, yea necessaries, of human life'.[132] If this was the case, Vitoria concluded that:

> there is no doubt that [colonisation by Spain] would not only be a permissible, but also a highly proper, course to take; nay, our sovereigns would be bound to take it, just as if the natives were infants. The same principle seems to apply here to them as to people of defective intelligence; and indeed they are no whit or little better than such so far as self-government is concerned.[133]

In Vitoria's view, then, the Spaniards would only be justified in taking over 'the administration of the country' *if* those institutions had proved incapable of enforcing the pre-existing rights of *dominium* which the Spanish individuals carried with them, as rational beings and hence as subjects of the *jus gentium*, to the 'new world'. For if the Indians were not capable of enforcing the *jus gentium* for themselves, then only through colonisation could the natural law principle of commutative justice be vindicated.[134]

In essence, Vitoria here was arguing that as rational beings, individual members of Indigenous communities were by defintion subjects of the *jus gentium*, meaning that their property could not be legitimately confiscated, nor their persons be enslaved, *unless* they violated that law; but since their rationality was still underdeveloped, the Spaniards would be justified in subjugating them *collectively* for their own good. Vitoria's argument here may be understood as resolving one of the main paradoxes in the Aristotelian idea of 'natural slavery', upon which, like many of his contemporaries, he based his argument. Certain individuals, Aristotle had argued in Book One of *The Politics*, were 'barbarians', who lacked reason or *logos*, as he called it – a term that referred both to language (Greek being the language of civilisation in Aristotle's view) and logic, encompassing the ability to identify 'the advantageous from its opposite, and thus the just from the unjust'. Such individuals were 'natural' slaves, whose enslavement would be as beneficial to them as it would be to their master in that it would expose the slave to the civilising influence of the master.[135]

[132] Ibid., 160–1.

[133] Ibid., 160–1

[134] On commutative justice, see Section 2.1.3, above.

[135] For a summary, see Nicholas D. Smith, 'Aristotle's Concept of Natural Slavery', 37 *Phoenix* (1984): 110–14. Aristotle was ambivalent, however, as to whether 'natural slaves' were, for him, completely without rationality and thus excluded from the realm of mankind (whom he defined as a 'rational animal') completely. William Fortenbaugh argued in the 1970s that Aristotle denied slaves 'the logical or reasoning half of the bipartite soul but not the alogical or emotional half'; such slaves were capable of making 'the judgements involved in emotional responses and therefore have at least a minimum share in the cognitive capacity

However, although Aristotle explained why, in his view, 'some human beings are only actualised as human beings through the guidance of others', he neglected to explain 'why some human beings deserve to suffer continuing despotic rule' after their 'actualisation' as human beings through the acquisition of *logos*.[136] It is *this* problem that Vitoria's thesis resolved. It did so by establishing a link between the rights of the rational individual, as a subject of the *jus gentium*, on the one hand, and the collective rights of the 'self-governing' community, on the other, with 'self-government', here referring to the capacity to 'administer a lawful State up to the standard required by human and civil claims' – i.e. to the existience of a legal and institutional structure capable of protecting 'universal' rights of *dominium* and enforcing the *jus gentium*. To the extent that the Indians did possess such institutions and were willing to enforce that law, they were rational, and should be regarded as collectively independent. To the extent they did not, they could, and should, be colonised for their own good, until the Spanish had succeeded in imparting *logos* to them. As Vitoria explained:

> Aristotle certainly did not mean to say that such as are not over-strong mentally are by nature subject to another's power and incapable of dominium alike over themselves and other things; for this is civil and legal slavery, wherein none are slaves by nature. Nor does the Philosopher mean that, if any by nature are of weak mind, it is permissible to seize their

peculiar to men in relation to other animals' (quoted in Smith, 'Aristotle's Concept', 114). However, Nicholas Smith counters that Aristotle understood the relationship between reason and emotion in terms of a 'regal' (paternalistically benign) relationship, whereas the relationship between master and slave is, in Aristotle, 'despotic'. The central concept at work must therefore be *logos*, rather than emotion – for Aristotle denied *logos* both to beasts (such as beasts of burden, over which man exercises an obviously despotic form of domination) *and* to 'natural' slaves. It was in this sense that Aristotle identified 'natural slaves' with 'barbarians – those who could not communicate in Greek, for him the language of civilisation, but only using brutish, unintelligible noises ('*bar-bar-bar*...'). The Greek word βαρβαρος is defined as 'A. barbarous, i.e. non-Greek, foreign ...; originally all non-Greek-speaking peoples, then specially [*sic*] of the Medes and Persians'. See Henry George Liddell and Robert Scott, *A Greek-English Lexicon* (Oxford: Clarendon Press, 1940). 'Barbarians' were 'natural' slaves who could legitimately be subjugated, because, as Smith explains 'when a barbarian/natural slave is captured and enslaved, he finally has the opportunity to come into contact with the proper use of *logos* – reasoned arguments designed to identify right from wrong'. But in the absence of a master (and hence in the absence of the institution of slavery) 'the barbarian would lack at least the full actualisation of the thing that distinguishes him from non-human animals, if not all of it'. Because 'he' lacks 'the capacity to deliberate, the barbarian/natural slave fails, when left among his own kind, to be in any actual way distinct from the beasts that all would allow are rightfully owned as property' in Aristotle's view. Smith, 'Aristotle's Concept', 114–20.

[136] Ibid., 122.

> patrimony and enslave them and put them up for sale; but what he means is that by defect of their nature they need to be ruled and governed by others and that it is good for them to be subject to others, just as sons need to be subject to their parents until of full age, and a wife to her husband.[137]

It is at this point, I suggest, that an intermediate category of subject was born: neither citizen (legal subject) nor slave (legal object) but 'natural slave', or (to use a term more familiar from the practice of European colonialism) 'native'. Such partially rational subjects were human and could not, therefore, be enslaved without cause; yet towards such individuals the duty existed to subject them *collectively* in order to expose them to *logos*. The question remained, of course, as to whether this period of training would ever come to an end – the analogy of child and father suggesting that it might; but the analogy of wife and husband suggesting, on the contrary, that the 'defect of their nature' was permanent.

2.2.2 The 'Self' in Self-Government: Abolition as Legal Non-Objectivity

The same assumptions were not, however, being applied to the tens of thousands of African individuals already being captured, appropriated as objects and shipped into the 'new world' by 1502.[138] Though he later changed his mind, even Las Casas, 'Protector of the Indians', began by arguing that the misery of the supposedly semi-rational 'Indians', whose labour was being shamefully exploited by the Spaniards, could best be ameliorated by importing supposedly sub-rational African slaves in larger numbers.[139] Though slavery and Blackness were not, at first, connected,[140] the more Africans were enslaved and imported into the Americas, the closer the association became. The unpaid labour supplied by the African slave trade contributed enormously to the economic viability of the first European colonies.[141] For

137 Vitoria, *De Indis*, 128.

138 Roger Anstey, *The Atlantic Slave Trade and British Abolition, 1760–1810* (London: Macmillan, 1975), 5.

139 See e.g. Lawrence Clayton, 'Bartolomé de las Casas and the African Slave Trade', 7 *History Compass* (2009): 1526–41.

140 Liliana Obregón, 'Spanish Colonial Critiques of African Enslavement', in 8 *Beyond Law* (2002): 41–66, at 42–3.

141 On the contribution of the slave trade to the evolution of the system of finance capital, see Ian Baucom, *Specters of the Atlantic: Finance Capital, Slavery, and the Philosophy of History* (Durham, NC: Duke University Press, 2005). On the contribution of the slave trade and of colonialism more generally to the concept of private property, see Brenna Bhandar, 'Property, Law, and Race: Modes of Abstraction', 4 *UC Irvine Law Review* (2014): 203–18, and, in particular, *Colonial Lives of Property: Law, Land and Racial Regimes of Ownership* (Durham, NC: Duke University Press, 2018).

the purposes of unpacking the relationship between individual and international legal subjectivity, however, what is striking is how persistently that Vitorian understanding of the relationship between race, rationality and 'self-government' endured, even as slavery's 'logic of contradiction' played out in the abolition first of the slave trade and then, in 1926, largely in connection with Ethiopia, of slavery itself. Thanks to that persistence, abolition had the paradoxical effect of rendering the collective subjugation of non-European polities *more*, rather than less, legitimate as matter of international law.

The reversal in attitudes to slavery was the outcome of a long and convoluted process.[142] Until the mid nineteenth century, even jurists who deplored slavery had been forced to admit that, whatever the domestic law of a particular state might say, the almost universal participation in the slave trade by states and other collectivities from the beginning of human history demonstrated that it was permitted under the *jus gentium*.[143] By the time the Final Act of the Congress of Vienna was concluded in 1815, Britain, the most powerful and vocal of the abolitionist states after 1807, had already concluded dozens of bilateral anti-slavery conventions.[144] In the first multilateral condemnation of the slave trade, the Vienna Convention condemned it as 'repugnant to the principles of humanity and universal morality'.[145] This was followed up with much stronger provisions toward the end of the century. In particular, the 1885 Berlin Act, which brought into being a regime of free trade in the Congo Basin, pledged its signatories 'to strive for the suppression of slavery and especially of the negro slave trade'.[146] Five years later the Brussels Act of 1890 dedicated its

[142] Seymour Drescher and Paul Finkelman, 'Slavery', in Fassbender and Peters (eds.), *The Oxford Handbook of International Legal History*, 890–916; *Convention to Suppress the Slave Trade and Slavery*, Geneva, 25 September 1926 ('Slavery Convention'), Art. 2.

[143] As Sir William Scott (later Lord Stowell) argued in the *Le Louis* case, which came before the British High Court of Admiralty in 1817, while the trade in African slaves may have violated English law, it would have been 'a most extravagant assumption in any Court of the Law of Nations, to pronounce that this practice, the tolerated, the approved, the encouraged object of law, ever since man became subject to law, was prohibited by that law'. *Le Louis* [1817] 12 Dods 210, 165 ER 1464 at 1477, cited in Drescher and Finkelman, 'Slavery', 891.

[144] Drescher and Finkelman, 'Slavery', 902.

[145] *Declaration of the Eight Powers on the Abolition of the Slave Trade*, 8 February 1815, annexed to *General Treaty between Great Britain, Austria, France, Portugal, Prussia, Russia, Spain and Sweden*, Vienna, 9 June 1815.

[146] *General Act of the Conference of Berlin Concerning the Congo, between Austria-Hungary, Belgium, Denmark, France, the German Empire, Great Britain, Italy, Netherlands, Ottoman Empire, Portugal, the Russian Empire, Spain, Sweden and Norway, the United States*, Berlin, 26 February 1885 ('Berlin Act'), Art. 6.

signatories to 'counteracting the slave trade in the interior of Africa'.[147] But it was only in 1926 that the signatories of the Slavery Convention finally determined, 'each in respect of the territories placed under its sovereignty, jurisdiction, protection, suzerainty or tutelage', not only to suppress the slave trade but also '[t]o bring about, progressively and as soon as possible, the complete abolition of slavery in all its forms'.[148]

Underlying this process was the emergence of a gradual, though paradoxical, consensus. As we have already seen, the republican contention that 'all men' are are 'born and remain free and equal in rights' left open the question of which human beings were to be classified as 'men'. The abolition of slavery did nothing to change this. Indeed, while abolition functioned very differently in different jurisdictions, the consensus that emerged as to its legal implications was not that all slaves everywhere should immediately be transformed into full legal subjects. It was, instead, that no human being should be treated as a legal *object*, as the private property of another. When considering how to allocate territorial sovereignty, this body of practice suggested the purpose of international law should be to enforce a juridical floor beyond which no human being should be allowed to fall – a floor which would allow all humans to own and exchange property, but not to be bought and sold themselves.

Thus, we saw, above, that the signatories of the Berlin Act of 1885 pledged 'to strive for the suppression of slavery and especially of the negro slave trade', but also that this was not the main purpose of the convention. Instead, that purpose was, as Matthew Craven has shown, to set up the legal regime necessary for the orderly extension of conditions of free trade to the Congo Basin.[149] The tool which was used to achieve both ends simultaneously was a new principle called 'effective occupation'. According to this new principle, territorial claims made by states in this area would be considered legitimate only if it was clear that a governing authority 'sufficient to cause acquired rights to be respected' had been established.[150] This was, in other words, precisely the kind of 'effectiveness' that (as we saw above) Judge Huber later referred to in the *Island of Palmas* case. The rights to be protected by those states which did obtain 'rights of

[147] *Convention Relative to the Slave Trade and Importation into Africa of Firearms, Ammunition, and Spiritous Liquors*, Brussels, 2 July 1890, Art. 1.

[148] *Slavery Convention*, Geneva, 25 September 1926, Art. 2.

[149] See Matthew Craven, 'Between Law and History: The Berlin Conference of 1884–1885 and the Logic of Free Trade', 3 *London Review of International Law* (2015): 31–59.

[150] *Berlin Act*, Art. 35.

sovereignty or Protectorate' in this area included property rights;[151] rights to 'freedom of trade and transit' for themselves and for their individual citizens;[152] as well as rights of '[f]reedom of conscience and religious toleration', which were also to be 'expressly guaranteed to the natives'.[153] The gesture which connected territorial sovereignty to the 'effective' extension, into the Congo Basin, of the rights and duties of legal subjects (the citizens of the signatory states), was thus precisely the same gesture which prohibited individual legal objectivity (slavery), and in doing so transformed the Congo Basin from a territory inhabited by potential slaves into one inhabited by 'natives', whose collective subjugation would be in their own interests in the sense that it was expected to trigger their transformation into rational beings. In the process of prohibiting slavery (presented as a humanitarian act designed to 'ameliorate' Africans' 'moral and material conditions of existence'[154]), international law simultaneously denied their capacity to claim any form of collective rights and duties of their own over their territory. Just as Vitoria had argued in relation to the Indigenous peoples of the 'Americas', the Indigenous peoples of the Congo could not lawfully be enslaved, according to the Berlin and Brussels Acts, but *for precisely that reason* they could and should be colonised for their own good. Rather than being actual or potential slaves, in other words, the post-Berlin Act 'natives' of the Congo Basin were now akin to Vitoria's 'natural slaves'.

Similarly, the much more ambitious Brussels Act of 1890, ostensibly dedicated to stamping out the slave trade per se, clarified at Article 1 that 'the most effective means of counteracting the slave-trade in the interior of Africa' entailed the '[p]rogressive organisation of the administrative, religious, and military services in the African territories placed under the sovereignty or protectorate of civilized nations'.[155] To this end, the Act's signatories pledged to bring about the 'extinction of barbarous customs, such as cannibalism, and human sacrifices' and to prohibit the importation of firearms into a large 'prohibition zone', which included the whole of West, Central and East Africa, with the explicit aim of reducing the capacity of local slave-raiders.[156] They also committed to setting up and guaranteeing a new regime of private property rights in Africa, for the purpose of

[151] Ibid., Art. 5.
[152] Ibid., Art. 35.
[153] Ibid., Art. 6.
[154] Ibid., Art. 6.
[155] Brussels Act, Art. 1.
[156] Ibid., Art. 8.

opening up the continent to capitalist enterprise. This included the building of roads, railways and telegraph lines, and the 'initiation' of African 'tribes' into the practices of 'agricultural labour' and the 'industrial arts', but also giving 'aid and protection to commercial enterprises'.[157] In particular, the state parties to the Brussels Act pledged to 'watch over [the] legality' of such commercial enterprises by 'especially controlling contracts for service with the natives', with the aim of 'prepar[ing] the way for the foundation of permanent centres of cultivation and of commercial settlements'.[158] Again, the emerging international law prohibition against slavery went hand in hand with a renewed international legal commitment to the 'complete liberty' of the 'commerce of all nations',[159] and with the reinvigorated project of 'new imperialism' to that end.

Thus, in contrast to the domestic experience of legal emancipation in the United States, for example, where slaves were in theory converted into citizens overnight,[160] the primary effect of abolition in the international legal context was to reinvigorate the colonial project by investing it with a 'humanitarian' rationale. However, in reconstructing non-state, non-European and, in particular, Black individuals as 'natives' invested with an extremely partial form of legal subjectivity, rather than as slaves who were legal objects – that is, in reconstructing them as territorially defined communities in need of tutelage, rather than as a mass of resources to be exploited directly – the emergent prohibition against slavery left firmly in place a well-established set of assumptions. These, of course, were the assumptions that individual legal subjectivity should be allocated on a hierarchical basis, with that hierarchy determined on the basis of the rationality of the individuals involved, which was in turn to be assessed collectively on the basis of the presence or absence of institutions of 'self-government'. It was, thus, no coincidence that the legal instruments that were developed to abolish slavery were often the same legal instruments which put in place the framework within which 'free trade' among self-governing states could flourish and expand. For the transformation of slaves into colonial subjects, capable of owning rather than of

[157] Ibid., Art. 2.

[158] Ibid., Arts. 1–2.

[159] Ibid., Preamble.

[160] Black citizenship, however, constitutionalised in the Thirteenth, Fourteenth and Fifteenth Amendments, was soon undermined by the passage, in the southern states, of a raft of legislation aimed at restricting the rights of African-Americans – legislation which later became known as the 'Jim Crow' laws. See e.g. Theodore Branter Wilson, *The Black Codes of the South* (Tuscaloosa, AL: University of Alabama Press, 1965). See Item 3, Section 5, below.

being property, was seen as desirable not only on humanitarian grounds. That transformation was also advocated on the basis of a strong economic rationale – and one that would be strengthened still further after the First World War.[161] On the one hand, the universalisation of the right to own and trade property (at least up to a point) brought into view a potentially enormous new market of emancipated slaves turned consumers. On the other hand, it was argued by many leading economists that just as much, if not more, and much higher-quality labour would be sold 'freely' by individual labourers than could be extracted coercively from individual slaves. Adam Smith had already argued in 1793, for example, that the 'labour of the slave proceeds from no other motive but the dread of punishment', meaning that slaves 'have no motive to industry'.[162] By contrast, '[f]reemen who have a stock of their own, can get anything accomplished which they think may be expedient for carrying on labour'.[163] Indeed, as many slaves, emancipated *en masse* in the Americas and the Caribbean, for example, often without land, income or education, found to their cost, a large part of the economic rationale for emancipation was predicated on the creation of an army of low-wage labourers. Just as Marx had spelled out in 1849,[164] and as we saw Edelman argue in the Frame,[165] in material terms, the distinction between slavery and liberty was hard to detect.[166] Or in the words of Patsy Mitchener, a former slave, 'slavery' and 'freedom' were, for emancipated African-Americans, just '[t]wo snakes full of p[o]ison'.[167]

The gradual reversal of slavery's legitimacy under international law therefore did not signal the emergence of an international legal order in which 'all men' possessed an equal right to be free. Instead, the French Declaration's injunction that '[m]en are born and remain free and equal in rights' requires to be qualified; for only humans deemed fully 'rational' counted as 'men' for this purpose. Excluded from this category were

[161] See below, Item 3, Section 4.1.

[162] Adam Smith, *Lectures on Justice, Police, Revenue and Arms*, ed. Edwin Cannan (Oxford: Clarendon Press, 1896), 234.

[163] Ibid., 231.

[164] Karl Marx [1849], *Wage Labour and Capital*, available at www.marxists.org/archive/marx/works/1847/wage-labour/ (accessed 4 November 2017).

[165] See Frame, Section 2.2.

[166] There is a huge literature on this debate. See e.g. Frank McGlynn and Seymour Drescher (eds.), *The Meaning of Freedom: Economics, Politics, and Culture After Slavery* (University of Pittsburgh Press, 1992).

[167] Patsy Mitchener, interview conducted at Raleigh, North Carolina, 24 July 1937, Federal Writers' Project of the Works Progress Administration for the State of North Carolina, *Slave Narratives: A Folk History of Slavery in the United States from Interviews with Former Slaves*, Vol. II, Part 2 (Washington DC: Library of Congress, 1941), 116–23, at 123.

not only women, children and the mentally unwell or unorthodox, but also large swathes of the world's male population. Certainly, the outright denial of individual legal subjectivity in the form of slavery did gradually come to be prohibited under international law. Indeed, so powerful did this prohibition become by the mid-nineteenth century that territories in which slavery was still practised – such as the Ethiopian Empire and the Confederate States of America between 1861 and 1865 – were recognised only on the condition that they would commit to abolishing slavery in the future, and in fact denied recognition altogether in the case of the Confederacy.[168] Even as legal objectivity came to be outlawed, however, this same process reinforced the idea that human beings could be ranked on a scale of rationality, which was to be measured on the basis of their possession (or not) of 'self-governing' institutions capable, as such, of protecting the universal rights of 'all (rational) men' to life, liberty and property. The transition from the seventeenth-century contractarian, natural law context inhabited by Vitoria to the increasingly republican political context, mirrored by an increasingly positivist international legal doctrine, made little difference to the structure of this justification. As the assumptions of social Darwinism gradually took hold of the European/neo-European psyche, the argument that non-European communities were rational, but not rational enough to merit the collective liberty offered by sovereign statehood, simply morphed into the argument that such communities were human but not 'evolved' or 'developed' enough for independent statehood.

Crucially, it is at this point that race, the 'ultimate trope of difference',[169] enters the picture, standing in as a proxy for use in that process of assessing 'rationality' on a collective basis. Precisely as sociologist Stuart

[168] See Don H. Doyle, 'Slavery or Independence: The Confederate Dilemma in Europe', in Cornelis A. van Minnen and Manfred Berg (eds.), *The U.S. South and Europe: Transatlantic Relations in the Nineteenth and Twentieth Centuries* (Lexington, KT: University Press of Kentucky, 2013), 105–24. The US had, of course, itself been recognised, following its declaration of independence in 1776, many years prior to its total abolition of slavery in 1865. The same goes for Brazil, recognised in 1822, more than 60 years before its own act of abolition in 1888. Mexico and all the other Latin American republics also abolished slavery after their recognition as independent states. By 1860, however, Doyle points out that the situation had changed, and – unlike the Empire of Brazil and the Spanish Empire in Cuba and Puerto Rico, for instance, where slavery continued to be justified, but only as a 'necessary evil' which would be brought to an end as soon as it had the means – the Confederacy set itself apart by 'defend[ing] slavery as a positive good that should be perpetuated forever' (ibid., 113–15).

[169] Henry Louis Gates, 'Editor's Introduction: Writing "Race" and the Difference It Makes', 12 *Critical Inquiry* (1985): 1–10, at 5.

Hall would later argue, race began to operate, in the practice of international law, as a 'floating signifier' – as a 'badge, a token, a sign' of some deeper material or 'biological' failure, thus allowing nature and culture to 'operate metonymically'.[170] It could simply be assumed that black and brown people, having failed as a matter of historical and anthropological 'fact' to establish 'self-governing' institutions of their own accord – having failed, in effect, to be Western European polities – were therefore incapable of organising themselves in any 'rational' way without help and guidance from outside. The idea that other systems of collective self-organisation and normative ordering might be recognised as equivalent, respectively, to 'governments', though considered by a small minority of European scholars, did not survive the process of generalisation and abstraction that was embarked on by the international lawyers of the late nineteenth century and beyond. In the abstract criteria for statehood, and in the theories of recognition and international personality developed by Oppenheim,[171] Dionisio Anzilotti,[172] Westlake,[173] Franz von Liszt[174] and others at this time, 'effective' institutions of 'government' meant one thing and one thing only: that the individual rights of those who already *had* such rights (citizens of existing, i.e. primarily European and American, states) could be enforced and, if possible, extended. The 'self' in the term 'self-governing' is, in other words, somewhat misleading, as we shall see further in the following section. For as both Vitoria's work and, centuries later, the *Island of Palmas* case have already demonstrated, these institutions of 'self-government' did not need to 'belong' to the population of the territory in question in order to function 'effectively'. On the contrary, they could very well belong to another entity, as long as that entity was itself a 'self-governing' state.

170 As Hall put it: 'It is the function of … race as a signifier, to make these two systems – nature and culture – correspond with one another in such a way that it is possible to read off the one against the other. So that once you know where the person fits in the classification of natural human races, you can infer from that what they're likely to think, what they're likely to feel, what they're likely to produce, the aesthetic quality of their productions, and so on.' In sum, 'the function of race as a signifier' constitutes 'a system of equivalencies between nature and culture'. Stuart Hall, 'Race, the Floating Signifier', talk at Goldsmiths College, London, directed by Sut Jhally, Media Education Foundation, 1997.

171 Oppenheim, *International Law*, 30–4, 99–101.

172 Dionisio Anzilotti, *Cours de droit international*, trans. Gilbert Gidel (3rd edn Paris: Recueil Sirey, 1919), 129.

173 John Westlake, *The Collected Papers of John Westlake on Public International Law*, ed. Lassa Oppenheim (Cambridge University Press, 1914), 82–3.

174 Franz von Liszt, *Le droit international: exposé systématique*, trans. Gilbert Gidel and Leon Alcindor (Paris: Pedone, 1927), 52–3.

2.3 *Colony/State*

This 'Item' has argued, so far, that if we place the figure of the individual legal subject at the centre of our investigation into the question of how the sovereign state emerged and came to be universalised, the topography of the historical landscape with which we are dealing looks altogether different. In effect, both in the early theory and practice of the state (Section 2.1) and during the centuries of Europe's 'discovery' and appropriation of the 'new world' through conquest, trade (including the trade in slaves) and later the enforcement of emancipation (Section 2.2), the state as a 'universal' form turns out to have emerged, not only through a dialectic between Europe and the non-European world, but in fact through a tri-alectic process.

Having inserted the figure of the individual into the equation in subsections 2.1 and 2.2, the purpose of this this subsection, 2.3 – the third side of the 'triangular story' of government – is to revisit the relationship between state and colony in and through a body of theory and practice that will, for many readers, be familiar. When viewed against the previous components of this item, and in conjunction with Item 1 and with the Frame, my hope is that this familiarity will evaporate.

2.3.1 Hegelian Recognition and the First Generation of European International Lawyers

As we have already seen in Section 1.1, the central doctrinal issue when it comes to the question of what Crawford calls 'the creation of states in international law' is that of recognition and its effects. With that in mind, it is, perhaps, surprising that Hegel's thinking on recognition – which has been investigated ceaselessly by political philosophers,[175] intellectual historians,[176] post-colonial theorists[177] and others, and which had a profound influence on the doctrinal developments of the late nineteenth century – has been probed so little by historians of international law.

[175] See e.g. Glen Coulthard, *Red Skin, White Masks: Rejecting the Colonial Politics of Recognition* (Minneapolis, MN: University of Minnesota Press, 2014); Patchen Markell, *Bound by Recognition* (Princeton University Press, 2003), esp. 90–122.

[176] See e.g. Susan Buck-Morss, *Hegel, Haiti and Universal History* (University of Pittsburgh Press, 2009).

[177] See e.g. Frantz Fanon, *Peau Noire, Masques Blanc* (Paris: Editions de Seuil, France, 1952), English translation: Frantz Fanon, *Black Skin, White Masks*, trans. Charles Lam Markmann (London: Pluto Press, 1986); generally, Timothy Brennan, 'Hegel, Empire, and Anti-Colonial Thought', in Graham Huggan (ed.), *The Oxford Handbook of Postcolonial Studies* (Oxford University Press, 2013), 142–61.

In *Elements of the Philosophy of Right* (1820), Hegel set out (in many ways like Vitoria) to understand the nature of the normative relationship between individual and society. For him, the ultimate form of society was, quite simply, the European nation-state. The 'philosophy of right' he developed in response to this relationship posited an analogy between what he called the 'self-consciousness' or 'personality' of the individual (these were two terms he used interchangeably),[178] and the 'self-consciousness' or 'international personality' (as he called it – a term adopted by international lawyers in the nineteenth century) of the state. Hegel argued, in explicitly teleological terms, that these two dimensions of 'self-consciousness' were inextricably linked together by a particular understanding of the notion of 'freedom'. As Allan Wood explains, Hegel's *Philosophy of Right* is 'founded on an ethical theory which identifies the human good with the self-actualisation of the human spirit. Hegel's name for the essence of this spirit is freedom', meaning 'action in which we deal with nothing that is external to our own objective nature'.[179] Importantly,

> Hegel insists that 'absence of dependence on another is won not outside the other but in it, it attains actuality not by fleeing the other but by overcoming it'.[180] Thus Hegel describes freedom as 'being with oneself in another', that is, actively relating to something other than oneself in such a way that this other becomes integrated into one's projects ... This means that freedom is possible only to the extent that we act rationally, and in circumstances where the objects of our action are in harmony with our reason. The most spiritual of such objects is the social order in which we live ... Freedom is actual, therefore, only in a rational society whose institutions can be felt and known as rational by individuals who are 'with themselves' in those institutions.[181]

Individual self-consciousness was, in other words, unattainable unless it could be 'won' in and through the process of pushing against and being recognised by the self-consciousness of others – i.e. in the absence of a 'rational' society full of other 'rational' individuals. This kind of formal, mutual, and therefore constitutive recognition, however, could only take place, Hegel insisted, in the process of a 'life-and-death struggle' – that is, a material struggle – between two as-yet-unrealised 'consciousnesses',

[178] See e.g. G. W. F. Hegel [1820], *Elements of the Philosophy of Right*, ed. Allan W. Wood, trans. H. B. Nisbet (Cambridge University Press, 1991), 67–9.

[179] Wood, 'Editors Introduction', in Hegel [1817], *The Philosophy of Mind*, vii–xxxii at xi–xii (references omitted).

[180] This quote is from G. W. F. Hegel [1817], *The Philosophy of Mind*, trans. William Wallace and A. V. Miller (Oxford University Press, 1971), para. 382A.

[181] Wood, 'Editor's Introduction', in Hegel [1817], *The Philosophy of Mind*, xii.

each itself divided between two conflicting 'wills'. These Hegel famously personified as those of 'Master' (the 'will to independence') and 'Bondsman' (the 'will to dependence').[182]

Much attention has been paid to the 'master–slave dialectic'. Less attention, however, has been focused on its relationship to a parallel, and almost identically constitutive relationship which Hegel then went on to posit between the mutual recognition of states and the constitution of what he called the 'personality of the state'.[183] The state was, in Hegel's view, 'the absolute power on earth'.[184] On the surface, this created a problem for his constitutive understanding of recognition, for if the state was by definition 'a sovereign and independent entity in relation to others',[185] as he argued, then how could its 'personality' or 'self-consciousness' simultaneously be understood as depending on external recognition? This, of course, is simply an early articulation of the classic positivist problem of how to create order between two sovereign states. Recognition, Hegel insisted, could only function properly if it took place simultaneously and mutually between two already sovereign nation-states.[186] This condition appears to obviate its defining function, leading to the apparent paradox that the only true sovereigns were, in effect, always-already sovereign, having arrived – rather like Althusser's 'Absolute Subject', discussed in the Frame – out of nowhere.

When transposed out of an abstract/philosophical and into a material/historical register, however, this paradox could be, and was, resolved, by Hegel in his *Lectures on the Philosophy of World History* (1837). As we have already seen, Hobbes, Machiavelli, Grotius and others derived their philosophy of the 'civil' state from the characteristics of the handful of early states and proto-states which were already in existence by their day, all of which were to be found in Western Europe. Three centuries later, with declarations of independence having been made and recognised in many parts of what had once been the Spanish, Portuguese, British, French and Ottoman Empires, Hegel was able to assert that 'world history' itself not only *should* tend, but *was* actually tending towards the nation-state, 'sovereign' externally and 'civil' in its internal institutional structure. Recognition, Hegel insisted in these lectures, just as he had

[182] G. W. F. Hegel [1807], *Phenomenology of Spirit*, trans. A.V. Miller (Oxford, New York: Oxford University Press, 1977), 111–38.

[183] Hegel, *Elements of the Philosophy of Right*, 317, 366–7.

[184] Ibid., 366.

[185] Ibid., 366.

[186] Ibid., 368.

done in *Elements of the Philosophy of Right*, could only be undertaken by always-already free and equal sovereigns, meaning that 'full' recognition in this 'true', mutual sense was precluded between unequal entities. In this 'historical' context, however, he cast inequality explicitly in terms of the possession or lack of (European) 'civilisation'. To underscore the point, Hegel illustrated it with a discussion of what he saw to be the opposite of the fully rational, fully 'self-conscious' individual, namely 'the African'. Unlike 'the European', 'the African', Hegel asserted, was incapable of distinguishing 'between himself as an individual and his essential universality' and was therefore also incapable of being free.[187] Africans therefore could not be recognised as rational and therefore self-conscious because they were not *already* rational and self-conscious, and could not therefore enter into the reciprocal process of mutual recognition which true freedom demanded. This, in turn, was connected in Hegel's thinking to the failure of Africans to organise their societies 'rationally'; that is, as 'self-governing' states.[188] This failure, Hegel argued, meant that 'civilised nations' (i.e. states) were not only entitled but actually bound to 'treat as barbarians other nations which are less advanced than they are', denying them both recognition and, therefore, any degree of 'international personality'.[189] In this way, Hegel arrived, via a different route, at a very similar conclusion to the one Vitoria had reached centuries before.

Given the marked resemblance between Hegel's language and logic on the one hand, and that employed by the first generation of 'professional' international lawyers on the other, to whom the task fell during the last quarter of the nineteenth century to theorise the apparently inexorable transformation of the world into a series of states and colonies, it seems highly likely that Hegel's work had a profound and direct influence on the evolution of the new 'positivist' international legal doctrine of this era, and on the practice described and influenced by that doctrine.[190] See, for

[187] G. W. F. Hegel [1837], *Lectures on the Philosophy of World History*, trans. H. B. Nisbet (New York: Cambridge University Press, 1975), 177.

[188] Ibid., 177.

[189] Hegel, *Elements of the Philosophy of Right*, 376.

[190] See Armin von Bogdandy and Sergio Dellavalle, 'George Wilhelm Friedrich Hegel (1770–1831)', in Fassbender and Peters, *The Oxford Handbook of the History of International Law*, 1127–31. See C. H. Alexandrowicz, 'The Theory of Recognition in Fieri', 34 *British Yearbook of International Law* (1958): 176–98, at 195. For a contrary view, see Nicholas Onuf and Peter Onuf, *Nations, Markets and War: Modern History and the American Civil War* (Charlottesville, VA: University of Virginia Press, 2006), 69. It is submitted, however, that Onuf and Onuf base their criticism of this hypothesis on a misunderstanding of the role of recognition in Hegel's *Philosophy of Right*.

example, the second edition of the American jurist Henry Wheaton's influential *Elements of International Law* (1863), one of the first international law texts to be translated into Chinese and Japanese.[191] According to Wheaton, the 'internal sovereignty of a State' did not 'depend on its recognition by other States'.[192] However, a state's 'external sovereignty', on the other hand, would 'require recognition by other States in order to render it perfect and complete'.[193] This argument appears to have been taken directly – much like the title of Wheaton's treatise – from Hegel's *Elements of the Philosophy of Right*.[194] Or, to cite another example, Thomas Lawrence's argument that 'the older states of Europe' constituted a special class of international person who together formed 'the nucleus of international society' likewise has clearly Hegelian overtones.[195] These states, Lawrence argued, had been international persons 'since time immemorial'. 'Modern International Law' had '[grown] up among them. There was never a time when they were outside its pale. Their influence helped to mould it. Many of them existed before the great majority of its rules came into being.'[196] Unlike other states, therefore, there was 'no need for them to be formally received among its subjects'.[197] Their international personality was original, unconditional and 'full' in a way that no other could hope to be.

Echoes of Hegel's (pseudo-)anthropological assumptions regarding the capacity of different races for subjectivity, both individual and collective, can be found in the writings of many other European jurists of this era. Johann Kaspar Bluntschli, one of Germany's most important international lawyers and theorists of the state at the turn of the nineteenth century, made use of overtly Hegelian language to claim that in fact 'the Negro' was so immune to the ideas of 'freedom' and 'equality' that 'he' collaborated willingly in the process of his enslavement. Just as Hegel had argued that '*Negroes* ... are sold and allow themselves to be sold without any reflection as to the rights or wrongs of it',[198] Bluntschli declared that

[191] Henry Wheaton, *Elements of International Law* (2nd edn London: Sampson Low, 1863). For a brilliant analysis, see Lydia H. Liu, *The Clash of Empires: The Invention of China in Modern World Making* (Cambridge, MA: Harvard University Press, 2004).

[192] Wheaton, *Elements of International Law*, 36–9.

[193] Ibid., 36–9.

[194] See Hegel, *Elements of the Philosophy of Right*, 317, 366–7.

[195] T. J. Lawrence, *The Principles of International Law* (London, New York: MacMillan, 1895), 84.

[196] Ibid., 84.

[197] Ibid., 84.

[198] Georg W. F. Hegel [1827–28], *Hegel's Philosophy of Subjective Spirit*, Vol. 2, ed. and trans. M. J. Petry (Dordrecht, Boston, MA: D. Reidel Publishing Company, 1979), 53.

'the Negro' would willingly prostrate himself and 'lift his master's foot himself onto his head'.[199]

Unlike Bluntschli, who for all his universalistic assumptions about freedom, equality and statehood, saw himself as a positivist, the Scottish neo-naturalist jurist James Lorimer in many ways inhabited the rift between the old and new thinking of this period.[200] This difference in approach, however, left his prejudices unaffected. 'As a political phenomenon,' Lorimer asserted, 'humanity, in its present condition, divides itself into three concentric zones or spheres – that of civilized humanity, that of barbarous humanity, and that of savage humanity.'[201] European and American states inhabited the first category; the Ottoman, Chinese, Japanese and Siamese Empires inhabited the second, together with the 'Separate States of Central Asia'; while African, American and Pacific 'natives' inhabited the third 'zone'.[202] Lorimer argued, with what seems to be a clear nod to Hegel, that in order for states to be recognised as subjects of international law, two things were required: both the 'will' (desire) and the 'power' (capacity) to 'reciprocate' that recognition. Assumptions about rationality and its connection to 'freedom', moreover, lay (as in Hegel) at the core not just of 'reciprocal will' but also of 'reciprocal power', since 'it is rational will alone that is free and capable ... of exhibiting itself as power'.[203] 'Savage' communities, therefore, could not lawfully be recognised as states because, even if they desired recognition, they were by definition collectively incapable of 'reciprocating' it. Lorimer further divided 'savage' communities into three categories, derived from domestic law: those of 'nonage', 'imbecility' and 'criminality'.[204] European states were duty-bound to colonise and 'civilise' communities which fell into the first category. With regard to 'imbecile' communities, their backwardness formed 'a permanent bar to recognition', thereby establishing a relation 'of perpetual pupilarity and

199 Johann Kaspar Bluntschli [1879], 'Arische Völker und arische Rechte', quoted in Koskenniemi, *The Gentle Civilizer of Nations*, 103.

200 See e.g. Gerry Simpson, *Great Power and Outlaw States: Unequal Sovereigns in the International Legal Order* (Cambridge University Press, 2004), 238–42; Martti Koskenniemi, 'Race, Hierarchy and International Law: Lorimer's Legal Science', 27 *EJIL* (2016): 415–29. See Stephen Tierney and Neil Walker (eds.), 'Symposium: The European Tradition in International Law: James Lorimer', 27 *EJIL* (2016): 409–92 (issue 2, with contributions from Martti Koskenniemi, Gerry Simpson, Karen Knop and Stephen Neff).

201 James Lorimer, *The Institutes of International Law: A Treatise of the Principles of Jurisprudence as Determined by Nature* (Edinburgh: T & T Clark, 1872), 101.

202 Ibid., 101.

203 Ibid., 156.

204 Ibid., 56–62.

guardianship'.[205] In the case of 'criminal' communities, '[t]he presence of a criminal intention, to the extent which it exists, is ... a proof of the absence of a rational will', and hence also of 'reciprocating power'.[206]

Lorimer also employed a similar understanding of freedom to that of Hegel. 'Freedom from external control will not satisfy the requirements of international law', he argued. 'The international State must be free from itself; it must possess subjective as well as objective freedom; it must be autonomous or self-ruling.'[207] That is to say, even more explicitly than Vitoria, Lorimer insisted that 'sovereignty' (the right to equal 'external freedom' of 'nations' in the context of the 'family of nations') was capable of being recognised and constituted only where institutions of 'self-rule' or self-government (indicating the equal freedom of individuals in the domestic context) were present. Only if it possessed the trappings of 'internal freedom' could an entity be understood as 'clothed with the conditions which render the exercise of reciprocating freedom *possible*'.[208]

Lorimer's thesis here also offers a useful illustration of the peculiar logic of international legal reproduction as a general process which, nonetheless, plays out very differently at different times and in different places. For unlike Hegel, who as we have already seen took a strict view as to the permanent incapacity of 'the African' and his community when it came to recognition and self-consciousness, Lorimer saw no reason why entities in his second or third 'zones' should not be recognised if they managed to become 'civilised' enough to be able to 'reciprocate' that recognition.[209] Discussing the case of Algeria, for instance, Lorimer argued that France's annexation in 1834 of this former 'barbary state' (an entity which was not only Arab, but whose engagement in piracy had rendered it 'criminal' for the purposes of the law of nations) had been lawful, as an act of 'discipline' in the absence of an international 'police'.[210] But, he went on, 'International Law attaches no bastard-badge even to States which have come into existence by means which it repudiates. Had Algeria come to respect the [individual] rights of life and property, its history would not

205 Ibid., 158.
206 Ibid., 160.
207 Ibid., 155.
208 Ibid., 155. Emphasis in the original.
209 To this extent, Lorimer's naturalism, 'embod[ying] a hierarchical view of races, states and individuals, was no less 'positivist' than Bluntschli's or Oppenheim's. Koskenniemi, '*Race, Hierarchy and International* Law', 416.
210 Lorimer, *Institutes of International Law*, 161.

have deprived it of the right to recognition'.[211] Algeria was not, in other words, permanently barred from recognition on account of the race of its population. On the contrary, had it successfully interpellated (to return to Althusser/Edelman's language) as a self-governing state, and transformed its institutions accordingly, such that individual 'rights to life and property' were indeed protected, this transformation would have been welcomed. As Ntina Tzouvala puts it, despite the 'racist or religious rhetoric' associated with the discourse of 'civilisation', in Lorimer and in the state practice on which he based his claims, the focus 'at the end of the day … [was] on specific institutional reform', including 'the protection of certain rights closely linked to the market'.[212]

At the same time, there were also certain 'civilised' European states from which recognition ought to be withheld or withdrawn, at least temporarily, according to Lorimer.[213] In particular, states possessed of 'intolerant theocratic systems', as he put it, were 'necessarily unrecognisable', as were 'intolerant' monarchies, republics and 'anarchies'.[214] Lorimer listed as respective examples the German Empire, the erstwhile revolutionary French Republic (which he despised; Lorimer was no republican) and a hypothetically 'nihilistic' Russia.[215] These states, he argued, possessed the 'power' to reciprocate recognition but lacked a 'reciprocating will'.[216] Since they *could* have recognised the other subjects of the law of nations but chose not to, they should themselves (reciprocally) be denied recognition. Importantly, however, and unlike 'barbarous' and 'savage' communities, states with merely 'intolerant' forms of government such as these had only to relinquish them for recognition once again to be legitimate. For instance, Lorimer argued that '[i]t was not till the restoration of a limited monarchy that the presumption of a reciprocating will, on the part of France, was regarded as sufficient to re-establish her right to readmission into the family of nations'.[217] As we shall see in Item 3, this is a surprisingly precise description of how the former German Empire was actually treated in the wake of the First World War – until its withdrawal from the League of Nations in 1933 under its new Chancellor, Adolf Hitler.

[211] Ibid.
[212] Tzouvala, *Letters of Blood and Fire*, 44.
[213] See Simpson, *Great Powers*, 239–41.
[214] Lorimer, *Institutes of International Law*, 126–33.
[215] Ibid., 127.
[216] Ibid., 109.
[217] Ibid., 132.

2.3.2 Between State and Colony I: Hybridity and the Chinese Empire

As this examination of recognition in Hegel and Lorimer suggests, while the international legal justification for deciding where a polity should be placed on the continuum from legal object (colony) to legal subject (sovereign state) was clearly imbued with racist thinking, this question was not only about race. Hypothetically, according to the doctrine of the late nineteenth century, it was possible that a self-governing Arab state might come into existence and be found eligible for recognition, if it could generate a set of governing institutions 'effective' enough to reproduce the rights of existing legal subjects to life, liberty and property – and, at the same time, if it could go one step further and transform its own population into 'free' and 'equal' citizens. Even Hegel conceded at one point that 'Negroes ... cannot be said to be uneducatable' on the grounds that 'in Haiti they have even formed a state on Christian principles' of 'freedom'.[218] Returning to Stuart Hall's idea of race as a 'signifier', one might say that race here did not determine a community's eligibility for recognition and sovereignty directly. Rather, it provided those who set out to assess that eligibility (namely, state officials and international lawyers) with a conceptual shortcut on the basis of which it could be assumed that the community in question did, or did not, possess 'rational' institutions of 'self-rule'. However, the use of race – or rather, of racist assumptions – as a shortcut indicator of capacity for self-government did not necessarily preclude the emergence of certain communities which defied such assumptions and managed successfully to transform themselves into – or 'mimic' we might say, echoing Bhabha[219] – the paradigm of self-governing statehood.

As Tzouvala has argued, in other words, the term 'civilisation' in international legal practice referred not so much to cultural superiority as to the particular set of 'institutions and legal norms' deemed 'essential for the development and reproduction of the capitalist mode of production'.[220] I have suggested that this particular assemblage of institutions and norms corresponded very precisely to the system of self-organisation known as 'government' – or, more specifically, as 'effective' government', 'self' government, 'civil' government or 'responsible' government – regarded and treated in international legal practice as the most important 'criterion' for statehood. It was in this spirit that John Westlake, writing in the 1880s,

[218] Hegel, *Philosophy of Subjective Spirit*, 54.
[219] See Frame, Section 3.2.
[220] Tzouvala, *Letters of Blood and Fire*, 56.

asserted that '[w]hen the people of European race come into contact with American or African tribes, the prime necessity is a government under the protection of which the former may carry on the complex life to which they have become accustomed in their homes'. He went on: 'Can the natives furnish such a government or can it be looked for from the Europeans alone? In the answer to that question lies, for international law, the difference between civilization and the want of it.'[221] Looking back on this body of doctrine and practice in the 1950s, it was Georg Schwarzenberger who coined the phrase 'standard of civilisation' precisely to describe this system of government. As he wrote: 'The test whether a State was civilised and, thus, entitled to full recognition as an international personality' was quite simply, 'whether its government was sufficiently stable to undertake binding commitments under international law and whether it was able and willing to protect adequately the life, liberty and property of foreigners.'[222] These 'minimum standards' were elaborated, Schwarzenberger pointed out, in 'a multitude of treaties' which 'codified [them] in meticulous detail and gradually developed [them] into rules of customary international law'.[223]

The effects of this nineteenth-century iteration of the process of international legal reproduction were felt perhaps most keenly in the so-called 'semi-sovereign states' – the most obviously hybrid members of the 'family of nations' at this time.[224] From the Ottoman Empire to the Chinese, Siamese and Japanese Empires, jurists were confronted with entities that met all the criteria for statehood but one: their 'governments', though in 'exclusive' control of their 'territories', were not considered to be 'effective' when it came to protecting foreigners' rights to life, liberty and property. This came to be resolved in two ways. One involved the creation of a

[221] Westlake, *Collected Papers*, 143. For a similar view, see Oppenheim, *International Law*, 99–110.

[222] Georg Schwarzenberger, 'The Standard of Civilisation in International Law', 8 *Current Legal Problems* (1955): 212–34, at 220.

[223] Ibid., 220.

[224] See generally e.g. Richard S. Horowitz, 'International Law and State Transformation in China, Siam, and the Ottoman Empire during the Nineteenth Century', 15 *Journal of World History* (2004): 445–86; Onuma Yasuaki, 'When was the Law of International Society Born? An Inquiry into the History of International Law from an Intercivilisational Perspective', 2 *JHIL* (2000): 1–66; Crawford, *The Creation of States*, 282–328. On Siam, see Francis Bowes Sayer, 'The Passing of Extraterritoriality in Siam', 22 *AJIL* (1928): 70–88. On Egypt, see Malcolm McIlwraith, 'The Declaration of a Protectorate in Egypt and its Legal Effects', 17 *Journal of Social and Comparative Legislation* (1917): 238–59. On China, see Quincy Wright, 'The End of Extraterritoriality in China', 37 *AJIL* (1943): 286–9 and, with, a brilliant and very particular take, Teemu Ruskola, 'Raping Like A State', 57 *UCLA Law Review* (2010): 1477–536.

system of extraterritorial jurisdiction, which ensured that European individuals would be subject to the jurisdiction not of the state in question but of their own state, with violations administered by their consulates rather than local courts.[225] The other was the system of 'unequal treaties'[226] containing special rights, negotiated on a treaty-by-treaty basis, but extended from one European state to the other via 'most favoured nation' and 'national treatment' principles.

Given the vast array of bilateral treaties negotiated between these 'Eastern Empires',[227] on the one hand, and Britain, France, Russia, Germany, Italy, the US and others on the other, over a period of 200 years (or indeed several centuries, in the case of the capitulations in the Ottoman context[228]), the consistency of their terms is remarkable. Invariably, these treaties included protections for individual rights to private property (with restitution if necessary); provisions for free (or freer) trade; protections for freedom of movement and of religious practice (particularly for Christian minorities); and, via the obligatory extraterritorial jurisdiction clause, guarantees of formal equality for Europeans (i.e. the citizens of states), and in some cases also for their local interlocutors.[229] Crucially, moreover, these treaties were only gradually abandoned as the Japanese, Chinese, Siamese and other 'semi-sovereign' states provided institutional proof of their capacity to 'furnish' Europeans (and, if necessary, their trading partners) with these rights independently – for instance, with the promulgation of the 'Meiji Constitution' in Japan.[230] Only after these entities had 'voluntarily' interpellated as self-governing states of their own accord were they re-recognised, as it were, as 'full' (or fuller) subjects of international law. Here, the example of the Chinese Empire's transformation from 'Middle Kingdom', a subject in a category all of its own, into a 'sovereign state', is particularly helpful in illustrating the peculiar combination, in the process of international legal reproduction, of the use of coercive force and the generation of desire.

[225] For an excellent analysis of the type of individual created by practice such as this, using Lorimer's work as a jumping-off point, see Knop, 'Lorimer's Private Citizens', 447–75.

[226] See esp. Matthew Craven, 'What Happened to Unequal Treaties? The Continuities of Informal Empire', 74 *Nordic Journal of International Law* (2005): 335–82; Dong Wang, *China's Unequal Treaties: Narrating National History* (New York: Lexington Books, 2005).

[227] Westlake, *Collected Papers*, 6.

[228] See e.g. Feroz Ahmad, 'Ottoman Perceptions of the Capitulations 1800–1914', 11 *Journal of Islamic Studies* (2000): 1–20; Özsu, 'The Ottoman Empire'.

[229] See Ahmad, 'Ottoman Perceptions'.

[230] See *Constitution of the Empire of Japan*, 29 November 1890, Arts. 18–32, guaranteeing, among other things, equality before the law, property rights and religious freedom.

The economy of the Chinese Empire, once tightly controlled from the imperial centre, was forcibly 'opened up' by two treaties – the Treaty of Nanking (1842)[231] and the Treaty of Tientsin (1858),[232] concluded in the wake of the two 'Opium Wars' with Britain. These wars had begun when the United Kingdom attacked the Chinese Empire in retaliation for the latter's seizure of large amounts of opium produced in the British Empire and destined for the Chinese market in its effort to ban the opium trade. As both treaties showed, Britain's aim was explicitly that of forcing the Chinese economy to become more 'open'.[233] It had, until that point, been axiomatic to the Chinese Empire's world view (as the Qianlong Emperor explained in 1793 to George III) that the 'Celestial Empire possesses all things in prolific abundance and lacks no product within its own borders', such that 'there was therefore no need to import the manufactures of outside barbarians in exchange for our own produce'.[234] What interaction did take place between China and the outside world in the form of trade had therefore been carefully limited and controlled throughout the Empire's history. That it existed at all was understood to be a matter of imperial 'beneficence', guided by the principle of 'treat[ing] strangers from afar with indulgence', and by this means 'exercis[ing] a pacifying control over barbarian tribes, the world over'.[235] The 'Celestial Empire' possessed no equivalent of the principle sovereign equality, for the Emperor was considered to be sovereign over the entire cosmos.[236] While those countries closest in culture and loyalty were given names, such as *Chaoxian* (Korea) and *Riben* (Japan), those on the semi-periphery and periphery – the latter stretching so far as to encompass Europe – were referred to

[231] *Treaty between Her Majesty the Queen of the United Kingdom of Great Britain and Ireland, and His Majesty the Emperor of China*, Nanking, 29 August 1842.

[232] *Treaty between Her Majesty the Queen of the United Kingdom of Great Britain and Ireland, and His Majesty the Emperor of China*, Tientsin [Tianjin], 26 June 1858. On the treaty port of Tianjin as an 'imperial location', see Luigi Nuzzo, 'The Birth of an Imperial Location: Comparative Perspectives on Western Colonialism in China', 31 *Leiden Journal of International Law* (2018): 569–96.

[233] For a short summary of the political and economic background to the Opium Wars, see Harold M. Tanner, *China, a History, Vol. II, From the Great Qing Empire through The People's Republic of China*, 1644–2009 (Cambridge, MA: Hackett, 2010), 72–7.

[234] Emperor Qianlong of China (r. 1735–96), Imperial Mandate to King George III of Britain (r. 1760–1801), in E. Backhouse and J. O. P. Bland, *Annals and Memoirs of the Court of Peking* (Boston, MA, New York: Houghton Mifflin, 1914), 322–34.

[235] Qian Long to George III. See Edward Q. Wang, 'History, Space, and Ethnicity: The Chinese Worldview', 10 *Journal of World History* (1999): 285–305, at 289.

[236] See John King Fairbank (ed.), *The Chinese World Order: Traditional China's Foreign Relations* (Cambridge, MA: Harvard University Press, 1968), 1–19.

simply as *yi*, *fan*, or *man*, all various terms for 'barbarian'.[237] By the time of the arrival of the Manchu-led Qing Dynasty in the seventeenth century, an earlier cultural organisation of the sphere of Chinese influence into Han/non-Han (civilised/barbarian) had given way to a more spatialised structure, based on a dichotomy between centre (*zhongguo*) and frontier (*bianjiang*).[238] Nonetheless, this structure remained a holistic one, encompassing the entire universe understood as a giant peripheral 'white' surrounding an indisputably Chinese 'yolk'.[239]

Clearly, with the 'Son of Heaven' ruling over the entire cosmos, and with international trade conducted by means of a complex tribute system (that which Earl McCartney, British Envoy to China, snubbed with his notorious refusal to kowtow to the Qianlong Emperor in 1792), 'the strict distinction between the "international" and the "domestic" seen in modern international law did not exist'.[240] By the same token, notions of 'civil' government and 'independence' made little sense in a context in which all other rulers and their peoples were subordinate by definition.[241] However, with the conclusion of the 'unequal' treaties of Nanking and Tientsin (between the Chinese Empire and France,[242] Russia[243] and the United States,[244] in addition to Britain) this began to change, as this extract from the British Treaty of Tientsin indicates:

> Article 3. His Majesty the Emperor of China hereby agrees that the [British] Ambassador ... [represents] the Sovereign of an independent nation, on a footing of equality with that of China ... [H]e shall use the same forms of ... respect to His Majesty the Emperor as are employed ... towards the Sovereigns of independent and equal European nations.
>
> Article 8. The Christian religion ... inculcates the practice of virtue and teaches man to do as he would be done by. Persons teaching it, or professing it, therefore, shall alike be entitled to the protection of the Chinese authorities ...

237 Wang, 'History, Space, and Ethnicity', 290.

238 Ibid., 303.

239 As described by the *huntian shuo* or 'organic heaven theory' developed at this time, visualising the universe as an egg. Ibid., 291–303.

240 Onuma, 'When was the Law of International Society Born?', 14.

241 See Horowitz, 'International Law and State Transformation', 457.

242 *Treaty of Peace, Friendship and Commerce between the Republic of France and the Chinese Empire*, Tientsin, 13 April 1885.

243 *Treaty between His Majesty the Emperor and Autocrat of All the Russias, and His Majesty the Emperor of China*, Tientsin [Tianjin], 13 June 1858.

244 *Treaty between the United States of America and the Chinese Empire*, Tientsin [Tianjin], 18 June 1858.

> Article 9. British subjects are hereby authorized to travel for their pleasure or for purposes of trade, to all parts of the Interior ...
>
> Article 11. [Five more cities and ports will be opened up to British trade. There, British subjects] are permitted to carry on trade with whomsoever they please, and to proceed to and fro at pleasure with their Vessels and Merchandise. They shall enjoy the same privileges, advantages and immunities at the said towns and Ports as they enjoy at the Ports already opened to trade, including the right of residence, of buying or renting Houses, of leasing Land ...
>
> Article 15. All questions in regard to rights, whether of property or person, arising between British subjects, shall be subject to the jurisdiction of the British authorities.
>
> Article 54. The British Government and its subjects are hereby confirmed in all privileges, immunities, and advantages conferred on them by previous Treaties; ... [They] will be allowed free and equal participation in all privileges, immunities, and advantages that may have been or may be hereafter granted by His Majesty the Emperor of China to the Government or subjects of any other nation.[245]

What is interesting about this treaty, as with the Treaty of Nanking,[246] is that while it certainly *was* 'unequal' in many senses (Chinese 'subjects' were not granted reciprocal rights in the British Empire, for example, while British subjects were to be (non-reciprocally) subject to British rather than Chinese law), it is significant that the emphasis of the treaty's language is, above all, on the establishment of a relationship of formal *equality* between the two states.

Most obviously, as this extract shows, the two 'Sovereigns' recognised each other mutually as the rulers of 'independent nation[s] on a footing of equality' both with one another and with 'the Sovereigns of independent and equal European nations' in general. But the individual enters the picture here, too. British 'subjects' were the ones granted rights to trade, travel, worship and own property freely, after all. And it was clear, moreover, that they could hardly exercise these rights effectively without, in doing

[245] *Treaty of Tientsin* (British), Arts. 3–14.

[246] In a very similar way, the Treaty of Nanking had secured the opening of five treaty ports in addition to Canton (Art. 2); the cession of Hong Kong and an indemnity of US$21 million (Arts. 3–7), permitted British merchants 'to carry on their mercantile transactions with whatever persons they please' instead of being restricted, as before, to trading only with licensed 'Hong' merchants (Art. 5); and at the international level bound the Empire to relinquish its insistence on the inferiority of the foreign 'barbarians' and to recognise its relationship with Britain as existing, henceforth, 'on a footing of perfect equality' (Art. 11). The *General Regulations for Trade and Tariff* concluded between the British and Chinese Empires in 1843, also guaranteed that tariffs would vary for the most part between 2.5 and 5 per cent, rising at the very most to 10 per cent for silk products.

so, setting in motion a process which would create reciprocal rights to freedom of travel, trade and worship on the part, at least, of those Chinese individuals with whom they interacted. Or to put it differently, it would be pointless for British individuals to possess a right to 'carry on trade with whomsoever they pleased', to 'proceed to and fro at pleasure with their Vessels and Merchandise', or to proselytise, if at least those Chinese individuals whose goods and services they sought to buy, whose 'vessels' they sought to hire, and to whom they sought to 'teach' the Christian 'virtue' of 'do[ing] as [one] would be done by', and so on, were not themselves at liberty to trade, travel and worship freely, at least up to that point. The result of the treaties' emphasis on formal individual equality and negative freedom, in other words, was just as 'unequal' as their more overtly exploitative clauses. For the consequence of the reproduction of such rights on the part of British citizens in China was to trigger a demand for those rights on the part of many of the Chinese individuals who stood to benefit, for example, from selling their wares to, hiring their boats to or sending their children to the mission schools set up by the British and other foreigners. Up until that point, it was not that these rights had been denied to Chinese individuals by the Celestial authorities; it was that they simply *did not exist* in the strictly hierarchical social and normative order of the Chinese Empire.

As this suggests, if we approach the unequal treaties from the perspective of international legal reproduction, we can start to make sense of them as a device through which the Chinese Emperor was forced, effectively with a gun to his head, to make a commitment, at the *international* level, to reproducing and protecting a particular kind of *individual* legal subjectivity domestically – *both* for foreigners and, to the extent they interacted with them on a legal basis, for Chinese subjects, in a process that was as much a result of the constitution of desire as it was a consequence of the deployment of violence. Those Chinese individuals became, in effect, the hybrid subjects (at once citizens and not-citizens) of an equally hybrid international subject – the Chinese Empire of the late nineteenth century, increasingly both 'sovereign' and less-than-sovereign. This dynamic became clearer and clearer as time went on. Further 'unequal treaties' were concluded with Britain, the United States, France, Sweden and Norway, Prussia, the German Confederation, Portugal and Japan over the next century. These treaties were characterised, like the Treaties of Tientsin, by their provisions for foreign property rights, extraterritorial jurisdiction and 'most favoured nation (MFN)' treatment – precisely that legal structure which would allow the citizens of China's treaty partners to carry their legal subjectivity with them into a jurisdiction which was not, otherwise, set up to make that possible, and to trigger a reciprocal demand for such rights among the 'natives'.[247]

The response of Chinese individuals to the 'unequal treaties' and their repercussions went in one of two directions. Some found the unequal treaties to be an unbearable humiliation, and demanded the expulsion of foreigners and a return to isolation on the part of the Celestial Empire.[248] Others, however, argued that the best way forward was, in effect, to beat the foreigners at their own game. For example, a movement known as the 'self-strengthening' (*tzu-ch'iang*) movement gained influence on the imperial authorities after the Opium Wars and especially after China's trouncing by Japan in the war of 1894–95. On the back of the slogan 'learn the superior technology of the barbarian in order to control him',[249] the Imperial authorities set out to reduce China's dependence on hostile foreign states,[250] and to increase its capacity to suppress the internal rebellions that were then breaking out all over the Empire under the influence of (and in reaction to) Western ideas, through a programme that came to be known as the 'Hundred Days of Reform'. However, the Boxer Rebellion (1899–1901) and the catastrophic reaction to it pushed the Empire to breaking point. In June 1900 the Yihetuans (Militia of Those United in Righteousness, or 'Boxers' as they became known in Europe in connection with their practice of martial arts) – a mystical, violently anti-imperial, anti-foreign, anti-Christian sentiment whose slogan was 'support the Qing dynasty and kill all foreigners!' – converged on Peking (Beijing), persuading the Empress Cixi (who had ousted the Guangxu Emperor) to declare war on China's eleven treaty partners: Great Britain, France, Japan, Russia, Italy, Spain, Belgium, the Netherlands, Austria-Hungary, Germany and the United States. The foreign legations were besieged for two months, until finally, on 14 August 1900, a force of 20,000 men, supplied by an eight-nation alliance of states (Britain, France, Austria-Hungary, Germany, Russia, the United States and Japan), arrived in Beijing to free them (see

247 Wang, *China's Unequal Treaties*, 11.

248 Jerome Ch'ên, 'The Nature and Characteristics of the Boxer Movement – A Morphological Study', 23 *Bulletin of the School of Oriental and African Studies, University of London* (1960): 287–308.

249 'The Self-Strengthening Movement in China, 1898', in Anthony Snyder and Sherri West (eds.), *Readings in Global History*, Vol. 2 (2nd edn Dubuque, IA: Kendall-Hunt, 1997), 166. See also Tanner, *China, a History*, Vol. 2, 86–97.

250 William M. Speidel, 'The Administrative and Fiscal Reforms of Liu Ming-ch'uan in Taiwan, 1884–1892: The Foundation of Self-Strengthening', 35 *The Journal of Asian Studies* (1976): 441–59, at 441–2.

Figure 4). The resulting 'Boxer Protocol' was perhaps the most unequal of all the 'unequal treaties'.[251]

The Empress's efforts to get 'self-strengthening' back on track with the 'New Policies' of 1901, which included proposals to transform the imperial government into a constitutional monarchy,[252] were overwhelmed by the number and strength of the popular uprisings of all descriptions which were by then taking place all over China. The demands of these groups varied wildly, from virulently racist calls to overthrow the 'furry and horned Manchu race' to radical feminist appeals to women's solidarity from the Foot Emancipation Society. However, calls for the replacement of the imperial system with a European-style republic were by far the most powerful, issuing from groups including the China Revival Society (Huaxinghui), the Restoration Society (Guangfuhui) and the Independence Army, who together formed the foundation of what would soon become the Nationalist Party (Guomindang). Significantly, by 1911, regions making up more than half the territory of China, including Jiujiang, Anhui, Fujian and Guandong, had declared their independence from the Chinese Empire in the form, not of various modes of collective organisation indigenous to Chinese history and culture, but instead of new sovereign states.[253] The attempted secessions were unsuccessful, however, and these multiple rebellions eventually coalesced in the Xinhai Revolution. With the abdication of the six-year-old Puyi Emperor on 12 February 1912, an empire that had endured for more than 2,000 years was terminated, and in its place a republican nation-state was declared, modelled explicitly on the self-governing state. The Constitution of the new Chinese Republic transformed eligible Chinese individuals (adult males over the age of twenty-one who were educated or who owned property and paid taxes) into Chinese 'citizens',[254] and made them 'equal'

[251] Among other things, the 'Boxer Protocol' included a commitment to punish by death or exile all those responsible for the killings and to '[prohibit] for ever, on pain of death, membership in any anti-foreign society'; to transfer the legation quarter of Peking to the 'exclusive control ... which may be made defensible of the Legations'; and to pay an indemnity of 450 million taels (16 million kilograms) of silver in compensation for damage to or loss of life and property. *Peace Agreement between Austria-Hungary, Britain, France, Germany, Italy, Japan, Russia and the United States and China*, Peking [Beijing], 7 September 1901 ('Boxer Protocol'), Arts. 1–10.

[252] See Tanner, *China, a History*, Vol. 2, 99–192.

[253] David Curtis Wright, *The History of China* (2nd edn Santa Barbara, CA: Greenwood, 2011), 123.

[254] Denis Twitchett and John K. Fairbank (eds.), *The Cambridge History of China*, Vol. 12, Pt. 1 (Cambridge University Press, 1983), 222–3.

before the law, bestowing on them, among other things, rights to 'security of their property and the freedom of trade' and 'freedom of religion'.[255]

International recognition of the new republic was not immediately forthcoming, however, notwithstanding its very overt efforts to meet the criteria for statehood. Instead, a long and strikingly explicit debate took place among the European powers and the United States over how recognition might be used as a tool to ensure the foreign 'interests' that had so far been secured by the treaty regime (since 1899, under the aegis of the so-called 'open-door policy'), even as China's 'territorial and administrative integrity and political independence' was formally acknowledged, constituted and guaranteed.[256] Reacting against Russia's attempt to extract special concessions for Manchuria back in 1902, the United States had already described this peculiar, both sovereign and less-than-sovereign quality of China's personality under international law:

> Any agreement by which China cedes to any corporation or company the exclusive right and privilege of opening mines, establishing railroads, or in any other way industrially developing [a particular part of Chinese territory] constitutes a monopoly, which is a distinct breach of the stipulations of treaties concluded between China and foreign powers, and thereby seriously affects the rights of American citizens; it restricts their rightful trade and exposes it to being discriminated against ... strongly tends towards permanently impairing the sovereign rights of China in this part of the empire, and seriously interferes with her ability to meet her international obligations.[257]

As this statement underscores, like the text of the unequal treaties themselves, the legal traction of China's international personality was understood, as a matter of international law, to depend directly on China's willingness and capacity to protect the rights of foreign citizens to be equally 'free' in the sense of possessing formally equal access to China's resources. When, in 1912, following the collapse of imperial rule and China's self-identification as a self-governing and therefore sovereign state, the Western powers were confronted with the question of how to manage their recognition of the new Chinese Republic, it was decided, in this spirit, that a 'Financial Consortium' should be convened to resolve the issue, consisting of the banks of the main concessionary powers

[255] *Provisional Constitution of the Republic of China*, 10 March, 1912, Arts. 5–6.

[256] Dean Acheson (ed.), *United States Relations with China, with Special Reference to the Period 1944–1949* (Washington, DC: US Department of State, 1949), 1.

[257] US circular to treaty powers, 1 February 1902, cited in Acheson, *United States Relations with China*, 3–4.

(Britain, France, Japan, Belgium, Russia and on some occasions also the the US). The European states agreed, in consultation with the banks, that recognition would be withheld until evidence of a 'regularly constituted parliamentary regime' arrived; until the Republic had made 'a formal guaranty [*sic*] of treaty stipulations and rights of foreigners in China'; and until it had signed up to a 'reorganization loan' aimed at 'enabl[ing] the Chinese Government to reorganise its administration on an effective modern basis', to 'pay off its large outstanding debts and build Chinese credit', and to 'protect the interests of American and European investors'.[258] Recognition was duly extended in October 1912, after a GB£25 million loan contract had been signed with the Six-Power Group, composed of Britain, France, Russia, Germany, Japan and the United States in April. Six years later, China would be welcomed into the League of Nations as an 'original' and hence unconditional member.

Crucially, then, the many 'unequal treaties' which had been concluded with the Chinese Empire under the 'open-door' policy, and which were later concluded with the Chinese Republic, were at no point understood as having undermined China's rights and duties as a person of international law. On the contrary, it was those very treaties which had first constituted China as a person of international law. In China, consequently, the more individual legal subjectivity was protected – and, indeed, extended, after the Republic rolled these rights out to Chinese individuals as well – the more 'sovereign' China was understood to be. The new Woodrow Wilson government was quite candid about this. As Wilson put it, shortly before US recognition was extended (on 2 May 1913).

> The awakening of the people of China to a consciousness of their responsibilities under free government is the most significant, if not the most momentous, event of our generation. With this movement and aspiration the American people are in profound sympathy. They certainly wish to participate and participate very generously in opening to the Chinese and to the use of the world the almost untouched and perhaps unrivaled resources of China.
>
> The Government of the United States is earnestly desirous of promoting the most extended and intimate trade relationship between this country

[258] US Department of State Press Release, 19 March 2012, annexed to William Straight, 'China's Loan Negotiations', 3 *Journal of Race Development* (1913): 369–411 at 411. Reform of China's currency and taxation systems, plus various projects of industrial development, characterised the first set of conditions, and the latter was to be achieved by the appointment of foreign agents to 'assist' the work of administration and foreign auditors with executive powers 'to effective expenditure of the loan funds borrowed for the purposes specified'. See Straight, 'China's Loan Negotiations', 393–4.

> and the Chinese Republic. The present Administration will urge and support the legislative measures [in China] necessary to give American merchants, manufacturers, contractors, and engineers, the banking and other financial facilities which they now lack and without which they are at a serious disadvantage as compared with their industrial and commercial rivals. This is its duty. This is the main material interest of its citizens in the development of China. Our interests are those of the Open Door – a door of friendship and mutual advantage. This is the only door we care to enter.[259]

The fact that this regime of conjoined individual and international 'freedom' and 'equality' – the regime known as 'self-governing statehood' or simply 'statehood' – could, when transplanted to the Chinese context, have no other result than to exacerbate China's materially subordinate position in relation to the world's other nation-states did not escape the notice of V. I. Lenin,[260] or, of course, Mao Tse-Tung.[261] As China's experience reveals, formal equality and liberty could themselves prove to be the most precise instruments of domination, even when 'freely' demanded by those struggling for emancipation.

2.3.3 Between State and Colony II: Hybridity and the Gradual Fragmentation of the European Empires

China's fate at the hands of the European powers and the United States was, of course, far from unique. Indeed, that fate was mirrored by that of the Ottoman, Japanese, Siamese and other 'Eastern empires'.[262] However, while the experience of transformation into a state, or proto-state, was

[259] Statement of the American Government in Regard to Support Requested by the American Group, 18 March 1913, cited in John V. A. MacMurray (ed.), *Treaties and Agreements with China, 1894–1919*, Vol. II (New York: Oxford University Press, 1921), 1025.

[260] Watching these events carefully from afar, Lenin wrote of the 'robber consortium': 'The point is that the Chinese revolution did not evoke among the European bourgeoisie any enthusiasm for freedom and democracy – only the proletariat can entertain that feeling, which is alien to the knights of profit; it gave rise to the urge to *plunder* China, partition her and take away some of her territories. This "consortium" of the six Powers (Britain, France, Russia, Germany, Japan and the United States) was trying to make China bankrupt in order to weaken and undermine the republic.' V. I. Lenin, 'Big Achievement of the Chinese Republic', trans. George Hanna, 68 *Pravda*, 22 March 1913, Marxists' Internet Archive, available at www.marxists.org/archive/lenin/works/1913/mar/22.htm (accessed 8 September 2017).

[261] See e.g. Mao Tse-Tung [1939], 'The Chinese Revolution and the Chinese Communist Party', in *Selected Works of Mao Tse-Tung*, Vol. II (Peking: Foreign Languages Press, 1967), Marxists' Internet Archive, available at www.marxists.org/reference/archive/mao/selected-works/volume-2/mswv2_23.htm (accessed 8 September 2017).

[262] On the Japanese and Ottoman Empires, see e.g. Tzouvala, *Letters of Blood and Fire*, 64–81.

certainly far more intense and traumatic in the non-European world, we should not then assume that the process had no effect in Europe.

For example, one set of contemporary illustrations can found in the provisions of the Treaty of Berlin, concluded in 1878 by Great Britain, Austria-Hungary, France, Germany, Italy, Russia and the Ottoman Empire.[263] This treaty provided for the 'conditional' recognition of the independence of Montenegro, Servia (Serbia) and Roumania (Romania) from the Ottoman Empire in the course of revising the territorial settlement that had been laid out in the Treaty of San Stefano, which ended the Russo-Ottoman War of 1877–78. The conditions placed on the sovereignty, or subjectivity, of these new states involved, in each case, terms that are not dissimilar to those of the 'unequal treaties' in their overwhelming emphasis on the establishment of conditions of formal equality and equal freedom.[264] In granting independence to Romania, for instance, it was pledged that '[t]he subjects and citizens of all the [signatory] Powers, traders or others' would be 'treated ... without distinction of creed, on a footing of perfect equality',[265] and forbade any moderation of the pre-existing regime of extraterritorial jurisdiction without the mutual consent of the 'parties concerned'.[266] 'Absolute freedom of communication' was 'guaranteed' in Montenegro,[267] and the treaty established a new regime of extraterritorial jurisdiction in Serbia.[268] In addition, provisions for the creation and protection of property rights for non-Muslims were guaranteed in both Montenegro and Serbia.[269] Meanwhile, Bulgaria was 'constituted' separately by the signatory powers as an 'autonomous and tributary Principality under the suzerainty of His Imperial Majesty the Sultan', with 'a Christian Government and a national militia'.[270]

As these illustrations indicate clearly, the concerns deployed by the existing states in constituting these new international persons directly were primarily commercial. In the case of the 'unequal treaties' imposed on 'Eastern empires' like China (as in the case of the establishment of 'effective' territorial sovereignty over colonies like the Island of Palmas and parts of the Congo Basin), these existing states prioritised the protection of

[263] *Final Act of the Congress of Berlin between Great Britain, Austria-Hungary, France, Germany, Italy, Russia and Turkey*, Berlin, 13 July 1878, Arts. 24–7 ('Treaty of Berlin').

[264] Ibid., Arts. 8 (Bulgaria); 37 (Serbia); 48 (Romania).

[265] Ibid., Art. 44.

[266] Ibid., Art. 49.

[267] Ibid., Art. 29 (Montenegro).

[268] Ibid., 37.

[269] Ibid., Arts. 39 (Serbia); 30 (Montenegro).

[270] Ibid., Art. 1.

'civil' rights on the part of visiting 'foreigners', i.e. foreign citizens. It was only after China had made the decision to identify itself 'freely' as a 'civil state' – only after its 'people', in declaring China a republic in 1912, had finally 'awaken[ed] ... to a consciousness of their responsibilities under free government', as Wilson put it – that the question of the extension of free and equal legal subjectivity to *all* (eligible) Chinese individuals also came up as the condition upon which an extended form of recognition would be granted. In the European context, however, the very similar set of conditions imposed by the signatories of the Treaty of Berlin on Serbia, Romania and Montenegro mandated the rolling-out of legal subjectivity to all their (eligible) inhabitants straight away. The Treaty imposed constitutional provisions on all of these new sovereigns, in exchange for their constitution as such, mandating the protection of 'civil and political rights' in general, with particular stress (in the context of Muslim-Christian clashes) laid on 'freedom of religious worship', and on freedom of trade via the prohibition of 'transit duties'.[271] Unlike China (which as we have just seen took until 1911 to get to this point) and unlike Vitoria's 'Indians', but *like* the Dutch Republic and the Republic of Haiti, to refer back to some earlier examples, these new European states had interpellated, independently and willingly, as subjects of international law, thereby demonstrating their 'rationality' (in European/Hegelian terms), their 'reciprocating will' and their capacity for 'self-government and mutual recognition'. Nonetheless, since 'will' was arguably more in abundance than 'power' at this point, the recognition of these sovereigns was conditioned in the Treaty of Berlin on their commitment to setting up the legal regime necessary to ensure that individual legal subjectivity would, indeed, be universally protected – the regime otherwise known as 'self-government'.[272]

[271] Ibid., Arts. 24–7 (Montenegro); Arts. 34–5 (Serbia); Arts. 43–4 (Romania).

[272] This point is reinforced if we look at the implications of the Treaty of Berlin for the 'sovereignty' of the Ottoman Empire from which these new states seceded – a 'semi-sovereign state' whose self-governing questions were being increasingly called into question at this time. If the Treaty brought Romania, Serbia and Montenegro into being as new 'civil' states, it also divested the Ottoman Empire of a large amount of territory and compelled it to implement 'civil' legal regimes not only in Bulgaria but also in Eastern Rumelia, Crete and elsewhere. For example, the 'administrative, judicial and financial system' of Eastern Rumelia, now placed under a 'Christian Governor-General', was to be 'determined' by a 'European Commission', with the 'immunities and privileges of foreigners' and religious liberty 'to be guaranteed' (Arts. 28–30). Meanwhile in Crete the 'Organic Law' of 1868, granting religious and political freedom to the Christian population, was to be 'scrupulously' enforced (Art. 23). The question of what rights the European powers possessed in relation to the Ottoman Empire if the latter violated any of the Treaty's terms was left largely alone. Nonetheless, the idea that military intervention in the Ottoman Empire

Torpedoing, as it did, the assumptions of European 'civilisation',[273] one might have expected the First World War to have been a setback for advocates of the idea that international personality should be conditioned on individual personality. On the contrary, however, the outbreak of the War served only to reinforce this connection, at least for jurists belonging to the Allied and Associated Powers. Unlike the Central Powers, led by three territorial empires – the German, Hapsburg and Ottoman Empires – the Allied side was composed almost exclusively (with the important exception of the Russian Empire) of self-consciously self-governing – that is, 'responsible' – nation-states, from Britain and France to the US and other newer states, including Italy, Greece and Romania. As we shall see further in the following chapter, these states narrated their war aims explicitly and consistently in terms of a struggle for 'freedom' against the supposedly outdated 'imperialism' and absolutism of the Central Powers.

It was no coincidence, for example, that the American Institute of International Law (AIIL) adopted its *Declaration on the Rights and Duties of Nations* in December 1915, just as the United States was debating whether or not to offer military support to its European allies. Three months later, in his opening address to the AIIL's annual meeting, its President, Elihu Root, voiced grave concerns over 'the principles of action upon which the war was begun', which he described as a 'repudiation of every element of fundamental right upon which the law of nations rests'.[274] Root was, of course, referring, among other things, to the alacrity and brutality with which the German Empire had invaded Luxembourg, Belgium and France. Above all, he noted, the behaviour of certain states in the War had violated the Declaration's understanding of international law as the body of rules governing 'a democratic community of nations in which

---

was justified if it proved necessary to enforce protections for Christian minorities had a long practical basis, such interventions having been carried out in Greece (1821–33), Lebanon and Syria (1860–61) and Crete (1866–69 and 1896–1900). See generally Davide Rodogno, *Against Massacre: Humanitarian Interventions in the Ottoman Empire, 1815–1914* (Princeton University Press, 2012).

273 See generally Jan Ifversen, 'The Crisis of European Civilization: An Inter-War Diagnosis', in Mehdi Mozaffari (ed.), *Globalization and Civilizations* (London, New York: Routledge, 2002), 151–77. For the contemporary perspective see e.g. Paul Valéry, 'La Crise de l'esprit' (1919), at https://biblio.wiki/wiki/La_Crise_de_l'esprit (accessed 27 January 2018); Francesco Saverio Nitti, *La Decadenza dell'Europa: le vie dell ricostruzione* (Florence: R. Bemporad & Figlio, 1922); Hilaire Belloc, *The Crisis of Our Civilization* (London etc.: Cassell, 1937).

274 Elihu Root, Opening Address as President of the American Society of International Law, Washington, 27 April 1916, 'The Declaration of the Rights and Duties of Nations adopted by the American Institute of International Law', 10 *AJIL* (1916): 211–21 at 215.

individual nations have the same rights and the same full liberty for their enjoyment, limited and limited only, by the equal rights of every other member of the community'.[275] The superiority of this order, Root argued, was underscored by 'the vast progress of civilization since the Peace of Westphalia, with the general advance of mankind in comfort, intelligence, [and] individual freedom and opportunity'.[276] All of this stood to be lost, he warned, if the 'nation[s] belonging to the society of nations' were not prepared to defend the rule of international law against those who sought to violate its fundamental principle: the 'independent equality of states'.[277]

This apparently unambiguous statement of the equal right of all 'nations' to adopt their own institutions, methods and principles of collective self-organisation is belied, however, by the implicit normativity of the Declaration's language, and that of Root himself. Contrasting the rule of international law (the 'scheme of organization of the civilized inhabitants of the earth') with 'the conditions of tribal hostility which prevailed during all the early part of human history', Root 'denied' that 'any aggregation of human beings in any state, under any form of government can be superior' to international law's 'duties of good faith, of justice, and of humanity'.[278] Yet Root went on to clarify that the phrase 'any state, under any form of government' actually meant that every state, as such, must have 'government based upon the rights of men'.[279] Seen through a lens provided by the process of international legal reproduction, what appears simply to be a deeply hypocritical statement – blind to the realities of Native American dispossession, slavery and ongoing racial oppression in the United States itself, not to mention its then-ongoing actions overseas in the Philippines, Haiti and elsewhere – is in fact, from an international legal perspective, perfectly legitimate and straightforward. Non-states, organised on the basis of norms and forms of authority that were not 'governments based upon the rights of men' did not '[belong] to the society of nations' as Root put it; did not fall 'within the confines of civilization'.[280] In addition to defining 'liberty' and 'equality' in such a way as to exclude almost the entirety of Asia, Africa and the Pacific from the scope of international law, this allowed Root to target his criticisms of barbarous international law-violation exclusively at those states (namely the Central Powers) which

275 Ibid., 213–14.
276 Ibid., 214.
277 Ibid., 216–17.
278 Ibid., 214.
279 Ibid., 219.
280 Ibid., 219–20.

were acting in so tyrannical a fashion as to place themselves voluntarily beyond what he called the 'confines of civilization'/'society of states'.

3 Conclusion: Race, Legal Subjectivity and Capitalist Reproduction

Following in the footsteps of the Russian Formalists and Futurists,[281] as taken up by critical scholars of international law today such as Sundhya Pahuja[282] and Susan Marks,[283] the objective of this chapter has been to 'make strange' something that is so familiar as to have become invisible. This is the truly revolutionary transformation, inconceivable until a few hundred years ago, involved in the division of virtually the entire surface of the earth into a series of states and state-administered territories – that is, into a series of international legal subjects and objects. By looking, not so much at these subjects and objects themselves as at the process which lay behind this transformation, my aim has been to 'impart the sensation of things' (in this case, the coercive 'pushes' and interpellative 'pulls' involved in driving this process forward) 'as they [were] perceived and not as they are known'.[284]

Although this global metamorphosis was only completed towards the end of the twentieth century, already by 1914 a pattern had been set over the course of several centuries' worth of theory and practice – articulated and set in motion (it might be well to point out, in the spirit of defamiliarisation) almost exclusively by property-owning white men. One result was the emergence of a new discipline, international law, ostensibly 'the body of rules prevailing between states'.[285] Yet if we examine the small print of the treatises of these theorists and scrutinise the fine details of the practice which their arguments responded to and, in turn, influenced, we see that international law also did something else; that it was, in fact, deeply

[281] For one of the most famous elaborations of the technique of 'defamiliarisation', see Viktor Shklovsky [1917], 'Art as Technique', in Lee T. Lemon and Marian J. Reis (eds. and trans.), *Russian Formalist Criticism: Four Essays* (Lincoln, NE: University of Nebraska Press, 1965), 3–24. Shklovsky was also a contemporary of Bakhtin's. See e.g. Viktor Shklovsky, 'Fransua Rable i kniga M. Bakhina,' in *Tetiva: O neskhodstve skhodnogo* (Moscow: Sovietskii pisatel, 1970), 257–96.

[282] Conversations and lectures, 2010–18.

[283] Susan Marks, *The Riddle of All Constitutions: International Law, Democracy and the Critique of Ideology* (Oxford University Press, 2000); Marks, 'Big Brother is Bleeping You – With the Message that Ideology Doesn't Matter,' 12 *EJIL* (2001): 109–23.

[284] Shklovsky, 'Art as Technique', 12.

[285] John Westlake, *Chapters on the Principles of International Law* (Cambridge University Press, 1894), 1.

committed to doing something else. This 'something else' concerned the transformation, as far as possible, of all human beings into subjects of a particular kind. The mechanism through which this was achieved involved the attachment of certain conditions to the assumption of international rights and duties by would-be sovereign states, and (something that the next chapter will attend to more closely) by means of interventionary measures aimed at disciplining those subjects of international law whose success in meeting these conditions began to wane.

The type of subjectivity in question is, as I have shown, precisely that of the 'free' and 'equal' *legal* subject discussed by Pashukanis and Edelman.[286] As we saw in the Frame, Edelman's central argument is that '[t]he red thread running through juridical ideology is freedom and equality. Every man is a subject (in law), that is, free and equal with respect to all other subjects (in law)'.[287] That freedom and equality, he continues, is constantly reaffirmed and reconstituted in the 'sphere of circulation' – the sphere in which citizens go about exercising their rights to life, liberty and property as though the miseries associated with the 'sphere of production' did not exist. For Edelman, the 'sphere of circulation' is therefore none other than the sphere of 'civil society'. Bearing this understanding of legal subjectivity in mind when we look at the history of what eventually became the discipline of international law, we find that at no point did states (in their practice) or international lawyers (in their doctrine) view it as a normative requirement that the assumption of international personality should be conditioned on measures aimed, for example, at achieving a more equal distribution of resources among the inhabitants of any sovereign-to-be. Nor did this emerging body of international legal theory and practice suggest that sovereign rights and duties should be bestowed solely on those entities which had committed themselves, say, to ensuring that the interests of non-human organisms would not be subordinated to human desires. On the contrary, such considerations were (and still are, as we shall see) treated as entirely irrelevant to the process of reproducing new international persons (as they had come to be known by the First World War, where this chapter ends). By contrast, what international legal theory and practice did (and does) insist upon was that international rights and duties would only be constituted if, and to the extent that, aspiring sovereigns proved to be both willing and able to protect the rights of the existing legal subjects within their jurisdiction to 'freedom'. For 'full' sovereignty, meanwhile (and as we shall see further in

[286] See Frame, Section 2.2.

[287] Edelman, *Ownership of the Image*, 144–5.

Item 3), that equal right to freedom had to be extended to all the individuals within the territory of any prospective state. Freedom, in this context, was understood in an exclusively negative sense, as the liberty of the individual to buy and sell commodities, including her own labour-power, on the 'free' market, and in doing so to accumulate resources without threat of compulsory, state-sanctioned redistribution. By reproducing this narrow set of individual rights, and in doing so forming and maintaining a 'level playing field' upon which competition for resources could take place 'freely', new states committed themselves to extending legal subjectivity to all the individuals within their jurisdiction.

This is not, of course, to deny the many differences that existed, for instance, between the scholastics and the positivists, or the contractarians and the republicans, about which a great deal has been written.[288] It is, instead, to point out that, across this long period of history, running roughly from 1532 to 1916, there were also similarities among them as well. In particular, from the natural law emphasis on subjective rights and commutative justice to the positivist emphasis on 'civilisation' and state sovereignty, we have seen that 'freedom' was understood, and consistently narrated, right across this period as something that belonged 'naturally' to 'all men' equally. What is crucial to note, however, is that in none of the treatises or instruments discussed above did 'all men' mean 'all human beings', or even 'all male human beings'. On the contrary, what this phrase meant was 'all *rational* human beings', with rationality understood as the capacity to weigh up costs and benefits with a view to maximising 'utility' in the manner of the *homo economicus*. Locke, for instance, described the 'wild Indian' (i.e. the Indigenous 'American' individual) 'who knows no enclosure, and is still a tenant in common' as being for this reason a pre-rational individual, who did not possess a right, for instance, to exclude British colonists from the land inhabited by her community as private property.[289] Having failed to enclose their land, 'mix' their labour with it with the aim of producing a surplus, and in doing render its produce capable of being accumulated, the Indigenous peoples of the Americas, Locke argued, had demonstrated their lack of rationality, their incapacity for freedom, and therefore their ineligibility for rights.[290] Whatever particular rights and duties may have belonged to particular groups of

[288] See e.g. Annabel S. Brett, *Liberty, Rights and Nature: Individual Rights in Later Scholastic Thought* (Cambridge University Press, 1997).

[289] Locke, 'Of Civil Government', 271.

[290] Ibid., 272.

Figure 5 Gutzon Borglum inspecting work on his 18m high profile of President George Washington during the creation of Mount Rushmore, South Dakota, 31 May 1932. Between 1927 and 1941, Borglum, his son and his team of 400 technicians dynamited 450,000 tonnes of stone out of e *Sápa* (the Black Hills), one of the holiest sites for the *Oceti Sakowin* (the Great Sioux Nation). This territory was seized from the *Lakȟóta* (Lakota) people in 1876, in violation of the 1868 Treaty of Fort Laramie, which had guaranteed Indigenous sovereignty over the mountains in perpetuity. Photograph by Rise Studio, Rapid City, South Dakota. Courtesy of the US Library of Congress Prints and Photographs Division, ref: LC-USZ62-63648.

individuals under the jurisdiction of particular states, empires, protectorates or colonies, in other words, for the purposes of international law's central task of deciding which entities should or should not be included among its subjects, it was the reproduction of *individual* legal subjectivity that provided the critical benchmark. It was to this capacity, I have argued, that the criterion of 'government' referred.

As the history presented in this chapter suggests, the relationship between international and individual legal subjectivity should be understood as conditional rather than as analogical (as in the 'domestic analogy'). The connection is, in other words, material rather than formal in nature. Equally, this history also reveals something about the peculiar nature of international legal reproduction as a process that is general (in the sense that the 'standard of statehood' has been applied to all aspiring sovereigns) but also inherently racialised, in a way that neither Pashukanis nor Edelman appears to notice. Thus, as Robert Knox has argued persuasively, 'when Pashukanis argued that the legal subject represented "the abstract commodity owner elevated to the heavens" he missed a crucial qualification: this abstract commodity owner was both white and European. Abstract formal equality obtained between these subjects only.'[291] As Knox points out, international law operates by 'mediat[ing] and articulat[ing] the expansion of capital through racialising certain territories and societies', thereby 'open[ing] them up for the penetration of capital, and facilitat[ing] their control and management'.[292] The history that I have laid out in this chapter builds on this critique by fleshing out the way in which race has operated historically as a signifier or marker of rationality, which was in turn seen as something that could only be assessed collectively, on the basis of the presence (or absence) or 'self-governing' institutions.

Item 3 takes up these suggestions and tests them further by zooming in on the process of international legal reproduction as it played out under the League of Nations and during the inter-war period more generally.

[291] Robert Knox, 'Valuing Race? Stretched Marxism and the Logic of Imperialism', 4 *London Review of International Law* (2016): 81–126, at 109. Knox applies Frantz Fanon's insistence – that Marxism requires to be 'slightly stretched' in order to take account of the peculiar character of the relations of production in the colonies – to international law itself. Cf. Frantz Fanon, *The Wretched of the Earth* (New York: Grove Press, 1963), 40.

[292] Knox, 'Stretched Marxism', 112.

Item No. 3

International Legal Reproduction and the League of Nations

On 5 February 1919, a group of statesmen met for the third time in the Peace Palace at Versailles, three months after the armistice which ended the First World War. Among those seated around the table were representatives of the 'Big Five' Allied Powers – United States President Woodrow Wilson; Japanese Minister for Foreign Affairs Baron Makino Nobuaki; Italian Prime Minister Vittorio Emanuele Orlando; Head of the British Delegation, Lord Robert Cecil; and former French premier Léon Bourgeois – together with Belgian Foreign Minister Paul Hymans; Serbian Minister at Paris Milenko Vesnić; and South African General Jan Smuts. Together, these men made up the Commission on the League of Nations, whose task it was to design what many, at the time, considered to be nothing less than a new 'world government'.[1]

On that particular freezing morning, the members of the League Commission were thrashing out the wording of what would become the second paragraph of Article 1 of the Covenant of the League of Nations. It had already been decided that twenty-eight of the 'Allied and Associated Powers' which had together won the War would become the League's founding members and would not, therefore, be required to meet any admission criteria, with the 'Big Four' (Britain, France, Italy and Japan) obtaining permanent seats on the League's Council, or executive body. Conversely the Central Powers were to be excluded from the League, initially at least. The question the Committee was then debating was therefore which other entities would be permitted to join. More specifically, the question they were wrestling with was whether or not League membership should be open exclusively to 'self-governing' entities. About halfway through the meeting, frustrated by his colleagues' hesitation over how specific the entry criteria should be, Wilson was moved to make an impassioned intervention:

> We have said that this war was carried on for a vindication of democracy. The statement did not create the impulse but it brought it to consciousness.

[1] See Mark Mazower, *Governing the World: The History of an Idea* (London: Allen Lane, 2012).

> So as soon as it was stated that the war was being waged to make the world safe for democracy, a new spirit came into the world. People began to look at the substance rather than at the form. They knew that governments derived their just powers from the consent of the governed. I should like to point out that nowhere else in the draft [of the League Covenant] is there any recognition of the principle of democracy. If we are ready to fight for this, we should be ready to write it into the covenant.[2]

For Wilson (just as for Elihu Root, as we saw at the end of Item 2[3]), the War had been a war of enlightenment – a baptism by fire – through which the truth of the 'new spirit' of democracy, already 'created', was at last 'brought to consciousness'. The Allied victory in the First World War represented – for this devout Presbyterian, born to a Confederate, slave-owning family, and the architect, at home, of 'federal segregation' between black and white Americans[4] – nothing less than a global, if not an eschatological, victory for 'liberty' against 'tyranny'.

This articulation no doubt struck many of Wilson's colleagues as hyperbolic, and even the US Senate refused, eventually, to approve US entry into the League he had done so much to create. Deep divisions existed both inside and outside the committee-room as to the priority that should be attached to the various pressing issues that were at hand – what consequences the 'enemy states' should face; how to respond to the 1917 revolution and the Russian civil war then under way; what should fill the 'sovereignty vacuum' in Central and Eastern Europe and West Asia, and many other questions which took months of negotiations to resolve.[5] Yet all members of the League Commission were united in one conviction: that the War marked a historical turning point, and that their victory, as an alliance of 'self-governing' sovereign states, had pitched the four defeated 'absolutist' empires forever into the 'dustbin of history'.[6] As the German-British jurist (inventor of the term 'standard of civilisation') Georg Schwarzenberger pointed out in 1936, for example, the emphasis

2 Third Meeting of the Commission (Notes of Mr Shepardson), in David Hunter Miller, *The Drafting of the Covenant* (New York: G. P. Putnam & Sons, 1928), 165.

3 See above, Item 2, Section 2.3.3.

4 See Eric S. Yellin, *Racism in the Nation's Service: Government Workers and the Colour Line in Woodrow Wilson's America* (Chapel Hill, NC: University of North Carolina Press, 2013).

5 For a detailed account of the tussles between Wilson, France's Georges Clemenceau and Britain's David Lloyd George and the delegations they led, see Margaret MacMillan, *Peacemakers: Six Months that Changed the World* (London: John Murray, 2001).

6 This is Leon Trotsky's almost contemporaneous phrase. Quoted in Bertrand M. Patenaude, *Stalin's Nemesis: The Exile and Murder of Leon Trotsky* (London: Faber & Faber, 2009), 194. Trotsky, a Bolshevik, levelled it at the Mensheviks at the All-Russian Congress of Soviets on 25 October 1917.

on 'self-government' did not stem exclusively from Wilson's conviction of 'the superiority of the American form of government'. On the contrary, like Wilson, 'continental politicians ... whether of the countries of the former Central Powers, or of those of the Allied and Associated Powers, deemed constitutional uniformity indispensable for the future League' because 'the people are firstly more sincere, and secondly peaceful than the statesmen who control their government, and particularly their foreign policy'.[7]

For example, in a heated discussion as to whether those states which remained neutral during the war should be offered 'original' League membership or whether they should be required to join later only after being assessed as 'self-governing', Orlando argued that if all the neutral states were allowed in unconditionally then 'you would have to invite Abyssinia which is a neutral state but not a fully self-governing state', insisting that neutral states must be forced 'to carry out the conditions [*sic*] that they enjoy liberty'.[8] To this Larnaude replied, however, that it was

> unthinkable that we should say to a country like Switzerland or Norway or like Denmark which enjoy greater liberty than ourselves [i.e. which had in place stronger protections for individual freedoms than France]: 'We are inclined to admit you into the League of Nations but it is first necessary that you enjoy full powers of self-government and that you guarantee that you will loyally carry out your engagements.' Such a condition can only be imposed upon countries which have acted against every rule of law.[9]

As this exchange underlines, the benchmark of 'self-government' (or internal 'liberty') as the condition which all entrants into the League would have to meet was considered so important, and so objective (if difficult to define[10]), that the French delegate to the League of Nations was even prepared to rank his own state lower than three others on that scale.

However, if the Versailles Conference seemed to hold out, to these men, the architects of a new global order, an unprecedented opportunity to reconstitute the world in a form which reflected this victory of 'liberty' over 'absolutism', the situation they confronted in the attempt to

[7] Georg Schwarzenberger, *The League of Nations and World Order: A Treatise on the Principle of Universality in the Theory and Practice of the League* (London: Constable and Co., 1936), 29.

[8] In Miller, *The Drafting of the Covenant*, 240.

[9] Ibid., 240.

[10] See, in particular, the account of the debates within the League Commission as to how to define this term, including the problems involved in conducting the debate in both French and English, and Wilson's declaration: 'I have spent twenty years of my life lecturing on self-governing states, and trying all the time to define one. Now whereas I haven't been able to arrive at a definition, I have come to the point where I recognize one when I see it.' 'Third Meeting of the Commission', 154–67.

realise that opportunity was a deeply paradoxical one. The negotiators at Versailles turned immediately to international law as their primary tool of reconstruction.[11] Yet in doing so they were also aware that the elevation of the sovereign state to a position of 'supreme authority' in the practice and positivist jurisprudence of the late nineteenth century was at least partly responsible for having dragged the world into a killing spree unprecedented in human history. In his famous Address on the Fourteen Points of early 1918, for instance, Wilson had declared that '[t]he day of conquest and aggrandizement is gone by' and that 'so is also the day of secret covenants entered into in the interest of particular governments and likely at some unlooked-for moment to upset the peace of the world'.[12] This dilemma was resolved by means of a tacit consensus: it was not the state itself that should be singled out for blame, but rather a perversion of it, manifested in the *autocratic* (as opposed to liberal) imperialism of the Central Powers. The primary sin of these 'Central Empires', as Wilson called them, was their refusal to 'accept a place of equality among the peoples of the world'.[13] They had refused, in other words, to accept the fundamental principle of sovereign equality. How was it possible that a set of supposedly 'civilised' states had embarked on such a wantonly destructive quest for world 'mastery', as Wilson put it?[14] As we are about to see, for the world's leaders, and for many contemporary international lawyers, the answer lay in the tyrannical forms of 'government' these 'Central Empires' had adopted.

In the case of that most heinous of all the enemy states, the German Empire, for example, Wilson argued that its foreign policy – its contempt for Belgian, Luxembourgian and French rights of political independence, territorial integrity and, for the first two, neutrality – had been beholden to 'the military party and the men whose creed is imperial domination' and not, as it should have been, to 'the Reichstag majority'.[15] The German-British jurist Lassa Oppenheim, whom we met in Item 2, made a very similar argument in a series of three lectures on the nascent League of Nations, which he delivered in 1918 at Cambridge University, where he was then Whewhell Professor of International Law. '[U]nless Germany be utterly defeated,' Oppenheim insisted, 'the spirit of militarism, which is not compatible with a League of

[11] Ibid., 115–242.

[12] Woodrow Wilson, 'The Fourteen Points', Address to Congress, 8 January 1918, available at http://avalon.law.yale.edu/20th_century/wilson14.asp (accessed 11 August 2016).

[13] Ibid.

[14] Ibid.

[15] Ibid.

Nations, will remain a menace to the world'; for '[a] military State submits to International Law only so long as it serves its interests, but violates International Law ... wherever and whenever this law stands in the way of its military aims.'[16] Oppenheim contrasted such 'military States' with what he called 'civilised States'.[17] Spelling out this distinction, he went on:

> [A]ll States were originally founded on force ... [and up] to the time of the French Revolution ... all wars were fought for the increase of the territory ... or [were] so-called colonial wars ... It was not until the nineteenth century that wars for the purpose of national unity broke out, ... and some kind of constitutional government was everywhere introduced ... It is for this reason that the outbreak of the present war is epoch-making, because ... at bottom this World War is a fight between the ideal of democracy and constitutional government on the one hand, and autocratic government and militarism on the other.[18]

Like Root, then – but also like Lorimer, Hegel, Jefferson, Locke, Hobbes and even Grotius and Vitoria – neither Wilson (undoubtedly the most famous statesman at the time[19]) nor Oppenheim (one of international law's most eminent professors[20]) had any hesitation when it came to viewing the past in terms of a continuously unfolding teleology. This teleology viewed the nation-state and the naturally 'free' and 'equal' individual as the twin pinnacles of world history. The 'Great War', it implied, signified the arrival of the 'epoch-making' moment at which the two dimensions of legal subjectivity had finally come together, such that any form of 'government' which did not connect them through institutionalised channels of responsibility could now definitively be judged illegitimate. The Central Powers were cast as the hopelessly anachronistic opponents of this unfolding liberal teleology, both in their irresponsible, and hence tyrannical, internally imperialistic domestic legal and institutional arrangements, and, for this reason, in their expansionist international relations.

[16] Lassa Oppenheim, *The League of Nations and its Problems: Three Lectures* (London, Bombay etc.: Longmans, Green & Co., 1919), 15.

[17] Ibid., 11.

[18] Ibid., 10–11.

[19] Wilson's influence on the peace negotiations, which dragged on throughout 1919, and on the eventual form taken by the League of Nations, is difficult to overstate. As British writer H. G. Wells wrote in his semi-fictional 'future history', *The Shape of Things to Come*, 'for a brief interval' Wilson 'seemed to stand for mankind'. 'So eager was the situation that all humanity leapt to accept and glorify Wilson', Wells continued. 'It seized upon him as its symbol. He was transfigured in the eyes of men. He ceased to be a common statesman; he became a Messiah.' H. G. Wells, *The Shape of Things to Come* (New York: Macmillan, 1936), 82.

[20] For a discussion of Oppenheim's ideas about statehood and recognition, see above, Item 2 (introduction) and Section 1.2.

This eschatological narration of the War served a useful purpose in allowing the mass slaughter of roughly 11 million individuals,[21] many of them conscripted, and the unprecedented destruction of cities, villages, factories and farmland by trench warfare and aerial bombardment, to be cast, not as a catastrophic repudiation of the sanctity of individual 'life, liberty and property', but rather as its vindication.[22] Equally, the idea that only the gradual universalisation of 'responsible' government could ensure that there would 'never again' be such a war offered a sense of purpose to the architects of the League – a normative framework within which their many disagreements could, at least initially, be contained. One question remained, however – the same question that had confronted the jurists, practitioners and philosophers we met in Item 2. Who should count as an individual, and who should count as a collectivity, for the purposes of legal subjectivity in this new chapter of human history? In the immediate aftermath of the First World War – a period in which the possibilities and risks of nationalism have perhaps never been more furiously debated – this question took on a particular sheen. Nonetheless, as this chapter will demonstrate, the parallels between the arguments which played out during the inter-war period and those which came before and after are striking.

Take, for example, the principle that Wilson is best known for introducing into the vocabulary of international law: that of 'national self-determination'. Every 'peace-loving nation', he declared in 'The Fourteen Points', had the right 'to live its own life, [and] determine its own institutions' in the 'assurance of justice and fair dealing by the other peoples of the world as against force and selfish aggression'.[23] As Antonio Cassese points out, it was clear to Wilson that '[s]elf-determination meant self-government', and hence that 'national self-determination' was 'synonymous with the principle that governments must be based on "the consent of the governed"'.[24] However, like many historians of the right of self-determination, Cassese argues that this principle was applied so selectively in the peace settlement that 'in the era after the First World War self-determination, although in vogue as a political postulate and a rhetorical slogan (chiefly in the Wilsonian version), was not a part of the

[21] See the analysis at http://necrometrics.com/20c5m.htm (accessed 10 August 2017).

[22] Luis Eslava, 'The Materiality of International Law: Violence, History and Joe Sacco's The Great War', 5 *London Review of International Law* (2017): 49–86.

[23] Wilson, 'The Fourteen Points'.

[24] Antonio Cassese, *Self-determination of Peoples: A Legal Reappraisal* (Cambridge University Press, 1995), 19.

body of international legal norms'.[25] As is often noted, Wilson failed to convince his colleagues to include a reference to self-determination in the Covenant, encouraging the view, among present-day international lawyers like Cassese and Malcolm Shaw, that 'it was clearly not regarded as a legal principle'.[26] The fact remains, however, that nationalism was the obsession of state representatives and international laywers during this period – a heady and paradoxical mixture of fear and fascination, as Berman has shown.[27] As we are about to see, moreover, obsession was, in fact, tempered, for the most part, by a much more mundane, more habitual impulse: the impulse to link international rights and duties to individual rights and duties in a particular way. Or, to put it another way, the question of *who* made up the 'self' of self-determination tended to be decided in conjunction with another question, that of *what* 'self-determination' should entail in terms of international rights and duties, in a way that embeds 'national self-determination' firmly in a very long, very well-established practice in international law of conditioning international legal subjectivity on a commitment to reproducing individual legal subjectivity. This juridical continuity, I suggest, renders the debate over whether 'national self-determination' was a right or a 'mere' political pinciple somewhat obsolete.

With this in mind, Section 1 will revisit the significance of the inter-war principle of self-determination, taking Cassese's observation into account. For as we shall see, this notoriously slippery principle cannot be understood in isolation from its much more mundane flip-side: the principle of 'self-government'. This re-examination also involves a challenge to the tendency of many histories of the Versailles Conference to narrate it as an exceptional moment, which 'changed the world' forever, and whose contours were determined as much by the 'likes and dislikes' of the individuals involved as they were by the '[a]rmies, navies, railways, economies, ideologies, [and] history'.[28] Contingent as events between 1919 and 1939 certainly were, there is, arguably, also a sense in which these outcomes were entirely predictable – particularly when approached from the viewpoint of those (colonised, exploited individuals

[25] Ibid., 27. See also e.g. Ulrike Barten, *Minorities, Minority Rights and Internal Self-Determination* (Cham etc.: Springer, 2015), 140, 189 and, from a different perspective, Bill Bowring, *The Degradation of the International Legal Order: The Rehabilitation of Law and the Possibility of Politics* (Abingdon: Routledge-Cavendish 2008), 18.

[26] Malcolm N. Shaw, *International Law* (6th edn Cambridge University Press, 2008), 251.

[27] See generally Berman, *Passion and Ambivalence.*

[28] MacMillan, *Peacemakers*, 1.

and communities) who began and ended the War at the bottom of the pile in material terms.[29] This predictability, or continuity, becomes easier to see if we place these events, as it were, inside the shadow-box, allowing them to be seen in relation to the various components of Items 1 and 2. To this end, five mechanisms through which the Allied and Associated Powers, in many cases acting through the League of Nations, influenced the conditional construction of a whole series of new 'international personalities' during the inter-war period will be examined below: the Covenant's entry criteria for new members; the 'minorities treaties'; the treatment of 'enemy states'; the Mandates System; and the League's response to recalcitrant 'original members'.[30]

1 'Self-Governing' Colonies? The League and its Entry Criteria

After many meetings and heated arguments, the members of the League Committee eventually agreed on the text of Article 1, paragraph 2 of the Covenant. It read as follows:

> Any fully self-governing State, Dominion or Colony ... may become a Member of the League if its admission is agreed to by two-thirds of the Assembly, provided that it shall give effective guarantees of its sincere intention to observe its international obligations, and shall accept such regulations as may be prescribed by the League in regard to its military, naval and air forces and armaments.

The formulation employed here seems particularly paradoxical. How could a dominion, let alone a colony, be 'fully self-governing'? As we have already

[29] Only women – provided they were of European descent and possessed of a certain amount of capital – might appear, superficially, to have moved closer to emancipation, obtaining the vote and work in several European and neo-European states at the end of the War. For example, propertied women over the age of thirty received the vote in the UK in 1918; in Canada in 1917; and in the United States in 1920. This was hardly a universal phenomenon, however. In Spain the date was 1931; in France, 1944; in Italy, 1946; in Greece, 1952; and in Switzerland, 1971. The false prize of legal subjectivity for women – including even these privileged women – whose 'right' to sell their labour-power has never been supplemented by a cancellation of their duty to perform domestic work, including the reproduction of human life, without pay, has been well documented by Silvia Federici, among others. This unpaid work of human reproduction – only more poorly remunerated since the universalisation of legal subjectivity – is nothing less than an ongoing mode of primitive accumulation, according to Federici, upon which capitalism continues to thrive. Silvia Federici, *Caliban and the Witch: Women, the Body and Primitive Accumulation* (New York: Autonomedia, 2004).

[30] See Natasha Wheatley, 'Spectral Legal Personality in Interwar International Law: On New Ways of Not Being a State', 35 *Law and History Review* (2017): 753–87.

seen, however, 'self-government', at least at this moment in history, referred more to a particular internal legal and institutional structure than it did to independence per se. In the eschatological atmosphere of the immediate post-First World War period, this emphasis seems to have become even more pronounced, such that several clearly non-independent entities were welcomed into the League, and allowed to accede to the rights and duties laid out in the Covenant, including Article 10's duty to 'respect and preserve as against external aggression the territorial integrity and existing political independence of all Members of the League'.[31] Five British dominions (Australia, Canada, India, New Zealand and South Africa) were granted 'original' membership of the League, while a sixth, the Irish Free State, was granted membership in 1923, along with the Kingdom of Egypt in 1937 (when it was still, in practice, a British protectorate) and the Kingdom of Iraq in 1932 (a very ambivalent sovereign discussed in section 4.2). Nonetheless, while the League's emphasis on and codification of 'self-government' as a benchmark against which to assess eligibility for international rights and duties was certainly more radical, it remained to a large extent in line with the practice we have already examined. As this practice indicates,[32] the first step for 'self-government', and therefore the first step towards some kind of international personality, involved the protection of the rights of *existing* legal subjects ('foreign citizens') such that those rights could be 'effective' in the territory in question. Only if an entity was itself claiming the *full* set of sovereign rights and duties was it necessary to reconstitute *all* the individuals within its jurisdiction, including 'natives', as legal subjects. If we view the Covenant in the light of the history offered in Item 2, in other words, we can see that, far from being paradoxical, in fact it made perfect sense for the League to consider a colony, a dominion or a mandated territory to be 'fully self-governing'. What was necessary, at a minimum, for a territory to be assessed as 'self-governing' was that it should be *governed by a 'self-governing' state* – a state that was both willing and able to render 'effective' the rights of other states and their citizens.

Bearing out this suggestion, many jurists at the time interpreted the process of acquiring membership of the League as having both constitutive and interpellative effects – effects which were explicitly aimed at ensuring that the world would become increasingly 'self-governing' in character, through the mechanism of the Covenant's conditions of accession.

[31] *Covenant of the League of Nations*, Versailles, 28 June 1919, Art. 10.

[32] See e.g. Item 2, Section 2.3.2., discussing the transition of the Chinese Empire from 'semi-sovereign' to 'sovereign' state.

Of these commentators, Georg Schwarzenberger was one of the most explicit. In his long-forgotten 1936 treatise, *The League of Nations and World Order*, Schwarzenburger set out to understand the operation of the 'principle of universality in the theory and practice of the League'.[33] Here he argued that for an international organisation like the League to succeed in its aim of eliminating war, it had to make decisions about what type of members it would welcome ('homogeneous' v 'heterogeneous' universality); whether it was necessary to include all members of the international community or only some of them ('absolute' v 'relative' universality); and how its decision-making should work ('imperial' v 'co-operative' universality).[34] As Schwarzenberger demonstrated, the League over the course of its first six years of existence placed different emphasis on the different poles of these three continuums at different times. Crucially, however, in tracking the debates of the architects of the Covenant and the practice of the League, Schwarzenberger drew attention to the principle of 'self-government' as the central principle around which concerted efforts were made to create a 'homogeneous' League of Nations. 'Article 1, paragraph 2, of the Covenant ... embodied the principle of constitutional homogeneity for future applicants ... inasmuch as it made self-government within the applying State a condition of membership'.[35] The criteria for membership were, in other words, for Schwarzenberger, intended to be constitutive both in an external and an external sense.[36]

This argument was also made by other contemporary scholars and practitioners of international law. For instance, João Chagas, Portugal's delegate to the League during the 1920s, noted that 'requests for admission [into the League] may be divided into two classes, those from states already constituted ... and those from states which desire to confirm their existence by being admitted'.[37] As the drafters of the Covenant were aware, Chagas suggested, membership of the League held out a powerful incentive to the weaker states of the family of nations, and therefore offered an equally powerful tool through which such states could be encouraged to become (more) 'self-governing'. Similarly, Lilian Friedlander, writing in the *British Yearbook of International Law*, argued that 'admission to the League is ... what "recognition of a sovereign state" was before 1920'.[38] To

[33] Schwarzenberger, *The League of Nations and World Order*.

[34] Ibid., 5.

[35] Ibid., 59.

[36] For instance, the customary right to self-defence was augmented, by the Covenant, via its procedures for the 'collective security' of League members. Covenant, Arts. 10–16.

[37] Quoted in Lilian M. Friedlander, 'The Admission of States to the League of Nations', 8 *British Yearbook of International Law* (1928): 84–100, at 92–3.

[38] Ibid., 100.

Friedlander, this indicated precisely that 'the qualifications laid down in Article 1 of the Covenant ... are the essential qualities of any independent state today'.[39] And Edward Phelan, who would later become Director-General of the International Labour Organization (ILO), made a similar point. 'The qualifications which a community must possess, before it can be admitted to cooperate on a footing of equality with other states', Phelan noted, 'are to be found defined in Article 1 of the Covenant. In the first place, two-thirds of the Assembly of the League must recognise that the qualifications exist. This is the equivalent of the old "recognition". But it is more definite and more impressive, because it must be collective.'[40] Phelan's argument, as he went on to clarify, was 'not that membership in the League alone confers effective international status', but that 'only states which fulfil the qualifications required for membership, and which can accept the obligations involved in it, are to-day full international persons'.[41] While several evidently 'full international persons' (not least the United States) remained outside the League for all or part of the inter-war period, the benchmark offered by Article 2, paragraph 1, according to Phelan, made it possible to assess their credentials for admission – and hence the 'fullness' of their personality – hypothetically. For all these scholars, in different ways, then, 'self-government', as codified in Article 1, paragraph 2 of the Covenant, was – and was designed to be – constitutive; and not only of the 'objective' exoskeleton (as it were) of states and other international persons, but also, and just as importantly, of their internal normative character.

2 Constitutive Minorities: The 'National States'

A second vantage point from which to examine the process of international legal reproduction in action during the inter-war period concerns the new 'national states' that were created as part of the peace settlement in Central and Eastern Europe. Famously, these new states were compelled to undertake a new set of obligations in relation to individuals belonging to certain communities within them – communities that became known as 'national minorities'.[42]

The 'national states'/'national minorities' scheme has become one of the most notorious of all the League's experiments in the creation and

[39] Ibid., 100.

[40] E. J. Phelan, 'The Sovereignty of the Irish Free State', 1 *The Review of Nations* (1927): 39–45, at 45–6.

[41] Ibid., 45–6.

[42] See Mohammad Shahabuddin, *Ethnicity and International Law: Histories, Politics and Practices* (Cambridge University Press, 2016), 98–135.

manipulation of sovereignty, not least because of Nazi Germany's instrumentalisation of its contours in relation to the German minority in the Sudetenland region of Czechoslovakia as a pretext for invasion of that country in September 1938. From the perspective of international legal reproduction, the significance of the minorities treaties – concluded in 1919 between the Allied and Associated Powers and the new, revived and/or newly enlarged states of central and eastern Europe (the Serb-Croat-Slovene State, soon to be Yugoslavia; Czecho-Slovakia [Czechoslovakia], Roumania [Romania] and Poland)[43] – is not that they represented the 'first attempt' to 'codify' and 'enforce minority rights on the international level', as many historians of human rights have argued.[44] Instead, what is so interesting about these treaties is the fact that their minority rights provisions formed only a tiny aspect of the constitutive and constitutional apparatus which they bound their signatories to implement. Even though the 'minorities treaties' have been referred to as such from the time of their conclusion onwards,[45] these instruments actually had a far more generally constitutive set of functions than this epithet suggests. Not only did the new national states commit to providing a particular set of cultural rights to their ethnic minority groups; they were also – and, in fact, more emphatically – required to put in place a set of norms and institutions which would ensure that *all* their individual inhabitants would be treated, and would treat each other,

[43] As discussed below, minority protection commitments were also included in many of the peace treaties (for example, with Austria, Bulgaria, Hungary and the Ottoman Empire, though not with Germany). In the case of the Treaty of Sèvres, concluded with (and later renounced by) the Ottoman Empire, these included minority protection commitments imposed on Greece. *Treaty of Peace between the Allied and Associated Powers with Turkey*, Sèvres, 10 August 1920. Note that the very same article of this 433-article treaty bound Greece to 'embody in a separate Treaty such provisions as may be deemed necessary to protect freedom of transit and equitable treatment for the commerce of all nations' (Art. 86). See Section 2.3, below, for a discussion of international legal reproduction in the context of the 'enemy states'. Connecting with the argument regarding self-government made in Section 2.1, above, Albania, Lithuania, Estonia, Latvia and Iraq were all forced to accept minorities commitments as the condition of their accession to the Covenant.

[44] Barten, *Minorities, Minority Rights*, 141–2. This is not, in any case, an accurate portrayal of the function of these treaties. As discussed in Item 2, the codification and enforcement of the rights of Christians in the Ottoman Empire, for example, had a long history, culminating in the Treaty of Berlin of 1878, which laid down an elaborate system of minority protections for the subjects of international law brought into being by the Treaty, such as Montenegro and Serbia. See generally Carole Fink, *Defending the Rights of Others: The Great Powers, the Jews, and International Minority Protection, 1878–1938* (Cambridge University Press, 2004).

[45] See e.g. Permanent Court of International Justice. *Questions relating to Settlers of German Origin in Poland, Germany* v. *Poland*, Advisory opinion, PCIJ Series B, No. 6, 10 September 1923 ('German Settlers in Poland Case'), 19.

as (negatively 'free' and formally 'equal') legal subjects. Indeed, as we are about to see, the objective of the former was to enable the effective implementation of the latter.

In short, the 'minorities treaties' constituted the new national states as 'self-governing' states as the condition upon which they obtained their sovereignty. One useful illustration can be found in the experience of Poland during its first years of post-War independence.

2.1 *Minorities and Citizens: The Case of Poland*

In 1919 Poland, which had been partitioned between the German and Russian Empires throughout the previous century, became an independent state again. By the end of the War, the administration of Ignacy Jan Paderewski had already been recognised as the Provisional Government of an independent Poland by the Allied and Associated Powers. The German Empire, however, still claiming sovereignty over Poland, only extended its recognition when forced into this as part of the Treaty of Versailles on 28 June 1919. It was only at this point, followed immediately by the conclusion of the 'Polish Minorities Treaty', later the same day, that the Polish Government's claim to exert 'exclusive' control over Poland's territory came to be formalised.

These two treaties went out of their way to guarantee that this governmental control would be 'effective' in the sense outlined in Item 2. That is to say, they worked together to ensure that Poland's legal and institutional structures would be dedicated to protecting the core rights and duties of existing legal subjects, *and* that it would reconstitute its own inhabitants as legal subjects themselves, including inhabitants belonging to ethnic minorities. Thus, in the first place, the Treaty of Versailles – the peace treaty between Germany and the Allied and Associated Powers, including Poland – specified that the Polish Minorities Treaty would include provisions for the protection of 'the interests of inhabitants of Poland who differ from the majority of the population in race, language, or religion', and provisions for 'freedom of transit and equitable treatment of the commerce of other nations'.[46] The Polish Minorities Treaty itself then went on to do precisely this, by committing Poland to 'conform[ing] her institutions to the principles of liberty and justice, and to giv[ing] a sure guarantee to the inhabitants of the territory over which she has assumed sovereignty'.[47]

[46] Treaty of Versailles, Arts. 87, 93.

[47] *Treaty between the Principal Allied and Associated Powers (the British Empire, Italy, Japan and the United States) and Poland*, Versailles, 28 June 1919 ('Polish Minorities Treaty'), Preamble.

The structure of the Polish Minorities Treaty is worth spelling out in some detail, not least because it was reproduced almost exactly not only in all the other 'minorities treaties' with the other 'national states', but also in almost all of the 'peace treaties' with the 'enemy states'. At Article 1, Poland agreed to recognise the subsequent seven articles as 'fundamental laws' with which 'no law, regulation or official action' would 'conflict or interfere' – that is to say, as integral elements of its constitutional framework. These were: an undertaking 'to assure full and complete protection of life and liberty to all inhabitants of Poland without distinction of birth, nationality, language, race or religion' (Art. 2); undertakings to offer Polish nationality to all 'German, Austrian, Hungarian or Russian nationals' now resident within its territory (Arts. 3–6); a guarantee that '[a]ll Polish nationals shall be equal before the law and shall enjoy the same civil and political rights without distinction as to race, language or religion' (Art. 7); and (only at Art. 8) a series of special rights to be afforded to Poland's 'racial, religious or linguistic minorities', regarding education, religion, charities and so on.[48] Even here, however, it is crucial to notice that the primary stipulation was that such minorities should 'enjoy the same treatment and security in law and in fact as the other Polish nationals'.[49] Though not included in the list of 'fundamental laws', Poland undertook, nonetheless, to make provisions for freedom of trade and transit, and in particular 'most favoured nation' procedures that the signatories insisted be extended by Poland to all the Allied and Associated Powers, and to join the 'general agreement for the equitable treatment of the commerce of other States', which the League planned to conclude within five years.[50] In return, the United States, the British Empire, France, Italy and Japan began by confirming their recognition of Poland as 'a sovereign and independent member of the Family of Nations'.[51]

While the terms of the rights accorded to different minority groups varied, the structure of the treaties subsequently concluded with the new Serb-Croat-Slovene State (later renamed the Kingdom of Yugoslavia),[52]

[48] Ibid., Arts. 2–8.
[49] Ibid., Art. 8.
[50] Ibid., Arts. 14–18.
[51] Ibid., Preamble.
[52] Ibid., Arts. 2, 7, 13.

Czecho-Slovakia,[53] Roumania,[54] Hungary[55] and others was almost identical with one exception. Unlike the 'national states', Hungary and the other 'enemy states', initially barred from the League, were not just forced to commit to signing a future free trade treaty; they were also prohibited outright from putting up any trade barriers.[56] As this suggests, the tendency either to celebrate these 'minorities treaties' as a first step towards the establishment of a universal human rights regime, or to castigate them for their exacerbation of ethnic tensions, runs the risk of obscuring the objective of their legal architecture. This was to distinguish the rights of ethnic minorities from those of regular citizens, not in order to give them a *different* type of legal subjectivity, but rather to ensure that their legal subjectivity would be ('effectively') *identical* to that of the majority of citizens.

This objective was not easily achieved in practice, however, and in Poland the question of the objectives of the League-era minorities regime was brought before the new Permanent Court of International Justice (PCIJ) almost immediately. The case concerned the Polish Government's attempt to 'oust'[57] members of Poland's German minority from their land as part of a more general policy of 'de-Germanization'.[58] The Court found this action to be a violation of Poland's commitments under the Minorities Treaty:[59]

> By the Minorities Treaty Poland has agreed that all Polish nationals shall enjoy the same civil and political rights and the same treatment and security in law as well as in fact. The action taken by the Polish authorities is contrary to the principle of equality in that it subjects the settlers to a discriminating and injurious treatment to which other citizens holding contracts of sale or lease are not subject.[60]

In the opinion of the Court, then, the Polish nation had been 'liberated' by means of its recognition by the Allied and Associated Powers as a

[53] *Treaty between the Principal Allied and Associated Powers and Czecho-Slovakia*, Saint-Germain-en-Laye, 10 September 1919, UKTS 020/1919: Cmd. 479 ('Treaty of Saint-Germain'), Arts. 2, 7, 17.

[54] *Treaty between the Principal Allied and Associated Powers and Roumania*, Paris, 9 December 1919, UKTS 006/1920: Cmd. 588 ('Treaty of Paris'), Arts. 2, 8, 13.

[55] *Treaty of Peace between the Principal Allied and Associated Powers and Hungary*, Trianon, 4 June 1920, UKTS 010/1920: Cmd. 896 ('Treaty of Trianon'), Arts. 55, 58.

[56] E.g. Treaty of Trianon, Arts. 200–01. See Section 3.1, below.

[57] German Settlers in Poland Case, 15.

[58] Ibid., 24.

[59] Ibid., 20.

[60] Ibid., 35.

sovereign state, at the same moment, and by means of the same legal instrument as that in which it had undertaken to guarantee the 'liberty' of its constituent population, including members of ethnic minorities. Article 8 of the Treaty was 'designed', the Court argued, further, to create 'equality in fact as well as ostensible legal equality in the sense of the absence of discrimination in the words of the law'.[61] It underscored this point in a second advisory opinion handed down only five days later:

> Poland ... at the moment of her final recognition as an independent state ... signed provisions which ... in so far as they are inserted in the Minorities Treaty, are recognized by Poland as fundamental laws ... Though, generally speaking, it is true that a sovereign State has the right to decide what persons shall be regarded as its nationals, it is no less true that this principle is applicable [in Poland] only subject to the Treaty obligations referred to above.[62]

In other words, as Berman points out, 'Polish sovereignty' was regarded by the PCIJ as 'coeval with its obligations to its minority'.[63] When this second advisory opinion is read in conjunction with the case that came before it, however, it transpires that Polish sovereignty was *also* coeval with Poland's obligations to the rest of its ('majority') population. Poland's special obligations towards the ethnic minorities functioned, then, as a corrective measure designed to ensure that its constitutive commitment, made in 1919, to guaranteeing 'free' and 'equal' subjectivity to all its inhabitants would be fulfilled.

As Poland's representatives recognised all to clearly, the Court's 'generally speaking' referred to the conditional nature of the external rights and duties that the new Polish state had acquired in 1919. Paderewski, Poland's Prime Minister between January and November 1919, had in fact protested strongly, prior to signing the Minorities Treaty, that these commitments constituted a violation of Poland's 'sovereign rights'.[64] In response, France's President Georges Clemenceau had retorted:

> It has been the established procedure of the public law of Europe that when a state is created or even when large accessions of territory are made to an established state, the joint and formal recognition of the Great Powers should be accompanied by the requirement that such State should, in the

[61] Ibid., 24.

[62] *Acquisition of Polish Nationality*, Advisory Opinion, PCIJ Series B, No. 7, 15 September 1923, League of Nations, 16.

[63] Berman, 'But the Alternative is Despair', 1838.

[64] Memorandum by M. Paderewski, 25 June 1919, in *La Documentation international: La Paix de Versailles, Vol. X: Commission de nouveaux Etats et des Minorités* (1932), 129, cited in Berman, 'But the Alternative is Despair', 435.

> form of a binding international convention, undertake to comply with certain principles of government.[65]

To Paderewski's dismay, the precedents cited by Clemenceau in support of this argument were drawn from the settlement instituted in the 1878 Treaty of Berlin.[66] Paderewski, indeed, protested that Poland was being treated as a 'Balkan' entity, and that the conditions contained in the minorities treaty were 'equivalent to regarding the Polish nation as a nation of inferior civilisation'.[67] Nor was this reaction limited to Poland. Ion I. C. Brătianu, the Romanian delegate, for example, walked out of the Versailles negotiations when Romania's own minorities treaty was first proposed 'in order to protest at what was perceived as an international control over Roumanian sovereignty'.[68]

The representatives of the new 'national states' were, of course, correct to point out that the practice of conditioning the bestowal of international personality on a pledge to create and protect a particular set of individual rights was far more explicit and more coercive in the case of supposedly 'uncivilised', viz. non-European, entities. Yet as the Balkan states and the American states had, indeed, discovered, European and neo-European sovereigns and aspiring sovereigns had hardly been exempted from this process. The sanction for reneging on this pledge might have changed, with the involvement of the League and with the PCIJ now empowered to enforce the commitment of the international community to the 'principle of equality' (as the Court put it), but these provisions were hardly new, as Item 2 demonstrated. Nowhere was this continuity clearer, during the League's early years, than in relation to the thorny question of what to do with the 'enemy states'.

3 Misguided Barbarism: The 'Enemy States'

While the fate of Germany in the wake of the First World War has been the subject of many histories, historians of international law have tended to refrain from looking closely at the collective fate of the 'enemy states'

[65] Clemenceau, Letter Addressed to M. Paderewski by the Conference, 24 June 1919, in *La Paix de Versailles*, 162, cited in Nathaniel Berman, 'The International Law of Nationalism: Group Identity and Legal History', in David Wippman (ed.), *International Law and Ethnic Conflict* (Ithaca, NY: Cornell University Press, 1998), 25–57, at 46.

[66] See Item 2, Section 2.3.3.

[67] Paderewski Memorandum, 47.

[68] Giuseppe Motta, *Less Than Nations: Central-Eastern European Minorities after WW1*, Vol. 1 (Newcastle-upon-Tyne: Cambridge Scholars Publishing, 2013), 256.

at Versailles.[69] One reason for this might have something to do with the reputation of the peace treaties, held up as punitive and therefore (in retrospect) as less-than-fully legitimate – as the epitome of 'victors' justice'. Speaking of the Treaty of Versailles, for example, Jan Klabbers notes that its terms are 'difficult to reconcile with sovereignty'.[70] When the peace treaties are viewed in relation to the other items in the shadow-box, however, the treatment of the former Central Powers from 1919 to 1923 begins to appear not as a digression from normal practice in relation to international personality, but instead as one of the most dramatic illustrations of the hybrid character of sovereignty.

As noted above, the conditional logic of the peace treaties mirrored that of the so-called minorities treaties closely – so much so that it is tempting to redescribe both as treaties of constitution (or re-constitution). Most obviously, all these peace treaties, with the important exception of the Treaty of Versailles, included a series of clauses in which the state in question undertook 'to assure full and complete protection of life and liberty to all [its] inhabitants ... without distinction of birth, nationality, language, race or religion'; to provide for the 'free exercise, whether public or private, of any creed, religion or belief'; to ensure that all its 'nationals' would be 'equal before the law' and 'enjoy the same civil and political rights without distinction as to race, language or religion'; to guarantee 'racial, religious or linguistic minorities ... the same treatment and security in law and in fact as other ... nationals'; and to recognise these clauses as 'fundamental laws' – that is, as constitutional provisions.[71] The clauses were identical not only to each other – from the Treaty of Saint-Germain with Austria (1919)[72] and the Treaty of Neuilly with Bulgaria (1919),[73] to the Treaty of Trianon with Hungary (1920)[74] and the Treaty of Sèvres with Turkey (1920), and even to the far less punitive Treaty of Lausanne (1923) which succeeded it[75] – but also to the relevant clauses in the minorities treaties.

[69] See Natasha Wheatley, *The Temporal Life of States: Sovereignty, Legal Knowledge, and the Archive of Empire in Central Europe* (under review).

[70] Jan Klabbers, *International Law* (2nd edn Cambridge University Press, 2017), 23.

[71] Treaty of Sèvres, Arts. 140–1, 145, 147.

[72] Treaty of Saint-Germain, Arts. 62–3, 66.

[73] *Treaty of Peace between the Allied and Associated Powers and Bulgaria, and Protocol and Declaration*, Neuilly-sur-Seine, 27 November 1919 ('Treaty of Neuilly'), Arts. 49–50, 53.

[74] Treaty of Trianon, Arts. 54–5, 58.

[75] Treaty of Sèvres, Arts. 140–1, 145 and 147; *Treaty of Peace between the British Empire, France, Italy, Japan, Greece, Roumania and the Serb-Croat-Slovene State and Turkey*, Lausanne ('Treaty of Lausanne'), 24 July 1923, Arts. 37–9.

As in the minorities treaties, moreover – though in this context far more explicitly and powerfully – the Allied and Associated Powers also drafted the peace treaties in such a way as to ensure that their own rights to own and trade property, and those of their nationals, would be protected and, if possible, extended via drastic programmes of mandatory trade liberalisation in the domestic and international spheres. In the case of the 'enemy states', these clauses were far more extreme than the 'free trade' provisions inserted into the minorities treaties, on the rationale that these states had incurred gigantic liabilities over the course of the War and hence had a duty to make reparation. Indeed, most of the text of the peace treaties, which in all cases ran into their hundreds of clauses, was dedicated to questions concerning property rights, insurance, trade, navigation, communications and financial reorganisation, and the 'detachment' of entire provinces and communities. Not only were the enemy states stripped of their overseas economic interests and 'possessions', along with enormous amounts of core territory.[76] Not only were their resources placed at the 'disposal' of the Allied and Associated Powers.[77] In addition, their waterways, railways, ports, stations and communications networks were opened up for Allied use without restriction, and their economies thrown open to trade via a quasi-universal regime of 'most favoured nation' and national treatment (including all the Allied and Associated Powers but excluding the other 'enemy states'.)[78]

In addition to determining questions of partition, reparations and minorities protection, then, an equally consequential but often overlooked function of the peace treaties was to expand the depth and breadth of individual legal subjectivity by facilitating the capacity of the Allied states, together with their citizens and companies, to access and exploit both the resources and markets of the 'enemy states'. By making the international personality of the new ('national') *and* the successor ('enemy') states (the former, of course, having been 'constituted' on the territory of the latter) conditional on the domestic reproduction of individual legal personality both for nationals (including 'minorities') and 'foreigners', the effect of the peace treaties was twofold. They ensured that the rights of existing (Allied) legal persons would be enforceable throughout Central and Eastern Europe as well as large areas of Southern Europe and West

[76] See e.g. Treaty of Trianon, Arts. 27–35; Treaty of Saint-Germain, Arts. 27–35; Treaty of Neuilles, Arts. 27–35; Treaty of Sèvres, Arts. 27–35; Treaty of Versailles, Arts. 27–41.

[77] See e.g. Treaty of Sèvres, Arts. 231–60.

[78] See e.g. Treaty of Trianon, Arts. 180–238; Treaty of Saint-Germain, Arts. 177–331; Treaty of Neuilles, Arts. 121–296; Treaty of Versailles, Arts. 27–41.

and Central Asia. However, they also brought about a change within these former 'autocracies' by ensuring that those within them would either remain or be transformed into individual subjects of law and hence into exchangers and consumers of commodities.[79]

Upon being presented with the text of their respective treaties, the former enemy states protested bitterly (as national states had done) at what they saw as a discriminatory and flagrant violation of their own right to 'national self-determination'. The representatives of Germany's new Weimar Republic, for example, pointed out that 'the legal basis agreed upon for the negotiation of peace' had been Wilson's 'Fourteen Points'.[80] But with the stroke of a pen, the peace treaties had crippled the economies of Germany and its former allies and triggered the transfer of millions of their 'nationals' to the jurisdiction of other states, often without any form of popular consultation. Partly because of centuries of *Ostsiedlung* ('East-settling'), heavily encouraged by the Imperial German government under the slogan *Drang nach Osten* (the 'race to the East'), which had made its extraterritorial population particularly large and partly on the basis of straightforward discrimination, German-speaking communities were by far the most numerous of those new 'minority' communities.[81] And as the German Delegation protested:

> Our enemies have repeatedly professed that they are not making war on the German people but on an imperialistic and irresponsible Government. Our enemies have repeated again and again that this war without parallel

[79] A close reading of these treaties throws up many other illustrations of the conditional relationship between international and individual legal personality envisaged by those who drafted them. To give just one illustration, eight clauses in the original Treaty of Sèvres provided for the independence of two further (very short-lived) 'national' states: Armenia and Hejaz (now part of Saudi Arabia). The Republic of Armenia was required to 'embody' a fresh treaty with the Allies containing 'such provisions as these Powers may deem necessary to protect freedom of transit and equitable treatment for the commerce of other nations' (Treaty of Sèvres, Arts. 88–93; the First Republic of Armenia lasted for a matter of months until it was invaded simultaneously by Turkey and by the Soviet Eleventh Army, arriving from Azerbaijan). Hejaz, meanwhile, whose independence was effected in just two clauses, was required to undertake that 'in commercial matters the most complete equality of treatment [would] be assured ... to the persons, ships and goods of nationals' of all members of the League (Treaty of Sèvres, Arts. 98–100; the Kingdom of Hejaz, in the Western part of what is now Saudi Arabia, a Hashemite Kingdom, lasted only until 1925 when it was conquered by the Sultanate of Nejd to create the Kingdom of Hejaz and Nejd). See e.g. Yücel Güçlü, 'Turkey's Entrance into the League of Nations', 38 *Middle Eastern Studies* (2003): 186–206, at 186–8.

[80] 'Comments by the German Delegation on the Conditions of Peace', 6 *International Conciliation* (1919): 1203–337, at 1206.

[81] Motta, *Less than Nations*, 83–7.

> should be followed by a new kind of peace, a peace of right and not a peace of might ... Germany's position among the nations should not be destroyed, and the right of self-determination should be recognized for all nations ... [However, the] conditions of peace which have been presented to us are an obvious contradiction of all such assurances from the mouths of the enemy statesmen.[82]

From the Allied perspective, however, the territories, peoples, individuals and resources which the enemy states had lost had been transferred from the jurisdiction of a series of decrepit 'absolutist' states to that of a series of modern 'self-governing' states. Viewed from this angle, the treatment meted out to the 'enemy states' by the Versailles settlement could very well be understood, not as a violation of the principle of self-determination but, on the contrary, its vindication. To make this suggestion is not to deny, of course, that the 'enemy states' had been regarded as sovereign prior to the War. It is, instead, to argue that they had violated, over the course of the First World War, an obligation that had come to be much more clearly defined by the end of the nineteenth century and over the course of the War itself, namely, the obligation, contained in the 'criteria' for statehood, to be 'self-governing'; to have a proper government. This point can be made even more precisely if we turn to a more detailed examination of the international legal fate of Germany, that most notorious of all the Central Powers.

3.1 *Germany and the Treaty of Versailles*

There was, as we have seen, no question for the architects of the Versailles Settlement as to the connection between Imperial Germany's 'autocratic' form of government and its willingness to violate the principle of sovereign equality without qualm. This opinion found perhaps its most biting expression in the lengthy response of the Allied and Associated Powers to the German Delegation's protests at the punitive terms of the Treaty of Versailles. The German Empire, they declared, in starting the War, had committed 'the greatest crime against humanity that any nation, calling itself civilized, has ever consciously committed'.[83] In the international sphere, Germany was accused of acting, unconstrained by any sense of responsibility towards its citizens, as a kind of super-sovereign, intent on

[82] 'Comments by the German Delegation', 1206.

[83] Allied and Associated Powers, Reply to the Comments of the German Delegation on the Conditions of Peace, 16 June 1919, in 6 *International Conciliation* (1919): 1341–424, at 1341.

trampling on the rights of other states, just as it trampled on the rights of its citizens. This was an unconscionable transgression of international law, the Allies retorted in their 89-page reply:

> [T]he rulers of Germany, true to the Prussian tradition, strove for a position of dominance in Europe. They were not satisfied with that growing prosperity and influence to which Germany was entitled, and which all other nations were willing to accord her, in the [international] society of free and equal peoples. They required that they should be able to dictate and tyrannize to a subservient Europe, as they dictated and tyrannized over a subservient Germany.[84]

Positioning Germany in this way as the prototypical 'rogue state' (as Gerry Simpson has put it),[85] allowed the Allies to insist that the War had been fought on behalf of 'practically the whole of civilized mankind', driven on by the inexorable 'rising tide of democracy'.[86]

In essence, the Imperial German government's abuse of the institutions of 'responsible' government it possessed on paper was here equated (in keeping with Oppenheim's taxonomy) with a wilful abandonment of 'civilization'.[87] Winston Churchill (British Secretary of State for War at the time of the Paris Peace Conference) had, in fact, made an almost identical argument back in 1914. 'If the Germans were decisively defeated so that they lost faith in their present governing system', he had declared, 'if they became, as it were, a grown-up nation like the liberated democracies of the world', then that world would no longer be one 'divided by fear and mistrust in consequence of the desire of one nation to raise itself above the others'.[88] Or, to put it in James Lorimer's language,[89] we could say that, according to the Allies, the German Empire, with its unvarnished contempt for the principle of sovereign equality, had become unwilling to 'reciprocate' the recognition that other sovereign equals accorded it.[90]

[84] Ibid., 1341.

[85] Gerry Simpson, *Great Powers and Outlaw States: Unequal Sovereigns in the International Legal Order* (Cambridge University Press, 2004), 261.

[86] Ibid., 1341, 1382.

[87] See generally James N. Retallack (ed.), *Imperial Germany, 1971–1918* (Oxford University Press, 2008).

[88] Quoted in 'Comments Made by the German Delegation', 1206–7.

[89] See above, Item 2, Section 2.3.1.

[90] This contempt was manifest in many aspects of German foreign policy prior to the war, from the notorious 'Schlieffen Plan' for an invasion of France via Belgium and Luxembourg, followed by an invasion by Russia (although see Terence Zuber, *Inventing the Schlieffen Plan: German War Planning, 1871–1914* (Oxford University Press, 2002) for the thesis that the 'Schlieffen Plan' was a post-War fabrication on the part of the Allies); to German attempts to induce Mexico to declare war on the United States (see e.g. Thomas Boghardt,

Having abandoned its 'reciprocating will', Germany could be treated as having forfeited at least some of the rights associated with international personality – at least until such time as it proved willing, again, to 'recognise' its fellow sovereigns as equals.

This retaliative impulse was reflected in the famously punitive terms of the Treaty of Versailles, which under normal circumstances would have constituted flagrant violations of Germany's sovereign rights.[91] Germany lost all overseas possessions and a huge amount of its core territory, including Alsace-Lorraine, Northern Schleswig and Posen. Union with Austria was forbidden and the Saarland, Germany's industrial centre, was placed under League control for 15 years, pending a plebiscite.[92] Germany's military capacity was severely restricted;[93] its rivers internationalised;[94] and its Kaiser 'publicly arraign[ed]' by the Allies for a 'supreme offence against international morality and the sanctity of treaties'.[95] In addition to a host of other in-kind forms of reparation, Germany was ordered, 'pending the full determination of their claims', to pay the Allies '20,000,000,000 gold marks'[96] (equivalent to roughly US$400 billion in 2010, the year in which Germany made its final repayment).[97]

Importantly, moreover, the terms of the Treaty stripped German citizens of their rights in many ways no less directly than they did the German state. Nor was this only the case for those who found themselves no longer German citizens but 'national minorities' within another state. For example, Germany also agreed to supply an Allied-controlled Reparation Commission with 'all the information which the Commission may require relative to the financial situation and operations and to the property, productive capacity, and stocks and current production of raw materials and manufactured articles of Germany and her nationals'.[98] Equally, Germany was also forced to renounce 'all rights accorded to her

---

The Zimmermann Telegram: Intelligence, Diplomacy, and America's Entry into World War I (Annapolis, ND: Naval Institute Press, 2012).

91 Treaty of Versailles, Art. 231; Thomas W. Lamont, 'The Final Reparations Settlement', *Foreign Affairs* (1930): 338.

92 Treaty of Versailles, Arts. 42–114.

93 Ibid., Arts. 159–210.

94 Ibid., Arts. 321–64.

95 Ibid., Art. 227.

96 Ibid., Art. 235.

97 Isabelle de Pommereau, 'Germany Finishes Paying WWI Reparations, Ending Century of "Guilt"', *Christian Science Monitor*, 4 October 2010, available at www.csmonitor.com/World/Europe/2010/1004/Germany-finishes-paying-WWI-reparations-ending-century-of-guilt (accessed 28 May 2016).

98 Treaty of Versailles, Art. 240.

or her nationals by treaties, conventions or agreements ... to representation upon or participation in the control or administration of commissions, state banks, agencies or other financial or economic organisations of an international character, exercising powers of control or administration, and operating in any of the Allied or Associated States, or in Austria, Hungary, Bulgaria or Turkey, or in the dependencies of these States, or in the former Russian Empire'.[99] In other words, Germany was compelled to renounce, on the part of its nationals, precisely that treaty-based claim to extraterritorial property rights which (as we saw in Item 2) gave legal subjectivity its universality. Moreover, Germany's economy was opened up fully and immediately to trade with Allied states, with 'most favoured nation' and 'national treatment' provisions implemented universally – that is, not only in relation to products and services, but also in relation to the 'property, rights or interests' of foreign nationals *within* Germany.[100]

Nonetheless, dramatic though its consequences may have been, what is so interesting about Germany's alleged lapse into barbarity/abandonment of 'reciprocating will' is that it was constructed as temporary from the outset, in a way that an alleged lack of 'reciprocating power' could never have been. The Allies made this clear when they insisted that '[i]t is only justice that restitution should be made and that those wronged peoples [the Allies] should be safeguarded *for a time* from the competition of a nation [Germany] whose industries are intact'.[101] And sure enough, in 1926, under the explicitly 'self-governing' or 'responsible' Weimar administration of Gustav Stresemann, Germany was not only welcomed into the League but offered a place among the 'great powers' of the League Council immediately. Further evidence of the resilience of its 'great power' status can also be found in the fact that, in contrast with the other peace treaties, the Treaty of Versailles with Germany did not include any 'fundamental laws' concerning minority rights.[102]

3.2 *The 'Poison of Bolshevism' and the 'Peace Offensive'*

Another very important example of the process of international legal reproduction in operation under the League of Nations concerns a state that is often left out of the equation, not having itself participated in the Paris Peace

[99] Ibid., Art. 258.

[100] Ibid., Arts. 264–312.

[101] 'Reply of the Allies,' 1344–5. Emphasis added.

[102] Contrast e.g. Treaty of Saint-Germain, Art. 63.

Conference. This is, of course, post-1917 Bolshevik Russia (from 1922 the Union of Soviet Socialist Republics or USSR). The Russian Empire fought doggedly on the side of the Allies during the First World War until the conclusion of the Treaty of Brest-Litovsk in March 1918. In this short-lived treaty, the new Soviet authorities had reneged on their commitments under the Triple Entente (Russia's defensive alliance with France and Britain, and by extension the other Allies, in place since the early 1900s) and signed a crippling armistice with the German Empire.[103] By the time the Versailles Conference commenced in January 1919, therefore, its participants had been faced with a new 'enemy state' – not a former wartime enemy, but even more worryingly, an enemy of their vision of the peace.

This enemy was the entity of uncertain international status which the Soviets had been creating, since October 1917, through their occupation of the heartland of the former Russian Empire, and their attempts to conquer the rest of it. In a memo written shortly before the the end of the First World War, Robert Lansing, then Secretary of State and later Head of the US Commission at Versailles, made explicit the Allies' reasons for considering 'Bolshevism' (the 'poison of Bolshevism', to use Wilson's phrase) an enemy no less dangerous for the emerging global order and its core normative principles than any member of the Quadruple Alliance had been. As Lansing declared:

> There are at work in Europe two implacable enemies of Individual Liberty and its guardian, Political Equality and Justice. These enemies are Absolutism and Bolshevism. The former is waning. The latter is increasing ...
>
> [Bolshevism's] appeal is to the unintelligent and brutish element of mankind to take from the intellectual and successful their rights and possessions and to reduce them to a state of slavery ...
>
> Bolshevism is the most hideous and monstrous thing that the human mind has ever conceived ... [and it] finds its adherents among the criminal, the depraved, and the mentally unfit ... Yet this monster which seeks to devour civilised society and reduce mankind to the state of beasts is certainly spreading westward ...
>
> A Bolshevik Germany or Austria is too horrible to contemplate. It is worse, far worse, than a Prussianized Germany, and would mean an even greater menace to human liberty.[104]

[103] *Treaty of Peace between Russia and Germany, Austria-Hungary, Bulgaria and Turkey*, Brest-Litovsk, 3 March 1918 ('Treaty of Brest-Litovsk').

[104] Robert Lansing, confidential memo to Wilson, 26 October 1918, cited in John M. Thompson, *Russia, Bolshevism, and the Versailles Peace* (Princeton, NJ: Princeton University Press, 1966), 15.

As the Commission on the League of Nations met at the Palace of Versailles in February 1919, its members can seldom have managed to rid their minds of the Soviet uprisings then in progress throughout the former Russian, German and Austro-Hungarian Empires, from Bavaria to Finland to Slovakia. Rosa Luxemburg and Karl Liebknecht had been murdered, and the German Revolution suppressed, only a few weeks before the Commission's meeting with which this chapter began. At the same time, there were no fewer than 13,000 American, over 23,000 Greek, 2,500 Italian, 12,000 Japanese, more than 2,000 Chinese and nearly 1,000 British and Australian troops on the ground in Siberia, Poland, Crimea, Bessarabia, Arkhangelsk and elsewhere in the Russian Empire between mid 1918 and late 1920, intervening directly on the side of the 'Whites' in an attempt to defeat the Red Army.[105] Wilson, Nobuako, Cecil, Orlando, Bourgeois, Larnaude and Smuts must certainly have been receiving regular updates on the progress of this massive military intervention into what was still, from the perspective of the White Army, the territory of the Russian Empire – a desperate new front in the First World War, still in crisis more than three months after the War's end. These statesmen were acutely aware that what they were facing at that moment was not just the possibility of a consolidated communist Russia or of further unrest within their own borders, but something that was, from their point of view, far worse: the emergence of a full-blown rival to the League of Nations – a rival international community.

However strange it might seem today, the idea that the Russian Civil War was a war between two rival international orders was a highly plausible reading of this situation at the time.[106] It would have been especially plausible immediately after March 1919, when the Communist International (Comintern) was launched with the specified aim of 'conduct[ing] an unyielding struggle against the ideas of Wilson's League of Nations' and of employing 'all available means, including armed force, for the overthrow of the international bourgeoisie and for the creation of an international Soviet republic as a transition stage to the complete abolition of the State.'[107] V. I. Lenin, head of the new Russian Soviet Federative Socialist Republic, saw the clash in precisely these terms, referring fre-

[105] See generally Ian C. D. Moffat, *The Allied Intervention in Russia, 1918–1920: The Diplomacy of Chaos* (Basingstoke, New York: Palgrave Macmillan, 2015); Norman Davis [1972], *White Eagle, Red Star: The Polish-Soviet War 1919–1920 and the 'Miracle on the Vistula'* (London: Pimlico Press, 2003).

[106] *Constitution of the Union of Soviet Socialist Republics*, 31 January 1924, Art. 1.

[107] Invitation to the First Congress of the Communist International, 24 January 1919, in Jane Degras (ed.), *The Communist International, 1919–1943: Documents*, Vol. 1 (Oxford University Press, 1956), 1.

quently to the 'alliance of capitalist States, which are banding together against the revolution under the hypocritical banner of the "League of Nations"'. Or, as Comintern's 1919 *May Day Manifesto* declared:

> In Paris the imperialist extortioners are trying to create their own black 'inter-national', the so-called League of Nations. Conscious workers throughout the world know perfectly well that the so-called League of Nations is in fact a league of bourgeois robbers for the oppression of nations, for the division of the world, for the enslavement of workers, for strangling the proletarian revolution.[108]

Two Soviet jurists, Evgeny Korovin and Evgeny Pashukanis, were then in the process of theorising international law's 'transitional period',[109] as international law travelled, they argued, from its pre-Soviet position as the body of law regulating 'the struggle between capitalist states', to an 'inter-class law', regulating a 'temporary compromise between two antagonistic class systems'.[110] As Schwarzenberger pointed out in the 1930s, this understanding held even after 1922 when the USSR Constitution integrated the six Soviet Republics into a single federated state. As he put it, 'at the very time when the [League] Covenant was launched [the Soviet authorities] laid down a counter-covenant in their constitution which gave entry into the U.S.S.R. to all existing and all future Socialist Soviet Republics which were eventually to form the Socialist World Soviet Republic'.[111]

The opposite side held a very similar view. As Wilson wrote to Lloyd George in March 1919:

> If we are to offer Europe an alternative to Bolshevism we must make the League of Nations into something which will be both a safeguard to those nations who are prepared for fair dealing with their neighbours and a menace to those who would trespass on the rights of their neighbours, whether they are imperialist empires or imperialist Bolshevists. An essential element, therefore, in the peace settlement is the constitution of the League of Nations as the effective guardian of international right and international liberty throughout the world.[112]

[108] In Degras (ed.), *The Communist International*, Vol. 1, 51.

[109] Evgeny A. Korovin, *International Law of the Transitional Period* [Международное право переходного времени] (Moscow: Gosudarstvennoe Izdatel'stvo, 1924). On Pashukanis, see Frame, Section 2.1.

[110] Evgeny Pashukanis, 'International Law', in Piers Beirne and Robert Sharlet (eds.), Peter B. Maggs (trans.), *Selected Writings on Marxism and Law* (London, New York: Academic Press Inc., 1980), 168–83, at 184–5.

[111] Schwarzenberger, *The League of Nations and World Order*, 40, citing *Declaration in regard to the Constitution of Socialist Soviet Republics*, Moscow, 30 December 1922.

[112] Wilson to Lloyd George, 25 March 1919, quoted in Charles Prince, 'The USSR and International Organizations', 36 *AJIL* (1942): 427–8.

As Wilson's apparently tautological phrase 'imperialist empires' reminds us, the word 'imperialism' for the engineers of the Versailles Settlement and of the League often indicated, not the 'enlightened' colonialism of the Allied powers (government by 'self-governing' states, as I have called it), but rather a government which had reneged on its duties to vindicate the supposedly natural 'equality' and 'freedom' of all its citizens and lapsed into ('non-reciprocating') autocracy. It was in this sense that Wilson could make an equivalence between 'imperialist empires' (the Central Powers) and 'imperialist Bolshevists' (referring to the efforts of Comintern and the Red Army to expand the territorial reach of the revolution). For these, as we have seen, were viewed as the 'two implacable enemies of Individual Liberty and its guardian, Political Equality and Justice' – as the nemesis of 'self-governing' statehood. Indeed, as the Allied and Associated Powers assembled at Versailles confronted the very real threat that the Soviet 'menace' would radiate out from Leningrad through the ranks of hungry workers, returning troops, displaced minorities and disaffected colonies, the emphasis they placed on the paradoxical and explosive notion of 'national self-determination' at last makes sense as an effort to head off, if not to usurp, one of the most tantalising promises offered by the leaders of the Bolshevik revolution. This was, of course, the offer of 'peace to all the peoples of all the belligerent countries upon the basis of Soviet terms – no annexations, no indemnities, and the right to self-determination of peoples',[113] combined with the extension of this promise to colonised and racially oppressed peoples throughout the world.[114] In this context, the assertion by Smuts in December 1918 that 'the fundamental policies which must guide the [L]eague in its territorial policy as the general heir and successor of the defunct empires' were contained in 'the general formula of "No annexations, and the self-determination of nations"' can readily be understood as a strategy of straightforward normative appropriation.[115]

[113] Vladimir Lenin, speech to the Second All-Russia Congress of Soviets of Workers' and Soldiers' Deputies, 26 October 1917, quoted in Murray Bookchin, *The Third Revolution: Popular Movements in the Revolutionary Era*, Vol. 3 (London, New York: Continuum, 2014), 245. See also Lenin's 'Report On Peace', introduced during the same meeting by that speech, at www.marxists.org/archive/lenin/works/1917/oct/25-26/26b.htm (accessed 13 October 2015).

[114] See e.g. Leon Trotsky, 'Manifesto of the Communist International to the Proletariat of the Entire World', 6 March 1919, in Jane Degras (ed.), *The Communist International*, Vol. 1, 38–47; 'Theses of the Fourth Comintern Congress on the Negro Question', 30 November 1922, in Ibid., 398–401.

[115] Jan C. Smuts, *The League of Nations: A Practical Suggestion* (London, Toronto, New York: Hodder & Stoughton, 1918), 12. See Section 4.1, below.

There were many strategic disagreements among the Allied states in the immediate post-armistice period over whether the military intervention into Russia should be reinforced (the option favoured by France), or whether the Soviet 'monster' should be deprived of sustenance through the provision of economic aid designed to lure its support away (favoured waveringly by Wilson, though certainly not by Lansing). Nonetheless, the Allied position on whether or not to recognise Soviet Russia and offer it membership of the League was clear. Even though the Allied and Associated Powers formed the core of the League of Nations, and were all offered unconditional membership of that organisation, and even though Russia had, until March 1918, been one of the staunchest of those Powers, suffering incomparable losses over the previous four years, 'Bolshevism' was the polar opposite of everything the League stood for in normative terms. It was therefore decided by the League Commission that '[d]efinitely untrustworthy and hostile States, e.g. Russia, should the Bolshevist government remain in power, should be excluded'.[116] Importantly, however, as with Germany, Russia's exclusion was always considered to be reversible provided that it was prepared to embrace 'Individual Liberty and ... Political Equality'. For instance, both Schwarzenberger and, in the 1960s, the political scientist Donald Buzinkai noted the significance of the fact that explicit provisions were made during the Versailles Conference for the admission of Russia to the League should its Bolshevik administration be overthrown and replaced by an administration that could be classified as 'self-governing'.[117] Buzinkai pointed out that '[a] "democratic Russian republic" was not only considered a friend and an ally, but a Great Power as well'.[118] Schwarzenberger, meanwhile, argued that, unsuccessful as they may have been, the 'interventions' made by the Allies in the attempt to 'enforce' the principle of homogeneity were fully 'consistent with the general principle adopted by the Paris [Peace] Conference to base membership of the League on the principle of self-government', and should be taken as 'proof that the will then existed to achieve [a normatively homogeneous League of Nations] in reality'.[119]

116 Early draft of the Cecil Plan, cited in Miller, *The Drafting of the Covenant*, 61 inc. n. 2.

117 Donald I. Buzinkai, 'The Bolsheviks, the League of Nations and the Paris Peace Conference, 1919', 19 *Soviet Studies* (1967): 257–63, at 260; Schwarzenberger, *The League of Nations and World Order*, 38–40. See e.g. account of amendments to the Covenant proposed at a meeting between Wilson, Colonel House and Cecil in March 2019, in Miller, *The Drafting of the Covenant*, 296.

118 Buzinkai, 'The Bolsheviks, the League of Nations and the Paris Peace Conference', 260.

119 Schwarzenberger, *The League of Nations and World Order*, 40.

The USSR did not, of course, disintegrate until the 1990s; and yet it was recognised, during the inter-war period, by most of the League's members,[120] and even, in 1933, by the United States. The following year the Soviet Union was not only welcomed into the League itself, but, like Germany, offered a seat on the Council immediately.[121] Given that this decision was taken at the height of Stalin's purges, and in the wake of the death of up to 10 million people in a famine induced by the USSR's botched policy of collectivisation, this decision evidently did not stem from the observation of the recognising states that the USSR had committed itself to protecting the 'life, liberty and property' of all its citizens. Running counter to much of their early rhetoric, what the Soviet authorities had signalled they were prepared to do by this time, however, was to protect the rights (and in particular the property rights) of foreigners within the USSR. As the historian John Thompson relates, as early as October 1918, with the Russian Civil War and the Allied intervention, Lenin had initiated what became known as the 'peace offensive'. From this point onwards, according to Thompson, the increasingly desperate authorities of the Russian Socialist Federal Soviet Republic (RSFSR, as it was then) proposed peace to the intervening Western governments no fewer than seven times, in each case offering economic concessions to the Allied states and their nationals in Russia as a bargaining chip.[122] A revealing moment came in early February 1920, when the Allies had finally swallowed the bait and invited the Soviet administration (though unofficially) to join several other factions in the Russian Civil War on the Principo Islands to participate in collective negotiations. When, in its formal reply to this quasi-invitation, the RSFSR made note of 'the great inclination which foreign capital has always displayed to exploit Russia's natural resources for its own advantage',[123] the Allied representatives were mortally offended. On hearing the news, the British Prime Minister Lloyd George, for example, is reported to have cried out: 'But the Bolsheviks ... [a]re the most consummate sneaks in the world! We are not after their money or their concessions or their territory, but are their friends who want to help them.

[120] H. L. 'The U.S.S.R. and the League of Nations', 11 *Bulletin of International News* (1934): 3–12, at 11.

[121] See Manly O. Hudson, 'Afghanistan, Ecuador and the Soviet Union in the League of Nations', 29 *AJIL* (1935): 112–16.

[122] Thompson, *Russia, Bolshevism and the Versailles Peace*, 88ff.

[123] Soviet reply of 4 February 1920, cited in Thompson, *Russia, Bolshevism and the Versailles Peace*, 115.

I suppose, because they know they have no high motives themselves, they do not believe anybody else has.'[124]

Professed 'high motives' notwithstanding, what events shortly revealed was that the Allied states were not prepared to halt a military intervention in pursuit of what we might now call 'regime change' until protections for foreign property rights had been restored, and trading relations re-established. Thus, British recognition of Soviet Russia, for example, was eventually forthcoming, in 1924, only after the conclusion of the 1921 Anglo-Soviet Trade Agreement. Negotiated in the same year as Lenin's notorious 'one step back for two steps forward' – the 'New Economic Policy', which introduced an element of controlled capitalism into the Soviet economy in an effort to boost its recovery from the famine – this treaty amounted to a tacit recognition between the two governments, who agreed 'to remove forthwith all obstacles hitherto placed in the way of the real trade between the United Kingdom and Russia in any commodities which may be legally exported from or imported into their respective territories to or from any other foreign country, and not to exercise any discrimination against such trade, as compared with that carried on with any other foreign country'.[125] Another illustration can be found in the decision of the United States to recognise the USSR some twelve years later, on a similarly conditional basis. Some of the US's conditions were *sui generis*,[126] but many others will now be familiar. The USSR was required to establish the procedures necessary to settle debts to the US, both public and private, resulting from its nationalisation of foreign property and repudiation of loans inherited from the Tsarist regime;[127] to offer US nationals 'the same freedom of conscience and religious liberty which they enjoy at home'; and to negotiate a 'consular convention' in which US nation-

[124] Wilson's description, cited in Thompson, *Russia, Bolshevism and the Versailles Peace*, 115.

[125] *Anglo-Soviet Trade Agreement*, 16 March 1921, Art. 1.

[126] For example, the US required the USSR to give a guarantee of non-intervention in US internal affairs, and to cease all revolutionary propaganda aimed at 'establishing subservient soviet nations in Latin America and in the United States'. 'Correspondence between US President Franklin D. Roosevelt, and Maxim Litvinov, People's Commissar for Foreign Affairs, Union of Soviet Socialist Republics', 16 November 1933 (Roosevelt-Litvinov Conversations), *US National Security Archives Online*, at http://nsarchive.gwu.edu/coldwar/documents/episode-1/fdr-ml.htm (accessed 16 October 2015).

[127] One of the new Soviet authority's first Declarations abolished private property by decree, which entailed the nationalisation of foreign property, the confiscation of foreign assets and repudiation of all bonds issued by the Tsarist government. See Vladimir Ilich Lenin, 'Declaration of Rights of the Working and Exploited People', 4 January 1918, approved 12 January 1918 by the Third All-Russia Congress of Soviets, at www.marxists.org/archive/lenin/works/1918/jan/03.htm (accessed 28 May 2016).

als would obtain the right 'to a fair, public and speedy trial and ... to be represented by counsel of their choice'.[128] These fragments from the early legal history of Soviet foreign relations suggest that, as a matter of international law, the RSFSR and later the USSR were recognised as 'sovereign' on the basis of a very similar rationale to that which was applied in the non-European world. If it was prepared to reproduce foreign legal subjectivity within its borders, then the Soviet state could be – and was – treated as sovereign, up to a certain point. However, that the Soviet authorities were not prepared to reconstitute their *own* citizens as legal subjects of this kind – that they were not prepared, in short, to embrace capitalism wholeheartedly – arguably left a question mark hanging over the USSR's rights and duties under interntional law throughout what became, after 1945, the Cold War. Indeed, from this point onwards, it becomes increasingly difficult to contend that any of the states on either side of the 'iron curtain' saw the sovereign rights of their adversaries as inviolable in any meaningful way. [129]

With these mainly European examples of the League's experiments in the field of international personality in mind, the next section will turn to the non-European context, to examine perhaps the most notorious of these experiments: the Mandates System. As we are about to see, the organisation of the Mandates System bore similarities to, as well as differences from, the way in which the League approached the question of the rights and duties of inter-war states, whether 'national' states, 'enemy' states or states of any other kind. All states were equal during the inter-war period, as we have just seen in Sections 1, 2 and 3, but some states were more equal than others – namely those whose 'self-governing' credentials, as 'effective' and 'responsible' enforcers and reproducers of individual legal subjectivity, could be clearly ascertained. 'Most' equal (as it were) were

[128] Roosevelt-Litvinov Conversations.

[129] The USSR violated its commitments to the US in a matter of months. According to the Office of the Historian, US Department of State: 'Unfortunately, the cooperative spirit embodied in the Roosevelt-Litvinov agreements proved to be short-lived. Shortly after his arrival in Moscow in December 1933, Bullitt [William C. Bullitt, the first US Ambassador to the Soviet Union] became disillusioned with the Soviets as an agreement on the issue of debt repayment failed to materialize. Moreover, evidence emerged that the Soviet Government had violated its pledge not to interfere in American domestic affairs. Finally, the killing of the Leningrad Communist Party boss, Sergey Kirov, launched the first of the "Great Purges" that led to the death or imprisonment of millions of Soviet citizens as the Stalinist regime liquidated any potential critics of the government. The wide scope and public nature of the purges horrified both American diplomatic personnel stationed in the Soviet Union, and the world at large.' See https://history.state.gov/milestones/1921-1936/ussr (accessed 16 October 2015).

those sovereign states which had just triumphed over the absolutism of the Central Powers during the First World War. 'Less' equal, meanwhile, were the new 'national states' of Central and Eastern Europe and the 'enemy states' (and even, to some extent, the USSR), whose commitment to the reproduction of 'free' and 'equal' individual subjectivity the Allies had attempted to codify in a series of explicitly conditional multilateral treaties concluded between them and the states in question. In the context of the Mandates System, however, set up to institutionalise and supervise the 'tutelage' of certain non-European colonies towards 'self-government', the hierarchy put in place by the League was far more explicit, and, in terms of its consequences, far more damaging. In terms of the substance and logic of conditionality, however, the difference was one of degree rather than substance.

4 'Sacred Trusts of Civilisation': Mandated Territories and Mandatory Powers

The Mandates System was devised, in the words of its first director, the Swiss lawyer William Rappard, as a 'compromise between the proposition advanced by the advocates of annexation, and the proposition put forward by those who wished to entrust the colonial territories [of the defeated Central Powers] to an international administration.'[130] Its starting point, spelled out in Article 22 of the Covenant, was that this very specific group of colonies – namely the non-European territories stripped from the German and Ottoman Empires in the wake of the War – were, by definition, 'inhabited by peoples not yet able to stand by themselves under the strenuous conditions of the modern world.'[131] Echoing the concerns of the Berlin and Brussels Acts, Article 22 laid down that 'the well-being and development of such peoples form[ed] a sacred trust of civilisation',[132] such that the 'tutelage of such peoples' was to 'be entrusted to advanced nations', who were charged with exercising this responsibility 'on behalf of the League.'[133]

These 'mandated territories' were then divided into three 'classes'. All, it was assumed, were incapable of 'stand[ing] by themselves under the

[130] Quoted in Quincy Wright, 'Sovereignty of the Mandates', 17 *AJIL* (1923): 691–703, at 691. See further Wright, *Mandates under the League of Nations* (University of Chicago Press, 1930).

[131] Covenant, Art. 22.

[132] Covenant, Art. 22.

[133] Covenant, Art. 22.

strenuous conditions of the modern world'.[134] However, the Arab, former Ottoman territories (which had, only a few years earlier, been promised independent statehood by the British in return for their support in fighting the Ottoman Empire during the First World War)[135] were deemed sufficiently 'developed' such that 'their existence as independent nations' could be 'provisionally recognized subject to the rendering of administrative advice and assistance'.[136] These became the 'Class A' mandates. 'Class B' mandates, by contrast – primarily former German territories in Central Africa – were deemed to be:

> at such a stage that the Mandatory must be responsible for the administration of the territory under conditions which will guarantee freedom of conscience and religion, subject only to the maintenance of public order and morals, the prohibition of abuses such as the slave trade, the arms traffic and the liquor traffic, and the prevention of the establishment of fortifications or military and naval bases and of military training of the natives for other than police purposes and the defence of territory, and will also secure equal opportunities for the trade and commerce of other Members of the League.[137]

Finally, at the bottom of the scale, 'Class C' mandates (mainly former German territories in the Pacific, as well as South-West Africa) were to be 'administered under the laws of the Mandatory as integral portions of its territory' subject to the same 'safeguards' as outlined for 'Class B' territories.[138] Sovereignty in the mandates was (as the jurist Arnold McNair famously described it) to be regarded as being 'in abeyance' until such time as 'the inhabitants of the Territory obtain recognition as an independent state', whereupon sovereignty would 'revive and invest in the new State'.[139] It was in this gap between 'abeyance' and 'investment' that the conditional and therefore flexible nature of 'sovereignty' emerged, for the first time, right out into the open.

134 Covenant, Art. 22.

135 See correspondence (esp. Letters 1–4) between Sharif Husayn of Mecca and Sir Henry McMahon, British High Commissioner at Cairo, 14 July–10 March 1916, available at *World War One Document Archive* (Brigham Young University Library), at https://wwi.lib.byu.edu/index.php/Letters_between_Hussein_Ibn_Ali_and_Sir_Henry_Mcmahon (accessed 13 September 2017); Geoffrey R. Watson, 'Before Oslo: A Brief Legal History of the Arab-Israeli Conflict,' in *The Oslo Accords: International Law and the Israeli-Palestinian Peace Agreements* (Oxford University Press, 2000), 3–40.

136 Covenant, Art. 22.

137 Covenant, Art. 22.

138 Ibid.

139 *International Status of South-West Africa*, Advisory Opinion, 11 July 1950, Separate Opinion of Arnold McNair, 154.

The Mandates System has justifiably been the subject of a great deal of interest in the field of international law and inter-war history. At the time, as Quincy Wright, later President of both the American Society of International Law and the American Political Science Association, explained: 'advocates ... looked upon it as a revolution in the relations of civilized and backward peoples which, if successful in these limited areas, may furnish an example for the government of other areas of similar character'.[140] Likewise, in 1950, at the very start of the process of decolonisation, McNair (then a judge on the International Court of Justice) described it, in retrospect, as an entirely 'new institution ... a new species of international government, which does not fit into the old conception of sovereignty and which is alien to it'.[141] The Mandates System, McNair went on, had been brought into being by the 'desire' of a 'large part of the civilized world' to '[open] a new chapter in the life of between fifteen and twenty millions of [colonised] people'.[142] Still today, continuing with this progressivist trajectory, the Mandates System is often described as a first step towards the creation of a right of colonised peoples and peoples under foreign occupation to self-determination in the form of a right to opt for independent statehood.[143]

As critics like Anghie, Eslava,[144] Ralphe Wilde[145] and others have pointed out, however, the suffering and exploitation of the populations of mandated territories was scarcely less than that of those peoples whose territories continued to be regarded as 'overseas possessions' of foreign states. Anghie, for example, offers the example of Nauru, which was administered by Great Britain and two British dominions, Australia and New Zealand, first as a mandated and then as a trust territory. By the time it became independent in 1968, approximately one-third of the island had been mined out in the form of phosphates, generating an estimated profit of GB£165 million. In 1928, only 2.8 per cent of these profits were being shared with the islanders.[146] For Anghie, then,

[140] Wright, 'Sovereignty of the Mandates', 691.

[141] *South-West Africa Case (McNair)*, 150.

[142] Ibid., 154.

[143] See e.g. the trajectory traced in Shaw, *International Law*, 224–5.

[144] Luis Eslava, 'The Moving Location of Empire: Indirect Rule, International Law and the *Bantu Educational Kinema Experiment*', 31 *Leiden Journal of International Law* (2018): 539–67.

[145] Ralph Wilde, *International Territorial Administration: How the Civilizing Mission Never Went Away* (Oxford University Press, 2008), 317–43.

[146] Antony Anghie, '"The Heart of My Home": Colonialism, Environmental Damage, and the Nauru Case', 34 *HIJL* (1993): 445–506, at 446; Anghie, *Imperialism, Sovereignty and*

far from representing a break with colonialism, the Mandates System should be regarded as its continuation in another form – the form of a 'fantastic universalizing apparatus that, when applied to any mandate territory … would be directed to the same ideal of self-government and, in some cases, transformed sufficiently to ensure the emergence of a sovereign state'.[147] However, Anghie continues, the type of sovereignty that emerged from this apparatus was of a particular character; for '[t]he Mandate System had devised a set of technologies that would compromise that independence and maintain – indeed, entrench – the division between advanced and backward States'.[148] This particularity stemmed from the 'contradiction' at the heart of its programme of tutelage 'between attempting to promote self-government while establishing an economic structure that recreated colonial relations', making 'real self-government impossible because government is made subservient to unequal economic development'.[149] Sovereignty in the mandates, according to Anghie, like 'non-European sovereignty' in general, came into the world, and remained, 'economised'.[150]

There is, however, another layer that we could add to this analysis, which becomes apparent when its origins and legal contours are laid, as it were, against the other fragments of history that have already been thrown into the shadow-box. From this three-dimensional perspective, as we might call it, what was 'fantastic', 'new' and 'revolutionary' about the Mandates System was the frankness with which it articulated and policed a particularly stringent version of the conditionalities that had *always* been attached in the theory and practice of international law to the assumption of sovereign rights. Or, to put it another way, it is not necessary to claim (as does the historian Susan Pedersen, for example[151]), that the Mandates System was 'a discursive arena and not an administrative system', or that the 'type of sovereignty' the League created for the mandated territories was 'unique' (as does Anghie),[152] in order to criticise the particularly profound and long-lasting damage this system inflicted on the societies and

the Making of International Law, 175, n. 236. For an excellent new analysis, see Cait Storr, *Nauru: International Status, Imperial Form and the Histories of International Law* (PhD thesis, Melbourne Law School, 2017).

147 Anghie, *Imperialism, Sovereignty and the Making of International Law*, 148.

148 Ibid., 192.

149 Ibid., 192–3.

150 Ibid., 157.

151 Susan Pedersen, 'The Meaning of the Mandates System: An Argument', 32 *Geschichte und Gesellschaft* (2006): 560–82, at 581.

152 Anghie, *Imperialism, Sovereignty and the Making of International Law*, 199.

ecosystems it touched. To concede that the Mandates System was, genuinely, in both a normative and material sense, a mechanism for creating independent, 'self-governing' states does not undermine the conclusion that it was also, and at the same time, a mechanism for ensuring that those states would remain drastically and forever subordinate to their erstwhile 'mandatory powers'. On the contrary, as we have already seen, and as we are about to see once again, the process of transforming these territories and their inhabitants on a conditional basis into more-or-less 'free' and 'equal' legal subjects was precisely the process which, in doing so, transformed their material elements into 'resources' to be extracted for their own benefit and for the collective benefit of the 'international community'. This point becomes clearer if we trace Article 22 back to its roots.

4.1 Origins: The 'Smuts Plan' and the 'Cecil Plan'

The origins of Article 22 lie in two proposals suggested by two members of the League Committee whom we met at the start this chapter: soon-to-be South African Prime Minister General Jan Smuts, an unabashed white supremacist 'whose segregationist policies at home paved the way for the apartheid state';[153] and the Conservative politician, Lord Robert Cecil, Head of the British Delegation to the Paris Peace Conference. Interestingly, both proposals envisaged the application of what became the Mandates System to certain non-European *and* to certain European territories.

The purpose of the Mandates System, for Smuts, was that of 'nursing towards economic and political independence' the 'peoples left behind by the decomposition of Russia, Austria, and Turkey', who were 'untrained politically' and 'either incapable [at present] of or deficient in power of self-government'.[154] Importantly, then, the 'Smuts Plan', a memorandum submitted in December 1918, entitled, *The League of Nations: A Practical Suggestion*,[155] applied both more widely and more narrowly than the Mandates System itself eventually did. Smuts' plan was wider in that, if Smuts had had his way, League control would have been exercised not just

[153] Mark Mazower, *No Enchanted Palace: The End of Empire and the Ideological Origins of the United Nations* (Princeton, Oxford: Princeton University Press, 2009), 19. Mazower also points out that it was Smuts whose 'soaring rhetoric' on the 'fundamental rights of man' came to form the basis of the UN Charter's preamble (28–31).

[154] Smuts, *A Practical Suggestion*, 11.

[155] Ibid.

over the former Ottoman territories of the Middle East,[156] but the whole of the former Ottoman, Russian and Austro-Hungarian Empires (territories which were, in the end, excluded from the reach of Article 22). Yet it was also narrower in that Smuts sought to exclude 'the German colonies in the Pacific and Africa' (which eventually became 'Class B' and 'C' mandated territories) on the grounds that they were 'inhabited by barbarians, who not only cannot possibly govern themselves, but to whom it would be impracticable to apply any idea of political self-determination in the European sense'.[157]

The benchmark which Smuts used to make these decisions about which of the world's 'peoples and territories' should be included within the system and which should be excluded, and about how these territories and communities should be ranked against one another, is also very interesting. For instance, the Smuts Plan laid out detailed provisions for reallocating sovereignty within Central and Eastern Europe (those territories which eventually became the 'national states' with 'national minorities' within them) and Central Asia (which were soon 'lost' to 'Bolshevism' and thus to the League's jurisdiction). Smuts argued that 'the rule of self-determination, or the consent of the governed to their form of government' should be 'fairly and reasonably applied'.[158] Finland, Poland, Czechoslovakia and Yugoslavia, he considered, 'would probably be found sufficiently capable of statehood to be recognised as independent states from the beginning'.[159] However, other communities, in the 'Transcaucasian or Transcaspian provinces of Russia [present-day Armenia plus most of Georgia, Azerbaijan, Turkmenistan and other parts of Central Asia]', 'Upper and Lower Mesopotamia [present-day Iraq], Lebanon and Syria' were 'as yet deficient in the qualities of statehood', and capable only of 'internal autonomy' under 'the guiding hand of some external authority to steady their administration'. This 'deficiency'

[156] According to Pedersen, Smuts 'restricted international control to the Middle East alone' in this proposal, which she therefore reads as 'an effort at containment'. Yet a close reading of the text of his *Practical Suggestion* in fact reveals the opposite. Smuts sought to bring not only West Asian, but also Central Asian and Eastern and Central European territories under varying degrees of League control. See Susan Pedersen, *The Guardians: The League of Nations and the Crisis of Empire* (Oxford University Press, 2015), 27.

[157] Smuts, *A Practical Suggestion*, 28. Interestingly, Smuts also excluded Alsace-Lorraine, whose annexation to France would in his view amount to a 'disannexation' (28). This suggests that even a German/French territory could potentially have been considered a mandated territory, according to Smuts.

[158] Smuts, *A Practical Suggestion*, 29.

[159] Ibid., 29

varied, however. Mesopotamia/Iraq, for instance, Smuts saw as being 'barely capable of autonomy', whereas Syria, he thought, was 'very close' to 'complete statehood'.[160] Smuts reserved a third category for communities whose 'administration would have to be undertaken to a very large extent by some external authority'. This was not, in his reasoning, because the populations of these territories were, in his view, racially inferior, but rather because they were so heterogeneous as to be incapable of 'administrative cooperation', as in Palestine and the 'Armenian vilyets'.[161]

The Smuts Plan is, therefore, of interest to the legal history of the expansion of the states system not only because of the frank and unsettling racism with which he dismissed Africans as 'barbarians, who not only cannot possibly govern themselves', but also because of its apparent inconsistency, which reveals something very important about the role of race in the process of international legal reproduction. Once again, the Smuts Plan is underpinned by a curiously violent universalist commitment, anchored in an unbending faith in the institutions of 'self-government' (or simply 'government' as it was coming to be known by this point) as the test by means of which to decide *how* 'sovereign' any particular entity should be. Both non-European and European peoples appear to have been ranked, in Smuts' mind, on the basis of their (presumed) willingness and capacity to protect the rights of existing individual subjects of law. Thus, Smuts insisted that the 'nursing' towards self-government of all these territories, both European and non-European, involved a responsibility, on the part of the nascent League and its representative mandatory powers, 'to maintain the policy of the open door, or equal economic opportunity for all'.[162] This principle, translated root and branch into Article 22, offers further evidence to support the suggestions made in Item 2. Smuts' exclusion of certain African territories, inclusion of certain European territories, and wildly varying assessments of certain Arab and Slavic territories, indicates that, in the process of international legal reproduction, race operated, not directly, but rather indirectly (and extremely subjectively) as a marker of a community's (in)capacity for self-government, itself taken as an indicator of the utility-maximising 'rationality' of its individual members.

In addition to the exclusion of former Russian and Austro-Hungarian territories, and to the inclusion of the German Empire's African colonies, the other major departure from the Smuts Plan concerned the rather more

[160] Ibid., 29.
[161] Ibid., 29.
[162] Ibid., 33.

detailed set of institutional prescriptions regarding 'self-government' that eventually found their way into Article 22. This detail was derived from a separate proposal put forward by the British Delegation at Versailles, headed by Cecil, on 24 January 1919.[163] In thinking out how to classify the territories which fell into the post-War 'sovereignty vacuum', the 'Cecil Plan' distinguished between what it called 'vested territories' and 'assisted states'. Though few specific examples were given, Cecil was clear that his proposal envisaged the inclusion both of 'territories which formerly belonged to Austria-Hungary and Turkey' (largely European territories) and of 'the Colonies formerly under the dominion of the German Empire' (Pacific and African territories).[164] On the one hand, territories with inhabitants 'not yet capable of nominating or explicitly approving the State appointed as mandatory of the League' were to become 'vested territories'.[165] Sovereignty over such territories should be 'transferred to any state' which had signed the Covenant and which could be trusted to 'afford to their inhabitants peace, order and good government'.[166] 'Assisted states', on the other hand (presumably located in Central and Eastern Europe, although perhaps also in West Asia), should, Cecil argued, be permitted to 'obtain their independence' and would be 'entitled to such assistance as they may desire for the purpose of securing peace, order and good government'.[167]

Above all, the principle of 'good government' (to use Cecil's term) hinged – as it did for Smuts, as it did in Article 1, paragraph 2 of the Covenant, and as it did both in the 'national' and 'enemy' states – on the capacity of the territory in question to protect the rights of existing legal subjects. Thus, both the states in control of 'vested territories' and the 'assisted states' were charged with 'maintaining', within their jurisdictions:

i. Freedom of conscience or religion, subject only to the maintenance of public order and morals;
ii. [T]he policy of the open door or equal opportunity for the nationals of all the states Members of the League in respect of the use and development of the economic resources of such territories;
iii. [F]reedom of transit and equality of trade conditions ...
iv. [T]he provisions of the Arms Traffic Convention.[168]

[163] *Draft Convention Regarding Mandates*, 24 January 1919, in Miller, *The Drafting of the Covenant*, 106–8.
[164] Ibid., 108.
[165] Ibid., 106.
[166] Ibid.
[167] Ibid.
[168] Ibid., 107.

Any state in control of 'vested territories' was also charged with prohibiting 'slavery and forced labour', 'traffic' in 'intoxicants' and 'native armed forces', and with resisting the temptation to stray from the principle of the 'open door' 'for the benefit of its own nationals'.[169]

If we place this plan into the shadow-box along with the rest of its contents up to this point, the particular perspective this gives us makes it seem unlikely that Cecil was being facetious in declaring these provisions to be fully in accord with 'the rule requiring the consent of the governed to their form of government'.[170] For 'self-government' (or 'good government', as he put it) hinged, for him, once again, on the extension of the rights and duties of *existing* individual subjects of law into the territory in question. The point at which a territory had managed to transform all its inhabitants into legal subjects ('citizens') was the point at which it was to be recognised as a state, but that did not preclude the possibility that it could have been considered 'self-governing', to some degree, before that point. As long as slavery, or human objectivity, had been outlawed, the question of whether the individuals within a non-state territory were to be allocated rights under international law was not an 'on/off' question, but a matter of degree. In effect, the logic behind the Cecil Plan was a logic which saw the 'mandatory power' as being entitled, as a 'self-governing' entity (state or dominion), to consent to its own rule on behalf of communities which were not yet capable of consenting themselves. After all, the term 'government' pointed to a relationship between an international legal subject on the one hand and individual legal subjects on the other. Arguably, therefore, the individuals who mattered, at this point, were the existing legal subjects of the 'family of nations' as a whole – the citizens of self-governing entities, i.e. sovereign states. It was *their* rights (to trade, own property, travel, worship freely and so on) which it was the duty of the Covenant, and of the League of Nations, to protect, while also 'assisting' the gradual spread of such full legal subjectivity to those individuals which had not, yet, been so transformed. If we quote the Cecil Plan more fully, this logic is clear:

> All policies of administration or economic development shall be based primarily upon the well considered interests of the peoples themselves. Although, in such territories, the inhabitants are not yet capable of nominating or explicitly approving the State appointed as mandatary of the League, it is recognized that the rule requiring the consent of the governed to their form of government should nevertheless be fairly and reasonably applied, and that the Mandatary should take into full and friendly

[169] Ibid.

[170] Ibid., 108.

consideration any expression of the desires of the inhabitants or of any section of them, with the object of determining their best interests, in view of all the circumstances of their situation and development.[171]

Cecil here was explicit: the consent of 'inhabitants ... not yet capable' of giving their consent could be inferred from their expressed 'desires', by the officials of 'self-governing' states, to the extent that these desires accorded with their 'best interests' – which were, of course, that they should be 'self-governing' and therefore 'open' to the markets of the world.

These proposals from the British Delegation found their way almost word for word into Article 22 of the Covenant. From there, they were incorporated directly into the text of the individual 'mandates' – the individual agreements concluded between the League and the 'mandatory powers', including not only the major European Empires, Britain (charged with the tutelage of Mesopotamia and Palestine) and France (mandatory power for Syria and Lebanon), but also Japan (South Pacific Mandate), and the most powerful British dominions, Australia and New Zealand (New Guinea; Nauru; Western Samoa) and South Africa (South-West Africa). Unlike the 'national states', in other words, the signature of the 'mandated territories' was not required on the treaties which brought their hypothetical international personality into being.[172] Nor did their 'native' populations possess the full set of 'liberties' which full legal subjectivity implied, including most notably the right to vote. Instead, as elsewhere in the colonial world, the mandatory powers set about making their administration of these territories 'effective'. And as elsewhere in the colonies, this 'effectivity' involved opening up the resources (both 'natural' and 'human') and the markets of the territories in question to the world.[173]

[171] Ibid., 108.

[172] See e.g. 'French Mandate for Syria and the Lebanon', Geneva, 12 August 1922, in 17 *AJIL*, Supplement: Official Documents (July 1923), 177–82, esp. Arts. 1, 5, 6, 8, 10, 11 and 12; 'British Mandate for Palestine', Geneva, 24 July 1922, in Ibid., 164–71, esp. Arts. 9, 11, 12, 15, 18 and 19. The British Mandate for Palestine was, of course, complicated by Britain's paradoxical double-commitment to establishing 'in Palestine a national home for the Jewish people' while at the same time doing 'nothing ... which might prejudice the civil and religious rights of existing non-Jewish communities in Palestine'. Ibid., Preamble.

[173] As Pedersen points out: 'Two economic principles marked the mandates regime from the start. The first, imposed on all Middle East and African mandate territories save South West Africa, was the principle of the "open door". Nationals of all League member states were to have an equal right to work, travel, reside, and hold property; "complete economic, commercial and industrial equality" was to prevail; and concessions for the economic development of the territory were to be granted "without distinction on grounds of nationality". The second (albeit qualified) principle was that labour should be "free".' Pedersen, *The Guardians*, 233.

Thus, as Frederick Lugard, British representative on the League's Permanent Mandates Commission, argued in his influential manual *The Dual Mandate in British Tropical Africa*,[174] 'the tropics' were to be regarded as 'the heritage of mankind' such that 'neither, on the one hand, has the suzerain Power a right to their exclusive exploitation, nor, on the other hand, have the races which inhabit them a right to deny their bounties to those who need them'.[175] Instead, the idea of 'dual mandate' was designed to indicate that '[t]he responsibility for adequate development rests on the custodian on behalf of civilisation – and not on behalf of civilisation alone, for much of these products is returned to the tropics converted into articles for the use and comfort of its peoples'.[176] 'Need', this text revealed, moreover, was something to be determined by the market – meaning that those territories whose populations had not yet been sufficiently 'developed' to have formed a market of their own – including the territories from which the products in question had been extracted – had a small claim on those resources. It was in this sense that mandatory and colonial peoples fell outside Lugard's sphere of 'civilisation'. But this, of course, did not in any way undermine the central commitment of the idea of the mandates to the principle of freedom and equality embodied in the 'open door', through which Britain (as an exemplary mandatory power) had 'secured to their inhabitants an unrestricted market for their produce, and to all engaged in their development, of whatever nationality, equality of commercial opportunity and uniform laws'.[177]

By 'of whatever nationality', Lugard quite clearly meant 'citizen of whatever state'. 'Natives' did not participate in the development of their territories; they were, instead, precisely that which was being 'developed' through their exposure to 'civilisation', in the form of law and commercial exchange, and their ensuing transformation into legal subjects. It was, as Lugard put it, 'the task of civilisation to put an end to slavery, to establish Courts of Law, to inculcate in the natives a sense of individual responsibility, of liberty, and of justice, and to teach their rulers how to apply these principles'.[178] Again, as this suggests, Lugard's definition of 'civilisation' was more or less interchangeable with that of 'self-government', and, as we saw Tzouvala argue, above, can thus be seen as directly bound

[174] Frederick Lugard, *The Dual Mandate in British Tropical Africa* (Edinburgh, London: W. Blackwood and Sons, 1922).

[175] Ibid., 60–1.

[176] Ibid., 61.

[177] Ibid., 60.

[178] Ibid., 5.

up in the reproduction of capitalist institutions. As Tzouvala,[179] Anghie[180] and Eslava[181] have all pointed out in different ways, the gradual transformation of the 'native' into a legal subject – into a 'free' and 'equal' individual who would willingly offer her labour-power in response to market incentives, and in exchange for wages, which she would then exchange willingly for goods manufactured using the resources extracted from her territory – was just as important in this logic as the extraction of the 'natural' resources themselves. Again, Lugard was quite candid about this. On the one hand, healthy 'natives', he argued, should be 'regarded as the greatest "asset" of the country [mandated territory or colony] because of their potential value as labourers', and should be cared for on the basis of the same principle that 'applies to the good treatment and good feeding of a horse or a plough-ox or to the increase of stock'.[182] On the other hand, however, Lugard argued that the African 'native' displayed an encouraging propensity to be 'tempted to earn wages by his desire to purchase the attractive goods offered for his choice'.[183] The 'free life' of a 'wage-earner', away from 'the discipline and restraint of his elders', was, he said, one to which many Africans could easily be attracted. In order to inculcate the rationality of the consumer/wage-labourer which Lugard (congratulating himself on his open-mindedness) held to be latent in all human beings, including Africans, he suggested (in the context of 'native' labourers employed by European mining companies, for example) that 'wage[s] should be paid in full ... into the hand of each man ... in cash ... [and] at short intervals',[184] and that a 'native market' should be set up close to the 'native' wage-labourer's 'camp', in which imported 'useful articles such as enamel-ware utensils, blankets, &c' should be 'exhibited'. The objective, of course, was to tickle into action the supposedly inherent impulse to 'truck, barter, exchange' (as Adam Smith put it) – and above all to own – on the part of the 'native'.[185]

To the disappointment of the mandatory powers and of the Permanent Mandates Commission (PMC), however, the 'natives' did not always respond 'rationally' to such incentives. Administrators frequently

179 Tzouvala, *Letters of Blood and Fire*, 53–6.

180 Anghie, *Imperialism, Sovereignty and the Making of International Law*, 167–8.

181 Eslava, 'The Moving Location of Empire', 565–7.

182 Lord Lugard, Response to Note by Friere d'Andrade, in Permanent Mandates Commission, *Minutes of the Seventh Session*, League of Nations Doc. C.648 M.237 (1925) VI, 206, quoted in Anghie, *Imperialism, Sovereignty and the Making of International Law*, 166.

183 Lugard, *Dual Mandate*, 405.

184 Ibid., 405.

185 Ibid., 405–6.

lamented, for example, that the 'natives' lacked sufficient 'foresight' to 'induce them to produce the foodstuffs indispensable for their elementary needs' and that the mandatory powers were therefore compelled, for the natives' own benefit, to force them to undertake this work.[186] This argument was used to justify the widespread use of forced labour in the mandated territories, notwithstanding the arrival, in 1930, of the ILO's celebrated Forced Labour Convention, whose signatories sought to 'suppress the use of forced or compulsory labour in all its forms within the shortest possible period'.[187] The Convention, however, specified four exceptions to this rule, including 'any work or service which forms part of the normal civic obligations of the citizens of a fully self-governing country', and, during the 'transitional period' leading to abolition, forced labour used 'for public purposes'.[188] These exceptions permitted the widespread use of forced labour in the mandates by mandatory powers in the interests of 'tutelage'.

Equally coercive measures were also introduced on behalf of the 'natives' collectively. As Pedersen's work has shown, for example, in September 1925 the PMC passed a new regulation guaranteeing that 'contracts and titles acquired in a mandated territory' would be 'as valid as if the territory were held in full sovereignty', with the aim of encouraging investment into the territories. This measure was backed up by a pledge that independence would not be permitted unless and until the League Council had received assurances from the new authorities of any former mandated territory 'that the financial obligations regularly assumed by the former mandatory Power will be carried out and that all rights regularly acquired under the administration of the former mandatory Power shall be respected'.[189] In other words, even though the '[m]andatory powers were, strictly speaking, *not sovereign*', Pedersen points out, with these measures 'the League had accepted that [it] had the right to alienate their charges' resources and land virtually in perpetuity'.[190]

In the mandates, then, just as in the 'national' and 'enemy' states, international legal subjectivity was predicated on the reproduction

[186] Halewyck de Heusch, Director General of Political and Administrative Affairs at the Belgian Colonial Ministry, 22 October 1925, quoted in Pedersen, *The Guardians*, 233.

[187] *Convention Concerning Forced or Compulsory Labour*, Geneva, 28 June 1930 ('Forced Labour Convention'), Art. 1.

[188] Ibid., Arts. 1–2.

[189] Pedersen, *The Guardians*, 235, quoted from the Minutes of the Permanent Mandates Commission, 35th session, 12th meeting, 15 September 1925.

[190] Ibid., 235. Emphasis in the original.

of individual legal subjectivity in the form of individual rights to own, obtain and exchange private property, to be implemented first for the nationals of the League member states via the Mandate System's 'open door' provisions, and supposedly, later on, upon independence – Article 22's tantalising offer – for all individuals within the territory. Yet in the mandates, as in the colonies (especially those subject to what the British called 'indirect rule'), the capacity of the peoples in question to reach this benchmark had been pre-assessed, during Article 22's conceptualisation, using race to benchmark their aptitude for 'self-government'. This pre-assessment, in turn, rendered it perfectly legitimate for those recently victorious 'self-governing' states and dominions to whose 'tutelage' these territories and communities had been entrusted, to consent 'rationally' on their behalf – to the extraction of the resources of their territories, to the transformation of their relationships and communities, and to the usurpation of their own normative systems, not in violation of, but rather in vindication of, the pursuit of 'self-government'. It is, perhaps, unsurprising, therefore, that only one mandated territory was ever permitted to accede to the Covenant. That territory was Iraq, or Mesopotamia as it was then known, a 'Class A' mandate whose status as such was ambiguous and contested from the beginning.

4.2 Iraq: From Mandated Territory to League Member State

Although it did not join the League until 1932, Iraq was first recognised as a sovereign state of sorts in October 1922 after its conclusion of a Treaty of Alliance with Great Britain.[191] Britain had been awarded the mandate for Mesopotamia at the April 1920 San Remo Conference of the Allied Supreme Council, at which, as Pedersen puts it, 'the Allied powers confirmed Britain's mandates over Mesopotamia and Palestine and France's over Syria and Lebanon and hammered out a secret agreement on the distribution of Iraqi oil'.[192] So strong was the resistance of Iraq's inhabitants to the idea of incorporation into the British Empire, and to the imposition of rules concerning land ownership and taxation, however, that in May 1920 a rebellion broke out demanding independent statehood immediately. It was swiftly and brutally suppressed by the British, allegedly with the use

[191] *Treaty of Alliance between Great Britain and 'Irak*, Baghdad, 10 October 1922 ('1922 Iraqi-Anglo Treaty').

[192] Susan Pedersen, 'Getting out of Iraq – in 1932: The League of Nations and the Road to Normative Statehood', 115 *The American Historical Review* (2010): 975–1000, at 978–9.

of chemical weapons. However, the mandate agreement itself was never signed and instead, even though the League continued to regard Iraq as a 'Class A' mandate, the relationship between Britain and Iraq was in fact consolidated by means of the Alliance of 1922. This treaty represented an effort to find a compromise between the League's expectations of a standard mandatory relationship on the one hand, and nationalist elements within Iraq on the other, and was forced through 'only after High Commissioner Percy Cox shut down nationalist newspapers, proscribed opposition parties, and deported key Shi'i leaders', and made a number of key concessions, including a promise to consider Iraq's candidacy for League membership every four years until it was achieved, starting from 1928.[193]

In effect, this treaty constituted Iraq as a British protectorate. It committed Iraq to British guidance 'on all important matters affecting … international and financial and fiscal policy'.[194] However, it also installed and recognised Faisal Ibn Hussein as the 'constitutional king of Iraq',[195] and drew up the outlines of a new 'Organic Law' – that is, of a constitution for the new Iraqi state. The Organic Law was to include, among other things: 'complete freedom of conscience' (Art. 2); minority rights (Art. 3); 'a sound financial and fiscal policy', to be determined with British assistance (Art. 4); judicial measures to 'safeguard the interests of foreigners' following the adumbration of the [Ottoman] 'capitulations regime' (Art. 9); 'national treatment' for British nationals and firms; MFN provisions; and 'freedom of transit' for all League states (Art. 11). In other words, the treaty's priorities were as much concerned with the protection of foreign and, in particular, British rights to property, commercial exchange, travel and religion as they were with reconstructing the population of Iraq as legal subjects themselves, and far more concerned with both of these than they were with bestowing a meaningful form of independence on Iraq.

By the time the Organic Law was actually passed two years later, however, further concessions had had to be granted in the face of growing unrest. Crucially, however, those concessions took the form of a more robust form of legal subjectivity for Iraqis and Iraq. Thus, Iraq was declared 'a sovereign State, free and independent', possessed of 'inalienable' 'sovereign rights' and a 'representative' government (Art. 2). All Iraqis were declared equal in rights and equal before the law (Arts. 6, 7,

[193] Ibid., 980.
[194] *1922 Iraqi-Anglo Treaty*, Art. 4.
[195] Ibid., Art. 1.

9 and 18), endowed with rights of personal security (Art. 7), freedom of expression and religion (Arts. 12–13), private property rights (Art. 10) and the right (so long as they were male and over 30 years old) to stand for election.[196] The Organic Law, in other words – strikingly similar both in structure and content to the body of 'fundamental laws' laid down for 'national' and 'enemy' states in the post-War minorities and peace treaties – was designed to reconstitute the individuals in the nascent state of Iraq as legal subjects. As the political scientist Adeed Dawisha describes, however, this double 'liberation' for Iraq and Iraqi individuals did little to limit British control over Iraq's political process or economic resources.[197] On the contrary, this control was secured in 1930, in anticipation of Iraq's entry into the League, by a second treaty concluded 'on terms of complete freedom, equality and independence which will become operative upon the entry of Iraq into the League of Nations'.[198] Interestingly, this second treaty, like the Organic Law of 1922, contained no mention of foreign property rights or free trade agreements. However, it did include numerous military commitments concerning two British airbases, the right to move British troops over Iraqi soil, jurisdictional and fiscal immunities for British forces, among other privileges,[199] while the following year, in 1931, the British-owned Iraqi Petroleum Company negotiated a new agreement permitting it to build a new pipeline and extend its exploration rights for a further 25 years.[200] And even if Britain had failed to ensure that the transformation of Iraqis into legal subjects would be accompanied by formal, constitutional protections for the legal subjectivity of 'foreigners', the League itself took up that baton, making Iraq's accession to the Covenant conditional on precisely such commitments.[201] Noting the PMC's conclusion that 'if [a] mandated territory had been required to grant equal economic access to all League states (as Iraq had been), it should grant those states most favored nation status at least for a time' fol-

[196] *Organic Law of Iraq*, annexed to Letter from the British Government to the Secretary-General of the League, 5 August 1924, in *LNOJ* (November 1924): 1759.

[197] See generally Adeed Dawisha, *Iraq: A Political History* (Princeton University Press, 2004), 15–36.

[198] *Treaty of Alliance between His Majesty in respect of the United Kingdom and His Majesty the King of Iraq*, Baghdad, 30 June 1930, Preamble ('1930 Iraqi-Anglo Treaty').

[199] Ibid., Arts. 4–5 and Annexure to Treaty of Alliance.

[200] Pedersen, 'Getting out of Iraq', 989.

[201] Ibid., 989. See Count de Penha Garcia (Portugal), 'General Conditions that must be fulfilled before the mandate regime can be brought to an end in respect of a country placed under that regime', *Minutes of the Permanent Mandates Commission*, 19th Session, 4–19 November 1930, Annex 8.

Figure 6 An official sorts intellectual property titles during the final years of the Chinese Empire, Trades Marks Registration Office, Tientsin (Tianjin), c. 1903–1906. Courtesy of the SOAS Library (Archives and Special Collections), University of London, ref: PP MS 82/2/1/171, by kind permission. Photograph by Reginald Follett Codrington, Commissioner of the Chinese Maritime Customs Service, 1898–1930 © Estate of R. F. C. Hedgeland.

lowing independence, Pedersen describes the Mandates System's 'mix of protections for existing European privileges ... and genuine humanitarian motives' as distinctly 'odd'.[202] Yet when viewed in relation to the shifting, three-dimensional 'background' offered here, the PMC's approach seems, not 'odd', but entirely predictable. For as we have seen, such conditions were typical, not only of the practice of creating new international personalities under the League, but of international legal reproduction in general.

Anghie's key argument with respect to the Mandates System concerns the way in which it allowed 'the discipline of economics itself [to become] all-pervasive', representing 'a new and powerful way of conceptualising and managing mandate territories and their peoples'.[203] This process, which Anghie characterises as the 'economization of sovereignty', ensured, he argues, that Third World international personality came into the world in a 'unique', already less-than-sovereign form.[204] This argu-

[202] Pedersen, 'Getting out of Iraq', 987.
[203] Lugard, *The Dual Mandate*, 581.
[204] Anghie, *Imperialism, Sovereignty and the Making of International Law*, 157.

ment has been criticised quite severely by historians of the Mandates System like Pedersen for depicting the work and impact of the Permanent Mandates Commission as having been far more consistent than it actually was.[205] Yet if my attempt to weave this history into a much longer and wider set of processes is justified, it suggests that if there is any criticism to be made of Anghie here it is that he *under*estimates the consistency with which 'sovereignty' was 'economised' by international legal norms and practices relating to the constitution of new international 'personalities'. 'Sovereignty', on this account, was not 'economised' only in the mandated territories, or indeed only under the League. 'Sovereignty' is 'economised' by definition.

This comes through particularly clearly if we examine the one remaining category of inter-war state which might be expected to have escaped this logic of conditionality altogether, namely the League's 'original' member states, whose claim to be 'self-governing' could – as we saw at the start of this chapter – simply be taken for granted. As the final section will show, however, the conditional nature even of their rights and duties could, in certain circumstances, be revealed.

5 Disciplining the Originals: Liberia and the 'Road from Serfdom'

One might have expected that the League's original members – the 48 Allied and Associated Powers – would have been insulated, by their automatic right to accede to the Covenant, from the kind of intervention experienced by the 'national states' like Poland, 'enemy states' like Germany and 'mandated territories' like Iraq, as well as by later entrants like the Ethiopian Empire, aimed at policing their commitment to the reproduction of 'free' and 'equal' legal subjectivity among their citizens. However, in spite of the fact that more than half of them were non-European,[206] events soon demonstrated that the League's non-European members – even very powerful ones, like Japan, a permanent member of the Council[207] – were more likely than European members to be accused

[205] Susan Pedersen, 'Back to the League of Nations', 112 *American Historical Review* (2007): 1091–117, at 1103–5.

[206] The League's non-European original members were Bolivia, Brazil, Chile, China, Colombia, Costa Rica, Cuba, El Salvador, Guatemala, Haiti, Honduras, Japan, Liberia, Nicaragua, Panama, Paraguay, Persia (Iran), Peru, Siam (Thailand), Uruguay and Venezuela, making up 44 per cent of the total. If the British dominions (Australia, Canada, India, New Zealand and South Africa) are included, the percentage rises to 54 per cent.

[207] Though Japan was one of the 'Big Five' Allied Powers, the Japanese delegation was consistently sidelined during the Paris Peace Conference, and failed in its efforts to have a 'racial

of derogating from the central norm of self-government and hence to have the resilience of their sovereign rights tested. What possible legal basis can there have been for the League to discipline its original members in this way? For reasons of space, I will explore this question through an examination of the disciplinary measures with which the League threatened one such member, the Republic of Liberia.

In 1930, the League of Nations launched an international investigation into allegations that slavery was still being practised systematically in Liberia. The grisly irony of this allegation was not lost on the League's Commission of Inquiry, let alone on Liberians themselves or on members of the African diaspora in the United States, in Latin America, in the Caribbean and elsewhere.[208] Established gradually as a colony from 1822, through the offices of the American Colonisation Society and a series of subsequent organisations (including, at one point during the mid 1920s, Marcus Garvey's Universal Negro Improvement Association), Liberia had been founded, at least in part, for the purpose of offering former slaves in the United States a more genuine form of emancipation than it was possible for them to enjoy at home. It was on this basis that Liberia had declared its independence on 26 July 1847,[209] in order to offer African-Americans the opportunity to become citizens in an independent Black Republic of their own.

The reasons behind Liberia's establishment first as a colony and then as a state are complex; yet in many ways they encapsulate the very precise ideological quality of the promise of legal subjectivity. In the first place, as is well known, the freedom obtained by slaves in the United States following the passage of the Thirteenth Amendment on 31 January 1865 was freedom of a particular kind. Emancipated slaves were offered precisely the

---

equality' clause inserted into the Covenant. See generally Thomas W. Burkman, *Japan and the League of Nations: Empire and World Order, 1914–1938* (Honolulu, HI: University of Hawai'i Press, 2008).

208 For example, both Marcus Garvey and W. E. B. Du Bois took a particular – though severely disaligned – interest in the fate of Liberia. See e.g. Frank Chalk, 'Du Bois and Garvey Confront Liberia: Two Incidents from the Coolridge Years', 1 *Canadian Journal of African Studies / Revue Canadienne des Études Africaines* (1967): 135–42. Du Bois in particular became heavily involved in Liberia's affairs, even becoming Envoy Extraordinary and Minister Plenipotentiary to Liberia on behalf of the Coolidge Government and visiting Liberia several times in a diplomatic capacity. See e.g. W. E. Burghardt Du Bois, 'Liberia, the League and the United States', 11 *Foreign Affairs* (1933): 682–95. For a strong critique of Du Bois's involvement, see Cedric Robinson, 'DuBois and Black Sovereignty: The Case of Liberia', 32 *Race and Class* (1990): 39–50.

209 See Ibrahim Sundiata, *Brothers and Strangers: Black Zion, Black Slavery, 1914–1940* (Durham, NC, London: Duke University Press, 2003), 48–78.

stripped-down form of legal subjectivity associated with 'self-government', including rights to own property, travel, trade, and worship without interference from the state, including, of course, the freedom to offer their labour in exchange for wages. In order to create this liberty, moreover, the right of white individuals to take possession of Black individuals and force them to work against their will and without pay was revoked, giving rise to bitter legal disputes in the US (as in France after the loss of its colony, Saint-Domingue) regarding the question of compensation for the loss of their property.[210] What legal subjectivity for former slaves in the United States did not include (consistently, again, with the idea of 'self-government') was any concession to the idea that the capacity to exercise it would, in practice, be determined by the unequal material resources which these new citizens found at their disposal, or any rights aimed at correcting this imbalance. Indeed, from 1865 onwards, many Southern US states enacted legislation – known at first as the 'Black Codes' and later as the 'Jim Crow' laws – that was designed to have precisely the opposite effect by restricting even these 'civil' rights, thereby guaranteeing that a pool of low-wage or debt-driven labour would remain available to white, settler capital. In this context, creating an independent Black state, Liberia, with a constitution and legal system entirely of its own construction, readily came to seem one of the few, if not the only, feasible means of realising even the strictly negative understanding of freedom that was outlined in the US Constitution – a freedom which emancipation *within* a structurally racist state would evidently continue to thwart.[211]

In the colonial context into which Liberia (like the United States) was born, however, between the now-prohibited legal objectivity of the slave and the materially disadvantaged legal subjectivity of the Black citizen,

[210] Haiti, for example, also a republic of freed slaves, was granted recognition by France only after it agreed to pay France (and French slave-owners) 150 million francs in compensation. In order to do this, Haiti was forced to borrow 24 million francs from private French banks, which lent only at extortionate rates of interest, increasing the overall debt to such an extent that the last repayment was only made in 1947. Peter Hallward, 'Operation Zero in Haiti', 27 *New Left Review* (2004): 23–47, at 28. For two excellent accounts of Haiti's encounter with international law, see Robert Knox, 'Valuing Race? Stretched Marxism and the Logic of Imperialism', 4 *London Review of International Law* (2016): 81–126, esp. 112ff., and Liliana Obregón, 'Empire, Racial Capitalism and International Law: The Case of Manumitted Haiti and the Recognition Debt', 31 *Leiden Journal of International Law* (2018): 597–615.

[211] According to Ibrahim Sundiata, approximately 1,000 African-Americans emigrated to Liberia between 1890 and 1910. 'By the late 1920s,' he writes, '12,000 to 15,000 "Americo-Liberians" lived surrounded by an indigenous population of perhaps 1.5 million.' Sundiata, *Brothers and Strangers*, 28, 24.

there lay an in-between status: that of the 'native', whose collective tutelage towards the attainment of *logos* and full legal subjectivity it was the duty of the 'self-governing' metropole to undertake. It was, arguably, in capitulating to the universalist aspirations of the 'free' and 'equal' subject, with its clearly assimilationist and transformative implications, that the paradox and the tragedy of the Liberian state lay. For in spite of its identification as a Black republic, Liberia's legal order rested from the very beginning on a constitutional division between 'civilised' and 'uncivilised', 'citizens' and 'natives'. Thus, for example, the first Liberian Constitution of 1847, based explicitly on the American Constitution, declared at Article 1 that:

> All men are born equally free and independent, and have certain natural, inherent and unalienable rights; among which, are the rights of enjoying and defending life and liberty, of acquiring, possessing and protecting property and of pursuing and obtaining safety and happiness.[212]

Not all human beings in Liberia, however, were considered to be 'men' for the purposes of the Constitution. On the contrary, only male African-American immigrants and their descendants ('Americo-Liberians') were eligible for citizenship, and only propertied Americo-Liberian men counted as 'men' when it came to the right to vote.[213] 'Natives' or 'aborigines' of the West African land upon which the colony of Liberia had been established did not, whether male or female.[214] Instead, in an echo of the Berlin Act, the 1847 Liberian Constitution pronounced '[t]he improvement of the native tribes and their advancement in the arts of agriculture and husbandry' to be 'a cherished object of [the Liberian] government'.[215] That Liberia's Indigenous peoples, composed of at least sixteen separate ethnic groups, each belonging to one of three linguistic units corresponding to three languages (Mel, Mande and Kwa), possessed long and complex histories of interaction both with each other and with the peculiar characteristics of Liberia's natural environment (simultaneously sandy,

[212] *Constitution of the Commonwealth of Liberia*, 26 July 1847 ('1847 Liberian Constitution'), Art. 1, Section 1 ('1847 Liberian Constitution').

[213] Ibid., Art. 1, Sec. 11.

[214] The Commission contrasted the Liberian government's 'gross exploitation and subjugation' of its 'natives' with the situation in 'other tropical African administrations' in which, it insisted, 'the native hinterland community of tribes has received first consideration'. *Report of the International Commission of Inquiry into the Existence of Slavery and Forced Labour in the Republic of Liberia*, Monrovia, 8 September 1930 (Washington: US Department of State, 1931), 139 ('Liberia Commission Inquiry').

[215] 1847 Liberian Constitution, Art. 5, Section 15.

swampy and mountainous) – giving rise to equally complex and well-weathered systems of production and reproduction centred on yam cultivation, fishing and limited stock-raising, held together with a patrilineal system of land allocation – was of no consequence to a nascent legal system centred on the negative freedom and formal equality of 'rational' individuals.[216] The 'natives' of the new Liberian colony-turned-state, in other words, lacked not only property itself (a prerequisite for voting, as we have seen), but also a concept of private property along European lines. Confronted with this fact, the authors of the 1847 Constitution apparently took a dim view of their capacity to develop the 'rationality' necessary for them to appreciate the benefits of 'these wholesome branches of industry', let alone for formal political participation and citizenship.

After Liberia declared its independence in 1847 on the basis of this Constitution, few states, with the exception of the US, had any hesitation in recognising it. Indeed, by 1861 it had been recognised as a sovereign equal by Britain, France, the Hanseatic Republics, Belgium, Denmark, Italy, the Netherlands, Holland, Sweden, Norway, Haiti, Portugal and Denmark. How is this recognition to be explained, given what we know about the contempt in which the leaders and officials of these states, together with the legal scholars and social scientists of their time, held individuals of African descent? One element of the legal history of Liberia's transformation into a sovereign state which might help make sense of this counter-intuitive recognition practice concerns the commitment displayed by the new Liberian Government to guaranteeing the legal subjectivity of Americo-Liberians (at least) as well as foreign citizens.

British recognition, for example, was forthcoming in the form of a Treaty of Friendship and Commerce, concluded with Liberia on 21 November 1848.[217] The main purpose of this treaty was spelled out in Article 2:

> There shall be reciprocal freedom of commerce between the British dominions and the Republic of Liberia. The subjects of Her Britannic Majesty may reside in, and trade to, any part of the territories of the Republic to which any other foreigners are or shall be admitted. They shall enjoy full protection for their persons and properties; they shall be allowed to buy from and to sell to whom they like, without being restrained or prejudiced by any monopoly, contract or exclusive privilege of sale or purchase whatever; and they shall moreover enjoy all other rights and privileges

[216] Sundiata, *Brothers and Strangers*, 50–1.

[217] *Treaty of Friendship and Commerce between the United Kingdom of Great Britain and Ireland and Liberia*, London, 21 November 1848.

> which are or may be granted to any other foreigners, subjects or citizens of the most favoured nation. The citizens of the Republic of Liberia shall, in return, enjoy similar protection and privileges in the dominions of Her Britannic Majesty.[218]

This was standard practice, of course, as we shall see further in the following chapter's examination of the Ethiopian Empire's transformation into a sovereign state. Great Britain was concluding almost identical treaties, at the time, to confirm its recognition of Costa Rica (1849), following its 1838 declaration of independence;[219] Peru (1850), following the re-establishment of constitutional government in the wake of the civil war of 1842–45;[220] El Salvador (1862);[221] the United States of Colombia (1866), in the wake of its promulgation of the liberal 'Constitution of Rionegro' of 8 May 1863;[222] Paraguay (1884), following the introduction of a liberal constitution in 1870;[223] and Honduras (1887), following its adoption of a liberal constitution in 1880,[224] in a process that has been described by John Gallagher and Ronald Robinson as the 'imperialism of free trade' in and through the establishment of 'informal empire'.[225] The effect, in this case, was to ensure that the legal subjectivity of British and Liberian citizens (though not of Liberian 'natives') would be 'effective' in both jurisdictions. The treaty went on to reiterate the prohibition on slavery which was then making its way into customary international law, specifying that Liberia would 'perpetually [abolish]' both '[s]lavery and the slave trade', indicating that at the very least its 'natives' would be permitted to earn wages and own/exchange property, rather than being appropriated and commodified themselves.[226] Unusually, when compared with these other jurisdictions, the 1847 Liberian Constitution restricted citizenship to

[218] Ibid., Art. 2.

[219] *Treaty of Friendship, Commerce and Navigation between the United Kingdom of Great Britain and Ireland and Costa Rica*, San José, 27 November 1849.

[220] *Treaty of Friendship, Commerce and Navigation between the United Kingdom of Great Britain and Ireland and Peru*, London, 10 April 1850.

[221] *Treaty of Friendship, Commerce and Navigation between the United Kingdom of Great Britain and Ireland and El Salvador*, Guatemala, 24 October 1862.

[222] *Treaty of Friendship, Commerce and Navigation between the United Kingdom of Great Britain and Ireland and Colombia*, London, 16 February 1866.

[223] *Treaty of Friendship, Commerce and Navigation between the United Kingdom of Great Britain and Ireland and Paraguay*, Buenos Aires, 16 October 1884.

[224] *Treaty of Friendship, Commerce and Navigation between the United Kingdom of Great Britain and Ireland and Honduras, and Protocol*, Guatemala, 21 January 1887.

[225] John Gallagher and Ronald Robinson, 'The Imperialism of Free Trade', 6 *The Economic History Review* (1953): 1–15.

[226] *Treaty of Friendship and Commerce between Great Britain and Liberia*, Art. 9.

'Negroes or persons of Negro descent',[227] and limited the right to hold 'real estate' to such citizens.[228] In practice, however, this had little effect on the provisions for formal equality that underpinned the Anglo-Liberian treaty. As the Firestone Tire and Rubber Company discovered in 1926, for example, this restriction on fee simple property rights did not rule out its right to obtain a renewable 99-year lease on one million acres of Liberian land, together with exclusive rights to the extraction of resources and sweeping tax exemptions.[229]

From the United States, however, recognition of Liberia was not forthcoming until 5 February 1862. As the historian Charles H. Wesley pointed out as early as 1917, Liberia's treatment here was on a par with Haiti's.[230] Though Haiti had also been recognised by many states by this point, including (at an extortionate price) even by France,[231] the US held off until 1862, in spite of the pleas of US industrialists.[232] The reason in both cases was clear. Prior to and for some months after the presidential victory of Abraham Lincoln in 1860, which triggered the attempted secession of the Southern slaving states in February 1861, pro-slavery Senators in Congress voiced powerful arguments against the recognition of Liberia and Haiti, pointing out that to recognise these states would also be to recognise the 'freedom' and 'equality' of individual Liberian citizens. In recognising the equality of Liberia and Haiti as international personalities, the United States (these representatives pointed out) could not avoid acknowledging Liberia's citizens as legal subjects. For example, as Senator Garrett Davis (Kentucky) had argued in response to a bill of 4 February

227 1847 Liberian Constitution, Art. 5, Section 13.

228 Ibid., Art. 5, Item 12.

229 Du Bois, 'Liberia, the League and the United States', 684.

230 For an excellent account of Haiti's path to 'sovereign statehood' see Knox, 'Stretched Marxism', 112–26.

231 As noted above (Item 2, Section 2.1.4), the condition upon which French recognition of Haiti was granted was Haiti's accession to an 'ordinance' issued directly by Charles X in which it agreed to pay France 150 million francs in compensation for the loss of the latter's slaves, in addition to opening its ports up 'to the commerce of all nations', and setting up a tariff regime in which 'duties levied in these ports either on ships or merchandise at the times of their entry or departure shall be equal and uniform for all nations except for the French flag, on behalf of which these duties are to be reduced to half the amount'. Ordinance of 17 April, 1825, accepted by Haiti on 4 July 1825, cited in Jacques Nicolas Léger, *Haiti: Her History and Her Detractors* (New York, Washington, DC: The Neale Publishing Company, 1907), Pt. I, Ch. 12, para. 184.

232 Charles H. Wesley, 'The Struggle for the Recognition of Haiti and Liberia as Independent Republics', 2 *The Journal of Negro History* (1917): 369–83. According to Wesley, 'in 1860, out of sixty countries trading with the United States, Haiti stood 27th and Liberia 29th'. Ibid., 378, n. 46.

1862 calling for the joint recognition of Haiti and Liberia: 'If a full-blooded Negro were sent in that capacity [of Minister Plenipotentiary or Chargé d'Affairs] from either of the two countries, by the laws of nations he could demand that he be received precisely on the same terms of equality with the white representative from the powers on the earth composed of white people.'[233] And if that were permitted to happen, he went on, how, then, could such recognition be denied to the newly emancipated Black citizens of the United States, let alone to those who remained enslaved? Such a contradiction, these Senators warned, would call forth an anger borne of injustice – a fury of interpellative rage, one might say – that would be impossible for the existing system to contain.

Eventually, however, commercial considerations won the day and both Liberia and Haiti were recognised by the US in the early 1860s.[234] The terms upon which recognition was granted were much the same as they had been in the British case:

> There shall be reciprocal freedom of commerce between the United States of America and the Republic of Liberia. The citizens of the United States of America may reside in, and trade to, any part of the territories of the Republic of Liberia to which any other foreigners are or shall be admitted. They shall enjoy full protection for their persons and properties, they shall be allowed to buy from and to sell to whom they like without being restrained or prejudiced by any monopoly, contract, or exclusive privilege of sale or purchase whatever; and they shall moreover enjoy all other rights and privileges which are or may be granted to any other foreigners, subjects or citizens of the most favoured nation. The citizens of the Republic of Liberia shall, in return, enjoy similar privileges in the United States of America and in their territories.[235]

The thinking which lay behind this recognition was articulated succinctly by the American Colonization Society (ACS) a few years later, in a memorial to Congress.[236] 'Africa at this day attracts the attention of the whole

[233] Senator Garrett Davis (Kentucky), 37th Congress, 2nd Session, quoted in Wesley, 'The Struggle', 380–1.

[234] *Treaty of Commerce and Navigation between the United States of America and the Republic of Liberia*, London, 21 October 1862 ('US-Liberia Treaty of Commerce and Navigation'); *Treaty of Amity, Commerce, and Navigation; Extradition between the United States of America and the Republic of Hayti* [*sic*], Port-au-Prince, 3 November 1864 ('US-Haiti Treaty of Amity, Commerce, and Navigation').

[235] US-Liberia Treaty of Commerce and Navigation, Art. 2. For the equivalent, see US-Haiti Treaty of Amity, Commerce, and Navigation, Arts. 2, 5 and 6.

[236] H. B. Latrobe (President), *Memorial of the American Colonization Society praying An Appropriation for the Purpose of Making Explorations and Surveys on the Western Coast of Africa, and from Liberia into the Interior of that Continent, with a View to Building Up*

civilized world because of the vast market that it affords for the relief of both Europe and America from the overproductiveness of manufacturing industry.'[237] Underscoring once again the connection between state recognition and commerce, the ACS noted that Britain had been 'the first to recognise the independence of the colored republic, and make a commercial treaty with it'.[238] Nonetheless, it continued, 'Liberia is of America, though her people are the descendants of Africans', and it urged the US Government to allocate new funds to the exploration of Liberia's 'interior', which it described as a 'fertile and thickly-inhabited country', resplendent not only with natural resources but also with 'natives' whose labour-power, and 'vast market' the United States should not miss the opportunity of exploiting.[239]

As in the case of the Chinese Empire (as we saw in Item 2) and as with the Ethiopian Empire (as we shall see in Items 4, 5 and 6), however, the reciprocal recognition afforded both to the sovereign rights of Liberia and to the individual rights of Liberian citizens in these commercial treaties masked a relationship of ongoing subordination. Few Liberians, after all, possessed the resources to claim these reciprocal rights in the United States, and Liberia's only significant export – rubber – left not only its economy but also its political establishment uncomfortably exposed to the demands of those rare foreign corporations that were willing to risk their capital on a Liberian enterprise. So desperate was the need for foreign investment by the mid 1920s that Firestone Co. was able to condition the Concession Agreement it eventually negotiated with the Liberian Government on the latter's assumption of a loan of US$5,000,000, from a bank (the Finance Corporation of Liberia) established by Firestone itself specifically for that purpose. Under that Concession Agreement, the Liberian Government leased Firestone one million acres of land (nearly 10 per cent of the country's arable land), offered it a tax exemption in perpetuity and undertook to guarantee the Company an adequate supply of labour.[240] Many Liberian officials were already, by this time, profiting from their role in supplying 'native' labour, often under duress and in appalling conditions, to the nearby Spanish colony of Fernando Pó (Bioko, today part of Equatorial Guinea). This new

American Trade and Commerce Therewith, 12 February 1879, Senate of the United States, 45th Congress, 3rd Session, Mis. Doc. 65: 1–3 at 1.

[237] Ibid., 2.

[238] Ibid., 2.

[239] Ibid., 2.

[240] Sundiata, *Brothers and Strangers*, 115.

demand therefore put enormous pressure on the 'native' labour supply, and created new sources of rent for Americo-Liberian middle-men, who took it upon themselves to 'encourage' men from the villages to work on Firestone's rubber plantations. Within a few years, Firestone's insatiable demands for labour, its establishment, in its Liberian plantations, of its own racially segregated 'white imperium in the Black Republic',[241] and the near-impossible burden represented by the repayments due both on the Firestone loan and on two other equally burdensome international loan agreements had thrown the Liberian Government into an acute crisis.[242] Events came to a head when, after his defeat in the openly fraudulent 1927 presidential elections, Thomas J. R. Faulkner published a harrowing exposé of labour conditions in Liberia.[243] According to the historian Ibrahim Sundiata, it was in order to deflect attention from Firestone's role in creating these conditions, and hence from its own role in supporting the company, that the United States launched a 'pre-emptive strike' by insisting on a full-scale League of Nations investigation into slavery in Liberia.[244]

The Report of the League's International Commission of Inquiry, delivered on 30 December 1930, offers a remarkable testament not only to the conditional nature of international personality in the Liberian context but also to the nature and purpose of that conditionality. The Commission found that 'classic slavery carrying the idea of slave markets and slave dealers no longer exists as such in the Republic of Liberia'.[245] However, the Liberian Government was reprimanded for having failed to stamp out several other forms of human servitude. Most important among the Commission's targets in this context was the recruitment, with the complicity of government officials and 'under conditions of criminal compulsion scarcely distinguishable from slave raiding and slave trading', of thousands of 'native' Liberian 'boys' for export, primarily to Fernando Pó.[246] The practice of human 'pawning' and the persistence of 'domestic' slavery, along with the widespread use of forced labour for private rather

241 Ibid., 226.

242 See Fred P. M. van der Kraaij, *The Open Door Policy of Liberia: An Economic History of Modern Liberia* (Bremen: Im Selbstverlag des Museums, 1983), 12–46. These loan agreements, dating from 1871 and 1906, had been agreed with a British company, the Liberian Development Company, run by Sir Harry Johnston. For Sir Harry's opinions about slavery in the Ethiopian Empire of the 1920s, see Item 5, Section 1.1.

243 Sundiata, *Brothers and Strangers*, 123–4.

244 Ibid., 124.

245 Liberia Commission Report, 83.

246 Ibid., 84.

than permitted (ILO-sanctioned) purposes, was also condemned.[247] More generally, the Liberian Government was castigated for its systematic mistreatment of its 'native' population. 'In order to suppress the native', the Commissioners wrote, 'and prevent him from asserting himself in any way whatever, for the benefit of the dominant and colonising race, although originally of the same African stock as themselves, a policy of gross intimidation and suppression has for years been systematically fostered and encouraged.'[248]

One crucial thing to note about the Report, moreover, is that while the League Commission did acknowledge certain problems concerning the Firestone plantations, it placed no responsibility whatsoever for the conditions which were then being inflicted on Liberia's labour force with Firestone itself, or with Liberia's wholly unmanageable external debt (much of it, as we have seen, likewise owned by Firestone). On the contrary, the Liberian Government's failure to employ 'modern' techniques of colonial administration in relation to this 'native' population was the circumstance singled out for blame. The problem, according to the Commission, was not that the 'natives' had been exploited by Firestone or excluded from the rights associated with citizenship. Rather, it was that they were not being properly trained by the Liberian Government in the rationality which eventual citizenship within this (already) self-governing state would require.[249] To return to Vitoria's Aristotelian logic, outlined in Item 2, the natives were not being properly exposed to *logos*, thus undermining the legitimacy, and therefore the sovereign rights, of Liberia as a person of international law. As this suggests, the Commission agreed wholeheartedly with the Liberian Government's assumption that the country's 'natives' lacked the rational capacity to hold and exercise the civil rights laid out in the Constitution. The problem, for the Commission, was that they would *continue* to lack it unless Liberia was prepared to take proper responsibility for their 'advancement'.[250] It was, moreover, self-evident, for the Commission, that the Liberian Government's 'policy of the "closed door"' lay at the 'root of the financial and other major difficulties in which the country is now involved', 'imped[ing] development by masking maladministration, discouraging research, delaying civilization and education, preventing competition and generally stifling commercial

[247] Ibid., 83.
[248] Ibid., 86.
[249] Ibid., 84–5.
[250] Ibid., 86.

enterprise'.[251] This 'policy of suppression and seclusion for fear of competition', the Commission insisted, could only lead 'to a condition of delayed development, bankruptcy, and final failure', and was 'bound to foster ill-treatment, extortion, and coercion of the natives'.[252] Under such a policy, 'the native must continue his harried existence with a feeling that he is really and truly a slave'.[253]

Having made this connection between the absence of commercial 'freedom' on the one hand and human bondage on the other, the Commission put its 'plan of assistance' on the table – a plan remarkably similar, as we shall see in Item 6, to that devised for the Ethiopian Empire in an effort to compromise with fascist Italy's demands. Liberia was to undertake a 'complete and urgent reorganisation of the government of the interior' along the lines of the familiar 'open-door policy', and this reorganisation was to be overseen by a series of League-appointed 'foreign advisors'.[254] Only by this means could 'the future stability of the Republic ... be secured, or alternatively saved from failure'.[255] Central to this internationally supervised plan for 'reorganisation' would be a programme of extensive internal economic integration, designed to connect the 'interior' with the coastline through the establishment of internal trading routes. Indeed, this imperative of 'opening up' the 'interior' to commerce was an even more urgent imperative, for the Commission, than the abolition of forced labour in Liberia.[256] For there was, it argued, 'a certain educative advantage in compulsory labour' when 'advanced and backward cultures are in contact'.[257] However, once this educative effect had taken root and a 'rational' labour force of willing, self-allocating workers created, the advantage would be even greater.[258] A programme of 'native' education was therefore to be undertaken at the earliest opportunity, aimed specifically at transforming the 'native' mentality into that of a freely participating market actor, who no longer needed to be coerced into meeting the legitimate demand

[251] Ibid., 84.
[252] Ibid., 137.
[253] Ibid., 137.
[254] Ibid., 141.
[255] Ibid.
[256] Sundiata, *Brothers and Strangers*, 223–8; Doreen Lustig, 'The Loss of Slavery as a Humanitarian Cause? The League of Nations and the Case of Firestone in Liberia', available at http://weblaw.haifa.ac.il/en/Events/IntlLaborLaw/Documents/Doreen.pdf (accessed 11 September 2017).
[257] *Liberia Commission Report*, 47.
[258] Ibid.

for labour of multinational companies like Firestone.[259] Education, the Commission argued, to underscore the point:

> heads the list where enterprising development is to be considered. Schools are of the first importance ... for broadening [the native's] ideas, teaching him market values, and the use he can make of the innumerable economic products and raw materials around him. With such incentives, trade and peaceful intercommunication follow. The unsophisticated native learns something of the world and his wants are increased. The missionary, school teacher, and the trader teach him what he may buy for his money, and he then wants to learn what he can grow, what he should do, or where he should work to make some, with the result that trade increases, the coast merchant flourishes, the revenues of Government expand, and money is forthcoming for more educational centres, for the construction of roads and transport facilities, and the payment of salaries, and the institution of further methods of general development.[260]

The Report then delivered its *coup de grace* by reminding Liberia that its rights and duties as a sovereign state were not held unconditionally. On the contrary, those rights and duties, the Commissioners insinuated, had been allocated to Liberia in exchange not only for its commitments to protecting the 'free' and 'equal' rights of its own citizens and those of visiting foreign citizens, but also to the gradual tutelage of its 'natives' such that they, too, might become (as Eslava has put it) 'self-disciplining' or 'self-ruled' legal subjects themselves.[261] In short, Liberia was under an obligation to live up to its self-identification as a 'self-governing' state in order that Liberians (including, eventually, 'the natives') should become 'self-governing' subjects. If it refused to accede to this League-supervised programme of 'reorganisation', the League Commission warned, Liberia

[259] See e.g. Ibid., 84.

[260] Ibid., 137.

[261] Discussing the *Bantu Education Kinema Experiment*, an inter-war project involving the production of silent educational films to be screened to 'native' people in the British protectorates and mandates in Tanganyika, Kenya, Uganda, Northern Rhodesia and Nyasaland, Eslava argues that '[t]he transition from colonial subjects and territories to citizens and nations could be seen ... as the final fulfilment' of the 'modern form of international administration that emerged in the interwar period', based on the idea of 'indirect rule'. This era 'brought into being ... a world in which direct commands have largely been replaced by a whole plethora of tightly-supervised processes of individual self-disciplining, which are increasingly more decentralized, localized and individualized'. However, at the same time, 'it also generated an increasingly multi-located and dynamic system in which relations of command continue to occur, but in such a way that the chains of causality become progressively more difficult, if not impossible, to define'. Eslava, 'The Moving Location of Empire', 565.

might 'discover that its place in the community of civilised nations is jeopardised'.[262]

In proposing the expansion of the 'free' market explicitly as the antidote to human bondage, the Commission juxtaposed formal economic liberty against physical servitude, not just metaphorically but materially. In doing so, it travelled precisely the same path, though in the opposite direction, as Friedrich Hayek would 14 years later in *The Road to Serfdom*.[263] This, perhaps, is only to be expected, given the very close relationship between those of the League considered to be experts on non-European governance, notably Rappard, and Hayek himself.[264] Like Vitoria's 'Indians', Liberia's 'aborigines' occupied the position of 'natural slaves' in this logic, entitled to be 'free' in the sense of being permitted to participate in the market as wage-earners and consumers, but not considered capable of being 'free' or 'sovereign' at the collective level without external and mandatory 'tutelage' from a state that was already 'self-governing' – in this case, the Republic of Liberia itself. Their continued colonisation could only benefit them, therefore, as long as that colonisation was not dedicated to straightforward exploitation, but rather to imparting to them, gradually, the mentality of the *homo economicus*, whose participation in the 'free' market would arise voluntarily, rather than requiring them to be coerced. If Liberia reneged on its commitments, not only towards its citizens and foreign citizens, but also towards its proto-citizens, in this sense, its *own* 'self-governing' credentials as a sovereign state would find themselves hanging in the balance.

Against all the odds, however, the Liberian Government managed to fend off the imposition of the League's 'plan of assistance' – to the bitter disappointment of Indigenous groups within Liberia, who welcomed the prospect of League intervention against a government by whom they had for so long been systematically excluded and exploited. For

[262] *Liberia Commission Report*, 144.

[263] Friedrich A. Hayek [1944], *The Road to Serfdom* (University of Chicago Press, 1994).

[264] For example, William Rappard, Director of the League's Mandates Section, a member of the Permanent Mandates Commission throughout its existence, and Swiss Representative at the ILO, delivered the keynote address at the inaugural meeting of the Mont Pelerin Society after the War, on 10 April 1947. Founded by Hayek, the Mont Pelerin Society was the first and remains the most influential international neoliberal organisation. Its objective is to counter the threat posed to 'human dignity and freedom' (described as the foundations of the 'civilisation' of 'Western Man') by what it saw, in 1947, as the 'growth of theories which question the desirability of the rule of law' and by 'a decline of belief in private property and the competitive market'. See 'Statement of Aims', The Mont Pelerin Society, at www.montpelerin.org/statement-of-aims/ (accessed 22 February 2018).

example, Senyon Juah Nimley, Paramount Chief of Sasstown, the largest of the five original Kru towns (established on the south-eastern coast of what became Liberia possibly as early as the 1500s), and a personal victim of the Liberian Government's coercive practices, wrote to Cecil in February 1934: 'our hearts are broken since we heard that the Liberians have rejected the League's Plan'.[265] Notwithstanding intense diplomatic pressure (though falling short of the military invasion which Firestone had demanded repeatedly from the US Government since 1932 when, under the Presidentship of Edwin Barclay, Liberia had announced a moratorium on repayments on the Firestone loan), Liberia rejected the plan in 1934. In spite of the urgings of Lord Lugard and the British Minister for Foreign Affairs, Anthony Eden, among others, it was agreed that Liberia's expulsion from the League should not be put before the Council, as a unanimous decision could not be guaranteed.[266] The 'plan of assistance' was accordingly withdrawn on 18 May 1934.

By this time, however, the Liberian Government had taken matters into its own hands, presenting Firestone suddenly with $100,000 in debt repayments in February of that year,[267] and issuing its three-year 'development plan' the following year. This was, in effect, a watered-down version of the League 'plan of assistance', complete with six appointed 'foreign specialists' who (as Firestone had long been demanding) were all US citizens. Enticed by rising rubber prices, the company came back to the negotiating table, and in March 1935 it signed a 'supplementary' loan agreement[268] and a new plantation agreement[269] with the Liberian Government. In return for reducing the interest rate on Liberia's loan, Firestone was given further sweeping tax exemptions, together with an exclusive right to explore and mine minerals on the land it had under lease, subject to a royalty of no more than 10 per cent on 'precious metals and precious stones', and a right to set up its own airfields and operate a radio communications

[265] Nimley to Cecil, 28 February 1934, quoted in Sundiata, *Brothers and Strangers*, 270.

[266] Sundiata, *Brothers and Strangers*, 183–4.

[267] Ibid., 194.

[268] *Agreement between the Government of Liberia and the Finance Corporation of America*, 16 March 1935, 882.6176F51/4118/*11*, in *Foreign Relations of the United States Diplomatic Papers*, 1935, General, The Near East and Africa, Vol. I, available at https://history.state.gov/historicaldocuments/frus1935v01/d810 (accessed 10 September 2017).

[269] *Agreement between the Government of Liberia and Firestone Plantations Company*, Freetown, 20 March 1935, 882.6176F51/41110/11, in *Foreign Relations of the United States*, at https://history.state.gov/historicaldocuments/frus1935v01/d811 (accessed 10 September 2017) ('Supplementary Plantations Agreement').

system.[270] Barely eight weeks later, the United States granted co-ordinated diplomatic recognition to the Edwin Barclay administration (which had previously been withdrawn in 1932 in response to the moratorium) on the grounds that this would be the most effective means by which to 'encourag[e] President Barclay to carry out his proposals, and ... [seek] their amplification along the lines laid down in the League Plan'.[271] Britain followed suit in December 1936.

As Liberia's encounter with the League's nascent disciplinary apparatus underscored, slavery, or legal objectivity, was indeed no longer tolerable for international law within a sovereign ('self-governing') state. Yet it was the prospect of fresh profits that new legal protections for international capital and trade would guarantee which determined when Black individuals would be treated as 'self-governing' legal subjects, and when they would be treated merely as 'natives', whose engagement with the market required external 'encouragement'. Liberia, a Black polity which had unilaterally identified as a 'self-governing' state, and which had proved its determination to protect the rights of foreign individuals and corporations, was encountered – ultimately – as sovereign (if, perhaps, not quite *as* sovereign as, say, the United States or Britain). When combined with its efforts to avoid repaying its vast international debts, Liberia's brutal exploitation of its Indigenous population was nearly enough to trigger its expulsion from the League. Yet the problem here was not the exploitation per se, but rather its objective. Forced labour for the personal gain of corrupt government officials was frowned upon, but forced labour aimed at educating the 'native' in market forces was regarded as quite another thing. In this context, the compulsory integration of the 'native' into national and international labour and commodity markets became, not a violation of the universal right to equal freedom, but rather a training in the art of rationality, and hence an apprenticeship for 'free' and 'equal' legal subjectivity or citizenship, whose universal uptake it was the Liberian Government's responsibility to ensure.

[270] Ibid., Art. 2, paras. (a)–(g).

[271] British Ambassador (Ronald Lindsay) to the Secretary of State, Washington, 17 January 1935, in *Foreign Relations of the United States Diplomatic Papers, 1935, General, The Near East and Africa*, Vol. I, available at https://history.state.gov/historicaldocuments/frus1935v01/d806 (accessed 10 September 2017); Minister in Liberia (Lester A. Walton) to the Secretary of State, Monrovia, 19 December 1936, in *Foreign Relations of the United States Diplomatic Papers, 1935, General, The Near East and Africa*, Vol. I, available at https://history.state.gov/historicaldocuments/frus1936v03/d500 (accessed 10 September 2017).

6 Conclusion: Sovereignty, Always-Already 'Economised'

In her recent and very important history of the Mandates System, Pedersen describes the League of Nations as 'an association of sovereign states that many of its supporters hoped would evolve into something much greater – a genuine association of peoples, an embryonic world government'. Unfortunately, she argues, '[t]hose hopes were always utopian, for the League was founded upon and remained devoted to the principle of state sovereignty'.[272] This is a familiar critique of the League, common both to early scholarship, emphasising its supposed 'failure', and to more recent work like Pedersen's, focused on its objectives and its debates over their implementation. When the various fragments of League-era history that I have glued together in this 'item' are stacked into the shadowbox, however, this critique appears somehow to miss the mark. Far from being 'devoted to the principle of state sovereignty', what is so interesting about the League, is, on the contrary, its dedication to the task of bringing into being and policing an incredibly complex and intricate hierarchy of greater and lesser 'sovereigns', some of which were states, and some of which were not. Certainly, the sovereign state provided the template against which all the League's experiments in the field of international legal reproduction were measured. However, if we direct our spotlight, not at the question of statehood itself, but instead at the process through which the League's many and diverse subjects obtained their 'sovereign' rights and duties, and subsequently came to be held to the commitments they made during this process, the theory and practice of the League of Nations starts to look not only remarkably successful, but also distinctly continuous with the practice of the previous era – and, indeed (as the Lid will suggest), with the practice of our own era.

The project of bringing into being and policing a self-governing hierarchy of international legal subjects (disciplinable from outside if necessary) was not one that the League invented for itself, as Item 2 has already shown. On the contrary, what was revolutionary about the League was the enthusiasm with which it devoted itself to intensifying and perfecting an international legal process that had been foundational to the discipline's doctrine and practice since its first stirrings in the late-fifteenth century. This process, as we have seen, concerns the gradual extension, consolidation and reproduction of the very specific constellation of rights and duties which not only create the ideal conditions for unhampered

[272] Pedersen, 'Back to the League', 1116.

capital accumulation, but also ensure that participation in the market no longer requires coercion but is, on the contrary, entered into 'freely' by the micro and macro subjects involved. Returning to Anghie's analysis of the Mandates System, one might characterise this as a process aimed at ensuring that sovereignty is *inherently* 'economised' – not only in the case of former mandated territories, but in all but the most primordial of international law's 'personalities'.[273]

Having laid this League era background into the theoretical Frame, on top of the 'long' background contained in Item 2, itself juxtaposed against the standard account of the Abyssinia Crisis offered in Item 1, the following three Items are concerned with the legal history of the Ethiopian Empire, tracking its transformation from a *sui generis* East African polity into a sovereign state, only to have that sovereignty extinguished (temporarily) by another such state. Like the other illustrations we have encountered so far, from Vitoria's 'Indians' to the Chinese Empire to the Republic of Liberia, Ethiopia's encounter with international law underscores the material nature of the connection between international and individual subjectivity, and the role of the criteria for statehood, and of 'government' in particular, in constituting this connection. Attending to this process, I will suggest, offers us a new and potentially much more radical response to the question of why the sovereignty of some international 'people' seems more resistant in some situations, and at some moments, than that in others.

However, Items 4, 5 and 6 will also focus much more strongly on two aspects of the process of international legal reproduction that have, so far, only been hinted at. These are, firstly, the inevitably hybrid nature of international personality as constituted in and through that process of international legal reproduction; and secondly, the question of what space this process leaves for resistance, and what shape that resistance is able to take. As we shall see, one of the things that Ethiopia's experience of passing through the process of international legal reproduction illustrates very clearly is how inherently uncompletable this process is, both in theory and in practice. As post-colonial theorists including Frantz Fanon,[274] Gayatri Chakravorty Spivak,[275] Homi Bhabha and

[273] Anghie, *Imperialism, Sovereignty*, 157.

[274] Frantz Fanon [1952], *Black Skin, White Masks*, trans. Charles Lam Markmann (London: Pluto Press, 1986).

[275] Gayatri Chakravorty Spivak, 'Can the Subaltern Speak?' in Cary Nelson and Lawrence Grossberg (eds.), *Marxism and the Interpretation of Culture* (Urbana, IL, Chicago, IL: University of Illinois Press, 1988), 271–313.

others have pointed out at the level of the individual 'colonial subject', the process of being forced to transform oneself from something 'other' into an approximation of the (supposedly universal, but in fact fundamentally European) 'self' in order to be 'recognised' is an unrelentingly violent one which the 'other' – compelled to meet standards which are inherently foreign – can never fully achieve by definition.[276] Similarly, Ethiopia's experience of attempting to transform itself into an international legal 'self' or subject which other such subjects could 'recognise' left it marked by indelible flecks of alterity. In practice, since only a tiny handful of the world's polities are, in fact, Western European, what this means is that the process through which the vast majority of the world's states were 'emancipated' is one and the same process as that which ensures their ongoing subjection to a process of relentless resource extraction. It is in this sense that we can think about international legal subjectivity as fundamentally mixed, split or hybrid. However, in arguing that this experience of conditionality and hybridity is the norm rather than the exception for international law's subjects, my intention is not to sideline the clearly racialised dimensions of international legal reproduction. It is, instead, to work out precisely how race and racism operate in this process – not as a condition or 'standard of civilisation' per se, but instead as the marker which stands in for another criterion: the benchmark of 'self-government', or, simply, 'government'.

The purpose of the following three items is to demonstrate that the claim of hybridity does in fact, as Bakhtin proposes,[277] operate in the material sphere, beyond the sphere of metaphor. That is to say, the term 'hybrid' describes a central aspect of what the Ethiopian Empire actually *was*, in an ontological sense, from the perspective of other states, their officials, their official documents, and therefore for international law itself. For as we are about to see, throughout the eighteenth, nineteenth and early twentieth centuries, Ethiopia was consistently encountered and narrated as a hybrid entity, not only by the European social scientists who took it upon themselves to produce the knowledge about this polity upon which state officials then based their own assessments, but also by the Ethiopian ruling class itself. These two bodies of knowledge were taken up both by state officials and by international lawyers themselves, to become embedded, in a material sense, in the personality of the Ethiopian Empire itself in a process that was expressly designed to transfigure this outlandish polity

[276] See above, Frame, Section 3.2.

[277] See above, Frame, Section 3.

into something more familiar and, therefore, more accessible to foreign individuals and firms and to their capital. Yet, as Bakhtin's insights also suggest, hybridity as a condition also brings with it a potential for resistance – a potential which Ethiopian officials re-deployed in their efforts to resist international law's demands that they relinquish their own norms and institutions and transform their Empire ever more fully into that supposedly universal legal and institutional apparatus: the 'self-governing' state.

Item No. 4

Empire des Nègres Blancs: The Emergence of the Ethiopian Empire as a Subject of International Law

This, the fourth item in the shadow-box, begins with a brief introduction to the history and historiography of the Ethiopian Empire. Together, Sections 1 and 2 underscore the way in which Ethiopia has been 'depicted with multiple personalities' in the scholarly tradition, as the historian Teshale Tibebu has argued.[1] Section 3 then analyses the Ethiopian Empire's encounter with international law from the mid nineteenth century up to the First World War – an encounter which, I argue, transformed it into a hybrid subject of international law not just metaphorically, but also juridically. Finally, in Section 4, I examine the impact of this encounter on Ethiopian understandings of what it was, in the Abyssinian normative universe, to be the Ethiopian Empire. As we shall see, the Ethiopian Empire's metamorphosis from a polity defined on its own terms into a 'sovereign state' was brought about both by the threat or use of force *and* through the production of desire on the part of Ethiopia and Ethiopians themselves. This case, though in many ways deeply idiosyncratic, is capable nonetheless of offering us a paradigmatic illustration of the process of international legal reproduction in action.

1 A Brief History of the Ethiopian Empire

The modern-day state of Ethiopia traces its descent back to the Aksumite Empire – an empire which, at the height of its powers between the first and seventh centuries CE, stretched from the core northern Ethiopian territories of Amhara and Tigre right across to the Arabian Coast. The Aksumite Empire officially adopted Orthodox Christianity in the 330s CE, and in about 1270 Emperor Yekunno-Amlak, an Amhara, established

[1] Teshale Tibebu, *The Making of Modern Ethiopia, 1896–1974* (Lawrenceville, NJ: Red Sea Press, 1995), xiv. The phrase '*empire des nègres blancs*' is taken from the book Alejandro Liano, *Éthiopie: Empire des Nègres blancs* (Paris: Pierre Roger, 1929), discussed below.

(or, according to some, re-established) the Solomonic dynasty of which Haile Selassie I was the last in line.[2]

With Yekunno-Amlak began a period of Christian imperial expansion. By the end of the fifteenth century, several neighbouring Muslim principalities had been conquered.[3] However, in 1527, the first in a series of dramatic incidents, each of which left a lasting scar on Ethiopia's collective consciousness, took place in the form of a *jihad* waged against the Christian empire by Ahmad ibn Ibrahim al Ghazi (known in Ethiopia as Ahmad 'Gragn', the left-handed), a general of the Adal Sultanate, which, from 1415 to 1577, existed in what is today the eastern part of Ethiopia, Djibouti and the north-western part of Somalia, with its capital at Zeila. Lasting from 1529 to 1543, this war pushed Ethiopia's borders right back to the edge of its core Christian highlands, bringing some three-quarters of what had been the Empire's land under Muslim control.[4] Ahmad Gragn's forces might well have destroyed Ethiopia had it not been for the arrival of a Portuguese force led by Cristóvão Da Gama, the son of Vasco da Gama. Portuguese missionaries had first arrived in 1520 in search of the legendary lost Christian king, Prester John,[5] and this new force of 400 men arrived at Massawa on 10 February 1541.[6] Although Da Gama was killed in action, Ahmad Gragn's army of Somalis, Hararis, Afars, Arabs and Ottoman Turks had been defeated by the combined Christian forces by March.

This first near-miss for the Empire, according to mainstream Ethiopian history, was followed closely by a second. This concerned the Oromo people (or *Galla*, as they were called by Ethiopian Christians, pejoratively), who are said to have 'swept across the highlands like a tidal wave',[7] capitalising on and consolidating the damage wrought by Ahmad Gragn. As we shall see, however, the image of the (non-Christian) Oromo[8] as invading hordes intent on destroying Ethiopia's Christian heritage and identity – an idea which continues to serve 'as a lightning rod for political responses to

[2] Bahru Zewde, *A History of Modern Ethiopia, 1855–1991* (2nd edn Oxford, Athens, OH, Addis Ababa: Addis Ababa University Press, 2001), 8.

[3] Ibid., 9.

[4] See Sihab ad-Din Ahmad ibn 'Abd-al-Qadir [c. 1537], *Futuh al-habaša (The Conquest of Abyssinia)*, trans. Paul Sternhouse (Hollywood, CA: Tsehai Publishers, 2005).

[5] Bahru, *A History of Modern Ethiopia*, 9

[6] See R. S. Whiteway [1902], *The Portuguese Expedition to Abyssinia in 1541–1543* (Nendeln, Liechtenstein: Kraus Reprint Limited, 1967).

[7] Bahru, *A History of Modern Ethiopia*, 9.

[8] The traditional Oromo religion is Waaqeffannaa. See Tasema Ta'a, 'Religious Beliefs among the Oromo: Waaqeffannaa, Christianity and Islam in the Context of Ethnic Identity, Citizenship and Integration', 8 *Ethiopian Journal of the Social Sciences and Humanities* (2012): 87–111.

Oromo nationalism' in 'Ethiopia's political discourse today'[9] – has been strongly disputed by Oromo and other historians.

The third historical trauma concerned the Portuguese once again. Attempting to capitalise on the goodwill that attended their intervention against Ahmad Gragn, Portugal deployed many more Jesuit missionaries to Ethiopia after 1541. Their success in converting Emperor Susenyos I (1572–1632) to Catholicism in 1622 triggered a terrible civil war.[10] Upon the latter's abdication, his son Fassiledes (1603–67), crowned Emperor Alam Sagad, immediately expelled the Jesuits,[11] who carried back with them to Europe the taint of Catholic perfidiousness and religious imperialism.

Ethiopia's characteristically decentralised system of government,[12] engendered by the mountainous terrain, lack of roads and long rainy season, was already, by this time, well established. Thanks, in part, to a series of regional religious schisms which undermined the central authority of the Ethiopian Orthodox Church, the Emperor's power declined markedly in relation to the regional nobility from the late eighteenth century until 1855, when the Emperor Tewodros assumed the throne.[13] This period of instability, known as the *Zemene Mesafint* ('era of princes'), threw into sharp relief the practical, as well as biblical meaning of the Emperor's title: *negusa nagast* ('king of kings'). Although, as the elect of God (*Siyyume Igze'abiher*), the Emperor was in theory all-powerful, many outlying areas of the empire operated as more-or-less independent fiefdoms. It was in this context that three successive Ethiopian emperors emerged in the nineteenth century, each determined to unify (or, according to some, 're-unify'[14]) the Empire.

The first of these, Tewodros II (1818–68), began his political career as a *shefta* (bandit) in border skirmishes with the Egyptians.[15] His bid for unification took the form of a 'head-on collision with regionalism'.[16] He centralised and modernised Ethiopia's armies and weaponry,[17] making efforts to enlist

[9] Mohammed Hassen, 'Revisiting Abba Bahrey's "The News of the Galla"', 34 *International Journal of African Historical Studies* (2012): 273–94, at 273.

[10] Bahru, *A History of Modern Ethiopia*, 9–10.

[11] Ibid.

[12] Sven Rubenson, *The Survival of Ethiopian Independence* (London: Heinemann, 1976), 30–2.

[13] Izabella Orlowska, 'Re-imagining Empire: The Coronation of Yohannis IV as an Expression of Historical Memory', in Witold Witakowski and Laura Lykowska (eds.), *Wälättä Yohanna: Ethiopian Studies in Honour of Joanna Mantel-Niećko* (Warsaw University Oriental Institute, 2006), 173–80, at 174.

[14] See Zewde Gebre-Sellassie, *Yohannes IV of Ethiopia: A Political Biography* (Oxford: Clarendon Press, 1975).

[15] Bahru, *A History of Modern Ethiopia*, 28–9.

[16] Ibid., 43–4.

[17] Ibid., 33.

the support of the Christian European states against the threat of Egyptian expansionism,[18] to which end he consistently 'evoke[d] the principle of Christian solidarity against Muslim Egypt'.[19] Tewodros's aspirations met with disaster in 1864 when, irritated at Queen Victoria's failure to reply to a letter,[20] he imprisoned the British Envoy, Charles Duncan Cameron, and his party, demanding compensation (*kasa*) in the form of technical assistance. As Tewodros is supposed to have articulated his demands, 'I don't want gold or silver; I want people who will open my eyes, because I am blind'.[21] Instead, the British sent a force of 32,000 men, led by Sir Robert Napier.[22] Tewodros met it at Meqdela (now Amba Mariam in central Ethiopia) where, hopelessly outnumbered, he committed suicide on 13 April 1868.[23] In a move they later regretted, the British force withdrew immediately on the grounds that it was not necessary 'that Abyssinia should be conquered in order to [ensure] its civilisation, and the development of its resources'.[24]

Tewodros was succeeded by Yohannes IV on 21 January 1872.[25] As Bahru argues, 'Yohannes followed a more cautious approach' to unification, viewing himself as 'a *negusa nagast* ... in the strict sense'.[26] However, this title was being claimed simultaneously by the ruler of one of the Empire's most important regions, *Negus* Menelik of Shewa (1844–1913). Following two punishing victories inflicted on the invading Egyptians,[27] Yohannes defeated Menelik's Shewan forces at Manz in January 1878,[28] but was killed on 9 March 1889 at the Battle of Matamma against the invading Mahdist Sudanese army, allowing Menelik to take the throne.

Menelik II's vision of unification was much more ambitious than that of his predecessors. Most of Ethiopia's southern territories had been conquered, often with great violence, by Menelik's armies towards the end of the nineteenth century (Map 1).[29] One of Menelik's most effective centralising innovations,

[18] Ibid., 34.
[19] Ibid., 36.
[20] Rubenson, *The Survival*, 225.
[21] Quoted in Rubenson, *The Survival*, 248.
[22] Bahru, *A History of Modern Ethiopia*, 40.
[23] Rubenson, *The Survival*, 268.
[24] Quoted in Ibid., 269.
[25] Bahru, *A History of Modern Ethiopia*, 42. On Yohannes IV, see, in particular, Izabela Orlowska, 'Re-imagining Empire: Ethiopian Political Culture under Yohannis IV, 1872–89' (PhD thesis, SOAS, University of London, 2006).
[26] Bahru, *A History of Modern Ethiopia*, 43–4.
[27] Ibid., 52–5.
[28] Ibid., 46 (n. 77). See also Harold G. Marcus, *The Life and Times of Menelik II of Ethiopia: 1844–1913* (Lawrenceville, NJ: Red Sea Press, 1995), 56.
[29] For a detailed description of this expansion see Seyoum H. Hameso, 'Notes on the Ethiopian Empire: Myth and History', in Seyoum H. Hameso, Trevor Trueman and Temesgen Mutela

aimed at bringing the Empire's peripheral areas under centralised control, was the so-called *neftenya* ('riflemen') system, involving the compulsory billeting of armed members of the Northern Christian, Amharic-speaking elite on impoverished southern peasant families.[30] It was Menelik II who finally anchored down the Empire's 'roaming capital', founding Addis Ababa in 1866 on the site of an Oromo village named Finfinne.[31] Menelik also undertook extensive European-style changes to the bureaucracy and military, with the help of foreign advisors like his Swiss assistant, Alfred Ilg,[32] attempted to abolish slavery in Ethiopia, and sought to increase Ethiopia's contact with Europe, especially after Ethiopia's famous trouncing (discussed below) of invading Italian forces at Adwa on 2 March 1896.[33] Menelik died in 1913, whereupon the short and highly controversial reign of his son, known as *Lijj* Iyassu, commenced.

Iyassu's multiple reforms included an attempt to abolish the *quragna* system, whereby plaintiff was chained to defendant and creditor to debtor until justice had been delivered.[34] He also led numerous slave raids on the Empire's peripheral communities, sometimes capturing tens of thousands of individuals at a time.[35] In 1916, the Shewan nobility led a coup against him, accusing him of having converted to Islam, and Menelik's daughter, Zewditu, took the throne, with *Ras* Tafari Makonnen (later to be crowned Emperor Haile Selassie I) as prince regent.[36] Zewditu headed a staunchly traditionalist faction, which included many members of the regional and ecclesiastical nobility. Tafari, however, was both interested in the potential of modern technologies and anxious about the European powers whose colonies, by now, completely surrounded the Empire. He gathered around him a group of reformist intellectuals who became known as the 'Young Ethiopians' (or, as Addis Hiwet has called them,[37] the 'Japanisers', who sought to emulate the Japanese Empire's self-transformation into the

Erena (eds.), *Ethiopia: Conquest and the Quest for Freedom and Democracy* (London: TSC Publications, 1997), 17–18.

30 Teshale, *The Making of Modern Ethiopia*, 44.

31 See e.g. Oromo Liberation Front, 'Finfinne ("Addis Ababa") is an Oromo Land', 6 May 2017, at http://oromoliberationfront.org/english/finfinne-addis-ababa-is-an-oromo-land/ (accessed 24 October 2017).

32 See Marcus, *Menelik II*, 178–213.

33 Ibid., 13.

34 Bahru, *A History of Modern Ethiopia*, 122–3.

35 Ibid., 122.

36 Ibid., 123–4.

37 Addis Hiwet, *From Autocracy to Revolution* (London: Review of African Political Economy, Occasional Publication No. 1, 1975).

first non-European 'great power').[38] Thereupon began the clash between conservative and modernising forces that would define Ethiopian politics until the Second World War.[39]

As Ethiopia became increasingly hemmed in by British, French and Italian colonies, perhaps the most obvious dispute concerned the question of whether the Empire should maintain its traditional policy of isolation or whether a more effective policy would be to gain acceptance as an equal by the European powers. This power struggle intensified but remained unresolved until Zewditu's death on 2 April 1930. Tafari was crowned His Imperial Majesty Haile Selassie I, King of Kings, Conquering Lion of the Tribe of Judah, and Elect of God on 2 November in a huge ceremony, attended by representatives of Britain, France, Belgium, Egypt, Sweden, Japan, Turkey, France, Italy and Germany, among others.[40]

2 A Brief Historiography of the Ethiopian Empire

If these are the bare facts of the Ethiopian Empire's history up to 1930, their interpretation is highly contested. As Teshale has pointed out, two main 'paradigms' dominate the interpretation of Ethiopian history. The 'Orientalist-Semiticist paradigm', as Teshale calls it, was developed by European commentators from the nineteenth century onwards, while the 'Aksumite paradigm' was derived from the religious texts of the Ethiopian Orthodox Church by the nobility of the Christian North. The following three subsections will unpack these two paradigms in the light of a third, more radically materialist paradigm, labelled the 'Radical Left paradigm' by Teshale. This is the Ethiopian historiography that has been developed, since the 1970s, by historians affiliated with those classes and ethnicities within Ethiopia that have traditionally found themselves on the losing end of this idiosyncratic yet incontestably imperial state.[41]

[38] See e.g. J. Calvitt Clarke III, 'Seeking a Model for Modernisation: Ethiopia's Japanizers', 10 *Selected Annual Proceedings of the Florida Conference of Historians* (2004): 35–51. See generally, Bahru Zewde, *Pioneers of Change in Ethiopia: The Reformist Intellectuals of the Early Twentieth Century* (Oxford, Athens, OH, Addis Ababa: James Currey, Ohio University Press, Addis Ababa University Press, 2002).

[39] Bahru, *A History of Modern Ethiopia*, 130–1.

[40] For an account of this 'most splendid affair', reported by British novelist Evelyn Waugh, among others, see Anthony Mockler, *Haile Selassie's War* (New York: Olive Branch Press, 2003), 12–13.

[41] Teshale, *The Making of Modern Ethiopia*, xii–xiv. See also, and in particular, Tsegaye R. Ararssa, 'Presenting Absence: The Figure of the Oromo in the Constitutions of Ethiopia' (PhD thesis, Melbourne Law School, in progress) (chapter summary on file with the author).

2.1 *Ethiopian History through European Eyes (the 'Orientalist-Semiticist Paradigm')*

The most striking characteristic of the 'Orientalist-Semiticist' narration of Ethiopian history is its deep sense of confusion. The intense European and American fascination with the Ethiopian Empire in the nineteenth and early twentieth centuries stemmed directly from this confusion. The 'Ethiopianist' scholars, diplomats, missionaries and journalists of this era simply could not get a handle on a country that seemed to them to be both European and African, both Christian and apostate, both 'civilised' and 'barbaric' – ultimately, familiar and different simultaneously. Through their eyes, as Teshale writes, Ethiopia's customs, society, language, political institutions, racial composition and even its geography were 'unique in and outlandish to Africa'.[42] The Ethiopian Empire, 'Christian, literate, civilised, handsome and sovereign for millennia', was, to these observers, 'an outpost of civilisation, the south western end of the Semitic world in Africa'.[43] The Ethiopian Empire was, from this perspective, an often infuriating, sometimes horrifying but always thrilling anomaly: as an independent African empire within a continent of European colonies; as an autochthonous Christian country which had survived for centuries by warding off attacks from surrounding Muslim and animist polities; as a united kingdom fragmented into countless regional 'fiefs'; as a lush, mountainous 'centre' ruling over an arid, desert 'periphery'; as an African state whose armies had been victorious over those of a European state, and yet in which slavery was still rife, and so on. Nonetheless, however they made sense of this puzzle, European and American scholars and officials at this time (and sometimes still today) had one thing in common: a tendency to conflate the whole of Ethiopia, in all its ethnic and religious complexity, into a single unit, known as 'Abyssinia', a Europeanisation of the Amharic word *habesha*, referring to the Christian northerners, Amhara and Tigreans in particular, who had ruled over the Empire's 'other' peoples for centuries, sometimes with great brutality.

As Teshale notes, European anthropologists from this period attempted to make sense of this supposed anomaly by tracing Ethiopia's history back to 'sometime during the first millennium [BCE], when a group of Sabeans crossed from Yemen to Africa ... [bringing] with them civilisation, script, and the knowledge of agriculture'.[44] The Caucasian Sabean migrants are then supposed to have 'mixed with the indigenous Negroid peoples'.[45] European

[42] Ibid., xvi.
[43] Ibid., xvi.
[44] Ibid., xvii.
[45] Ibid., xvii, quoting the British ethnologist Charles Gabriel Seligman.

legal scholars put forward a parallel argument about the mixed origins of Ethiopia's legal traditions.[46] Most importantly, they argued that the *Fetha Nagast* ('Book of Kings') – Ethiopia's most important legal code (brought from Egypt and translated from Arabic into Ge'ez during the reign of Zar'a Yaqob (1399–1468)) – bore within it clear traces of the influence of Roman civil law.[47] As early as 1841, for example, Sir William Cornwallis Harris, leader of the British diplomatic mission to the region of Shewa which concluded one of the first commercial treaties with Ethiopia, described the *Fetha Nagast* as 'an Aethiopic translation of the code of Justinian.'[48] Much later, in 1917, the Yale law professor Charles Sherman was still claiming that 'the present legal system of Abyssinia' was 'based on the Roman law of Justinian.'[49] Bearing in mind the contemporary obsession (noted in the Frame) with the effects of racial 'miscegenation,'[50] Sherman's language here is worth noting. Ethiopia's legal code had, he argued, 'deteriorated from its original Roman purity' over the course of Ethiopia's 'separation of centuries from the outside civilized world and the long continued struggle against Moslem neighbouring nations.'[51] The *Fetha Nagast* was also hybrid in another way,[52] with the first half of it (largely relying on the Old and, to a lesser extent, New Testament) pertaining to religious matters such as fasting, alms, and so on, and the second half (now known to be derived from a combination of four handbooks of Roman-Byzantine, Syro-Roman and other law, originally written in Latin, Arabic and Greek, as well as, again, the Old Testament) laying out the rules on secular matters such as

[46] This was a subject they became particularly interested in after eleven copies of the *Fetha Nagast* were looted by the Napier expedition in 1868 from the royal treasure-house at Magdala, together with countless other treasures, and found their way into the British Museum. Peter H. Sand, 'Roman Origins of the Ethiopian "Law of Kings" (*Fetha Nagast*), in Peter Strauss (ed.), *The Fetha Nagast: The Law of the Kings* (Durham, NC: Carolina Academic Press, 2009), xxxix–l, at xl. See further: Yirga Gelaw Woldeyes, 'Reflections on Ethiopia's Stolen Treasures on Display in a London Museum,' The Conversation, 5 June 2018, at https://theconversation.com/reflections-on-ethiopias-stolen-treasures-on-display-in-a-london-museum-97346 (accessed 3 Oct. 2018).

[47] For the text seems to have 'derived from an Arabic work known as *Mağmū al-quānīn* ('Collection of Canons'), written in the year 1238 by the Christian Egyptian jurist Abū'l-Fadā'il Ibn al'Assāl as-Safī, a contemporary of Patriarch Cyril III of Alexandria (1235–43)'. For a detailed genealogy, see Sand, 'Roman Origins,' l.

[48] William Cornwallis Harris, *The Highlands of Æthiopia, Described, During Eighteen Months' Residence of a British Embassy at the Christian Court of Shewa*, Vol. II (London: Gilbert & Rivington, 1844), 92.

[49] Charles Phineas Sherman, *Roman Law in the Modern World*, Vol. 1 (Boston, MA: The Boston Book Co., 1917), 177.

[50] See Frame, Section 3.1.

[51] Sherman, *Roman Law*, 177–8.

[52] Sand, 'Roman Origins,' xxxix–xlix.

diet, clothing, marriage, slavery, punishment and property. This structure reflected an interconnection between religious and secular law which had gradually been discarded, from the late eighteenth century onwards, by emerging secular European states.

The Ethiopian Empire and its inhabitants, then, were imagined, by European scholars, travellers and diplomats, as hybrid constructions in almost every sense during that period – racial, topographical, cultural, religious; even juridical. In 1885, for example, the French agent and explorer Denis de Rivoyre (who established the first Ethiopian-French trading firm, the *Compagnie Franco-Ethiopienne*, in 1881) described the (northern) Ethiopians he met as 'men' (he did not trouble himself with the women) 'of quick intelligence with pure traits, although bronze, with an elegant appearance, with a graceful carriage [and] civilised customs'. 'Bronzeness' of skin notwithstanding, Rivoyre therefore concluded that they must be members of the 'great Caucasian family'.[53] Similarly, more than half a century later, in 1910, Austrian anthropologist Friedrich Julius Bieber described 'Abyssinians' as belonging to 'the only [nation] that is civilised without wearing trousers and shoes'.[54] And as Tafari's determination to 'modernise' his country began to attract the attention of Europeans in the 1920s, this traditional/modernist dichotomy, too, became part of the hybridised paradigm used by Europeans to make sense of what was, as they saw it, the paradox of the Ethiopian Empire. In 1930, for example, German traveller and author Hermann Norden described Ethiopian painting as being 'so completely primitive as to seem ultra-modern'.[55] James Baum, a member of the 1926 'Abyssinian Expedition' organised by Chicago's Field Museum of Natural History, described the country in similar terms in his 1928 book, pointedly entitled *Savage Ethiopia*. Alluding to Menelik's famous description of Ethiopia as 'an island of Christians in a sea of pagans', he declared: 'we came away with the conviction that Tafari Makonnen is the one island of intelligence in a sea of black, barbarian ignorance'.[56] A year later, in 1929, Spanish traveller Alejandro Liaño went

[53] Denis de Rivoyre, 'L'Abyssinie pittoresque et commerciale', quoted in Harold G. Marcus, 'Racist Discourse about Ethiopia and Ethiopians Before and After the Battle', in Abdussamad H. Ahmad and Richard Pankhurst (eds.), *Adwa: Victory Centenary Conference, 26 February–2 March 1996* (Addis Ababa University Press, 1998), 391–402, at 396.

[54] Quoted in Marcus, 'Racist Discourse', 397.

[55] Hermann Norden, *Africa's Last Empire: Through Abyssinia to Lake Tana and the Country of the Falasha* (London: H. F. & G. Witherby, 1930), 10.

[56] James E. Baum, *Savage Abyssinia* (London: Cassell, 1928), 45–6.

so far as to entitle his volume *Éthiopie: Empire des Nègres Blancs*.[57] And in the same year, the US anthropologist Robert Gale Woolbert was still likening Tafari's 'anti-feudal, centralizing' efforts to those of 'the Valois and the Tudors in fifteenth- and sixteenth-century France and England', concluding that '[t]he political evolution of Ethiopia' was 'just about five hundred years behind that of Europe'.[58]

What is important about this narrative, and the body of knowledge it created, is the way in which it came to be drawn upon and echoed by the jurists, diplomats and other state officials who sought to make sense of the Ethiopian Empire's capacity to exercise rights and duties under international law. As we shall see in Section 3, below, given the very particular way in which international law is created, through the gradual accumulation of 'state practice' and '*opinio juris*', this perception of Ethiopia as an unfathomably mixed-up entity filtered directly into Ethiopia's own subjectivity as a person of international law. First, however, let us turn to a competing Ethiopian historiography, germane to the Ethiopian imperial elite themselves.

2.2 Ethiopian History through the Eyes of the Abyssinian Elite (the 'Aksumite Paradigm')

Much more familiar to Ethiopians at this time was the narrative propagated by the Ethiopian Orthodox Church and Abyssinian nobility. This narrative, Teshale's 'Aksumite paradigm', is outlined in a sacred fourteenth-century text called the *Kabra Nagast* ('Glory of Kings'), described by the historian and Semitic philologist Edward Ullendorff as 'the repository of Ethiopian national and religious feelings', equivalent to the Torah or Qur'an.[59] According to the *Kabra Nagast*, Ethiopian history begins in about 950 BCE with the birth of King Menelik I. According to this account, Menelik's birth was the result of a brief encounter between the biblical King Solomon and the Ethiopian Queen Makeda (better known outside Ethiopia as the Queen

[57] Liaño, *Éthiopie*. Interestingly, both the latter and Baum's *Savage Ethiopia* were among the cache of books which the Italian Delegation sent to the Secretary-General of the League of Nations in September 1935, urging him to put them 'at the disposal' of the Members of the League as proof of Ethiopia's barbarous way of life, and hence of the legitimacy of Italy's pending colonisation of the country. Italian Representative at Geneva, 'Letter to the Secretary-General, Transmitting Other Books Concerning Ethiopia', 16 September 1935, *LNOJ* (November 1935): 1586.

[58] Robert Gale Woolbert, 'Feudal Ethiopia and Her Army', 14 *Foreign Affairs* (1935): 71–81, at 73–4.

[59] Edward Ullendorff, *Ethiopia and the Bible* (Oxford University Press, 1968), 75.

of Sheba) on the latter's visit to Jerusalem.[60] All *Habesha* are descended from Menelik I from this perspective – who, having visited his father, returned from Jerusalem, taking with him the Ark of the Covenant (the *Tabot*), which he placed in the holy city of Aksum, symbolising the transference of God's preference from the Jews to the Ethiopians.[61] The identity of *Habesha*/Abyssinians is thus a hybrid one from the perspective of the Aksumite paradigm just as much as it is from the Orientalist-Semiticist perspective. However, rather than the intermingling of the Caucasian Sabeans and Ethiopia's Black African population, it is the mythical union between Makeda and Solomon which is understood to have founded not only a new, mixed-blooded people, but also a strongly Judaic strand of Christianity (and, of course, a divinely ordained imperial dynasty).[62]

The Aksumite paradigm, working in an ideological sense through the *Fetha Nagast* and the *Kebra Nagast*, corresponded to, and legitimated, a complex social order. To summarise it very schematically, power, in the Ethiopian Empire, can be described as having emanated outwards from a central point, the Emperor or Empress, whose sole right it was to distribute individual (and theoretically non-hereditary) *gult* rights.[63] These were rights related to land, but not rights 'to' land, as in the European feudal system. Instead, Ethiopian peasants or *gebbar* were considered, by and large, to own their land on the basis of hereditary production rights known as *rist*. *Gult* rights were rights over those (*gebbar*) who worked the land, and over that portion of their resources and products which was due to the *gult*-holder (as to local church officials) in the form of tribute and corvée labour.[64] Grants of *gult* rights by the Emperor also included certain judicial rights and the right to raise a private army, to be put at the disposal of the Emperor on demand.[65] The *Fetha Nagast* provided the normative backbone both to this hierarchical social system and to the power of the Church. Referring to St Paul's letter to the Romans, it was written that:

> God has provided for the appointment of judges and rulers to take place, so that the world may become beautifully calm ... since equality of forces can cause many wars. And God in his wisdom has established many kinds

[60] The meeting (although not the sex) is also described in the Bible, 1 *Kings* 10:1–13.

[61] Teshale, *The Making of Modern Ethiopia*, 14.

[62] Ethiopian Orthodox Christianity shares many features with Judaism. See Teshale, *The Making of Modern Ethiopia*, 7–10 (n. 103).

[63] Bahru, *A History of Modern Ethiopia*, 14.

[64] Ibid., 14.

[65] Donald D. Donham, 'Old Abyssinia and the New Ethiopian Empire: Themes in Social History', in Donald D. Donham and Wendy James (eds.), *The Southern Marches of Imperial Ethiopia: Essays in History and Social Anthropology* (Oxford, Athens, OH, Addis Ababa: James Currey, Ohio University Press and Addis Ababa University Press, 2002), 3–50, 9.

> of authority, such as that of man in respect to woman, the father in respect to the son, the old in respect to the young, the master in respect to the slave, the teacher in respect to the disciple, and, more so, the chief in respect to the one who is placed under him. The Lord acted in the same way with the body, [creating] the head and placing the other parts under it; he also did this with other animals, such as bees, raza, ants, antelopes, eagles, buffaloes, and all kinds of fish – every one has its chief and when there is no authority there is confusion and lack of order ...
>
> For the spiritual and corporal benefits which we derive from the ruler, let us give him tribute and presents in payment for them ... And if you say that you are better than [your] ruler by faith and by works, know that this is not your time since now you are a pilgrim and feeble. Your time will come.[66]

In stark contrast to the idea of the 'self-governing' state, arising in turn from the idea of a social contract among formally equal individuals, aimed at stemming violence through a once-and-for-all and limited relinquishment of 'freedom' to a state beholden to its citizens, whose power was then adminstered through a 'responsible' government, the legal code articulated in the *Fetha Nagast* involved an entirely different understanding of the relationship between ruler(s) and ruled. Rather than functioning as a transmitter whose purpose it was to organise the compromise between state (public macro-subject) and individual (private micro-subject), 'government' in the Ethiopian Empire worked through a multifaceted normative hierarchy which bound all individuals into a web of complex, interlocking relationships of authority and submission, including many rulers and judges, each with differing levels of authority and hence with different rights and responsibilities. The premise was precisely the opposite of that of 'responsible' government in the European sense. 'Equality of forces' was something that caused, rather than prevented wars in the Ethiopian Empire. In order to make the world 'beautifully calm' it was considered necessary, not to maximise the freedom of every individual up to the point at which that freedom impinged on that of another individual (something that would only lead to 'confusion and lack of order'), but instead to establish 'many kinds of authority', pertaining to many kinds of social relationship, each with 'its own chief'. This chief (from the Emperor through to the regional *Ras* or *Shum* down to the individual *neftenya* or *balabbat*) should be rewarded for his trouble, not in the form of an official salary offered to a public servant, but in the form of 'tribute and presents' offered to him directly by those over whom he exercised authority. Those who found themselves in a lowly position were urged not to assert themselves as equals, but instead to submit to God's

[66] Strauss (ed.), *The Fetha Nagast*, 271–2.

will, content in the knowledge that, if not in this life, then in the next one, their time (to dominate and extract) would come.

As the historical anthropologist Donald Donham notes, one of the most important of these divinely sanctioned systems of devolved authority, the *gult/neftenya* system, supplied one of the primary expansionary pressures on the Empire, as highland areas 'filled up', requiring the conquest of lands further and further to the south. By the time of the Italian invasion in 1935, he argues, the 'core' highland Christian areas of the Empire had been supplemented by three different types of territories to the south. A very few semi-independent kingdoms were permitted to remain, in exchange for tribute paid to the Emperor in the form of ivory, gold and other valuable resources. However, most southern lands had been settled via the interlocking systems of *neftenya* and *gult*. Nonetheless, in the southernmost lowland areas, unsuitable for plough cultivation as demanded by the *gult* system, local leaders (*balabbat*) were appointed in return for a fixed tax, usually in the form of cattle or sometimes slaves.[67]

As this very brief description of the normative underpinnings of the Aksumite paradigm and the social order which it legitimated suggests, 'Abyssinian' civilisation – the civilisation of the Ethiopian Empire's ruling class – was founded (not entirely unlike its European counterpart) upon a Christian/non-Christian, civilised/barbaric dichotomy, which mapped, in turn, onto a geographical-political split within the Empire itself. These divisions had an ethnic and religious dimension, with the Abyssinian 'self' defined against a set of 'others' or *yal-tatamqu ahzab* ('unbaptised heathens').[68] Until the second half of the twentieth century, however, ethnicity in the Ethiopian Empire functioned according to a peculiar logic of its own. Unlike the (pseudo)anthropological European conception of 'civilisation', which (as described in the Frame) guaranteed that 'full' selfhood would always remain just out of reach for the colonial subject,[69] the process of 'becoming Abyssinian' in Ethiopian society was, at least potentially, one that *could be completed*. As Donham puts it, the category 'Amhara' (or, more broadly, we could say *Habesha* or 'Abyssinian') was a flexible one, denoting 'a particular position within the core-periphery structure' rather than 'a traditional tribal identity that depends primarily on descent'.[70] Yet the price, for those 'others', such as Oromo or '*Galla*', who did 'become' *Habesha*, was

[67] Donham, 'Old Abyssinia', 37–44.

[68] Teshale, *The Making of Modern Ethiopia*, 13.

[69] See Frame, Section 3.2.

[70] Donham, 'Old Abyssinia', 12.

'Abyssinianisation'. This meant three things above all: accepting the *rist* system of hereditary production rights; learning Amharic; and converting to the Orthodox Christian faith.[71] Thus, Donham argues,

> [a]lthough 'Galla' carried overtones of race and slavery – particularly to Abyssinians in the far north – its primary meaning seems to have been focused on religion and culture, not on race. 'Galla were pagans. They were uncivilized. *Ye-Galla ch'ewa ye-gomen ch'oma yelem* ('It's as impossible to find a Galla gentleman as it is to find fat in greens ...') But in fact, some Galla ... were finally 'civilized'; over time, they became Amhara.[72]

This incorporative, and yet relatively flexible approach to entry into the Ethiopian Empire's dominant ethnicity was facilitated by a similarly flexible approach to what we might call social status. In European feudal society, lords, peasants and serfs were engaged in fixed, hierarchical, functionally interdependent tasks. In the social order of the Ethiopian Empire, by contrast, although it was equally hierarchical, 'all men were thought to be basically the same, even if chance and personal destiny had rendered them temporarily unequal'.[73] Thanks to the constant bestowal and withdrawal of *gult* rights by the Emperor, especially after Menelik's ascent to power, no stable class hierarchy was able to develop. Thus, according to the anthropologist Allan Hoben:

> In the northern Ethiopian model all men are ultimately seen as pursuing the same goals in a rather Hobbesian manner, and social integration and order depend on men's being firmly controlled through a pyramidal network of personal dyadic ties of subordination and superordination. These differing conceptions of social order are expressed metaphorically in statements about the relationship between the segments of society. In the European metaphor the parts of the body politic are linked to the parts of the body; in the Ethiopian metaphor the relationship of the élite to the peasantry is one of horseman and horse.[74]

Violence, as this suggests, was central in a system in which *neftenya*, for example, were simply foisted on peasant families without any duty

[71] Ibid., 10–12.

[72] See Ibid., 13.

[73] Donham, 'Old Abyssinia', 5, disagrees with Teshale on the issue of whether or not these three divisions, characteristic of medieval European society, are also applicable to Ethiopian society.

[74] Allan Hoben, 'Family, Land and Class in Northwest Europe and Northern Highland Ethiopia', in Harold Marcus (ed.), *Proceedings of the First United States Conference of Ethiopian Studies* (East Lansing, MI: Michigan State University Press, 1975), quoted in Donham, 'Old Abyssinia', 6. See also Allan Hoben, *Land Tenure among the Amhara of Ethiopia: The Dynamics of Cognatic Descent* (University of Chicago Press, 1973).

towards them which might have mitigated the right of these armed officials to extract tribute.[75] However, if violence held this Abyssinianised social hierarchy together, it also promised a way out. The dream, however unlikely, of rising through the military ranks to become a lord or even the Emperor had been personified by a sufficient number of famous figures (including Emperor Tewodros himself) to remain a potent one for many a low-grade regional militiaman.[76] In this centralised-but-fragmented, deeply hierarchical socio-political system, ties were personal, flexible (at least in principle) and brutally enforced – a situation summed up in the famous aphorism: 'a dog knows his master but not his master's master'.[77]

If Ethiopia's combination of traditional and modern was something many Europeans found exotic and fascinating, it was the resilience of Ethiopian slavery which evolved into a European obsession in the first decades of the twentieth century. As we saw in Item 2, between the late fourteenth century and the mid nineteenth century, European states and neo-European settler colonial states had overseen the kidnapping and enslavement of some 11 million African individuals for the purpose of extracting and accumulating enormous quantities of capital from the lands they had appropriated and settled during this period. From the second half of the nineteenth century onwards, however, these states – for equally self-interested reasons – gradually came to accept, and to establish through their practice as part of customary international law, the idea that slavery and the slave trade were unlawful. From this point onwards, these states, and the international law their practice and statements established, turned the spotlight back on those African individuals and communities themselves where slavery continued to be a significant aspect of social life – individuals and communities which could thus be cast as

[75] This system did possess an ideological justification, supplied by the Orthodox Church. It was thought necessary to the maintenance of social order among essentially similar individuals that material 'satisfaction' should be avoided. Those who are satisfied, according to this perspective, were those without the kind of social ties that might restrain them, and were therefore considered likely to take more than their fair share. Thus, the same word, *hudad*, described both the gruelling Lenten fast, designed to discipline the peasants' essentially sinful nature, and that area of the lord's fields which was worked by the peasants' corvée labour. Similarly, the Amharic word for nobility, *mekwannint*, derives indirectly from the verb *konene*, meaning to discipline, constrain or inflict pain. Donham, 'Old Abyssinia', 6.

[76] Peter P. Garretson, 'Vicious Cycles: Ivory, Slaves, and Arms on the New Maji Frontier', in Donald D. Donham and Wendy James (eds.), *The Southern Marches of Imperial Ethiopia: Essays in History and Social Anthropology* (Oxford, Athens, OH, Addis Ababa: James Currey, Ohio University Press and Addis Ababa University Press, 2002), 196–218, at 200.

[77] Quoted in Donham, 'Old Abyssinia', 9.

backward, uncivilised and in need (whether they knew it or not) of foreign 'assistance'.

The Ethiopian Empire, where a particular kind of slavery had been entrenched for centuries, was one such polity. The *Fetha Nagast*, indeed, makes many mentions of slavery, at one point devoting an entire chapter to its justification and proper regulation. The chapter begins as follows:

> [The state of] liberty is in accord with the law of reason, for all men share liberty on the basis of natural law. But war and the strength of horses bring some to the service of others, because the law of war and of victory rendered the vanquished slaves of the victors.[78]

As this suggests, those conquered populations which were incorporated into the Ethiopian Empire, particularly during the expansionist reigns of Yohannes IV and Menelik II, supplied this institution with a relatively consistent flow of new bodies in the mid and late nineteenth century. Menelik, for example – notwithstanding his proclamation of 1876, which transformed the *Fetha Nagast*'s prohibition on Christian engagement in the slave trade into 'hard' law, and his decree of 1889 abolishing slavery *per se* – made an exception for prisoners-of-war, who were still permitted to be captured and enslaved.[79]

The exchange of slaves in Ethiopia, moreover, formed part of a complex barter economy in which value was determined far more importantly by social and moral or religious factors than by the supposedly 'rational' determinants of demand and supply. Indeed, money did not come into widespread use in Ethiopia before the start of the nineteenth century, and profit maximisation was explicitly prohibited in the *Fetha Nagast*, which laid down that 'after having gathered thy grapes, thou shalt not turn back and gather the remaining, but shalt leave it to the poor and strangers'.[80] In social terms, and in contrast to the plantation system introduced in the 'new world', Ethiopian slaves were not put to work on the basis of a 'market rationale' but rather as a 'status symbol'.[81] For example, Abba Jifar II, the ruler of Jimma province, is said to have had more than 10,000 slaves and Menelik II some 70,000 of his own.[82] In 1901, this state of affairs

[78] Richard Pankhurst, *An Introduction to the Economic History of Ethiopia*, Vol. 1 (Addis Ababa: Haile Selassie I University Press, 1961), 372–3. See Miguel F. Brooks (ed. and trans.), *A Modern Translation of the Kebra Nagast: The Glory of Kings* (Lawrenceville, NJ: Red Sea Press, 1996).

[79] See Bahru, *A History of Modern Ethiopia*, 60–8.

[80] Pankhurst, 'Ethiopia and the Great Transformation', 7 *Aethiopica* (2004): 84–113, 87.

[81] Ibid., 94.

[82] Jamie Stokes, Anthony Gorman and Andrew Newman (eds.), *Encyclopaedia of the Peoples of Africa and the Middle East* (New York: Facts on File, 2008), 516.

caused the British journalist Herbert Vivian to voice his astonishment at discovering a system in which every man, however impoverished, had 'as many retainers as possible, who go with him and eat with him as members of his family': 'one carries his gun, another his sword, another his purse, and the fourth ... carries nothing at all'.[83] This connection with the accumulation of social rather than financial capital made Ethiopian slavery a particularly difficult institution to abolish, as the dilemma faced by Abba Jifar in the 1880s illustrates. Ordered by Menelik II to abolish slavery and the slave trade in his jurisdiction, his reluctance to do so stemmed in large part from the enormous tribute he was forced to pay the Emperor in exchange for Jimma's continued state of semi-independence – annually including 60 horses, 60 mules, 100 vases of honey, 30 elephant tusks, 60 slaves, 100 sacks of coffee, 20 lion/tiger skins, and a certain amount of money in Maria Theresa thalers. Only through the capture and exchange of slaves was Abba Jifar able to procure such goods.[84]

The dynamics of Ethiopian slavery were, then, quite different from those of the chattel slavery system entrenched in the Caribbean and the Americas in the seventeenth and eighteenth centuries for the purpose of generating profits. Ethiopian slavery was a key aspect of a distinctively non-capitalist (or, by the turn of the nineteenth century, barely capitalist) social order, regulated by a mixture of local customary law and the natural law precepts of the *Fetha Nagast*. Moreover, and significantly, while slaves were certainly looked down upon, being a slave in the Ethiopian Empire of the nineteenth and early twentieth centuries was merely the lowest of several other extremely lowly statuses in Ethiopian imperial society.[85] Several notable members of the Ethiopian elite rose all the way up from the position of slave to that of lord. One example is *Dejazmatch* Balcha Safo (1863–1936), who was discovered on the battlefield by Menelik's troops in Gurageland, having already been castrated (a customary punishment for defeated soldiers), and then enslaved. Balcha rose to become

[83] Herbert Vivian, *Abyssinia. Through the Lion-Land to the Court of the Lion of Judah* (London: C. Arthur Pearson, 1901), 216.

[84] Seid A. Mohammed, 'A Social Institution of Slavery and Slave Trade in Ethiopia: Revisited', 7 *African Journal of History and Culture* (2015): 85–90, at 86, citing Tekalign Woldemariam, 'The Slave Trade in the Economy of Jimma', in Taddese Beyene (ed.), *Proceedings of the Eighth International Conference of Ethiopian Studies, 1984*, Vol. I (Addis Ababa: Institute of Ethiopian Studies, 1989), 309–16. Maria Theresa thalers were a silver bullion coin, first minted in 1741 and named after Empress Maria Theresa, ruler of the Austro-Hungarian Empire from 1740 to 1780. Though it lost its currency status in Austria in 1858, the thaler remained in use throughout the Arab world, in Ethiopia, Indonesia, India and elsewhere, until after the Second World War.

[85] Cited in this context by Teshale, *The Making of Modern Ethiopia*, 54.

one of Menelik's leading officers,[86] becoming *Shum* of the Sidamo region at a time of rapidly expanding coffee production, and obtaining thousands of slaves of his own.[87] Similarly, Zewditu's Minister of War, *Fitawrari* Habte Giorgis Dinagde (1851–1926) – reputedly an awe-inspiring if not utterly terrifying figure – is alleged to have been born a slave.[88] Perhaps even more importantly, as Teshale explains, the term *barya* ('slave') served a key symbolic function:

> [t]o sign a letter with the words *baryawe* (your slave), was standard procedure. The person who signed *baryawe* was not a slave at all. He *considered* himself to be one. In this context, the entire population was treated as the 'slave' of the *negusa nagast* ... [who] spoke of himself as We ... to emphasize his singular ultimate power over his 'slave' subjects.[89]

In a discursive sense, in other words, the concept of slavery pervaded those parts of Ethiopia that had been successfully 'Abyssinianised'. Everyone but the *Negusa Nagast* her/himself was in some sense a slave.

2.3 The Materialist Critique of Ethiopian Historiography

Taken together, this constellation of social, economic and normative forces – Ethiopia's in some ways flexible and in other ways inflexible class structure; its largely non-capitalist economy based on ties of tribute rather than commodity exchange and wage-labour; its united-but-fragmented administrative structure; the pervasive moral and legal force of the Ethiopian Orthodox Church backed up by the *Fetha Nagast* – can help explain both why so many of Ethiopia's emperors, from Susenyos onwards, sought to outlaw slavery, and why they consistently failed to do so.[90] These factors also underscore, however, the way in which the 'Aksumite' understanding of the Ethiopian Empire dovetailed with the Orientalist-Semiticist understanding in viewing the Empire as an entity that was, in some fundamental way, *mixed*, and therefore ambivalent, unclassifiable, exceptional and, above all, legitimate in its expansionist-assimilationist impulse.

[86] Paul B. Henze, *Layers of Time: A History of Ethiopia* (New York: C. Hurst & Co., 2000), 190, n. 8.

[87] Haile Selassie I, *My Life and Ethiopia's Progress*, Vol. 2 (London: Research Associates School Times, 1999), 79.

[88] Marcel Griaule, 'Comments by M. Marcel Griaule on Some of the Questions Dealt with in the Italian Government's Memorandum on the Situation in Ethiopia', 14 September 1935, in *LNOJ* (November 1935) 1588–95, at 1588.

[89] See Teshale, *The Making of Modern Ethiopia*, 63–4. Emphasis in the original.

[90] Pankhurst, *An Introduction to the Economic History of Ethiopia*, Vol. 1, 378.

As 'radical left' scholars note, Abyssinians are understood as a hybrid people in both the 'Orientalist-Semiticist' and 'Aksumite' paradigms, born of an intermingling between an extra-African ('civilised') element on the one hand, and an indigenous African ('uncivilised') element on the other. It is on this exceptionalist basis that both paradigms explain Ethiopia's success in becoming the only polity in Africa to have escaped colonialism (apart from a five-year period of partial Italian occupation resisted tooth and nail throughout). Yet, as they also note, the Aksumite assumption that *Habesha* constitute a common religious community, defined against Ethiopia's non-Christian 'others', obscures the degree to which Christian peasants were *themselves* ruthlessly exploited. Both the Church and the nobility extracted tribute from the peasant or *gebbar* – a system illustrated by the Amharic maxim *gabare yamibalaw enjie yamikaflaw ayatum* ('the peasant may have nothing to eat, but he always has something to pay').[91] Moreover, when it came to the 'exaggerated forms of exploitation that developed in the western periphery, the predatory expansion of the state affected particularly the women and children of the subjugated populations'.[92] As Wendy James points out, for instance, many historical sources attest to the fact that 'sexual access was among the rights an owner of *gebbar* might expect' as his due from female peasants under the grant of *gult*.[93]

In material terms, these critical scholars point out, this meant that the life of a slave and that of a *gebbar* were sometimes difficult to distinguish in material terms. The stem-word itself, *geber* – a name given to peasants, as well as to servants and slaves – refers both to the concept of work itself, and to the tribute (due in both labour and produce) levied from the peasant, often to the point of starvation.[94] Moreover, when *gult* rights became unstable and confused, or where conditions were so bad that peasants had simply fled, individuals who were, in theory, *gebbar* were sometimes simply enslaved so as to make up the missing tribute with their own bodies – either being carried off by departing governors, or sold (sometimes by neighbours in a desperate effort to ward off their own enslavement, and/or in exchange for arms for the same purpose).[95] This 'cycle of violence', as the historian Peter Garretson has described it, stemmed directly from

91 Teshale, *The Making of Modern Ethiopia*, 71.

92 Wendy James, 'Lifelines: Exchange Marriage among the Gumuz', in Donham and James (eds.), *The Southern Marches*, 119–47, at 120.

93 Ibid., 120.

94 Teshale, *The Making of Modern Ethiopia*, 4. See also Bahru, *A History of Modern Ethiopia*, 14.

95 Garretson, 'Vicious Cycles', 106–218.

the parasitic nature of the Ethiopian Empire's economy – something that became more and more acute over the course of the nineteenth century. Lords who had been granted *gult* rights (which, particularly in the south, could be withdrawn at any time) sat above the production process, skimming off any surplus produced by their *gebbar*.[96] If they had little interest in the kind of long-term investments that would increase productive efficiency on their land, peasants, too, were hardly incentivised to produce more than the bare minimum, when producing more would only render them liable to further exploitation.[97] This was, in other words, a primarily extractive, non-market system of production and appropriation, only marginally supplemented by exchange, existing in a largely non-monetary economy driven not by profit but by the expansionist logic of the *neftenya-gebbar* system.[98]

Adding to the Ethiopian imperial economy's resistance to the idea of commodity production and market exchange was the fact that the supposedly 'low-status and niggardly merchant' was generally treated by Ethiopian society as a social outcast. Indeed, 'the very word for merchant, *negadē*, was synonymous with Islam – that which was outside, in opposition to, Abyssinian society'.[99] Artisans, too, such as blacksmiths, ironmongers and potters, were socially shunned.[100] Abyssinians were permitted neither to eat nor to intermarry with them, and such groups were prohibited from owning land.[101] Manual labour, in other words, let alone wage labour, was regarded as a low-status activity. The result was that those commodities which were traded (usually by Muslims or foreign intermediaries) up to

[96] Donham, 'Old Abyssinia', 16.

[97] Donham, 'Old Abyssinia', 15. For an analysis in the context of Gedeo region, see Charles W. McClellan, 'Coffee in Centre-Periphery Relations: Gedeo in the Early Twentieth Century', in Donham and James (eds.), *The Southern Marches*, 175–95, at 179–80. The designation *gebbar* or peasant applied not to the individual her/himself but rather to a proportion of her/his output that was capable of being appropriated. Thus '[a] "full" gebbar was one able to pay the highest amount' while '[o]ther "lesser" *gebbar* were grouped together to create "full" *gebbar* and paid their tax collectively'. Ibid., 180, citing Gebre-Wold-Ingida Worq, 'Ethiopia's Traditional System of Land Tenure and Taxation', 5 *Ethiopian Observer* (1962): 302–39, and Mahteme Sellassie Wolde Maskel, *Zikre Neger* (Addis Ababa: Netsanet Press, 1942).

[98] In 1904 only about one-third of state revenues were received in cash, and Menelik II established Ethiopia's first bank the following year, via a concession granted to the (British-controlled) National Bank of Egypt. Donham, 'Old Abyssinia', 27–9.

[99] Donham, 'Old Abyssinia', 15.

[100] Marcel Griaule, 'Labour in Abyssinia', 23 *International Labour Review* (1931): 181–202, at 188.

[101] Donham, 'Old Abyssinia', 5.

1917, when the opening of the Djibouti–Addis Ababa Railway made the export of coffee a profitable activity, were for the most part slaves, ivory and gold – articles that, rather than being 'produced', were rather 'the booty products of Abyssinian predation'.[102] In a context in which the *gebbar*'s situation was one of 'ownership' of her land, but not of its product or of her own labour-power, the line between the appropriation of her grain, the appropriation of her body and the appropriation of her person became, in practice, increasingly thin as Ethiopia's transformation into a recognised state (described in the next subsection) came to be consolidated.[103]

Beyond this discussion of the Christian peasant's exploitation, a second, equally radical critique of the two standard accounts of Ethiopian history concerns the collusion of the Orientalist-Semiticist and Aksumite paradigms in normalising the forced assimilation of non-Christian peoples, justified in terms of an evangelical (internal) civilising mission.[104] For the dominance of the Abyssinian imperial elite was distinctly racialised from the point of view of many of Ethiopia's peoples. And of course, as Teshale points out in relation to the Orientalist-Semiticist account of the anthropological origins of 'Abyssinia', '[t]o say that Ethiopian history starts with the Sabeans, and not with [Ethiopia's Indigenous peoples, such as] the Agaw, Beja, etc., is tantamount to starting with the invaders'.[105] However close the status of *gebbar* and slave may have been in terms of the impoverished and coerced quality of their daily lives, moreover, it remained the case in terms of the Aksumite world view that even 'the poorest peasant from the north considered himself superior to any southerner'.[106] For the Nilo-Saharan peoples of the far south, in particular (in provinces like Maji on the Sudanese border) – peoples whose skin colour was typically darker than that of many Northerners – race was indisputably a factor in legitimating their subjection. The pejorative Amharic term that was applied to such peoples, *Shankilla*, meant 'quite simply, blacks',[107] and for these peoples, only

[102] Ibid., 27.

[103] The wretched life of the *gebbar* was perhaps most famously described by Asbé Hailu, one of *Ras* Tafari's closest associates among the Young Ethiopians, in an essay of 1928. The essay ends with two neighbours who spy the corpse of a *gebbar*, worked to death by his master, being carried from the compound 'on a stick' while someone makes off with the peasant's donkey. 'Who was it that died?' one asks. The other replies: 'Don't mind him, sister ... he was not human born; he was only a gebbar.' Quoted in Donham and James (eds.), *The Southern Marches*, v.

[104] Teshale, *The Making of Modern Ethiopia*, xv–xvii.

[105] Ibid., xiii–xiv.

[106] Donham, 'Old Abyssinia', 24.

[107] Ibid., 12.

(forcibly) incorporated into the Empire in the late nineteenth century (see Map 1), the relatively open channels for (conditional) social mobility were blocked. In Donham's words, the Ethiopian Empire's 'Southern marches' constituted 'a permanent periphery that was never incorporated into the Abyssinian core', containing 'essentially, reservoir populations of potential slaves, seen almost as part of the natural environment of the Abyssinian state',[108] rather like Ethiopia's elephants, which, by 1910, had already been hunted to the point of extinction.[109] According to Mordechai Abir, slaves from these areas were assigned the hardest work and were worth less, whereas enslaved 'non-Black' individuals of, say, Oromo or Sidama ethnicity, often captured as prisoners-of-war on the field of battle, were considered much more valuable, and were taken on by Christians as personal servants or, in the case of women, as wives or concubines.[110] This racialised class system within the categories of slave and *gebbar* was also meshed with a religious hierarchy, for the *Fetha Nagast* prohibited the sale of Christian slaves to non-believers. Immunising Ethiopia's Christian population, however impoverished, from enslavement, this norm also reinforced the existing social hierarchy between Christians and non-Christians. One consequence was that '[f]or those on the frontiers [of the Empire] Christian identity promised an escape from the worst aspects of Abyssinian domination', such that 'at times peoples on the southern periphery begged northern emperors to make them Christian'.[111] In this way, slavery both fuelled, and was fuelled by, Ethiopia's characteristically fragmented form of unity, in a dynamic that relied both on the enforced transformation of the 'other' into an approximation of the 'self', and on the creation of a desire for such transformation as the better of two evils. As this suggests, we should not assume that those who could potentially 'become Amhara' (to borrow Donham's phrase) necessarily fared any better than *Shankilla*, or any better than the same individuals would have done in the context of European colonialism, with its 'scientific' assumptions about race. As with the European 'colonial subject', the 'choice' for any Oromo or Sidama, for example, was essentially one between annihilation by voluntary assimilation or annihilation by force.

One particularly vivid illustration of the collusion between the Orientalist-Semiticist and Aksumite arguments with respect to oppressed

[108] Ibid., 12.

[109] McClellan, 'Coffee in Centre-Periphery Relations', 177.

[110] Mordechai Abir, *Ethiopia: The Era of the Princes: The Challenge of Islam and Re-Unification of the Christian Empire, 1769–1855* (New York: Praeger, 1968), 57.

[111] Donham, 'Old Abyssinia', 11.

groups within the Empire concerns the Oromo – in the 1930s, as today, Ethiopia's most populous ethnic group. Common to both paradigms, as we have seen above, is the assumption that the Oromo 'hordes' invaded the Empire in the wake of Ahmad Gragn's invasion. The most famous account of this alleged invasion is *Abba* Bahrey's *The History of the Galla* (*Zenahu Lagalla*), written in the midst of the Oromo migration in 1593. Bahrey wrote: 'I have begun to write the history of the Galla in order to make known the number of their tribes, their readiness to kill people, and the brutality of their manners.'[112] A. M. H. Jones and Elizabeth Monroe, in their (for many years definitive) 1935 *History of Abyssinia*, reproduced this assessment without question. Abyssinian 'civilisation' was 'wrecked' by this 'invasion', they assert, for the '*Gallas*' possessed 'raiding parties [which] moved with great rapidity, looting and destroying everything they passed.'[113]

As Oromo historians and their colleagues insist, however, the idea that their ancestors immigrated into Ethiopia from outside 'is a myth perpetuated by confusing historical Abyssinia and modern Ethiopia, the boundaries of which were determined in the last two decades of the nineteenth century.'[114] According to some, Oromo inhabited 'core' Abyssinian areas from at least the fourteenth century CE, and perhaps even as early as the tenth century CE, including parts of northern and eastern Ethiopia and Shewa in the Abyssinian heartland.[115] From this perspective, the migration of Oromo settlers is more accurately understood as a re-occupation of originally Oromo lands appropriated by invading Abyssinians.[116] Equally, the idea that (as Ullendorff wrote in 1975) the Oromo 'had nothing to

[112] In Charles F. Beckingham and G. W. B. Huntingford (eds. and trans.), *Some Records of Ethiopia, 1593–1646: Being Extracts from 'The History of High Ethiopia or Abassia' by Manoel de Almeida together with Bahrey's 'History of the Galla'* (London: Hakluyt Society, 1954), 109–29.

[113] A. M. H. Jones and Elizabeth Monroe, *A History of Abyssinia* (Oxford: Clarendon Press, 1935), 9; see also 65, 105.

[114] Mohammed Hassen, *The Oromo and the Christian Kingdom of Ethiopia: 1300–1700* (Woodbridge: Boydell & Brewer, 2015), 10.

[115] See e.g. Alemayehu Haile, *History of the Oromo to the Sixteenth Century* (2nd edn Finfinne: Oromia Culture and Tourism Board, 2006); Mohammed Hassen, *The Oromo of Ethiopia: A History, 1570–1860* (Cambridge University Press, 1990); Mekuria Bulcha, 'Conquest and Forced Migration: An Assessment of the Oromo Experience', in Seyoum H. Hameso and Mohammed Hassen (eds.), *Arrested Development in Ethiopia: Essays on Underdevelopment, Democracy, and Self-Determination* (Lawrenceville, NJ: Red Sea Press, 2006), 38–82; P. T. W. Baxter, Jan Hultin and Alessandro Triulzi, eds., *Being and Becoming an Oromo: Historical and Anthological Enquiries* (London: Africa Book Centre, 1996).

[116] See especially Alemayehu, *History of the Oromo*.

contribute to the civilisation of Ethiopia'[117] is belied, among other things, by the *Gaada* system of age and generation grading,[118] which has for a long time been well-known among anthropologists for its democratic nature,[119] remarked on also by the otherwise deeply prejudiced British Envoy, Walter Plowden.[120] The parallel narratives of hybridity as peaceful assimilation supplied, in tandem, by the Orientalist-Semiticist and Aksumite perspectives, have in recent years been confronted with the argument that their combined exceptionalism serves to mask the systematic and often brutal suppression of difference. As Seyoum Hameso puts it, for example:

> Such nations as the Oromo, Sidama, Shekecho, Wolaya and their corresponding traditional, democratic authority structures were subordinated to anachronistic northern autocracy, feudalism, force and tradition tied by manipulative marriage. By imposing itself, the Abyssinian colonial rule corrupted the [*Gaada*] system of the Oromo, the *Luwa* of the Sidama and similar cultures of other nations.[121]

This alternative and deeply critical history should alert us, therefore, to the way in which both European *and* Abyssinian imperialism, though opposed on the issue of the 'sovereignty' of the Ethiopian Empire as a whole, have conspired against Ethiopia's structurally subordinate peoples within the territorial boundaries of the Empire.

Bearing this in mind, the next two components of this chapter will examine the encounter between international law (demonstrating how it drew on the body of knowledge associated with the 'Orientalist-Semiticist' paradigm) and the Ethiopian Empire (which, as we shall see, operated in its foreign relations on the basis of a mixture of 'Orientalist-Semiticist' and 'Aksumite' knowledge) during this period.

117 Edward Ullendorff, *The Ethiopians: An Introduction to Country and People* (2nd edn London: Oxford University Press, 1975), 76.

118 P. T. W. Baxter, 'Ethiopia's Unacknowledged Problem: The Oromo', 77 *African Affairs* (1978): 283–96, at 284.

119 Under the rules of the *gaada* system, Oromo men were grouped 'by age and genealogical generation' into an organisation which combined ritual, political and military elements. The *gaada* system 'maintained a strongly democratic and egalitarian ethos and restrained the exploitation of office, wealth and power', with 'no office holder, nor set of elders in office, [able to] retain office for longer than a ritually prescribed period, usually of eight years'. Baxter, 'Ethiopia's Unacknowledged Problem', 284–5.

120 Walter Chichele Plowden, *Travels in Abyssinia and the Galla Country: An Account of a Mission to Ras Ali in 1848* (London: Longmans Green & Co., 1868), 307, 286, 129. See Section 3.1, below. See further Asafa Jalata, 'The Struggle for Knowledge: The Case of Emergent Oromo Studies', 39 *African Studies Review* (1996): 95–123, at 98.

121 Seyoum, 'Notes on the Ethiopian Empire: Myth and History', 22–3.

3 The Orientalist-Semiticist Paradigm and the Treaty Regime: Re-Producing the Ethiopian Empire as a Sovereign State

Mentions of the Ethiopian Empire, though rare, crop up with some regularity in the international law treatises of the nineteenth and early twentieth centuries. Against the background presented in Sections 2 and 3, the astonishment voiced by the authors of these treatises at Ethiopia's simultaneously familiar and unfamiliar aspects makes sense as an astonishment derived from precisely that body of knowledge which Teshale describes as the 'Orientalist-Semiticist paradigm'. As we are about to see, the response of these jurists was to classify the Ethiopian Empire as a paradox – recognisable and unrecognisable, same and other, and therefore somehow sovereign *and* less-than-sovereign at the same time.

One example is provided by John Westlake's blunt assertion in 1896, that while 'international society' included 'a few Christian states' outside Europe and the Americas (such as 'the Hawaiian Islands, Liberia and the Orange Free State'), the same '[could not] be said of all Christian states, not for instance of Abyssinia'.[122] Lassa Oppenheim, writing two decades later, was slightly more generous, though no less condescending. His conclusions were also extremely muddled. Having noted that international law had 'ceased to be a law between Christian States solely' thanks to the (conditional) recognition of the Ottoman Empire and Japan, Oppenheim asserted that '[t]he position of such States as Persia, Siam, China, Korea, Abyssinia, and the like' was 'doubtful'.[123] These states were 'certainly civilised States, and Abyssinia is even a Christian State', but 'their civilisation [had] not yet reached that condition which is necessary to enable their Governments and their population in every respect to understand and to carry out the command of the rules of International Law'.[124] However, Oppenheim considered that, while all of them had made 'efforts to educate their populations, to introduce modern institutions, and thereby to raise their civilisation to the level of the Western', to the extent that they had failed to '[accomplish] this task', they would remain 'for some parts within the circle of the Family of Nations' but 'for other parts outside'.[125] Oppenheim elaborated further on this theme later in his famous treatise, in

[122] In John Westlake [1896], 'The Principles of International Law', reprinted in *The Collected Papers of John Westlake on Public International Law*, ed. Lassa Oppenheim (Cambridge University Press, 1914), 82.

[123] Lassa Oppenheim, *International Law: A Treatise*, Vol. 1 (London: Longmans, 1905), 33.

[124] Ibid., 33.

[125] Ibid., 33–4.

his discussion of the 'international personality' of 'non-Christian states' – a heading under which he included 'Abyssinia' even though (by his own admission) it was a Christian state.[126] In Africa, he declared, 'the Negro Republic of Liberia and the Congo Free State' were 'the only real and full members of the Family of Nations'. Egypt (under 'Turkish suzerainty') and 'Tunis' (a 'French protectorate'), for their parts, were only 'half-Sovereign', while Abyssinia and Morocco, Oppenheim considered, were 'both full-Sovereign States, but for some parts only within the Family of Nations'.[127]

Oppenheim's bewilderment no doubt stemmed, in part, from the fact that many treaties had already been concluded with 'Abyssinia' by the turn of the century, when he was writing. As the next section will describe, the Ethiopian Empire had been consistently and explicitly recognised as a sovereign equal in all of these treaties. However, these agreements also, and in the same breath, extracted conditions in return for that recognition which crystallised its status as a sovereign 'unequal'. It was in this way that the Ethiopian Empire was 'born' into the 'family of nations' as a hybrid international person – as a juridical 'nègre blanc'.

3.1 The Treaty and Concession Regime of the Late Nineteenth Century: Ethiopia as Both Subject and Object of International Law

One of the earliest of these treaties was the 1841 Treaty of Amity and Commerce negotiated, during the *Zemene Mesafint*, between the British Empire and the core region of Shewa, then led by *Negus* Sahle-Selassie (1795–1847).[128] In common with many of the treaties which Britain and others were concluding then with non-European empires in other parts of the world,[129] this treaty emphasised the formally equal standing of both 'sovereigns', placing a particularly strong emphasis on reciprocity.[130] For instance, it provided for the reciprocal freedom of travel and residence both for British subjects within Shewa and for Shewan subjects throughout the British Empire (Arts. 13–15). The signatories agreed limits to the taxation of 'British merchants', who obtained the right to import and export goods in and out of Shewa without any further restrictions (Arts. 5, 7 and 8), in

[126] Ibid., 148.
[127] Ibid., 156–7.
[128] *Treaty of Amity and Commerce between Great Britain and Shewa*, Angollah, 15 November 1841.
[129] See Item 2, Section 2, above.
[130] See Matthew Craven, 'What Happened to Unequal Treaties? The Continuities of Informal Empire', 74 *Nordic Journal of International Law* (2005): 335–82.

return for 'national treatment' provisions for the 'goods and merchandize of all subjects of Shewa who may visit Great Britain' (Art. 9). In addition to further equivalent measures aimed at securing reciprocal freedom of trade, contract, travel and residence for both British and Shewan individuals, Sehle Selassie undertook 'to keep open and secure the avenues of approach betwixt the sea-coast and Abyssinia', for 'the better security of merchants [both British and Shewan] and their property' (Art. 12).

The purpose of establishing relations of formal equality not only between the British Empire and Shewa but also between British and Shewan individuals in the two countries' respective jurisdictions is clarified if we turn to the account, published shortly after his return to Britain, by the treaty's British negotiator, William Harris. 'British commerce', Harris observed,

> has not only forced its way, but created markets and customers in many a wilder and more inaccessible portion of the globe than highland Abyssinia, and its operation promises to open the only means of improvement and civilization ... [T]he living ship of the desert is a machine of transport adequate to the most important traffic; and, if once established, that traffic would in a few years doubtless bind both people and ruler in the strongest chains of personal interest. It would rapidly change the pursuits of the people – convert the rude hut into a comfortable dwelling – limit, if not extinguish, the slave trade with Arabia, and if not reform, at least enlighten, the clouded Christianity of Æthiopia.[131]

As Harris's observations confirm, the treaty's painstaking constitution of reciprocal 'freedom' and 'equality' between Shewa and the British Empire should not be taken as reflecting a British belief that the two countries were of equal standing. It was, as its negotiator suggested, hardly likely that a kingdom which was unable to draw the line between individuals and commodities, whose architectural imagination was still restricted to the 'rude hut', and whose manufacturing output consisted (as Harris also pointed out) exclusively of hand-woven goods, would offer any serious competition to the firms or goods of the world's leading industrialised power, whether inside Shewa or elsewhere. In a context of material inequality on this scale, as Harris well knew, the institution of a regime of *formal* equality between Britain and Shewa, and between British and Shewan individuals, would have had a double advantage: that of flattering the Negus, while also creating a formal 'level playing field' upon which the strongest would find it easy to win.[132] In return, Sehla Selassie was

[131] Harris, *The Highlands of Æthiopia*, Vol. 2, 384.

[132] For further details of the treaty negotiations, see Rubenson, *The Survival*, 152–9.

left with the impression he would have access to 'a steady supply of arms, ammunition' – always an important concern for Ethiopian rulers.[133]

Eight years later the British concluded a second treaty, with the imperial regent, Ras Ali II of Begemder. This treaty of 1849 reproduced the Shewan treaty almost word for word, but with some extras included.[134] These included the addition of a 'most favoured nation' (MFN) clause 'grant[ing] to the subjects of Her Britannic Majesty, and to the produce and commerce of her dominions, all favours, privileges, advantages, or immunities, either as regards duties, imposts, or charges, or in any other respect whatsoever, which His Majesty of Abyssinia has already granted, or may hereafter grant, to the subjects, produce, or commerce of any other foreign country' (Art. 4). The national treatment clause was widened from Shewa to include the Empire as a whole, with the addition of an MFN clause for Ethiopians 'in the United Kingdom' (not this time in the whole British Empire (Art. 9)). A new clause provided that 'commercial intercourse shall be allowed and encouraged betwixt the subjects of Abyssinia and of the countries beyond that kingdom, on the one hand, and the subjects of Great Britain, on the other' (Art. 10). The most radical alteration was a non-reciprocal provision for British consular jurisdiction (Art. 17). Again, account of the conclusion of the treaty with *Ras* Ali II given by the British mission's head, Walter Plowden, offers a sharp contrast to this emphasis in the text, on formal equality and reciprocal recognition.

> [O]ne morning, I went into [Emperor Ali II's] inner tent, and had the Treaty read to him by my scribe. After the Abyssinian manner, he kept talking to his favourite shoomeree [*sic*] about a horse that was tied in the tent, and that was nearly treading me under foot half a dozen times (we all sat on the ground, the Ras inclusive) ... I begged his attention to what was being read, to which he assented, and yawned exceedingly; however, it was got through, some points having been explained and dwelt upon by me. Whereupon, the Ras said that he saw no harm whatever in the document; on the contrary, that it was excellent, but appeared to him exceedingly useless, inasmuch as he did not suppose, as Abyssinia was then constituted, that one English merchant would or could enter it in ten years.[135]

[133] Rubenson, *The Survival*, 155.

[134] *Treaty of Friendship and Commerce between Great Britain and Abyssinia*, Ennowga, 2 November 1849.

[135] Plowden, *Travels in Abyssinia*, 429. Plowden having been murdered between Gondar and the Red Sea coast on his way back to Britain, his memoirs were edited and published by his brother, Trevor Chichele Plowden. For a similar view, see the account of Lord Edward Gleichen, leader of the next British diplomatic mission to Ethiopia in 1897: Count Gleichen, *With the Mission to Menelik, 1897* (London: Edward Arnold, 1898), esp. 3, 152.

In this, Ali II was quite correct. But for the British that was precisely the point: not immediately to flood the country with British goods, for which the Ethiopian economy was clearly unready, but to ensure that, when the time came, Britain would have the advantage.

As Plowden well knew, the 'merchants' of a country like Ethiopia (of which, as we have seen, there were not very many in any case) were unlikely to arrive in Britain at all, let alone in sufficient numbers as to require their reciprocal rights to be engaged. Plowden, in any case, had already noted the absence of profit-maximising rationality among Ethiopian individuals, remarking on the latter's (in his view) peculiar habit of giving and receiving favours without payment being exchanged. 'Among equals', he noted, 'it is the custom to beg for anything that they may fancy ... A chief of the highest rank will ask, without shame, for the merest trifle.'[136] The only class of person relatively 'free from this habit', he noted, were '[t]he principal merchants'.[137] Other than that, 'from the king to the beggar' this was a custom 'in universal use', he said, such that 'it may be said that Abyssinia is a nation of beggars in various disguises'.[138] Ethiopia, after all, produced almost nothing the European market desired beyond coffee, the production of which for export began only after 1917.[139] There was no danger that a balance of payments crisis like that caused by European demand for Chinese silk, porcelain and tea would develop in this context (Britain was, of course, between the two Opium Wars at this point). What Ethiopia did possess, however, was water – a prime consideration for the British, considering the dependence in Anglo-Egyptian Sudan on the water which flowed along the Blue Nile from Lake T'ana. Ethiopia also possessed a potentially enormous market and, relatedly, a potentially unlimited supply of free labour. In order to unlock this potential, however, two things were required: on the one hand, protections for the basic rights to life, liberty and property on the part of British traders, including a regime of free travel, trade and contract, as well as consular or some other form of extraterritorial jurisdiction; on the other, the abolition of slavery, which would simultaneously swell the size both of the labour market and the market for commodities from the British Empire.

These episodes from British practice were replicated in an escalating sequence of treaties concluded between the leading members of the

[136] Plowden, *Travels in Abyssinia*, 408.
[137] Ibid.
[138] Ibid.
[139] Donham, 'Old Abyssinia', 27.

'family of nations' and various Ethiopian regions or with the Ethiopian Empire as a whole over the next fifty years.[140] Moreover, Menelik II's reign (from 1889 to 1913) coincided, as we saw earlier, with the construction of a new normative regime in Africa, stemming (in the wake of the Berlin and Brussels Acts) both from the operationalisation of the principle of 'effective occupation', and from the impulse to eliminate slavery while also expanding the conditions necessary for the introduction of European commerce into Africa.[141] Together with the opening of the Suez Canal in 1869, these factors rapidly 'transformed the Horn of Africa into a highly strategic region' for European trade.[142] The British gradually established protectorates of varying degrees of formality over 'British Somaliland' (1888), Egypt (1882), Sudan (1899) and over British East Africa, later Kenya (1895). French control over French Somaliland (Djibouti) was formalised in 1896, while Italian Somaliland was confirmed as a protectorate in the 1880s, during which period Italy was also in the process of gaining the foothold, initially commercial, on the Ethiopian coast (see Map 2).[143] In this process, the initial concerns of these three states to nail down relations of formal equality with the Empire (including establishing provisions for extraterritorial jurisdiction and the abolition of slavery in Ethiopia[144]) came increasingly to be tied in with the desire to extend such relations to one another. This extension would ensure that, even if Ethiopia did not, at that moment, offer much in terms of resources and

[140] See e.g. *Treaty of Peace, Friendship and Commerce between France and the Sultan of Gobad*, Obock, 9 April 1884, with provisions, among other things, for French freedom of movement (Art. 2), freedom of contract and freedom of exchange for French merchants (Art. 5); *Treaty of Friendship and Commerce between Shewa and Italy*, Ancober, 21 May 1883, with provisions for reciprocal appointment of ambassadors (Art. 2), free trade (Art. 3), national treatment (Art. 4), freedom of movement for Italian nationals (Art. 7), a 5 per cent flat-rate import tax on Italian goods (Art. 8) and consular jurisdiction for all disputes involving Italians (Art. 12), MFN (Art. 14); *Treaty to Regulate Commercial Relations between the United States of America and the Ethiopian Empire*, Addis Ababa, 27 December 1903; *Treaty between the Austro-Hungarian Empire and the Ethiopian Empire*, Addis Ababa, 21 March 1905.

[141] See Item 2, Section 2.2.2, above.

[142] Kevin Shillington (ed.), *The Encylopaedia of African History*, Vol. 1 (New York: Fitzroy Dearborn, 2005), 613.

[143] *Convention between Berehan Dini, Sultan of Raheita, and the Rubattino Company for the Cession of the Islands of Ommel-Buchar, Ras-er-Raml, and the Darmachie Group*, Raheita, 30 December 1879; *Convention between Danakil Chiefs and Rubattino Company for the Cession of the Island of Sennabor and the Continental region between Ras Darmab and Ras Lumah*, Assab, 15 May 1880.

[144] For an excellent analysis, see Hailegabriel G. Feyissa, 'European Extraterritoriality in Semicolonial Ethiopia', 17 *Melbourne Journal of International Law* (2016): 1–28.

markets, British, French and Italian citizens and goods would at least be able to find a way *through* Ethiopia (both in terms of transport and of taxation) on favourable terms. The three powers were also concerned, of course, to formalise the boundaries of their newly extended possessions, which in turn implied the formalisation of the traditionally flexible limits of the Ethiopian Empire itself.[145]

Again and again, however, even as their negotiators proceeded on the basis of a frankly racist and predatory rationale, the Ethiopian Empire was recognised in these treaties as a sovereign equal of equivalent standing to its co-signatories.[146] As this suggests, far from being a response to ('declaration of') a pre-existing relationship of formal equality existing (i) between the Ethiopian Empire and other states, and (ii) between individual Ethiopian and European diplomats and traders, these treaties quite clearly sought not just to 'constitute', but actually to *call into being* that relationship of formal equality – that is, to 'hail' Ethiopia and Ethiopians as legal subjects. Returning to the language of Althusser and Edelman,[147] we might say that the aim of these treaties was to trigger – through a combination of material necessity and 'specular' desire – a legal transformation that operated simultaneously in two dimensions: reconstructing the Ethiopian Empire as a state; and reconstructing the individuals over whom the Ethiopian Emperor exercised power as its citizens. If this suggestion is plausible, then it allows us to make sense of Harris's observation that by opening Ethiopia up to international commerce, the 1941 Anglo-Shewan Treaty would 'doubtless bind both people and ruler in the strongest chains of personal interest' and in doing so 'extinguish' slavery. Firstly, the function of this and virtually all the other treaties that were subsequently concluded with Ethiopia over the next

[145] Treaties combining these two interests were concluded with respect to French and British Somaliland (1897), Sudan (1902), British East Africa (1907), Italian Somaliland (1908) and beyond during Menelik's reign – perhaps most dramatically, with Eritrea, the annexation of which by Italy was confirmed on 10 July 1902. See Rubenson, *The Survival*, 111–12; *Treaty between Italy and Ethiopia, for the Delimitation of the Frontier between Eritrea and Ethiopia*, Addis Ababa, 10 July 1900; *Treaty between Great Britain and Ethiopia, and between Great Britain, Italy, and Ethiopia, relative to the Frontiers between the Soudan* [*sic*], *Ethiopia, and Eritrea*, Addis Ababa, 15 May 1902.

[146] See e.g. *Treaty of Commerce between the United States and the Ethiopian Empire*, Addis Ababa, 27 June 1914. This treaty was virtually identical in its terms to all the others described above, providing, for example, to 'citizens of the two Powers' the freedom to 'travel and transact business throughout the extent of the territories' of the two signatories (Art. 1); for 'security of those engaged in business therein, and of their property' (Art. 2); most favoured nation treatment for the 'citizens' of both signatories (Art. 3); and so on.

[147] See Frame, Section 2, above.

century was to extend the rights of existing legal subjects (the citizens of sovereign states like Britain) into Ethiopian territory. Secondly, these treaties recognised that in order to be realised 'effectively', the European/American individual rights they caused to be reproduced in Ethiopia (to trade freely, to equality before the law and so on) would need to constitute similar rights at least for those Ethiopians with whom European legal subjects interacted, in a kind of mirror-process that was (precisely as Althusser suggests) '*doubly* speculary'.[148] Finally, efforts to abolish slavery would – in principle – have the effect of transforming an enormous underclass of right-less slaves and *gebbar* into a class, if not of 'citizens', then certainly of 'natives' in the European colonial sense – wage-labourers capable (at least) of owning and exchanging property, and to this end prohibited from being owned and exchanged themselves.[149]

Ethiopia and Ethiopians did not, however, prove as responsive to the interpellative effects of this logic as had been hoped. This, perhaps, can help to explain why it was that, even as the European powers repeatedly reaffirmed their recognition of Ethiopia's status as a sovereign equal,[150] they were also, and simultaneously, concluding agreements among themselves which described (and in doing so, constituted) Ethiopia as something less than 'fully' sovereign. Perhaps the most notorious concerns the 1889 Treaty of Wich'alle (or 'Uccialli', in the Italianised version) concluded between Ethiopia and Italy.[151] In typical fashion, this treaty was devoted to resolving boundary questions (Art. 3), setting up reciprocal diplomatic relations (Art. 2), establishing consular jurisdiction for disputes involving Italians (Arts. 10, 12 and 13), prohibiting the slave trade (Art. 14), and establishing a scrupulously reciprocal regime for 'the subjects of each of the two Contracting Parties', who were mutually empowered to 'freely enter, travel, and [exit] with their effects and merchandise' the territories under the other's jurisdiction (Art. 7) as well as to 'buy or sell, let or hire, and dispose of their property in any other way, similarly to natives' (Art. 8). However, this apparently watertight evidence of Italy's recognition both of Ethiopia and of Ethiopians as full and equal legal subjects

[148] Louis Althusser, 'Ideology and Ideological State Apparatus (Notes towards an Investigation)', Ben Brewster (trans.), in Althusser, *Essays on Ideology* (London: Verso, 1984), 54. Emphasis in the original. See Frame, Section 2.2, above.

[149] Harris, *The Highlands of Æthiopia*, 384.

[150] See, among others, e.g. *Convention Additional to the Treaty of Friendship and Commerce signed at the Camp of Ucciali*, Naples, 1 October 1889, Art. 1: 'The King of Italy recognises King Menelek [*sic*] as Emperor of Ethiopia'.

[151] *Treaty of Perpetual Peace and Friendship between Ethiopia and Italy*, Wich'alle, 29 September 1889 ('Treaty of Wich'alle').

is belied by two peculiarities. First, the treaty permitted the sale of arms and ammunition only to Menelik himself (Art. 6) – a restriction in keeping with European commitments under the Brussels Act.[152] Secondly, and more radically, there was a mismatch (deliberate, as it turned out) between the Amharic and Italian versions of Article 17. This became evident on 11 October 1889, when Italy notified the signatories of the Berlin Act, 'in conformity with' Article 34 of that Act, that Menelik II had agreed, under Article 17 of the Treaty of Wich'alle, 'to avail himself of the government of H.M. the King of Italy for any negotiations which he may enter into with the other Powers or Governments'.[153] In submitting this notification, Italy made clear its intention that Ethiopia should now be recognised as an Italian protectorate, for Article 34 of the Berlin Act committed its signatories to making any new claims of sovereignty 'effective' (as Articles 7 and 8 of the Treaty arguably did) and to notifying the others of such claims.[154] In the Amharic version of the treaty, however, Ethiopia's use of Italy as a conduit for its foreign affairs was optional. Italy, in other words, had attempted to trick Ethiopia into signing away its independence in the small-print of a treaty which, in almost all of its other clauses, affirmed it as a sovereign equal.

Menelik's response was to write a letter of his own to the European heads of state in October 1890, declaiming Italy's duplicity as 'degrading' to his 'independent kingdom'.[155] These protests were, on the surface, very successful.[156] President Carnot of France wrote to Menelik expressing sympathy for his efforts to 'develop the greatness and the prosperity of the proud nation which has so courageously defended its independence and Christian faith for centuries'.[157] Russia likewise refused to recognise Italy's claims, declaring that 'she regards Menelik as an independent sovereign'.[158] Only a few years later, however, France was persuaded to stop supplying Ethiopia with arms in the middle of the first Ethio-Italian War (1895–6), discussed below, on the grounds that no one could wish for the success of this 'brave but barbarous foe' at the 'price of the

[152] See Item 2, Section 2.2.2.

[153] Rubenson, *The Survival*, 389.

[154] See further Item 2, Section 2.2.

[155] Menelik to President Carnot of France, 30 October 1890, quoted in Rubenson, *The Survival*, 392.

[156] Rubenson, *The Survival*, 389–92.

[157] Ibid., 397.

[158] Quoted in Rubenson, *The Survival*, 397. Menelik had already appealed to the Tsar for arms on the basis of Orthodox Christian solidarity. See also Marcus, *Menelik II*, 116.

discomfiture of a civilised nation'.[159] Meanwhile, barely a year after the 'Uccialli' debacle, Britain had for its part embarked on a series of negotiations with Italy whose fruit was a series of 'Protocols' of March and April 1891 and May 1894 (Map 2) in which they divided Ethiopia into two potential 'spheres of influence' – a smaller British one in the south-west and in a narrow strip of the east, and a huge Italian 'zone' covering almost the entire Empire, from the northern plateaux down to the Ogaden desert in the south-east.[160] These Protocols contained no clue whatsoever as to what would trigger the activation of these 'spheres of influence', or indeed what that 'influence' might entail. Nonetheless, on the day before the second of them was published, the heads of state of Italy and Britain wrote to Menelik assuring him that 'nothing was closer to [their heart[s]' than to see the Ethiopian crown 'honoured and independent'.[161]

Menelik terminated the Treaty of Wich'alle on 27 February 1893,[162] writing to King Umberto of Italy:

> it is with much dishonesty that he [Umberto], pretending friendship, has desired to seize my country. Because God gave the crown and the power that I should protect the land of my forefathers, I terminate and nullify this treaty. I have not, however, nullified my friendship. Know that I desire no other treaty than this. My kingdom is an independent kingdom and I seek no-one's protection.[163]

Italy, still insisting on the 'legality' of its proclaimed protectorate, as it would continue to do even in 1935,[164] responded with a 'defence plan' which aimed to exploit Ethiopia's characteristic united-but-fragmented system of government. Pretenders to the throne would be encouraged, and it was hoped that with Menelik's elimination, 'the empire could be divided into two kingdoms, one in the north, another in the south, under Italy's lofty protection'.[165] This idea, again underscoring the hybridised nature of

[159] Rubenson, *The Survival*, 395–7.

[160] *Protocol between the British and Italian Governments for the Demarcation of their respective Spheres of Influence in Eastern Africa, from the River Juba to the Blue Nile*, Rome, 24 March 1891; *Protocol between Great Britain and Italy for the Demarcation of their respective Spheres of Influence in East Africa, from Ras Kasar to the Blue Nile*, Rome, 15 April 1891; *Protocol between Great Britain and Italy defining their respective Spheres of Influence in Eastern Africa*, Rome, 5 May 1894 (see Map 2).

[161] King Umberto to Menelik II, 15 April 1891, quoted in Rubenstein, *The Survival*, 393.

[162] Rubenstein, *The Survival*, 394.

[163] Quoted in Ibid., 394.

[164] 'Situation in Ethiopia. Memorandum by the Italian Government, and Documents Relating Thereto', 4 September 1935, in *LNOJ* (November 1935): 1355–417, at 1357.

[165] Roberto Battaglia, *La prima guerra d'Africa* (Torino: Einaudi, 1958), 572–4.

contemporary perceptions of the Ethiopian Empire, that Ethiopia's non-Christian, colonised 'periphery' might legitimately be amputated from its northern Christian, imperial core, would emerge again and again in the years leading up to 1935. Meanwhile, from December 1894 onwards, fighting between Italian and Ethiopian forces slowly escalated into the First Ethio-Italian War.

3.2 The Bombshell of Adwa and the Whitification[166] *of Menelik II*

Ethiopia's resounding defeat of the invading Italians first at Dogali[167] (26 January 1887) and then, even more resoundingly, at Adwa (1 March 1896) threw Europe into chaos.[168] Newspapers in Britain and France expressed their fears that the defeat 'must diminish European prestige throughout Africa whenever civilisation is brought into contact with barbarism',[169] while the Austria-Hungarian and German Empires (Italy's partners in the Triple Alliance) urged Italy to settle the score with Ethiopia immediately, so as to reinstate its 'rightful' position among the European powers.[170] Rioting broke out in all major Italian cities, and Francesco Crispi's government resigned in disgrace.[171]

The language used by Europeans to make sense of this shock defeat of a European state by an African polity is, again, revealing. Initially, as the historian Birhanu Teferra has shown, officials and commentators sought to rationalise the outcome of Adwa by narrating it as a 'disaster' which (like an earthquake or a tsunami) had 'befallen' Italy.[172] Over time, however, as

[166] On the concept of 'whitification', from critical race theory, see in particular Michelle Wallace, *Invisibility Blues: From Pop to Theory* (London, New York: Verso, 1990), 19.

[167] Ironically, the origins of the Battle of Dogali lie in Britain's decision to renege, strategically, on its treaty with Ethiopia of 3 June 1884, ceding Massawa to Italy rather than restoring it from Egypt to Ethiopia and thereby demonstrating its own inability to 'carry out the command of the rules of International Law' cited by Oppenheim as being demonstrative of Ethiopia's unreadiness for international personality. See Richard Pankhurst, 'Ras Alula, Dogali and the Beginnings of Italian Colonialism on the Horn of Africa', in Taddesse Beyane, Taddesse Tamrat and Richard Pankhurst (eds.), *The Centenary of Dogali: Proceedings of the International Symposium*, Addis Ababa-Asmara, 24–25 January 1987 (Addis Ababa: Institute of Ethiopian Studies, Addis Ababa University, 1988), 123–6.

[168] See respectively Taddesse et al., *The Centenary of Dogali*; Abdussamad and Pankhurst (eds.), *Adwa*. These two defeats also marked the beginning of the Italian anti-colonial movement.

[169] *The Times*, 6 March 1896, quoted in Birhanu Teferra, 'European Press Reactions to Adwa', in Abdussamad and Pankhurst (eds.), *Adwa*, 441–77 at 445.

[170] Birhanu, 'European Press Reactions', 463–4.

[171] Ibid., 445.

[172] Marcus, 'Racist Discourse', 441.

another historian, Harold Marcus notes, European commentators, unable to abandon their white supremacist assumptions, adopted a different strategy: they began increasingly to characterise Ethiopians as Caucasian or, at least, as not entirely Black. Above all, they began to describe Menelik as an African leader of such exceptional quality as to have proven himself, as it were, an honorary white person. Count Gleichen, negotiator of the 1897 Anglo-Ethiopian Treaty, for example, described Menelik as a military 'genius', who had by 'an almost superhuman activity and attention to every detail … succeeded … in consolidating the country'.[173] Robert Skinner, who as chief of the first US mission to Ethiopia, negotiated the Commercial Treaty of 1904, had a similar reaction.[174] Menelik, he wrote, had single-handedly 'created the United States of Abyssinia – a work for which he was endowed by Nature with the constructive intelligence of a Bismarck, and the faculty of handling men by sheer amiability of a McKinley'.[175] From this 'basically racist' viewpoint, Marcus points out, '[i]f usually inferior people accomplished anything, they necessarily had to be superhuman, extraordinary, and astonishing'.[176]

This new way of making sense of Ethiopia's exceptionality by attributing the Empire's successes to its extraordinary Emperor made it possible, in 1896, for Italy to swallow its pride and conclude a peace treaty in which it recognised 'without reserve' the 'absolute independence of the Ethiopian Empire as a sovereign and independent state'.[177] The following year, meanwhile, both Britain and France concluded fresh treaties with the Ethiopian Empire, providing, as usual, for mutual recognition, 'freedom of intercourse', MFN treatment and other now-familiar clauses dedicated to constructing an 'open door' into Ethiopia.[178] Indeed, according to the legal historian Theodore Vestal, 1896 became the 'year of the *ferenj* [foreigner]' in Ethiopia, with European states 'rushing' to conclude

[173] Gleichen, *With the Mission to Menelik*, 3, 152. For the treaty, see below, note 178.

[174] *Treaty to Regulate Commercial Relations between the United States of America and Ethiopia*, Addis Ababa, 27 December 1904.

[175] Robert P. Skinner, *Abyssinia of To-Day: An Account of the First Mission Sent by the American Government to the Court of the King of Kings (1903–1904)* (New York: Longmans, Green & Co., 1906), 141, cited in Marcus, 'Racist Discourse', 397. William McKinley was US President from 1897–1901.

[176] Marcus, 'Racist Discourse', 396–7. See also Harold G. Marcus, 'The Black Men Who Turned White: European Attitudes Towards Ethiopians, 1850–1900', 39 *Archiv Orientální* (1971): 155–265.

[177] *Treaty of Peace between the Kingdom of Italy and the Ethiopian Empire*, Addis Ababa, 26 October 1896, Art. 3 ('Treaty of Addis Ababa').

[178] *Treaty between Great Britain and Ethiopia (Frontiers of British Protectorate on Somali Coast)*, Addis Ababa, 14 May 1897, Arts. 1, 2 and 4.

treaties and 'set up consulates throughout the country and [to aid] foreign merchants and investors seeking concessions and royalties'.[179] Many of the mainly mining, agricultural and commercial concessions that were granted by Menelik to foreign corporations during this period remained 'of paper value' only.[180] A few of them, however, became extremely important, such as the railway concession granted on 9 March 1894 to Ilg, Menelik's long-time Swiss advisor, from which grew the Addis Ababa–Djibouti Railway,[181] and a banking monopoly given to the British on 10 March 1905, thanks to which Ethiopia's first bank, the Bank of Abyssinia, was set up.[182] As Bahru notes, '[t]he former provided the infrastructure for imperialist penetration of [Ethiopia], the latter its financial arm'.[183]

3.3 *Imperial Sovereignty as Spheres of Influence: The Tripartite Agreement and the Treaty of London*

This rhetorical solution to the paradox of a strong African state could only be temporary, however. For if Ethiopia's success as a subject of international law rested solely on Menelik's quasi-white subjectivity, the question of how Ethiopia's status would be regarded after his death remained unresolved. Among European scholars, heads of state, diplomats and other officials, the consensus that Ethiopia's independence would not last long after Menelik went virtually unchallenged. This projected precariousness was attributed not to their own imperial desires but to Ethiopia's internal state of 'sickening disorder', as one commentator later put it[184] – a state which would force the European powers to intervene as soon as Menelik was out of the way.

179 Theodore M. Vestal, 'Reflections on the Battle of Adwa and its Significance Today', in Paulos Milkias and Getachew Metaferia (eds.), *The Battle of Adwa: Reflections on Ethiopia's Historic Victory Against European Colonialism* (New York: Algora Publishing, 2005), 21–36, at 32.

180 Bahru Zewde, 'Concessions and Concession-Hunters in Post-Adwa Ethiopia: The Case of Arnold Holz', 45 *Africa: Rivista trimestrale di studi e documentazione dell'Istituto italiano perl'Africa e l'Oriente* (1990): 365–83, at 366.

181 See Shiferaw Bekele, 'The Ethiopian Railway and British Finance Capital, 1896–1902', 46 *Africa: Rivista trimestrale di studi e documentazione dell'Istituto italiano perl'Africa e l'Oriente* (1991): 351–74.

182 See Charles Schaefer, 'The Politics of Banking: The Bank of Abyssinia, 1905–1931', 25 *The International Journal of African Historical Studies* (1992): 361–89.

183 Bahru, 'Concessions and Concession-Hunters', 366.

184 Harry Johnston, 'Letter to the Editor,' included in 'Abyssinian Slaves – Prof. Murray on League Action – Import of Arms', *Westminster Gazette*, 2 May 1922, in FO 371/7141 Political (Abyssinia) 1922 (UKNA).

Perhaps the most powerful and juridically potent illustration of this tendency is to be found in the 1906 'Tripartite Agreement' concluded between Britain, France and Italy,[185] shortly after news arrived that Menelik II had suffered a serious stroke.[186] Treating Ethiopia's eventual disintegration as a foregone conclusion, the three signatories began the Preamble by reaffirming their recognition of the Ethiopian Empire as a full subject of international law, and declaring it to be in their 'common interest' to 'maintain intact the integrity of Ethiopia',[187] pledging '[i]n the event of rivalries or internal changes in Ethiopia' to 'observe a neutral attitude'.[188] They also declared that the Agreement did not 'in any way infringe the sovereign rights of the Emperor of Abyssinia'.[189] In the same breath, however, the three powers also pledged to 'come to a mutual understanding in regard to their attitude in the event of any change in the situation arising in Ethiopia, and to prevent the action of the three States in protecting their respective interests ... resulting in injury to the interests of any of them'.[190] At Article 1 they agreed to 'cooperate in maintaining the political and territorial *status quo* in Ethiopia', defining this status quo, however, not on the basis of Ethiopia's internal order, but on their own interests in that country. These interests were then set out in a series of eleven boundary and commercial treaties, with the Anglo-Italian Protocols of 1891 and 1894 coming first on the list (see Map 2). At Article 2 of the Agreement, the three powers also agreed that new 'demands for agricultural, commercial, and industrial concessions in Ethiopia' would be made collaboratively, and extended protections for the individual rights of British, Italian and French nationals, including in particular their rights to trade and travel freely and to own and trade private property in Ethiopia.[191] At Article 3, however, the signatories revealed that what their

[185] *Agreement between the United Kingdom, France, and Italy respecting Abyssinia*, London, 13 December 1906, 001/1907: Cd. 3298 ('Tripartite Agreement').

[186] Antoinette Iadarola, 'Ethiopia's Admission into the League of Nations: An Assessment of Motives', 8 *International Journal of African Historical Studies* (1975): 601–22, at 603.

[187] Tripartite Agreement, Preamble.

[188] Ibid., Art. 3.

[189] Ibid., Art. 1.

[190] Ibid., Preamble.

[191] For example, the Tripartite Agreement's clauses relating to railway concessions permitted such individuals to travel, as legal subjects, along all the railway lines which were at that time under construction from ports and settlements in their colonies into Ethiopia under the auspices of various concessions granted, or expected to be negotiated, with the Ethiopian authorities. On these railways it was agreed that 'the nationals of the three countries [would] enjoy in all matters of trade and transit absolute equality of treatment', and that goods would not 'be subject to any fiscal transit duty', in effect establishing a free trade regime among the three of them along these lines of communication. The three

decision to commit to a policy of 'abstaining from all intervention in the internal affairs of the country' in the event of internal disruptions in the future actually amounted to was a pledge to restrict such intervention 'to such action as may be, by common consent, considered necessary for the protection of the Legations, of the lives and property of foreigners, and of the common interests of the three Powers'.

In sum, then, Britain, France and Italy committed themselves to a policy of non-intervention with respect to Ethiopia except when such intervention was deemed necessary to protect their interests, and those of their citizens. Britain's major concern was to secure the flow of the Blue Nile through Ethiopia to Egypt and Sudan from Lake T'ana.[192] France's objective concerned the Djibouti–Addis Ababa Railway, a French concession.[193] Italy's plans began with a desire to secure a 'territorial connection' through Ethiopia between Eritrea and Italian Somaliland[194] and ended, as we have just seen, with the dream of establishing a protectorate over the entire country.[195] In sum, the effect of the Tripartite Agreement was to divide Ethiopia up into three 'spheres of influence' (rather than two, as in the Anglo-Italian Protocols): for the British 'in the Nile Basin'; for the French in 'the French Protectorate on the Somali Coast [Djibouti], the hinterland of this Protectorate and the zone necessary for the construction of the railway'; and for Italy in 'the hinterland of her possessions and the territorial connection between them to the west of Addis Ababa'.[196] This ambivalent, not to say schizophrenic, attitude to Ethiopia's 'sovereignty' was underscored in a second agreement concluded by the same powers on the same day with respect to 'the importation of arms and ammunition into Abyssinia'.[197] This made specific reference to the Brussels Act and to the 'pernicious and preponderating

signatories also agreed 'to extend to the nationals of all other countries the benefit of the [Treaty's] provisions ... relating to equality of treatment as regards trade and transit' (Tripartite Agreement, Arts. 6–9).

192 Ibid., Art. 4a. See also *Treaty between Great Britain and Ethiopia, and between Great Britain, Italy and Ethiopia, relative to the Frontiers of the Soudan, Ethiopia, and Eritrea*, Addis Ababa, 15 May 1902, Art. 3. The same treaty also altered and/or confirmed a number of other Ethiopian borders, including the border with the Italian colony of Eritrea.

193 Ibid., Arts. 4c and 5. The realisation of this goal, in 1917, 'gave France virtual control over Ethiopian trade with the outside world'. Iadarola, 'Ethiopia's Admission', 604.

194 Tripartite Agreement, Art. 4b.

195 Iadarola, 'Ethiopia's Admission', 604.

196 Tripartite Agreement, Arts. 4a–4c.

197 *Agreement between the United Kingdom, France and Italy Respecting the Importation of Arms and Ammunition into Abyssinia*, London, 13 December 1906 ('1906 Arms and Ammunition Agreement').

part played by firearms in operations connected with the slave-trade'.[198] Replicating the hybridised narrative of the Orientalist-Semiticist paradigm, then, these two 'tripartite' treaties treated Ethiopia simultaneously as a sovereign state *and* as a territory that could be divided into European 'spheres of influence'.

Menelik's response was to write immediately to the signatories emphasising those aspects of the Treaty that were favourable to Ethiopia, and downplaying those that were not. As he put it in his letter to Italy: '*Io le ringrazio dell'avermela partecipata e della loro volontà di consolidare e mantenere l'indipendenza del Nostro regno. Ma questa attuale convenzione nelle parole di qualunque di esse (Potenze), è sottoposta al Nostro potere sovrano e sia noto che essa non Ci vincola in qualunque Nostra parola*'.[199] He also defied the 'tripartite' powers by staying alive for a further seven years. When he eventually did die, on 12 December 1913, the Ethiopian Empire entered the prolonged succession crisis described above, but Europe's attention was soon consumed by the outbreak of the First World War and its various dilemmas, including the need to entice Italy away from the Triple Alliance and onto the Allied side. In April 1915, a secret agreement was concluded with Italy to this end by Britain and France, together with Russia. 'In the event of France and Great Britain increasing their colonial territories in Africa at the expense of Germany', Italy was promised 'in principle' an 'equitable compensation, particularly as regards the settlement in her favour of the questions relative to the frontiers of the Italian colonies of Eritrea, Somaliland and Libya and the neighbouring colonies belonging to France and Great Britain'.[200] After the War, however, when Italy's demands were eventually presented to the Committee for the Application of Article 13 on 16 May 1919,[201] Italy was left, as *The Times* put it, 'in the plight of Old Mother Hubbard's dog'.[202] These demands were

[198] *Convention Relative to the Slave Trade and Importation into Africa of Firearms, Ammunition, and Spiritous Liquors*, Brussels, 2 July 1890, Art. 8.

[199] 'I thank them [the three Powers] for giving me notification and for their desire to consolidate and maintain the independence of our Government. But this arrangement in the words of each of the Powers is subordinate to our sovereign power and let it be noted that in no way does it bind our word.' Menelik II, Letter to the Government of Italy, 4 December 1906, in *Ministero degli affari esteri, Trattati, convenzioni, accordi, protocolli ed altri documenti, relative all'Africa (1825–1906)*, Vol. 2 (Rome: Italia Direzione Centrale degli Affari Coloniali, 1906), 1257.

[200] *Agreement between France, Russia, Great Britain and Italy*, London, 26 April 1915 ('Treaty of London'), Art. 13.

[201] Robert L. Hess, 'Italy and Africa: Colonial Ambitions in the First World War', 4 *Journal of African History* (1963): 105–26 at 123–4.

[202] Quoted in Iadarola, 'Ethiopia's Admission', 605.

based on Colonial Minister Gaspare Colosimo's *programma massimo* for Italian imperial expansion.[203] That programme, hypothetical to the point of delusion, called upon Italy's partners in the Tripartite Agreement to renounce all their interests in Ethiopia, which should be designated an almost exclusively Italian sphere of influence.[204] Britain and France, however, refused – and the inauguration of the Mandates System[205] gave them good grounds for doing so by ensuring that, in a formal sense, Britain and France had not in fact enlarged their own empires, but had simply taken on responsibilities of colonial 'tutelage ... on behalf of the League'.[206]

Ethiopia's independence thus survived yet another potentially terminal threat, leaving a question mark, once again, over its 'split personality', as constituted in and through the international legal practice of this era. As the reaction of Westlake and Oppenheim attests, in many ways international law responded to the Ethiopian Empire in the same way it had responded to the other 'eastern empires', such as the Chinese, Japanese and Ottoman Empires.[207] The particular problem that confronted international law when it came to Ethiopia, however – a problem that neither Westlake nor Oppenheim mentioned, but which obsessed diplomats and state officials throughout the late nineteenth and early twentieth centuries – was not only that Ethiopia was a Black state (as, indeed, were Haiti and Liberia), but that it was also a 'slave state'. According to international law's teleological narrative of 'progress' towards 'free' and 'equal' subjectivity, in other words, it was a moral and legal anachronism. It is in this context that commentators like the British journalist Herbert Vivian saw fit to remark (to give only one particularly disturbing example) that while it was 'no doubt reasonable that a nation of niggers, possessing three hundred thousand rifles, should take a tone different from that of niggers who are not permitted to possess any', Ethiopia's officials went 'too far when they presume[d] to arrogate to themselves a superiority over civilised countries against which they could not possibly stand up'.[208] As we

[203] See Hess, 'Italy and Africa', 105–8.

[204] Hess, 'Italy and Africa', 108.

[205] See Item 3, Section 4, above.

[206] *Covenant of the League of Nations*, annexed to *Treaty of Peace between the British Empire, France, Italy, Japan and the United States (the Principal Allied and Associated Powers), and Belgium, Bolivia, Brazil, China, Cuba, Czechoslovakia, Ecuador, Greece, Guatemala, Haiti, the Hedjaz, Honduras, Liberia, Nicaragua, Panama, Peru, Poland, Portugal, Roumania, the Serb-Croat-Slovene State, Siam, and Uruguay, and Germany*, Versailles, 28 June 1919, Art. 10 ('Covenant'), Art. 22.

[207] See Item 2, Section 2.3.

[208] Vivian, *Abyssinia*, 248.

have seen, the concern to abolish slavery in Ethiopia surfaced constantly, both in dedicated[209] and commercial treaties.[210] As this suggests, however 'defined' the Ethiopian Empire's boundaries may have become, however 'settled' its population, and however 'recognised' its independence, it remained difficult, if not impossible, to consider its 'system of barbaric government' (as Vivian put it) – in which the line between human 'subject' and human 'object' remained indistinct and permeable – a true 'government' for the purposes of statehood. The resilience of its rights as a subject of international law waxed and waned accordingly.

4 Complicity as Resistance: Sovereign Statehood from the Aksumite Perspective

The previous section has just drawn attention to the vacillating, sometimes actively duplicitous, but above all constitutive response of other members of the 'family of nations' to the question of Ethiopia's status. This response created, for the Ethiopian Empire, what was, in effect, a bipolar form of international legal subjectivity. The question that remains to be answered, however, is what effect this process had on Ethiopia's own sense of its status and place in the world, and on the distribution of wealth, power and pleasure within the Empire itself. Bearing in mind the 'Aksumite paradigm', Teshale's distillation of the imperial Ethiopian world view of this period, the following subsection will tackle this question by examining the official Ethiopian response to these changes, together with the internal critique that arose of this response within Ethiopia, asking how these mapped on to the four criteria for statehood in practice.

4.1 *The Aksumite Paradigm meets the Standard of Statehood*

Whatever the Ethiopian Empire was from the 'Aksumite' perspective, it was not an individual legal subject 'writ large'. The Emperor/Empress, as we have seen, occupied the pinnacle of an enormously complex subjective hierarchy, and it was in the imperial person – in his/her direct, 'Solomonic', connection with God – that the normative force of Ethiopia's 'sovereignty' lay. Nor

[209] See e.g. *Treaty between Great Britain and Abyssinia for the Suppression of the Slave Trade*, Adwa, 3 June 1884.

[210] See e.g. *Treaty of Friendship and Commerce between Ethiopia and Italy*, Wich'alle, 2 May 1889, Art. 14; in relation to the Ethiopian Empire's former coastline, shortly to become Eritrea, *Convention between the Sultan of Aussa (Danakils) and Italy for the Opening of the Assab-Aussa-Shewa Road*, 7 July 1887, Art. 1; *Treaty of Friendship and Commerce between Italy and the Sultan of Aussa (Danakils)*, Adelé Gubó, 9 December 1888, Art. 7.

Figure 7 Secretary-General Ban Ki-moon (left) briefs the UN General Assembly on his visit to Libya, New York, 10 November 2011, UN Photo #494130 © UN Photo/J.C. McIlwaine.

did the Aksumite understanding of the Empire's physical extent have much in common with the international legal idea of state 'territory'. For centuries, Ethiopia's borders had been regarded, not as fixed and unchanging, but rather as a moving front line in the eternal cosmic battle between Orthodox Christianity on the one hand, and Islam/Ethiopia's other non-Christian religions on the other. The Ethiopian Empire ended, from this official perspective, where civilisation stopped and barbarity began.[211] As Donham puts it:

> The idea of a delimited border was ... new to Abyssinian notions, and it was one to which governors in peripheral areas adapted only slowly ...

[211] Menelik II, 'Letter to the Heads of State of Britain, France, Germany, Italy and Russia', 10 April 1891, in Ian Brownlie, *African Boundaries: A Legal and Diplomatic Encyclopaedia* (Berkeley and Los Angeles, CA: University of California Press, 1979), 777–8. As early as the first decade of the nineteenth century, Welde Selassie, ruler of Tigre, had written to King George III as one Christian ruler to another, stressing, 'that he was surrounded by pagans (*aremi*, which here includes Muslims) on all sides, including the coast, and thank[ing] George III for the opportunities of communication provided by the presence of British ships in the Red Sea' (Rubenson, *The Survival*, 50). Similarly, Yohannes IV had appealed to the European heads of state on the basis of 'Christian solidarity with Ethiopia, who found herself under threat of Islami[s]ation and enslavement by Ishmail', then ruler of Egypt. Bahru, *A History of Modern Ethiopia*, 50.

> [T]raditionally there was no idea of a fixed territory in which all the inhabitants could be counted equally as 'citizens'. Abyssinians, that is, those who spoke Semitic languages and who were Orthodox Christians, lived in a certain territory ... But Abyssinian power ... was never thought to be limited to that sphere. Rather, it radiated out from the centre. The people who happened to reside in the far peripheries were not Abyssinians, but they were reserved for Abyssinian domination. This whole history appears to be encapsulated in the word that eventually came to mean citizen, *zēga*, 'subdued', 'subject', 'obedient'. Gradually *zēga* came to be applied to anyone within the boundaries of the modern state, under the domination of the nation.[212]

Likewise, the Ethiopian Empire's 'population' could not be understood, from the imperial perspective, as something that ought to be 'settled'. For generations, as we have seen, successive Ethiopian Emperors had regarded it as their duty to subjugate, convert and incorporate as many peripheral communities as possible. Whether 'Abyssinian' or not, the subjects of the Emperor were not regarded as citizens until the mid twentieth century. Until that time, they were, instead, imperial subjects, tied to the centre by strongly decentralised chains of coercion and tribute (or, in the case of slaves, simply in their capacity as imperial objects which could form part of that tribute).

As this suggests, the 'government' of the Ethiopian Empire in some ways bore a stronger resemblance to a European colonial administration than it did to the kind of 'responsible' government whose powers had, by the end of the First World War, been laid out in the constitutions of new nation-states from Peru to Serbia to Germany to China to Romania. Such colonial administrations, as we have seen, were considered 'effective' to the extent that they bound themselves (often, like Ethiopia, through the conclusion of numerous commercial treaties) to protect the legal subjectivity of visiting foreigners and abolishing slavery. Yet the resemblance was superficial. If Ethiopia's was a colonial administration, where did 'metropolitan' power end and 'native' institutions begin? In any case, the Ethiopian Empire's claim was to be a sovereign state, not a colonial administration. To this claim, its decentralised, fragmented system of authority – a system in which no clear line could be drawn between subjectivity and objectivity, public and private, formal rights and material power, secular and religious law – contributed little that seemed, from an international legal perspective, like a government. Its independence – proven at the

[212] Donham, 'Old Abyssinia', 42–3.

Battle of Adwa – provided, on close inspection, almost the only solidly 'recognisable' feature of the Ethiopian 'state'.

Starting in the late nineteenth century, however, several things began to happen which compelled Ethiopia's sovereigns quite literally to 'come to terms' with the normative system with which they were confronted – that is, international law. On the one hand, the establishment of European colonial jurisdictions on the peripheries of the Empire forced upon them the need to fix the boundaries of the Empire, and rendered more urgent the need to obtain the modern weapons that, post-Adwa, would be necessary to fend off further advancement. On the other hand, the strategy of the European and American states, in simultaneously recognising the Ethiopian Empire's sovereignty and making plans to undermine it, triggered an understandable sense of outrage, giving rise to numerous protests in which it was asserted that the Ethiopian Empire was, indeed, the sovereign equal of its neighbours. Equally, however, there was also the deep-rooted and characteristically Aksumite sense of Ethiopia as a Christian Empire, different from and yet bearing a fundamental affinity with the Christian states of Europe. The result, as outlined above, was a slew of treaties and concession agreements and an influx of foreigners. The rights of these foreigners were increasingly subject to European jurisdiction, especially in the wake of the 1908 'Klobukowski Treaty' with France,[213] whose MFN provisions ensured that its extraterritorial jurisdiction clause would be extended to foreign citizens 'and their protégés', including, as Hailegabriel Feyissa points out, the 'Africans, Arabs, Indians and East Europeans, who monopolised foreign trade in Ethiopia for much of the first half of the 20th century'.[214] Some of the frustrations generated by this gradual and partial transformation – part-coerced, part-voluntary, part-external, part-internal – into something more 'recognisable' to international law, can be heard in a song that is supposed to have been sung by some of Menelik II's soldiers, accustomed to living off the land and hence to pillaging as far afield as proved necessary and possible, now subjected to a claustrophobic new treaty regime:

> By a little scrap of paper [a treaty]
> Many countries have been lost.

[213] *Treaty of Friendship and Commerce between Ethiopia and France*, Addis Ababa, 10 January 1908 ('Klobukowski Treaty'), esp. Art. 7. Later, after 1922, a Special Court was set up to try cases arising between Ethiopians and foreigners. See Heinrich Scholler, *The Special Court of Ethiopia, 1920–1935* (Stuttgart: Äthiopistiche Forschungen, 1985).

[214] Hailegabriel, 'European Extraterritoriality in Semicolonial Ethiopia', 7.

> In the morning we had nothing to eat,
> How can we live if there is no food in the evening also?
> From Kaffa to Wallega and Joti's country[215]
> And all along the frontier you make treaties.
> Why do you do this?
> You have us and we are brave soldiers.
> From Massowah to Asmara runs the railway
> And from Jibuti to Dire Dawa;
> From Khartoum runs the boat to Gambela.
> Officers let us think this over.
> If we do not throw off this load which presses us
> In the evening it will be too late.[216]

Much like the 'Boxers' in China, Menelik's soldiers here were describing some of their anxieties about the opportunities which were gradually being given to the Empire's European treaty partners to gain control over Ethiopia's own resources. After all, Massowah (Massawa) and Asmara were now both, since the 1889 Treaty of Wichalle, within the Italian colony of Eritrea, formerly Ethiopia's coastline. The only railway in Ethiopia itself was the French-controlled railway, running from the French colony of Djibouti to Dire Dawa, and eventually extended to Addis Ababa some time later, in 1917 (see Map 3). Khartoum was then in Anglo-British Sudan, with the river route described by the soldiers running to the British concessionary port and customs station at Gambela. However, if this song indicates some of the frustrations felt by ordinary Ethiopians, it also draws our attention to some of the ways in which this transformative process sometimes served the imperial centre rather well. In particular, the new treaty regime allowed Menelik II to consolidate his nineteenth century territorial conquests over numerous previously quasi-independent rulers by drawing on the formal recognition and latent enforcement capacities of his powerful European neighbours. If we look, for example, at the letter Menelik circulated to European heads of state in April 1891

215 *Dejazmatch* Joti was one of the rulers of Welega ('Wallega') at this time.

216 Song sung by Menelik's soldiers, found in the UK Foreign Office Archives by Peter Garretson, FO371/1043/9302, 27 July 1911. Cited in Garretson, 'Vicious Cycles', 196. See Maps 1–3. Gambela was founded in 1907 by the British as a trading station along the river Baro. The concession had been granted to the British on 15 May 1902 by Menelik II in a series of treaties in which the border with Anglo-Egyptian Sudan was defined. It was thus to the British authorities at Gambela that the representatives of the Western Oromo Confederation sent their delegation in May 1936 (see Item 6, Section 2.3).

laying out the borders of the Ethiopian Empire,[217] it is evident that, rather than simply mapping Ethiopia's territorial extent, this letter was actually a 'a programme, a statement of aspirations, based upon ancient historical claims', put forward as a 'basis for expansion' – or, to put it differently, a land-grab.[218] Menlik wrote:

> While tracing today the actual boundaries of my Empire, I shall endeavour, if God gives me life and strength, to re-establish the ancient frontiers [tributaries] of Ethiopia up to Khartoum, and as far as Lake Nyanza with all the Gallas. Ethiopia has been for fourteen centuries a Christian land in a sea of pagans. If Powers at a distance come forward to partition Africa between them, I do not intend to be an indifferent spectator. As the Almighty has protected Ethiopia up to this day, I have confidence He will continue to protect her, and increase her borders in the future. I am certain He will not suffer her to be divided among other Powers.[219]

As this statement underscores, it would be inaccurate to describe Menelik as having internalised the doctrinal assumption that a 'defined territory' should constitute a definitive feature of Ethiopian statehood and hence a prerequisite for sovereign rights. On the contrary, while capitulating to this idea in principle, Menelik also stated unequivocally that, having 're-established' Ethiopia's 'ancient frontiers', he aspired to expand them in the future – a project he regarded as his divinely sanctioned duty. If international law was determined to narrate the Empire as both 'self' and 'other' simultaneously, then Menelik seems to have taken this ambivalence as an opportunity to adopt the language of international law (the language of sovereignty, independence, territorial boundedness, MFN and so on) *only* insofar as it served his own interests, and his own identity, as Ethiopian Emperor.

Menelik's letter, which received no reply, was followed up a few years later by Ethiopia's crushing victory over the Italians at Adwa. According to Vestal, this victory allowed him to preserve and extend 'the territories of ancient Ethiopia' (excepting its coastline) and to 'implement the idea of a central government that might supplant the Ethiopian Orthodox Church as the symbol of national unity', thus laying the groundwork which would allow Ethiopia, at last, to become 'part and parcel of a globalized world that recognizes sovereignty – a value for which the heroes of Adwa

[217] Menelik II, Letter to the Heads of State of Britain, France, Germany, Italy and Russia, 10 April 1891, in Brownlie, *African Boundaries*, 777–8.

[218] Menelik II, Letter to the European Heads of State, 777.

[219] Ibid.

sacrificed their lives.'[220] Yet the idea that Ethiopian 'sovereignty' developed as an ontological reality, then to be straightforwardly 'recognised' by the 'world', is problematic. Menelik did set up ministries for the first time in 1907, for example, having 'expressed his dismay at hearing Europeans say that Ethiopia was a country without law and that it had a government without rules and regulations'.[221] It remains the case, however, that his new ministers (threatened with excommunication if they disobeyed the rules) were primarily for show.[222] Menelik's objective in making this concession 'to the outward norms of European government' was not, Bahru argues, to make his country more like a European state, but instead to boost his reputation in relation to his neighbours, and therefore internally, 'in the difficult years ... [he] foresaw following his stroke'.[223]

Even in 1931, when Ethiopia's first constitution was drafted during the first year of the reformist Emperor Haile Selassie's reign by *Bäjerond* Täklä-Hawaryat Täklä-Maryam (who served as head of the Ethiopian Delegation to the League of Nations at the height of the Abyssinia Crisis[224]), Ethiopian institutions of 'government' bore only a partial resemblance to the idea described by the criterion of 'government', as laid down by the Montevideo Convention less than two years later. This constitution, based in many ways on the Japanese 'Meji' Constitution of 1889 (itself based on the Constitution of the German Empire), began by asserting that: '*Le territoire d'Ethiopie, dans son ensemble, est d'un bout à l'autre soumis au Gouvernement de Sa Majesté l'Empereur. Tous les natifs de l'Ethiopie sujets de l'Empire forment ensemble la nation éthiopienne*.'[225] It then went on, at virtually every step, to insist that 'in virtue of his imperial blood' ('*en vertu de son sang impérial*'), the Emperor, Haile Selassie, was '*droit à tous les honneurs qui lui sont dus conformément à la tradition et à la présente constitution*'.[226] His power ('*pouvoir*') was absolute ('*incontestible*'). As this suggests, individuals within the Empire were not described as 'citizens', but rather as 'natives' and 'subjects'. On the one hand, the Constitution

220 Vestal, 'Reflections on the Battle of Adwa', 31–5.

221 Bahru, *Pioneers of Change*, 176.

222 Ibid., 176.

223 Ibid., 175.

224 See Items 5 and 6, below.

225 'The territory of Ethiopia, in its entirety, is, from one end to the other, subject to the government of His Majesty the Emperor. All the natives of Ethiopia, subjects of the Empire, together form the Ethiopian Empire.' *Constitution of the Empire of Ethiopia*, Addis Ababa, 16 July 1931, Art. 1 ('1931 Ethiopian Constitution'), Art. 1.

226 '[E]ntitled to all the honours due to him in accordance with tradition and with the present Constitution.' 1931 Ethiopian Constitution, Art. 5.

bestowed on them an equal right not to be 'deprived' of their 'moveable or landed property'.[227] On the other, the law was subject entirely to the 'supreme power' of the Emperor himself.[228] Meanwhile, members of both the new Senate[229] and the new Chamber of Deputies were to be selected from the nobility, 'until the people are capable of electing them for themselves'.[230] In short, the 1931 Constitution re-inscribed all the hierarchies celebrated by the Aksumite paradigm, but did so by gesturing, in some places, to the language of 'self-government'. Bearing this in mind, the next section will turn, finally, to the impact of the process of becoming a 'sovereign state' on the question of what it was, in both a normative and a material sense, to be an individual within the Ethiopian Empire.

4.2 *Legal Subjectivity on Aksumite Terms*

Prior to the mid nineteenth century, as we have seen, ideas of formal equality and negative freedom played little part in Ethiopian society. Whether noblemen, clergymen, *gebbar*, merchants, artisans, slaves and/or women, individuals within the Ethiopian Empire clearly cannot be said to have regarded their relationship to the imperial administration as a social contract to which they had, in however theoretical a way, 'consented'. Nor do they seem to have regarded themselves as existing in a relationship of formal equality to one another, such that the encroachment by one on the liberties of another represented the limits of individual 'right'. On the contrary, individual liberty in the Ethiopian Empire, as we have seen, was a precarious thing, capable of being lost partially, or even altogether, for those unlucky enough, for example, to find themselves on the losing side of an imperial war or slave raid. In terms of property rights, as noted in Section 2.3, above, members of the peasantry (not the holders of *gult*) were the owners of their own land; yet the *gebbar* was not permitted to sell her land, and left it unattended at her peril. Nor did the *gebbar* exercise rights to dispose 'freely' of her produce or labour, which was subject to formalised approbation by her social superiors. With exchange for the purpose of generating profit (the very process which, according to Pashukanis and Edelman, gives rise to the formally free and negatively equal interpersonal relations which constitute law) very much frowned

[227] Ibid., Art. 27.
[228] Ibid., Art. 29.
[229] Ibid., Art. 31.
[230] Ibid., Art. 32.

upon, commercial interaction was, by all accounts, far less important than tribute or straightforward extraction. Ethiopian imperial society was, as John Markakis describes it, a 'stratified, highly authoritarian social system with its ranked allocation of authority, status and privilege' – one which varied in its details depending on the influence of local customs and on the 'spiritual legitimacy' accorded to it by the Church, which in turn guaranteed its 'acceptance by the peasant mass'.[231]

Nonetheless, the period of transformation described above also witnessed the emergence of a very powerful internal critique of Ethiopia's traditional mode of self-organisation. This critique was partly inspired by European ideas (almost all of Ethiopia's 'reformist intellectuals', as Bahru Zewde calls them, had obtained a European education, either having been sent abroad or to the Swedish, French, Italian, Armenian, Greek or other missionary and community schools set up in Ethiopia from the 1840s onwards). However, its authors also sought to defend aspects of Ethiopian imperial society from the ills associated with Westernisation, and with the introduction of capitalism in particular.[232] For example, in 1912 Gäbra-Heywät Baykädañ[233] lamented that '[i]n our country, it is shameful to earn your bread by the sweat of your brow', and honourable 'to be called a soldier ... following a chief like a dog'. And whereas in 'civilized societies' a soldier was 'someone who protects the peasant and the *gäbbar*', in Ethiopia 'the soldier [is] the sworn enemy of the peasant. Hence, our fertile land lies fallow. And hence our poverty.'[234] With a logic not dissimilar to that of the Chinese Empire's exactly contemporary 'self-strengthening movement', Gäbra-Heywät concluded that Ethiopia's only chance of survival was to learn to become something that Europeans respected. 'In the old days, Ignorance held sway', he wrote. 'Today, however, a strong and unassailable enemy called the European mind has risen against [Ethiopia]. Whoever opens his door to her [i.e. to the European mind] prospers; whoever closes his door will be destroyed. If our Ethiopia accepts the European mind, no one would dare attack her; if not, she will disintegrate and be enslaved.'[235] Yet Gäbra-Heywät and his colleagues

[231] John Markakis, *Ethiopia: The Last Two Frontiers* (Martlesham: Boydell & Brewer, 2011), 34.

[232] Bahru, *Pioneers of Change*, 29.

[233] Described by his translator, Tenkir Bonger, as 'one of the early theorizers of the dependency theory'. See Gabrahiwot Baykadagn, *State and Economy in Early Twentieth Century Ethiopia*, trans. Tenkir Bonger (London: Karnak House, 1999), xix.

[234] Gäbra-Heywät Baykädañ, 'Até Menilek-na Ityopya' ('Emperor Menilek and Ethiopia'), *Berhan Yehun*, Asmara, 1912, quoted in Bahru, *Pioneers of Change*, 122.

[235] Gäbra-Heywät, 'Até Menilek', 254, quoted in Bahru, *Pioneers of Change*, 110

were, simultaneously, all too aware of the hypocrisies that lay behind the language of 'freedom' and 'equality' which was then being smuggled into Ethiopia's internal regulatory structures via dozens of treaties and concession agreements with European companies.[236] They lamented, for example, the destruction of traditional crafts, rapidly being wiped out by cheap imported 'clothing, household utensils and even ploughshares'.[237] Gäbra-Heywät also worried intensely about the changes that were being wrought to his fellow Ethiopians' wants and desires by their exposure to the new practices and norms associated with commodity production and exchange. 'Unless the [Ethiopian] government gives it proper guidance', Gäbra-Heywät wrote, the Ethiopian people, rapidly falling in love with 'glamour and comfort', and 'acquir[ing] many tastes' without any 'ability to satisfy them', confronted a 'disastrous' fate.[238] His concern, in other words, was precisely with the alteration in the 'pursuits of the people' he was witnessing. This was, of course, precisely the same alteration that Harris had gleefully predicted in consequence of the opening-up of Ethiopia to European commerce, which, he foresaw, would generate a new desire to 'convert the rude hut into a comfortable dwelling'.[239]

As a new generation of critical historians, anthropologists and sociologists has noted, however, it was, of course, the poor and the ethnically excluded who faced the most serious material consequences of Ethiopia's transformation into a state. Most dramatically, perhaps, these scholars have noted that the Battle of Adwa was a victory over the Ethiopian Empire's internal 'others' just as much as it was a triumph over its external enemies. Reflecting on this victory, the sociologist Siegfried Pausewang has made the point that it would be 'no exaggeration to say that Ethiopia escaped colonialism by participating in it'.[240] In the ensuing rush to obtain concessions and conclude commercial treaties, 'Menelik's state in effect

[236] For two accounts of Europeans attempting to trick or straightforwardly defraud the Ethiopian Empire, see Rubenson, *The Survival*, 159–63, on the 1843 Franco-Shewan 'Treaty' of Commerce of 1843, and Bahru, 'Concessions and Concession-Hunters', 365–83, at 366, on the fraudulent exploits of the German 'concession-hunter', Arnold Holz, during Menelik's reign.

[237] Bahru, *Pioneers of Change*, 101.

[238] Gäbra-Heywät Baykädañ, *Mangest-na YäHezb Astädadär* ('Government and Public Administration'), Addis Ababa, 1952 EC, trans. and quoted in Bahru, *Pioneers of Change*, 101. The book, *Mangest-na YäHezb Astädadär*, was written around 1909, and published posthumously.

[239] Harris, *The Highlands of Æthiopia*, 384. See Section 3.1, above.

[240] Siegfried Pausewang, 'Local Democracy and Central Control', in Abebe Zegeye and Siegfried Pausewang (eds.), *Ethiopia in Change: Peasantry, Nationalism and Democracy* (London, New York: British Academic Press, 1994), 209–30, at 228.

joined the ranks of the colonial powers to become the only African colonial power Europe hesitatingly recognized'.[241] Indeed, the very (European) weapons Menelik had used to defeat the Italians were soon redeployed to 'subjugat[e] pastoral or peasant communities to a centralised political structure which follow[ed] the principles of European colonial rule'.[242] This allowed '[t]he interests of the centre' increasingly to be 'given priority over those of the local community, and the interests of export over those of home consumption', gradually destroying 'indigenous systems of social security' and forcing local communities 'to conform to economic rules that did not accommodate the needs of collective responsibility'.[243] To put it differently, the more the Ethiopian Empire came to resemble a state in the international legal sense, the more effectively it was able to subjugate those within its jurisdiction whom it had been subjugating for decades, if not for centuries.

The legal scholar Tsegaye Ararssa makes a similar point when he argues that the victory at Adwa legitimised and concretised not only the Italian annexation of Eritrea, but also the many other occupations and conquests that had been made by Menelik's armies:

> The[se] other peoples' land and identity was alienated (from their own land and own subjectivity as collectivities) irredeemably after Adwa. Their occupation by conquest was internationally legitimized by, because of, and after Adwa. Adwa was indeed a very divisive moment ... [I]t was also the first moment of division between citizen and subject. It was the moment that defined the outer bounds of citizenship in the Ethiopian polity. It was a moment that putatively defined the cleavage between the core and the periphery, the citizen and the subject, the *rist* land and the *gebbar* land, the north and the south, the Ethiopian and his (and much less her) others. It was the moment of inauguration of state violence, looting, plunder, pillage, genocide, alienation, dispossession, and displacement right before a watching colonial-imperial world. Almost all evils of the modern Ethiopian state are rooted in the Adwa moment.[244]

From the perspective of Ethiopia's 'others' ('all the Gallas', as Menelik refers to them sweepingly in his boundary-defining letter of 1891), then,

241 Ibid., 228.

242 Seyoum, 'Notes on the Ethiopian Empire', 21–2. See also Baxter, 'Ethiopia's Unacknowledged Problem', 283.

243 Pausewang, 'Local Democracy and Central Control', 228.

244 Tsegaye R. Ararssa, 'Did Menelik II Really Say he is Caucasian? A Call for Caution – Lest We Rewrite History in the Name of Contextual Interpretation', *Addis Standard*, 7 June 2016, at http://addisstandard.com/opinion-menelik-ii-really-say-caucasian/ (accessed 18 October 2017).

and perhaps also from that of even impoverished Abyssinian *gebbar*, the members of this generation of scholars argue that the Ethiopian Empire participated in the 'scramble for Africa' no less enthusiastically, and no less successfully, than the European powers did themselves. Both aspects of the Ethiopian Empire's hybrid identity – part-state (in a formal sense), part-empire (in an Abyssinian sense) – conspired to legitimate their ongoing domination. Ironically, in other words, the more the Ethiopian Empire became a state *and* the more it resisted becoming a state – the more it became 'self' to international law *and* the more it remained 'other' and stayed true to its own 'self' – the more its *own* 'others' could be disciplined and dominated.

5 Conclusion

The aim of this item to be deposited inside the shadow-box was to examine what happened, in a legal and material sense, to the 'inside' and to the 'outside' of the Ethiopian Empire when international law extended its state-centric jurisdiction over East Africa and came up against this partly familiar, and partly unfamiliar polity. By the time of Menelik's death in 1913, the Empire clearly bore some resemblances to the international legal conception of statehood. Yet it also continued to manifest certain other traits which European officials and lawyers found impossible to 'recognise' as belonging to a state. Putting it rather schematically, we might say that the encounter between international law and the Ethiopian Empire resulted in the latter's partial metamorphosis. Ethiopia, familiar but also disconcertingly different, was narrated, and constituted, quite literally, as a simultaneously sovereign and less-than-sovereign entity by the authors of the treaties, diplomatic memoranda, concession agreements, letters and other manifestations of state practice that have been discussed above. In both the doctrine and practice of treaty-making and diplomatic intercourse, the Empire became a subject of international law whose hybrid nature – whose 'traces' of otherness – proved incapable of being fully erased, and yet which gave its rights and duties an inherently pliable quality. Most obvious among these traces was the continuance of slavery – an institution which was, as we have seen, incompatible with the idea of 'government' as a 'criterion' of statehood, according to the international legal norms of the era. These concerns – underpinned, one and all, by an anxiety about the capacity of capital to 'progress' beyond the boundaries of the Ethiopian Empire and into its 'interior'– became only more acute in the aftermath of the First World War, as we are about to see.

Item No. 5

Interpellation and Resistance: Ethiopia and the Allure of the League

The previous chapter added a fourth element into the shadow-box, a composite of three different histories, based on three different historiographies, of the Ethiopian Empire. Positioning this fourth item within the theoretical Frame laid out at the start of the book, and against the three other items that were already inside it, allowed a very particular story – of the (partial) transformation of the Empire into a subject of international law, and of the (even more partial) transformation of the subjects of the Ethiopian Emperor into individual legal subjects – to be juxtaposed against a more general account of the process of international legal reproduction. Now, on the point of adding a fifth item into the box, we find ourselves, in temporal terms, in the middle of the First World War, armed with an understanding of some of the peculiarities of the Ethiopian Empire's international personality. In spatial terms, meanwhile, we find ourselves in possession of an awareness of some of the connections (or *correspondances*, to use Walter Benjamin's term) between that idiosyncratic and distinctly split personality on the one hand, and that of many (if not most) of the other members of the 'family of nations' on the other.

These *correspondances* between the particular, contingent story of Ethiopia's transformation into a sovereign state and the general, 'necessary' or structural story of international legal reproduction within which that story unfolded, become even more visible if we examine the events which led to the Ethiopian Empire's conditional accession to the Covenant of the League of Nations in September 1923. Having addressed the question of fascism's very specific impact on international law elsewhere,[1] I focus here on

[1] See e.g. Rose Sydney Parfitt, 'The Anti-Neutral Suit: International Legal Futurists, 1914–2017', 5 *London Review of International Law* (2017): 87–123; Rose Parfitt, 'Fascism, Imperialism and International Law: An Arch Met a Motorway and the Rest is History …' 31 *Leiden Journal of International Law* (2018): 509–38. 'Is Fascism Making a Comeback?", *StateOfNatureBlog.com*, 3 December 2017, available at http://stateofnatureblog.com/one-question-fascism-part-one/ (accessed 17 December 2017); and the work of the 'Fascism and the International' workshops, Mexico City, 18–20 June 2018 and Melbourne, 22–25 May 2018.

the task of contrasting two broad, and very different, understandings of the Ethiopian Empire's status in the 1920s and 30s. What I have called the 'view from Geneva' encompasses the debates which informed the decision-making process at the League of Nations, typically within a familiar set of parameters provided by international law. The 'view from Addis Ababa', meanwhile, refers to the hybrid and/or deliberately hybridised arguments which took place within and were deployed by Ethiopia and its officials, based in the Ethiopian capital. Section 1 therefore examines the events and arguments leading up to Ethiopia's accession to the League from 'Geneva', while Section 2 probes them from 'Addis Ababa', in order to juxtapose one against the other.

1 The View from Geneva I: League Membership with Strings Attached

From the mainstream international legal perspective, reflecting that of the states which made up the 'international community' of the early twentieth century, the main sticking point when it came to the question of the Ethiopian Empire's international personality concerned the ongoing practice of slavery in that country. Just as the failure to appropriate and cultivate land 'productively' (that is, for profit) had long been taken as evidence of the irrationality of Indigenous populations in the Americas, Australasia and elsewhere, so a parallel argument seems to have been applied to slavery. The resource that those who (irrationally) continued to engage in the practice of slavery left undeveloped and running wild was, in this context, rationality itself. For as Lord Lugard (British representative on the League's Permanent Mandates Commission) and his colleagues among the ideologues of 'indirect rule' insisted, only 'free' individuals could develop this kind of utility-maximising rationality.[2] Paradoxically, however (and in another echo of Vitoria's version of the Aristotelian institution of 'natural slavery'), this suggested to Lugard and others, not that colonialism was illegitimate, but quite the opposite: that those belonging to 'sub-rational' races should be gradually and deliberately exposed to the incentives of the market, as wage-labourers, consumers and perhaps even farmer-entrepreneurs. This exposure required that they should be governed, not according to local norms and institutions, but rather by an external 'self-governing' state.

In the context of the Ethiopian Empire, the issue of slavery and its impact on the question of whether the Ethiopian 'government' really was

[2] See Item 3, Sections 4 and 5 above.

capable of governing 'effectively' reached a head in the wake of Emperor Menelik's death on 12 December 1913. In the aftermath of the First World War, the glory of the Battle of Adwa – a shock victory, yet one achieved with spears, swords and antiquated rifles rather than with tanks, chemical weapons and aerial bombardment – faded quickly. Meanwhile, international law's longstanding preoccupation with the 'effective' government had, as we saw in Item 3, reached its apotheosis, in the eschatological ethos of the immediate post-1918 period, in the principle of 'self-government'. In this context, imbued with the conviction that 'tyranny' had just been forever vanquished by 'liberty', a kind of macabre fascination with slavery in Africa, and in particular in Ethiopia, swept across Western Europe and North America, nourished by regular reports of ongoing slave raids on Ethiopia's borders coming from an increasingly voracious and mobile international press.[3]

1.1 *Self-Government and the Slavery Scandal of 1922*

In January 1922 the issue hit the headlines as never before with the publication of three anonymous stories in the *Westminster Gazette*, a Liberal London-based newspaper.[4] These articles (written, as it turned out, by Major Henry Darley, a British Frontier Agent at Maji and author of the book *Slaves and Ivory*,[5] and Dr Dyce Sharp, a former physician to the British Legation at Addis Ababa) branded the Ethiopian Empire simultaneously 'the only remaining free and independent native State in Africa' and 'the last home of open slavery'.[6] Beyond their lurid description of the conditions endured by Ethiopian slaves, these articles sparked off a scandal of gigantic proportions with the allegation that the British legation itself – legally British terrain – was 'full of slaves', some of whom might well be British colonial subjects seized in raids into neighbouring Anglo-Egyptian

[3] See e.g. Peter P. Garretson, 'Vicious Cycles: Ivory, Slaves, and Arms on the New Maji Frontier', in Donham and James (eds.), *The Southern Marches*, 196–218, at 200.

[4] 'Abyssinia To-Day – 1: The Home of Slavery', *Westminster Gazette*, 18 January 1922; Anon., 'Abyssinia To-Day – 2: Impossibility of Trade', *Westminster Gazette*, 19 January 1922; 'Abyssinia To-Day – 3', *Westminster Gazette*, 20 January 1922 (filed in FO 371/7141 Political (Abyssinia) 1922 (UKNA)). The slaves were owned by the Legation's servants. See also J. H. Dodds Memorandum, 24 January 1922, A 486/486/1, FO 371/7141 Political (Abyssinia) 1922 (UKNA). For an account of this episode, see Suzanne Miers, *Slavery in the Twentieth Century: The Evolution of a Global Problem* (Lanham, MD: Altamira, 2003), 66–86.

[5] Henry Darley, *Slaves and Ivory* (London: Mellifont Press, 1925).

[6] 'Abyssinia To-Day – 1'.

Sudan.[7] How could such a situation possibly have arisen? The authors' explanation is telling. Deprived of the 'natural capacity and enlightenment of the Emperor Menelik', they explained, Ethiopia had 'relapsed into a state that approaches barbarism'.[8] The country was now 'decaying' to the point at which '[t]he Central Government exercises no authority that is worth mentioning at a greater distance than ten miles from the Palace'.[9] Even Addis Ababa's inhabitants enjoyed 'little or no security either for their persons or their possessions'.[10] Meanwhile 'Abyssinian justice' continued to be 'mediaeval in its methods' and deeply biased against foreigners, such that '[n]o Abyssinian Judge, however heavily he has been subsidised' would ever 'give a decision in favour of a European against a local Governor in Chief'.[11] The only 'remedy' for these 'evils', they suggested, was to ration the importation of arms into the country such that 'the Emperor' (by which they meant the Regent, *Ras* Tafari; like many of their European contemporaries, they ignored the fact that Empress Zewditu had assumed the throne in 1916) 'has no longer a margin to sell to the slave-traders'. Only this action would promote the mutual interests both of 'Abyssinians' and of 'British [colonial] subjects over the Abyssinian borders, who are free to-day but who may be slaves to-morrow'.[12] The assumption that 'natives' subject to the jurisdiction of a 'self-governing' state like Britain were 'free', in contrast to the subjects of a tyrannical African empire such as Ethiopia,[13] did not, in other words, take long to surface in this debate.

The aftershocks of this scandal, reported and discussed everywhere from the House of Lords to the *New York Times*, continued throughout 1922 and 1923.[14] So loud was the outcry that, under pressure from a number of influential organisations, including the British League of Nations Union (headed by Lord Robert Cecil), the Anti-Slavery (and Aborigines' Protection) Society (the ASS), and the *Ligue Suisse pour la Défense des Indigènes* (Swiss League), the issue was placed on the agenda of the

[7] 'Abyssinia To-Day – 1'. Foreign Office records reveal that this was, in fact, the case. According to Dodds, then British Minister in Addis Ababa, 'It is true that Abyssinian servants at the British as well as the French and Italian Legations possess slaves'. Dodds, Memorandum, 24 January 1922.

[8] 'Abyssinia To-Day – 1'.

[9] Ibid.

[10] Ibid.

[11] 'Abyssinia To-Day – 2'.

[12] 'Abyssinia To-Day – 3'.

[13] See Item 3, Section 2.1.

[14] Antoinette Iadarola, 'Ethiopia's Admission into the League of Nations: An Assessment of Motives,' 8 *The International Journal of African Historical Studies* (1975): 601–22, at 608.

Assembly of the League of Nations in 1923.[15] The British Government was horrified. For if Ethiopia had indeed 'degenerated' into a state of disorder in the wake of Menelik's death then partition would soon be on the horizon under the terms of the 1906 Tripartite Treaty, and Britain stood to gain very little from it; far less than Italy.[16] Britain's fear, that is, was not that international law would be violated were intervention into Ethiopia to be perceived as necessary; it was that international law (in the form of the Tripartite Treaty) would be enforced. As Rowland Sperling, then head of the African Department in Whitehall, put it, Britain had 'the most to lose by partition', not only because Britain's 'share [was] the smallest', but also because 'Italy and France ... would discriminate in favour of their own trade in their spheres', whereas '[a]t present the trade of all three countries enjoys equality of opportunity in Abyssinia, so far as it can be assured by [the] treaties'.[17]

It was in an attempt to square this circle of eliminating slavery within the Ethiopian Empire without, in doing so, placing the 'open-door' regime guaranteed by the existing treaty regime at risk that the idea of admitting Ethiopia to the League on a conditional basis emerged. The ASS first placed this potential solution on the table, initially in private meetings with British Foreign Office officials,[18] and then in a well-publicised petition addressed to Sir Eric Drummond, Secretary-General of the League. The petitioners (among them Ramsay MacDonald, Sidney Webb, Lady Violet Bonham Carter, and the playwright and champion of 'positive' eugenics George Bernard Shaw) argued that:

> The widespread nature of the evil [of slavery] can, we believe, only be adequately dealt with by giving to Abyssinia such advice and assistance as she may need in evolving a strong African Government ... We suggest ... offering to Abyssinia a form of Mandate of an advanced type under guarantees as to sovereignty and territorial integrity by the League, or possibly by a form of collective Mandate placed in the hands of more than one Power. If to this could be added a conditional invitation to Abyssinia to enter the League of Nations as a Sovereign State, the League of Nations might thereby confer upon Africa the greatest blessing which has yet visited the Dark Continent – namely, entirely disinterested but effective

[15] Iadarola, 'Ethiopia's Admission', 609.

[16] See e.g. Roland Sperling, Memorandum, 3 March 1922, A 1475/136; Harris to Curzon, 28 August 1923; Sperling to Harris, 4 September 1923, all in FO 371/8406: Political (Abyssinia) 1923 (UKNA). On the Tripartite Treaty, see Item 4, Section 3.

[17] Roland Sperling, Memorandum, 10 February 1922, FO 371/7147/A1475/486/1 (UKNA).

[18] Arthur Balfour, Telegram to Claud Russell, 6 June 1922, FO 371/7148: Political (Abyssinia) 1922, A. 3428/486/1 (UKNA).

> assistance in evolving a self-governing African State, free from the institution of Slavery.[19]

As in the *Westminster Gazette* articles, slavery was presented here as the antithesis of individual liberty, and hence as the greatest evil which could result from the absence or 'decay' of a country's institutions of government. Such institutions *could*, according to the petition's logic, be transformed into 'evolved' and 'effective' institutions from the outside – that is, by the 'disinterested assistance' of the League. But however it was achieved, eliminating slavery was the *sine qua non* if a polity's legal and administrative institutions were to be considered those of a state.

The petition reached the League headquarters in Geneva, unofficially, in August 1923, together with several other reports making similar arguments with respect to Ethiopia. These included an independent report from the Swiss League[20] and an investigation by the French Government into slavery in Africa, with a special Annex on Ethiopia.[21] The latter reproduced the assumptions of the 'Orientalist-Semiticist paradigm'[22] faithfully and discussed certain precepts of the *Fetha Nagast*, according to which it was 'strictly forbidden to sell a Christian to an infidel'. The *Westminster Gazette* articles, the French Government said, contained 'inexactitudes', but the 'main part remain[ed] unfortunately true'.[23] Erasing more flexible Abyssinian/Aksumite attitudes to ethnicity[24] through the superimposition of a distinctively European racial essentialism, the French report asserted that:

> *Les Abyssins, dont la religion est toute imprégnée des préceptes hébraïques, se trouvèrent, dès début de leur conquête de l'Étiopie, en contact avec des races issues, suivant eux, de la descendance de Cham que Noé, en le maudissant, avait destiné à être l'esclave de ses frères. C'était déjà là pour eux un motif de réduire en servitude les tribus négroïdes, kouchitiques et kamitiques contre lesquelles ils eurent à combattre et qui ne suivaient pas la loi mosaïque. Celle-ci ne contrenait-elle pas du reste cette ordonnance: 'Les esclaves que tu*

19 *Slavery and the League of Nations: The Appeal of the Anti-Slavery and Aborigines Protection Society*, 9 August 1923, FO 371/8406: Political (Abyssinia) 1923, A. 3428/486/1 (UKNA).

20 *L'Esclavage en Abyssinie, Rapport rédigé à la demande de la Ligue Suisse pour la Défense des Indigènes* (Geneva, 1923), in Société des Nations, Assemblée 4 (1923), Documents 41–144, League of Nations Archives, Geneva (LONA).

21 See 'Renseignements communiqués par le gouvernement française', in *Société des Nations: La question de l'esclavage*, 10 August 1923, A.18.1923.VI, 2–11, in dossier 'League of Nations: Documents on Slavery' (no dossier number), Box R.64, 8–11 (LONA).

22 See Item 4, Section 2.1.

23 'Renseignements communiqués par le gouvernement française', 2.

24 See Item 4, Section 2.2.

> *auras, hommes ou femmes, tu les prendras des nations qui t'entourent; c'est d'elles que vous achèterez serviteurs et servantes'.*[25]

Likewise, the Swiss League report began with '*un exposé succinct geographico-ethnique des conditions de l'Ethiopie ou Abyssinie*',[26] complete with maps onto which ethnic 'zones' had been drawn in coloured pencil.[27]

As we have already seen, it made very little sense to characterise the Ethiopian Empire as an empire in this highly racialised European sense. Not only was it possible to 'become' Abyssinian; it was also the case that even Christian *gebbars* were mercilessly exploited by the imperial centre – the more so as prospects for selling surplus tribute on the international market began to open up.[28] However, France's (very typical) assessement of the Ethiopian Empire on the basis of a European model of imperialism, involving a semi-Caucasian metropole, whose duty it was to assume responsibility for a racially differentiated 'negroid' periphery, served a crucial ideological purpose. For if Ethiopia was a European-style empire that had, since the glory days of Menelik II, 'decayed' to the point at which its Christian-Caucasian elite could no longer be understood as fulfilling their imperial duties, and were now subjecting their 'negroid' imperial subjects to a 'savage' tyrannical regime, then two pieces of the puzzle fell into place. Firstly, Ethiopia became more comprehensible as a 'barbaric' (rather than exceptional) African polity. Secondly, a new solution to the problem of slavery emerged, which involved emancipating Ethiopia's oppressed 'colonies' from the Empire's pre-Menelikian 'core' on humanitarian grounds, and transferring them to the jurisdiction of one of Ethiopia's neighbouring, and by definition 'self-governing', states (namely Britain, France or Italy). This 'solution' (first mooted by Italy at the time of the Treaty of Wich'alle debacle, as we saw

[25] 'The Abyssinians, whose religion is completely imbued with Hebraic precepts, found themselves, at the beginning of their conquest of Ethiopia, in contact with races derived, like them, from the offspring of Shem who, having been cursed by Noah, became the slave of His brothers. They had, therefore, a pre-existing motive to reduce the Negroid, Cushitic and Hamitic tribes against whom they had to fight and who did not follow Mosaic law. The latter did not constrain this ordinance: "The Slaves you will have, men or women, you will take from the nations that surround you; it is from them that you will buy [your] servants and maids"'. 'Renseignements communiqués par le gouvernement française', 6.

[26] '[A] succinct geographical-ethnic exposé of the conditions of Ethiopia or Abyssinia', *L'Esclavage en Abyssinie*, 1.

[27] The maps indicated that this 'ethnic' information had been gathered first-hand by, among others, Major Darley, co-author of the *Westminster Gazette* articles. The Swiss League report provoked an outcry both in Ethiopia and Britain with its allegation that Britain was seeking to use the cause of abolition in its own 'zone' (according to the Tripartite Treaty) as an opportunity to annex 'Abyssinia' outright. *L'Esclavage en Abyssinie*, 17.

[28] See Item 4, Section 4.2.

above[29]) – one of territorial amputation justified on the racialised grounds of a failing civilising mission – would later play a crucial role in the crisis of 1935.

The furore triggered by these petitions and reports in Geneva culminated in a motion 'to refer to the appropriate Committee the question of the recrudescence of slavery in Africa in order that it may consider and propose the best methods for combating the evil'.[30] It was this resolution that led to the formation of the League's Temporary Slavery Commission in 1924, whose far-reaching investigation into slavery on the continent of Africa led ultimately to the landmark Slavery Convention of 1926.[31] There still remained, however, the question of what to do about Ethiopia. Given what we now know, both about perceptions of the Empire as a hybrid entity and about contemporary European concerns relating to racial 'miscegenation',[32] the language used throughout the debate is, again, revealing. For example, the *Westminster Gazette* stories, with distinct echoes of the 'racial degeneration' theory of human hybridity,[33] suggested that Ethiopia was 'reverting back' to its more typically 'African' traits (such as slavery), and leaving behind those pseudo-European traits it had only flukishly managed, temporarily, to mimic.[34] In a similar vein, Sir Harry Johnston – author of a book unambiguously titled *The Backward Peoples and Our Relations with Them* (1920)[35] and director of the shady Liberian Development Company,[36] argued that the 'power and energy of the Abyssinians of Semitic speech' had 'degenerated' so abjectly since 1913 that it left 'such government as there is to chieftains of Negroid Gala [*sic*] stock'.[37] Johnston declared himself to be 'sceptical about the power of any Negro or Negroid people (Abyssinia nowadays is virtually a Negroid State) to rise to a settled order of civilisation without "white" control, a "white" education'. The 'only practicable cure' for Ethiopia's state

[29] See Item 4, Section 3.1.

[30] League of Nations, 'Slavery in Africa', Motion Proposed by Sir Arthur Steel-Maitland, Delegate for New Zealand, 7 September 1922, Third Assembly of the League of Nations, in File 1/23252/23252, Box R61 (LONA).

[31] *International Convention with Object of Securing the Abolition of Slavery and the Slave Trade* ('Slavery Convention'), Geneva, 25 September 1926, 60 LNTS 253. See Item 1, Section 2.1.

[32] See Frame, Section 3.1.

[33] See Frame, Section 3.1.

[34] 'Abyssinia To-Day – 2'.

[35] Harry H. Johnston, *The Backward Peoples and Our Relations with Them* (London, New York: Oxford University Press, 1920).

[36] See Item 3, Section 5 on the activities of the Liberian Development Company.

[37] Harry Johnston, Letter to the Editor, in 'Abyssinian Slaves – Prof. Murray on League Action – Import of Arms,' *Westminster Gazette*, 2 May 1922. The letter begins 'Sir, I have never been in Abyssinia'.

of 'sickening disorder', Johnston concluded, was that the country should be partitioned among the Tripartite powers.[38] Likewise using the the trope of 'human hybridity' as his template, John Harris, organising secretary of the ASS, was of the opinion that 'purely native government' in Africa had so far 'failed to satisfy modern standards', whereas 'the happiest experiments' had proved to be those in which 'Native African Governments are being evolved by the aid of disinterested white advisors'.[39] It was, in his view, obvious that no one wished to see Ethiopia 'reverting to the barbarous level of a slave State'.[40] Declaring the Tripartite Agreement to be 'in the closest harmony with the main principles of the League', Harris therefore suggested that Ethiopia should be encouraged to apply for League membership, but that its admission should be 'postponed pending an abolition of slavery, and the re-establishment of ordered government' – two sides, for him, of the same coin.[41]

The veteran diplomat Claud Russell, British Minister in Addis Ababa during the first half of the 1920s, came to the opposite conclusion using the same, 'miscegenation' inspired logic. Slavery, Russell suggested, wasn't such a bad institution in a society where 'needs' were 'limited to food, clothes and shelter', necessities supplied to slaves by their owners. 'In the labour of these slaves there is nothing comparable to what is associated in our minds with the slavery of the American plantations … In Abyssinia men either do not work at all, or they work a little. No one toils. The fact of being unpaid presents little hardship when men's wants are so few as they are in this country.'[42] For Russell, then, the failure of Ethiopians to develop the mindset of the consumer-producer went hand in hand with their failure to develop the mindset of the wage-labourer.[43] The problem was thus not one of the continuance of slavery in a gradually modernising nation-state, but rather

[38] Johnston, Letter to the Editor.

[39] In John Harris, 'Slavery in Abyssinia – How the League Could Help – a Modern Gordon Needed – Weakness of 1906 Agreement', *Westminster Gazette*, 28 April 1922.

[40] Harris, 'Slavery in Abyssinia'. Having masterminded the suppression of the Taiping rebellion in China, the slave trade in Sudan (unsuccessfully) and the Basuto uprising in South Africa, Gordon was killed while back in Sudan, attempting to suppress the Mahdist rebellion. Cynthia F. Behrman, 'The After-Life of General Gordon', 3 *Albion: A Quarterly* (1971): 47–61, 47.

[41] Harris, 'Slavery in Abyssinia'.

[42] Claud Russell to the Marquis Curzon of Kedleston, 16 March 1922, A1799/486/1, FO 371/7141 Political (Abyssinia) 1922 (UKNA).

[43] Ibid. Russell here is quoting from Vergil: *parcere subjectis et debbelare superbos* means 'spare the vanquished and subdue the arrogant', a principle associated with Roman imperialism.

of a perverted reversal of the civilising mission which should be stopped in its tracks as quickly as possible. As Russell put it:

> The *fons et origo* of slavery [in Ethiopia] is the domination by the Amharas of races of inferior development to themselves. The remedy for this is the self-determination of the races in question, or their protection by a civilised Power. *Parcere subjectis* is not a principle of Abyssinian rule, and as long as there are negroid tribes included in the Empire, it is likely that they will be exploited and enslaved. What is wrong is that the Amharas, being black, have taken up the white man's burden.[44]

Genuine emancipation could only be brought about by one of two options, Russell concluded: the 'self-determination' of these 'negroid tribes'; or their transformation into European protectorates ('England might someday find it possible to give her protection to the oppressed tribes of the south ... and west ... in the lands that they inhabit'). On the other hand, since League membership would complicate matters in this case, it was therefore to be discouraged.[45]

Though deeply counter-intuitive from the perspective of mainstream international legal doctrine, Russell's posited equivalence between 'self-determination' and 'protection' makes sense if examined in light of this book's 'modular' history of international legal reproduction. For the 'remedy' in either case was expected not only to abolish human property as a matter of law. It was also, in doing so, expected to transform the Ethiopian Empire's entire 'social system' from one in which 'wants' were 'few' and in which 'no-one toils' to one in which '[t]he native is tempted to earn wages by his desire to purchase the attractive goods offered for his choice'.[46] Indeed, Russell's position here echoes Lugard's suggestions in his exactly contemporaneous manual, *The Dual Mandate in British Tropical Africa*.[47] '[W]here a native conquering race holds an aboriginal people in control', Lugard wrote, 'a system of slavery and forced labour becomes practically inevitable by reason of mutual mistrust and the absence of such social organisation as renders possible a written contract, and a payment for services in a recognised medium.'[48] Sperling was of a similar view. As he put it, '[a] form of slavery undoubtedly exists in Abyssinia as is perhaps inevitable in a country in which a very slightly civilised governing race has imposed

44 Ibid.

45 Quoted in Iadarola, 'Ethiopia's Admission', 609.

46 Frederick Lugard, *The Dual Mandate in British Tropical Africa* (Edinburgh: William Blackwood and Sons, 1922), 402.

47 See Item 3, Section 2.

48 Lugard, *The Dual Mandate*, 390.

its rule on the original and still less civilised inhabitants'.[49] As this suggests, once again, in 1922 it was entirely plausible to describe the colonisation of a 'backwards' people by a 'self-governing state' (such as Britain or France) as 'self-government' in and of itself. Indeed, in the case of 'negroid' societies in which it could be assumed that market rationality had to be inculcated from the outside, this was understood to offer the only means by which 'self-determination' could be rendered 'effective'.

A parallel view was offered by Darley in a follow-up to the *Westminster Gazette* articles. Upon Menelik's death, he argued, 'Abyssinia ... reverted to a state of savagery'. Ruled 'under the feudal system as was Europe in the Middle Ages', this 'beautiful land', 'potentially the richest in Africa', remained shamefully underexploited. 'The Abyssinians', he insisted, 'toil not neither do they spin, but live in squalor on the labour of their slaves.' The only hope Darley saw for 'the almost extinct races of the southern part of this beautiful land' was that the League 'might be persuaded ... to "do something"'.[50] Captain Tracy Philipps (until recently Britain's Chief Political Officer in the Uganda Military Area) then responded in a letter to *The Times*. 'Men of the ruling race' in Ethiopia, he declared, were 'generally a mass of untrained, undisciplined, soldier-parasites into whose hands the subject peoples are delivered, in lieu of pay and maintenance.'[51] The 'only efficacious remedy [must] be economic', he concluded. Zewditu and Tafari would surely 'realise the immense advantage to the Country of financial re-organisation by neutral advisers, as in Persia', and then, '[o]nce the army and provincial officials were properly paid & controlled, the negroid subject peoples would cease to be farmed out like cattle & sold into slavery'.[52]

However, while these interventions were widely discussed not only in the British Parliament but also in the League,[53] it was Lugard himself who

[49] Roland Sperling, 'Slavery in Abyssinia: Origin of Present Agitation', 23 May 1922, A. 3326/486/1, in FO 371/7148: Political (Abyssinia) 1922 (UKNA).

[50] Major Henry Darley, 'Abyssinia of To-Day', 22 *Outward Bound* 1922: 689–96, in FO 371/8406: Political (Abyssinia) 1923 (UKNA).

[51] Captain J. E. T. Philipps, Letter to the Editor, *The Times*, 10 April 1923, in *La question de l'esclavage*, File 1/27748/23252, Box R.62, LONA.

[52] Ibid.

[53] Philipps also sent this letter directly to William Rappard. Rappard replied that his 'suggestion that a financial reorganisation of Abyssinia should form the basis of any effective suppression of slave trading is a novel one and I read your argument with particular interest'. Rappard, letter to Philipps, 11 April 1923, in *La question de l'esclavage*, File 1/27748/23252, Box R.62, LONA. See also e.g. 'Slavery in Abyssinia', HL Deb, 30 July 1923, *Hansard*, Vol. 54, Col. 1461, Earl Beauchamp speaking.

drew up the most detailed and influential plan for the elimination of slavery in Ethiopia – a plan in which the Ethiopian Empire was represented, simultaneously, as an empire, a colony, a sovereign state and collection of 'spheres of influence'. This plan[54] involved nothing less than 'a complete change in the social life of the people of Abyssinia'.[55] Ethiopia should be transformed into a special form of 'Class A' mandated territory under the direct 'tutelage' of the League.[56] Ethiopia's 'existence as an independent nation would be provisionally recognised', but it would be the League itself rather than a mandatory power which would '[render] Administrative advice and assistance', acting through a disinterested 'Agent' whose 'sole object would be to bring order out of chaos and to liberate a people now held in slavery'.[57] Failing this, 'partition between the [Tripartite] Powers' might well become 'inevitable'.[58] Lugard noted that the League had no jurisdiction ('no *locus standi* whatsoever') in regard to any sovereign state which was not one of its members.[59] However, this problem might be overcome through recourse to the provisions of the Berlin and Brussels Acts (updated in 1919),[60] whose signatories could 'authorise the League, acting on their behalf, to depute' a European officer to lead an inquiry into the suppression of slavery in Ethiopia.[61]

It was a fact, according to Lugard, that Ethiopia was 'immensely rich, with an adequate population, and is capable of great wealth and prosperity'. However, he continued, 'Abyssinians' were an 'ignorant, turbulent and very conceited people, suspicious of, and hostile to, Europeans'.[62] Ethiopian society was bifurcated both racially and politically – a 'duality' which was

[54] For a summary, see 'Slavery in Abyssinia – Views of Sir Fredrick Lugard', Westminster Gazette, 5 May 1922.

[55] Annex to Sir F. Lugard's Memorandum on 'Slavery and Systems of Restrictive Liberty for the Temporary Slavery Commission' of 4 December 1922, Note on Conditions in Abyssinia, in *League of Nations, Assembly 4 1923, Committees 4-6*, LONA, 104 ('Lugard Memorandum'). See also Lugard, 'Slavery in Abyssinia'.

[56] Lugard Memorandum, 10. See Item 3, Section 4.

[57] Ibid., 10. Lugard wrote 'B. class Mandate' in the original memo. This is amended in red pencil in the margin with an 'A!'

[58] Ibid., 7–8.

[59] Lugard Memorandum, 4.

[60] *Convention Revising the General Act of Berlin, February 26, 1885, and the General Act and Declaration of Brussels, July 2, 1890*, Saint-Germain-en-Laye, 10 September 1919. The signatories of these treaties had 'pledged themselves' to employ 'all means at their disposal for putting an end to the Slave-trade' and, to this end, to prohibit the sale of arms within a specified zone, in which much of Africa, including Ethiopia, fell. Lugard Memorandum, 1. On the Berlin and Brussels Acts, see Item 2, Section 2.2.2.

[61] Lugard Memorandum, 5–6.

[62] Ibid., 8.

'chiefly responsible for the present abuses'. On the one hand, the 'dominant race' considered 'work of any kind ... abhorrent', and 'depended' on the slave labour of 'the bulk of the people', namely 'Gallas and other tribes' whom they held 'in subjection as slaves and serfs'.[63] As a result, 'large areas in Abyssinia' had been completely 'depopulated by Slave-raiding', a state of affairs that had been exacerbated by 'the system of appointment of Provincial Chiefs, whose aim it is to make as much profit as they can during their term of office.'[64] On the other hand, Lugard argued that imperial politics within the Empire were themselves split between Zewditu, with her 'clique of reactionary chiefs who oppose all reform, and detest Europeans', and Tafari who, though 'lacking in boldness and initiation', was a French-speaker and 'not without intellectual ability'.[65] Above all, Tafari, who 'recognis[ed] that reform [was] necessary if the independence of his country is to be preserved', was therefore to be 'approached' directly, persuaded to usurp the throne from Zewditu, and then 'accept the advice of a European Councillor, to re-organise the Administration'.[66] Ongoing support for the hypothetical new Tafari regime, to be installed by what was in effect a League-orchestrated coup, was to be made conditional, Lugard proposed, on Tafari's 'suppression of the slave trade, reasonably good government, and protection of foreigners, with equal commercial opportunity to all', with the threat of 'coercion in order to remove obstruction, and compel fulfilment of pledges' to lie in the background. If Tafari refused to accept the plan, meanwhile, he would be presented with 'a threat that each of the [Tripartite] Powers would temporarily occupy a post in Abyssinian territory'.[67]

Lugard was candid about the plan's objectives here. The 'cession of the Slave trade' was expected to lead to 'the inauguration of other reforms which would undoubtedly promote the material interests of the Powers'.[68] His only worry was that if 'reform would bring commercial prosperity', the 'resulting benefits' would have to be 'shared equally by the three Powers'.[69]

[63] Ibid., 3.

[64] Ibid., 2.

[65] Ibid., 8.

[66] Ibid., 8, 13, n. 7.

[67] Ibid., 10. Written in the memo's margins, in pencil, are comments from both Drummond, the League's Secretary-General, and William Rappard, Director of the Mandate Department, calling it '[a] very interesting note which will be of great value', and 'a most interesting, ingenious and bold suggestion'. Note from William E. Rappard, Director of the Mandates Section, to the Secretary-General forwarding a Memorandum from Lord Lugard on Slavery in Abyssinia, 4 December 1922, Dossier 1/24628/23252, Box R.61, LONA.

[68] Lugard Memorandum, 7.

[69] Ibid., 10.

This scheme to abolish slavery was, in other words, also a plan to transform the Ethiopian Empire into a more profitable place within which Britain, France, Italy and their nationals could do business. Once again, in the logic of 'self-government', abolition and profit-seeking (personal and economic 'liberty') went hand in hand. Neither this, nor his insistence on the involvement of European or American 'advisors' in the creation of a new Ethiopian 'Central Force' and budgetary apparatus,[70] affected the conviction with which Lugard assured his audience at the League that his plan was highly likely to be accepted, given that his 'proposals' 'would not threaten the integrity and independence of the [Ethiopian] Kingdom' in the least.'[71]

1.2 Conditional Membership: Ethiopia's 'Special Obligations'

Thwarting Lugard's predictions, however, Ethiopia did apply for League membership, in September 1923. In that month, as we saw in Item 1,[72] the League's Sixth Committee on Political Questions met to assess that application on the basis of its standard questionnaire, reflecting the criteria articulated in Article 1, paragraph 2, of the Covenant:

i. Is Abyssinia's request for admission into the League of Nations in order?
ii. Is Abyssinia recognised *de jure* or *de facto* and by what states?
iii. Does the country possess a stable government and well-defined frontiers?
iv. Is it self-governing?
v. What have been the acts and declarations of Abyssinia (a) as regards her international obligations, (b) as regards the stipulations of the League with reference to armaments?[73]

As Item 4 laid out in some detail, Ethiopia had been 'recognised' by many states by this time. Yet the three states which, above all, had helped to 'define' the Empire's 'frontiers', in regards to which most of Ethiopia's 'international obligations' had been made over more than half a century of 'acts and declarations', and which had for many decades been selling

[70] Ibid., 9, 16 n. 14

[71] Ibid., 7.

[72] See Item 1, Section 1.

[73] 'Annex 5: Abyssinia's Application for Admission to the League', Report of the Second Sub-Committee, Revised Text, adopted by Sixth Committee 20 September 1923, Minutes of the Sixth Committee (Political Questions), Meetings of the Committees, Records of the Fourth Assembly, *LNOJ* Sp. Supp. No. 19, in *League of Nations, Assembly 4 1923, Committees 4–6*, 34–5 (LONA).

'armaments' to the Ethiopian Government (notwithstanding the provisions of the Brussels Act), were its neighbouring 'powers', Britain, France and Italy. All three were permanent members of the League Council at this time, and all three (Britain via Australia) sat on the Sixth Committee.[74] The latter's determinations, in other words, cannot be understood as having been straightforwardly 'disinterested'. Equally, the previous Section's discussion of the debates over how best to solve the problem of slavery in Ethiopia offers some insights into the genesis of the 'special obligations' which the Sixth Committee imposed on Ethiopia as a condition of its accession to the Covenant. Interestingly, these 'special obligations' were, in fact, significantly less interventionist than almost any of the plans for the Empire's transformation into a self-governing entity we have just examined; plans which were then in circulation in the parliaments, press and 'non-governmental organisation' reports of Britain, France, Switzerland and elsewhere. Rather than attempting to 'downgrade' Ethiopia to a special form of 'Class A' mandate (Lugard's scheme), these obligations (as the ASS had urged[75]) conditioned the Empire's accession to the Covenant on three rather contradictory obligations. Firstly, Ethiopia, represented at Geneva by a Delegation headed by *Ras* Nadew Aba Wollo (see Figure 8), was asked to accede to Article 11 of the *Convention Revising the General Act of Berlin, February 26, 1885, and the General Act and Declaration of Brussels, July 2, 1890* (1919). In doing so, Ethiopia assumed the role of a metropolitan state in relation to its overseas colonies, undertaking (in the wording of these treaties) to 'watch over the preservation of [its] native populations and to supervise the improvement of the conditions of their moral and material well-being' by securing 'the complete suppression of slavery ... and of the slave trade'.[76] Secondly, the Ethiopian Empire was required to accede to Article 6 of the *Convention for the Control of the Trade in Arms and Ammunition*. In accepting this condition, Ethiopia agreed to be regarded, like the rest of colonised Africa which fell within the Brussels Act's 'prohibition zone', as inhabited by individuals so habituated to slave-raiding that

[74] Until Italy withdrew from the League on 11 December 1937, all three of Ethiopia's limitrophe powers, Britain, France and Italy, occupied permanent seats on its executive body, the League Council, and as such possessed special responsibilities regarding the settlement of international disputes under the Covenant. Covenant, Arts. 10–16.

[75] Item 1, Section 1.

[76] *Convention revising the General Act of Berlin, February 26, 1885, and the General Act and Declaration of Brussels, July 2, 1890*, Saint-Germain-en-Laye, 10 September 1919, UKTS 018/1919: CMD. 447, Art. 11(1).

they were not to be trusted with weapons.[77] This position was reinforced by a third 'special obligation', according to which Ethiopia agreed to the League's supervision of its implementation of the other two. Thus, according to the first 'special obligation', Ethiopia was an imperial power charged, much like the European empires, with the 'tutlelage' of its less-than-civilised 'natives'. According to the second and third 'special obligations', however, Ethiopia was itself an uncivilised polity requiring further tutelage before it could be trusted with the kind of weapons that were required by fully sovereign states in order to exercise their rights – notably the right of self-defence.

As we saw in Item 1, the tendency of those international law and international relations scholars who have made note of the 'special obligations' has been to cast them as an example of international law's Eurocentric 'standard of civilisation' in action.[78] And indeed, there was at least one member of the Sixth Committee which devised the 'special obligations' for Ethiopia who had found the very idea of Ethiopia's candidature repugnant on straightfowardly 'civilisational' grounds. This was Sir Joseph Cook, the Australian Delegate. Cook had been indignant at the idea that League membership would allow 'Abyssinia' to 'examine and criticise countries whose civilisation was more advanced than her own'.[79] Yet the records from the Sixth Committee's meetings also show that Cook was challenged by the other Committee members for his antiquated assumption that Ethiopia's (to them) evident lack of 'civilisation' rendered it permanently 'backward' and, thus, definitively less-than-sovereign.[80] One faction, including the Chinese, Venezuelan and Portuguese delegates, had opposed the idea of placing any conditions on Ethiopia's accession. Would this not, Freire d'Andrade (Portugal) had asked (recalling that over 'five centuries' his country had twice helped Ethiopia defend 'her threatened independence'), 'constitute an encroachment on [Ethiopia's] sovereignty [*sic*] rights?'[81]

77 *Convention for the Control of the Trade in Arms and Ammunition, and Protocol*, Saint-Germain-en-Laye, 10 September 1919, Art. 6.

78 See Item 1, Section 1.

79 'Abyssinia's Request for Admission', Fourth Meeting, 19 September 1923, Records of the Fourth Assembly, Meetings of the Committees, Minutes of the Sixth Committee (Political Questions), in *LNOJ*, Special Supplement no. 19 (1923): 12–16, 15.

80 Put squarely on the defensive, Cook eventually voted in favour of the conditional accession plan, which passed unanimously at the Committee's fifth sitting. 'Abyssinia's Request for Admission', Fifth Meeting, 20 September 1923, Records of the Fourth Assembly, 21.

81 Comments of M. Freire d'Andrade (Portugal), 'Abyssinia's Request for Admission', Fourth Meeting, at 13. See also the comments of the Chinese and Venezuelan delegates, Ibid., 14–15.

The most numerous and powerful voices, however, took a more complicated position, arguing, in effect, that Ethiopia was somewhere in-between a sovereign equal and a sovereign unequal, and should therefore be admitted into the League in order to assist 'her' to become 'more' self-governing, and thus more sovereign. Thus, as M. Louwers (Belgium) had argued, conditionality under the League had many 'precedents', and even '[c]ountries with advanced civilisations had also had to give, on their entry into the League, special undertakings'. 'The prestige of the ancient African Empire could not therefore be affected by the signature of the proposed undertakings'.[82] Similarly, Count Bonin-Longaire (Italy) had insisted the Committee's request 'contained nothing to wound Abyssinia's susceptibilities, since other States, which had arrived at a higher degree of civilisation, had already consented to undertake special engagements not included in the Covenant'. In his view, accession, in facilitating the League's assistance 'in its fight against slavery', would allow Ethiopia 'to become an ever more active and effectual pioneer of civilisation in Central Africa'.[83] Likewise, M. De Jouvenal (France), had pointed out that 'many [European] Governments found themselves faced with similar difficulties in their African territories', and had gone on to note that 'the abolition of serfdom in one of the most important European countries, namely, Russia, had taken place less than a century ago'.[84] The concern that the Ethiopian government did not possess 'adequate means of exercising its authority as far as the confines of its territory' could doubtless be extended to 'all Colonial Governments', but there were only 'two ways of placing a government in possession of adequate strength'. A 'choice had to be made between a policy of conquest [of Ethiopia] and one of cooperation [with Ethiopia]', and the latter was 'certainly preferable, by virtue of the very principles which the Members of the League had pledged themselves to respect'. Ethiopia's 'national liberty', he had concluded, as well as its 'domestic liberty', could best be 'strengthened' through its admission into the League.[85] It was, of course, this argument that won the day.

Once again, as this debate underlines, it is clear that the 'special obligations', though tailor-made for Ethiopia, were cut from a familiar fabric. It is also clear, however, that race was hardly an inconsequential factor in

[82] Comments of M. Louwers (Belgium), 'Abyssinia's Request for Admission', Fourth Meeting, 14.

[83] Comments of Count Bonin-Longaire (Italy), 'Abyssinia's Request for Admission', Fifth Meeting, 19.

[84] Comments of M. De Jouvenal (France), Ibid., 17–21, 20.

[85] Ibid., 20.

this process. Nonetheless, far from operating as a condition *per se*, such that Ethiopia, failing to be fully white, could not therefore be fully sovereign, race here operated as a 'floating signifier'[86] of the capacity to meet a more general condition (or criterion) of statehood. Ethiopia's blackness 'signified', not that it was incapable of sovereignty, but rather that it would need external 'assistance' in order to develop its institutions of 'self-government' before it could be regarded as having met the 'standard' of statehood. Since the sole purpose of these institutions was to protect and, ideally, extend the 'natural' rights of 'all men' to 'freedom' and 'equality', their suitability and desirability could simply be presumed, just as it had been presumed on a universal basis from the sixteenth century onwards.

2 The View from Addis Ababa I: League Membership as Self-Defence

The archives examined in order to reach these conclusions reveal a great deal about why and how Ethiopia's application to the League came to be seen as an opportunity to transform Ethiopia into a self-governing state, and hence as a space amenable to capitalist penetration. Yet these archives reveal almost nothing about the rationale that lay behind Ethiopia's own decision to apply for League membership. As might be expected, the Empire's decision to lodge the application was, of course, the product of a different debate, conducted, at least in part, with the aid of a different set of normative principles. Indeed, the application itself, which took the form of a letter sent by *Ras* Tafari Mackonen on behalf of the Ethiopian Empire (*Mängestä Ityop'p'ya*) can even be said to have landed on the League Secretary-General Eric Drummond's desk at two different moments, which were experienced differently in Geneva and Addis Ababa. In Geneva time, defined by the Gregorian calendar, this moment was September 1923. In Addis Ababa time, defined by the solar calendar used in Ethiopia (*yä'Ityop̂p̂ya zämän aḳoṭaṭär*, closely related to that of the Coptic Orthodox Church in Alexandria), the letter arrived in Mäskäräm 1916.[87]

[86] Stuart Hall, 'Race, the Floating Signifier', talk at Goldsmiths University, London, directed by Sut Jhally, Media Education Foundation, 1997. See Item 2, Section 2.2.2.

[87] The timing of the Ethiopian day also differs from that of the European day. It begins at dawn, the equivalent in European time to 6 a.m.

2.1 *To Be, or Not to Be (and on Whose Terms?): Debating League Membership*

By the time this double moment had arrived, the split between the conservative supporters of Empress Zewditu and *Ras* Tafari's Young Ethiopians was already well entrenched. To characterise this (as did many European analysts, as we have seen) as a split between African traditionalism and aspiring European modernism would, however, be a mistake. As the heir to the Solomonic throne, *Ras* Tafari had, of course, received an education steeped in the precepts of the *Fetha Nagast* and *Kebra Nagast*. Yet, as the son of *Ras* Mäkonnen Wäldä-Mikaʾél (1852–1906), a leading patriot-moderniser, he had also been educated by a French monk, André Jarossuau.[88] This combination was not uncommon among his supporters. *Bäjerond* Täklä-Hawaryat Täklä-Maryam (1884–1977), for example, who drafted Ethiopia's first Constitution in 1931,[89] and in early 1933 travelled to Geneva to head the Ethiopian Delegation to the League,[90] provides one illustration. Having accompanied *Ras* Mäkonnen (Tafari's father) on the Adwa campaign at the age of 11,[91] Täklä-Hawaryat was entrusted to Count Leontieff, a member of the Russian Red Cross team which had travelled to Ethiopia to care for the wounded,[92] and taken back to Russia, where he was adopted by the grandson of the Decembrist Prince Sergey Volkonsky and sent to military school in St Petersburg. He later spent time in Paris and London. Of his return to Ethiopia, Täklä-Hawaryat wrote that he 'could see that my countrymen would face certain humiliation unless they modernised'.[93] He did not, however, equate modernisation with straightforward Europeanisation. Instead, in the company of Gäbrä-Heywät,[94] and likewise with the Japanese Empire as his model,[95] he was deeply committed to the reorganisation of Ethiopia's administrative structures on the basis of 'fair and equitable' principles, and to the abolition of slavery (to

[88] Harold G. Marcus, *Haile Selassie I: The Formative Years, 1892–1936* (Lawrenceville, NJ: Red Sea Press, 1995), 2–3.

[89] See Item 4, Section 4.1.

[90] Bahru Zewde, *Pioneers of Change in Ethiopia: The Reformist Intellectuals of the Early Twentieth Century* (Oxford, Athens, OH, Addis Ababa: James Currey, Ohio University Press, Addis Ababa University Press, 2002), 210.

[91] *Ras* Mäkonnen is likely to be one of the mounted figures at the centre of the painting of the Battle of Adwa, which is reproduced on the cover of this book.

[92] Bahru, *Pioneers of Change*, 57.

[93] Täklä-Hawaryat Täklä-Maryam, unpublished autobiography, Vol. 1, 168, translated by and cited in Bahru, *Pioneers of* Change, 100.

[94] See Item 4, Section 4.2, above.

[95] See Item 4, Section 4.2.

the chagrin of more conservative elements in the imperial administration),[96] and remained acutely aware of the dangers that throwing open the Ethiopian economy would pose to Ethiopia's agriculture, crafts and – ultimately – independence. In the context of the debate over foreign loans and mining concessions, for example, Täklä-Hawaryat argued that 'exchanging pure gold for dubious money' flowing in from Europe and the United States was akin to 'mortgaging the fortunes of future generations'.[97]

All too acutely aware of the furore over slavery in the European press and of the many voices calling for intervention to suppress it, Tafari and his supporters soon concluded that League membership held out the best guarantee for Ethiopia's sovereignty, as well as the best source of what we might now call 'development assistance'. This task of realising this decision was far from easy, however, for 'the empress [Zewditu] and Habte Giorgis ... were opposed to foreign alliances and to negotiations in Europe'. They were also 'in total conflict with Tafari's conclusion that national survival depended on policies that extricated Ethiopia from the pull of the tripartite powers and opened it to the other nations of the globe'.[98] Looking back, in the 1930s, on his predicament, Tafari – by that time Emperor – wrote: 'my own ideas and the people fond of old customs squeezed me like wood between two pieces of iron'.[99] His first move was to follow up an earlier anti-slavery edict with another, issued in *Hämle* 1914 (July 1922), instructing all regional governors to ban slave trading within their jurisdictions.[100] In the same month, Tafari summoned officials and governors from all corners of the Empire, and the Council of the Realm met continuously for six days and nights to discuss the idea of applying for League membership.[101]

Convincing the conservative clergy and nobility was no easy matter, however, as historian Zewde Retta argues.[102] Using primary documents

[96] Bahru, *Pioneers of Change*, 117–18, 128. *Näggadras* Haylä-Giorgis, *de facto* Prime Minister from 1911 to 1916, is supposed to have said of him: 'What I want is a box that closes when it is closed and opens when it is opened. I have no need for someone like Täklä-Hawaryat who opens and closes of his own volition.' Täklä-Hawaryat, unpublished autobiography, cited in Ibid., 59.

[97] Täklä-Hawaryat, unpublished autobiography, cited in Ibid., 101, 115.

[98] Marcus, *Haile Selassie I*, 44 (n. 3). Emphasis added.

[99] Quoted in Ibid., 45.

[100] Ibid., 48. Upon hearing news of the edict, *Fitawrari* Habte Giorgis Dinagde – who, it will be recalled, may have been born into slavery himself – is reported to have exclaimed: 'What is this? [My wife] Altayework will have to go to the river to collect water and I will have to chop wood?' Quoted in Ibid., 49–50.

[101] Ibid., 53.

[102] Zewde Retta, *Tafari Makonnen: The Long Journey to Civilisation and during Menelik, Iyassu and Zewditu 1884–1922* (Addis Ababa: Central Publishing, 1998), 421–34. Zewde's

and the oral testimony of his father, *Kenyazmach* Retta, who served under both Emperor Menelik II and Zewditu,[103] Zewde explains that the nobility put three questions to Tafari:

> One. Would not membership in the League [*Mah'bär*] of Nations make it very easy for the foreigners [*ferenji*] to come to our country freely and spy on us, and to invade us as soon as they found it advantageous? It would be impossible to forbid a fellow-member from coming to our house (*bet*) by closing the door.
>
> Two. As is recorded in our history, *ferenji* can never be true friends to us; if for the sake of seeking civilisation [*silit'ane*] we open our hearts to them, it might ultimately be more harmful than advantageous. And then what would be our defence?
>
> Three. If the number of foreigners coming to our country increased because of our membership [of the League of Nations], would this not give them the opportunity to convert our children to the faith of the Roman Bishop [i.e. Catholicism] using the unscrupulous methods they [always] bring with them?[104]

Two Amharic terms deserve special attention here. The first is *silit'ane*. This term, though translated as 'civilisation', in fact has a very different resonance from the highly racialised, evolutionist European understanding of 'civilisation'. Indeed, 'civilisation-as-*silit'ane*' might be better translated as 'accumulated knowledge gained through modern education'. Yet even that definition was in dispute, as we shall see. For conservatives in the Ethiopian Empire of the early twentieth century, such education invariably invoked the teachings of the Ethiopian Orthodox Church, seen as the traditional custodian of the education of the Empire's youth.[105] For the Young Ethiopians/Japanisers, by contrast, the desire for *silit'ane* was a desire for the most advanced forms of technical knowledge – agricultural, military, institutional, educational and so on. Unlike the unattainable goal of 'civilisation-as-whiteness',[106] then, 'civilisation-as-*silit'ane*' was,

book is available in Amharic only. I am hugely grateful to Tilaye Gebre-Medhin (Addis Ababa) and Abebaw Yigzaw (London) for translating parts of this text for me.

103 In addition to interviews with his father, Zewde used sources found in America, England and France, as well as the unpublished memoirs of *Ras* Imru (Haile Selassie's cousin, who grew up with him), the unpublished work of *Fitawrari* Tekle Hawaryat, and *Blatte* Merze Hazane Walde Qirquos's account of Zewditu's reign.

104 Zewde, *Tafari Makonnen*, 421–5.

105 This understanding of the term *silit'ane* emerged from conversations with several friends and colleagues, including Tilaye Gebre-Medhin and Asfaw Damté in Addis Ababa, Abebaw Yigzaw in London, and Tsegaye Ararssa in Melbourne, to whom I will be eternally grateful. Notes on file with the author.

106 See Frame, Section 3.1, above.

in principle, a process which the Empire's non-Abyssinian 'others' *could* complete – though still, of course, at the cost of relinquishing any alternative identities. This suggests that the debate in Addis Ababa in late 1916/1923 was not a discussion about whether or not to 'become more European', but rather how to obtain those aspects of European existence which might allow the Empire *to remain what it already was*. Perhaps the most important thing it needed, in this respect, was a claim to independence which European and other states, Britain, France and Italy in particular, would respect. In short, international recognition of Ethiopia as a sovereign state required reconfirmation, and allies were needed – ideally allies prepared to recognise the principle of collective self-defence. In addition, the reformists also sought to improve the material conditions experienced by the vast majority of Ethiopia's population; hence the need for 'modern' agricultural, engineering and other techniques.[107] According to Täklä-Hawaryat, indeed, the Amharic language at that time contained no word for 'progress', meaning that the word *silit'ane* may simply have been the best translation available.[108]

A second linguistic issue here concerns Tafari's decision to translate the term 'League of Nations' into Amharic as '*Mah'bär* of Nations'. The *mah'bär* was, and remains, an extremely important Abyssinian social institution.[109] The members of a *mah'bär*, in the context of the Ethiopian Orthodox tradition, are those members of a community who identify with a particular patron saint of the Ethiopian Orthodox Church (*Yäityop'ya ortodoks täwahedo bétäkrestyan*).[110] In this context, the *mah'bär* can be seen as a covenanting group of Christians, with a common patron saint – often that of their local parish church, whose *tabot* (a wooden replica of the original Ark of the Covenant, at Aksum) was kept in the church's inner sanctum or 'holy of holies'. According to custom, the members of a *mah'bär* would meet once a month, on their Patron Saint's day, in the

[107] For two penetrating critiques of international law's relationship to the development project, see Sundhya Pahuja, *Decolonising International Law: Development, Economic Growth and the Politics of Universality* (Cambridge University Press, 2011) and Luis Eslava, *Local Space, Global Life: The Everyday Operation of International Law and Development* (Cambridge University Press, 2015).

[108] Bahru, *Pioneers of Change*, 210.

[109] See Abraha Weldu, '*Mahebär*: Dynamics of a social self-help association', 9 *African Journal of History and Culture* (2017): 27–33; Anne Britt Flemmen, 'Religious *Mahbär* in Ethiopia: Ritual Elements, Dynamics, and Challenges', 46 *Journal of Religion in Africa* (2016): 3–31.

[110] Stéphane Ancel, 'Maḫbär et Sänbäte: Associations Religieuses en Éthiopie', 8 *Aethiopica* (2005): 95–111, at 95.

house of each member of the association in turn.[111] The monthly transfer from one house to another would be marked by a procession in which the group would carry a symbolic chalice (*tsiwwaa*) from one member's house to the next. When they arrived, they would break bread and drink wine from the *tsiwwaa* (symbolising Christ's broken body and spilled blood) to commemorate Christ. However, '[b]eyond their ceremonial functions, [*mah'bärs*] were organised to provide mediation and mutual assistance for their membership, for instance, to help rebuild a house that had burned down, or lend seed during times of crop failure'.[112] The relationships among members of these covenanting fraternities were for this reason experienced as being just as close, if not closer, than blood relationships.[113]

Bearing in mind the decision (at Woodrow Wilson's insistence) to call the founding treaty of the League of Nations a 'Covenant' in a deliberate invocation of the Judaeo-Christian idea of God's 'covenant' with his chosen people, this translation ('league' as *mah'bär*) is, I suggest, critical to a proper understanding of Ethiopia's position in relation to the League. In the first place, the word 'Covenant' in the Aksumite world view could not but refer to the most sacred of Christian agreements. This term explicitly invoked the image of the 'tablets of the covenant' (the tablets on which the ten commandments were written), which, according to the traditions of the Ethiopian Orthodox Church (described in Item 4), had been kept in the *Tabot* in the holy city of Aksum since the first Solomonic Emperor, Menelik I, returned from Jerusalem. Secondly, if to join the League was to join a *Mah'bär* of Nations, then in joining, Ethiopia would, by definition, lose the right to refuse anything at all that might be asked of it by other members of the League, including access to the Ethiopian 'house' or 'home'. To translate this back into the language of international law, the noblemen feared – quite correctly, as it turned out – that Ethiopia's independence was just as likely to be weakened by accession to the Covenant as it was to be strengthened.[114]

After the nobility had directed their questions to Tafari, Zewde relates, it was the turn of the *Ich'ege*, the Abbot of the monastery of Däbrä

[111] Charles Schaefer, 'Maĥbär', in Siegbert Uhlig (ed.), *Encyclopaedia Aethiopica*, Vol. 3, He–N (Wiesbaden: Harrassowitz Verlag, 2007), 649–50. My thanks to Peter Garretson for sending me this reference.

[112] Ibid., 649–50.

[113] Zewde, *Tafari Makonnen*, 421–34.

[114] My thanks to Tsegaye Ararssa for his insights on this question. Notes on file with the author.

Libanos,[115] the second-highest ecclesiastical position in the Ethiopian Orthodox Church, to ask his question. Referring to the procession in which the *Tsiwwaa*, symbolising the *tabot* of the local Patron Saint, was carried from one *mah'bär*-member's house to the next, he asked: 'When we prepare to be a member of the *Mah'bär* of States, which Patron Saint are we going to take with us into the League?'[116] According to Zewde, this question was a 'headache' for Tafari, in that it engaged an additional aspect of the *mah'bär* concept: that of *dirib tabot* ('double saint'), arising from a practice in which certain parishes adopted not one, but two patron saints (and therefore two *tabots*).[117] In essence, the *Ich'ege* was asking what aspect – if any – of the Ethiopian Empire's epistemology and normativity would be able to coexist with that of its fellow League members in a single covenanting community: in a single *mah'bär*. On Zewde's reading, the *Ich'ege* was trying, in other words, subtly to scupper Tafari's chances of persuading the other more conservative members of the Council of the Realm of the desirability of League membership by drawing attention to the incommensurability of these two normative universes and therefore also to the risk that League membership would pose to Ethiopia's identity – to the survival of the cultural, religious, administrative and other idiosyncrasies which made the Empire what it was.

The *Ich'ege*'s question returns us to Bakhtin's distinction posited earlier between 'authoritative' and 'dialogical' (or 'internally persuasive') modes of understanding.[118] The central issue, from his perspective, was whether equality would be predicated on sameness. Would embarking on the quest to guarantee Ethiopia's status as the formal equal of the European states mean that Ethiopia would be forced to relinquish precisely those characteristics that equality was sought in order to preserve? Or, to put it in the language of the Frame, would League members be capable of understanding Ethiopia as an 'unfinalised' subject among other unfinalised subjects, or would they insist on 'finalising' it as the necessary consequence of its transformation from object into subject (of international law)? Seen in this light, the point was clearly not that the Ethiopian nobility and clergy

[115] In one of the most notorious massacres of the Italian occupation, 297 of the monastery's monks and 23 laymen were killed on 21 May 1937, in retaliation for the attempted assassination of Rodolfo Graziani, then Viceroy of Italian East Africa. See Ian Campbell, *The Addis Ababa Massacre: Italy's National Shame* (London: Hurst, 2017).

[116] Zewde, *Tafari Makonnen*, 421–34.

[117] Ibid., 421–34. On the *tabot*, see Teshale Tibebu, *The Making of Modern Ethiopia, 1896–1974* (Lawrenceville, NJ: Red Sea Press, 1995), 8.

[118] Frame, Section 3.2.

misunderstood the League's function in the debate of 1916/1923. On the contrary, the nobility put forward a different, 'Abyssinian' understanding of the Covenant, and of the implications of becoming 'recognisable' to other states. Their (well-founded) suspicions were that League membership would make it harder, rather than easier, to fend off intervention on the part of Ethiopia's fellow League members. They were, unfortunately, quite correct. Those League members *did* insist that Ethiopia transform its internal institutions to become more like their own, as we shall see in Item 5. They *were* prepared, when they judged it necessary, to sacrifice Ethiopia's independence in order to protect their own. The task of defending Ethiopia's identity and independence simultaneously *would* be impossible. Though the language of the Ethiopian aristocracy and ecclesiastical nobility might have sounded anachronistic (even to Tafari, it seems), the nobility's only 'mistake' lay in their retention of the outdated sixteenth-century association between Europeans and perfidious Catholic missionaries. Nonetheless, while it was international law's capitalist evangelism that posed the greater risk by the 1920s, the terminal threat did, ironically enough, come from 'Rome'.

Against Tafari's arguments for League membership, then, voiced in the language of sovereign equality and collective security, the imperial nobility and clergy deployed a traditional Abyssinian vocabulary of belligerent imperial isolation. French-educated descendant of King Solomon as he was, however, Tafari was more than capable of swimming in both discursive streams. Taking advantage of his bilingualism, shared by many in his faction, Tafari's response was to adopt what Bakhtin would have recognised as a strategy of 'intentional hybridisation', splicing an Aksumite discourse together with an international legal discourse in such a way as to render them mutually more distinctive, while at the same time attempting to expose one as inferior to the other. The starting point of his response to the *Ich'ege* was to argue that '[w]henever there is conflict between countries, the *Mah'bär* of Nations will investigate the matter and give its judicial verdict', for under its rules 'if one aggressive government tries to invade another weak government, with arms, the member countries of the *Mah'bär* of Nations will fight it together'. This was, of course, a straightforward restatement of the Covenant's collective security principle under Article 16. In the same breath, however, Tafari also reminded his audience of that Abyssinian truism, that '[w]e the Ethiopian Nation, live surrounded by Animists and Muslims' who 'look at us as enemies because we are Christians'. The bond of Christianity did not, he admitted, guarantee that all foreigners could be counted upon as friends, since 'many of them, being jealous of our independence, would want us to perish'. However,

Tafari continued, there was 'no reason why our religion should be affected', or any indication that it would not be possible to 'live together in harmony as Catholics and *Tewahidos*, honouring each others' faith'. He concluded: 'if we will have closer relations with the European countries, who are more advanced in the modern civilisation and who are Christians, the advantage will be more than the disadvantage'.[119] He side-stepped the 'double-saint' issue by declaring (not entirely accurately) that '[a]ll the other independent [*neza*] countries, numbering over fifty, are members of the *Mah'bär* of Nations', and all were 'ardent believers like us who fulfil their religious obligations'. Once Ethiopia had obtained its 'seat beside the other free governments', he promised to 'work hard to ensure that our *täwahedo* faith, inherited from our fathers' would be 'honoured and recognised throughout the world'.[120]

As this exchange makes clear, the importance of the Ethiopian Orthodox Church to Ethiopia's conception of its own sovereignty cannot be overstated. The Abyssinian notion of civilisation was predicated on the conviction that Ethiopian Orthodox Christianity was the only true form of Christianity. Thus, when the nobility stressed their 400-year-old suspicion of Europeans as underhand Catholic proselytisers, Tafari countered with a vision of Ethiopia as a member of a worldwide Christian civilisation,[121] within which the norms of the League itself were rooted. To back up this vision of Ethiopia and Europe as members of a common Christian family, rather than as Orthodox 'self' to Catholic 'other', Tafari appealed to two different but equally longstanding 'others': Islam and paganism. When defined against these common enemies, he suggested, Christianity's different factions were unimportant. From the perspective of the Ethiopian Empire's aristocracy, of which Tafari was soon to be the leader, the civilised world *was* the Christian world, just as it had been for Francisco de Vitoria, Francisco Suárez, Hugo Grotius, Thomas Hobbes, and all the early natural law theorists of the *jus gentium* right up to the second half of the nineteenth century.

2.2 Double-Voiced Diplomacy: Ethiopia's Application for League Membership

Tafari's efforts to portray the League of Nations as the most recent, most highly institutionalised version of an ancient Christian 'family of

[119] Marcus, *Haile Selassie I*, 4.
[120] Ibid., 4.
[121] See Item 2, Section 2.1.2.

nations' can be observed even more clearly in his letter to Drummond of 1916/1923.[122] In Zewde's account Tafari, faced with the need to persuade the League of Ethiopia's desire and capacity to carry out reforms such as the abolition of slavery, while at the same time persuading the imperial nobility of the League's willingness to refrain from interfering with Ethiopia's culture and traditions, resorted to a strategy that can only be described as 'hybridised' in the Bakhtinian sense.[123]

Having at last secured the consent of the Empress and her supporters to apply for League membership, Tafari began his letter to the Secretary-General with a clear statement of Ethiopia's sense of itself as an isolated and embattled Christian polity, deserving of the support of other Christian nations:

> As the Holy Scriptures bear witness, since the year 1500 after Solomon we have ... been contending with the heathen – by whom ... we are surrounded – for the true faith and the laws of God, and to maintain the independence of our country and the freedom of our religion. With God's help we have baptised thousands of heathen, who have become our brothers, and only in the time of our Emperor [Menelik II] have we had peace.[124]

Here, Tafari again produced the well-worn Abyssinian image of Ethiopia as a Christian island surrounded by an ocean of unbelievers. He drew Drummond's attention to the disruption caused by *Lijj* Iyassu's 'leanings towards the religion [i.e. Islam] against which we had so energetically fought', and blamed this disruption for Ethiopia's subsequent failure to 'continue along the path of progress' that Menelik II had initiated. Tafari sought, then, to emphasise Ethiopia's role in the defence and expansion of Christianity in the Horn of Africa as against its aggressive Muslim neighbours. He also stressed the Empire's internal civilising mission, in

[122] I am relying on the official League translation here: *Appendix III: Request for Admission to the League of Nations from Abyssinia* (6 September 1923) A.55.1923.VI, in *Société des Nations, Assemblée 4 (1923)*, Documents 41–144 (LONA), n. p. ('Request for Admission from Abyssinia').

[123] According to Zewde, Tafari wrote two letters, one in Amharic, the other French – ostensibly translations of one another, but in fact saying very different things – and sent them off to Geneva, relying on the inability of Zewditu to speak French and of anyone at the Palais Wilson to speak Amharic. Zewde, *Tafari Makonnen*, 421–34. Having compared the two – a translation of the Amharic letter, as reproduced by Zewde, and the letter, in French, which arrived in Geneva – I have not been able to find many differences between them. That does not mean, however, that Tafari's strategy was not one of hybridisation, as I argue below. For the French version, dated 12 August 1923, see '*Demande d'admission à la Société des Nations présentée par l'Empire d'Ethiopie*', Geneva, 6 September 1923, A.55.1923.VI, bound in *Société des Nations, Assemblée 4* (1923), Documents 41–144, LONA.

[124] Request for Admission from Abyssinia.

Figure 8 The Ethiopian Delegation to the League of Nations, Geneva, September 1923. From left to right: Robert Linant de Bellefonds, *Ras* Nadew Aba Wollo Nadeon, *Ato* Fasika. © United Nations Archives at Geneva, by kind permission.

which 'thousands of heathen' had been changed, as it were, from 'others' into 'brothers' through their (often forcible) conversion to Ethiopian Orthodox Christianity.[125]

Yet at other points in the letter, Tafari switched from the Aksumite vision of the Ethiopian Empire's unity and purpose to a narrative founded on the doctrinal international legal criteria for statehood. The Empire, Tafari pointed out, had 'endeavoured to establish bonds of friendship [with

[125] Ibid.

other states]; we built a railway, we adhered to the Brussels Convention, we joined the Universal Postal Union (UPU), and we signed treaties, which we have always observed, with the Powers which cooperated to found the League of Nations'.[126] The signature of treaties, strict adherence to their terms and the joining of international organisations like the UPU were, of course (as we saw in Section 1, above) precisely the kind of evidence of Ethiopia's recognition by other states, and of its 'sincere intention to observe its international obligations', that the Sixth Committee required of new candidates for League membership. But Tafari also meshed these doctrinal arguments in with Aksumite equivalents. For example, he again insisted to Drummond, just as he had insisted in his responses to the nobility, that the normative roots of the Ethiopian Empire and the League sprang from the same soil. As he wrote:

> As we [the Ethiopian Empire] received the Gospel at the same time as you [the League of Nations], we should genuinely have liked, despite the difficulties with which we are surrounded, to bring our laws into agreement with yours. We are confident that all that we have done will serve as a guarantee that this objective will be carried out, and we trust that you will recognise our efforts. We know that the League of Nations guarantees the independence and territorial integrity of all the nations in the world, and maintains peace and agreement among them; that it is anxious to remove all the obstacles to friendship which give rise to wars when one country is offended; that it causes truth and loyalty to be respected. These principles specially befit a nation which has always been firmly Christian. The perpetual desire of this Christian Government is to govern its people in peace and tranquillity, and to develop its country under prosperous conditions.[127]

Here, Tafari painted a picture in which Ethiopia had 'received the Gospel' at the same moment as the other member states of the League, but had then fallen behind in modernising its 'laws' because of the country's difficult practical circumstances, as a Christian country surrounded by hostile elements. More than that, he characterised the principles of international law and those of the League members themselves, including the foundational principles of non-intervention, territorial integrity, the non-use of force and *pacta sunt servanda*, as specifically *Christian* principles. Ethiopia's ability to understand and implement these principles was therefore not to be doubted, because Ethiopia's own culture and the international legal culture of the League sprang from the same source.

[126] Request for Admission from Abyssinia.
[127] Request for Admission from Abyssinia.

Ethiopian normativity (based on the teachings of the Ethiopian Orthodox Church) and League normativity (based on the Covenant and on international law more generally) were siblings.

3 Conclusion

Bearing in mind the translations mentioned above – *mah'bär*/league and *silit'ane*/civilisation – we are now in a position to place these two (Orientalist-Semiticist/European and Aksumite/Abyssinian) evaluations of the Ethiopian Empire as a subject of international normativity side-by-side and inspect them together. Tafari's letter to Drummond, as we have seen, provided evidence that the Ethiopian Empire's government had been 'stable' for several millennia and that the Empire had been consistent in fulfilling its international obligations. It made no mention of armaments. As to the criterion of 'self-government', the letter certainly articulated a vision of Ethiopia's ancient claim to self-rule, but this centred, not on any institutionalised social contract between ruler and ruled or any rights pertaining to all individuals, but rather – in the spirit of the 'Aksumite paradigm' – on the expansion of Ethiopian Orthodox Christianity. Equally, the conception of Ethiopia's physical extent put forward in Tafari's letter was very different from the League's own understanding. Far from being 'well-defined' in the territorial sense intended by the Sixth Committee, and in spite of the fact that they had been confirmed in numerous treaties with the European powers, Tafari depicted Ethiopia's frontiers, as Menelik II had done before him in 1891,[128] as the moving front line in an ongoing, perhaps eternal cosmic battle between the Ethiopian Orthodox Church and its religious enemies. These borders were by definition *flexible* rather than fixed – expanding when the empire was strong (as in the late nineteenth century under Menelik II) and contracting when it was weak (as in the early sixteenth century during the war against Ahmad Gragn).

Interestingly, the effect of this letter on its audience in Geneva must have been almost exactly as Tafari had hoped. This becomes especially clear when we consider the intrusiveness of the suggestions then in circulation (outlined in Section 1, above) as to what his Empire's fate deserved to be – suggestions ranging from wholesale League-sponsored administrative reconstruction to racially determined partition among the 'tripartite' powers. Certainly, for years after Ethiopia's entry into the League in September 1923, Tafari fought against the restrictions placed

[128] Item 4, Section 4.

Map 1 Extent of the Ethiopian Empire's political and economic control during the first half of the nineteenth century compared with its borders in 1935.

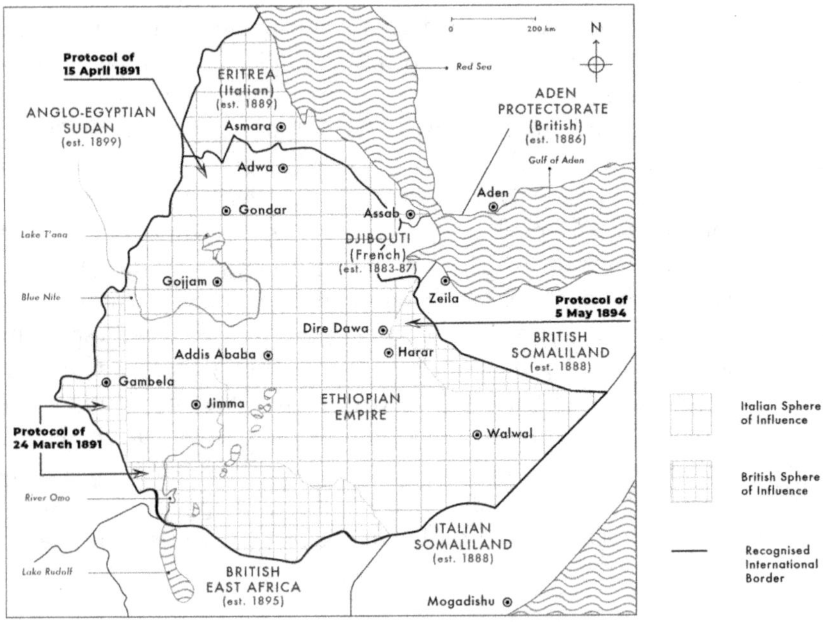

Map 2 The Anglo-Italian Protocols of 1891 and 1894.

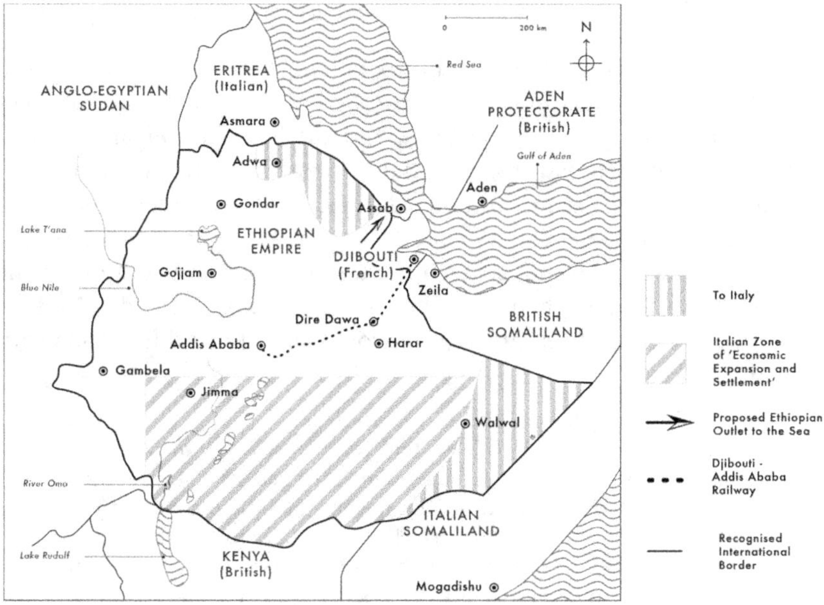

Map 3 The 'Hoare-Laval Pact' of December 1935.

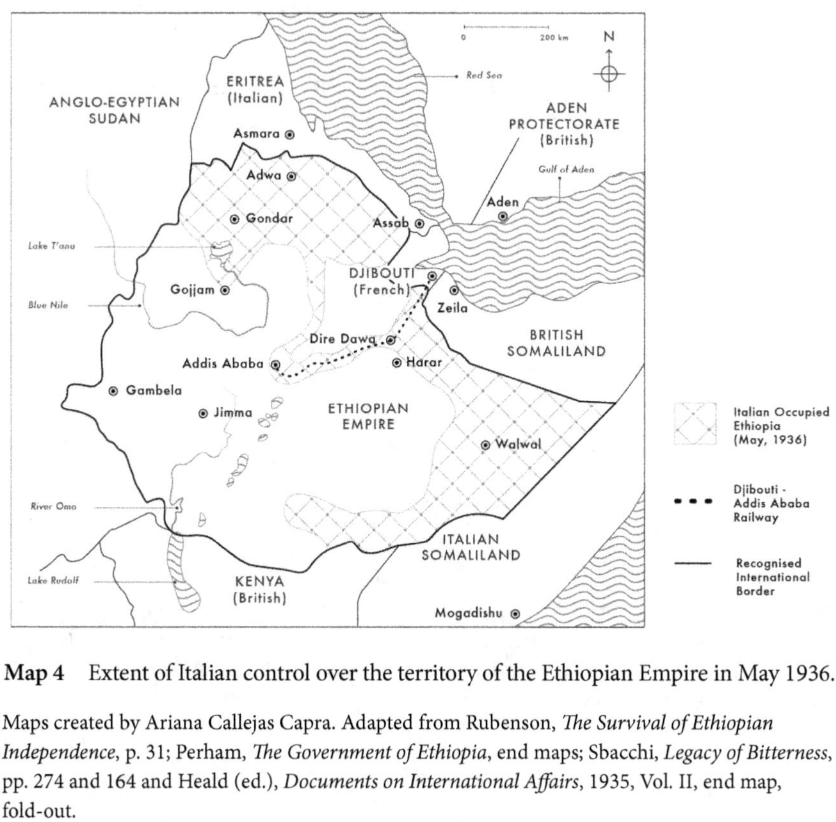

Map 4 Extent of Italian control over the territory of the Ethiopian Empire in May 1936.

Maps created by Ariana Callejas Capra. Adapted from Rubenson, *The Survival of Ethiopian Independence*, p. 31; Perham, *The Government of Ethiopia*, end maps; Sbacchi, *Legacy of Bitterness*, pp. 274 and 164 and Heald (ed.), *Documents on International Affairs*, 1935, Vol. II, end map, fold-out.

by the 'special obligations' on Ethiopia's capacity to obtain arms.[129] Nonetheless, Ethiopia's request for admission *was* granted, the protections of the Covenant *were* secured, and the 'special obligations' concerning slavery even had the potential to strengthen the position of the Young Ethiopians as against the Zewditu faction. *Ras* Nadew Aba Wollo (see Figure 8), who, as Head of the Ethiopian Delegation to Geneva at that time, signed both the Covenant and the declaration containing the 'special obligations' on behalf of the Empire, communicated this sense of satisfaction in the telegram he sent from Geneva to Addis Ababa with news of the decision:

> To Your Royal Highness, the Crown Prince,
>
> Because your Creator is with you the decisive case which you have been labouring over for long has been approved by the nations of the world and the decision that Ethiopia is to become member of the honoured and great *Mah'bär* of Nations has been passed. History has been fulfilled by the miracle of God ... This manifestation of the miracle of God is not only on this one. For among those who advocated for, and helped Ethiopia to become a member of the League of Nations in equality, Italy was the forerunner. We did not think or dream a country that was our enemy would ever help us this much. Hereafter, rejoice our Queen [Zewditu] and Our Crown Prince [Tafari]! We your servants are also extremely happy.[130]

Sadly, however, as we shall see in the next and final historical item, Ethiopia's new sense of security lasted barely two years.

[129] Harold G. Marcus, 'The Embargo on Arms Sales to Ethiopia, 1916–1930', 16 *The International Journal of African Historical Studies* (1983): 263–379; *Treaty between Ethiopia, France, the United Kingdom and Italy concerning the Importation of Arms*, Paris, 21 August 1930.

[130] Zewde, *Tafari Makonnen*, 434.

Item No. 6

Reconnecting the Crisis

Having circled away from it – to the Aksumite Empire of the 330s; to the lands that later became the Americas of the sixteenth and seventeenth centuries; to the European empires of the 'Middle Ages'; to the French, Haitian and Liberian Republics of the late eighteenth century; to the Chinese Empire, post-Ottoman Balkans and Congo Basin of the nineteenth century; to the Eastern European 'enemy' and 'national' states and West Asian 'mandates' of the early twentieth century and beyond – we now arrive back at the point in space and time where we began: at 5 a.m. on 3 October 1935, on the southern shore of the Mareb as Italian troops poured across the Eritrean border into Ethiopia. Having introduced the standard account of the Abyssinia Crisis back at the very start of this process of assemblage,[1] the task of this final item to go into the box is to offer a new telling of the (hi)story which, when set against this complex, multilayered background, causes certain obscure elements of it suddenly to leap out into the foreground. This item, Item 6, will be composed of a series of x-ray images taken at key moments during the Crisis. Their purpose, as with x-rays in general, is not to eliminate or damage the soft tissue (in this case, the contingent historical detail), but rather to filter through it, in order to produce an image of the denser matter (here, the enforceable rights and duties at issue during the Crisis) which gave the Empire form and, perhaps, structured its fate. Viewed at close range, these 'hard' rights and duties might well appear no less contingent, and therefore no less indeterminate, than the personalities, appetites and dispositions of the individuals involved, from Haile Selassie to Benito Mussolini to Frederick Lugard. However, by the end of the chapter we will be in a position to view this series of legal x-rays not only in relation to one another, but also in relation to the other items that are already stacked together. If, at the end of this account, we stand back and squint in order to take in

[1] See Item 1, above.

the shadow-box and its contents as a whole, a series of *correspondances* between these disparate elements will, I hope, be clearly visible.

Beginning with the 'Walwal Incident' of late 1934 and ending with the near-unanimous *de jure* recognition of Italian sovereignty over Ethiopia in late 1938, a familiar pattern emerges to Ethiopia's treatment by other states. This pattern is common both to the efforts that were made (primarily by Italy) to undermine Ethiopia's rights as a sovereign equal, and to those efforts (on the part of the League of Nations and its other members) that ostensibly sought to 'resolve' the impending conflict with Italy. More specifically, in the various agreements and attempted agreements that were made with respect to Ethiopia during this four-year period, a similar set of concerns surfaced again and again. Using a mode of analysis that is indebted to the work of Nathaniel Berman,[2] in particular, these elements can be listed as follows:

(i) an 'adjustment' of territories between Ethiopia and its colonial neighbours, Britain, France and Italy (I: TERRITORIAL 'ADJUSTMENTS');
(ii) Ethiopia's partition into two racially determined 'zones', in one of which (Ethiopia's recently conquered southern regions) Ethiopia's 'government' was considered to be less legitimate, and less 'effective', than the other (so-called 'Ethiopia proper', i.e. the Abyssinian highlands) (II: RACIALISED PARTITION);
(iii) a League-administered scheme of 'assistance' aimed at 'reorganising' Ethiopia's internal administrative and legal structures and abolishing slavery, in order to transform the Ethiopian Empire into a better approximation of a 'self-governing' state, and its inhabitants into better approximations of legal subjects (III: LEAGUE-SUPERVISED 'REORGANISATION');
(iv) the protection, and ideally the extension, within Ethiopia, of the 'established rights' of British, French, Italian and other existing ('foreign') legal subjects (individuals and corporations), under the existing, treaty-based regime (IV: PROTECTION/EXTENSION OF FOREIGN RIGHTS); and
(v) the requirement of formal Ethiopian consent to the implementation of any scheme (though not of Ethiopian participation in the negotiations leading to any such scheme) (V: ETHIOPIAN 'CONSENT').

Taken together, these features, which are reproduced again and again in different combinations, shift our understanding of the Crisis profoundly.

[2] See esp. Nathaniel Berman, '"But the Alternative is Despair": European Nationalism and the Modernist Renewal of International Law', in Nathaniel Berman, *Passion and Ambivalence: Colonialism, Nationalism and International Law* (Leiden: Martinus Nijhoff Publishers, 2012), 115–242.

Far from being a 'failure' for international law and for the League, from inside the shadow-box, the Crisis looks more like a minor success.

1 The View from Geneva II: The Ethiopian Dilemma

For over a decade after its entry into the League in late 1923, Ethiopia appeared to enjoy a period of calm in its international relations. In 1928, for example, it concluded a Treaty of Friendship, Conciliation and Arbitration with Italy,[3] its mortal enemy, together with a Convention granting Ethiopia a concession for the construction of a 'free zone' on the Eritrean coast at Assab.[4] The language of the 1928 Treaty of Friendship will be familiar. The two states pledged 'reciprocally ... not to take ... any action which may prejudice or damage the independence of the other' (Art. 2); to 'promote ... commerce' between them (Art. 3); to maintain Italian extraterritorial jurisdiction (Art. 4); and (more exceptionally) to submit any disputes to conciliation or arbitration 'without having recourse to arms' (Art. 5). Even this tense calm, however, turned out to be entirely superficial.[5]

1.1 Eleven Years in the Life of a Conditional Sovereign: From the Anglo-French Exchange of Notes to the Walwal Arbitration

The first worrying moment came as early as 1925, when Britain and Italy, in an initially secret exchange of notes, agreed to resurrect a 1919 Italian proposal designed to implement the terms of the secret Treaty of London, with which Italy had been lured onto the Allied side in the First World War in 1916.[6] In that Italian proposal (initially rejected by the UK), Italy had

[3] *Treaty of Friendship, Conciliation and Arbitration between Italy and Abyssinia*, Addis Ababa, 2 August 1928.

[4] *Convention between Abyssinia and Italy for the Construction of a Motor Road from Assab to Dessieh and the Concession of an Abyssinian Free Zone at Assab*, Addis Ababa, 2 August 1928. The concession was never operationalised. See W. B. Stern, 'The Treaty Background of the Italo-Ethiopian Dispute', 30 *AJIL* (1936): 189–203, at 202.

[5] As Marcus's research has shown, the treaty was in fact 'the master-piece of Italy's durable minister in Addis Ababa, Giuliano Cora, who convinced Mussolini that it would make Italy supreme in Ethiopia, which would be transformed thereby into a de facto dependency'. Cora to Mussolini, Addis Ababa, 30 March 1928, cited in Harold G. Marcus, 'The Embargo on Arms Sales to Ethiopia, 1916–1930', *The International Journal of African Historical Studies* 16 (1983): 263–379, at 271.

[6] *Exchange of Notes between the United Kingdom and Italy, Respecting Certain British and Italian Interests in Abyssinia*, Rome, 14 and 20 December 1925, in 50 *League of Nations Treaty Series* (1926): 282–93 ('*Anglo-Italian Exchange of Notes*'). On the Treaty of London, see Item 4, Section 3.3.

offered to support Britain's ongoing quest to obtain permission to construct a dam on Lake T'ana (which fell within the Italian 'zone' according to the Anglo-Italian Protocols; see Map 2), and to obtain a related road-building concession (IV: PROTECTION/EXTENSION OF FOREIGN RIGHTS).[7] In return, Italy sought British support in pursuit of an Italian concession to build a railway through Italy from Eritrea to Italian Somaliland; for the establishment of 'an exclusive economic influence in the west of Ethiopia and in the whole of the territory to be crossed by the above-mentioned railway' (that is, for the establishment of Italian economic dominance over a vast area, encompassing roughly the entire southern half of Ethiopia, including the two British 'spheres of influence' in the west) and for a number of other 'economic concessions regarding the Italian zone' (II: RACIALISED PARTITION; IV: PROTECTION/EXTENSION OF FOREIGN RIGHTS).[8] Britain wrote to Italy on 14 December 1926 to resuscitate this proposal, and the two states agreed to undertake 'common action with the Abyssinian Government in order to obtain that the [desired] concessions ... should be granted' by Ethiopia (V: ETHIOPIAN 'CONSENT').[9]

The reaction in Ethiopia was, understandably, one of horror. Reports arrived from Addis Ababa of 'highly emotional meetings, often in tears', organised by the Young Ethiopians, and of roadblocks lifted only for foreign cars not belonging to Britons or Italians.[10] Tafari made a formal protest immediately, first to Britain and Italy, then to the League.[11] Britain and Italy, in response, insisted that theirs had been no more than an 'undertaking to afford each other support when the consent of the Abyssinian Government is sought for the construction in Abyssinia of certain public works',[12] in an agreement that was 'of a purely economic character',[13]

[7] *Anglo-Italian Exchange of Notes*, 283.

[8] Ibid., 283–4.

[9] Ibid., 285.

[10] Bahru Zewde, *Pioneers of Change in Ethiopia: The Reformist Intellectuals of the Early Twentieth Century* (Oxford, Athens, OH, Addis Ababa: James Currey, Ohio University Press, Addis Ababa University Press, 2002), 196.

[11] *Covenant of the League of Nations*, annexed to *Treaty of Peace between the British Empire, France, Italy, Japan and the United States (the Principal Allied and Associated Powers), and Belgium, Bolivia, Brazil, China, Cuba, Czechoslovakia, Ecuador, Greece, Guatemala, Haiti, the Hedjaz, Honduras, Liberia, Nicaragua, Panama, Peru, Poland, Portugal, Roumania, the Serb-Croat-Slovene State, Siam, and Uruguay, and Germany*, Versailles, 28 June 1919 ('Covenant'), Art. 20.

[12] 'Letter from the British Government to the Secretary-General of the League of Nations', 3 August 1926, *LNOJ* (November 1926): 1519–23.

[13] 'Letter from the Italian Minister at Addis Ababa to His Highness Tafari Makonnen, Heir to the Throne of Abyssinia', 9 June 1926, *LNOJ* (November 1926): 1520.

and therefore self-evidently 'in the interests of Abyssinia' itself.[14] This the Ethiopian authorities did not swallow. Deploying a straightforward international legal argument, yet one permeated with the 'Aksumite' understanding of the League as a '*Mah'bär* of Nations', Tafari retorted that:

> on our admission to the League of Nations we were told that all nations were to be on a footing of equality within the League, and that their independence was to be universally respected, since the purpose of the League is to establish and maintain peace among men in accordance with the will of God.[15]

He also expressed doubts as to whether agreements 'stipulat[ing] that part of our Empire is to be allotted to the economic influence of a given Power' were helpful to the delicate task of 'convinc[ing] our people that foreigners who wish to establish themselves for economic reasons in our country ... are genuinely innocent of concealed political aims'.[16] These dignified protests were ignored.

The turning point came in December 1934. An Anglo-Ethiopian Boundary Commission assigned to delimit the border with British Somaliland had arrived on site with an Ethiopian escort to discover that Walwal, an area in the Ethiopian province of Ogaden, was occupied by Italian troops.[17] The Commission withdrew under Italian pressure,[18] and in the ensuing violent 'incidents',[19] some 130 people were killed, mostly Ethiopians.[20] Italy and Ethiopia blamed one another, with Italy insisting – in true fascist style – on a formal apology, reparations, a salute to the Italian flag and punishment of the alleged offenders.[21] Ethiopia requested that the issue be placed on the League Council's agenda,[22] but Italy demanded that it go to arbitration under Article 5

[14] 'Letter from the Italian Government to the Secretary-General of the League of Nations', 7 August 1926, *LNOJ* (November 1926): 1525.

[15] 'Protest sent by His Imperial and Royal Highness Tafari Mackonen, Regent and Heir to the Throne of Abyssinia, to the States Members of the League of Nations', 19 June 1926, *LNOJ* (November 1926): 1517–18.

[16] Ibid., 1518.

[17] 'Dispute between Ethiopia and Italy: Report of the Council of the League of Nations under Article 15, paragraph 4 of the Covenant', adopted 7 October 1935, *LNOJ* (November 1935): 1605–32, 1606 ('Report of the Council').

[18] Christian Curle (ed.), *Letters from the Horn of Africa, 1923–1942: Sandy Curle, Soldier and Diplomat Extraordinary* (Barnsley: Pen & Sword Military, 2008), 136. See also 'Unanimous Award of the Italo-Ethiopian Commission of Conciliation and Arbitration', 3 September 1935 (extracts), in 'Report of the Council', 1610.

[19] 'Report of the Council', 1606.

[20] Pitman B. Potter, 'The Wal Wal Arbitration', 30 *AJIL* (1936): 27–44.

[21] 'Report of the Council', 1606.

[22] 'Request by the Abyssinian Government under Article 11, Paragraph 2, of the Covenant of the League of Nations: Inclusion of this Item in the Agenda of the Session of 17 January 1935', *LNOJ* (February 1935): 124.

of the 1928 Treaty.[23] Italian obstructionism, together with Mussolini's dispatching of war material and troops to East Africa, led Ethiopia to insist that the dispute be brought 'in its entirety' before the Council under Article 15 of the Covenant.[24] Italy pleaded self-defence.[25] Ethiopia then agreed to return to the table on condition that Italy halt military operations and transfer arbitral responsibility to the League Council if negotiations failed.[26] With tensions running extremely high, Italy and Ethiopia in April appointed two arbiters each, including several of the leading lights of inter-war international law, such as Albert de La Pradelle and Pitman Potter (both acting for Ethiopia).

A fifth arbiter, the lawyer and veteran diplomat Nikolaos Politis, then Greek representative at the League, was appointed in early August, after months of deadlocked negotiations, entrusted with the casting vote.[27] The negotiations did fail, stumbling over two issues in particular: Italy's objections to Ethiopia's appointment of non-Ethiopian arbitrators, supposedly indicative of the Empire's 'backwardness'; and the question of whether the arbitrators were competent to determine under whose sovereignty Walwal lay. On the latter question, the League Council took Italy's side, deciding on 3 August 1935 that the Arbitration Commission was not competent to determine what was, essentially, the central question under consideration.[28] On 3 September, the Arbitration Commission gave its award. Although Italian troops and hardware were already pouring into Eritrea by this time, casting serious doubt on Italy's commitment to a peaceful resolution, the Commission decided that the Walwal Incident was 'due to an unfortunate chain of events' for which neither Italy nor Ethiopia bore responsibility.[29] The League Council was already scheduled to meet the

23 *Treaty of Amity, Conciliation and Arbitration between Italy and Ethiopia*, Art. 5.

24 'Letter from the Ethiopian Government to the Secretary-General', 17 March 1935, *LNOJ* (May 1935): 572.

25 'Telegram from the Italian Government to the Secretary-General', 22 March 1935, *LNOJ* (November 1935): 573.

26 'Letter from the Ethiopian Government to the Secretary-General', 29 March 1935, *LNOJ* (November 1935): 576.

27 See Linos-Alexander Sicilianos and Thomas Skouteris (eds.), 'Special issue: The European Tradition in International Law: Nikolaos Politis', 23 *EJIL* (2012) (issue 1): 215–73.

28 'Dispute between Ethiopia and Italy: Request by the Ethiopian Government', 3 August 1935, *LNOJ* (August 1935): 967. As John Spencer, then legal advisor to the Ethiopian Government, later remarked, 'it might be queried whether the Council had not somewhat exceeded its role by defining the competence of the Commission'. John H. Spencer, 'The Italian-Ethiopian Dispute and the League of Nations', *31 AJIL* (1937): 614–41, at 620.

29 'Italo-Ethiopian Commission of Conciliation and Arbitration, Award of 3 September 1935', 29 *AJIL* (1935): 690–8 at 697.

following day, on 4 September, to 'undertake the general examination ... of the relations between Italy and Ethiopia'.[30]

The story of the Walwal Incident is related, at some length, in the League Council's official report on the Crisis, delivered on 7 October 1935, four days after the invasion began.[31] As that report indicates, the Arbitration Commission and the League Council, though nominally separate, were in fact working together closely from March 1935 onwards. According to the former, the incident itself was 'settled' by the arbitration, but unfortunately 'a growing tension in the relations between Italy and Ethiopia' had arisen nonetheless, resulting from 'Italian and Ethiopian military preparations' and 'insecurity' on Ethiopia's frontiers – that is, from the actions of *both* parties. What this report, painstakingly balanced between two formal equals, does not reveal, however, are the various 'solutions' that were proposed and then rejected during the negotiations, thereby forcing the issue onto the desk of the Council. Archival sources cast some light on this matter. For example, an examination of the telegrams sent back to Rome by Italy's various ambassadors during the summer of 1935 reveals that Politis had been attempting to persuade Haile Selassie to accept the suggestions of France and Britain since April 1935, that is, for several months before his official appointment as fifth arbiter. Such an examination also reveals the content of those suggestions. Specifically, Politis's proposal (following direct consultations, in Paris, with French and British officials) was that Haile Selassie should make a formal request to the League of Nations, asking for the Ethiopian Empire to be taken on as a mandated territory under Article 22 of the Covenant (V: ETHIOPIAN 'CONSENT'/III: LEAGUE-SUPERVISED 'REORGANISATION'). '*[S]e Etiopia tiene a conservare sua indipendenza,*' Politis argued, '*non c'è che un solo mezzo, quello di chiedere, finchè c'è ancora tempo, mandate Inghilterra o Francia*'.[32] By 13 August (ten days after he had accepted the role of fifth arbiter) Politis was urging Haile Selassie not only to request that his Empire be downgraded from a recognised sovereign state to a mandated territory, but also to accept that Ethiopia's mandatory power should be, not Britain or France, but

[30] 'Dispute between Ethiopia and Italy: Request by the Ethiopian Government', 3 August 1935, *LNOJ* (August 1935): 967–8.

[31] 'Report of the Council', 1605–10.

[32] '[I]f Ethiopia wants to preserve its independence, there is only one way of doing so, that of asking, while there is still time, to be placed under an English or a French mandate.' Telegram (marked 'secret' and initialled by Mussolini) from the Italian Ambassador in Addis Ababa: Guido Vinci, 'Incidente di Ualual: Politis e Commissione Arbitrato' (telegram), Addis Ababa, 26 April 1935, in Gabinetto 249, Busta 566 (MAE Archives).

Italy.[33] In a telegram, intercepted by the Italian legation in Addis Ababa, to Jacovos Zervos, personal physician to Haile Selassie, Politis begged Zervos to use his influence to convince the Emperor that '*L'Abbisinia sarebbe salvata come Stato; la S.d.N. avrà la sua alta protezione con la garanzia della Francia e dell'Inghilterra*'.[34] In Politis's view, this plan would also '*aiuterà l'Etiopia economicamente, civilizzerà l'Etiopia e conservà l'integrità di tutto il paese*'.[35] Politis concluded by offering to attempt to secure for Ethiopia a seaport, either at Zeila or, strangely, at the closely guarded French port of Djibouti in return (I: TERRITORIAL 'ADJUSTMENTS').[36]

Politis, then, one of the most highly respected international lawyers of his generation, regarded it, in a juridical sense, not only as possible, but also as necessary, that Ethiopia, a recognised sovereign state, could and should consent to the downgrading of its rights under international law. Ethiopia's ongoing status as a state was, for Politis, wholly compatible with its transformation. Indeed, it was understood to be necessary precisely to 'save' Ethiopia's statehood from destruction. Two years later, in 1937, Politis was elected President of the *Institut de Droit International* – international law's oldest and most influential engine of normative development.

1.2 Juridical Skeletons in the Closet: From the Mussolini-Laval Accords to the Maffey Report to the Zeila Plan to the Tripartite Negotiations

Another incident which not only ratcheted up the tension over the course of the Walwal Arbitration but also pushed France in Italy's direction took place in March 1935.[37] In that month it emerged that the

[33] Telegram (marked secret and initialled by Mussolini) from the Italian Ambassador in Paris: Morano Pignetto, 'Commissione Conciliazione – Quinto [A]rbitro', Paris, 6 August 1935, in Gabinetto 249, Busta 566 (MAE Archives).

[34] 'Abyssinia would be saved as a State; the League of Nations will have [the] highest protection, with France and England's guarantee.' Nikolaos Politis, telegram to Dr. Zervos, intercepted by Ambassador Vinci, in Guido Vinci, 'Telegramma Ministro Politis al Dr. Zervos', Addis Ababa, 13 August 1935, in Gabinetto 249, Busta 566 (MAE Archives).

[35] '... assist Ethiopia economically, civilise Ethiopia, and preserve the integrity of the country as a whole'. 'Telegramma Ministro Politis al Dr. Zervos.'

[36] 'Telegramma Ministro Politis al Dr. Zervos'.

[37] Alex ('Sandy') T. Curle, 'They Hold a Secret of International Importance[:] They will Not Disclose It', unpublished memoirs, Vol. 1, 55. The personal archives of Sandy Curle, political officer and assistant British commissioner on the Anglo-Ethiopian Boundary Commission, shed some light on this: 'The Survey staff were all engaged then on a Top Secret operation carrying out a survey of three possible narrow corridors, of varying width, connecting Ethiopia with the town of Zeila, a small rapidly decaying port on the Gulf of Aden some 28 miles from Jibuti. It was a part of a proposal then under consideration by the Emperor Haile Silassie by which the British would cede Zeila to Ethiopia

Anglo-Ethiopian Boundary Commission caught up in the Walwal Incident back in December 1934 had been engaged in some clandestine activities of its own. In addition to marking out Ethiopia's border with Sudan, the Commission had also been mapping out the contours of a potential transfer of territories, in which Britain planned to give Ethiopia the port of Zeila (in British Somaliland) in exchange for a large area of the Ogaden region (I: TERRITORIAL 'ADJUSTMENTS').[38]

When they got wind of the plan, the French were outraged at this potential challenge to the dominance of the (Franco-Ethiopian) Djibouti–Addis Ababa Railway, which had received explicit protections in the 1906 Tripartite Agreement. Coming, as it did, in the wake of Nazi Germany's withdrawal from the League October 1933, this news of Britain's untrustworthiness as an ally provided one trigger for the so-called 'Mussolini-Laval Accords', concluded in in Rome in January 1935.[39] The main body of the Accords was dedicated to 'recruit[ing] Italy into a French security arrangement against Germany'.[40] However, French and Italian 'interests' in East Africa provided some of the most important bargaining chips in the negotiations (IV: PROTECTION/EXTENSION OF FOREIGN RIGHTS). Mussolini and Laval (then the French foreign minister, later to succeed Philippe Pétain as Prime Minister of Vichy France) congratulated themselves on having tackled several unresolved issues, '*notamment de toutes les questions relatives à l'application de l'article 13 de l'accord de Londres du 26 avril 1915*', and undertook to develop '*les relations économiques de leur territoire métropolitain avec leurs colonies en Afrique et les pays voisins*'.[41]

with a narrow corridor across British Somaliland and in return, the British would receive a part of the Ogaden region in Ethiopia in which British Protected tribes exercised their right of trans-frontier seasonal grazing under the 1897 Anglo-Ethiopian Treaty. Absolute secrecy was most important since the French would be very angry as it allowed Jibuti to be by-passed and goods could be transported to Ethiopia by means other than the Franco-Ethiopian [Djibouti-Addis Ababa] Railway.' My thanks to Curle's daughter, Christian Curle, for allowing me access to this archive.

38 The operation was discovered in March 1934 when the son of the French Minister in Addis Ababa, a wireless operator, broke the British codes and uncovered the operation. Curle, 'They Hold a Secret', 55.

39 *Treaty between France and Italy regarding the Settlement of their Interests in Africa*, Rome, 7 January 1935, in Stephen Heald and John W. Wheeler-Bennett (eds.), *Documents on International Affairs 1935*, Vol. 1 (Oxford University Press, 1936), 19–24 ('Mussolini-Laval Accords').

40 G. Bruce Strang, 'Imperial Dreams: The Mussolini-Laval Accords of January 1935', 44 *The History Review* (2001): 799–809, at 800.

41 'Notably of all questions relating to the application of Article 13 of the Treaty of London of 26 April 1915'; 'the economic relations between their metropolitan territory and their colonies in Africa and hinterlands'. Mussolini-Laval Accords, 24.

As in the Anglo-Italian Exchange of Notes of 1925, in other words, the wartime Treaty of London – in which France (among others) had promised large areas of Ethiopian territory to Italy, in secret, and entirely without Ethiopia's consent – continued, in 1935, to provide Italy's claims with a legal backbone that these states (both of them also, of course, permanent members on the League Council) found legitimate.

The publication of the Mussolini-Laval Accords on 7 January 1935 caused a fresh outcry in Ethiopia,[42] which, although not mentioned by name, was conspicuously the only 'hinterland' (*pays voisin*) of their existing colonies which did not already fall under European sovereignty. This outcry was exacerbated by rumours (later confirmed) that France, in return for Italy's guaranteed support against Germany, had given Italy a 'free hand' in Ethiopia, though whether this was directed towards territorial expansion or 'only' economic domination remained unclear.[43] Certainly, in Italy's view, France, in the Mussolini-Laval Accords, had renounced all its interests under the Tripartite Agreement other than those relating to the Djibouti–Addis Ababa Railway, and had indeed agreed explicitly to '*dare mano libera all'Italia per soddisfare i suoi bisogni di espansione in Africa Orientale e regolare una volta per sempre ogni questioni col Governo etiopico*'.[44] France was certainly aware of this interpretation, given Italy's own letter, of 18 June 1935, which had informed it of its '*intendimenti nella questione etiopica, che erano di ottenere il domino diretto sulle zone periferiche dell'Impero ed il protettorate sul nucleo amharico centrale*'.[45] Though sceptical, France gave its assent to this plan for Ethiopia's division into a more sovereign 'core' and a less sovereign 'periphery' (II: RACIALISED PARTITION) while insisting that '*non si deve parlare di guerra e non si deve mettere a repentaglio l'esistenza della S.d.N.*'[46]

As this suggests, the Mussolini-Laval Accords incorporated a long-standing assumption, deeply rooted in the 'Orientalist-Semiticist'

[42] Anthony Mockler, *Haile Selassie's War* (New York: Olive Branch Press, 2003), 44–5.

[43] See William C. Askew, 'The Secret Agreement between France and Italy on Ethiopia, January 1935,' 25 *Journal of Modern History* (1953): 47–8, at 48.

[44] '[G]ive Italy a free hand to satisfy her need for expansion in East Africa and to resolve once and for all questions relating to the Ethiopian Government', *Francia: Situazione politica nel 1935* (Rome: Ministro degli Affari Esteri, 1935), document no. 11, cited in Askew, 'The Secret Agreement', 9.

[45] '[I]ntentions in the Ethiopian question, which were to obtain [a regime of] direct control over the peripheral zones of the Empire and a protectorate over the central Amharic nucleus', *Francia: Situazione politica nel 1935*, cited in Askew, 'The Secret Agreement', 9.

[46] '[T]here must be no mention of war, and the existence of the League of Nations must not be placed in jeopardy.' *Francia: Situazione politica nel 1935*, cited in Askew, 'The Secret Agreement', 9.

interpretation of Ethiopian history, and funnelled directly into the realm of diplomacy, parliamentary debates, official reports, committee resolutions and, of course, treaties. This was the assumption that Ethiopia was not a unitary entity, but rather a racial, cultural, geographical, political *and therefore* legal hybrid. As such, the option of splitting the country in some way between its 'central Amharic nucleus' and the 'peripheral zones', which had only recently been forcibly incorporated into its territory under Menelik II, remained, it seems, on the table in terms of legitimate international legal options. This notion of a relatively sharp distinction between the Abyssinian highlands and the Empire's 'Southern marches' was, as we have seen, not entirely a European fiction.[47] What is important about this for our understanding of the Abyssinia Crisis itself, however, is the manner in which that racialised distinction between areas of the Empire over which the Ethiopian authorities were 'more' or 'less' sovereign came to be woven into an international legal rationale which viewed Ethiopia simultaneously as a colonial power akin to its European neighbours, *and* as a 'half-caste' sub-sovereign whose rights and duties could legitimately be downgraded, if necessary, in the interests of protecting the rights of more genuinely 'self-governing' states and their citizens.

An equally plastic understanding of Ethiopian international legal subjectivity was articulated in a governmental report, seldom mentioned in histories of the Crisis,[48] which exerted an important influence on British policy in relation to Italy and Ethiopia. This, the 'Maffey Report' (prepared by the Inter-Departmental Committee on British Interests in Ethiopia, chaired by John Maffey) was commissioned by the Foreign Office on 6 March 1935, in response to an Italian offer of negotiations aimed at 'exploring the possibility of the development of [British and Italian mutual interests in Ethiopia] in a harmonious manner' (IV: PROTECTION/EXTENSION OF FOREIGN RIGHTS).[49] The Maffey Committee's task was to investigate 'how the absorption of the whole or part of Ethiopia by Italy would react upon the existing treaty rights and obligations of this country with respect to Ethiopia and the two foreign limitrophe Powers

[47] See Item 4, Sections 2.2 and 2.3, above.

[48] The work of Alberto Sbacchi is an exception here, although Sbacchi appears to base his analysis on official Italian responses, rather than on the report itself. See e.g. Alberto Sbacchi, *Legacy of Bitterness: Ethiopia and Fascist Italy, 1935–1941* (Lawrenceville, NJ: The Red Sea Press, 1997), 279–81.

[49] Quoted in 'Report of the Inter-Departmental Committee on British Interests in Ethiopia', 18 June 1935, in W. N. Medlicott, Douglas Dakin and M. E. Lambert (eds.), *Documents on British Foreign Policy, 1919–1939*, Second Series, Vol. 14 (London: HMSO, 1976), Appendix II, 743–77, at 743 ('Maffey Report').

(i.e. Italy and France)'.[50] Its primary conclusion was that '[n]o ... vital British interest is concerned in and around Ethiopia as would make it essential for His Majesty's Government to resist an Italian conquest of Ethiopia'.[51] Therefore, Maffey and his colleagues went on, while 'an independent Ethiopia would be preferable', there was little to fear from Italy.[52] The Report's authors were anxious to clarify that its findings should not be taken as suggesting that Britain 'should condone, or should connive at, an Italian absorption of Ethiopia, the integrity of which His Majesty's Government has undertaken to maintain' through its signature of the League Covenant and the 1906 Tripartite Agreement.[53] However, the very fact that the Report was commissioned in the first place suggests rather strongly that Britain was in two minds, at the very least, about how rigorously to oppose Italy's annexation of Ethiopia.[54]

A first point to make about this assessment is that Britain's wavering commitment to the defence of Ethiopia's sovereignty evidently cannot be subsumed entirely within the wider policy of fascist 'appeasement'. For the Maffey Committee, after all, there was nothing to appease in 1935, at least insofar as Italy was concerned. Certainly, the Report confirms that Britain did feel bound by the Covenant, and wished if possible to avoid confronting Italy over Ethiopia. Yet it also makes clear that the Covenant was only one among many longstanding international legal instruments influencing the normative character of Britain's relationship with the Ethiopian Empire at that time. The decision of the Maffey Committee to begin its history of Ethiopia with the reign of Emperor 'Theodore' (Tewodros II), for example, was justified on the grounds that it was he who first 'began to assert the power of the Emperor and the Central government against the great Rases', and who made 'the first important contact between Ethiopia and European Powers' in the form of various commercial treaties.[55] In this account, Ethiopia is narrated as having fallen into 'confusion' at the end of Tewodros's reign; as having been subjected to a 'frustrated' programme of centralisation under 'John' (Yohannes IV); as having progressed to a high-point under Menelik II (during which period Ethiopia's borders were 'defined' by treaty, European railway and banking concessions were

[50] Maffey Report, 743.
[51] Ibid., 775.
[52] Ibid., 775.
[53] Ibid., 744.
[54] See e.g. Samuel Hoare, speech to the Sixteenth Assembly of the League of Nations, 11 September 1935, in Heald (ed.), *Documents*, 100–5.
[55] Maffey Report, 751–2.

allocated, governmental power was asserted over the 'Rases' and 'slavery was nominally abolished'); as having then collapsed again into 'complete confusion' under 'Lij Yassu' and 'Zauditu' before arriving, finally, at an uneasy calm under Haile Selassie.[56] It did not seem 'just', the Committee conceded, 'to write off the Ethiopian Empire as irremediably barbarous and uncivilised without any hope of eventual reform'; yet Maffey worried about the limited 'power of the central Government over the great feudal chiefs' – a lack of effective and exclusive control which was fuelled by the 'absence of anything in the nature of a public impulse towards good government'.[57] In the event of Haile Selassie's death, the Committee opined, Ethiopia was likely to descend again into 'complete anarchy', which, under the Tripartite Agreement, would 'necessitate action by the neighbouring European Powers in order to produce a more settled state of affairs'.[58] The opinions of British governmental officials had, in other words, altered little since the early 1920s.[59]

One of the interesting things about the Maffey Report, for our purposes, is the absence of any sense that Ethiopia's subjectivity under international law should be taken as fixed or absolute. The Report discussed the need to protect established British 'interests' in Ethiopia by reference both to the many agreements in which Ethiopia had been carved up into 'spheres of influence' and to the no less numerous agreements in which Britain and others had recognised Ethiopia's equal rights as a sovereign state.[60] This, apparently, made it possible for those rights to be treated, in the Maffey Report, as waxing and waning in strength, with the degree of their plasticity hinging once again on 'effective' or 'self' government.

The issue, then, does not seem to be that Britain desired to conquer Ethiopia, or even to establish direct access to its resources (beyond Lake T'ana's waters), for this was not something the Committee felt to be worthwhile. Ethiopia's deposits of gold and platinum were declared to be small, 'low-grade', largely inaccessible and therefore unprofitable.[61] Ethiopians, meanwhile, were described variously as 'cruel', 'crude', 'proud', 'suspicious', 'intolerant', 'indolent', given over to feuding and reluctant to abandon the 'anachronism' of slavery.[62] All in all, the Maffey Report concluded, the

[56] Ibid., 751–2.
[57] Ibid., 758.
[58] Ibid., 758.
[59] See Item 5, Section 1, above.
[60] Maffey Report, 752–7.
[61] Ibid., 747.
[62] Ibid., 751–2.

population was characterised by a 'deplor[able] inefficiency and lack of discipline, and was largely bereft of any orderly or commercial instinct'.[63] The result, in a country of 'extraordinary fertility ... susceptible of great agricultural development', was that techniques of 'agriculture and stock-raising' remained completely 'primitive', such that '[o]nly three products [were] sold abroad in any quantity: Coffee, hides and skins and beeswax'.[64] According to the Maffey Report, Ethiopia and Ethiopians had (to put it in the language of the Frame) proved themselves to be remarkably resistant to the interpellative 'call' of legal subjectivity. The problem then, was not that Britain found its own ambitions in Ethiopia challenged by Italy, but rather that the British were being forced to decide how to respond now that another power was in pursuit of what Britain had disdained. In such a context, the Report urged, the British should (as the French had done two months earlier in the Mussolini-Laval Accords) cut their losses and leave the hard work of transforming Ethiopians into efficient, rational market actors to Italy.

This being the case, the Maffey Report's only outstanding anxiety was fascist Italy's *own* potential for irrationality as a potential colonial neighbour. 'Normally in peace,' the Committee argued, 'a frontier with a first-class European Power is to be preferred to a frontier with a semi-civilised nation since the strong Power will more effectively control the inhabitants.'[65] Similarly, 'it might be urged that an Italian conquest of Ethiopia would provide new openings for British commerce hitherto closed owing to the backward state of Ethiopia'.[66] Yet Italy was not your 'normal' 'first-class European Power'. Importantly, it was not Italy's fascism that worried the Committee here. Maffey, in fact, never mentioned the word 'fascism', and in any case, as the British Foreign Secretary Samuel Hoare was shortly to underline in Parliament, the British Government '[had] always understood and well understand Italy's desire for overseas expansion' and was fully prepared 'to endeavour to ensure for Italy some territorial satisfaction' in Abyssinia.[67] Nonetheless, Italy's expansionist desires in pursuit of its *spazzio vitale* (or in its Nazi version, *Lebensraum*), and, in particular, Italy's autarkical tendencies, did tip the balance marginally in favour of Ethiopian independence, the Report said. In the event that this preference was not realised and Italy did conquer Ethiopia, the

[63] Ibid., 759.
[64] Ibid., 747.
[65] Ibid., 765.
[66] Ibid., 769.
[67] Samuel Hoare, Secretary of State for Foreign Affairs, Speech to the House of Commons, *Hansard*, HC, col. 516–18, 11 July 1935.

Committee made two suggestions. Firstly, 'every effort should be made' to ensure that 'British subjects have, as now [under the existing treaty regime], equal opportunities for trading in Ethiopian territory, i.e. efforts should be made to maintain the "open door" in Ethiopia' (IV: PROTECTION/ EXTENSION OF FOREIGN RIGHTS). Secondly, Britain 'should not neglect any opportunity', if an invasion materialised, to obtain certain Ethiopian territories for itself, in the region of Lake T'ana and on the borders with British Somaliland, Kenya and Sudan (I: TERRITORIAL ADJUSTMENTS), on the basis of the Anglo-Italian Protocols.[68]

For the British, as for the French, then, Ethiopia's rights and duties were both more complex and more flexible than the terms of the Covenant suggest when taken on their own. This attitude did not stem solely, or even mostly, from the external 'political' pressure which the growing power of fascism was then exerting on their legal obligations under the Covenant.[69] On the contrary, the attitude of Britain and France was founded on an international legal regime that, as this *opinio juris* demonstrates, had been in construction since 1841. In that regime, the Ethiopian Empire had been recognised repeatedly as a sovereign state. Yet this recognition had carried with it a number of extra conditions relating to the legal regime *inside* Ethiopia (conditions then mirrored by the 'special obligations' attached to its accession to the Covenant in 1923). The more Ethiopia was understood to have violated these obligations, the less resilient its sovereign rights became.[70]

On 23 June 1935, with a first draft of the Maffey Report in hand, Anthony Eden, British Minister for League of Nations Affairs, was propelled to Rome by a flurry of anxiety set in motion by Germany's reintroduction of military conscription in March, together with Italy's belligerent behaviour at a recent meeting of Stresa Front members.[71] In the attempt to encourage Italy to settle the 'Abyssinian question' without recourse to arms, Eden

[68] Maffey Report, 770–6.

[69] See Item 1, Section 1, above.

[70] Maffey Report, 754.

[71] In April 1935, Britain, France and Italy had formed the Stresa Front in response to Hitler's repudiation, in March, of Versailles' key disarmament clauses. In this new agreement, three 'tripartite' states pledged to reaffirm the Locarno Pact of 1925 (see *Treaty of Mutual Guarantee between Germany, Belgium, France, Great Britain and Italy*, Locarno, 16 October 1925) and to defend Austria's independence. Though Italian troops were already massing on its Eritrean border, Italy was, in other words, in a strong bargaining position, and threatened to withdraw from the League at the first sign of support for Ethiopia. As a result, the issue of Ethiopia was glaringly absent from the Conference's Final Declaration of 14 April, which asserted that the three powers would oppose 'any unilateral repudiation of treaties, which may endanger the peace *of Europe*'. Emphasis added. According to Frank Hardie, 'Mussolini [had] asked for the addition of the words "of Europe" and this was

presented Mussolini with a new version of the Zeila Plan, upon which the Anglo-Ethiopian Border Commission had been engaged prior to the Walwal Incident in 1934. Britain, Eden suggested, would try to persuade Ethiopia to cede the Ogaden region to Italy (rather than to Britain as originally planned), in return for a corridor to the sea at Zeila through British Somaliland (I: TERRITORIAL 'ADJUSTMENTS').[72] Mussolini rejected the offer, arguing (in an oblique reference to the Brussels Act's 'prohibition zone' and to Ethiopia's second 'special obligation') that an Ethiopian outlet through which the Empire could import arms would be 'positively dangerous'.[73] According to Eden's account of the meeting, Mussolini had declared that:

> [i]f Abyssinia came to terms without war, he would be content with surrender of those parts of Abyssinia which had been conquered by her in the last fifty years and which were not inhabited by Abyssinians. In saying this, Signor Mussolini made a circular gesture which I took to mean that he regarded such territories as existing on all four sides of Abyssinia. The central plateau could, he continued, remain under Abyssinian sovereignty, but only on condition that it was under Italian control. If, however, Abyssinia could not come to terms with Italy upon these lines, then, if Italy had to fight, her demands would be proportionally greater. Signor Mussolini made a sweep of his hand indicating that Italy would then have the whole country.[74]

In return for refraining from an invasion, Mussolini, according to Eden, demanded that Ethiopia consent to being placed under an Italian protectorate 'over a circular area including about two-thirds of the population of Abyssinia – in fact over all Abyssinia except a central plateau' (II: RACIALISED PARTITION). However, 'if it came to a war he would wipe Abyssinia off the map'.[75] Meanwhile, with shipments of troops and weapons to Italian East Africa continuing, Ethiopia had begun to send a series of increasingly desperate communications to Geneva, calling attention to Italy's intention to launch, at any moment, 'the massacre of a people which constitutes a menace to none'.[76] Ethiopia's desperation was increased by the unilateral

accepted in silence by the British and French Ministers' (Frank Hardie, *The Abyssinian Crisis* (London: Batsford, 1974), 117).

72 Anthony Eden, Statement to Parliament, 3 September 1935, in Stephen Heald (ed.), *Documents on International Affairs 1935*, Vol. 2 (Oxford University Press, 1937), 35

73 Eden, quoted in Hardie, *The Abyssinian Crisis*, 124–5.

74 Eden, quoted in Hardie, *The Abyssinian Crisis*, 124–5.

75 Eden, quoted in George Scott, *The Rise and Fall of the League of Nations* (London: Hutchinson, 1973), 328–9.

76 'Letter from the Representative of Ethiopia to the Secretary-General, 12 August 1935', *LNOJ* (November 1935): 1602. See also e.g. 'Letter from the Representative of Ethiopia to the Secretary-General', 10 September 1935, *LNOJ* (November 1935): 1602; 'Telegram

decisions of Belgium, Switzerland and Czechoslovakia, under Italian pressure, to halt arms shipments to Ethiopia, and of France and Britain in July (followed by the United States in October) to place an embargo on arms shipments to *both* states as formally equal partners in an international dispute.[77] Italy's ambitions were soon fully out in the open, with Mussolini declaring in the newspaper *Il Popolo d'Italia* at the end of July: '*La soluzione del problema non può essere che totalitaria. Un espansione che non sia presidiata dalle armi, un protettorato che non sia accompagnato da misure militari ... [I]l problema non ammette – con Ginevra, senza Ginevra, contro Ginevra – che una soluzione*.'[78]

Like the Eden–Mussolini negotiations of June 1935, the negotiations which led to the next international effort to head off an Italian invasion did not include Ethiopia. In August 1935, Eden and Laval met their Italian counterparts in Paris under the auspices of the 1906 Tripartite Agreement. They did so (as the excluded Ethiopian representative, Täklä-Hawaryat, did not hesitate to point out in the *aide-mémoire* he handed to Eden in Paris, effectively as the committee room door was closed in his face) in spite of the fact that, like the 1925 Exchange of Notes and the Laval-Mussolini Accords of January 1935, the Tripartite Agreement had been invalidated by Article 20 of the Covenant.[79] Moreover, even though they took place explicitly under the auspices of a pre-League treaty, these negotiations took place with the League's blessing, with the Council's President, for one, expressing his hope that they would be 'crowned with

from His Majesty the Emperor of Ethiopia to the Secretary-General', 25 September 1935, *LNOJ* (November 1935): 1602; 'Telegram from His Majesty the Emperor of Ethiopia to the President of the Council', 28 September 1935, *LNOJ* (November 1935): 1603.

77 This move had little impact on Italy, which could produce its own arms and was, in any case, being supplied by Germany. However, it ensured that when war broke out (after which the embargo was lifted) Ethiopia, whose access to arms was still restricted even after the 1923 arms condition was modified in 1930, found itself virtually undefended. Only 20 per cent of Ethiopia's soldiers possessed working rifles, for example, with a maximum of 40 rounds of ammunition each. George W. Baer, *Test Case: Italy, Ethiopia, and the League of Nations* (Stanford, CA: Hoover Institution Press, 1976), 79. See also Marcus, 'The Embargo', 263–379.

78 'The solution of the [Ethiopian] problem must be totalitarian. Any action of expansion or any protectorate must be accompanied by military measures ... There exists – with Geneva, without Geneva, against Geneva – but one solution.' In *Il Popolo d'Italia*, 31 July 1935, cited in Giuseppe Rocco, *L'Europa verso la seconda guerra mondiale* (Milan: Greco & Greco Editore, 1997), 150.

79 '*Aide-mémoire* left with Mr Eden by the Abyssinian Minister in Paris', 15 August 1935, enclosed in Clerk to Hoare, 16 August 1935, in Medlicott, Dakin and Lambert (eds.), *Documents*, Vol. 14, 492–4.

success'.[80] Moreover, the direct involvement of the League was a prerequisite for one of the key substantive elements of the negotiations. As Täklä-Hawaryat clarified in his *aide-mémoire*, and as the British had already ascertained secretly from Haile Selassie, via the British Minister at Addis Ababa, Sidney Barton, Ethiopia had agreed to one concession in particular. Specifically, the Empire had signalled that it would be willing to implement an extensive programme of administrative, judicial and economic 'reform', supervised by foreign officials,[81] along lines not entirely dissimilar to Lord Lugard's 1922 proposals, as long as the Imperial authorities retained the power to select these officials, and as long as the programme was operating under the auspices of the League, meaning that *'la Souveraineté de l'Empire éthiopien ... [,] son indépendence politique ... [et] l'intégrité de son territoire'* were not undermined (III: LEAGUE-SUPERVISED 'REORGANISATION').[82] According to Barton, Haile Selassie might even be willing to cede Ogaden and some territory in Aussa to Italy in exchange for the corridor to Zeila, some further financial compensation, and for the accession of Ethiopia to a revised Tripartite Agreement (I: TERRITORIAL 'ADJUSTMENTS'). However, while Ethiopia 'desired to bestow on its people the benefits of progress and civilisation within the economic and social order', as Täklä-Hawaryat put it, it would only be 'disposed to give foreigners concessions on its territory' on a strictly 'open door' basis, 'without either discrimination or exclusive privileges on the basis of the nationality of the beneficiaries'. Any 'attribution, to one Power or to several Powers, of an exclusive political influence or economic advantages on Ethiopian territory' would be wholly unacceptable.[83]

The Anglo-French proposals eventually presented to Italy in Paris mirrored Haile Selassie's suggestions closely (perhaps, one might speculate, bearing in mind their resemblance to the 1922 proposals made by Lugard, Henry Darley, Captain Philipps and others,[84] because it was Barton who had originally suggested the idea to the Emperor). They spun them, however, with a particular bias towards the 'interests' of the three powers.[85]

[80] See *Report of the Council*, 1611.

[81] Barton to Hoare, Addis Ababa, 13 August 1935, in Medlicott, Dakin and Lambert (eds.), *Documents*, Vol. 14, 478–9.

[82] '[T]he Sovereignty of the Ethiopian Empire ...[,] her political independence and her territorial integrity.' '*Aide-mémoire* left with Mr Eden by the Abyssinian Minister in Paris', 493.

[83] '*Aide-mémoire* left by the Abyssinian Minister', 493–4.

[84] Item 5, Section 1.1.

[85] See 'Revised Draft prepared by United Kingdom Delegation as Amended after Discussion with French Delegation, 16 August 1935', enclosed in Clerk to Hoare, Paris, 16 August 1935, in Medlicott, Dakin and Lambert (eds.), *Documents*, Vol. 14, 496–7 ('Paris Proposals').

Britain, France and Italy would provide 'collective assistance' to Ethiopia for 'extensive reforms' to 'the most varied fields of national life' including 'economic, financial, commercial and constructional development; foreign settlement, modernisation of administrative services; anti-slavery measures and frontier and other police services' (III: LEAGUE-SUPERVISED 'REORGANISATION').[86] This was, they argued, a reform process to which these three states 'would be particularly well qualified ... to lend ... collective assistance'.[87] The proposed reforms were to be 'freely assented to by Ethiopia in the fullness of her sovereignty and without anything being imposed on her contrary to her independence or her integrity' (V: ETHIOPIAN 'CONSENT').[88] However, 'particular account' would be 'taken of the special interests of Italy, without prejudice to the recognised rights of France and the United Kingdom' (IV: PROTECTION/EXTENSION OF FOREIGN RIGHTS).[89] Meanwhile, Britain and France 'did not in any way exclude' the possibility of a redrawing of boundaries 'to which Italy and Ethiopia might agree' (I: TERRITORIAL 'ADJUSTMENTS').[90] Italy, however, flatly rejected the proposals once again, voicing particular objection to the idea that Ethiopia should become a signatory to a new Tripartite Agreement and in this way be 'placed on the same level as the three Great Powers'.[91]

1.3 Conditionality and the League's Proposals: The Committee of Five and its 'Charter of Assistance'

Meeting, as scheduled, on 4 September to undertake a 'general examination' of the troubled relations between Italy and Ethiopia, the League Council found a diplomatic grenade waiting on its bench in the form of Italy's 277-page memorandum, attacking Ethiopia's right to claim the rights associated with League membership.[92] Ethiopia, Italy insisted, in an argument backed up by copious 'evidence' including dozens of photographs of castrated children and other alleged barbarities (the verac-

A summary of the rejected Paris proposals, as presented to the League Council, forms Appendix 1 to *Report of the Council*, 7 October 1935, 1620 ('Summary of the Paris Proposals').

86 'Summary of the Paris Proposals', 1620.

87 Ibid., 1620.

88 Ibid., 1620.

89 Ibid., 1620.

90 Ibid., 1620.

91 Drummond to Hoare, Rome, 17 August 1935, in Medlicott, Dakin and Lambert (eds.), *Documents*, Vol. 14, 501–3, 502.

92 'Situation in Ethiopia. Memorandum by the Italian Government, and Documents Relating Thereto', 4 September 1935 ('Italian Memorandum') *LNOJ* (November 1935): 1355–417.

ity of which was strongly contested by the Ethiopian Delegation and others),[93] had failed to live up to its commitments under international law. This was not simply a complaint that Ethiopia had violated the principle of *pacta sunt servanda*, and that proportional 'countermeasures' were therefore justified. It was, instead, a claim that Ethiopia no longer displayed the objective characteristics of a state, and therefore could neither claim the customary set of sovereign rights to territorial integrity and political independence, for example, nor ask its fellow League members to fulfil their duties towards it under the Covenant's collective security provisions. This legal interconnection between the conditional nature of League membership and the conditional nature of statehood per se was made explicit in the memorandum's conclusion that '[t]he admission of Ethiopia to the League was a political act based on the belief that, through participation in the system of international co-operation represented by the League, Ethiopia could be led to make by herself the efforts necessary to approach, even though only gradually, the level of civilisation of the other peoples belonging to the international community'. However, Italy went on, 'Ethiopia has shown that she does not possess the qualifications necessary to enable her to obtain, through participation in the League, the impulse required to raise herself by voluntary efforts to the level of the other civilised nations'.[94]

Significantly, these alleged failures related almost exclusively to allegations regarding Ethiopia's (in)capacity to protect the individual rights associated with legal subjectivity. Thus, Part I of the memorandum (entitled 'Violations of Italo-Ethiopian Treaties by Ethiopia') devoted fully thirty-six pages to allegations that Italian 'lives, property and interests' had been actively 'menaced' by the Ethiopian state and its subjects. This was cast as a violation of the network of treaties that had been concluded over a series of decades,[95] and hence also of 'Ethiopian law itself', into which the rights and duties created in those treaties had been embedded.[96] Ethiopia was accused of systematic economic discrimination 'in violation of the most-favoured-nation clause' in the Klobukowski Treaty

[93] See e.g. Joseph van Molle (Belgian Representative at Geneva), 'Letter addressed to M. Jèze, posted on September 10th, 1935, and received at Geneva on September 12th, 1935', *LNOJ* (November 1935): 1587. The letter enclosed a protest sent to the Italian Delegation at the use of a photograph in the memorandum of Molle, which had been used without his consent and 'given an interpretation which [he] never attached to it'.

[94] Ibid., 1416.

[95] Ibid., 1352–88.

[96] Ibid., 1362.

Figure 9 The Council of the League of Nations meets to discuss the Abyssinia Crisis, Geneva, 22 January 1936. © United Nations Archives at Geneva, by kind permission.

and other agreements, both with respect to Ethiopians when it came 'the acquisition of landed property by foreigners', and with respect to other states (among those mentioned were France, the Netherlands, the United States and Britain). So systematic was this violation, Italy alleged, that 'the Treaty of Amity of 1928, which should have made Italy the *most favoured nation*, made her in practice the *least favoured nation*'.[97] Foreigners' guaranteed freedom of movement, the memorandum went on, was 'subject to limitations and vexations of every kind'.[98] Equally, Ethiopia's institutions for the 'administration of justice', said to '[occupy] first place among the functions of the State', were accused of ineptitude, inefficiency, ignorance, procedural chaos – and a systematic bias against foreigners, and hence of a failure to uphold the principle of equality before the law.[99]

[97] Ibid., 1361. Emphasis added. For a discussion of the treaty regime in question, see Item 4, Sections 3 and 4.

[98] Ibid., 1362–5.

[99] Ibid., 1365.

The memorandum's other major focus was the ongoing practice of slavery.[100] In addition to detailed descriptions of the horrors of slavery, and of the dependence of the Ethiopian economy on its perpetuation, the memorandum included copious references to British sources, including the report of Lord Noel Buxton, who in 1932 had led a mission sent by the Anti-Slavery and Aborigines' Protection Society to Ethiopia. According to Buxton, as quoted in the memorandum, slavery in Ethiopia 'goes with the absence of anything that we should call government. The State machinery is weak, being little more than mediaeval', while '[r]espect for law' in Ethiopia was 'in its infancy'.[101] Compounding the problem, Italy added, was the 'gebber system', itself 'a form of slavery'.[102] Italy insisted that Ethiopia was not, in fact, 'a national state' but was instead comprised of 'two distinct regions' – a core, the 'old Abyssinian State', and a periphery, Abyssinia's 'colonies', described as 'non-Abyssinian areas recently conquered by the arms of the Negus Menelik' and since administered, with great brutality, by what was, for the people involved, an alien colonial power.[103] 'Surely', Italy argued, it was 'in the interests of civilisation that the Harrari, Galla, Somali, Sidama and other people which for centuries have formed separate national entities, should be removed from Abyssinian oppression' (II: RACIALISED PARTITION). To 'rescue' them would, Italy said – making direct reference to Article 23 of the Covenant, which guaranteed 'fair and humane conditions of labour for men, women and children',[104] as well as an oblique reference to Article 22 – be 'in conformity with the spirit of the Covenant, which requires that colonisation should be carried out only by advanced States which are in a position to ensure the development and welfare of the native peoples'.[105] All in all, Italy concluded, 'the Ethiopian State to-day is in such a condition of internal disorder, and so politically, economically and culturally backward, that it cannot carry out, unaided, the thorough reorganisation without which it must remain a permanent danger to the Italian colonies' and was therefore incapable of offering any evidence of its ability to fulfil its undertakings satisfactorily.[106] Despite its League membership, Ethiopia was accused of having 'systematically violated the treaties she has signed and

[100] Ibid., 1399–415.
[101] Lord Noel Buxton, *The Times*, 9 April 1932, quoted in Italian Memorandum, 1404.
[102] Italian Memorandum, 1395.
[103] Ibid., 1393–4.
[104] Covenant, Art. 23; Italian Memorandum, 1398.
[105] Italian Memorandum, 1396.
[106] Ibid., 1389.

shown that she does not possess that degree of internal organisation which is indefensible to a member of the community of civilised nations'.[107]

The publication of the memorandum was, of course, a disaster for Ethiopia. The League reacted, two days later, by forming a Committee charged with 'seek[ing] for a pacific settlement' of the dispute: the so-called 'Committee of Five', consisting of delegates from Spain, Poland, Turkey and, of course, Britain and France.[108] The Committee of Five delivered its proposals just over a week later, on 24 September 1935. The structure of its report, again, is telling. The Report began by restating the the Committee's guiding principle, also that of the League itself: the 'obligation of respecting the independence, territorial integrity and security of all States Members of the League'.[109] But this was followed immediately, in paragraph two, by a reminder that upon admission to the League 'Ethiopia assumed special obligations regarding ... slavery and the traffic in arms'.[110] In paragraph three, the report then quoted part of a speech which the Ethiopian Delegate, Täklä-Hawaryat, had delivered to the League Assembly a week earlier, in which he had said:

> Any suggestion calculated to raise the economic, financial and political level of the nation to which I have the honour to belong, provided it proceeds from the League of Nations and is to be carried out in the actual spirit of the Covenant, will be regarded by Ethiopia as the action of sister nations which have reached a more advanced stage of civilisation and are sincerely desirous of guiding my country in the path to progress.[111]

The effect of this three-stage introduction was, of course, to reinforce Italy's core assertion that Ethiopia was an 'uncivilised' state which had failed to meet its international commitments. Additionally, Ethiopia was portrayed as having itself *admitted* – officially and recently – that its own grasp on 'civilisation' was tenuous, and as having thus consented in advance to any League-directed programme of reforms designed to rectify this state of affairs (v: ETHIOPIAN 'CONSENT'). The Committee then outlined what it called a 'Charter of Assistance' for the wholesale 'reorganisation' of Ethiopia's 'administrative, legal and judicial system (III: LEAGUE-SUPERVISED 'REORGANISATION'),[112] a scheme very much along

[107] Ibid., 1367.

[108] *Report of the Council*, 1612.

[109] 'Note from the Chairman of the Committee of Five', in *Report of the Council*, 1621.

[110] Ibid.

[111] Täklä-Hawaryat, speech to the League of Nations Assembly, 11 September 1935, quoted in 'Note from the Chairman of the Committee of Five', in *Report of the Council*, 1621.

[112] 'Charter of Assistance' proposed by the Committee of Five, in Report of the Council, Appendix II, 1622–5 ('Charter of Assistance').

the same lines as that which the League had attempted to impose on Liberia only a few years earlier.[113]

Notable throughout the Charter of Assistance is a heavy emphasis on the need for legal and institutional reform, aimed primarily at strengthening the rights of 'foreigners', especially in the commercial sphere, and at effecting the abolition of slavery among Ethiopians. For example, Section 1 ('Police and Gendarmerie') envisaged a new foreign-organised police force whose task would be: ensuring 'the application, throughout the Empire, of existing or future laws' relating to the suppression of slavery and arms-carrying in line with the 'special obligations'; '[p]olicing centres in which Europeans reside'; '[e]nsuring security in agricultural areas where Europeans may be numerous'; and '[m]aintaining order in the frontier territories of the Empire so as to safeguard neighbouring [i.e. British, French and Italian colonial] territories'.[114] Meanwhile, Sections 2 and 4 included headings such as: 'Possibility for foreigners to participate in the economic development of the country (land tenure, mining regulations, exercise of commercial and industrial activities)'; 'Foreign trade; economic equality on a basis of reciprocity'; and 'Reorganisation of mixed courts which try cases between foreigners and Ethiopians'. Section 3 ('Finance') dealt with the 'supervision' of public expenditure; the 'assessment' of taxes; the 'establishment and operation of fiscal monopolies'; 'studies in connexion with the loans which would be required for the development of the country or the carrying out of certain [proposed] reforms'; and 'control of [Ethiopia's] pledges assigned to the service of the loans' – all of which were to be carried out by 'foreign specialists' (IV: PROTECTION/EXTENSION OF FOREIGN RIGHTS). By contrast, the section entitled 'public services', referring to those services which would be directed towards the welfare of *Ethiopian* individuals and communities (such as 'education' and 'public health'), were listed only as headings, with no further detail included. The most senior 'foreign specialists', the Charter of Assistance went on, should be 'appointed by the [League] Council', with the Emperor's 'agreement', while the others would be 'nominated' by the 'assistance' mission's head and then 'appointed by the Emperor'. The latter's influence over his country's comprehensive 'reorganisation' was, in this way, limited to his right to 'submit to the Council any observations [Ethiopia] may wish' on the programme's progress.[115]

[113] See Item 3, Section 5, above.

[114] 'Charter of Assistance', 1622.

[115] Ibid., 1622–3.

The Committee of Five concluded its report by adding that it had been 'informed' by Britain and France of two things: first that they would be 'ready to facilitate territorial adjustments between Italy and Ethiopia' by making 'certain sacrifices in the region of the Somaliland coast', provided that Ethiopia's 'special obligations' regarding slavery and the traffic in arms would be extended to these new areas (I: TERRITORIAL 'ADJUSTMENTS'); and secondly that 'without wishing to impair the existing régime in regard to the treatment of foreigners and in regard to external trade', they were 'prepared to recognise a special Italian interest in the economic development of Ethiopia' and would 'consequently ... look with favour on the conclusion of economic agreements between Italy and Ethiopia, on condition that the existing rights of French and British nationals and protected persons are respected by the two parties, and that the recognised interests of France and the United Kingdom under all agreements already in force are safeguarded' (IV: PROTECTION/EXTENSION OF FOREIGN RIGHTS).[116]

Given that Britain and France were themselves both represented on the Committee of Five (not to mention sitting as permanent members, along with Italy, on the Council which was tasked with evaluating the proposal and, later on, providing disinterested oversight of the scheme), the decision of these two states to present themselves as having 'informed' the Committee of their support was somewhat disingenuous, to say the least. As for the Charter of Assistance itself, this was, in fact, little different in substance from those 'solutions' that were being debated in Britain and elsewhere more than a decade earlier, for the transformation of Ethiopia into a species of 'Class A' mandate, complete with all the provisions for the 'open door' which that status entailed, as urged by the Maffey Committee.[117] Importantly (and just as in the case of the 'Class A' mandated territories like Iraq and Syria), the Charter of Assistance in no sense regarded its proposals for downgrading the Ethiopian Empire's rights to territorial integrity and political independence, for example, as jeopardising its claim to be a state. On the contrary, in 1935 it was a fact that some states ('small states' in the League vernacular) possessed less reliant rights and more onerous duties than others, depending on their 'self-governing' capacities. As Hoare had put it in a speech to the Commons a fortnight earlier: '[w]e [in Britain] believe that backward nations [like Ethiopia] are, without prejudice to their independence and integrity, entitled to expect

[116] Ibid., 1623.
[117] Item 5, Section 1.1.

that assistance will be afforded them by more advanced peoples in the development of their resources and the building-up of their national life.'[118]

The solution laid out by the Committee of Five, whose task it was to 'seek for a pacific settlement' to the dispute between Ethiopia and Italy, makes little sense from the perspective of the standard account of the Abyssinia Crisis. If, as this account assumes, international law's exclusive concern was with the maintenance of peace, as threatened by the growing confidence of the lawless fascist states, one would surely have expected the Committee to outline a set of mutual concessions to be made both by Italy and by Ethiopia in a new round of League-supervised negotiations at the very least, if not also to have reprimanded Italy for its belligerence. Instead, however, the Committee's proposals consisted exclusively of an elaboration of the backwardness and inefficiency of Ethiopia's governing institutions, and of a programme of external intervention aimed at transforming them along predetermined lines. In short, the Committee responded to a two-sided international dispute (in the formal terms of the League) with a one-sided programme of structural adjustment (as we might now call it) aimed primarily at 'liberalising' its economy. This was, of course, simply a non-militarised, 'consensual' version of precisely what Italy was proposing.

Ethiopia accepted the Committee of Five's proposals cautiously 'as a basis for negotiations', stressing once again its rights as a sovereign state.[119] Italy, once again, rejected them. A month later, the invasion began.

1.4 Economic Sanctions and the Hoare-Laval Pact

If we were to take them by themselves, that is, ignoring their legal background, both 'long' and 'short', the developments which followed the invasion might be taken as suggesting that the collective security apparatus set up by the Covenant functioned reasonably well. Thus, on 7 October, four days after the invasion commenced, the League of Nations Council formed a 'Committee of Six', and decided that Italy had 'resorted to war in disregard of its covenants'.[120] Then, in its first (and only) use of Article 16, the League Assembly recommended that economic sanctions be imposed

[118] Samuel Hoare, speech to the Sixteenth Assembly of the League of Nations, 11 September 1935, in Heald (ed.), *Documents*, 100–5 at 101.

[119] 'Reply of the Abyssinian Government to the Suggestions and Communications of the Committee of Five', 23 September 1935, *LNOJ* (November 1935): 1626.

[120] 'Report of the League of Nations Council Committee', in 30 *AJIL*, Sp. Supp. (1936): 37–40, at 40 (informally known as the 'Committee of Six').

on Italy.[121] Importantly, the test employed by the Committee of Six – '(1) Does a state of war exist between Italy and Ethiopia? (2) If so, has the war been resorted to in disregard of Articles 12, 13, or 15 of the Covenant?'[122] – was a narrow one, based exclusively on the Covenant's collective security provisions. As Quincy Wright pointed out shortly afterwards in the *American Journal of International Law*, of which he was then on the Board of Editors, the League would 'seldom be confronted by so flagrant a case of aggression presenting so little difficulty in applying tests'.[123]

Yet another committee, the Coordination Committee, was then appointed by the Council to address the issue of sanctions.[124] It made five proposals. These included: an embargo on the importation of all Italian goods; the lifting of existing embargoes on the sale of arms and ammunition to Ethiopia; and embargoes on the export of arms and ammunition to Italy, along with several other important goods including animals, rubber and aluminium.[125] Notoriously, however, petrol, iron, coal and, most crucially, oil were excluded from the list of banned exports to Italy. Moreover, states outside the League, like Germany and the United States, were of course free continue trading with Italy as they chose. The US Neutrality Act of 31 August 1931 prohibited the export of arms to both Italy and Ethiopia, but excluded raw materials considered essential to the manufacture of arms and munitions, such as scrap iron, steel, cotton, copper and oil, from these limitations.[126] Despite President Franklin D. Roosevelt's several appeals to the 'American people' to 'so conduct their trade with belligerent nations that it cannot be said that they are seizing new opportunities for profit or that by changing their peacetime trade they give aid to the continuation of war',[127] US exports to Italian colonies in Africa had already risen, by November 1935, from a monthly average of US$25,403 in 1934 to one of $583,735, with crude-oil exports up from 61,708 to 414,474 barrels over the same period – increases of 37 per cent and 85 per cent respectively. [128]

[121] See 'Statement by the President [of the League Assembly], Dr. Beneš', 11 October 1935, in Heald (ed.), *Documents*, 191.

[122] Report of the Council Committee, 40.

[123] Quincy Wright, 'The Test of Aggression in the Italo-Ethiopian War', 30 *AJIL* (1936): 45–56, 53.

[124] Heald (ed.), *Documents*, 193 (commentary by the editor).

[125] Ibid., 193–4.

[126] Ibid., 265.

[127] Statement by President Roosevelt, 29 February 1936, in Heald (ed.), *Documents*, 293–4. A similar appeal was made in October 1935.

[128] Ibid., 265, n. 4.

By the end of 1935, blood-curdling reports were coming in of Italy's tactics against Ethiopian soldiers and civilians, including its use of illegal chemical weapons in the Takkaze Valley, where tear-gas grenades and asphyxiating gas were dropped in December, first in the form of gas-bombs and later using aerial spray-tanks.[129] Public pressure to ratchet up the sanctions regime, in particular by the inclusion of oil, was building. Mussolini, however, had made it clear that Italy would regard such sanctions as an act of war and respond by pulling Italy out of the League and opening negotiations with Germany. The result was a fourth and final reconciliation attempt: the notorious Hoare-Laval Pact, drawn up by the British and French Foreign Ministers on 10 December 1935.

Leaked to the press the following day to international shock and horror, the Hoare-Laval Pact[130] has been condemned, almost unanimously, by historians as having been formulated 'behind the back of the League';[131] as 'an act of blatant treachery towards the League';[132] and even as the event that 'killed the League'.[133] When examined inside the box, however, what is, in fact, so interesting about the Hoare-Laval Pact is how little it differed, in substance, from all the other plans which came before it, both for Ethiopia and for other 'backward' states and territories. Indeed, a close-up examination of the Hoare-Laval Pact undermines the idea that it was negotiated 'behind the back of the League' immediately. Britain and France had been entirely open with the League about their decision to embark on a new round of negotiations with Italy, arguing that in doing so they were only meeting the 'desire expressed … in the Council and the Assembly to see the conflict brought to an end by an agreed settlement'. They referred explicitly to the proposals of the League's Committee of Five as 'the basis of the settlement' they were aiming at.[134] At a meeting of the Coordination Committee a month earlier, for instance, both Laval and Hoare had updated the Committee on the progress of the negotiations, with Laval insisting, for example, that it was 'only within the

[129] Lina Grip and John Hart, 'The Use of Chemical Weapons in the 1935–36 Italo-Ethiopian War', *SIPRI Arms Control and Non-proliferation Program* (October 2009), 3, at www.sipri.org/sites/default/files/Italo-Ethiopian-war.pdf (accessed 5 December 2017).

[130] See 'Outline of an Agreed Settlement of the Italo-Ethiopian Conflict', Paris, 10 December 1935, in *LNOJ* (January 1936): 40–1 ('Hoare-Laval Pact').

[131] Baer, *Test Case*, 131.

[132] Scott, *The Rise and Fall of the League of Nations*, 350.

[133] A. J. P. Taylor, *The Origins of the Second World War* (London: Hamish Hamilton, 1991), 96.

[134] 'Letter from the Representatives of the United Kingdom (Anthony Eden) and France (Pierre Laval) to the Secretary-General communicating the Suggestions for an Agreed Settlement of the Conflict', Geneva, 13 December 1935, *LNOJ* (January 1936): 39–40.

framework of the League that proposals can be examined and decisions reached'.[135] Both men insisted the same after the scandal broke and they were forced to resign,[136] as did their parliamentary colleagues.[137] Equally, the Coordination Committee had given its blessing to their ongoing pursuit of a negotiated solution with Italy back in early November.[138]

What was different about the Hoare-Laval Pact, however, were the circumstances in which the plan was presented – to an unrepentantly aggressive invading power, whose invasion of Ethiopia had been confirmed as a violation of the Covenant.[139] The scale of the proposals was also more extreme, both in terms of the territory to be 'adjusted' and the way in which the extension of 'foreign rights' within the Ethiopian economy was skewed specifically towards Italian industry. Hoare and Laval had suggested that Italy should be allowed to expand the south-western border of Eritrea to incorporate a large area of eastern Tigre, including even the city (or 'wound', as it was referred to by Mussolini) of Adwa,[140] and that the western border of Italian Somaliland should be expanded to include the whole of Ogaden. In return, Ethiopia would obtain a narrow corridor of territory to the sea, leading not to Zeila but to the less desirable port of Assab (I: TERRITORIAL 'ADJUSTMENTS'), with the slavery and arms 'special obligations' to be enforced therein. It emerged that Britain had been prepared to offer Ethiopia Zeila, instead, with a corridor through British Somaliland, but only on condition that Ethiopia pledged 'not to construct from the port which it acquires any railway communicating

135 Pierre Laval, Statement to the Coordination Committee, 2 November 1935, and Samuel Hoare, Statement by Hoare to the Coordination Committee, 2 November 1935, in Heald (ed.), *Documents*, 336–7.

136 See e.g. Hoare, Statement to Parliament, 19 December 1935, in Heald (ed.), *Documents*, 386; Laval, 'Statement to the Committee of Eighteen', 12 December 1935, in Heald (ed.), *Documents*, 362.

137 Baldwin, Statement to Parliament, 10 December 1935, in Heald (ed.), *Documents*, 350; Eden, Statement to Parliament, 10 December 1935, in Heald (ed.), *Documents*, 351.

138 Paul van Zeeland, Statement to the Coordination Committee, 2 November 1935, in Heald (ed.), *Documents*, 338. The Committee's Chairman, Augusto de Vasconcelos, declared that he 'gave [this statement his] full approval'. Augusto de Vasconcelos, Statement by the Chairman to the Coordination Committee, 2 November 1935, in Heald (ed.), *Documents*, 341. According to Robertson, van Zeeland had been persuaded to make this intervention by Britain and France (see James C. Robertson, 'The Hoare-Laval Plan', 10 *Journal of Contemporary History* 10 (1975): 433–64, at 442.

139 See James C. Robertson, 'The British General Election of 1935', 9 *Journal of Contemporary History* (1974): 149–64.

140 Mussolini referred frequently to '*la ferita di Adua*' during the Crisis. See e.g. Antonella Randazzo, *L'Africa del Duce: I crimini fascisti in Africa* (Varese: Arterigere Editore, 2008), 176.

with the interior'. The reason for this was that such a railway would compete with France's Djibouti–Addis Ababa Railway, which both Britain and Italy had undertaken to protect in the 1906 Tripartite Treaty.[141] Britain would also be willing to 'conclude with the French Government all necessary arrangements to safeguard the interest of the port of Jibouti and the Franco-Ethiopian railway' (IV: PROTECTION/EXTENSION OF FOREIGN RIGHTS). Such a pledge would, of course, have obviated the purpose, for Ethiopia, of obtaining an outlet to the sea in the first place.[142] Moreover, what had in the Committee of Five's 'Charter of Assistance' been conceived as an Italian 'special interest' in Ethiopia's economic 'development' was transformed, in the Hoare-Laval Pact, into a gigantic zone of 'economic expansion and settlement reserved to Italy' covering almost the entire south of the country. All in all, the scope of the territory allotted either to Italian sovereignty or to Italian 'expansion and settlement' bore a strong resemblance to the scope of the territory which, under the Anglo-Italian Protocols and the Tripartite Agreement, had been allocated either to Italy's or to Britain's 'sphere of influence' since the last decade of the nineteenth century – long before the invention of the League, and long before the emergence of fascism (see Maps 2 and 3). And while the same could not be said of the zone contiguous with Eritrea, both of the southern areas earmarked for Italian control fell within the 'peripheral zone' which (according not only to the Italian memorandum of 4 September 1925, but also to the Maffey Report, the Mussolini-Laval Accords, the 1925 Anglo-French Exchange of Letters, the slavery reports of the French government, Swiss League and Anti-Slavery Society, Lugard's memorandum of 1922, and numerous other assessments and proposals) had been brutally incorporated on the basis of an illegitimate African pseudo-civilising mission and then left to descend into a state of increasingly barbaric anarchy (II: RACIALISED PARTITION).

The question of a scheme of 'foreign assistance' and the protection of 'foreign rights', moreover, were closely integrated into the plan for this Italian 'zone of economic expansion and settlement', which was to 'form an integral part of Ethiopia ... under the sovereignty of the Emperor'. Within it, however, Hoare and Laval proposed that 'Italy would enjoy exclusive economic rights' including 'the right of ownership of unoccupied

[141] See Sir R. Vansittart (Foreign Office), Memorandum, enclosed in 'Vansittart, letter to G. Clerk, 16 December 1935', in Medlicott, Dakin and Lambert (eds.), *Documents on British Foreign Policy, 1919–1939*, 784–90.

[142] White Paper, 14 December 1935, quoted in Baer, *Test Case*, 129.

territories, the monopoly of the exploitation of mines, forests, etc.'[143] The only qualification would be 'the acquired rights of natives and foreigners' within this zone, which Ethiopia would also be required to protect. Italy, in return, would be 'obliged to contribute to the economic equipment of the country and to devote a portion of its revenues to expenditure of a social character for the benefit of the native population'.[144] Yet the 'zone of economic expansion and settlement' was not *only* envisaged as being simultaneously an integral part of Ethiopian territory on the one hand, and an area which Italy could settle and exploit on the other; it was also to remain subject to League supervision. It was in spelling this out that Hoare and Laval connected their proposal explicitly with the Committee of Five's Charter of Assistance. Under nominal Ethiopian sovereignty, 'control' in the Italian zone was to be 'exercised ... by the services' of this League-supervised 'scheme of assistance', they insisted, the only difference being that Italians would be allowed to take 'a preponderating, but not an exclusive, share in these services'.[145] Hoare and Laval left the question of whether the Charter of Assistance would also apply beyond the Italian 'zone' up in the air. However, their statement that '[t]he services of the [Committee of Five's] scheme of assistance, in the capital [Addis Ababa] as well as in the reserved zone, would regard it as one of their essential duties to ensure the safety of Italian subjects and the free development of their enterprises' strongly suggests that this was, indeed, part of the plan.[146] In the version of the text that the two ministers communicated to the Ethiopian Government, moreover, an extra clause had been added to the sentence which described the extent of Ethiopian control over the Italian 'zone'. Thus, in the version of the plan sent to Ethiopia, it was stated that '[t]he control of the Ethiopian administration in the zone would be exercised, under the sovereignty of the Emperor, by the services of the scheme of assistance drawn up by the League of Nations *and already accepted by the Emperor as extending over the whole area of Ethiopian administration*'.[147] As we saw in the previous subsection, however, Ethiopian consent had been given to the use of the Charter of Assistance only 'as a basis for negotiations'.[148] Hoare and Laval, in other words, had attempted to

[143] Hoare-Laval Pact, 40.
[144] Ibid.
[145] Ibid.
[146] Ibid.
[147] Ibid., 41. Emphasis added.
[148] 'Reply of the Abyssinian Government to the Suggestions and Communications of the Committee of Five', 23 September 1935, *LNOJ* (November 1935): 1626.

predetermine Ethiopia's consent to the scheme (V: ETHIOPIAN 'CONSENT'). As more generally in the Abyssinia Crisis, this causes problems for the idea that the Hoare-Laval Pact was a 'political' act of sabotage visited from the outside on the otherwise innocent international legal framework.

1.5 De Facto v. *De Jure Recognition*

After seven months of war, and with Italian troops nearing Addis Ababa, Haile Selassie fled the country on the night of 1 May. He travelled first to Jerusalem, then to Geneva, finally ending up in Bath, where he remained in exile until 1941. Addis Ababa fell to the Italians a few days later, on 5 May 1936, and on 10 May Mussolini announced Ethiopia's formal annexation to Italy's giant fascist empire, shortly to be renamed *Africa Orientale Italiana*, investing Italian King Vittorio Emanuele III with the title of *Imperatore d'Etiopia*.[149]

A new question of international law now arose: whether or not to extend formal recognition to the annexation. Four years earlier, on 11 March 1932, in response to Japan's invasion of Manchuria, the League Assembly had declared it 'incumbent upon the members of the League of Nations not to recognise any situation, treaty or agreement which may be brought about by means contrary to the Covenant ... or the Pact of Paris'.[150] Yet on 15 May 1936, Austria became the first state to recognise Ethiopia as an Italian territory, followed closely by Danzig (then an international city) and San Marino. Germany (no longer a League member by that point) followed suit on 24 October 1936, citing its desire 'to look after German interests in Ethiopia, to keep existing German concessions, and at the same time receive reparation for damages suffered by German subjects during the Italo-Ethiopian War'.[151] Then followed Hungary, Albania and Luxembourg (all League members, like Austria), as well as Japan (which had withdrawn from the League in 1933), which, on 18 November 1936 in Rome, expressed its hope that this would '[safeguard] Japanese

[149] Heald (ed.), *Documents*, 9.

[150] Resolution of the League Assembly, 11 March 1932, in 'Letter from the Secretary-General to the United States Minister at Berne', Fourth Plenary Meeting of the Assembly, 11 March 1932, *LNOJ*, Special Supplement No. 101 (1932): 90. The 'Pact of Paris' or 'Kellogg-Briand Pact' refers to the *Treaty between the United States, Germany, Belgium, France, Britain, Italy, Japan, Poland and Czechoslovakia providing for the Renunciation of War as an Instrument of National Policy*, Paris, 27 August 1928.

[151] Sbacchi, *Legacy of Bitterness*, 209–10. See generally B. M. Telders, 'La reconnaissance de l'empire italien et le droit international', 9 *Nordisk Tidsskrift for International Ret* (1938): 3–13.

trade and commercial interests in Ethiopia.'[152] Switzerland's recognition was also made on 27 November 1936 'with an eye to maintaining its commercial and economic rights in Ethiopia.'[153] Other League member states, such as Ecuador, Canada, Belgium, Haiti, Chile, Honduras and Poland, though slower in extending *de jure* recognition to the annexation, had hurried to end their sanctions against Italy between April and June 1936, and on 4 July the League terminated the sanctions regime collectively, in response to a British resolution.[154] This evidence of the annexation's *de facto* recognition was reinforced, in Britain's case by its conclusion of a new Anglo-Italian Commercial Agreement (6 November 1936); a 'Gentleman's Agreement' (1 January 1937) with Italy concerning 'peaceful co-existence' in the Mediterranean; and a third Anglo-Italian agreement on the Mediterranean and Middle East, known as the 'Easter Accords', on 16 April 1938 (discussed below). By the end of November 1938, however, almost all the world's states, including Britain and France, had extended their *de jure* recognition to 'Italian Ethiopia.'

Given that Italy's invasion of Ethiopia had, only three years earlier, been condemned by almost every member of the international community barring Italy itself as a cut-and-dried violation of the Covenant, the question arises as to how this international legal U-turn can be explained. As we have already seen, the standard move made by historians of diplomacy or international law is to invoke the trope of appeasement. And it is certainly the case that the European members of the international community found themselves under enormous pressure to recognise Ethiopia as Italian in the aftermath of the annexations's announcement in May 1936. Italy and Germany had been drawing together in the wake of Hitler's remilitarisation of the Rhineland in March 1936, the conclusion of the Austro-German Treaty of 11 July 1936 (widely seen as a first step towards Anschluss, a move prohibited, like the Rhineland's remilitarisation, under the Treaty of Versailles), and finally with the outbreak of the Spanish Civil War on 17 July. On 11 December 1937, Mussolini further upped the ante by announcing Italy's withdrawal from the League, declaring: '*Non avevamo dimenticato e non dimenticheremo l'obbrobrioso tentativo di strangolamento economico del popolo italiano perpetrato a Ginevra!*'[155] However,

[152] Galeazzo Ciano, *L'Europa verso la catastrofe* (Milan: Mondadori, 1948), 23.

[153] Sbacchi, *Legacy of Bitterness*, 210.

[154] Sbacchi, *Legacy of Bitterness*, 210–11.

[155] 'We have not forgotten and we will never forget the disgraceful effort economically to strangulate the Italian people perpetrated by Geneva!' Cited in Renzo De Felice, *Mussolini il duce. Lo stato totalitario, 1936–1940* (Turin: Einaudi tascabili, 1996), 450.

the legal context in which the international community's *de jure* recognition of 'Italian Ethiopia' gradually took place was not composed exclusively of the 'external', 'political' pressure brought on by the growing power of fascism in Europe. This context also engaged a number of 'internal' and indisputably 'legal' considerations with which the rise of fascism was closely entangled. In 1937 and 1938, this entanglement became particularly visible thanks to one aspect of Haile Selassie's battle on all fronts to insist on Ethiopia's rights as a sovereign state and hence on the annexation's illegitimacy. One aspect of this personal battle involved the Emperor's repeated attempts to contest Italy's efforts, as new *de facto* (or *de jure*, for those states that had recognised the annexation) government of Ethiopia, to claim the royalties that were owed to the Ethiopian government by the various foreign companies which were operating there under concessions. The most important of these enterprises were the French-owned Djibouti–Addis Ababa Railway (controlled by the *Société Franco-Éthiopien de Chemin de Fer de Djibouti–Addis Abeba*) and salt monopoly (controlled by the *Société Franco-Éthiopien du Sel*) on the one hand, and, on the other, the Bank of Ethiopia. The latter had only recently gained its independence from the British-controlled National Bank of Egypt, to which the concession for the original Bank of Abyssinia had been granted by Menelik II in 1905, and which remained the latter's correspondent bank in Cairo and London.[156]

Over the first half of 1937 (that is, before *de jure* recognition of Italian Ethiopia by France and Britain), Italy had blocked several attempts by Haile Selassie and C. S. Collier, the Canadian Governor of the Bank of Ethiopia, to sell Ethiopia's shares in the railway and salt monopoly concessions or use them as collateral. However, on 9 June 1937, Haile Selassie brought an action against Italy in Paris, requesting the French courts to uphold his possession of some US$1,500,000 of stock in the railway. The Emperor's argument was that, unless and until France had recognised the conquest *de jure*, he remained 'the only legal ruler of Ethiopia as far as France was concerned' and was hence 'entitled to sole proprietorship of the shares'.[157] He brought a similar action in March 1937 against the *Société du Sel*.[158] According to the historian Alberto Sbacchi, the French directors of both the *Société de Chemin de Fer* and of the *Société du Sel*

[156] Charles Schaefer, 'The Politics of Banking: The Bank of Abyssinia, 1905–31', 25 *The International Journals of African Historical Studies* (1992): 361–89, at 364.

[157] 'Haile Selassie Moves in Paris to Sue Italy on $1,500,500 in Ethiopian Railway Stock', *New York Times*, 10 June 1937, 7.

[158] *Haïlé Selassié* v. *Gouvernement italien*, Tribunal civil de la Seine, GP.1937.II.924, as affirmed in *Haïlé Selassié* v. *Etat italien*, Cour d'appel de Paris, GP.1939.I.640.

feared that Italy would follow through on its repeated threats to nationalise these companies.[159] These men therefore petitioned the French courts to throw the cases out, while at the same time negotiating directly with Italian officials in Paris, to whom they expressed their willingness to pay their companies' dividends to Italy, and their wish that Haile Selassie would smooth the path for them to do so by abdicating.[160] In the end, the French courts avoided the issue by throwing both cases out on jurisdictional grounds after Italy claimed sovereign immunity. They then ordered Haile Selassie to pay costs.[161]

The British courts were faced with a similar situation in 1938, when Haile Selassie brought a case against the British company Cable and Wireless Ltd.[162] However, although their first decision, in March 1938, was to throw the case out, as in France on the grounds of sovereign immunity,[163] that decision was overturned on appeal.[164] Nevertheless, on 6 December 1938 the High Court ruled that the decision of the British Government to extend *de jure* recognition to 'Italian Ethiopia' a week earlier left it with no choice but to 'allow the appeal and dismiss the action'.[165] Its conclusion was not only that 'His Majesty the King of Italy as Emperor of Abyssinia [was now] entitled by succession to the public property of

[159] Sbacchi, *Legacy of Bitterness*, 248–52.

[160] The Bank of Abyssinia was established through a concession granted by Menelik II on 10 March 1905 to the National Bank of Egypt, a private bank under British control registered in Egypt. See Schaefer, 'The Politics of Banking'.

[161] Sbacchi, *Legacy of Bitterness*, 252.

[162] Cable and Wireless Ltd was formed in 1929 of a gigantic merger between the Eastern Telegraph Group (itself an 'amalgamation of British Indian Submarine, Falmouth, Gibraltar and Malta, and the Marseilles, Algiers and Malta companies with the Anglo-Mediterranean, which had been created in 1868 to link Malta, Alexandria, and the new Suez Canal') on the one hand, and Marconi's Wireless Telegraph and Signal Company, on the other. Company Histories, 'Cable and Wireless Plc', at www.company-histories.com/Cable-and-Wireless-plc-Company-History.html (accessed 8 December 2018).

[163] *Haile Selassie* v. *Cable and Wireless Ltd*, Chancery Division (Bennett J), 23 March 1937, 549–50.

[164] The appeal turned on the fact that, at the moment when the case was brought, '[t]he original sovereign [Haile Selassie I] was still recognized by the Government of this country [Britain] as de jure sovereign', even though 'the conquering power [Italy] was recognized as being in control de facto', and that since 'nothing had happened to divest the title formerly vested in the sovereign [Haile Selassie]' and 'the right to sue for the money and to recover it was vested in him', 'the fact that His Majesty the King of Italy cannot be brought before the Court cannot deprive the plaintiff of his right to have his claim adjudicated by the [British] courts'. *Haile Selassie* v. *Cable and Wireless Ltd*, Court of Appeal (Sir Wilfred Greene MR, Scott and Clauson LJJ), 30 June 1937, 182, 844.

[165] *Haile Selassie* v. *Cable and Wireless Ltd (No. 2)*, Chancery Division (Sir Wilfred Greene MR, Scott and Clauson LJJ), 6 December 1938, 198.

the State of Abyssinia, and [that] the late Emperor of Abyssinia's title thereto [was] no longer recognized as existent', but also – and much more radically – that Italy's 'right of succession' was to be 'dated back' to the moment of *de facto* recognition. This moment of *de facto* recognition the Court placed as far back as December 1936, even though at that time it was well known that Italian forces controlled less than half of Ethiopia's territory, little more than they had seven months earlier when the annexation was announced (see Map 4). In doing so the High Court not only deprived Haile Selassie of another year's worth of dividends, but also overturned the entire rationale behind the appeal.[166]

Haile Selassie v. *Cable and Wireless Ltd* has become a standard feature in textbook discussions of the doctrine of recognition. In such textbooks, the three cases involved are routinely held up as demonstrating the importance of *de facto* (as opposed to *de jure*) and governmental (as opposed to state) recognition as pragmatic diplomatic solutions which allow the day-to-day business of international relations to proceed even when important 'political' questions stand unresolved.[167] In this standard presentation, the task before the British courts was simply to work out who Cable and Wireless Ltd should, legally speaking, be paying their royalties too – whether to the *de facto* government (Italy), or to the *de jure* government-in-exile (represented by Haile Selassie). As counsel for Cable and Wireless Ltd insisted , for example, the company's 'only interest' in the case was 'to pay the money to the right person'.[168] If this really was its 'only interest', however, one would be justified in asking why it was that this private company, supposedly neutral between Italy and Ethiopia, argued so forcefully *against* the claims of Haile Selassie.

A very similar question arises if we examine a second British case, this time brought, not by Haile Selassie, but by Collier, to contest the legality of Italy's liquidation of the Bank of Ethiopia by a decree of 20 June 1936, and to claim for the imperial government, in the Italian Government's stead, those of the Bank's assets that were still in the hands of the National Bank of Egypt. As in *Haile Selassie* v. *Cable and Wireless Ltd*, one might have assumed that the National Bank of Egypt would have been uninterested in

[166] *Haile Selassie* v. *Cable and Wireless Ltd (No. 2)*, Chancery Division (Sir Wilfred Greene MR, Scott and Clauson LJJ), 6 December 1938, 197. For the rationale of the appeal, see above, note 164.

[167] See Hersch Lauterpacht, *Recognition in International Law* (Cambridge University Press, 1947), 329–48.

[168] Wynn Parry KC and H. G. Robertson for the respondents, *Haile Selassie* v. *Cable and Wireless Ltd*, Court of Appeal, 842.

the question of which party it should transfer the assets to as long as that party was, legally speaking, the correct one. Yet, just as Cable and Wireless Ltd had done, the National Bank of Egypt aligned itself *against* Collier during the case, arguing vigorously in favour of the validity of the liquidation. It was, counsel for the Bank insisted, 'immaterial whether it is as the *de facto* or *de jure* government of Abyssinia that His Majesty's government have recognized the Italian administration'. The point, according to the Bank, was that 'the decree purporting to dissolve the Bank of Ethiopia' had been made, and that it was 'valid according to the Italian Commercial Code' (that is, to the commercial code of the *de facto* government), which meant, they argued (presenting no evidence for this argument), that 'other governments cannot [legally] question its validity'.[169] The judge, Justice Clauson, agreed, arguing (incorrectly, both in factual and legal terms) that the Italian decree of liquidation had been 'made by a *de facto* government having the occupied territory completely under its control and therefore under its full governmental authority'.[170] The fact that Haile Selassie continued to be recognised *de jure* by the British Government at the time of the case meant nothing more than that the Emperor continued to have 'some right (not in fact at the moment enforceable) to reclaim the governmental control of which he has in fact been deprived'. At that time, however, Justice Clauson continued, these rights were merely 'theoretical' and therefore could not be taken into account in any way in any of Her Majesty's courts.[171]

Notwithstanding its doctrinal usefulness in revealing the power of *de facto* recognition, Justice Clauson's judgment has been widely criticised by international lawyers, including Quincy Wright, Arnold McNair and Hersch Lauterpacht, in particular for its rejection as 'fallacious' of the injunction of customary international humanitarian law in limiting the rights of occupying powers to acts that are 'necessary for preserving peace, order and good government'.[172] If, however, we place this case in amongst all the other items in the shadow-box, and approach it not as a question

[169] Wynn Parry KC and V. R. Idelson for the National Bank of Egypt, *Bank of Ethiopia* v. *National Bank of Egypt and Liguori*, 515.

[170] *Bank of Ethiopia* v. *National Bank of Egypt and Liguori*, Chancery Division (Clauson J), 11 May 1937, 513.

[171] *Bank of Ethiopia* v. *National Bank of Egypt and Liguori* (Clauson J), 522.

[172] *Bank of Ethiopia* v. *National Bank of Egypt and Liguori* (Clauson J), 522. The relevant provision is: Convention (IV) on the Laws and Customs of War on Land, 18 October 1907, Art. 43. See Arnold McNair, *Legal Effects of War* (Cambridge University Press, 1944), 341; Rkystyna Marek, *Identity and Continuity of States in Public International Law* (2nd edn Geneva: Libr. Droz, 1968), 266–7; Lauterpacht, *Recognition*, 286; Quincy Wright, 'The British Courts and Ethiopian Recognition', 31 *AJIL* (1937): 683–8.

of international humanitarian law, but instead as a question of statehood and international personality, a certain *correspondance* shows up which would otherwise be difficult to detect. This *correspondance* concerns the relationship between the supposedly pragmatic idea of *de facto* governmental control on the one hand, and governmental 'effectiveness' as the *sine qua non* criterion for statehood on the other.[173] It suggests, in other words, that the significance of the case for international law concerns not Clauson's poor grasp on the law of occupation, but rather its capacity to illustrate the way in which two apparently separate areas of international law have, historically, worked together to undergird the private rights of international capital over and against the recognised public rights of a non-capitalist (or insufficiently capital-friendly) state. Both Cable and Wireless Ltd and the Bank of Egypt would, after all, have been entirely correct if it had been their assessment that Ethiopia's *de facto* government (Italy) was capable of protecting their rights and interests more 'effectively' than its *de jure* government (under Haile Selassie) had ever been. And this was likewise Justice Clauson's concern.

This bias towards established individual or 'private' rights in Ethiopia is evident not only from vigorous preference of the French and British companies involved in these cases for the jurisdiction of the *de facto* ruler (that is, for fascist rather than Imperial Ethiopian 'government'). It is also evident from the contours of Clauson's rationale. See, for example, Clauson's argument that, even had he not determined the 'peace, order and good government' limitation on the rights of occupying powers to be 'fallacious', he would still have considered the Italian decree liquidating the Bank of Ethiopia to be valid. This was because of the 'confusion' which would have resulted, he said, 'if the only bank of issue in the country [the Bank of Ethiopia] were allowed to continue its business under the control of persons [i.e. Collier] who, until the last moment, seem to have been engaged in strenuous attempts to assist the displaced government [i.e. Haile Selassie's government] to resist the attacks of those [i.e. the Italians] who have become the *de facto* government'.[174] To put it more simply, for Clauson Italy's liquidation of the Bank of Ethiopia had to be regarded as valid because the Bank's authorities had previously supported the efforts of the internationally recognised Ethiopian Government to exercise its sovereign right of self-defence against the 'attacks' which Italy had launched against it during its illegal invasion of the country. The Bank's authorities, he reasoned, would therefore be ill-disposed towards co-operating with the

[173] See Item 2, Section 1.3.

[174] *Bank of Ethiopia* v. *National Bank of Egypt and Liguori* (Clauson J), 523.

occupying regime. Clearly, Clauson did not reach this opinion on the basis of a hidden Italofilism, any more than did the lawyers of Cable and Wireless Ltd, or the National Bank of Egypt. This bias, in the domestic French and British courts, against Haile Selassie, as representative of the exiled *de jure* government, and towards Italy as the in situ *de facto* government, does not appear to have stemmed from any particular inclination towards either Italy or its Fascist politics. What is important to note here, however, when it comes to explaining the pro-Italian leanings of the British and French companies involved and of the British and French courts, is that the deciding factor in all of these cases was that of 'effective' governmental control, understood as the capacity of the government to protect a particular set of private, individual rights – and above all property rights. Crucially, moreover, Italy's status as Ethiopia's *de facto* (thus 'effective') government had repercussions not only at the level of private rights, but also at the level of Ethiopia's international personality. To place this chain of events in the context of the 'long' history of international legal reproduction, it would seem that 'effective' government, in these cases judged to have been exercised, by definition, by the '*de facto*' government, was a criterion powerful enough to shift at least one sovereign right (to collect the royalties owed by companies operating under concessions granted by previous Ethiopian Emperors) to the government of a different state (Italy) altogether.

It is hard to know exactly how much influence these cases had on Britain, France or any of their allies. We do know, however, that with all but the final judgment in *Cable and Wireless* in his back pocket, the British Foreign Minister Lord Halifax travelled to Geneva in May 1938. The purpose of his visit was to put forward the proposal that the League's members should be allowed to decide individually, rather than collectively, whether or not to recognise Italian sovereignty over Ethiopia *de jure*, notwithstanding their collective commitment in 1932 to the non-recognition of situations brought about in violation of the Covenant. Halifax justified this proposal on the grounds (factually tenuous to say the least; see Map 4) that even though resistance was, at that time, still continuing' in certain parts of the country', there was no longer any 'organised native authority and no central native administration with the slightest prospect of reconquering the country.'[175] To fail to recognise the fact of effective and exclusive Italian control over the whole of Ethiopia's territory,

[175] 'Question of the Consequences arising out of the Existing Situation in Ethiopia' (Lord Halifax), Fifth Meeting of the Council (Public), 23 May 1938, *LNOJ* (May–June 1938): 333–47 at 334.

he said, would therefore be to 'live in an unreal world'. Such an attempt to take refuge in 'eternal and immutable moralities' rather than 'face facts' on the part of the Leauge's member-states would be to jeopardise not just the League but 'the ends which it exists to serve', among which the 'greatest of [all] is peace'.[176]

Haile Selassie had been granted permission to attend the debate, in spite of the uncertainty which hung over his Delegation's credentials, thanks to Italy's new status as Ethiopia's *de facto* government. For him, as well as for Lorenzo Taezez (Täklä-Hawaryat's successor as Head of the Ethiopian Delegation at Geneva), representatives of a country which had by this time been waging a war of resistance against Italy's occupation for more than two years, Halifax's insistence on the need to recognise the annexation in order to preserve 'peace' must have been difficult listening. Non-recognition of an astonishingly violent conquest was, after all, as the Emperor pointed out, by far 'the least onerous way of observing Article 10 [of the Covenant] since it call[ed] for nothing more than a passive attitude requiring no national sacrifice' and involved 'no risk of war or reprisals'.[177] In replying to Halifax the Emperor pointed, as so often before, to the hypocrisy of the 'world's most powerful States', which had 'unceasingly ... reiterated that the sanctity of international contracts is the basis of international morality', while simultaneously throwing Ethiopia to the lions.[178] The Emperor also brought the Council's attention to the fact that Lord Halifax, in presenting this proposal to the assembled representatives, was in fact acting on the basis of an undertaking that Britain had made to Italy a month earlier, promising that it would 'take steps' at this very meeting to remove any 'obstacles' which might 'impede the freedom of Member States as regards recognition of Italian sovereignty over Ethiopia'.[179] As the Emperor went on to elaborate, this British undertaking to Italy formed part of a new Anglo-Italian treaty (the 'Easter Accords'), in which the two states had agreed to open negotiations 'as soon as possible on the subject of commercial relations between Italian East Africa and the United Kingdom, India, and British colonies, overseas territories, protectorates and mandated territories ... to the whole of Italian East Africa [i.e. including

[176] Ibid., 335.

[177] 'Question of the Consequences' (Emperor Haile Selassie), 337.

[178] Ibid., 336.

[179] *Agreement between the United Kingdom and Italy, consisting of a Protocol with Annexes and Exchanges of Notes*, Rome, 16 April 1938 ['Easter Accords'], Enclosure No. 11: Exchange of Notes, Lord Perth to Count Ciano, Rome, 16 April 1938, quoted in 'Question of the Consequences' (Emperor Haile Selassie), 336.

Ethiopia] of the Treaty of Commerce and Navigation signed at Rome on the 15th June 1883'.[180] In addition, the Emperor noted, to this unmistakable signalling that Britain intended shortly to recognise the annexation, the Easter Accords included an Italian 'assurance' that it had 'no intention of overlooking or repudiating' its 'obligations' to Britain regarding Lake T'ana.[181] These, of course, were obligations that had been assumed in a series of agreements from which Ethiopia had been excluded, including the 1925 Exchange of Notes, and the 1906 Tripartite Agreement. Insofar as Ethiopia was concerned, then,[182] the United Kingdom had agreed to exchange *de jure* recognition for the protection of its existing, treaty-based interests in Lake T'ana, and for the immediate or future protection of the rights of British individuals and their enterprises in Ethiopia to freedom of trade, movement, exchange, property ownership and worship. In other words, Britain had conditioned its forthcoming recognition of the extension of Italian sovereignty over Ethiopia on the protection and further reproduction of the legal subjectivity of British individuals and companies within this territory. Adding salt to the wound was the fact that Lord Perth, British Ambassador to Rome since 1933 and the diplomat who had negotiated the Easter Accords with Mussolini, was a figure well known to Haile Selassie from the time of his first communications with the League in 1923. For Lord Perth was none other than Eric Drummond, then Secretary-General of the League, who had succeeded his late half-brother to become the seventh Earl of Perth in August 1937.[183]

[180] See *Treaty of Commerce and Navigation between Her Majesty and the King of Italy*, Rome, 15 June 1883. This treaty, as might be expected, and precisely in line with the Treaty concluded between Italy and Shewa less than a month earlier (see *Treaty of Friendship and Commerce between Shewa and Italy*, Ancober, 21 May 1883, discussed in Item 4, Section 3.1.), established conditions of 'reciprocal freedom of commerce and navigation' for the citizens and 'native subjects' of each of the parties throughout their territories and imperial possessions (Art. 1), under detailed most favoured nation (MFN) provisions (Arts. 11–12), and guaranteed rights of free movement, residence, contract, property, and equality before the law (Arts. 13–15). 'Italian East Africa' (Africa Italian Orientale) was announced by Mussolini as a unitary colony incorporating Libya, Eritrea, Italian Somaliland and Ethiopia on 9 May 1936, the same day Italy's annexation of Ethiopia was declared.

[181] Easter Accords, Annex 5: 'Declaration on Lake Tsana', Rome, 16 April 1938.

[182] The Easter Accords included clauses relating to many other issues, including perhaps most importantly Italy's agreement to undertake 'proportional evacuation of foreign volunteers from [the civil war in] Spain'. Easter Accords, Enclosure No. 11: Exchange of Notes, Count Ciano to Lord Perth, Rome, 16 April 1938.

[183] Eric Drummond was Secretary-General of the League of Nations from 1920 until his posting to Rome in 1933.

Confronted with this betrayal, as personal as it was political, Haile Selassie used this opportunity to underline again that '[a]s the lawful sovereign of the Ethiopian people', it was his 'duty to defend the political independence of the Ethiopian people and the territorial integrity of [his] country, as well as the life, property and liberty of each of the individuals and each of the religious or civil bodies of which the Ethiopian nation is made up'.[184] Though subtle, this argument conveyed a devastating point. For as the Emperor suggested, Italy's governmental control over Ethiopia might well have been 'effective' from the point of view of the protection of the material rights and interests of 'foreigners', as established in numerous treaties in concessions. However, from the point of view of Ethiopians themselves, the regime Italy had put in place was effective primarily in the activities of murder, torture, appropriation and destruction.[185] Nonetheless, it might be argued that Haile Selassie's intervention here was beside the point. For as the numerous reports, investigations and proposals examined in Items 5 and 6 had repeatedly underscored, the Ethiopian 'government' had not succeeded, according to its European peers, in protecting foreign rights in Ethiopia, let alone in transforming Ethiopia's entire population into a population of full legal subjects, possessed of 'effective' rights to 'life, property and liberty'. It was this failure which – for Mussolini as for Maffey, and for Laval as for Lugard – seems to have convinced the rest of the international community that the Emperor's 'government' ought not, or no longer, to be regarded fully as such for the purposes of statehood, and hence of the possession of sovereign rights. This conclusion is supported by the fact that by the outbreak of the Second World War, all but five of the world's states had chosen to formalise their recognition of Italian sovereignty over Ethiopia. They did so in a way that contrasted sharply with their treatment of the governments

[184] 'Question of the Consequences' (Emperor Haile Selassie), 337.

[185] As well as many acts of mass terror and destruction then underway, just over a year earlier the Italian administration had, in the wake of an assassination attempt on the Italian Viceroy, Rodolfo Graziani, unleashed 'three terror-filled days and nights of arson, murder and looting' upon Addis Ababa, in which 'thousands of innocent and unsuspecting men, women and children were roasted alive, shot, bludgeoned, stabbed to death, or blown to pieces with hand-grenades', resulting in the massacre of no fewer than 19,000 Ethiopians. Ian Campbell, *The Addis Ababa Massacre: Italy's National Shame* (London: Hurst, 2017). The assassination attempt took place on the steps of an imperial palace which Italians had taken over as their headquarters. The palace is now home to the Institute of Ethiopian Studies at Addis Ababa University, where much of the research for Items 1, 4, 5 and 6 was carried out. The massacre is known in Ethiopia as 'Yekatit 12' after its date in the Ethiopian calendar.

of the Netherlands, Greece, Norway, Poland, Belgium, Yugoslavia and Luxembourg, among others, which fled into exile in Allied states during the War (many of them, like Haile Selassie, to Britain) and continued to be recognised while there, notwithstanding their evident lack of 'effectiveness'.[186] Many factors were clearly at work here to construct this difference in treatment. At least one of them, however, seems to have been the logic of international legal reproduction.

2 The View from Addis Ababa II: Between Equality-in-Identity and Equality-in-Difference

Section 1 has suggested that it is not only possible but also, in a historical sense, necessary to revise our understanding of the significance of the Abyssinia Crisis for the discipline of international law. Far from offering us a textbook example of the need to enforce international law more effectively (as in the standard account), from this perspective the Crisis supplies us with a complex, idiosyncratic and yet informative illustration of the conditional nature of international personality and of the specific material effects of that conditionality. My argument is not that the Covenant's protections for Ethiopia's sovereign rights were considered by Britain, France, Italy or any of the world's other states and dominions to be without force. It is, instead, that – like virtually every other subject of international law at that time – Ethiopia's rights as such had been recognised, and constituted, in exchange for a series of undertakings in which

[186] Some twenty-five governments fled their occupied countries during the War and continued widely to be recognised as *de jure* governments-in-exile (see Stefan Talmon, *Recognition of Governments in International Law: With Particular Reference to Governments in Exile* (Oxford: Clarendon Press, 1998), 290). Arguably, however, at least two things distinguished Ethiopia's legal situation from theirs. Firstly, as we have just seen, the Haile Selassie administration was not considered to be 'effective' even before the invasion, so much so that powerful business interests both in Britain and France, not to mention the Maffey Committee itself, were of the opinion that Italian governance of Ethiopia would, even under normal circumstances, be preferable to continued Solomonic rule. This was not the case for the European governments-in-exile. Secondly, although the new Italian authorities in Ethiopia certainly did not, at first, treat foreign legations and business interests within Ethiopia with the kind of respect their home states might have wished, Italy was quick to use the termination of this ill-treatment as a bargaining chip. Greater respect would be shown to British, French and other diplomatic and business interests in Ethiopia, Italy suggested, when *de jure* recognition was forthcoming. It is unlikely, in Europe and thus outside the 'colonial' context then considered normal to Africa, that either Italy or Germany would have been able to employ such a bargaining chip in relation to business interests in occupied Europe. To investigate this speculation further, however, is beyond the scope of this book.

it committed itself, under international law, to alter its domestic institutions and its domestic normative structure. In this process, the coercive and voluntary aspects of which are difficult to disentangle, the Ethiopian Empire committed itself to ensuring that a particular set of already-established rights belonging to existing individual legal subjects (for the most part, British, French and Italian citizens and their commercial enterprises, together with those of other states) would be protected and in this way reproduced within its borders – rights, essentially, to be treated as equally 'free' in the negative sense. According to its treaty partners, however, Ethiopia failed to make good on these undertakings. Far from functioning as regular inter-state obligations, whose violation, though punishable with countermeasures, by definition leaves the 'sovereign' rights and duties of the contracting state unaffected, this particular set of (constitutive) undertakings operated very differently. For these undertakings together added up to a pledge to create and maintain a 'government', in the sense intended by the 1933 'Montevideo criteria' – one that was 'effective', 'responsible', 'self-governing' or simply (as the British described it) 'good'. This commitment was, in other words, the central element upon which the edifice of Ethiopia's international legal subjectivity (like that of almost any other state) balanced. The more that commitment was called into question, the more flexible, even permeable, Ethiopia's rights and duties as a subject of international law became.

However, even if the Ethiopian Empire did find itself caught in the hegemonic process referred to here as that of international legal reproduction, we should not make the mistake of casting the Empire as a mere passive victim in this scenario. As we have already seen, Ethiopia protested vigorously against what it understood to be the flagrant abandonment of the Covenant's principles by Britain, France, Italy and the other League states. In doing so, its officials displayed a mastery of international legal doctrine which few of their colleagues could match. Yet to reduce Ethiopia's strategy to the act of unsuccessfully speaking law to power would be to miss the most sophisticated aspect of its strategy of resistance. This, as this section will suggest, was its hybridised quality, with which the Ethiopian Empire sought to redeploy its part-sameness and part-otherness as a weapon of self-defence against the pressure to become something that it was not. Indeed, such an evaluation can only seem plausible if Ethiopia's own interventions are ignored completely – something that has, in general, been the situation in the field of international legal history. With this in mind, Section 2.1 will examine the Ethiopian Delegation's official response to the Italian memorandum of 4 September 1935 (29 Nähäse 1927 according to the

Ethiopian calendar), discussed above. Section 2.2 will then turn to the dossier of letters and petitions sent to Haile Selassie from the front line of the war of resistance which was then ongoing against Italy's occupation, and forwarded on to the Secretary-General in late December 1938. Finally, Section 2.3 will highlight the hegemonic character even of this counter-hegemonic strategy of hybridisation on the part of the exiled Imperial administration, turning to the struggle of certain Oromo groups within Ethiopia at this time simultaneously to resist Italian and Abyssinian imperialism, and the role of the trope of 'self-governing' statehood in their attempts to do so.

2.1 *Ethiopia's Response to the Italian Memorandum*

In response to Italy's devastating attempt to undermine Ethiopia's claim to be a state, entitled to an equal set of sovereign rights and duties under international law, the Ethiopian Delegation submitted two replies. One came from the head of the Ethiopian Delegation, *Bäjerond* Täklä-Hawaryat Täklä-Maryam.[187] The other was an invited expert response from Marcel Griaule, a well-known French anthropologist. Interestingly, the discursive impact which might be harnessed by splicing together elements of the language of international law, on the one hand, with elements of the 'Aksumite' vision of international normativity, was lost on neither Täklä-Hawaryat nor Griaule. In their submissions, both constructed compelling discourses of what we might call Ethiopia's 'equal otherness' – its claim to be 'equal' in a formal sense, in spite of being 'other' in a material or substantive sense. In doing so, they presented the members of the League with what was, in effect, a kind of macro 'mimic man' – with an image of Ethiopia that was at once *familiar* (in its state-like-ness) *and unfamiliar* (as a very different form of polity from the template on which the criteria for statehood were based), and therefore deeply unsettling. The idea, it seems, was through their juxtaposition of sameness and otherness, to throw the hypocrisies and biases of international law into sharp relief, and in doing so to reinforce Ethiopia's claim to be a sovereign state *even if* it refused to reconstitute itself entirely along the lines suggested by the criterion of ('good') government. This was, in other words, a strategy of straightforward 'intentional hybridisation', precisely in the Bakhtinian/Bhabhaian sense.

One of the Italian memorandum's most damaging elements, as we saw above, was Italy's attempt to refute Ethiopia's claim to be self-governing

[187] See Item 5, Section 2.1.

on the grounds that it was guilty of violating (or of allowing to be violated) the rights of individual foreigners and companies it had promised, in numerous international instruments, to protect. In effect, Italy argued that Ethiopia had not only violated international law, but had actually usurped, and in doing so sullied, the great European 'civilising mission', and was therefore unfit to remain a member of the family of nations. This was not, of course, the first time such an argument had been made. On the contrary, the idea that what was 'wrong' in the Ethiopian Empire was 'that the Amharas, being black, ha[d] taken up the white man's burden' had a long genesis in the history of Ethiopia's encounter with international law.[188] What distinguished the Italian memorandum was not its content, but its intention: to justify an invasion that would otherwise have been irrefutably illegitimate. In attempting to challenge this allegation, Täklä-Hawaryat and Griaule set out to prove Ethiopia's self-governing credentials without capitulating entirely to what they clearly perceived to be an external normative standard. Both responded using a complex strategy of simultaneously defending and denying Ethiopia's imperial self-identity. In doing so, they chose not to align Ethiopia with the many other African polities which had fallen victim to European imperialism, or even with the League's more ordinary 'self-governing' states, dominions, 'international cities' (like Danzig) and others. Instead, both Täklä-Hawaryat and Griaule classed the Ethiopian Empire as a comrade of the European 'great powers', and as possessed, for that reason, of a set of weighty domestic duties towards the civilisation of its 'native' population, as well as international rights in respect of other states. Just as remarkably, both coupled this image with an attempt to portray Ethiopian imperialism as ancient and exceptional – if not entirely unique – and hence as (formally) equal to but (substantively) different from the European empires.

Regarding the most problematic issue of slavery, for example, Griaule explained its persistence in the Ethiopian Empire both on the grounds that the latter's 'geographical situation' had 'kept [Ethiopia] aloof from the main trend of western civilisation', and on the grounds that Ethiopian slavery was qualitatively different from its European/American equivalent in that Ethiopian slaves (he argued) were fully 'received into the family'.[189]

[188] Claud Russell to the Marquis Curzon of Kedleston, 16 March 1922, A1799/486/1, FO 371/7141 Political (Abyssinia) 1922 (UKNA). See above, Item 5, Section 1.1.

[189] 'Comments by M Marcel Griaule on Some of the Questions Dealt with in the Italian Government's Memorandum on the Situation in Ethiopia', Geneva, 14 September 1935, LNOJ (November 1935): 1587–95 at 1592 ('Comments by Griaule').

Drawing on the incorporative and yet relatively flexible Abyssinian concept of civilisation as *silit'ane* ('accumulated learning')[190] Griaule also pointed out that '[a]ny Ethiopian, whether free or not, can rise to the highest honours in the Empire'.[191] In doing so, he implied that 'Abyssinian civilisation' (true to the Aksumite and Orientalist paradigms, he conflated the terms 'Ethiopian' and 'Abyssinian') was progressive and legitimate – at least as progressive and legitimate as the European civilisation – but in a specifically Ethiopian way. Equally hybridised, it might be argued, was Griaule's argument that the 'increased contact with Western civilisations' which continued membership of the League would afford Ethiopia would hasten its abolition of slavery. For, he said, the 'Christian Empire of Ethiopia, relying on the ancient liberalism which is the basis of its people's character, has ... realised the necessity for accelerating this evolution', which would 'proceed in the best possible conditions if the Ethiopian Empire remains mistress of its own destiny'.[192] Here, Griaule accepted that Ethiopia's 'primitive' institutional structures required Western 'assistance', as did Haile Selassie and the other Young Ethiopians (also operating, as I argued above, on an understanding of civilisation-as-*silit'ane*). As he did so, however, Griaule also reasserted the Empire's claim to equal otherness by embedding Ethiopia's 'ancient liberalism' (pointing to an original cultural affinity with Europe) *within* 'the people's character', rather than externalising that 'liberalism' as a separate 'legal' culture requiring to be imported from outside (as the Committee of Five's 'Charter of Assistance' was shortly to suggest). In this way, Griaule deployed the need for Ethiopia's 'hastened evolution' as an argument *against* any attempt to downgrade its rights and duties as a fully sovereign state.

For his part Täklä-Hawaryat, tackling Italy's allegation that Ethiopia's was a 'barbaric' and hence illegitimate form of imperialism, expressed surprise that, as a poor state by all accounts, the Ethiopian Empire should be expected to exercise 'on the desert confines of a vast empire, which that empire considers as a colony, a greater degree of authority than that exercised by a great Western Power over its own colonial territory'.[193] This excuse was, he pointed out, used consistently by European colonial administrators to justify their failure to suppress slavery in territories

[190] See Item 5, Section 1, above.

[191] 'Comments by Griaule', 1593.

[192] Ibid., 1593.

[193] 'Preliminary Observations of the Ethiopian Delegation on the Italian Government's Memorandum', 14 September 1935, *LNOJ* (November 1935): 1595–1601, at 1599.

under their control.[194] Similarly, Griaule argued that 'even if' it were accepted 'that Ethiopia forms a nucleus of conquerors living in the midst of conquered tribes', its 'international obligations concerning the exercise of effective authority over border districts must surely be viewed with the same tolerance as is extended to European [colonial] Powers'.[195] Yet having insisted that Ethiopia's imperialism ought to be judged on the same basis as Europe's, Griaule then determined the extent of the Ethiopian Empire, which he described as 'the oldest colonising enterprise in the world',[196] on a very Abyssinian basis – namely by means of the date at which the Empire's subject territories had 'become' Christian. In this he adhered to the Aksumite – that is, cosmic and flexible – understanding of the Empire's scope, as opposed to an international legal definition focused on territorial fixity.[197]

The Italian memorandum had also attacked Ethiopia's claim to possess sovereign rights and duties on the grounds of the latter's 'national' heterogeneity, with the institutions of slavery and of the *gebbar* system presented as evidence that Ethiopian individuals could hardly be described as rights-bearing citizens possessed of a government to whose rule they had consented. Griaule approached this part of the argument by giving an Orientalist-Semiticist explanation of the origins of the Abyssinians as a people (notably the only one of Ethiopia's numerous constituent peoples he felt it necessary to account for).[198] 'The Abyssinians', he argued, 'are descended from the Assyro-Babylonians. They have worked out their special destiny in one of the most isolated regions of the world ... where no echo from the civilisation developing in the plains could reach them.'[199] Having attached to his written submission a 'racial map', Griaule asserted that 'the Ethiopian type' dominated the Empire's core northern highlands, whereas its surrounding areas were inhabited primarily by 'a type which is still Ethiopian but contains a large proportion of black blood'.[200] He sought to turn this argument to the Empire's advantage by casting the

[194] As G. F. Archer, Governor General of Sudan, wrote to the Anti-Slavery Conference of 1926: 'I would, however, remind you that the Sudan is a vast area in which there is a great variety of tribes and conditions ... Thus ... I must deprecate undue acceleration or haste in the handling of this very difficult subject.' 'Submission of the Government of Sudan' (Anti-Slavery Conference, 31 January 1926), Dossier 1/49465x/46781, Box R.76 (LONA).

[195] 'Comments by Griaule', 1588.

[196] Ibid., 1590.

[197] Ibid., 1590.

[198] Ibid., 1591.

[199] Ibid., 1591.

[200] Ibid., 1592.

Ethiopian Empire in the role of a kind of self-tutoring entity – simultaneously mandatory power and mandated territory – rather than as a backward territory which should itself be transferred to European tutelage. Thus, Griaule asserted that '[i]n the same way as in Black Africa, Mohammedanism is more successful than Christianity because it is better suited to the needs of the natives, Abyssinian civilisation will succeed better than any other among peoples like those of southern Ethiopia'.[201]

In his own submission, Täklä-Hawaryat, in turn, mixed an 'Aksumite' understanding of Ethiopia's self-governing credentials together with a powerfully Wilsonian discourse which gestured to the rejuvenating power of nationalism in order to deny that the Ethiopian government was racially removed from, and therefore ruled without the consent of, large portions of its population:

> [T]he Ethiopians who came from the Yemen with Solomon's dynasty settled in the kingdom of Aksum, spread over the high plateaux and overflowed into the lower regions, where they intermarried with the Galla and formed a veritable nationality, which, according to the principles laid down by Mancini in his celebrated lesson at Florence in 1851 would be entitled to claim the whole country as far as the sea.[202]

Here, Täklä-Hawaryat overlaid Griaule's mix of Aksumite and Orientalist-Semiticist logic with a quintessentially inter-war, liberal nationalist international legal understanding of statehood as vehicle for 'national self-determination', even going so far as to root that understanding in the words of one of the most distinguished Italian international lawyers of the mid nineteenth century, Pasquale Mancini (1817–1888), who became the first President of the *Institut de Droit International* upon its formation in 1873.[203]

But it was ultimately Griaule who appealed to the most characteristically Abyssinian or 'Aksumite' vision of what self-government should mean. He did so by quoting *Ras* Hailu Täklä-Haymanot (1868–1950), former governor of Gojjam province and one of the most famous (if not infamous) members of the Ethiopian nobility at that time. *Ras* Hailu was quoted as having declared:

> It is said that the Prince enriches himself by grinding down the people, and this is proved by the number of his granaries. In very truth, there is no instance in the chronicles of a Prince who has grown thin through a

201 Ibid., 1590.

202 Ibid., 1590; 'Preliminary Observations of the Ethiopian Delegation', 1597.

203 Martti Koskenniemi, *The Gentle Civilizer of Nations: The Rise and Fall of International Law 1870–1960* (Cambridge University Press, 2001), 41 and see generally Ibid., 14–97.

> lack of grinding stones! But there is this that I would cast upon the mind: in hard times, the people make a hollow of the palms of their hands and stretch out their arms towards the granaries of the Prince, for the King is the people's steward.
>
> ... Know that at the bottom of my heart there is this great certainty. The power of my reign lies not only in my arms, in my finest machine-gun, it lies in the plough that I drive on the first day when the ground is broken, when I give my people the signal for work in the fields and when by driving a furrow I designate the Prince's paramount right of ownership over all land and domains. My royal crown is but the lash of labour around my brow.[204]

The image conjured up by *Ras* Hailu's words was of an Empire whose social fabric was made up of a web of irrefutably benign personal hierarchies, connecting every *gebbar* to his landowner, every landowner to his governor, and every governor to Emperor and Church through ties of custom, labour, tribute, land and – crucially – through the common endeavour of defending Ethiopia's cultural and religious identity and hence its independence.[205]

On the one hand, then, much of Täklä-Hawaryat's response was taken up by a series of extraordinarily fluent appeals not only to the doctrinal history of self-determination in international law, from Mancini to Wilson, but also to the cutting-edge social scientific languages of the time, from anthropology and psychoanalysis.[206] On the other hand, and juxtaposed against it, was Griaule's effort to ground Ethiopia's claim to international personality in an unrepentantly Abyssinian trope of hierarchical, anti-capitalist, divinely ordained political, social and economic ordering, the very opposite of 'self-government'.[207] If we were to interpret this persistent splicing of recognisably 'international legal' with recognisably 'Abyssinian' understandings of the standards which Ethiopia was accused of having violated as a strategy of intentional hybridisation (an idea which Bakhtin was, in fact, developing at exactly that moment, in the

[204] Quoted in 'Comments by Griaule', 1594.

[205] See Section 2.3, below.

[206] For example, at one point Täklä-Hawaryat made the argument that 'cruelty which appears indispensable to the severity of the punishment assumes different forms in different times and places without the people of one time or of one place having the right to regard this difference as representing stages in a hierarchy of culture when it is merely a case of psychological variations on the same plane of human conscience'. 'Preliminary Observations of the Ethiopian Delegation', 1599.

[207] Interestingly, this strategy of equalisation through juxtaposition is evident even within *Ras* Hailu's own declaration, where the technology of the 'grinding stone' is set against that of his 'finest machine-gun'.

mid-1930s[208]), it might be suggested that the aim of Täklä-Hawaryat and Griaule was to highlight the normative hollowness of the idea of 'sovereign equality' as a status conditioned on a culturally specific and normatively far from neutral standard, masquerading as an objective criterion.

2.2 Resistance on Many Fronts

Unfortunately, as we have already seen, this strategy had little effect. It seems, however, to have been the only one available to the Ethiopian Empire, especially after November 1938, when the legitimisation of Italian sovereignty over Ethiopia meant that the Ethiopian Delegation's credentials at the League were threatened.[209] This might explain why we can see this strategy at work again, in December 1938, when Haile Selassie transmitted a dossier to the League Secretary-General in Geneva, containing a series of reports and petitions that had been sent to him from the front line by some of the leaders of the Ethiopian resistance movement, together with a number of Italian propaganda items.[210]

The reports describe in chilling detail the atrocities that were still being inflicted upon Ethiopian soldiers and civilians more than three years after the conflict began. At the same time, they also display a similar interweaving of a recognisably 'international legal' with an unrepentantly 'Aksumite' normativity. One of these documents, for example, was a petition 'from the People of Ethiopia who are Striving for their Independence to the League of Nations and the Peoples of the Entire World', which was double-dated as '21st Maskerem, 1931 (October 1st, 1938)'. The petition began: 'Since the day that Italy infringed the independence of Ethiopia in violating the law ... we have continued to resist, up hill and down dale, against this Italy which never wearies of committing the most ignoble deeds of atrocity.'[211] 'You must', it continued, still addressing the 'entire world', 'have had word

208 For the argument that Ethiopia was, here, employing a distinctively 'modernist' formulation, see Nathaniel Berman, 'Beyond Colonialism and Nationalism? Ethiopia, Czechoslovakia, and "Peaceful Change"', in *Passion and Ambivalence: Colonialism, Nationalism and International Law* (Leiden: Martinus Nijhoff, 2012), 319–83, 350.

209 For an account of the battles that took place in 1938 over Ethiopia's right (or lack of it) to attend meetings at the League, including meetings at which its own fate was being discussed, see Gerald Chaudron, *New Zealand in the League of Nations: The Beginnings of an Independent Foreign Policy, 1919–1939* (Jefferson, NC: McFarland, 2011), 118–28.

210 'Communication from the Permanent Ethiopian Delegate Accredited to the League of Nations to the Secretary-General', London, 28 December 1938', *LNOJ* (January 1939): 8–22.

211 In 'Communication from the Permanent Ethiopian Delegate', 9.

from time to time ... of how our blood never ceases to flow ... [W]e say – if you will not accord justice to this Ethiopia which entreats you so piteously for aid, before she becomes childless – what, then, is the use of the League of Nations?'[212] Consistently conflated both in the petition and in the other reports (just as they had been in *Ras* Tafari's letter to Eric Drummond of 1923) were two very different understandings of international justice: on the one hand, the divine justice celebrated in the *Fetha Nagast*, and on the other, the procedural justice celebrated by international law.

To turn to another example, in his letter to the Emperor, included in the dossier, *Dejazmatch* Mangacha Djembere[213] of Gojjam wrote:

> Your Majesty,
>
> I pray that my Creator, who delivered Jonah from the belly of the whale, may bring you back from across the sea to Ethiopia, and that in preserving us, who are in anguish and tribulation, He may make us worthy to gaze upon your eyes and to kiss your shoes of gold again ... God in His goodness has given us Your Majesty, so that you might draw out of darkness into light your country, Ethiopia, which was backward in progress, remote from civilisation and living in the gloom of ignorance ... Instead of the happiness which your reign would have brought us, agony and tribulation have befallen us as a daily sacrifice. But ... we are certain that ... He will not allow Ethiopia to be lost for ever; for is it not said: 'God's anger and mercy walk hand in hand'?[214]

Similarly, in another of the dossier's documents, the 'civil, military and religious authorities' of Semien, Wollo, Begameder, Wag, Lasta, Gojjam and Shewa addressed Haile Selassie in a collective letter, in which they wrote:

> Your Majesty,
>
> We raise our hands towards Heaven to beseech the Almighty to accord life and health to Your Majesty, to deliver our country from our enemies, and to grant us the joy of seeing your radiant face in rejoicing and in peace.
>
> Your Majesty, it is now two and a half years since Italy, which had promised to respect the independence of Ethiopia, has been making war upon us, contrary to her word, and in transgression of the Covenant of the League of Nations ... Our sufferings are mitigated and our hopes are raised by the knowledge that Your Majesty is standing before the Assembly of Nations, the Sceptre of Solomon in your hand, to proclaim to the world how your defenceless people are being unjustly exterminated ...

[212] Ibid.

[213] Sometimes spelled Mangasha Jimbirre.

[214] 'Communication from the Permanent Ethiopian Delegate', 10.

> Woe to those nations which will not accord equitable justice to this Emperor of Ethiopia, respectful and loyal to his engagements, who stands before them in his pure majesty to demand justice, for they will incur the responsibility of inciting the wrath of God. If your sorrow and your efforts do not obtain an immediate result, God will accord His justice when it pleaseth Him ...
>
> But, Your Majesty, do not grieve too deeply, for in proportion to the furious efforts of the enemy to destroy us, our losses are not so great. The God of Ethiopia has not abandoned His people, and we have faith that He will accept as a burnt offering this innocent blood that is shed every day ... A nation that has not undergone trial forgets the kindness of its God and of its Sovereign and cannot know how dear is the price of liberty ...
>
> Let the Roman Caesar stay quietly in Rome; Ethiopia belongs to the Ethiopians.[215]

As these communications suggest, these resistance leaders were labouring under no illusions about the workings of international law. On the contrary, they all demonstrate an intricate knowledge of the terms of the Covenant; of the League's institutional structure; of international law's promise of 'equitable judgement' and 'equitable justice'; of the principle of *pacta sunt servanda*; of the customary prohibition of the commission of 'ignoble deeds of atrocity'; of the growing illegitimacy of the invasion of one country by another, and so on. However, for these 'civil, military and religious authorities' spearheading the battle against Italian occupation, this call for immediate law-enforcement was part of a much bigger story, with a far longer – indeed, biblical – timeframe. In these letters, God was beseeched to return to Ethiopia its absent Emperor just as He had returned Menelik I from Jerusalem. Haile Selassie's right to stand before the League of Nations was derived not only from his position as Ethiopia's 'Sovereign' head of state, but also, and more importantly, from his dynastic connection to King Solomon himself and from his Christian love for his people. As Haleka Hailu, 'Archpriest' of Debre-Tabor and Gondar, had written, 'Your Majesty is coveted like food in the midst of famine, and the love of your people for you will never dry up, but will spring forth unceasingly'.[216] 'Positive' international law and the natural law of the *Fetha Nagast* were deliberately mixed together, in these documents, as presented by Haile Selassie to the Secretary-General and transmitted to the League, in such a way as to present the Ethiopian Empire, rather than the 'great powers' at Geneva, as international law's one true disciple, all the more

[215] Ibid., 20.
[216] Ibid., 16.

faithful thanks to precisely to those elements of its culture which those 'great powers' had so often dismissed as barbaric. The image these letters conjured up of a harmonious and utterly benign imperial polity – one in which the most heartfelt wish of any Ethiopian would be to experience the joy of seeing the Emperor's 'radiant face' once again – cannot but have reminded their uncomfortable audience in Geneva how much blood-letting the establishment of 'effective' government had always entailed.

The power of these documents was further accentuated by the extracts from Italy's propaganda efforts with which they had been enclosed. Evidently the Italians had attempted to voice their instructions to the Ethiopians in a normative language to which they would be receptive. The result was entirely bogus – not (as in Bakhtin and, later, Bhabha) a deliberate hybridisation designed to throw the hypocrisy of one 'social language' into relief, but rather an accidental hybridisation which, far from convincing its audience, simply pushed Italy's mendacity into the spotlight. 'People of Gojam, hearken!' one of them read. '[B]y submitting entirely to Italy and her majestic Caesar, your country and your people would be well governed and protected by force of arms and peaceful administration.'[217] Another said: 'Oh people of Bagameder! I have already proclaimed my words of peace: let the merchant proceed with his business; let the labourer proceed with his ploughing!'[218] A third, dropped from an aeroplane somewhere in rebel territory in September 1938, was addressed 'To the Ballabat, the Kalitcha, the Chiefs and the People of Galla'. Displaying some knowledge of the sources of Oromo discontent, this leaflet declared that:

> Your enemies, seeing that the Italian Government respects and protects you, are endeavouring by lies to make you break your agreement with the [Italian] Government ... These people are wicked and false like the serpent. Remember how, in the past, they did you much harm and ... [made] you live like slaves ... The Italian Government has delivered you from their yoke ... People of Galla, hearken! The Italian army will not retreat from the territory it occupies without having destroyed to the last man, the rebels who seek to corrupt you and steal your goods.[219]

In addition to the faux-Old Testament language of serpents, hearkenings and wickedness, these proclamations betrayed a number of false assumptions. Most obviously, only a tiny minority of Ethiopians saw themselves

[217] Ibid., 19–21.
[218] Ibid., 20.
[219] Ibid., 19–21.

as 'merchants' and 'labourers'.[220] Very few had many 'goods' that could be 'stolen'. For as we saw in Item 4, Ethiopian society was not, for the most part, organised around wage-labour and private property at this time. Nor did the Italians seem to appreciate the historical resonance of references to 'the grandeur and justice of Rome'[221] and to the success of 'Caesar' in forcibly usurping Haile Selassie's throne.[222]

The Italians, in other words, seem to have expected the resistance eventually to submit to the *de facto* situation, just as international law itself had done. Playing out, almost to the letter, what Walter Benjamin had written in 1921, the 'origin of law' had again showed itself to be a 'violence crowned by fate'.[223] Following a linear course, like Benjamin's rosary beads, 'right' had legitimised 'might', disguising the painful consequences of war and occupation into a new status quo through the application of international legal principles firmly grounded in individual 'freedom' and 'equality' ('effectiveness', '*de facto*' authority and so on). From the mostly Aksumite perspective of these resistance leaders, drawn for the most part from the Abyssinian nobility, however, time and normativity were not connected in this linear fashion. On the contrary, Ethiopian Imperial time circled back continually to the foundation myths of the Empire – to the Jesuit crisis; to the reign of Solomon; even back to Jonah and the whale. Italy's mistakes, seen from the perspective of these propaganda efforts, were no more than the blunders of a new 'totalitarian' pomposity superimposed on top of the equally bloodthirsty, 500-year-old international legal teleology of the 'self-governing' state. As these badly hybridised injunctions rained down from the sky among shells and poison gas, they rang false in the ears at least of those who identified with the Aksumite paradigm.[224] In consequence, it was on the biases of international law itself, rather than the shortcomings of the Ethiopian Empire's dominant normative apparatus, that these scraps of fascist propaganda threw light.

220 See Item 4, Section 2.3.

221 'Communication from the Permanent Ethiopian Delegate', 19.

222 See Item 4, Section 1; Item 5, Section 2.1.

223 Walter Benjamin, 'Critique of Violence' [1921], in *Walter Benjamin: Selected Writings*, Vol. 1: 1913–1926 ed. Marcus Bullock and Michael W. Jennings, trans. Edmund Jephcott (Cambridge, MA: Harvard University Press, 2003), 236–52, at 242.

224 As Lij Yohannes Yasu replied to one of Bastiani's overtures, 'All the nations of the world know that you have been for a long while the enemy of Ethiopia. But our hearts are strong. A goat and a leopard, a lion and a calf, a lamb and a jackal, an infidel and a Christian, an Italian and an Ethiopian, can never be reconciled. On the day that all these are reconciled, then will we also become reconciled', 25 July 1928/16 Hamlé 1930, in 'Communication from the Permanent Ethiopian Delegate', 13.

2.3 Resisting the Resistance

As the extracts from Haile Selassie's dossier of December 1938 suggest, not least through the careful process through which they had been translated and abridged, the Emperor was at some pains to emphasise the unity of the resistance movement within Ethiopia. Above all, the message this dossier was intended to convey was that Haile Selassie retained the backing of the whole of Ethiopia's population, which remained implacably opposed to Italian rule.

However, as Britain, France and the other League states knew only too well, there were many in Ethiopia who had gone over to the Italian side. These collaborators included several distinguished members of the Abyssinian elite – in particular those put out by Haile Selassie's efforts to centralise the Empire's administrative system by abolishing the semi-independent status of many regions such as Tigray, Gojjam, Jimma, Begemder and Sidamo. Thus, as the historian Ezekiel Gebissa has argued, when the invasion began, many of the 'deposed hereditary rulers felt that their time had come to settle scores' and defected to the Italian side in return for the restoration of their lands.[225] Ironically, the most notorious of the aristocratic defectors was *Ras* Hailu of Gojjam himself, whose expressions of loyalty to the Emperor had, ironically enough, been cited in Griaule's 1935 submission to the League as proof of the united, harmonious and robust nature of the Ethiopian Empire's idiosyncratic system of imperial rule.[226] However, Italy's propaganda was also relatively effective when it came to those communities which had suffered for decades, if not centuries, at the hands of Abyssinian imperialism. For example, in Northern Shewa, ethnic tensions between local Amharic and Oromo populations were easily whipped up by the occupying power intent on

[225] Ezekiel Gebissa, 'The Italian Invasion, the Ethiopian Empire, and Oromo Nationalism: The Significance of the Western Oromo Confederation of 1936', 9 *Northeast African Studies* (2002): 75–96, at 75.

[226] Ironically, *Ras* Hailu – a longstanding thorn in Haile Selassie's side – having been charged with 'mendacity, corruption, tax evasion, and treason' in 1932, had been either under house arrest or in prison until the Italian invasion, when he had been cast out of the train on which Haile Selassie fled Addis Ababa, along with *Dejazmatch* Balcha Safo. While the latter, at the age of 73, went on to lead the resistance in Gurage, *Ras* Hailu became one of the Fascist regime's most high-profile collaborators, for which he was rewarded extensively with honours (such as *Ordine coloniale della Stella d'Italia*), special permissions (to build a house in the Italian district of Addis Ababa, for example) and wealth, including the restoration of his lands. See generally Sbacchi, *Legacy of Bitterness*, 144–5.

using 'the classic policy of "divide and rule" to strengthen [its] position',[227] as the historian Ahmed Hassan Omer shows. Thus, in the wake of the catastrophic Italian victory over Ethiopian imperial forces at the Battle of Maichew (31 March 1936), when Rayya and Azëbu Oromo guerrillas had attacked the retreating Imperial forces headed by Haile Selassie himself,[228] ethnic relations in the north had become increasingly fraught. The Italians soon realised that '[t]he most effective method' of striking at the resistance movement was to incite 'ethnic and religious conflicts between the Christian Amhara on the one hand and the [M]uslim Argobba, Amhara, Afara and Oromo inhabitants of the region on the other'.[229]

Yet many of these disaffected communities were, of course, acutely aware that Italian imperialism was hardly preferable, in the long run, to Abyssinian imperialism. Indeed, as Ezekiel points out, where many 'Africans in European-dominated territories saw the [Italian] invasion as a catastrophic event that dashed their hopes of regaining independence', for several peoples within the Ethiopian Empire who 'had been conquered and subjected to Abyssinian colonial rule, the event created a propitious moment to reassert their independence'.[230] One possibility which seemed to offer a way out of this trap was the option of appealing for outside help. According to Ezekiel, at least two Oromo factions – based in Jimma and Sayyo – appealed to Britain for the establishment of a protectorate over their territories.[231] However, the most organised attempt to escape this doubly imperialist pincer-grip came from an Oromo movement in the west of the country, led by Hambissa Kumsa (christened Habte Mariam Gebre Egziabher) of Leequaa Naqamtee, together with representatives from Qellem, Gidami, Jimma and Beni-Shangul.[232] On 25 May 1936, less

[227] Ahmed Hassan Omer, 'The Italian Impact on Ethnic Relations: A Case Study of a Regional Policy in Northern Shoa (Ethiopia), 1936–1941,' 16 *Annales d'Ethiopie* (2000): 147–59, at 151. Ahmed's arguments are based on extensive interviews with survivors from the 1936–41 period.

[228] Ahmed, 'The Italian Impact on Ethnic Relations', 157–8; Mockler, *Haile Selassie's War*, 121; Ezekiel, 'The Italian Invasion ... and Oromo Nationalism', 76.

[229] Ahmed, 'The Italian Impact on Ethnic Relations', 152. Ahmed also notes, however, that in the chaos of reprisals against guerrilla tactics, Oromo civilians in the area were soon suffering just as much as their Amhara neighbours, causing many former Oromo collaborators to switch sides again, and swelling the ranks of the resistance movement enormously. Ibid., 154–9.

[230] Ezekiel, 'The Italian Invasion ... and Oromo Nationalism', 77.

[231] Ibid., 78, 79. So, indeed, did Haile Selassie himself at a certain point. See George Baer, 'Haile Selassie's Protectorate Appeal to King Edward VIII', 9 *Cahiers d'Études Africaines* (1969): 306–12.

[232] Ezekiel, 'The Italian Invasion ... and Oromo Nationalism', 81.

than three weeks after the Italians had taken Addis Ababa, these rulers, having already ejected most Abyssinian officials from the area, agreed to form the 'Western Oromo Confederation' (WOC). Rather than declare themselves independent and invite the wrath of the Italians, these leaders decided to make a formal request of Britain, asking that the area be placed in trust as a mandated territory under the League of Nations, with Britain as its mandatory power.

As this indicates, the promise of 'provisional recognition' of their 'existence as [an] independent [nation] ... subject to the rendering of administrative advice and assistance by a Mandatory' seemed to offer the leaders of the WOC an escape route from both Abyssinian and fascist domination. These leaders also seem to have been absolutely clear about the kind of internal structures they would need to put in place in order for this self-identification to be taken seriously by other states. Thus, Ezekiel's research reveals that two of these leaders were careful to '[turn] their soldiers away from the French company properties at Youbdo platinum mine ... in order to show their good intentions', and 'did their best to protect local residents and expatriates' from the violence and disorder which accompanied their ejection of the area's former (Amhara) rulers.[233] They also set about organising a 'modern civil administration', first by putting the WOC's own police and army in control;[234] then, on 23 May, by drawing up a list of delegates with 'full power', Habte Mariam wrote, 'to conduct negotiations and to sign treaties with the British Government';[235] and finally by sending out a delegation to the British authorities at the British concession at Gambela, which arrived on 7 June 1936. The Delegation explained to the British District Commissioner that they wished the Western Oromo Confederation 'to be placed under a League of Nations mandate, the mandatory power of which will be exercised by Britain, until such time that the Confederation is ready to exercise full powers of a legitimate sovereign state'.[236] As its spokesmen explained, a British mandate was to be preferred in order to avoid a rupture of the already very important network of commercial relations that had grown up between the region now

[233] Ibid., 82.

[234] Ibid., 83.

[235] Habte Mariam to Captain Maurice, 23 May 1936 (UK Public Records Office, FO 371/20206), cited in ibid., 83. Captain Maurice was district commissioner of the Gambella enclave, a small area surrounding the port and customs station at Gambella, along the Baro (a tributary of the Nile), which Menelik II had granted to the British in a concession agreement of 15 May 1902.

[236] Habte Mariam to Captain Maurice, 23 May 1936, cited in Ezekiel, 'The Italian Invasion ... and Oromo Nationalism', 84.

claimed as the territory of the WOC and Anglo-Egyptian Sudan. At the same time, they explained, an international mandate directly under the League (as had been proposed for Ethiopia as a whole) would be likely to include Italians among its personnel and was therefore 'bound to prevent good governance and derail their ultimate goal of self-government'.[237]

Three days later, the leaders of the Western Oromo Confederation sent a formal letter to Anthony Eden, then the British Foreign Secretary, which read:

> At this critical moment of its existence pe [*sic*] people of Western gallas [*sic*] are faced with a problem of pulling itself out of the unfortunate circumstance in which it finds itself and for which it is in no way responsible. With this object in view they have formed a confederation under the le [*sic*] leadership of His Excellency Dejasmatch Habte Mariam to bring their cause before the bar of world public opinion. And they are confident to obtain justice with the help of Your Government. His Excellency Dajasmatch Habte Mariam is now busy in organizing civil administration. He has so far set up Health Office, Financial and Commercial Department, Political and Foreign Relations Department, Army and Police Department, and a Comunication [*sic*] Department.[238]

The efforts of the Western Oromo Confederation, however, were in vain. Eden, in a letter to the Secretary-General in September, did make note of the fact that he had received a petition sent by 'certain Galla chieftains', as he put it.[239] However, he explained (to the Secretary-General; not to the leaders of the Western Oromo Confederation) that Britain had declined to accept the invitation to take on 'Western Abyssinia' on the grounds that, '[a]s is well known ... the whole policy of His Majesty's Government in the Italo-Abyssinian question has been to fulfil the obligations of the United Kingdom as a Member of the League of Nations without seeking, or seeming to seek, any advantage for themselves'. What Britain *had* done in response to these communications, Eden reported, was to appoint a new British consular agent in the area 'with the duty of protecting foreigners'.[240] In spite of the evidence presented to Eden that the WOC had explicitly self-identified as a 'self-governing' state, then, it seems that race here was functioning – once again – as a stand-in. It seems, moreover, that

[237] Ibid., 83, citing notes, held in the National Archives, from a meeting at Gambella, 8 June 1926, PRO, FO 371/20206, 84.

[238] Yilma Deressa to Secretary of State for Foreign Affairs Anthony Eden, 11 June 1936, PRO, FO 371/20206, cited in Ibid., 85.

[239] 'Letter from the United Kingdom Delegation to the Secretary General', Geneva, 26 September 1936, *LNOJ* (December 1936): 1408.

[240] 'Letter from the United Kingdom Delegation to the Secretary General', 1408.

it was on the basis of this stand-in that Eden felt himself to be at liberty to pre-judge the Confederation's (in)capacity to offer 'effective' protection (protection, that is, that would be *more* 'effective' than Italy's) for 'foreigners' in the area and their rights.

The project for a Western Oromo Confederation presented as a self-governing state-in-waiting was, then, stillborn. Nonetheless, the fact that it was even attempted offers further evidence of the far-reaching interpellative 'pull' of the idea of 'free' and 'equal' legal subjectivity on both a 'macro' and a 'micro' scale. Just as the Ethiopian Empire had gradually come to self-identify as a sovereign state during the late nineteenth and early twentieth centuries, so, it seems, this group of Oromo leaders and communities developed a similar 'voluntary' response to a situation which offered no other viable way out. Aware that, in the absence of international recognition, any declaration of independence could only be counter-productive, with their own normative and institutional structures already in ruins thanks to many years of Abyssinian imperialism, and face-to-face with a highly militarised fascist power, those Oromo leaders laid out their aspirations almost exactly as the Committee of Five had laid out its plans to reform the self-governing credentials of Ethiopia as a whole. Making sure that their commitment to protecting the lives, liberty and property of foreigners was seen to be in earnest, they articulated their normative commitments in terms of a treaty and, in accordance with Article 22 of the Covenant, asked for the temporary assistance of Britain and the League in meeting this goal. Eden, however, with the Maffey Report's pessimistic assessment of the potential for development of Ethiopia's resources and markets still fresh in his mind,[241] seems barely to have given this invitation a second glance.

3 Conclusion

By the device of taking a series of historical x-ray images of the Crisis and its genesis at certain key moment and laying those images one on top of the other, this chapter has put forward an international legal history of the so-called Abyssinian Crisis which is quite different from the standard account discussed in Item 1. This (ac)cumulative process has shown, especially when these x-rays are examined alongside Items 4 and 5, to assume that international law was straightforwardly violated when one sovereign equal (the Ethiopian Empire) was invaded by another (fascist Italy) is to oversimplify

[241] See above, Section 1.2.

Figure 10 Archie Moore, *Blood Fraction*, 2015, one hundred individually framed pigment UltraChrome ink prints on Epson Archival Matte Paper, each 28 x 22.8 x 3.4 cm (framed) overall installed dimension 325 x 275 x 3.4 cm, edition 3 + 1 AP. Collections: edition 1/3, National Gallery of Australia. Photo: Jessica Maurer. Image courtesy of The Commercial, Sydney, by kind permission of the artist.

the international legal situation considerably. For as Items 4, 5 and 6 have now demonstrated, the Ethiopian Empire possessed a form of subjectivity under international law that was, as I have characterised it, hybrid – that was sovereign in some contexts, and less-than-sovereign in others. The Abyssinia Crisis therefore cannot function convincingly as a textbook example of what happens when 'good' international law allows itself to be tragically overcome by 'bad' power politics. Instead, the international legal history of the Crisis points us towards the rather alarming possibility that the annexation was just as 'legal' as it was 'illegal'. My intention in pointing this out is not to condone the invasion, or to apologise for the truly horrifying nature of its conduct. It is, instead, to draw attention to the way in which the norms and institutions of international law contributed to the events and justifications which led to Ethiopia's soon-to-be-recognised annexation by Italy.

When read as a self-contained piece of research, this chapter can be understood as offering quite a standard 'critical legal history' of the Crisis – one which reveals that international law was, in this episode, 'part of the problem' rather than 'part of the solution'.[242] In particular, this chapter has underlined how unique the Ethiopian Empire was, and how its particular history, culture, economy and set of political challenges came to be built into its 'personality' as a subject of international law in a way that renders standard assumptions about the functioning of its 'equal' status inaccurate. There is, however, another way of reading the conclusions of this chapter, and that is as a sixth 'item' stacked into the shadow-box this book has attempted to construct. Observing the Crisis at long range rather than at close range, in this way, suggests that while the Ethiopian Empire's idiosyncrasies are certainly a crucial part of the story, another equally important part of it concerns the similarities or affinities which its experience bears when viewed in relation to certain other, seemingly unrelated episodes drawn from the history of the sovereign state and its expansion. Held in place by the theoretical Frame constructed at the start, the pattern of *correspondances* that is revealed by this process offers us one way of responding to the question of 'structural bias'.[243] Specifically, this pattern encourages us to ask, not what states are, but how such a historically and geographically specific normative apparatus as the sovereign state came to be taken for granted as a neutral space capable of accommodating any number of different visions of human and non-human community.

The observations return us to the issue of the relationship between history and resistance which I raised at the very start of this book. In putting together the Frame, I sought to build into it a series of questions that are

[242] I take this formulation from David Kennedy's famous critique, 'The International Human Rights Movement: Part of the Problem?', 15 *Harvard Human Rights Journal* (2002): 101–26.

[243] Martti Koskenniemi, *From Apology to Utopia: The Structure of International Legal Argument* (Cambridge University Press, 2005), 562–617.

opened up for scholars and practitioners of international law by Benjamin's 'theses on the philosophy of history'. One of these concerned international law's relationship with the violence and inequality that Benjamin associated with 'progress', understood in terms of the progressive widening and deepening of the capitalist economy. This widening and deepening has 'progressed' so far since Benjamin's death in 1940 that, today, almost no pocket of gas inside a mountain, almost no tangerine on a fruit-seller's stall and almost DNA hiding in the cells of a cotton-seed is permitted to remain outside it.[244] Another of these questions concerned the possibility of applying Benjamin's critique of historicist time to the temporality of international law. As suggested in the Frame, Benjamin's description of law's violence as a violence 'crowned by fate' offers us another important instrument with which to tackle the apparent inexorability of 'progress'. It forces us to see how law balances its commitment to the norms of freedom and equality with a willingness to legitimate whatever has come to pass; to 'recognise' whatever *de facto* situation has become 'effective' (as occupied Ethiopia found to its cost).

The point, then, is not that international law oscillates constantly between 'utopia' and 'apology'.[245] The point is, rather, that international law is, structurally, hybrid: it is simultaneously utopian and apologistic. The consequences of this, in material terms, are anything but 'indeterminate'. On the contrary, international law – reproducing its subjects and its normativity in and through the process I have described in this book – in fact formalises a normatively very specific, 'progressive' understanding of the relationship between past and present. Not only does international law *narrate* history as a progress narrative, therefore; it also *causes history to unfold in this catastrophically 'progressive' way* – in a way that systematically transforms things (including humans and their energies) into 'resources' and then redistributes them towards a smaller and smaller fraction of the total number of human beings on the planet. In doing so, this particular, 'progressive' mode of historical unfolding continues to inflict irreversible damage on other humans, species and entities and ways of being and knowing. If this reading is correct, we can understand the violence of the 'secret agreement' which Benjamin posited between past and present generations as precisely that violence of 'progress' which is given material form by law – a violence whose past horrors we, the

[244] See Luis Eslava, Usha Natarajan and Rose Parfitt, '(Post)Revolutionary Interlinkages: Labour, Environment and Accumulation', 4 *Transnational Legal Theory* (2013): 108–25.

[245] See Koskenniemi, *From Apology to Utopia*, 600–16.

'present generation', have an obligation to acknowledge, if not also to redeem. In short, when placed in the shadow-box, the Abyssinia Crisis can, if we let it, become 'the small individual moment' in which we can see 'the crystal of the total event' of international law's ongoing implication in the global maldistribution of wealth, power and pleasure with which the planet is currently struggling.[246] There is, however, still one task left in order to complete the shadow-box – perhaps the most important task of all. That is, of course, the task of working out whether or not the world has changed so much since 1938 as to have rendered the process of international legal reproduction a thing of the past. The final element of the book, then, will attempt that leap – not Benjamin's 'tiger's leap' of historicism, backwards into the unfathomable 'thickets of long ago', but something that will try to approximate what he describes as a 'dialectical leap' in 'the open air of history'[247] – thereby depositing the argument in the 'now' of the early twenty-first century.

[246] Walter Benjamin, *The Arcades Project*, ed. Rolf Tiedemann, trans. Howard Eiland and Kevin McLaughlin (Cambridge, MA: Harvard University Press, 1999), 461.

[247] Walter Benjamin [1940], 'On the Concept of History', in *Walter Benjamin: Selected Writings*, Vol. 4: 1938–1940, ed. Howard Eiland and Michael W. Jennings, trans. Harry John (Cambridge, MA: Harvard University Press, 2003), 389–400, at 395.

Lid: Discipline, Resistance and the Process of International Legal Reproduction Today

Much has changed, in both institutional and material terms, since late 1938 – not least in Ethiopia itself. After five years of struggle, the resistance movement finally forced Italy out of Ethiopia with the help of British troops, after Britain, in the wake of Italy's entry into the Second World War on the German side on June 1940, withdrew the *de jure* recognition it had extended to 'Italian Ethiopia' less than three years earlier. Haile Selassie I was transported back from Bath to Addis Ababa and restored to the throne, and at the end of the War, Ethiopia became one of the founding members of the United Nations.

However, this gradual process of re-recognition and re-constitution as a 'sovereign state' should not be taken as evidence that Ethiopia's core rights and duties as a person of international law had become any less malleable in practice. For example, Britain did not, following Haile Selassie's re-instalment, treat Ethiopia as an Allied state, but instead, in the context of the ongoing War, classified it as 'occupied enemy territory'. This move facilitated Britain's appropriation of virtually all the infrastructure which the Italians had put into the country, which was then transported to nearby British colonies such as Kenya, on the reasoning that Ethiopians were not yet sufficiently 'developed' to make use of it efficiently.[1] Britain concluded a treaty with Ethiopia in 1942, recognising it (again) as a fully independent state, while also providing for the reinforcement of extraterritorial jurisdiction,[2] for British 'advisors' to most governmental ministries, and for British control over Ethiopia's currency and international trade as well as over the territories of Ogaden, the Djibouti–Addis

[1] See esp. Richard Pankhurst, 'Post-World War II Ethiopia: British military policy and action for the dismantling and acquisition of Italian factories and other assets, 1941–2,' 29 *Journal of Ethiopian Studies* (1996): 35–77; Harold G. Marcus, *The Politics of Empire: Ethiopia, Great Britain, and the United States, 1941–1974* (Berkeley, CA: University of California Press, 1983).

[2] See esp. Hailegabriel G. Feyissa, 'European Extraterritoriality in Semicolonial Ethiopia,' 17 *Melbourne Journal of International Law* (2016): 1–28, at 15–20.

Ababa Railway, Haud and elsewhere.[3] As Hailegabriel Feyissa notes, quoting from a British foreign policy paper on Ethiopia of 1941, 'despite acknowledging that the arrangement may be interpreted as envisaging a protectorate-like status for Ethiopia, the British insisted that their policy for Ethiopia was "that it shall be re-established as speedy [*sic*] as possible as a native state under its own ruler, involving [the British government] in a minimum political responsibility and as slight a burden as possible on the British exchequer".'[4] These measures were only partially superseded in a new treaty in 1944,[5] in part because of Haile Selassie's desire for British military support in order to quell a number of troublesome internal rebellions, notably in Woyane in Eastern Tigre and in Ogaden.[6]

Ethiopia, then, having been restored to full independence, retained its hybrid and therefore tractable form of sovereignty, and was still being encountered, narrated and engaged with simultaneously as a 'sovereign equal' *and* as a territory with some weaker set of rights, even after its 'liberation'. This same pattern of legal conditionality, hybridity and malleability continues to be evident throughout Ethiopia's journey since that time, from the increasingly autocratic Haile Selassie regime, to the notoriously oppressive communist regime of the Derg, which seized power in 1974, and on into its current, post-1991 formation as an ethnic federation 'founded on the rule of law and capable of ensuring a lasting peace, guaranteeing a democratic order, and advancing ... economic and social development'.[7] Speaking very generally, two elements in particular of the last eighty years of Ethiopian history stand out. On the one hand, Tsegaye

[3] *Agreement between His Majesty's Government in the United Kingdom and the Emperor of Ethiopia*, Addis Ababa, 31 January 1942. The Ogaden was handed back to Ethiopia only in 1955. See *Agreement between the Government of the United Kingdom of Great Britain and Northern Ireland and the Government of Ethiopia relating to certain matters connected with the withdrawal of British Military Administration from the territories designated as the Reserved Area and the Ogaden*, London, 29 November 1954.

[4] Hailegabriel, 'European Extraterritoriality in Semicolonial Ethiopia', 14.

[5] *Agreement between the United Kingdom and the Ethiopian Empire for the Regulation of Mutual Relations*, Addis Ababa, 19 December 1944.

[6] For example, as Hailegabriel notes, 'although after 1944 Britain no longer required Ethiopia to retain British judges in its courts, the extraterritorial application of British law in Ethiopia did not change a great deal', with British judges continuing to sit 'in its higher courts (including tax appeal commissions) until the 1960s'. Hailegabriel, 'European Extraterritoriality in Semicolonial Ethiopia', 19.

[7] *Constitution of the Federal Democratic Republic of Ethiopia*, Addis Ababa, 8 December 1994, Preamble. See generally Bahru Zewde, *A History of Modern Ethiopia, 1855–1991* (2nd edn Oxford, Athens, OH, Addis Ababa: James Currey, Ohio University Press, Addis Ababa: Addis Ababa University Press, 2002), 228–56.

Ararssa points out that while in 'the *longue durée* of Ethiopian history, the current federal arrangement can be told as a story of the first step in the unbreakable quest for freedom from the bondage of an ethnicized/racialized hierarchy imposed by the Abyssinian Empire on the "other" peoples of Ethiopia', the country's present system of 'authoritarian constitutional rule' means that the federation 'has not delivered the promised emancipation' Abiy Ahmed Ali's recent election as its first Oromo Prime Minister notwithstanding.[8] On the other hand, meanwhile, the fact that land remains (as under the Derg) the 'common property of the Nations, Nationalities and Peoples of Ethiopia' under the 1994 Constitution has not prevented the acquisition of gigantic tracts of Ethiopia's territory by foreign investors.[9] Indeed, as Gashahun Lemessa Fura has pointed out, state ownership of the land has in fact facilitated the government's capacity to offer long-term land leases to foreign companies, allowing local occupants to be easily, and legally, displaced.[10]

The willingness which Ethiopia's post-communist government has shown to open Ethiopia's resources up (again) to foreign investors has transformed the Ethiopian economy from a supposedly hopeless case (as the Maffey Committee saw it in 1935, for example, just as Sir William Cornwallis Harris had done in 1841[11]) into a global success story. According to the World Bank, the country has 'experienced strong, broad-based growth averaging 10.5% a year from 2005/06 to 2015/16, compared to a regional average of 5.4%'.[12] This is understood to be thanks,

[8] Tsegaye Ararssa, 'Ethiopia's Experiment with Federalism: Why it's not South Africa's Apartheid?' (Part I), *Addis Standard*, 29 September 2015, at http://addisstandard.com/ethiopias-experiment-with-federalism-why-its-not-south-africas-apartheid-part-i/. See also Tsegaye, 'The Official Narrative and the Federation to Come', *Addis Standard*, 20 September 2017, at http://addisstandard.com/commentary-ethiopias-experiment-federalism-eyeing-federalism-come/.

[9] *1994 Constitution of Ethiopia*, Art. 40.

[10] See in particular Gashahun Lemessa Fura, 'Transnational Land Acquisitions in Sub-Saharan Africa: Competing Claims and the Role of (International) Law' (PhD thesis, Melbourne Law School, 2017). As the Oakland Institute has documented, '[c]orporations, fund managers, and nations anxious to secure their own future food security have been scouting out and securing large land holdings for offshore farms or just for speculation'. As a result, according to the US-based Oakland Institute, more than 3,619,509 hectares of land were transferred to investors over just three years in the wake of the global financial crisis of 2008, with disastrous environmental and social consequences, not least for those who have been forcibly displaced from their land (Oakland Institute, *Understanding Land Investment Deals in Africa: Ethiopia* (The Oakland Institute, 2011), 3).

[11] See Item 6, Section 1.2; Item 4, Section 2.1.

[12] 'The World Bank in Ethiopia', updated 30 October 2017, at www.worldbank.org/en/country/ethiopia/overview (accessed 15 February 2018).

in particular, to Ethiopia's widely applauded implementation of a host (to quote the United States Department of State's Bureau of Economic and Business Affairs) of 'incentives for international investors' such as: '1) facilitation of repatriation of investment and profit, 2) ease in hiring expatriate personnel, [and] 3) temporary income tax exemptions for investments in selected sectors'.[13] Over the last decade, Ethiopia has also become a key regional ally in the global 'war on terror', with the United States, for example, giving it a 'green light and logistical support' in its 2006 invasion of neighbouring Somalia (seen as a haven for Islamic terrorists), in return for the use of its prisons as black holes into which terror subjects could be 'rendered', interrogated and possibly tortured.[14] Ethiopia's post-Cold War experience, in other words, has been very different from that of certain other, more recalcitrant Third World states whose still partially planned economies have recently been forcibly 'liberalised' on the back of armed interventions ostensibly carried out for other reasons, including self-defence and the protection of human rights. Here Iraq,[15] and Libya[16] are of course two of the most extreme examples. In the Ethiopian context,

[13] US Bureau of Economic and Business Affairs, *2017 Investment Climate Statements – Ethiopia*, 29 June 2017, at www.state.gov/e/eb/rls/othr/ics/2017/af/269733.htm (accessed 15 February 2018).

[14] See e.g. Christopher Thompson, 'Africa's Secret Prisons', *New Statesman*, 21 May 2007, at www.newstatesman.com/society/2007/05/ethiopia-rights-somalia (accessed 21 December 2017).

[15] Konstantina Tzouvala, 'Letters of Blood and Fire: A Socio-Economic History of International Law' (PhD thesis, Durham University, 2016), 190, and more generally 184–219. See also Kerry Rittich, 'Occupied Iraq: Imperial Convergences?', 31, *Leiden Journal of International Law* (2018): 479–508 and Matilda Arvidsson, 'The Subject in International Law: The Administrator of the Coalition Provisional Authority of Occupied Iraq and its Laws' (PhD thesis, University of Lund, 2016). As is well known, the 2003 invasion of Iraq was justified primarily on the basis of self-defence and/or on the grounds that existing Security Council Resolutions, passed under Chapter VII of the UN Charter, had already authorised the use of force. However, behind these arguments the need to protect the 'human rights' of individual Iraqis was continually invoked. Note, for example, British Prime Minister Tony Blair's effort to convince the House of Commons that the use of force was justified. The use of force, he insisted, was necessary to give 'the future government of Iraq ... the chance to begin the process of uniting the nation's disparate groups, on a democratic basis, respecting human rights'. Tony Blair, Speech to the House of Commons, 19 March 2003, *The Guardian*, at www.theguardian.com/politics/2003/mar/18/foreignpolicy.iraq1 (accessed 17 February 2018). For a brilliant analysis, see Charlotte Peevers, *The Politics of Justifying Force: The Suez Crisis, the Iraq War, and International Law* (Oxford University Press, 2014).

[16] On the neo-liberalising objectives of the 2011 NATO invervention, see Adam Hanieh, *Lineages of Revolt: Issues of Contemporary Capitalism in the Middle East* (Chicago, IL: Haymarket Books, 2013), 431.

however, a long series of ongoing and violently suppressed uprisings among the Oromo, in particular, as well as other ethnic groups excluded by the now Tigrayan-dominated government, has not elicited any desire among the more 'successful' members of the international community to use military force for the ostensible purpose of 'protecting' these communities from their government. On the contrary, even as human rights organisations continued to express grave concerns about the Ethiopian Government's propensity for authoritarianism and violence,[17] Barak Obama became the first American president ever to visit Ethiopia in 2016, when he praised the country for its contribution to the struggle against Al Shabab, and for its high rates of economic growth.[18] Meanwhile, aid and 'development' funding continues to pour into the country, with Ethiopia currently one of the top five global aid recipients, obtaining $1,984 billion in 2016, more than any other African state.[19] While this aid is designed to serve a variety of different purposes, prominent among them is the aim of 'fortify[ing] the rule of law throughout the country' so as to encourage 'human rights-based economic development'.[20]

As Ethiopia's recent experience suggests, then – particularly when compared with that of 'rogue states' like Iraq, Libya, Afghanistan and others – the 'human rights' which have, typically, been 'protected' by the international 'military and monetary interventions' of the last few years have not,[21] generally speaking, been the kinds of rights one might intuitively associate with the impulse to end the hardship of local individuals and communities suffering 'atrocities' at the hands of their governments,[22] such as rights to medical care, housing, food or a minimum income, for example. Individual rights certainly have been given much stronger legal protections, with strong encouragement from the world's most powerful states and from major international institutions. However, the narrow range

[17] See e.g. Human Rights Watch, *Ethiopia: Country Report, 2016*, at www.hrw.org/world-report/2017/country-chapters/ethiopia (accessed 15 February 2018).

[18] 'Obama praises Ethiopia over fight against al-Shabab', *BBC News*, 27 July 2015, at www.bbc.com/news/world-africa-33671340 (accessed 15 February 2018).

[19] Statistics from the Organisation for Economic Co-operation and Development, at https://public.tableau.com/views/AidAtAGlance/DACmembers?:embed=yand:display_count=no?and:showVizHome=no#1 (accessed 15 February 2018).

[20] 'Our Projects: Ethiopia', Irish Rule of Law International, funded by Irish Aid, at http://irishruleoflaw.ie/our-projects/ethiopia/ (accessed 15 February 2018).

[21] See Anne Orford, 'Locating the International: Military and Monetary Interventions after the Cold War', 38 *HIJL* (1997): 443–85.

[22] Ban Ki-Moon, *A Vital and Enduring Commitment: Implementing the Responsibility to Protect*, Report of the UN Secretary-General, GA/SC Res. A /69/981–S /2015/500, 13 July 2015, 1–2.

of internationally protected individual rights in question maps quite precisely onto the equally narrow range of individual rights which the Ethiopian Government has, arguably, been protecting – on the part of Ethiopian entrepreneurs and foreign investors in particular. These rights are, for the most part, limited to stronger property rights, protections for equality before the law, rights to trade freely, and so on – that is, to the suite of core rights which this book associates (following Pashukanis and Edelman) with legal subjectivity.[23] These are the rights which make it possible for 'citizens of the world' (as Karen Knop calls them),[24] including wealthy and mobile members of the local elite in 'developing countries', to appropriate local resources and transform them into personal capital, leaving the majority in the same predicament in which they began, if not worse. In a pattern we have already seen repeated many times, then, what seems to matter when it comes to the resilience of the territorial 'sovereignty' of a state such as Ethiopia is not so much the physical and psychological suffering of its citizens as its commitment to protecting a 'level playing field' which those citizens may or may not have the resources to access, but upon which all 'citizens of the world' are welcome to compete.

Nonetheless, even if this very brief overview of Ethiopia's tumultuous recent history reveals a familiar pattern, in which the durability of *international* legal subjectivity still seems to be connected to the protection and extension of *individual* legal subjectivity, the question remains as to whether this connection holds more generally. After all, and as noted at the start of this chapter, the changes which the world has been undergoing since the end of the Second World War are immense. Beginning with the institutional changes, quite apart from the imminent fall of fascism (as an official state ideology at least), communist rule was consolidated not only in the USSR but across a large portion of the globe before it collapsed in 1989, or came to be modified significantly, in all but a few states.[25] Meanwhile, over the 1950s, 1960s and 1970s, formal European colonial rule was finally shaken off after nearly half a millennium of expansion

[23] See esp. Orford, 'Locating the International'; Orford, *Reading Humanitarian Intervention: Human Rights and the Use of Force in International Law* (Cambridge University Press, 2003); Susan Marks, *The Riddle of All Constitutions: International Law, Democracy, and the Critique of Ideology* (Oxford University Press, 2010).

[24] Karen Knop, 'Lorimer's Private Citizens of the World', 27 *EJIL* (2016): 447–75. On Lorimer, see above, Item 2, Section 2.3.1.

[25] It is, of course, as ridiculous to deal with the history of the rise and fall of communism in once sentence as it is to deal so briefly with the rise and fall of fascism or colonialism. For an outstanding legal history of the 'Soviet world', however, see Scott Newton, *Law and the Making of the Soviet World: The Red Demiurge* (Abingdon: Routledge, 2015).

and consolidation. Nonetheless, one of the most interesting and peculiar things about this infinitely variegated and truly global series of institutional transformations is how consistent their outcome has been – namely 'sovereign statehood', along 'self-governing' lines.[26]

Equally momentous changes have, of course, been taking place in the material sphere over the same timespan. Indeed, according to the climate scientist Will Steffen, this period has 'without doubt seen the most rapid transformation of the human relationship with the natural world in the history of humankind'.[27] Today's economy is fuelled by depleted stocks of oil and gas, rather than by apparently unlimited supplies of coal, as in the inter-war period. It relies increasingly on digital rather than physical forms of information and communication. Its population is increasingly urban, exists on an increasingly meat- rather than plant-based diet, and travels increasingly by car and plane rather than on horse, boat or foot. The world's weapons are far more widely dispersed and powerful, from the assault rifle to the hydrogen bomb, with the long-term consequences of using nuclear weapons and nuclear power still to be fully calculated. Together, these shifts have given rise to what Steffen and others refer to as the 'great acceleration' – a term developed to describe 'the holistic, comprehensive and interlinked nature' of changes that have 'been simultaneously sweeping across the socio-economic and biophysical spheres of the Earth System' since the 1950s, with massive population growth, foreign direct investment, water use and fertiliser consumption mapped in direct correlation, for example, onto global warming, increasing ocean acidification, marine fish capture, terrestrial biosphere degradation and other indicators.[28] One result is that the world's non-human species are dying out at a rate unseen since the extinction of the dinosaurs.[29] Humans, for their part, may be living longer and, on average, becoming wealthier, but

[26] The most significant of these is the Antarctic, although territorial claims are increasingly being made here too. See e.g. Matthew Teller, 'Why Do So Many Nations Want a Piece of Antarctica?', *BBC News*, 20 June 2014, at www.bbc.com/news/magazine-27910375 (accessed 15 February 2018).

[27] See also Will Steffen, Regina Angelina Sanderson, Peter D. Tyson, Jill Jäger, Pamela A. Matson, Berrien Moore III, Frank Oldfield, Katherine Richardson, Hans-Joachim Schellnhuber, Billie L. Turner and Robert J. Wasson, *Global Change and the Earth System: A Planet Under Pressure* (Berlin, Heidelberg, New York: Springer-Verlag, 2004), 131.

[28] Will Steffen, Wendy Broadgate, Lisa Deutsch, Owen Gaffney and Cornelia Ludwig, 'The Trajectory of the Anthropocene: The Great Acceleration', 2 *Anthropocene Review* (2015): 81–98, at 82.

[29] 'The Extinction Crisis', Centre for Biological Diversity, at www.biologicaldiversity.org/programs/biodiversity/elements_of_biodiversity/extinction_crisis/ (accessed 6 October 2017).

human societies are becoming increasingly unequal.[30] Partly as a result of these changes, the human world today is experiencing perhaps its most intense set of interlocking crises since the late 1930s, including uprisings and armed conflicts that have engulfed not only Ethiopia, but much of the Middle East, North Africa, much of Asia and elsewhere over the past decade, as well as the global escalation in refugee flows, the re-emergence of far-right nationalism in mainstream European, North American and Asian politics, the growing frequency and scale of terrorist attacks launched by white supremacists, jihadist groups and others, the ongoing economic fallout from the 2008 global financial crisis, and far beyond.

The question this final chapter sets out to answer is what the relationship between these two sets of changes, institutional and material, might be, and specifically whether the idea of international legal reproduction might offer a useful framework when it comes to making sense of that relationship. I explore this question in three stages. Section 1 looks in more detail at some of the connections between the institutional and material changes just described, and at some of the debates that have emerged in response to them. Section 2 embarks on a rapid journey through the international legal history of the past eight decades to argue that the process of international legal reproduction does offer a useful critical lens through which to examine the major changes and continuities of this period. Finally, Section 3 turns to the question of resistance. Specifically, it engages the theory and practice of a crucially important front line in the 500-year-old battle against the transformations mandated and/or triggered by the process of international legal reproduction – namely the struggle of Indigenous peoples all over the world for self-determination on Indigenous terms. In making this gesture towards Indigenous ontological, epistemological and normative thought and practice, I am not seeking to 'tap into' Indigenous understandings of law and subjectivity as though these were yet another set of pristine natural resources which could and should be mined out and then exported for consumption on the global market.[31] Instead, what Section 3 will attempt to do is to juxtapose

[30] For an overview, see https://inequality.org/facts/global-inequality/ (accessed 15 February 2018).

[31] This idea of 'tapping into' Indigenous knowledge for the purpose of 'development' and 'sustainability' is, indeed, already firmly on the agenda of the 'international community' (see e.g. Douglas Nakashima, Lyndel Prott and Peter Bridgewater, 'Tapping into the World's Wisdom', 125 *UNESCO Sources* (2000): 11–12; World Bank, *Indigenous Knowledge for Development: A Framework for Action* (Washington, DC: World Bank Group, 1998), at http://documents.worldbank.org/curated/en/388381468741607213/pdf/multi-page.pdf (accessed 20 January 2018)), and the risk of commodification is already being

certain elements of the Indigenous struggle, as narrated and interpreted by Indigenous scholars and activists, against some of the book's earlier fragments from the history of the emergence and consolidation of the state system, with the aim of creating a space in which certain affinities might – or might not – jump out.

Given its function in relationship to the other elements of this book, I have suggested that it might be more helpful to think of this chapter as the lid of the shadow-box, rather than as a conclusion per se. Like the lid of any shadow-box, made of some transparent material like glass or Perspex, its aim is to give its viewers access to the box's contents, allowing them in this way to view what they find in there, and the relationship between its different components, from various different angles. Equally, and again like any lid of this kind, its purpose is to protect the components inside the box and in doing so to remind spectators of their material separateness (in both time and space) from what they see inside. In the case of *this* shadow-box, however, the lid is designed to be lifted, so that observers can move the elements they find in there around, fill in the gaps they find with items of their own, and play around with the contents of the box as they please. It is in this sense that the history I have presented in this book should be understood as modular, in the sense that it amounts – and can only amount – to a series of fragments of different pasts. They might have been arranged in a certain formation here, but there is no reason why that ordering should remain fixed. On the contrary, these fragments can and should be assembled and reassembled in any number of different ways.

1 Change and Continuity in the Institutional and Material Worlds

Many scholars of international law and international relations in the post-Cold War period have drawn attention to the fact that it is not just statehood that has come to be universalised over the past thirty years, but also a particular type of government. During the Cold War, this was usually referred to as 'democracy'. Now, the supposedly more technical and hence more neutral term 'governance' is more commonly used. If we turn, however, to the World Bank's 'Worldwide Governance Indicators' (WGI) project, established in 1996 to monitor the 'progress' of 'more than

realised – most obviously, perhaps, in relation to seeds and plant varieties in the biocultural sphere, as Rajshree Chandra has shown (Rajshree Chandra, *The Cunning of Rights: Law, Life, Biocultures* (Oxford University Press, 2016)).

200 countries' towards 'good governance', we find, as Jothie Rajah has demonstrated, that the term is in a normative sense far from neutral.[32] According to the Bank's definition, 'governance' refers to 'the traditions and institutions by which authority in a country is exercised'. Ecumenical as this definition may be in principle, the Bank regards only six 'traditions and institutions' as legitimate. These are: 'voice and accountability' (defined as 'the extent to which a country's citizens are able to participate in selecting their government'); 'political stability and the absence of violence'; 'governmental effectiveness'; 'regulatory quality' ('the ability of the government to formulate and implement sound policies and regulations that permit and promote private sector development'); 'rule of law' ('the extent to which agents have confidence in and abide by ... the quality of contract enforcement, property rights, the police, and the courts'); and 'control of corruption' (that is, control of 'the extent to which public power is exercised for private gain ... as well as "capture" of the state by elites and private interests').[33]

As the very existence of the WGI project suggests, the vast majority of the world's states are regarded by international institutions like the Bank, the UN and the European Union (and by the aid programmes of powerful states[34]) as being either 'well governed' or in the process of being internationally 'assisted' to become 'better governed' – often in conjunction with intensive 'development', 'statebuilding', 'peacekeeping' and other programmes.[35] That 'good governance' is understood, by the international institutions which fund and monitor progress towards it, as the opposite of – indeed, the antidote to – institutional systems which are dedicated to the redistribution of wealth is also explicit. On the Bank's 'The World Bank in Vietnam' webpage, for example, the strapline reads: 'Vietnam's shift from a centrally planned to a market economy has

[32] See, in particular, Jothie Rajah, '"Rule of Law" as Transnational Legal Order', in Terence C. Halliday and Gregory Shaffer (eds.), *Transnational Legal Orders* (Cambridge University Press, 2015), 340–73.

[33] World Bank, 'Worldwide Governance Indicators' (WGI) Project, at http://info.worldbank.org/governance/wgi/#doc (accessed 26 December 2017).

[34] See e.g. the UK Government's 'Good Governance Fund', established in 2015, to 'support a series of governance and economic reform initiatives ... in Ukraine, Georgia, Moldova, Serbia and Bosnia and Herzegovina' by offering funding for 'technical assistance' in areas including 'anti-corruption; improving the business environment; judicial reform; key sector reforms (e.g. banking and energy); strengthening the rule of law; and supporting an independent media'. See https://devtracker.dfid.gov.uk/projects/GB-1-205093 (accessed 27 January 2018).

[35] See Section 2, below.

transformed the country from one of the poorest in the world into a lower middle-income country' making 'Vietnam now ... one of the most dynamic emerging countries in the East Asia region.'[36] Similarly, in Ethiopia, where, as we saw above, state ownership in land is still enshrined in the constitution, World Bank economists worry that 'with a rapidly growing population, the pressure for land redistribution remains high in many areas of the country', with negative effects on investment and 'capital accumulation'.[37] The conclusion they draw is that 'the institutions of property rights matter for efficiency, investment and growth'.[38]

For supporters of developments like those taking place in Vietnam, Ethiopia and elsewhere, the recent institutional history of such states represents incontestable evidence that the world is steadily moving away from colonialism and totalitarianism towards ever-greater individual 'freedom' and 'equality' – a move that is narrated as indisputably progressive.[39] This perspective, both in its neoliberal manifestation (focused on straightforward privatisation, liberalisation and deregulation) and in its recent, ostensibly post-neoliberal manifestation (focused on correcting 'market failures' and achieving 'sustainability'), blames a particular kind of state, with a particular set of ('bad') norms and institutions, for the world's problems.[40] In this way, the 'good governance' framework is predicated firmly on ensuring not that state power should be reduced *per se*, but that it should be restricted to the performance of a limited but crucial set of tasks – namely, as Honor Brabazon puts it, 'facilitating market transactions through particular legal institutions, such as securing property rights and ensuring the enforcement of contractual obligations'.[41] 'Good governance'

[36] See www.worldbank.org/en/country/vietnam (accessed 17 January 2018).

[37] Daniel Ayalew, Ali Stefan Dercon and Madhur Gautam, 'Property Rights in a Very Poor Country: Tenure Insecurity and Investment in Ethiopia', *World Bank Policy Research Working Paper 4363* (Washington, DC: World Bank, 2007), available at http://documents.worldbank.org/curated/en/351491468036358289/pdf/WPS4363.pdf (accessed 17 January 2018), 2–3.

[38] Ibid., 24.

[39] See, perhaps most notoriously, Francis Fukuyama, *The End of History and the Last Man* (New York: Free Press, 1992). In the international legal sphere, see, most famously, Thomas M. Franck, 'The Emerging Right to Democratic Governance', 86 *American Journal of International Law* (1992): 46–91.

[40] For a good example from the Ethiopian context see e.g. Helen Epstein, 'Cruel Ethiopia', *The New York Review of Books*, 13 May 2010, at www.nybooks.com/articles/2010/05/13/cruel-ethiopia/.

[41] Honor Brabazon, 'Introduction: Understanding Neoliberal Legality', in Brabazon (ed.), *Neoliberal Legality: Understanding the Role of Law in the Neoliberal Project* (New York: Routledge, 2016), 1–20, at 5.

therefore excludes any but the most minimal role for the state in equalising resources, for instance by guaranteeing social rights such as the right to education, land, work, housing, social security, healthcare and so on. Instead, governance is 'good' when the state restricts its role to that of protecting a vision of the 'rule of law' which endows all individuals with the same limited set of formal rights (to private property, freedom of contract and trade, etc.), and in doing so provides a framework of 'equality of opportunity' within which they can (and must) compete against one another for resources. This 'ability to pursue individual self-interest through autonomous market transactions' is understood and celebrated, moreover, as the institutional epitome of 'freedom'.[42] This post-Cold War consensus regarding the need to restrict the power of the state has led some international institutions and academics to suggest that because 'good governance' (with its emphasis on the 'rule of law') is already being implemented more effectively by international institutions and local jurisdictions, the state is itself becoming an anachronism.[43]

By contrast, critics of these developments, like Susan Marks, Anne Orford, James Gathii and Luis Eslava, among others, insist that democracy cannot be reduced to 'good governance'. As their work shows, while using the word 'democracy' to describe these changes suggests that the world's states are becoming more responsive to their populations' needs and concerns, the institutions associated with 'good governance' and the 'rule of law' are in fact aimed at making states more responsive to the needs and concerns of international capital by reducing costs, augmenting profits and strengthening the rationale for further international interventions.[44] As Susan Marks argued, for example, 'good governance' or 'low-intensity democracy', as she calls it,

> is linked, on the one hand, to the goal of stabilizing existing positions in the global distribution of power and resources. It meets the immediate needs of anti-authoritarian crisis, easing tensions, and restoring order. Yet it does so in a manner that forestalls far-reaching structural change in peripheral and semi-peripheral regions. Thus, the concentration in these regions of relatively low wage, low profit, less monopolized economic activities is not endangered. On the other hand, low intensity democracy is linked as well to the project of expanding the reach of global markets

[42] Brabazon, 'Introduction', 3.

[43] See e.g. the World Bank's recent emphasis on 'resilient cities', at www.worldbank.org/en/results/2017/12/01/resilient-cities and on 'competitive cities' as a 'local solution to a global lack of growth and jobs', at www.worldbank.org/en/topic/trade/publication/competitive-cities-a-local-solution-to-a-global-lack-of-growth-and-jobs (accessed 17 January 2018).

[44] Marks, *The Riddle of All Constitutions*, 56–7.

> and eliminating remaining barriers to the transnationalization of capital. It facilitates the penetration and consolidation of capitalist relations of production in peripheral and semi-peripheral regions. Policies of economic liberalization, structural adjustment, exchange deregulation, and so on have greater legitimacy when pursued by elected governments than when imposed by unelected regimes.[45]

This kind of 'democracy', Marks concludes, constitutes a legal and institutional structure within which capitalism becomes the only possible way of organising social and economic relationships, and in fact 'differs little in substance from authoritarian rule'.[46]

Similarly, James Gathii, in a searing critique, pointed out in 1999 that the main function of the 'good governance' strategy was to wrap the World Bank's 'stigmatization of protective governmental interventions in the economy as necessarily inimical to economic growth and freedom' in a legitimising cloak of 'democracy' and 'human rights' rhetoric.[47] It is not just that the 'human rights' in question are restricted to those viewed as 'compatible or consistent' with this 'financial and economic mandate'; in colonising the language of democracy and human rights, the 'good governance' agenda also empties these concepts of their critical and emancipatory potential, and should therefore be understood as a counter-insurgency strategy on the part of the international institutions deployed against 'oppositional and transformative social projects'.[48]

Attending to a different aspect of this problem, in 1997 Orford drew attention to the connection between the economic and political priorities of international institutions like the UN, the World Bank, the International Monetary Fund and the World Trade Organization. As she argued, 'the increased trade and financial liberalization enabled by newly effective international economic institutions' and the 'expansion of the United Nations collective security', employed as 'a means for the liberal alliance of democratic states to bring human rights, democracy, and humanitarian principles to those in undemocratic or failed states', are widely understood as 'the two most significant changes in international politics resulting from the break-up of the Soviet Union'.[49] Yet 'the extent

[45] Ibid., 56–7.

[46] Ibid., 61.

[47] James T. Gathii, 'Good Governance as a Counterinsurgency Agenda to Oppositional and Transformative Social Projects in International Law', 5 *Buffalo Human Rights Law Review* (1999): 107–73, at 108, 163.

[48] Ibid.

[49] Orford, 'Locating the International', 443.

to which the activities of international institutions' have contributed to the many crises of the post-Cold War period, which the 'expanded collective security system' has then been called upon to resolve, continues to be drastically underestimated.[50]

In the intervening two decades, the 'good governance' project has shifted somewhat – though more in terms of the focus of its attention than the substance of its message. As Luis Eslava has pointed out much more recently, for example, the 'good governance' agenda is closely linked to processes of privatisation, liberalisation, deregulation and decentralisation, leading to a new emphasis on cities and other local jurisdictions, as opposed to states and national economies as before. However, this should not be taken as signalling the beginning of the end for the state, either as a political unit or as a subject of international law. Drawing on the work of Neil Brenner,[51] Stuart Elden,[52] Yishai Blank[53] and others, Eslava points out that the '[c]urrent international interest in the locality ... does not imply the disappearance of the nation-state, or that the social, economic and political lives of localities are freed from their territorial preconditions'.[54] Instead, what is taking place today is a 'reterritorialization of socioeconomic and political-institutional spaces', a reassignment of functions from the 'national' to the 'local' level, and a 'proliferation of levels of governance' and jurisdictional formations, from the 'free trade zone' to the 'global city' to the 'industrial park', which reorder the relationship between global, national and local, and between the public and the private.[55] The aim is to 'solidify instances of firm (yet flexible, in relation to market forces) sovereign control across Third World nations – places where development success can be attributed to the alignment of local, national and international aspirations'.[56]

Building on this body of work, the next section brings these arguments into conversation with the 'dynamic' or 'logic' of conditionality that I have sought to draw attention to in the earlier parts of this book.[57] In particular,

[50] Ibid.

[51] Neil Brenner, *New State Spaces: Urban Governance and the Rescaling of Statehood* (Oxford University Press, 2004).

[52] Stuart Elden, 'Missing the Point: Globalization, Deterritorialization and the Space of the World', 30 *Transactions of the Institute of British Geographers* (2005): 8–19.

[53] Yishai Blank, 'Localism in the New Global Legal Order', 47 *HIJL* (2006): 263–81.

[54] Luis Eslava, *Local Space, Global Life: The Everyday Operation of International Law and Development* (Cambridge University Press, 2015), 15.

[55] Eslava, *Local Space, Global Life*, 14–15.

[56] Ibid., 15.

[57] See Stand, above.

it will draw attention to a series of *correspondances* between 'good governance' in the late twentieth/twenty-first-century practice of states on the one hand, and the legal and institutional apparatus that has, historically, been referred to as 'self-government', 'effective' government, 'responsible' government, or, quite simply, as 'government', on the other. This suggests, in turn, that the promotion of 'good governance' by those members of the international community whose 'governments' are, by their own assessment, 'good', is not a new rubric of intervention developed in the post-Cold War period. On the contrary, it has always been available as a means of disciplining those too-obviously hybrid sovereigns which (whether through lack of desire or capacity) have failed to transform themselves fully from 'other' into 'self' in the manner laid down by the purportedly objective Montevideo criteria. The result, as we shall see, has been the creation of an increasingly unequal, increasingly volatile international order in which violence of various kinds is continually being brought to bear on those (humans and non-humans) who/which, historically, have already suffered the most. The end result of this process, in which the compulsory and the voluntary have become impossible to disentangle, is the slow obliteration of other ways of knowing and being in the world.[58]

To bring home this point, we need only recall US Secretary of State Hillary Clinton's 2011 speech to the UN Human Rights Council, discussed at the very start of this book, in the Stand. Clinton argued in that speech that Libya's Muammar Qadhafi government had, through its violation of 'universal rights', 'lost the legitimacy to govern', bestowing on the 'international community' both a right and a duty to use military force to displace it and assist the Libyan people in 'shaping' a 'new government'.[59] This assistance, she declared (over-confidently, as it turned out), would involve building 'strong institutions, including an independent judiciary that promotes the rule of law and helps ensure official accountability and transparency, and stands against corruption'. These, she cautioned, were not 'Western principles or American ideals' but 'truly universal ... lessons learned by people all over the world who have made the difficult transition to sustainable democracy'.[60] A fortnight later, accepting the logic of Clinton's argument, the UN authorised a coalition of NATO

[58] See esp. Arturo Escobar, 'Latin America at a Crossroads: Alternative Modernizations, Post-Liberalism, or Post-Development?', 24 *Cultural Studies* (2010): 1–65, discussed below.

[59] Hillary Clinton, Address to the UN Human Rights Council, New York, 3 March 2011, available at https://geneva.usmission.gov/2011/02/28/sec-clinton-hrc-geneva-2011/ (accessed 16 May 2018).

[60] Clinton, Address to the UN Human Rights Council.

states and allies (Belgium, Bulgaria, Canada, Denmark, France, Greece, Italy, Jordan, the Netherlands, Norway, Qatar, Romania, Spain, Sweden, Turkey, the United Arab Emirates, the UK and the US) to enforce what Orford notes was a 'radical and far-reaching' set of demands placed by the UN on the Qadhafi government and Libyan forces.[61]

As the Frame argued – a point that now, I hope, stands on firm ground – Clinton's rationale for 'Operation Unified Protector' clearly illustrates the material consequences of the conditional relationship this book has posited between individual and international legal subjectivity. If we pay attention to this relationship, I have suggested, it is hardly surprising to discover, simply from a glance at the list of coalition members, that those sovereign equals which either invented the very ideas of 'government', 'statehood', and the 'free' and 'equal' or 'sovereign' legal subject, or embraced them successfully, should be found in the role of international disciplinarians, enforcing other states' protection of 'universal rights', and those states (like Libya) on the receiving end of such disciplinary intervention. Indeed, the very fact that Libya *is* a state, when only a century before – prior to Italy's annexation of Tripolitania, Cyrenaica and the Fezzan from the Ottoman Empire in the Italo-Ottoman War of 1911–12 – there had been no such state, or even any single 'Libya', but rather an extremely complex array of different epistemological, ontological and normative frameworks, linked to an equally complex array of communities, many of them nomadic (including the Bedouin community to which Qadhafi himself belonged), merits consideration. So, too, does the selectiveness with which certain states have been singled out for intervention, whereas equally violent and authoritarian states have not.[62]

In order to understand how we have arrived at such a situation, in which 'all sovereigns are equal', to paraphrase George Orwell, but 'some sovereigns are more equal than others', it is necessary to link this book's argument, concerning the process of international legal reproduction and the hybridity of international personality, in with two bodies of literature in particular. The first of these is being produced by a new generation of Marxist and Marxian scholars of international law,[63] upon which this book

[61] Anne Orford, 'What Kind of Law is This?' *LRB Blog*, 29 March 2011, at www.lrb.co.uk/blog/2011/03/29/anne-orford/what-kind-of-law-is-this/ (accessed 17 January 2018).

[62] On the Middle East and North Africa region, see Hanieh, *Lineages of Revolt*, 443.

[63] See e.g. Grietje Baars, *Law, Capital and the Corporation* (Leiden: Brill, forthcoming, 2018); Honor Brabazon, '*The Master's Tools*': *The Possibilities and Perils of Law-Based Resistance to Neoliberalism* (manuscript under review); Irina Ceric, 'The Sovereign Charter: Security, Territory and the Boundaries of Constitutional Rights', 44 *Ottawa Law Review* (2013):

has already drawn substantially. While its various projects are extremely diverse, one common factor concerns the aim of drawing attention to international law's material dimensions and distributive implications, and to insist on the need to supplement a historiographical emphasis on agency/contingency with an attendance to structure/necessity. The second body of work (not necessarily separate from the first) which, in my view, offers us a very important set of tools in this context, emerges from the debates that are currently ongoing as to the significance of the material changes alluded to above. For many of the strongest voices in this debate, the changes associated with the 'great acceleration' are so significant as to have created a rupture, marking an entirely new geological epoch or 'anthropocene', beginning for many of these theorists just after the Second World War.[64] Critics like Jeremy Baskin, however, have pointed out the idea of the anthropocene 'normalises a certain portion of humanity as the "human" of the Anthropocene, reinserting "man" into nature only to re-elevate "him" above it', making it 'a paradigm dressed

353–40; B. S. Chimni, *International Law and World Order: A Critique of Contemporary Approaches* (2nd edn Cambridge University Press, 2017); Eslava, *Local Space, Global Life*; Michael Fakhri, *Sugar and the Making of International Trade Law* (Cambridge University Press, 2014); Onur Ulas Ince, *Colonial Capitalism and the Dilemmas of Liberalism* (Oxford University Press, 2018); Robert Knox, 'Marxist Approaches to International Law', in Florian Hoffmann and Anne Orford (eds.), *The Oxford Handbook of the Theory of International Law* (Oxford University Press, 2016), 306–26; Tor Krever, 'Law, Development, and Political Closure', in Honor Brabazon (ed.), *Neoliberal Legality: Understanding the Role of Law in the Neoliberal Project* (New York: Routledge, 2016), 22–42; Marks, *The Riddle of All Constitutions*; China Miéville, *Between Equal Rights: A Marxist Theory of International Law* (Leiden, Boston: Brill, 2005); Claire Mummé, 'Property in Labour and the Limits of Contract,' in Ugo Mattei and John Haskell (eds.), *Research Handbook on Political Economy and Law* (Cheltenham, Northampton, MA: Edward Elgar, 2015), 400–21; Umut Özsu, 'From the "Semi-Civilized State" to the "Emerging Market": Remarks on the International Legal History of the Semi-Periphery,' in Ugo Mattei and John Haskell (eds.), *Research Handbook on Political Economy and Law* (Cheltenham, Northampton, MA: Edward Elgar, 2015), 246–59; Nicolás M. Perrone, 'The Emerging Global Right to Investment: Understanding the Reasoning behind Foreign Investor Rights', 8 *Journal of International Dispute Settlement* (2017): 673–94; Akbar Rasulov, 'The Nameless Rapture of the Struggle: Towards a Marxist Class-Theoretic Approach to International Law', 19 *Finnish Yearbook of International Law* (2008): 243–94; Maïa Pal, *Jurisdictional Accumulation: An Early Modern History of Law, Empires and Capital* (Cambridge University Press, forthcoming); Ntina Tzouvala, 'Food for the Global Market: The Neoliberal Reconstruction of Agriculture in Occupied Iraq and the Role of International Law', 17 *Global Jurist* (2016): 1–27; Tzouvala, 'Letters of Blood and Fire'.

[64] The term was first popularised by the Nobel Prize-winning atmospheric chemist Paul J. Crutzon in the early 2000s. See e.g. Paul J. Crutzon, 'Geology of Mankind', 23 *Nature* (2002): 23.

as epoch'.[65] Similarly, the environmental historian/historical geographer Jason Moore and the philosopher and biologist Donna Haraway have pushed back, not against the idea that the changes which are transforming the world's ecosystems stem from the activities of humans,[66] but against the idea that 'man' (*anthropos*), the male of the human species, can be held responsible *per se* for these changes – changes which are caused by women as well as men and which, perhaps more importantly, stem from and impact on different communities at different historical moments very differently. The cause of these changes, they insist, is not 'man', but capitalism – that is, a very particular way of organising the relationship between humans and 'nature'.[67] Or as Haraway puts it, in very much the same spirit as Walter Benjamin, the culprit is our 'dark bewitched commitment to the lure of Progress', which continues to '[lash] us to endless infernal alternatives, as if we had no other ways to reworld, reimagine, relive, and reconnect with each other, in multispecies well being'.[68] For this reason, Haraway, Moore and others prefer the clunkier but, in their view, more accurate term 'capitalocene' (or, a term that Haraway also likes, 'Chthulucene'). Moreover, as they and their colleagues also point out, capitalism did not begin in the 1950s, or even with the industrial revolution (another popular starting date for the Anthropocene),[69] but emerged in tandem with the expansion of the European colonial project.[70]

Bringing these two bodies of literature together, meanwhile, critical international environmental lawyers have been pointing out, increasingly vociferously, that capitalism and colonialism did not sweep across

[65] Jeremy Baskin, 'Paradigm Dressed as Epoch: The Ideology of the Anthropocene', 24 *Environmental Values* (2015): 9–29, at 9.

[66] See e.g. Steffen et al., *Global Change and the Earth System*.

[67] See e.g. Jason W. Moore, *Capitalism in the Web of Life* (New York: Verso, 2015).

[68] Donna J. Haraway, 'Staying with the Trouble: Anthropocene, Capitalocene, Chthulucene', in Jason W. Moore (ed.), *Anthropocene or Capitalocene? Nature, History, and the Crisis of Capitalism* (Oakland, CA: PM Press, 2016), 32–76, at 54.

[69] See e.g. Crutzon, 'Geology of Mankind', 23.

[70] See e.g. the work of anthropologist Kent Lightfoot who, among others, argues on the basis of archaeological and palaeo-ecological evidence collected on the west coast of the US that early European colonialism 'driven by profit making incentives to exploit lucrative resources and to raise cash crops for world markets' resulted in 'fundamental transformations in both temperate and tropical ecosystems on a global scale well before the advent of full-scale industrialism in the 1800s'. In short, he concludes that 'these human modifications to marine, estuarine, and terrestrial ecosystems in pre-colonial and colonial times signal an early chronology for the Anthropocene' beginning in the late 1400s/early 1500s. Kent G. Lightfoot, Lee M. Panich, Tsim D. Schneider and Sara L. Gonzalez, 'European Colonialism and the Anthropocene: A View from the Pacific Coast of North America', 4 *Anthropocene* (2013): 101–15, at 113.

the world of their own accord, but did so in conjunction with the emergence and expansion of the state, of law (in the Western sense) and of international law.[71] Thus, as Usha Natarajan argues in a ground-breaking article co-authored with Kishan Khoday, the manifest failure of the many multilateral environmental agreements of the last few decades to halt or even slow the rapid pace of environmental deterioration cannot be put down simply to an absence of political will. At the same time, far from offering a solution to the catastrophic breakdown in the planet's ecosystems, international law has in fact played, and continues to play, 'an important role in universalizing certain dogmas that are barriers to imagining sustainable ways of life'.[72] They continue:

> Through particular disciplinary conceptualizations of sovereignty, development, property, economy, human rights, and other central disciplinary tenets, international lawyers have helped normalize a world-view where nature is understood predominantly as a natural resource, where humanity is at the centre of the environment and privileged above all else, where progress is defined by our degree of control over nature, and where this capacity to control is believed to be limitless.[73]

This argument dovetails neatly with the central argument of this book, which attempts to make sense of the transformation of the world from an expanse of land and sea inhabited by many different species, of which humans (organised in a huge variety of different ways) were only one, into an 'international community' of 'sovereign states' dedicated to subordinating the needs of the majority of humans and non-human species to the needs and desires of a small minority of humans. It was, as I have argued, and as Natarajan and Khoday's work also suggests, in the process of setting up a particular mode of identifying as an individual and a community – 'rational' on the one hand, and 'self-governing' on the other – as universal standards used to assess, dominate and incorporate all alternatives that capitalism and colonialism gathered their momentum. This is the process I have referred to here as that of international legal reproduction – a process which has advanced a project of systematic

[71] See, in particular, the works collected in Kishan Khoday, Vanessa Lamb, Tyler McCreary, Karin Mickelson, Usha Natarajan and Ileana Porras (eds.), 'International Legal Theory Symposium: Locating Nature', 27 *Leiden Journal of International Law* (2014) (issue 3): 571–660. See also the work of Julia Dehm, e.g. 'Carbon Colonialism or Climate Justice? Interrogating the International Climate Regime from a TWAIL Perspective,' 33 *Windsor Yearbook on Access to Justice* (2017): 129–61.

[72] Usha Natarajan and Kishan Khoday, 'Locating Nature: Making and Unmaking International Law,' 27 *Leiden Journal of International Law* (2014): 573–93, at 586.

[73] Ibid., 586.

redistribution, over the last 500 years, of wealth, power and pleasure away from disadvantaged individuals and communities and towards the world's most privileged human beings; along with an equally systematic redistribution of vital resources away from non-human species and things, and towards that same tiny minority of privileged humans. From this theoretical starting point, then, Section 2 offers some reflections on the usefulness of international legal reproduction as a framework for negotiating the relationship between 'now' and 'then' in a way that is both accurate and political – that is, in a way that is aimed explicitly at challenging this process of systemic upwards redistribution.

2 The New International Legal Reproduction

The most important piece of evidence which might, on the face of it, be mobilised *against* the idea that international personality is (still) conditional on the reproduction of individual legal subjectivity concerns the political diversity of the governments, and therefore of the states themselves, which came into being between the 1920s and the 1970s. Most obviously, in a very large-scale deviation from the norm of 'government' as 'self/effective/responsible government', many Cold War-era states either came into the world with, or later adopted, socialist or communist forms of self-ordering often inspired by or with the support of the USSR. Ethiopia, as we have just seen, was one of them, as of course were China, Vietnam, Serbia, Romania, East Germany, Libya and Iraq, among others.[74] Regardless of what happened in or after 1989, it can hardly be said that these states possessed a legal-institutional structure dedicated to the reproduction of individual legal subjectivity through strong protections for individual rights to life,[75] liberty in the negative sense, and private

[74] See above, Item 2, Section 2.3.2; Item 3, Section 4.2.

[75] From the USSR to Cambodia to Ethiopia itself, many if not most of the communist regimes of the twentieth century have been associated with systematic human rights violations, and in particular violations of the rights of their citizens to life and personal security. In the context of the USSR and the People's Republic of China, for example, see e.g. Anne Applebaum, *Gulag: A History* (New York: Broadway Books, 2003); Paul Lendvai, *One Day That Shook the Communist World: The 1956 Hungarian Uprising and Its Legacy* (Princeton University Press, 2008); Yangwen Zheng, Hong Liu and Michael Szonyi (eds.), *The Cold War in Asia: The Battle for Hearts and Minds* (Leiden, Boston: Brill, 2010). See generally Odd Arne Westad, *The Global Cold War: Third World Interventions and the Making of our Times* (Cambridge University Press, 2006); Elizabeth Schmidt, *Foreign Intervention in Africa: From the Cold War to the War on Terror* (Cambridge University Press, 2013). It should be noted, however, that the practice of 'free' states during and after the Cold War can hardly be said to have been more respectful of any 'inherent' right to life, especially if

property. How, then, can this divergence from what I have argued is the core 'criterion' of statehood – the pivot on which international personality turns – be explained?

The mainstream response to this question can be found in the standard – and largely retrospective – account of the emergence of the right of peoples to self-determination in and through the decolonisation practice of the 1950s and 60s. Famously, the emerging international persons whose words and actions constituted this right sought categorically to reject the conditionality which international law had attached for so long to the assumption of rights and duties under international law. As the General Assembly's 'Colonial Declaration' of 1960 stated in no uncertain terms:

> Inadequacy of political, economic, social or educational preparedness should never serve as a pretext for delaying independence ...
> Immediate steps shall be taken, in Trust and Non-Self-Governing Territories or all other territories which have not yet attained independence, to transfer all powers to the peoples of those territories, without any conditions or reservations, in accordance with their freely expressed will and desire, without any distinction as to race, creed or colour, in order to enable them to enjoy complete independence and freedom.[76]

In a revolutionary deviation from centuries of practice, this demand for an unconditional right to obtain international personality was accepted by the 'international community' – up to a point, at least. Many have therefore interpreted this as the moment when the non-European world struck back at the inherent Eurocentrism of international law, and terminated the assumption that non-European peoples should not be permitted to obtain rights and duties under international law until they had been deemed to

---

one also takes into account the willingness of the most powerful of these to use violence against the citizens of other states, and against their colonial subjects or former colonial subjects. On the intervention practice of the US, France, UK, Belgium and other 'free' states during the Korean, Vietnam, and Algerian wars, during the 'Troubles' in Northern Ireland, during Congo's and Kenya's wars and post-wars of liberation and elsewhere, for example, see e.g. Michael Cox, 'Northern Ireland: The War that Came In from the Cold,' 9 *Irish Studies in International Affairs* (1998): 73–84; David Percox, *Britain, Kenya and the Cold War: Imperial Defence, Colonial Security and Decolonisation* (London: I. B. Tauris, 2004); Antoine-Denis N'Dimina-Mougala, 'Les manifestations de la guerre froide en Afrique centrale (1961–1989)', 233 *Guerres Mondiales et Conflits Contemporains* (2009): 53–65.

[76] See e.g. *Declaration on the Granting of Independence to Colonial Countries and Peoples*, GA Res. 1514 (XV), 14 December 1960, paras. 3 and 5.

have met a 'standard of civilisation'.[77] Struck by the moral wrongness of colonialism, so the argument goes, according to mainstream scholars and practitioners of international law, the normative force of the emerging, soon-to-be *jus cogens* right of peoples to self-determination allowed many decolonising states to be recognised as full subjects of international law even in cases where they were clearly unable to meet the criterion of 'effective' government.[78]

To rearticulate this argument in the language of international legal reproduction, the standard account suggests that the criterion of 'effective' government was, in effect, relaxed, exceptionally, for territories and communities emerging out of situations of colonialism and military occupation. Combined with the political dynamics of the Cold War, this relaxation made it possible for many states to come into existence possessed of 'governments' which were not, in the legal sense, 'effective', including many socialist and communist administrations. However, it is of course precisely this argument, concerning the momentary relaxation of the criterion or standard of 'effective' government, which scholars and practitioners from the 1990s onwards invoke when they argue that many post-colonial states have 'failed' or – more recently (see Section 2.3) – that they have reneged on their 'responsibility to protect' their populations. These scholars, such as Gerald Helman, Steven Ratner, Robert Jackson, Carl Rosberg and, in the international legal context, Gerard Kreijen, not to mention Ian Spears in relation to the history of the Abyssinia Crisis itself (see Item 1), insist that the international community made a gigantic mistake when 'self-determination was given more attention than long-term viability'[79] during the decolonisation process. The result, they argue, was that many former colonies were allowed to become states even though 'the

[77] See e.g. Arnulf Becker Lorca, 'Petitioning the International: A "Pre-History" of Self-Determination', 25 *EJIL* (2014): 497–523.

[78] See Crawford, *Creation of States*, 56–8. For Crawford, 'norms that are non-derogable and peremptory [like self-determination] cannot be violated by State-creation any more than they can by treaty-making'. Crawford, *Creation of States*, 107.

[79] See esp. Gerald B. Helman and Steven R. Ratner, 'Saving Failed States', 89 *Foreign Policy* (1993): 3–20; Robert H. Jackson, *Quasi-states: Sovereignty, International Relations and the Third World* (Cambridge University Press, 1990); Robert H. Jackson and Carl G. Rosberg, 'Why Africa's Weak States Persist: The Empirical and the Juridical in Statehood', 35 *World Politics* (1982): 1–24; Gerard Kreijen, 'The Transformation of Sovereignty and African Independence', in Gerard Kreijen, Marcel Brus, Jorris Duursma, Elizabeth De Vos and John Dugard (eds.), *State, Sovereignty and International Governance* (Oxford University Press, 2002), 45–107. For a critique, see Ruth Gordon, 'Saving Failed States: Sometimes a Neocolonialist Notion', 12 *American University Journal of International Law and Policy* (1997): 903–74.

viability of their economic bases and their developmental potentiality were questionable'.[80]

There are several problems with the 'failed states' narrative, as its many critics have pointed out – not least the assumption that colonialism ended because colonial states such as France, Britain, Spain and Portugal, suddenly came to be convinced of its normative wrongness.[81] For the purpose of our examination of the process of international legal reproduction in the post-Cold War period, however, the most important issues to draw attention to, here, are two.

In the first place, even if the criterion of 'effective' government was relaxed, to a certain extent, in the context of the right of peoples to self-determination, that right can hardly be said to have been entirely unconditional. On the contrary, as Sundhya Pahuja, among others, has pointed out, decolonisation was structured entirely on the basis of the norm of statehood.[82] Colonial territories and peoples, to whom a right of 'external' self-determination was available, were presented with a list of only three options: emergence as a sovereign 'independent State'; 'free association' with another 'independent State'; or 'integration' with another 'independent State'.[83] The idea that a 'full measure of self-government' (as the General Assembly put it) might have been compatible with some *other* form of collective self-organisation simply was not on the table in the 1950s and 1960s; nor is it there today. Notoriously, moreover, when it came to two of the other criteria for statehood, 'fixed population' and 'defined territory', even the option of altering territorial boundaries inherited from colonialism was withheld thanks to the acceptance by states of the principle of *uti possidetis juris* ('as you possess under law'),[84] a principle of customary

[80] Jackson and Rosberg, 'Why Africa's Weak States Persist', 16.

[81] For a start, few of the colonial powers gave up their empires without a fight, as the Algerian and Angolan wars are not alone in demonstrating. In addition, a great deal of research exists to support the idea that, in finally countenancing the end of territorial imperialism, the colonial powers planned to extend – and did, indeed, extend – the duration of their control over the resources of their former colonies through less formal channels (see, among many other formative texts, Kwame Nkrumah, *Neocolonialism: The Last Stage of Imperialism* (New York: International Publishers, 1966); Andre Gunder Frank, *The Development of Underdevelopment* (Boston, MA: New England Free Press, 1966)).

[82] Sundhya Pahuja, *Decolonising International Law: Development, Economic Growth and the Politics of Universality* (Cambridge University Press, 2011), 44–94.

[83] GA Res. 1941 (XV), 15 December 1960, Principle VI.

[84] *Case Concerning the Frontier Dispute (Burkina Faso* v. *Republic of Mali)*, 22 December 1986, ICJ Rep. 1986, 554, para. 20.

international law since the emergence of the Latin American states.[85] In the process, communities which had been jammed together or split apart by colonial powers more interested in profit maximisation than in local needs and desires, lost the opportunity to opt for for reintegration or separation, while Indigenous territories and Indigenous forms of communal self-organisation, collective authority and ontology/normativity continued to be subordinated (as discussed in more detail in Section 3, below) to the regime of self-governing statehood.[86] Perhaps most important of all is the fact that the options of these territories and communities had, to a large extent, been predetermined by decades of colonial administration aimed precisely at destroying alternative modes of communal existence and ensuring that colonised individuals would have little choice but to identify as market actors. Ntina Tzouvala asserts:

> Whether through treaties or through the international administration of territories, international law assumed a proactive role in the transformation of colonial polities into centralised nation-states with capitalist economies. The dissolution of traditional modes of producing and living, and the gradual centralisation of power promoted by colonial international law, enabled the emergence of sovereignty as the hegemonic form of post-colonial communal organisation. Hence, sovereign statehood, far from being a self-evident truth or purely a discursive strategy, was in fact the very outcome of colonial social engineering, and international law had played a significant role in this process.[87]

A second issue with the assumption that the problems experienced by 'Third World' states stem from the international community's failure to attach any conditions related to viability to their emergence as independent states is linked to the developments of the last few decades. Even if it is accepted that, during the mid twentieth century, the geopolitical situation created by the Cold War, combined with the success of the anti-colonial struggle, ushered in an era of normative permissiveness when it came to the emergence of new states, it would be a mistake to follow Crawford in extrapolating from this a general rule to the effect that 'international law lays down no specific requirements' for what, in normative terms, should count as a 'government'.[88] Indeed, from the 1970s onwards,

[85] Organisation of African Unity Heads of State and Government, 'Cairo Declaration on Boundaries', Cairo, July 1964, AHG/Res.16(1) 1964. For a strong critique, see Makau wa Mutua, 'Why Redraw the Map of Africa? A Moral and Legal Inquiry', 16 *Michigan Journal of International Law* (1995): 1113–76.

[86] See Section 3, below.

[87] Tzouvala, *Letters of Blood and Fire*, 118–19.

[88] Crawford, *The Creation of States*, 56.

the major institutions of the 'international community', together with that community's most 'successful' states, have – acting through a wide variety of international legal instruments (including bilateral investment treaties, free trade agreements, regional customs unions, sovereign debt contracts, peace agreements, 'stand-by agreements', institution-building 'programmes', Security Council resolutions, the decisions of international 'dispute resolution mechanisms', and so on) — unleashed what can only be described as a relentless backlash. The aim of this backlash, it appears, is to compensate for, and if possible, to reverse, the effects of this (momentary) normative relaxation. This is achieved by threatening states whose 'governments' – that is, whose effective commitment to reproducing individual legal subjectivity within their borders – are found wanting. The scale of this backlash, as I characterise it, involving a concerted effort to re-condition the rights and duties of states on their willingness and capacity to protect and extend the rights and duties associated with legal subjectivity is enormous. The following three sub-sections will examine three areas in which this process of re-conditionalisation is most obvious: 'structural adjustment'; 'earned sovereignty'; and the 'responsibility to protect'. In relation to the first two of these paradigms, my focus will be primarily on the immediate post-Cold War period – the moment at which the aims of the backlash they formed part of first became evident. Returning, in Section 2.3, to the 'responsibility to protect' in its secret 'other life' of 'prevention', however, makes it possible to bring the analysis up to date.

2.1 'Structural Adjustment' as Reverse Engineering

The story of the evolution of the 'Washington Consensus' between the two international financial institutions (IFIs), the International Monetary Fund and World Bank, and their imposition of the precepts of that consensus on 'developing' states via 'structural adjustment policies' (SAPs), is well known. From the very beginning of the idea of structural adjustment in the 1950s, the direction of 'adjustment' was closely tied in with the geopolitical priorities of the Cold War. With the USSR in possession of a seat on the Security Council, and with a growing number of post-colonial states in the General Assembly, the two sides of the Cold War were relatively balanced in the UN. However, the IFIs, neither of which the USSR ever joined, and whose 'Chinese' seats were claimed by the People's Republic of China (PRC) from Taiwan only in 1980, proved much more amenable to domination by the states of the 'free' world – by the United States and the Western European states in particular.[89] This institutional balance of forces paved the way for SAPs to become one of the primary instruments used to promote 'freedom' in the emerging post-colonial states from the late 1950s right through to the 1980s. In parallel with the many 'illegal' interventions into post-colonial states that were being launched simultaneously by the states of the 'free world' during this period, in order to dislodge socialist governments in the name of 'democracy', dozens of 'legal' interventions were made by the IMF and World Bank in the name of 'structural adjustment'. These SAPs were, quite unapologetically, aimed at dismantling socialist economic structures and encouraging free-market economic institutions in their stead.[90] Unlike the military interventions of this period, these 'economic' interventions were 'consensual'. However, faced with an overwhelming debt crisis, particularly after 1974, post-colonial states had little choice but to request these loans and accept the conditions attached to them.

If we were to re-narrate this story in the idiom of international legal reproduction, we could say that SAPs in this way provided the 'free world' with a mechanism for 'disciplining' those states whose administrations had effectively refused to prioritise the reproduction of 'free' and 'equal' individual subjectivity and focused their attention, instead, on strategies of economic discrimination and industrial expropriation aimed at 'import-substituting industrialisation' and the protection of 'infant industries'. During the 1970s and 1980s in particular, thanks to the material 'incentives' provided by the debt crisis, and by the grinding poverty associated with post-colonial path dependency more generally, SAPs made it possible for the IFIs to force these delinquent states to reconstitute their legal and institutional frameworks in a number of key areas. These included improving fiscal policy 'discipline' and reducing public spending; engineering more 'competitive' exchange rates; radical trade liberalisation; the encouragement of foreign direct investment; privatisation of state enterprises; 'deregulation' with the aim of encouraging competition; and legal 'reforms' aimed at making property rights more 'secure'.[91] Drawing attention to the 'long' history of

[89] See 'China and the International Monetary Fund (IMF)', Permanent Mission of the People's Republic of China to the United Nations Office at Geneva, 19 April 2004, at www.china-un.ch/eng/zmjg/jgjblc/t85557.htm (accessed 18 January 2018).

[90] See also Ha-Joon Chang, *Kicking Away the Ladder: Development Strategy in Historical Perspective* (London: Anthem Press, 2005).

[91] John Williamson, *Latin American Adjustment: How Much Has Happened?* (Washington, DC: Institute for International Economics, 1990), 7–41.

international legal reproduction allows us to see here that these provisions were hardly new. On the contrary, while the mechanism of SAP enforcement was (and remains) primarily economic rather than military, these conditions added up to a set of provisions that were, in substance, remarkably similar to the provisions contained in the numerous instruments through which the Ethiopian Empire was recognised as a sovereign equal; through which the 'mandated territories' were administered; through which the post-First World War 'enemy states' and 'national states' were constituted and reconstituted; through which the 'door' of the Chinese Empire was 'opened'; through which the disintegration of the Ottoman Empire was settled, and so on.

The Cold War was, of course, eventually 'won' by the 'free world'. To this extent, the first phase of structural adjustment must be judged to have been a success. The social costs of this victory, however, were very high, and stood in sharp contradiction to the developmentalist language in which the virtues of structural adjustment were narrated. The response of the IFIs to the powerful criticism they had begun to receive was twofold. First, the 'failure' of structural adjustment to deliver 'development' was blamed on implementation rather than substance, opening the way for closer mechanisms of international scrutiny and oversight in relation to those domestic institutions of post-colonial countries that were responsible for implementing SAPs.[92] Secondly, a new, 'softer' rhetoric was developed, which was in theory more attentive to the broader political context than the narrowly economistic precepts of the Washington Consensus, and which took account of the differing local needs and of the need for local 'ownership' of restructuring programmes.[93] Together, these two responses to the criticism of 'hard' structural adjustment in the 1970s and 80s have dovetailed, from the late 1990s onwards, in a focus on the need for institutional as well as policy 'reform', articulated in terms of 'good governance', a key component of which is the 'rule of law'. Indeed, even in the more recent context of the 'War on Terror' and the counter-revolutions which have followed the 2011 'Arab Spring', the 'rule of law' and especially stronger and more widespread property rights protections are

[92] World Bank, *Effective Implementation: Key to Development Impact*, Portfolio Management Task Force, 22 September 1992 (Washington, DC: Bank Group, 1992) ('Wapenhans Report').

[93] Joseph E. Stiglitz, *More Instruments and Broader Goals: Moving Towards the Post-Washington Consensus*, World Institute for Development Economics Research Annual Lecture, January 1998 (Helsinki: UNU/WIDER, 1998).

regularly being invoked as the key preventative measure, capable of nipping revolutionary (and even terrorist) threats in the bud.[94]

From this point onwards, the IFIs (among other international lenders) have targeted their loan conditionalities even more precisely at the creation of 'an effective property rights system [to support] economic growth and wealth creation by rewarding effort and good economic judgement by actors in the market' and to bring about 'enhancement and liberalisation of the law of contract'.[95] Precisely what this means, both in 'development' and 'statebuilding' contexts, has been spelled out by the commercial law scholar, Jeswald Salacuse.[96] 'Emerging markets' in the post-Cold War period – a new name for 'developing states' deemed to be on the road to 'success' – are, according to Salacuse, shifting away from public law and planning with the encouragement and assistance of the IFIs, among other international institutions, and focusing instead on three areas much better suited to 'support[ing] economic growth and wealth creation'. Firstly, they have sought to 'strengthen the recognition and enforcement of property rights and the liberalization of the law of contract'.[97] Secondly, they have cut back on all but those regulations necessary 'to be sure that the rules of the game are clear and that the private players abide by those rules and play fairly', such that resources can be allocated exclusively by the market's logic of 'rewarding effort and good economic judgement'. Thirdly, sucessful 'emerging markets' have dedicated themselves to creating a strong,

[94] See, in particular, Ibrahim Shihata, 'Preface: Good Governance and the Role of Law in Economic Development,' in Ann Seidman, Robert B. Seidman and Thomas W. Walde (eds.), *Making Development Work: Legislative Reform for Institutional Transformation and Good Governance* (The Hague etc.: Kluwer Law International, 1999). There have been many excellent critiques of this process. See e.g. James T. Gathii, 'Good Governance as a Counter Insurgency Agenda to Oppositional and Transformative Social Projects in International Law', 5 *Buffalo Human Rights Law Review* (1999): 107–74; Pahuja, *Decolonising International Law*, 172–53; Alvaro Santos, 'The World Bank's Uses of the "Rule of Law" Promise in Economic Development', in David M. Trubek and Alvaro Santos (eds.), *The New Law and Economic Development: A Critical Appraisal* (Cambridge University Press, 2006), 268. For the argument that the lesson of the 'Arab Spring' is the need to extend property rights, thereby democratising (as it were) the right to participate in and accumulate capital through the global economy, see e.g. Hernando de Soto, 'What the Arab World Really Wants', *The Spectator*, 13 July 2013, at www.spectator.co.uk/2013/07/what-the-arab-world-really-wants/ (accessed 6 August 2018). For a critique, see Luis Eslava, Usha Natarajan and Rose Parfitt, '(Post)Revolutionary Interlinkages: Labour, Environment and Accumulation', 4 *Transnational Legal Theory* (2013): 108–25.

[95] Jeswald W. Salacuse, 'From Developing Countries to Emerging Markets: A Changing Role for Law in the Third World', *The International Lawyer* 33 (1999): 875–90, 887.

[96] Ibid., 876–90.

[97] Ibid., 887.

independent judiciary to 'become the final arbiters of conflict among private actors in the economy'.[98]

As economists like Ben Fine and legal scholars like Tor Krever and Kerry Rittich have pointed out, however, what was presented as an effort to soften the impact of structural adjustment, and to reduce the powers of the IFIs vis-à-vis their creditors, has actually greatly increased 'discretionary intervention under the guise of good governance', while at the same time making the intensity of intervention more palatable by 'wrap[ping] it up in terms of local ownership'.[99] Rittich, for example, has cast the more recent iterations of this 'softening' as nothing less than an 'incorporation of the social'. Loan conditionalities, she notes, are increasingly focused on ostensibly social concerns and on environmental 'sustainability'; yet their primary purpose is to secure local consent (and hence reduce the costs of implementation) by usurping the language in which dissent might most naturally be articulated. In this context human rights have been transformed from 'the terrain of struggle' into a particular set of juridicised, and therefore constrained, answers to the problems faced by vulnerable communities.[100]

Over the course of the 1990s, such 'economic' strategies of formally consensual intervention within sovereign states were given a political boost by the emergence of the 'failed states' paradigm introduced in the previous section.[101] So powerful has this idea become that since 2005 a US think-tank called the Fund for Peace has been publishing the 'Failed States Index' (renamed the 'Fragile States Index' in 2014), in collaboration with *Foreign Policy* magazine.[102] This 'index' was quickly followed by the annual 'States of Fragility' report from the Organisation for Economic Co-operation and Development (OECD),[103] and the World Bank's own 'Harmonized List of Fragile Situations' (as it has been known since

[98] Ibid., 888.

[99] Ben Fine, 'Neither the Washington nor the Post-Washington Consensus: An Introduction', in Ben Fine, Costas Lapavitsas and Jonathan Pincus (eds.), *Development Policy in the 21st Century: Beyond the Post-Washington Consensus* (London: Routledge, 2001), 1–27, at 14–15; Krever, 'Law, Development, and Political Closure under Neoliberalism', 22–42; Kerry Rittich, 'The Future of Law and Development: Second Generation Reforms and the Incorporation of the Social', 26 *Michigan Journal of International Law* (2004): 199–243.

[100] Ibid., 241.

[101] See esp. Helman and Ratner, 'Saving Failed States'; Jackson, *Quasi-states*; Jackson and Rosberg, 'Why Africa's Weak States Persist'; and for an international legal take, Kreijen, 'The Transformation of Sovereignty and African Independence'.

[102] See http://fundforpeace.org/fsi/ (accessed 18 January 2018).

[103] See www.oecd.org/dac/conflict-fragility-resilience/listofstateoffragilityreports.htm (accessed 5 June 2018).

2011).[104] However, whereas Helman, Ratner and their colleagues in the 1990s advocated nothing less than the implementation of a new version of the League of Nations' Mandates System ('conservatorship') as the most 'cost-effective' way of dealing with the problem of 'failed states',[105] the programmes that have actually been implemented by the UN and other international bodies since this time, in the form of 'peacekeeping', 'peacebuilding' and 'statebuilding' operations, have focused their energies, like the IFIs, on 'encouraging', at arm's length, the 'consensual' implementation of 'good governance' and the 'rule of law'.[106] Bearing in mind the rationale of late colonialism, this should come as no surprise. As we have already seen, the creation of 'self-governing' individuals who could (whether willingly or unwillingly) be relied upon to engage with labour and commodity markets of their own accord, rather than needing to be coerced into doing so through enslavement or forced labour, has (I have suggested in this book) been the objective of statehood, colonialism and more broadly of international law ever since the abolition of slavery in the mid-nineteenth century, if not since the conquest of the 'new world' in the sixteenth century.

Acting on the basis of formal sovereign consent in a material context which placed the backs of post-colonial communities against a concrete wall of poverty, debt and conflict, international law acted quickly, in the immediate post-Cold War period, to put the 'self-governing' back into statehood, in order, as it were, to reverse-conditionalise states' sovereign rights and duties in the wake of the normative hiatus of Cold War-era decolonisation. In moving beyond what was customarily understood as the sphere of the 'economy' into the political and social spheres associated with 'governance', supported (as Eslava demonstrates) by an increasingly close-up jurisdictional focus, increasingly trained on the level of the 'local', the IFIs – supported by the peacekeeping and statebuilding work of the UN and other international coalitions like the OECD and the EU – have obtained a far sharper set of legal tools with which to reverse-engineer self-government in recalcitrant states.[107] On the one hand, these

[104] See www.worldbank.org/en/topic/fragilityconflictviolence/brief/harmonized-list-of-fragile-situations (accessed 18 January 2018).

[105] Helman and Ratner, 'Saving Failed States', 20.

[106] David Chandler is the authority here. See e.g. David Chandler, *Peacebuilding: The Twenty Years' Crisis, 1997–2017* (New York: Springer, 2017); David Chandler, *International Statebuilding: The Rise of Post-Liberal Governance* (Hoboken, NJ: Taylor & Francis, 2010).

[107] See Thilo Bodenstein, Jörg Faust and Mark Furness (eds.), 'Special Issue: European Union Development Policy: Collective Action in Times of Global Transformation and Domestic Crisis', 35 *Development Policy Review* (July 2017): 439–597 (issue 4); Luis Eslava, *Local Space, Global Life*.

tools are being used to discipline 'bad' governments into abandoning redistributive programmes and instituting more effective protections for property rights, free trade, law and order. On the other hand, and as the work of Rittich and others indicates, their purpose is to encourage individuals within these states, their cities, and other local jurisdictions, to interpellate as legal subjects (and hence as market actors) by 'incorporating' the language of social rights into the 'free' and 'equal' rhetoric of the much more restricted range of rights associated with legal subjectivity. The effect is to usurp (first discursively, then practically) the need for genuinely redistributive measures aimed at reducing the social and environmental costs of capitalism.

2.2 Sovereignty and How to 'Earn' It

Another important illustration of the way in which the 'international community' has attempted to compensate for the loosening of the criterion of 'effective' government during the decolonisation era concerns the heightened emphasis that has been placed on this criterion in the practice of post-Cold War era statebuilding. Dozens of new states have come (or come back) into existence since the early 1990s, in an atmosphere eager to interpret the collapse of communism as a vindication of the universal superiority of 'market democracy'.[108] To give one now-classic illustration, the *Declaration on the Guidelines on the Recognition of New States in Eastern Europe and in the Soviet Union*, issued in 1991 by the foreign ministers of the European Community, famously affirmed the Community's 'readiness to recognise, subject to normal standards of international practice and the political realities of each case' *only* those 'new States' which had 'constituted themselves on a democratic basis' and 'accepted the appropriate international obligations ... especially with regard to the rule of law, democracy and human rights'.[109] Indeed, in a kind of reversal of the reduced emphasis on 'effective government' during the decolonisation era, Bosnia–Herzegovina – which was recognised as a sovereign state on 6 April 1992 – is not the only example of a state that was recognised on the basis of its commitment to implementing

[108] For a critique, see William I. Robinson, 'Promoting Polyarchy in Latin America: The Oxymoron of "Market Democracy"', in Eric Hershberg and Fred Rosen (eds.), *Latin America and Neoliberalism* (New York: The New Press, 2006), 96–119.

[109] EC Foreign Ministers, *Declaration on the 'Guidelines on the Recognition of New States in Eastern Europe and in the Soviet Union'*, 16 December 1991, in 61 *British Yearbook of International Law* (1991): 559.

'effective government' (increasingly narrated in the language of 'good governance' and the 'rule of law') in the midst of a devastating civil war which called into question its capacity to meet all four of the criteria for statehood.[110]

The war was brought to an end on 14 December 1995 with the 'Dayton Accords', overseen by the US, UK, EU and Russia.[111] In addition to spelling out the terms of the ceasefire and post-war political settlement, the Accords imposed on Bosnia a full-length constitution in a way that recalls the 'organic'/'fundamental' laws upon which Iraq's independence was conditioned in 1922, and upon which the independence of the 'national states' was conditioned in the 'minorities treaties' of 1918–19 (present-day Bosnia–Herzegovina, of course, having formed part of one of these, the 'Kingdom of Serbs, Croats and Slovenes', or Yugoslavia as it later became). The Preamble to Bosnia's externally mandated constitution begins: 'Based on respect for human dignity, liberty and equality ... Desiring to promote the general welfare and economic growth through the protection of private property and the promotion of a market economy ...'[112] The Dayton Accords also established a 'High Representative' to 'coordinate' its implementation in collaboration with the UN, World Bank and European Commission.[113] Belying, somewhat, its ostensibly 'international' character and the stated commitment of the UN and EU to the redistribution of racialised and gendered power, Office of the High Representative (OHR) has, since 1995, been occupied exclusively by white European men and the OHR deputy position by white men from the United States, in a manner not altogether dissimilar from the debate over and arrangements for 'foreign advisors' proposed in relation to Ethiopia and Liberia by the League of Nations during the 1930s.[114] Meanwhile, the OHR was given special powers to adopt binding decisions over the heads of local actors and to remove elected local representatives from office – powers which have been

[110] See Christian Hillgruber, 'The Admission of New States into the International Community', 9 *EJIL* (1998): 491–509.

[111] *General Framework for Peace in Bosnia and Herzegovina [proposed by the US, the UK, the EU and the Russian Federation]*, Dayton, 21 November 1995 ('Dayton Accords').

[112] *Constitution of Bosnia and Herzegovina*, Annex 4 to the Dayton Accords, at 59–80.

[113] *Agreement on Civilian Implementation of the Peace Settlement*, Annex 10 to the Dayton Accords, at 111.

[114] 'The HR and his Deputies', www.ohr.int/?page_id=1153 (accessed 8 January 2018). Indeed, of the 27 individuals who have occupied the position not only of High Representative, but also of Principal and Deputy High Representative so far, every one of them has been a white man.

severely criticised.[115] Nonetheless, the OHR remains in place today, over twenty years after its supposedly temporary initiation, suggesting that the implementation of 'reforms that ensure fiscal and economic stability' and 'establishing the rule of law' are greater priorities for the 'international community' than the actualisation of democratic procedure.

The example of Bosnia–Herzegovina serves to underscore the critiques discussed at the start of this chapter. Many international lawyers in the post-Cold War period, notably Thomas Franck, embraced these developments as evidence that 'democracy' was 'on the way to becoming a global entitlement, one that increasingly will be promoted and protected by collective international processes'.[116] However, an analytically more useful way of putting this would be to argue that 'good governance' (or what I have called 'self-government') is once again (after a short hiatus during the mid-twentieth century) the 'standard of statehood', adherence to which has always been (in Franck's words) 'promoted and protected by collective international processes'.

The evidence for this reinvigorated emphasis on the criteria of 'government' is also evident in the trend towards so-called 'remedial' secession. For advocates, this type of secession is permitted, exceptionally, under international law, where human rights violations have been serious and systematic enough to indicate that a people's right to 'internal' self-determination has been violated, thereby transforming it into a right to 'external' self-determination, normally possessed only in situations of colonialism and 'foreign military occupation'.[117] The most prominent legal argument associated with remedial secession is the so-called 'earned sovereignty' approach, also a child of the late 1990s. This 'conflict-resolution approach' is defined as involving 'the conditional and progressive devolution of sovereign powers and authority from a state to a substate entity under international supervision'.[118] Again, a close look

[115] See Tim Banning, 'The "Bonn Powers" of the High Representative in Bosnia Herzegovina: Tracing a Legal Figment', 6 *Goettingen Journal of International Law* (2014): 259–302.

[116] Franck, 'The Emerging Right to Democratic Governance', 46.

[117] *Reference re: Secession of Quebec*, Supreme Court of Canada, 2 S.C.R. 297, para. 138.

[118] See, among many other papers written by Paul R. Williams and his colleagues at the Public International Law and Policy Group (PILPG), a Washington-based think-tank, Paul R. Williams and Francesca Jannotti Pecci, 'Earned Sovereignty: Bridging the Gap Between Sovereignty and Self-Determination', 40 *Stanford Journal of International Law* (2004): 1–40 and the special issue in volume 31, issue 3 of the *Denver Journal of International Law and Policy* (2003). For a recent attempt to revive the paradigm, see Paul R. Williams, Abigail J. Avoryie and Carlie J. Armstrong, 'Earned Sovereignty Revisited: Creating a Strategic Framework for Managing Self-Determination Based Conflicts', 21 *ISLA Journal*

at the 'earned sovereignty' approach and at the practice existing so far in support of it indicates that the particular legal and institutional character of the international personalities envisaged as emerging from this process of secession is just as important, for advocates of 'earned sovereignty', as the desire to end the suffering of their populations. According to advocates of 'earned sovereignty', certain oppressed communities should be, and increasingly are being, offered a limited set of rights and duties under international law, but only if, and *to the extent* that, they have 'earned' it. In the first place, 'sovereignty' can only be 'earned' by communities through the experience of very severe human rights violations. In the second place, moreover, international rights and duties can only be 'earned' by polities that display a sufficient desire and capacity ('will' and 'power', we might say, recalling Lorimer) to implement a particular set of legal and institutional arrangements, under the 'supervision' of international institutions such as (again) the World Bank, IMF, UN, EU and NATO.

The go-to illustration of the 'earned sovereignty' approach in action is once again linked to the post-communist transition. This example concerns Kosovo, which seceded from Serbia after a NATO-led bombing campaign in 1999.[119] Over the course of a decade, Kosovo was subject to an intensive UN and NATO-led 'statebuilding' mission (UNMIK), underpinned by an unrepentantly conditional rationale known as 'standards before

of International and Comparative Law (2015): 1–26. For a critique, see Drew, 'The Meaning of Self-Determination'; Ralph Wilde, *International Territorial Administration: How Trusteeship and the Civilizing Mission Never Went Away* (Oxford University Press, 2008), 261–2.

[119] See e.g. Janusz Bugajski, R. Bruce Hitchner and Paul Williams, *Achieving a Final Status Settlement for Kosovo* (Washington, DC: Center for Strategic and International Studies, 2003). This report was produced in the wake of two conferences, the first held in November 2002 by the Center for Strategic and International Studies (CSIS) together with the National Albanian American Council and the Dayton Peace Accords Project; the second held in March 2003, sponsored by the Dayton Peace Accords Project and the Public International Law and Policy Group (PILPG), and attended by representatives of the National Albanian American Council and the Project on Ethnic Relations; Paul R. Williams, 'Earned Sovereignty: The Road to Resolving the Conflict over Kosovo's Final Status', 31 *Denver Journal of International Law and Policy* (2003): 387–425. Paul R. Williams, a professor of law and international relations, 'world renowned peace negotiation lawyer', and co-founder and president of the PILPG, has participated in negotiations for the Dayton Accord (Bosnia–Herzegovina), Rambouillet Agreement and Paris negotiations (Kosovo), Ohrid Agreement (Macedonia) and Podgorica/Belgrade negotiations (Serbia and Montenegro), in addition to advising parties during the negotiations to end the conflicts in Nagorno-Karabakh, Sri Lanka, Georgia/Abkhazia, Somalia and elsewhere. See www.drpaulrwilliams.com/ (accessed 10 January 2018).

status'.[120] Kosovo's readiness for statehood, and hence the robustness of the sovereign rights it was to obtain, was measured by the extent to which it had 'progressed', under the auspices of this mission, on 'eight standards': 'democratic institutions; rule of law; freedom of movement; returns and reintegration; economy; property rights; dialogue with [the Serbian Government in] Belgrade; and the Kosovo Protection Corps'.[121] Then, in March 2007, the UN Special Envoy for the Kosovo Status Settlement, Martti Ahtisaari, declared Kosovo to be ready, not for independent statehood *per se*, but for internationally 'supervised independence'. In return for 'status' (that is, for a limited range of 'sovereign' rights and duties under international law), Kosovo would be asked to commit to becoming 'a multi-ethnic society, which [would] govern itself democratically and with full respect for the "rule of law"', to creating 'an open market with free competition' and to remaining under the 'supervision' of the 'international community'.[122] The so-called Ahtisaari Plan featured prominently in Kosovo's declaration of independence the following year,[123] and in the decision of many Western European and North American states to recognise its independence.[124] However, the Ahtisaari Plan did not in the end receive the Security Council's support.[125] As a result, Kosovo's status remains up in the air. Meanwhile, the European Union Rule of Law Mission in Kosovo (EULEX), which took over 'supervision' of Kosovo's 'progress' towards 'good governance', remains active, its mandate having been extended several times since it was set up in 1999, along with UNMIK, by Security

[120] 'Implementing "Standards Before Status" Policy Core Political Project for UN Kosovo Mission, Security Council Told', UN Press Release SC/7999, 6 February 2004, at www.un.org/press/en/2004/sc7999.doc.htm (accessed 10 January 2018).

[121] Ibid.

[122] 'Report of the Special Envoy of the Secretary-General [Martti Ahtisaari] on Kosovo's Future Status', UN Security Council, S/2007/168, 26 March 2007 ('Ahtisaari Plan').

[123] *Declaration of Independence of Kosovo*, 17 February 2008, available at http://news.bbc.co.uk/2/hi/europe/7249677.stm (accessed 19 March 2012).

[124] For example, then-US Secretary of State Condoleezza Rice explained the US decision on the grounds that Kosovo had agreed 'to implement the Ahtisaari Plan, to embrace multi-ethnicity as a fundamental principle of good governance, and to welcome a period of international supervision'. Condoleezza Rice, 'US Recognises Kosovo as Independent State.' Statement by Secretary of State, 18 February 2008, at https://2001-2009.state.gov/secretary/rm/2008/02/100973.htm (accessed 5 June 2018). See also David Miliband, 'Political Developments in Kosovo', written ministerial statement by the Secretary of State for Foreign and Commonwealth Affairs, 28 February 2008, and Ahtisaari Plan, para. 4.

[125] 'Russia Rejects New Kosovo Draft', *BBC News*, 1 June 2007, http://news.bbc.co.uk/2/hi/europe/6710529.stm; 'China Expresses Concerns over Kosovo', *China Daily*, 19 February 2008, at www.chinadaily.com.cn/china/2008-02/19/content_6464411.htm (accessed 28 September 2012).

Council Resolution 1244.[126] As Paul R. Williams, earned sovereignty's most enthusiastic advocate, summarises the approach as follows, writing with Francesca Pecci,

> the most relevant aspect of the global conflict management trend [towards 'earned sovereignty'] is that it may indicate the emergence of a binding new set of values perceived as essential by states. The values shaping and inspiring the contemporary commitments of the international community include ending ethnic violence, stopping human rights atrocities, promoting democracy, and encouraging the rule of law.[127]

2.3 *Discipline as 'Responsibility' as 'Prevention'*

As Sections 2.1 and 2.2 have just shown, the 'structural adjustment'/'good governance' and 'failed states'/'earned sovereignty' paradigms remain extremely influential still today – perhaps more so than one might expect. Nonetheless, it is undeniable that their heyday has passed and that, by the early 2000s, the panicked international security rhetoric associated with the 'War on Terror' had taken over. The same cannot be said, however, of the 'responsibility to protect' (R2P) paradigm – very much a creature of the era of the present 'global security' era.[128] As mentioned in the

[126] SC Res. 1244, 10 June 1999, paras. 10–11.

[127] Williams and Pecci, 'Bridging the Gap', 23. This kind of negotiated 'peace process', whose terms are set and supervised by the 'international community', has also been employed in conflicts involving territories – notably Palestine and Western Sahara – whose recognised right to 'external' self-determination remains unrealised. Until the end of the 1990s, the predicament of these territories was generally understood to be one of an illegitimately thwarted 'external' right of peoples to self-determination. Since then, however, it has been increasingly re-narrated as one of straightforward civil conflict, in which the claims of all the parties involved must be balanced against one another in an egalitarian manner, and whose outcome must conform to a supposedly universal set of normative standards relating, once again, to 'good governance' and the 'rule of law'. See e.g. *A Performance-Based Roadmap to a Permanent Two-State Solution to the Israeli-Palestinian Conflict*, proposal from the United Nations, European Union, United States and Russian Federation ('the Quartet') 30 April 2003 ('Roadmap to Peace'). For an excellent critique, see Catriona Drew, 'The Meaning of Self-Determination: "The Stealing of the Sahara" Redux?', in Karin Arts and Piedro Pinto Leite (eds.), *International Law and the Question of Western Sahara* (Leiden: International Platform for Jurists for East Timor, 2007), 87–105, at 95–100. See also Catriona Drew, 'The East Timor Story: International Law on Trial', 12 *EJIL* (2001): 651–84.

[128] For a devastating critique of the way in which 'R2P' 'develops an ambitious conceptual framework aimed at systematising and giving formal expression to the protective authority exercised by international actors in the decolonised world since 1960', see Anne Orford, *International Authority and the Responsibility to Protect* (Cambridge University Press, 2011).

Frame, Operation Unified Protector is, at the time of writing, still the only major military intervention to have been launched under the rubric of the international community's posited 'responsibility to protect' civilian populations from their 'irresponsible' governments. Taken together with the chaotic fallout from the invervention in Libya, and in the face of the international community's manifest failure to carry out similar interventions to 'protect' civilians in arguably even more catastrophic humanitarian emergencies (in Syria, Palestine, Myanmar and Yemen, for example), this has led some commentators to declare the 'R2P' paradigm, though only endorsed officially by the United Nations in 2005, already dead.[129] This suggestion, however, is in fact profoundly misleading. Instead, what is crucial to recognise about the 'responsibility to protect' is that military intervention (whether multilateral or not) does not exhaust, and has never exhausted, the normative content of this idea, as laid out by its architects in the United Nations and elsewhere. On the contrary, such intervention is simply the extreme end of a much broader set of rationales, permissions and proposals which have been under development at the UN,[130] first under the rubric of 'sovereignty as responsibility',[131] and more recently under that of the 'responsibility to prevent'.[132]

In the wake of the 2001 World Trade Center attacks, and of the catastrophic consequences of the ensuing wars in Afghanistan and Iraq, this rationale of 'responsibility' and 'prevention' has found an increasingly central place in the language employed in the sphere of international relations by state officials, 'special advisors', 'special envoys' and international lawyers. Confronted, since 2001, not with a diminution but rather with a striking escalation of the 'terrorist threat' posed by radical Islam, and (though far lower on the agenda of the 'international community')

[129] See e.g. Tom Esslemont, 'As Syrian Deaths Mount, World's "Responsibility to Protect" Takes a Hit', *Reuters*, 25 October 2016, at www.reuters.com/article/us-mideast-crisis-syria-law/as-syrian-deaths-mount-worlds-responsibility-to-protect-takes-a-hit-experts-idUSKCN12O2S3 (accessed 10 January 2018).

[130] See e.g. Boutros Boutros-Ghali, *An Agenda for Peace: Preventive Diplomacy, Peacemaking, and Peacekeeping*, Report of the Secretary-General, A/47/277, 17 June 1992, 9.

[131] The 'sovereignty as responsibility' idea is associated in particular with Francis Deng, Special Advisor to the UN Secretary-General for the Prevention of Genocide. In one of its first iterations, see e.g. Francis M. Deng et al., *Sovereignty as Responsibility: Conflict Management in Africa* (Washington, DC: Brookings Institution, 1996). Or, more recently, see Francis M. Deng, 'From "Sovereignty as Responsibility" to the "Responsibility to Protect"', 2 *Global Responsibility to Protect* (2010): 353–70.

[132] See e.g. Ban Ki-Moon, *Responsibility to Protect: State Responsibility and Prevention*, Report of the Secretary-General, A/67/929–S /2013/399, 9 July 2013, 11.

by radical white nationalism, together with the closely connected global refugee crisis, those states and international institutions that have historically identified most closely with the paradigm of 'free' and 'equal' legal subjectivity are now positing an *absence* of 'good governance' in these regions as the root cause of such 'security threats'. In his 2015 report, for instance, 'tak[ing] stock of ten years of efforts to advance the responsibility to protect', outgoing UN Secretary-General Ban Ki-Moon placed particular emphasis on 'elevating prevention as a core aspect of the responsibility to protect'.[133]

Above all, as numerous 'high-level' reports of this nature underscore, this 'responsibility' is to be implemented through 'capacity-building' assistance, aimed at 'establish[ing] the foundations of good governance based on the rule of law, democratic principles and values, and accountability'. '[C]onstitutional protections' aimed at 'creating a society based on non-discrimination' together with 'free and fair' elections and a 'fair and inclusive transitional justice process' are assumed, of their own accord, to make people 'less likely to resort to violence to resolve their differences or make their voices heard'.[134] This is not to take away from the UN's recent acknowledgement (a step forward when compared with earlier iterations of R2P[135]) that 'business practices, particularly in extractive industries' can 'contribute to the commission' of 'atrocity crimes',[136] and that material inequalities are likewise 'risk factors' in this context.[137] As Anne Orford's work shows, however, the circular relationship suggested by this connection between the material fallout from international intervention on the one hand, and the problems which such intervention is designed to solve on the other, remains very much a peripheral consideration for the United Nations and for the other institutions (such as NATO and the EU) and states which have taken on the duty of implementing this 'responsibility to protect'.[138] Meanwhile, the 'risk management' tools proposed to tackle such 'threats' continue to be narrated in terms of instituting protections

[133] Ban Ki-Moon, *A Vital and Enduring Commitment*, 1–2.

[134] *State Responsibility and Prevention*, 8–11.

[135] See e.g. Kofi Anan, *In Larger Freedom: Towards Development, Security and Human Rights for All*, Report of the Secretary-General, A/59/2005, 21 March 2005.

[136] Ban Ki-Moon, *Fulfilling our Collective Responsibility: International Assistance and the Responsibility to Protect*, Report of the Secretary-General, A/68/947–S/2014/449, 11 July 2014, 7.

[137] *State Responsibility and Prevention*, 11.

[138] See generally Orford, 'Locating the International', 443, and Orford, *Reading Humanitarian Intervention.*

for 'equality of opportunity.'[139] In other words, the 'responsibility' of states – as policed by the 'international community' in the exercise of its own responsibility, through the use of force if necessary – is understood to lie fundamentally and, increasingly, exclusively in the reproduction of individual legal subjectivity.

3 Resisting International Legal Reproduction

The idea that all individuals everywhere are or should be free and equal – that they possess a 'fundamental' and 'universal' right to be equally free – is an appealing one. So, too, is the corresponding idea that the purpose of the state is to protect that right, and that the purpose of an international community is to take 'responsibility' for the enforcement of protection. As we have just seen in Section 2 and indeed throughout this book, this right to equal freedom within self-governing states has been demanded by different individuals and groups in all kinds of different contexts over the last five centuries. This demand, moreover, has become particularly loud in overtly oppressive situations in which the normative systems of particular groups have been stigmatised and suppressed – situations of colonisation, occupation, or totalitarian or patriarchal rule, for example. The vocabulary of a universal right for all individuals and all peoples to be 'free' insofar as they do not restrict the liberty of others, and 'equal' in their rights and duties under the law, provides a widely available, and widely understood vocabulary for condemning such intolerable situations, for demanding their termination, and for generating solidarity and support from external actors on the basis of a common set of norms.

This cycle, in which a particular situation of oppression is opposed, often very effectively, by recourse to a universalist language of emancipation, is one way in which individuals and communities from a wide variety of different backrounds and world views have found themselves identifying as, or aspiring to become, legal subjects. This point about the interpellative force of what she calls the 'juridical' idea of the human has been made brilliantly by Samera Esmeir in her essential study of Egypt and Egyptians under British Occupation, *Juridical Humanity*. 'Juridical

[139] *Fulfilling our Collective Responsibility*, 7.

humanity', Esmeir argues, is both 'a technology of colonial rule and a modern relationship of bondage'.[140] Moreover,

> with its claims of overcoming a despotic past, [it] was from start to finish a concept productive of subjugation to the state and its law. To escape bondage, to introduce a different concept of the human, or to abandon the human as a political concept, rebellion and continuous struggle may be the only course. But this will depend on the practice of rebellion and of struggle; struggles and rebellions may only end up reproducing the sovereignty of the state and its positive law. And yet, some rebellions and struggles carry the potential to introduce new texts and practices for losing the human in politics, or articulating other concepts of the human, while challenging the texts and practices of state law.[141]

On the one hand, as Esmeir suggests, the problems that stem from 'juridical humanity' – or from legal subjectivity more generally – are in some ways the same problems that Marx identified nearly 200 years ago. Marx characterised the demand for legal subjectivity (or 'political emancipation', as he called it) as the reduction of the human being to 'an egoistic, independent individual' on the one hand, and to 'a citizen, a juridical person' on the other.[142] The effect, Marx argued, was one of 'alienation' essentially from the material substance of one's body; from the things one makes and from one's fellow human beings (and, one might add, other creatures and things). As Pashukanis, Edelman and more recent critics have since shown, moreover, not only are individuals thereby forced to exchange their labour-power for wages in order to obtain commodities, but it is also the case that communities, in the form of states in particular, but also regions, cities and municipalities are increasingly coming to regard themselves as competing with one another for the resources necessary for 'sustainability'. In the twenty-first century, competition is no longer centred on the expansion of territorial sovereignty but, instead, on the arm's-length appropriation of resources, extracted from the earth but also, and much more subtly and indirectly, from the billions of minuscule profit margins that are to be found in almost every human (and increasingly non-human) undertaking, but which can only be detected and harnessed by those with access to the most sophisticated

[140] Samera Esmeir, *Juridical Humanity: A Colonial History* (Stanford University Press, 2010), 285.

[141] Ibid., 17.

[142] Karl Marx, 'On the Jewish Question' [February 1844], *Collected Works of Karl Marx and Friedrich Engels*, Vol. 3: March 1834–August 1844 (Lawrence & Wishart Electronic Book, 2010), 146–74, at 168.

technology around.[143] This type of market-based, often virtual interaction by which our world is coming increasingly to be determined, is understood to be 'free' in the sense that individuals respond, in the market place, to incentives on the basis of their own decision-making, rather than on the basis of commands issued by the state or from some other authority. Yet as critics have been pointing out for decades, behind this formal 'freedom' lies an astonishingly powerful set of coercive forces, which are grounded as much in desire as they are in violence. Above all, I have suggested, they are grounded in the figure of the 'self-governing' state – the dominance of which has been implored as much as it has been imposed – and its commitment to the reproduction of the 'juridical' human individual. This force stems not from the explicit command of an identifiable human authority, but instead from the material requirement of all living organisms of a minimal amount of resources to stay alive, in a distributive situation which denies that minimum to a large percentage of the world's (human and non-human) population. What is disputed, of course, is where that 'minimum' lies. Some 'desperately need' a holiday or a second car. Others desperately need somewhere to sleep or a cup of clean water. In an institutional context in which the only equality that matters is formal, and in which the only freedom that counts is negative ('freedom from'), both needs are registered as equally 'desperate'. This remains the case even though the capacity of the two 'needers' to satisfy them is (thanks not least to the substance of the needs themselves) unequally distributed, to a terminal degree.

Capital accumulation, in other words, hovers behind the alluring idea of a natural right of all individuals to be equally free at every point. The concrete and increasingly universal realisation of legal subjectivity, both macro and micro, in the form of the closely supervised self-governing state has forcibly transformed most human beings into self-producing, self-exchanging commodities, which really do 'freely' (and unlike loaves of bread or iPads) 'go to market and perform exchanges in their own right'.[144] At the same time, in an increasingly universal system of competition among 'free equals', the failure of those who lag behind in the accumulative race can be cast as stemming from personal laziness or ineptitude, rather than from long-term structural factors linked to race,

[143] See e.g. the World Bank's 'Global Platform for Sustainable Cities', at www.worldbank.org/en/topic/urbandevelopment/brief/global-platform-for-sustainable-cities (accessed 18 February 2018).

[144] Karl Marx, *Capital: A Critique of Political Economy*, Vol. 1, trans. Ben Fowkes (Harmondsworth: Penguin, 1978), 178.

gender, 'path dependency' and beyond. This failure to accumulate capital causes human beings and communities to be stigmatised as failures per se, triggering a range of disciplinary measures, from discriminatory language to military intervention, which in turn trigger a demand for the better enforcement of the right to be equally free. But today's 'losers' are just the twenty-first-century equivalent of the sixteenth century's 'natural slaves'.

As this flickering correspondance suggests, 'earned sovereignty', 'failed states', 'good governance' and the 'responsibility to protect' (understood as a responsibility to protect the rights of international capital) are hardly new phenomena. On the contrary, some of the 'constellations' we might find between 'now' and some of the 'thens' examined above stand out surprisingly clearly. For example, in Item 3 we observed how in 1919 the British Delegation to the Paris Peace Conference anchored its proposal on the nascent Mandates System in the language of 'good government'. This involved, to bring Lord Cecil's words back to mind, the construction of an 'open door or equal opportunity for the nationals of all the states Members of the League in respect of the use and development of the economic resources of such territories', together with 'freedom of transit and equality of trade conditions'.[145] Viewed against the complex and disparate background gradually assembled in this book, this reverse-echo of the present-day fixation on 'good governance' might seem less like a coincidence and more like a pattern. The same can also be said if we were to flip back to Francisco de Vitoria's use of the term 'self-government'.[146] Again, though writing in 1532, Vitoria used a remarkably similar term to describe a remarkably similar norm. For him, as we saw in Item 2, any right to 'self-government' on the part of the 'Indians' rested on their willingness and capacity to protect the 'natural' individual rights of the *Conquistadores* to travel and to obtain and trade private property freely. If the Indians failed in this regard, Vitoria concluded, the Spanish Crown was duty-bound to usurp their existing structures of self-organisation 'just as if the natives were infants', the latter having demonstrated that they were 'no whit ... better than such so far as self-government [was] concerned'. Even as they make enormous jumps across time and space, these affinities suggest that the idea and practice of the state, and of the 'international' norms which regulate its reproduction, have been implicated since their birth in a project of redistributing not only wealth and power but also pleasure (or,

[145] See Item 3, Section 4.
[146] See Item 2, Section 2.2.1.

perhaps more accurately, the absence of suffering) towards a tiny global minority of the world's human population.

This is not the end of the story, however, for as critics like Haraway, Moore and Natarajan point out, the problem is not just one of inter-human or inter-societal distribution. Far more pressing, in terms of the future of the planet's ecosystems, and hence of its capacity to sustain life, is a different kind of distributive question. This question concerns the distribution, between humans and non-human species, of the capacity to exist and to continue to exist. This problem, as we have seen, has become increasingly acute as the spaces on earth which lie beyond the jurisdiction of the 'self-governing' state become fewer and fewer. As I have argued elsewhere in relation to the fascist doctrine and practice of international law – and as the actions both of Mussolini and of other European leaders during the Abyssinia Crisis have already revealed – it was once considered obvious that 'successful' statehood would require territorial expansion at the expense of other states.[147] Today, however, the prospects for such expansion have run out, both formally and materially. This means that states seeking to match the demand for natural resources arising from their growing national 'markets' (whether growing in terms of population, wealth or both) are faced with only two options: either expunge their 'surplus populations' somehow,[148] or transform new 'virgin' areas of the material world (such as recyclable waste or carbon emissions) into tradable 'natural resources'.[149]

If nothing else, this book has already demonstrated that there can be no 'policy solution' to the distributive effects of the process of international legal reproduction because the very categories and legal/institutional structures which 'policy' must take for granted lie at the root of the problem. On the other hand, however, and as the passage above

[147] See e.g. Rose Sydney Parfitt, 'The Anti-Neutral Suit: International Legal Futurists, 1914–2017', 5 *London Review of International Law* (2017): 87–123; Parfitt, 'Fascism, Imperialism and International Law: An Arch Met a Motorway and the Rest is History …' 31 *Leiden Journal of International Law* (2018): 509–38; Parfitt,'Is Fascism Making a Comeback?', *StateOfNatureBlog.com*, 3 December 2017, available at http://stateofnatureblog.com/one-question-fascism-part-one/ (accessed 17 December 2017); and the work of the 'Fascism and the International' workshops, Mexico City, 18–20 June 2018 and Melbourne, 22–25 May 2018.

[148] Anne Orford, 'Surplus Population and the History of International Law', Kent Law School, Centre for Critical International Law Annual Lecture, 30 November 2017.

[149] See, in particular, the work of Aihwa Ong, e.g. Ong, *Fungible Life: Experiment in the Asian City of Life* (Durham, NC: Duke University Press, 2016) and the collection Ong and Nancy N. Chen (eds.), *Asian Biopolitic: Ethics and Communities of Fate* (Durham, NC: Duke University Press, 2010). My thanks to Genevieve Painter for this.

from Esmeir also suggests, the process of transforming the world into a series of universal 'juridical' subjects and subjecting it to their 'policy' has been challenged constantly, throughout its history, by 'rebellions and struggles' of every kind. Indeed, if the analysis presented here is correct, such rebellions and struggles stem directly from the fact that the transformation of 'other' into 'self' can never be complete. To rephrase the problem Esmeir flags up: the question is whether such resistance movements involve the demand to be recognised as 'same' (as in the case of newly independent Liberia, many of the Latin American states and the post-1918 'national states', for example) or whether (as I argued in the case of the Ethiopian Empire's relationship with the League) they involve the demand to be treated properly in spite of being (wholly or partly) 'other'. With this question in mind, the final section of this book will turn to one of the most radical and persistent efforts to stand up to the non-negotiable 'universality' of legal subjectivity. This is the struggle for 'self-determination' on Indigenous terms, ongoing since the very beginning of the state system itself and engaged in by many within the world's estimated 370 million Indigenous people.[150] As the very existence of this struggle demonstrates, however powerful the interpellative 'pull' of 'free' and 'equal' legal subjectivity may be, it has never been powerful enough to cancel out the space for resistance altogether. On the contrary, the very fact this process is by definition transformative, *and therefore* hybridised, in itself supplies the evidence that there are (still) alternatives 'out there' in the world which do not (as the logic of the Ethiopian Empire arguably did, like certain understandings of the Caliphate) simply offer an alternative form of imperialism.

In spite of the astonishing and prolonged violence that has been, and continues to be inflicted on Indigenous peoples,[151] many very powerful resistance movements remain in place. These movements take a wide variety of different positions on the nature of the problem, and on the question of how to respond to it – positions that do not always align with

[150] United Nations Permanent Forum on Indigenous Issues, 'Indigenous Peoples, Indigenous Voices', Factsheet, available at www.un.org/esa/socdev/unpfii/documents/5session_factsheet1.pdf (accessed 24 April 2017).

[151] See, in particular, the work of Paulo Illich Bacca, including Bacca, 'Indigenous Peoples and the Legacies of Colonialism in International Criminal Law: The Challenging Crime of Genocide', *Critical Legal Thinking*, 7 October 2015, at http://criticallegalthinking.com/2015/10/07/indigenous-peoples-legacies-of-colonialism-international-criminal-law/; Bacca, 'Indigenizing International Law from an Inverse Legal Anthropology', *Naked Punch*, 13 May 2017, at www.nakedpunch.com/articles/270 (both accessed 16 February 2018).

one another. However, there is a strong current among these very diverse movements, which insists on the connection between colonialism, capitalism and statehood as the source of the problems which these communities (and the world at large) are facing. It is this connection which has led the Kahnawà:ke Mohawk anthropologist Audra Simpson to call for what she characterises as a 'politics of refusal'.[152] At the centre of Simpson's ethnography of Indigenous resistance lies an idea that runs in parallel with this book's notion of the inevitably hybrid nature of legal subjectivity when imposed by (or demanded from) the self-governing state. The experience of being Kahnawà:ke, Simpson argues, is an experience split between two completely different mindsets. This, in her view, is both an oppressive condition predicated on the inevitable failure of 'other' to become 'self', and a bridge to a different set of subjective resources which cannot be burned by that mandatory process of transformation. This term, 'Indigenous', she writes,

> is embedded conceptually in a geographic alterity and a radical past as the Other in the history of the West. Although seemingly unable to be both things at once, the Mohawks of Kahnawà strive to articulate these modalities as they live and move within a territorial space that is overlaid with settler regimes that regulate or circumscribe their way of life. Their struggle with the state ... is a sign, also, of colonialism's ongoing existence and simultaneous failure. Colonialism survives in a settler form. In this form, it fails at what it is supposed to do: eliminate Indigenous people; take all their land; absorb them into a white, property-owning body politic.

With this potential affinity in mind, it is to Simpson's work, and to that of other scholars and activists involved in this struggle, that the final sections of the book turn. What I hope to achieve is not a reinterpretation of this thinking for my own purposes but, instead, a final act of colligation, in which some of the key arguments that are being made in the context of Indigenous resistance are set against some of the histories of resistance discussed earlier, in order to see what (if any) trans-historical affinities and solidarities hover into view.

What is different about *this* juxtaposition, however, is its scale. As we have seen, all the other fragments of the history of international legal reproduction examined so far, and of resistance to that process, refer to particular struggles that have taken place in particular times and places. By contrast, the history of Indigenous resistance to the processes of legal interpellation

[152] Audra Simpson, *Mohawk Interruptus: Political Life Across the Borders of Settler States* (Durham, NC: Duke University Press, 2014).

and subjectivisation, set in motion by the arrival of colonialism, capitalism and the state, *is* the history of colonialism, capitalism and the state – from 1492 until today, and from 'Colombia' ('Christened', of course, after the continent's 'discoverer', Cristóbal Colón – also known as Christopher Columbus) to 'New Zealand' (named, in 1642, by its Dutch 'discoverer', after a province, Zeeland, in the Netherlands). Just as the process of international legal reproduction is (or so I have argued) a general process, common to the formation of all but the 'original' states of the world, so the Indigenous struggle – so often positioned as a 'domestic' and 'historical' affair and therefore as a peripheral consideration both for international and state law – is a general struggle. It is not an aspect of the history of the expansion of state. It *is* that history – although it is also far more than that, and up to 59,500 years longer for the many of the peoples concerned.[153] It is no wonder, then, that we find radical Indigenous thinking and practice – which begins from the observation that the state, as the source of the problem, therefore cannot also be its solution – at the vanguard of the struggle against the ongoing effects of colonialism and capitalism.[154]

3.1 *Indigenous Self-Determination on Indigenous Terms*

Having appropriated Indigenous lands and recast them as its 'territory' (understood as an unlimited reservoir of 'natural resources' there for the taking), and then embarked on an (ongoing, though only partially successful) project to submerge Indigenous ideas and practices of communal self-understandings beneath its own vision of 'freedom' and 'equality' in order to achieve this, the state is an inescapably colonial formation from

[153] I am extremely grateful to Genevieve Painter for this point, and for the many conversations which led me to this argument. See Christopher Klein, 'DNA Study Finds Aboriginal Australians World's Oldest Civilization', *History.com*, 23 September 2016, at https://history.com/news/dna-study-finds-aboriginal-australians-worlds-oldest-civilization (accessed 7 August 2018), and also *Uluru Statement from the Heart*, 26 May 2017, at www.referendumcouncil.org.au/sites/default/files/2017-05/Uluru_Statement_From_The_Heart_0.PDF (accessed 7 August 2018).

[154] There are of course exceptions to this rejection of statehood as a solution to the problem of colonialism – in the Palestinian context, for example. (On the Israel-Palestine situation as one of settler-colonialism, see Mazen Masri, *The Dynamics of Exclusionary Constitutionalism: Israel as a Jewish and Democratic State* (Oxford: Hart Publishing, 2017).) However, unlike some other Indigenous peoples, the Palestinians, as inhabitants of a former British mandated territory, do possess an 'external' right to self-determination. For the classic case law explanation of the difference between 'external' and 'internal' self-determination, see *Reference re: Secession of Quebec*, Supreme Court of Canada, 2 S.C.R. 297, para. 138.

the Indigenous perspective. This is not, however, simply a question of competing claims to territorial sovereignty. On the contrary, at the centre of this struggle lies a concept of land, in many Indigenous cosmologies, that is very different from the criterion of 'fixed territory' that international law lays down as one of the essential elements of statehood. As the Cuban diplomat Miguel Alfonso Martínez, then UN Special Rapporteur on the Rights of Indigenous Peoples, put it in 1999, land embodies 'the essential elements of [Indigenous] cosmogony' and constitutes 'the ultimate source of life and wisdom'.[155] The idea that Indigenous lands might be divided up, sold off and thus legitimately and permanently 'alienated' is both metaphysically and morally wrong from a perspective which views land as something 'not "owned" but "preserved" for future generations'.[156] This means that the ontological basis upon which Indigenous ways of thinking and being are founded are, in many cases, entirely different from those which underpin the ideas of statehood, self-determination and 'free' and 'equal' legal subjectivity more generally. Writing in the Latin American context, for example, the anthropologist Arturo Escobar describes these 'relational' ontologies as being 'differentiated from the dualist ontologies of liberal modernity in that they are not built on the divides between nature and culture, us and them, individual and community'. Relationality, in this context, 'refers to a different way of imagining life (socio-natural worlds)'.[157]

Similarly, to take an example from what is now 'Canada', Indigenous communities in the Yukon 'have historically seen themselves as *part of* the land, rather than separate from it', according to the anthropologist Paul Nadasdy.[158] As human inhabitants of that land, they understand themselves as being 'enmeshed in a complex web of reciprocal relationships and obligations with the land and the animals upon it', such that their use of the land 'is completely contingent on their fulfilment of certain obligations to both land and animals'.[159] The Dene political theorist Glen Coulthard gives the term 'grounded normativity' to the 'ethical framework

[155] *Study on Treaties, Agreements and Other Constructive Arrangements between States and Indigenous Populations*, Final Report by the United Nations Special Rapporteur on Indigenous Peoples, UNESCO Commission on Human Rights, E/CN.4/Sub.2/1999/20, 22 June 1999, 40.

[156] Ibid.

[157] Escobar, 'Latin America at a Crossroads', 4.

[158] Paul Nadasdy, '"Property" and Aboriginal Land Claims in the Canadian Subarctic: Some Theoretical Considerations', 104 *American Anthropologist* (2002): 247–61, at 247–8. Emphasis in the original.

[159] Ibid., 247–8.

provided by [such] place-based practices and associated forms of knowledge'. [160]As Coulthard articulates it:

> Indigenous struggles against capitalist imperialism are best understood as struggles oriented around the question of *land* – struggles not only *for* land, but also deeply *informed* by what the land as a mode of *reciprocal* relationship (which is itself informed by place-based practices and associated form[s] of knowledge) ought to teach us about living our lives in relation to one another and our surroundings in a respectful, nondominating and nonexploitative way.[161]

Nor, of course, does the term 'land' here refer exclusively to the soil underfoot. On the contrary, 'land' in this context operates frequently as a shorthand for entire ecosystems comprising multiple non-human species and elements as well as humans themselves. As another anthropologist, Eduardo Kohn, has argued in his groundbreaking *How Forests Think* – an 'anthropology beyond the human' based on fieldwork conducted with the inhabitants of Ávila, a Runa/Quechua village in Ecuador's Upper Amazon – such ecosystems are not, from a Runa perspective, simply networks of organisms engaged, with the exception of its thinking humans, in instinctive patterns of behaviour. On the contrary, the relationships among the humans, dogs, leafcutter ants, jaguars, crab-eating racoons, trees, tobacco plants and other elements in and around this village comprise an 'ecology of selves' in which 'living semiotic dynamic, meaning (i.e., means–ends relations, significance, "aboutness," telos) is a constitutive feature of the world and not just something we humans impose on it'.[162] He continues:

> This colonially inflected, multispecies ecology of selves is real in an ethnographic and ontological sense. But it depends for its existence on the continuous flourishing of dense nonhuman ecologies just as it does on the humans who live by tapping into those ecologies. If too many of these elements that make up this ecology of selves disappear, a particular kind of life (and afterlife) will come to an end – forever. And we will have to find ways to mourn its absence.[163]

However, Kohn cautions, if that happens 'it is not as if all life will end. There will be other Runa ways of being human – ones that might well

[160] Glen Coulthard, *Red Skin, White Masks* (Minneapolis, MN: University of Minnesota Press, 2014), 60.

[161] Coulthard, *Red Skin, White Masks*, 60. Emphasis in the orginal.

[162] Eduardo Kohn, *How Forests Think: Toward an Anthropology Beyond the Human* (Berkeley, CA: University of California Press, 2013), 69. My thanks to Genevieve Painter for pointing me in this direction.

[163] Ibid., 631.

also entangle nonhumans, ones that might call forth other spirits. And we must find ways to listen for the hopes that that kind of reality houses as well.'[164] This argument dovetails with one of Audra Simpson's most powerful arguments: that one of the greatest threats to the Indigenous struggle involves (and has long involved) Western outsiders:

> fetishized, deeply controlled canonical approach to 'culture as the pure,' 'culture as tradition,' 'culture as what is prior to settlement' [which] disavows or pushes away its context of articulation: the political project of dispossession and containment, as it actually works to contain, to fetishize and entrap and distill Indigenous discourses into memorizable, repeatable rituals for preservation against a social and political death that was foretold but did not happen.[165]

The aim of those involved in this struggle, then, is not (these interventions underline) 'sovereignty' in the international legal sense. Nor is it simply about carving out a space within an existing sovereign jurisdiction (such as 'Canada' or 'Ecuador') in which Indigenous methods of hunting and fishing, for example, might be practised without interference. On the contrary, the very assertion that the legal permission of the state is required before Indigenous individuals can engage in practices which pre-existed the state's violent and, according to the law which pre-existed it, entirely unlawful appropriation of the land those practices relate to, is deeply problematic. Even where such 'cultural' rights have, for reasons of pragmatism, been accepted, they can quickly be emptied of meaning when the land, rivers and oceans in question are polluted or otherwise damaged by the state's other 'lawful' activities, such as mining and oil drilling.[166] But there is also an even deeper problem, given that for many Indigenous peoples, 'the land is the source of the law', as the Kombumerri/Munaljahlai legal scholar Christine Black has put it, succinctly.[167] If, as Black, Borrows, Simpson, Coulthard and many other Indigenous legal scholars attest, the law is not about the land but *in* the land, then one action (such as carving the profile of four heads of state into a mountain range – see Figure 5) that is perfectly lawful according to state law may amount to a very serious violation of another set of laws whose normativity is operational

[164] Ibid., 631.

[165] Simpson, *Mohawk Interruptus*, 99.

[166] See e.g Niobe Thompson and Tom Radford, *To the Last Drop*, 'Witness' documentary (Doha: Al Jazeera, 2012), available at www.aljazeera.com/programmes/witness/2011/06/20116227153978324.html (accessed 13 November 2017).

[167] C. F. Black, *The Land is the Source of the Law: A Dialogic Encounter with Indigenous Jurisprudence* (London, New York: Routledge, 2011).

in exactly the same space as the first. Black, for example, draws on the Indigenous concept of *Djang*, used by Senior Law Man Bill Neidjie (1920–2002), the last surviving speaker of the Gaagudju language from northern Kakadu, in what is now the Northern Territory of 'Australia', to make this point. '*Djang*, in a word, is Law', Black explains. 'But when it is tapped into inappropriately – as with mining – it becomes a disorganizing principle, confounding and confusing, blighting the Land.'[168]

Instead, the aims of this struggle, according to these scholars, are (at least) threefold. One of these aims, they argue, consists in defending (and, if necessary, re-establishing) conditions under which Indigenous communities can continue to exist lawfully on their own terms, not as relics of the past but instead as twenty-first-century inhabitants of dynamic, growing and changing modes of thinking and being. A second aim consists in these scholars' insistence on respect for Indigenous law *as* law (again, on its own terms). A third stems from the urgent need to relativise the epistemological, ontological and normative foundations of the state, state law and international law – not only in order to ensure that Indigenous ways of thinking and being can continue to thrive, but also to attend to the relationship between the 'dualist ontologies' of 'liberal modernity' (as Escobar calls them) and the escalating global environmental crisis.[169]

However, even if many Indigenous scholars and activists actively reject the paradigm of 'self-governing' statehood – even if they 'refuse' (the key term for Audra Simpson) fully to interpellate as legal subjects, individual and collective – this has not halted the state's efforts to draw them into the interpellative cycle that I characterise as the process of international legal reproduction. As an example, consider Coulthard's accounts of the efforts of the Dene to carve out a space in the territory of 'Canada' within which they might live more easily on Dene terms. In the 1970s, Coulthard explains, proposals put forward by the Dene for a new system of communal land custodianship were rejected by the Canadian Government. Such measures, the Government reasoned, 'would amount to the establishment of an exclusionary, indeed, "race-based" jurisdiction in northern Canada'.[170] The Canadian state, in other words, viewed the Dene's proposals as an effort to exclude an area of state territory from the domain

[168] Ibid., 48. See Bill Neidjie, *Story About Feeling* (Broome: Magabala Books, 1989).

[169] See, in particular, Julie Evans, Ann Genovese, Alexander Reilly and Patrick Wolfe (eds.), *Sovereignty: Frontiers of Possibility* (Honolulu, HI: University of Hawai'i Press, 2012); Olivia Barr, *A Jurisprudence of Movement: Common Law, Walking, Unsettling Place* (Abingdon: Routledge, 2016)

[170] Coulthard, *Red Skin, White Masks*, 70.

of individual property rights, free passage, free trade, and freedom of 'sojourn' (to recall Vitoria's language), and therefore as a violation, in principle, of the equal rights of all Canadian citizens, including non-Dene Canadian citizens (and indeed foreigners) to buy property or, perhaps, to obtain mining concessions, in the area regarded by the Dene as their lands. Since that time, as Coulthard details, Canada has made clear again and again that its willingness to constitute a limited set of collective rights for Indigenous peoples like the Dene would only be granted in return for a set of undertakings which allowed for the ongoing extraction, by private enterprises (whether Canadian or not), of the 'natural resources' existing on or within the lands in question.[171] Indeed, Canada has only been prepared to cede 'sovereign' rights, opposable to itself, to Indigenous peoples over part of its territory on condition that the Indigenous institutions which take over are committed to protecting the property rights of all existing legal subjects, as the work of a groundbreaking group of Indigenous scholars, including Coulthard, Taiaiake Alfred, John Borrows, Val Napoleon, Jeffery Hewitt and Audra Simpson, among others, has demonstrated.[172] As this suggests, among other things, the possibility that the concepts of legal subjectivity, self-government and statehood might themselves be, in a historical sense, 'race-based' cannot even be articulated in the language of self-government.

Similarly, in the 'Australian' context, a large body of critical scholarship and activism has emerged to indicate that a similar logic is at work in the common law principle of 'native title'.[173] The Australian Supreme Court's *Mabo* decision (formalised in the 1993 Native Title Act) was

[171] Ibid., 160.

[172] See e.g. Taiaiake Alfred, *Peace, Power, Righteousness: An Indigenous Manifesto* (Don Mills, Ontario, New York: Oxford University Press, 1999); John Borrows, *Freedom and Indigenous Constitutionalism* (University of Toronto Press, 2016); Coulthard, *Red Skin, White Masks*; Val Napoleon, 'Aboriginal Self-Determination: Individual Self and Collective Selves', 29 *Atlantis* (2015): 31–46; Simpson, *Mohawk Interruptus*; Ruth Buchanan & Jeffery Hewitt, 'Treaty Canoe', in Hohmann & Joyce (eds), *International Law's Objects* (Oxford: OUP, forthcoming 2018), among many other excellent scholars and works. I have concentrated on Indigenous scholars in this footnote; there are, of course, many non-Indigenous fellow travellers whose work has been extremely important in this context.

[173] Native title is defined as 'the communal, group or individual rights and interests of Aboriginal people and Torres Strait Islander people in relation to land and waters, possessed under traditional law and custom, by which those people have a connection with an area which is recognised under Australian law'. National Native Title Tribunal, available at www.nntt.gov.au/Pages/Glossary.aspx (accessed 2 May 2017).

widely hailed as a victory for Aboriginal peoples.[174] And indeed, the decision of the Australian state to recognise Aboriginal peoples in Australia as having had, prior to the arrival of the British, systems of law that included normative connections to Indigenous lands ('country'), constituting a form of collective legal subjectivity, was certainly an enormous step forwards when compared with the situation that preceded it.[175] However, as quickly became evident, not only is native title almost impossible to claim (thanks, in particular, to the procedural requirement that an unbroken connection of claimant communities to 'country' can be demonstrated); not only does it exclude the right to conclude treaties with the Australian government (although it is possible that this might be on the point of changing);[176] native title has also turned out to be very easily 'extinguished', whether in full (by the existence of freehold titles and other land leases) or in part (by pastoral leases).[177] In short, as many Aboriginal scholars have argued, including Black, Mark McMillan, Aileen

[174] See *Mabo and Ors* v. *Queensland (No. 2)* (1992) 175 CLR 1, esp. judgment of Justice Brennan, *Native Title Act* No. 100 (1993). On the assumption that, in reaching this decision, the Court 'reverses' the doctrine of *terra nullius*, see David Ritter, 'The "Rejection of Terra Nullius" in *Mabo*: A Critical Analysis', 18 *Sydney Law Review* (1996): 5–33.

[175] Depending on the nature of the claim, as the Central Land Council puts it, '[r]ecognition of native title may give Indigenous people the right to hold ceremony, gather bush tucker or have a say on what development can happen on the land'. Central Land Council, 'What is Native Title?', at www.clc.org.au/articles/info/what-is-the-native-title/ (accessed 2 May 2017).

[176] See, notoriously, the judgment of the Federal Court of Australia in *Members of the Yorta Yorta Aboriginal Community* v. *Victoria and Ors* [1998] FCA 1606, Federal Court of Australia, 18 December 1998, that the 'tide of history' had 'undoubtedly washed away any traditional rights that the indigenous people may have previously exercised in relation to controlling access to their land within the claim area' and denying the claim to native title on this basis. See also Australian High Court, *Members of the Yorta Yorta Aboriginal Community* v. *Victoria* (2002) 214 CLR 422. At the time of writing, the first steps have just been taken in Victoria, the Northern Territories and Western Australia to begin a process of treaty-making with Aboriginal communities. These developments come in the wake of the landmark National Constitutional Convention of May 2017. This Convention brought together more than 250 Aboriginal and Torres Strait Islander leaders at the foot of Uluru in Central Australia on the lands of the Anangu people. The 'Uluru Statement from the Heart' issued by the Convention calls, among other things, for the creation of a 'Makarrata Commission to supervise a process of agreement-making' between the Australian Federal and State Governments on the one hand, and Aboriginal peoples and Torres Straight Islanders on the other. *Makarrata* (a word from the language of the Yolngu people in Arnhem Land) means 'the coming together after a struggle'. See *Uluru Statement from the Heart*, 26 May 2017, at www.referendumcouncil.org.au/sites/default/files/2017-05/Uluru_Statement_From_The_Heart_0.PDF (accessed 7 August 2018).

[177] See e.g. David Ritter, *The Native Title Market* (Perth: UWA Publishing, 2009).

Moreton-Robinson, Irene Watson and others,[178] even after the creation of native title, Aboriginal land claims in Australia are only likely to be recognised in the Australian courts if, and to the extent that, any alternative arrangements for communal engagement with the land demonstrate their commitment to respecting, and therefore reproducing, existing property rights belonging to pre-established legal subjects, whether individual or corporate, Australian or 'foreign'.

If my attempt to draw this work together is justified, these connections suggest that the struggle for Indigenous self-determination on Indigenous terms can offer a present-day and extremely powerful illustration of the incorporative and destructive logic of the process of international legal reproduction. More important than this, however, this struggle also operates as an undeniable, concrete reminder that statehood and capitalism are neither universal nor inevitable, and that alternatives to a process whose function it is precisely to eliminate alternatives do (still) exist. With this in mind, the following subsections will finish by placing two elements of this struggle alongside two of this book's running themes: hybridity/hybridisation on the one hand, and time/history/legality on the other.

3.2 Recognition, Reconciliation, Hybridisation

Since the 1970s, the clash between Indigenous understandings of self-determination based on Indigenous law and the 'right of peoples' of

[178] Black, *The Land is the Source of the Law*; Mark Harris, *Human Rights, the Rule of Law and Exploitation in the Postcolony: Blood Minerals* (Abingdon: Routledge, forthcoming, 2019); Mark McMillan, 'Koowarta and the Rival Indigenous International: Our Place as Indigenous Peoples in the International', 23 *Griffith Law Review* (2014): 110–26; Aileen Moreton-Robinson, *The White Possessive: Property, Power, and Indigenous Sovereignty* (Minnesota, MN: University of Minneapolis Press, 2015); Irene Watson, *Aboriginal Peoples, Colonialism and International Law: Raw Law* (Abingdon: Routledge, 2015). As well as these Indigenous scholars, many fellow-travellers' work has had an important impact in this area. See e.g. Barr, *A Jurisprudence of Movement*; Ann Curthoys, Ann Genovese and Alexander Reilly, *Rights and Redemption: History, Law and Indigenous Peoples* (Sydney: UNSW Press, 2008); Kirsty Gover, *Tribal Constitutionalism: States, Tribes, and the Governance of Membership* (Oxford University Press, 2010); Dylan Lino, 'Thinking Outside the Constitution on Indigenous Constitutional Recognition: Entrenching the Racial Discrimination Act', 91 *Australian Law Journal* (2017): 381–5; Shaun McVeigh and Shaunnagh Dorsett, 'Conduct of Laws: Native Title, Responsibility, and some Limits of Jurisdictional Thinking', 36 *Melbourne University Law Review* (2012): 470–93; Sophie Rigney, 'The Hopes and Discontents of Indigenous-Settler Reconciliation', 11 *International Journal of Transnational Justice* (2017): 359–68.

self-determination as understood in international law, has been negotiated above all by reference to ideas of 'recognition' and 'reconciliation'. The aim, in Coulthard's words, has been to '[reconcile] Indigenous peoples' assertions of nationhood with settler-state sovereignty via the accommodation of Indigenous identity-related claims through the negotiation of settlements over issues such as land, economic development, and self-government'.[179] Yet, as Coulthard points out, and as the Pi'ilani/ Kahakumakaliua writer and political theorist Haunani-Kay Trask argues, likewise, in the Hawaiian context, 'ideologically, "rights" talk is part of the larger, greatly obscured historical reality of American colonialism'; so much so that 'by entering legalistic discussions wholly internal to the American system, Natives participate in their own mental colonization'.[180] Just as settler-colonialism is 'territorially acquisitive in perpetuity',[181] so, Coulthard argues, drawing on Mohawk political theorist Taiaiake Alfred and Anishinaabe feminist Leanne Betasamosake Simpson, does settler-colonial rule add up to what Michel Foucault called 'governmentality'. In other words, the settler-state comprises 'a relatively diffuse set of governing relations that operate through a circumscribed mode of recognition that structurally ensures continued access to Indigenous peoples' lands and resources by producing neocolonial subjectivities that coopt Indigenous people into becoming instruments of their own dispossession'.[182] According to this analysis, the power of the settler-state – and, I would add, of the state in general, since all states, in the logic of this book, are settler-states to some degree – 'works *through* rather than entirely *against* freedom'.[183]

One way we might bring this rejection of the 'recognition' paradigm into conversation with some of the earlier elements of this book is by

[179] Coulthard, *Red Skin, White Masks*, 151. In Australia, for example, the movement towards 'reconciliation' is led by the NGO Reconciliation Australia, which is leading the campaign to have Indigenous peoples recognised in the Australia Constitution. See www.reconciliation.org.au and www.recognise.org.au (accessed 19 April 2017). In the US, the process is both older and less apologetic. In 2010, the first Obama administration signed a 'Native American Apology Resolution', which was heavily criticised, among other things, for the lack of publicity attending to it. See e.g. Rob Capriccioso, 'A Sorry Saga: Obama signs Native American Apology Resolution; Fails to Draw Attention to it', *Indian Country Today*, 13 January 2010, available at http://indianlaw.org/node/529 (accessed 29 April 2017).

[180] Haunani-Kay Trask, *From a Native Daughter: Colonialism and Sovereignty in Hawaii* (Monroe, ME: Common Courage Press, 1993), 112.

[181] Coulthard, *Red Skin, White Masks*, 152. Emphasis removed.

[182] Ibid., 156.

[183] Ibid. Emphasis in the original.

placing it within the Bakhtinian framework of 'organic' versus 'intentional' hybridisation examined in the Frame and in the context of Ethiopia's interventions before the League of Nations.[184] As we have seen in several different contexts, and as Genevieve Painter points out in her work on the history of settler–Indigenous relations in North America,[185] not all 'social languages' as Bakhtin called them (not all jurisprudences, we might say, in the legal context) are equally powerful. For those less willing or less able, in a material sense, to impose their world view on others, the risk is that what Bakhtin saw as the relatively benign process of 'organic hybridisation' might collapse into straightforward domination by assimilation. This is the kind of risk highlighted by the Tanganekald/Meintangk/Boandik scholar of international law, Irene Watson, in her critique of the 2007 *United Nations Declaration on the Rights of Indigenous Peoples* (UNDRIP),[186] for example. UNDRIP's 'original intention', Watson points out, was to 'empower First Nations' self-determination in relationship to our law and lands', and in doing so to assert the right of Indigenous peoples 'to survive the policies of states, especially when those policies have an assimilationist agenda'.[187] However, 'under the pressure of UN member states, the UNDRIP focus shifted to a generalist individual human rights approach'.[188] For instance, Article 1 of the Declaration, which guarantees Indigenous peoples 'the right to the full enjoyment, as a collective or as individuals, of all human rights and fundamental freedoms as recognized in ... international human rights law', is reduced or 'read down' to the idea that Indigenous peoples have 'human rights and fundamental freedoms as collectives or as individuals', according to Watson.[189] This allows the idea that Indigenous peoples are 'law-full peoples' on their own terms to be systematically 'ignored',[190] or simply reinterpreted as a demand for 'self-determination' in international legal, rather than Indigenous, terms.

This totalitarian quality of legal subjectivity – the way in which it requires the subordination of all other ways of being and knowing on the part of all individuals and communities who choose (or are forced

[184] See above, Item 5, Section 2 and Item 6, Section 2.

[185] See esp. Genevieve Renard Painter, 'A Letter from the Haudenosaunee Confederacy to King George V: Writing and Reading Jurisdictions in International Legal History', 5 *London Review of International Law* (2017): 7–48.

[186] *United Nations Declaration on the Rights of Indigenous Peoples*, Annexed to GA61/295, 13 September 2007 (UNDRIP).

[187] Watson, *Aboriginal Peoples, Colonialism and International Law*, 38.

[188] Ibid., 38.

[189] Ibid., 38.

[190] Ibid., 38.

to choose) to articulate their emancipatory demands in the language of equal rights – is equally obvious if we examine some of the very first encounters between state law and Indigenous law. In the 'Canadian' context, for example, Painter points out that this encounter was marked from the very beginning by a material imbalance which predetermined which jurisprudence would dominate.[191] To illustrate, Painter describes a meeting, in October 1887, between two Canadian commissioners and Nisga'a and Tsimshian leaders, in which the former explained to the latter that all the land in the Naas River Valley now belonged to the Queen of England.[192] As she notes, on the basis of the archival records of this meeting, 'the Nisga'a did not simply disagree with the commissioners' words; they could not hear those words as lawful claims of ownership'; while the English commissioners, for their part, 'could not hear evidence of uninterrupted Nisga'a presence as lawful ownership of the land'.[193] The absence of an 'agreement about the conventional procedures for the speech act of "claiming the land"' seems, on the surface, to have affected both sides equally in the context of these bipartite negotiations. But while it was of virtually no consequence to the British Empire,[194] for the Nisga'a it was the beginning of what many members of that community regard as a catastrophic process of dispossession, displacement and incorporation.

This clash, simultaneously ontological, epistemological and normative, together with the underlying distributive bias of the encounter, continues to play out today. Nadasdy's work, also in 'Canada', for example, analyses some of the consequences of the decision of certain Indigenous leaders in the Yukon to re-narrate their communities' demands (for hunting rights, for example) in the language of property rights. As Nadasdy notes, while this decision has 'greatly expanded aboriginal people's access to the legal institutions of the state, allowing them to defend their interests in land and self-government more effectively',[195] the re-articulation of Indigenous claims in the language of 'rights' is also threatening to undermine the very purpose for which that language was deployed. Members of the Kluane (within the territory of Yukon), for example, 'see their relationship with animals as social in nature characterised by relations of mutual respect

[191] Genevieve Renard Painter, 'Law as Minor Jurisprudence: Is it a Mistake?', 21 *Law, Text, Culture* (2017): 276–300, at 289.

[192] Ibid., 278.

[193] Ibid., 279.

[194] Ibid., 279.

[195] Nadasdy, '"Property" and Aboriginal Land Claims', 252.

and reciprocity'.[196] For them, 'animals ... give themselves to hunters when and if the hunters prove themselves worthy, and with this gift comes heavy obligations and responsibilities'.[197] Applying the notion of property rights to animals is therefore 'inappropriate' in that it brings with it 'a sense of entitlement, an expectation that those rights will be fulfilled'.[198] By contrast, in Kluane epistemology, '[r]espectful hunters trying to understand their lack of success' will 'search within themselves for a lapse in character, rather than looking outward for someone or something that is depriving them of their rights'.[199] This means that the very 'expectation that would accompany someone's "right to kill" an animal is contrary to the proper attitude of respect that a hunter must have if he or she is to be successful in the hunt'.[200] In recent years, Nadasdy relates, 'many Kluane people ... have put aside their discomfort with the idea of "owning" land and animals, electing to participate in the land claim process because they see it as the only realistic chance they have to preserve their way of life against increasing encroachment by Euro-Canadians'. In doing so, however, 'they have been forced to express their interests and way of life in the language of property, a process plagued by problems of cultural translation and ridden with politics'. The paradox is thus that while 'First Nation people's strategy of expressing their claims in the language of property ... might indeed be the only realistic way for them to protect their own interests', this strategy helps to 'obscure the fact that there are other ways to conceive [the] relationship between humans and land/animals', and to ensure that 'property remains a hegemonic discourse in the arena of aboriginal-state relations'.[201]

If we were to stop, for a second, and place this strategy alongside the Ethiopian Empire's experience at the League, and/or the Chinese 'self-strengthening movement', or the Haitian Revolution, the paradox facing the Kluane might show itself to be a familiar one. Or, at least, this paradox might reveal itself to be as familiar as it is *sui generis* or 'different'. That paradox suggests, in line with Edelman's account of legal subjectivity, that the more Indigenous peoples attempt to make their demands comprehensible to the state by articulating them in the language of law,

[196] Ibid., 257.
[197] Ibid., 257.
[198] Ibid., 257.
[199] Ibid., 257.
[200] Ibid., 257.
[201] Ibid., 258.

the more powerful the interpellative 'pull' of that language becomes.[202] Or as Kirsten Anker puts it, 'whether claims to land, resources and jurisdiction are read in terms of equality or of the distinctiveness of Indigenous peoples, the mechanical process of deciding claims turns on the recognition of some fact of the claimants' lives as something "else": sometimes occupation, sometimes tradition, sometimes law' – 'a process of linguistic and cultural translation that requires Indigenous lives to be both legible and rendered into the terms of another law'.[203] Simply by voicing their demands in the idiom of negative freedom and formal equality, Indigenous individuals and communities – like individuals and communities everywhere – answer to, and in doing so identify with, at least to some extent, the 'Absolute Subject', that is, capital. What is different about this context, however, is the tenacity of the struggle to defend and continue to live by Indigenous ontological and normative systems, in defiance of such pressures to 'consent'. This means that the coercive and inevitably partial (or hybrid) nature of 'Indigenous legal subjectivity', as the product of this enforced process of interpellation is, for those who inhabit it, glaringly obvious.

In the attempt to avoid the incorporative bias associated with 'recognition' and 'reconciliation', some Indigenous scholars and activists have adopted a strategy that Bakhtin might have recognised as 'intentional' (as opposed to 'organic') hybridisation. These are interventions aimed not at mixing ('reconciling') Indigenous and non-Indigenous legal epistemologies, but rather at juxtaposing one against the other in order to highlight the biases and hypocrisies of the latter. Some examples of this kind of strategy can be found in the decision of critics like Watson, Audra Simpson, Alfred or Borrows to write in a combination of English and Nunga or Nishnaabeg, or introduce their lectures in Kahnawà:ke or Ojibwe; or in Borrows' recommendation that readers should skip the preface (*n'gii-pawauddjige*) to his book so as to 'struggle' with and 'more sharply encounter with greater intimacy [its] particular Anishinabek methodology' (founded as much in dreams, animal creation narratives, oral histories, landscapes, 'thunder and lightning' and recent histories of resistance, he argues, as it is in Canadian legal doctrines and comparative legal theory); or in the insistence of the authors of the 2017 *Uluru Statement from*

[202] See esp. James Martell, *The Misinterpellated Subject* (Durham, NC: Duke University Press, 2017).

[203] Kirsten Anker, *Declarations of Interdependence: A Legal Pluralist Approach to Indigenous Rights* (Burlington, VT: Ashgate, 2014), 191–2.

the Heart that the 'destiny' of future generations of Aboriginal and Torres Straight Islanders must be to 'walk in two worlds'.[204]

One connection we might see between these interventions and some of the other strategies of resistance examined earlier, then, concerns the way in which they alter the context in which (Western) 'legal' language is found, by pinning them (as it were) *against* the language (not always verbal; not always written) of Indigenous law.[205] In the process, words whose meaning we have been taught to take for granted, like 'rights' or 'self-determination', are stripped of their emancipatory pretentions, becoming 'double-voiced' (as Bakhtin might have argued), and therefore politicised, in a way that is arguably more effective, for example, than a discourse of reverse-racism directed against white settlers and their descendants. As Alfred insists, 'if the goal is to obliterate the oppressor's power altogether, any challenge will fail; if we seek instead to initiate a different kind of challenge, in the form of regenerating our own existences in the face of the oppressor's false claims to authority, legitimacy, and sovereignty, we cannot but succeed and, thus, force the state to transform itself'.[206] Or as the poet and activist Audre Lorde argued, famously, in 1979, in the context of a different struggle, and yet likewise pitched against the complacency of formal understandings of equality in conveniently overlooking difference and in doing so reinscribing inequality:

> [S]urvival is not an academic skill. [Survival] is learning how to stand alone, unpopular and sometimes reviled, and how to make common cause with those others identified as outside the structures in order to define and seek a world in which we can all flourish. It is learning how to take our differences and make them strengths. For the master's tools will never dismantle the master's house. They may allow us temporarily to beat him at his own game, but they will never enable us to bring about genuine change.[207]

[204] John Borrows (Kegedonce), *Drawing Out Law: A Spirit's Guide* (Toronto, Buffalo, London: University of Toronto Press, 2010), i.

[205] As an illustration, see Painter's juxtaposition of two legal texts – one written in 'pen-and-ink writing'; the other in 'wampum writing' – in a letter written by four Haudenosaunee families to King George V during the First World War. As she shows there, context is about language, and law-as-language is inextricable from that context. Painter, 'A Letter from the Haudenosaunee Confederacy', 49.

[206] Taiaiake Alfred, *Wasáse: Indigenous Pathways of Action and Freedom* (Peterborough, Ontario: Broadview Press, 2005), 395.

[207] Audre Lorde, 'The Master's Tools Will Never Dismantle the Master's House', in Audre Lorde, *Sister Outsider: Essays and Speeches* (Berkeley, CA: Crossing Press, 2007), 203–9, at 206. Lorde made these comments in the context of her searing take-down of the instrumentalisation of her subjectivity 'as a Black lesbian feminist ... invited to comment within

The willingness of some Indigenous peoples, acting on the authority of Indigenous law, to share their lands notwithstanding the manner in which they have been (and are still being) appropriated has radical implications, therefore, for (Western) law's claim to lawfulness. This point was well made by Philip Blake, a member of the Dene, in a statement to the McKenzie Valley Pipeline Inquiry (the 'Berger Inquiry'), commissioned by the Canadian Government in the mid 1970s to investigate the social, environmental and economic impact of the proposed pipeline.[208] As Blake argued, in a passage quoted by Coulthard:

> If our Indian nation is being destroyed so that poor people of the world might get a chance to share this world's riches, then as Indian people, I am sure that we would seriously consider giving up our resources. But do you really expect us to give up our life and our lands so that those few people who are the richest and most powerful in the world today can maintain their own position of privilege?
>
> That is not our way.
>
> I strongly believe that we do have something to offer your nation ['Canada'], however, something other than our minerals ... For thousands of years we have lived with the land, we have taken care of the land, and the land has taken care of us. We did not believe that our society has to grow and expand and conquer new areas in order to fulfil our destiny as Indian people ...
>
> I believe your nation might wish to see us, not as a relic from the past, but as a way of life, a system of values by which you may survive in the future. This we are willing to share.

And thanks, perhaps, to strategies of juxtaposition or 'intentional hybridisation' such as this, as well as to the straightforward 'refusal' of many Indigenous individuals to subsume their Indigeneity within the 'universal' subjectivity of the 'free' and 'equal' state citizen, signs have begun to emerge that Indigenous law is indeed beginning to be encountered, by law, on its own terms. For example, Law Schools in Canada are teaching Indigenous law not as a separate subject but as an integral part of the standard public law curriculum.[209] In South Africa, the concept of *ubuntu*, originally a Nguni Bantu term referring to the idea that 'a person

the only panel at this conference [the Second Sex Conference, New York, 29 September 1979] where the input of Black feminists and lesbians is represented'.

208 Philip Blake, 'Statement to the Mackenzie Valley Pipeline Inquiry' ('Berger Inquiry'), in Mel Watkins (ed.), *Dene Nation: The Colony Within* (University of Toronto Press, 1977), 5–9. Quoted in Coulthard, *Red Skin, White Masks*, 63.

209 See Jeffery Hewitt, 'Decolonizing and Indigenizing: Some Considerations for Law Schools', 33 *Windsor Yearbook of Access to Justice* (2016): 65–84.

is a person through other people', was included in the Epilogue of South Africa's 1993 Interim Constitution and is now being relied upon regularly in the judgments handed down by the South African Constitutional Court.[210] In Latin America, meanwhile, the Colombian Constitutional Court has halted numerous 'development' projects on the basis of their failure to comply with Article 330 of the 1991 Colombian Constitution, which regulates the self-government and territorial rights of 'Indigenous (Indian) territories'.[211] For example, in its T-129 ruling of 2011, the Court halted explorations by Gold Plata Corporation in Acandi, overturning favourable rulings by several lower courts on the grounds that '*no se puede obligar a una comunidad étnica a renunciar a su forma de vida y cultura por la mera llegada de una obra de infraestructura o proyecto de explotación*'.[212]

Also very significant – though, as in Colombia, bitterly contested – are the innovations made by the Ecuadorian Constitution of 2008 and the Bolivian Constitution of 2009. Drawing directly on the Quechua concept of *sumak kawsay*, meaning living well in harmony with community and nature in a way that promotes regeneration and growth, and referring directly to 'Pacha Mama', the earth goddess of Inca mythology who has the self-sustaining power to create and sustain life,[213] the Ecuadorian Constitution was amended to reflect the state's decision to 'build':

> *Una nueva forma de convivencia ciudadana, en diversidad y armonía con la naturaleza, para alcanzar el buen vivir, el* sumak kawsay;
> *Una sociedad que respeta, en todas sus dimensiones, la dignidad de las personas y las colectividades;*
> *Un país democrático, comprometido con la integración latinoamericana ... la paz y la solidaridad con todos los pueblos de la tierra ...*[214]

[210] See generally Drucilla Cornell and Nyoko Muvangua, *uBuntu and the Law* (New York: Fordham University Press, 2012).

[211] *Constitución de la República de Colombia*, Bogotá, 20 July 1991, Art. 330.

[212] '[A]n Indigenous community cannot be forced to renounce its way of life and culture by the mere arrival of a work of infrastructure or project of [resource] exploitation.' *Corte Constitucional de Colombia, Sentencia T-129/11, Acción de tutela ejercida por Oscar Carupia Domicó y otros, a nombre de los resguardos Chidima-Tolo y Pescadito pertenecientes a la etnia Embera-Katío contra los Ministerios de Transporte, Ambiente, Vivienda y Desarrollo Territorial, Interior y de Justicia, de Minas y Energía, de Agricultura, de Defensa, el Consejo Asesor de Regalías adscrito al Departamento Nacional de Planeación, las alcaldías de Unguía y Acandí, la Corporación Autónoma Regional del Chocó (Codechocó), el Ejército Nacional, la Brigada XVII y la Agencia Logística de las Fuerzas Militares*, 3 March 2011 (trans. Luis Eslava). The Court also halted construction on a highway and on an electric-power line project in the same ruling on the grounds of failure to obtain the consent of local Indigenous communities.

[213] See www.pachamama.org/sumak-kawsay (accessed 16 January 2018).

[214] 'A new form of public coexistence, in diversity and in harmony with nature, to achieve the good way of living, the *sumak kawsay*; A society that respects, in all its dimensions, the

To this end, the state of Ecuador endows '[*l*]*a naturaleza o Pacha Mama, donde se reproduce y realiza la vida*' with the right (*derecho*) '*a que se respete integralmente su existencia y el mantenimiento y regeneración de sus ciclos vitales, estructura, funciones y procesos evolutivos*'.[215] The 2008 Constitution also grants Indigenous and Afro-Ecuadorian peoples a host of special rights (Art. 56), including rights to 'keep ownership' (*mantener la posesión*) of their lands, to develop, maintain and apply Indigenous law, and to 'uphold, protect and develop' 'ancestral wisdom', with the appropriation of 'Indigenous knowledge, innovations and practices' being strictly forbidden.[216] In Bolivia, meanwhile, the 2009 Constitution begins as follows:

> *En tiempos inmemoriales se erigieron montañas, se desplazaron ríos, se formaron lagos. Nuestra amazonia, nuestro chaco, nuestro altiplano y nuestros llanos y valles se cubrieron de verdores y flores. Poblamos esta sagrada Madre Tierra con rostros diferentes, y comprendimos desde entonces la pluralidad vigente de todas las cosas y nuestra diversidad como seres y culturas. Así conformamos nuestros pueblos, y jamás comprendimos el racismo hasta que lo sufrimos desde los funestos tiempos de la colonia.*[217]

As in Ecuador, the Bolivian Constitution also puts in place a comprehensive set of protections for the rights of Indigenous peoples and Afro-Bolivians,[218] and grants the right to a 'healthy, protected and balanced environment' (*un medio ambiente saludable, protegido y equilibrado*) to 'individuals and collectives of present and future generations, as well as to other living things, so they may develop in a normal and permanent way' (*los individuos y colectividades de las presentes y futuras generaciones, además de otros seres vivos, desarrollarse de manera normal y permanente*).[219] More than this, however, Bolivia is declared to be a

dignity of individuals and community groups; A democratic country, committed to Latin American integration ... peace and solidarity with all peoples of the Earth ...' *Constitución de la República del Ecuador*, Quito, 28 September 2008, Preamble (official trans.)

215 'Nature, or Pacha Mama, where life is reproduced and occurs, has the right to integral respect for its existence and for the maintenance and regeneration of its life cycles, structure, functions and evolutionary processes.' 2008 Constitution of Ecuador, Art. 71.

216 2008 Constitution of Ecuador, Arts. 56–60.

217 'In ancient times mountains arose, rivers moved, and lakes were formed. Our Amazonia, our swamps, our highlands, and our plains and valleys were covered with greenery and flowers. We populated this sacred Mother Earth with different faces, and since that time we have understood the plurality that exists in all things and in our diversity as human beings and cultures. Thus, our peoples were formed, and we never knew racism until we were subjected to it during the terrible times of colonialism.' *Constitución Política del Estado de Bolivia*, Sucre, 7 February 2009, Preamble (official trans.).

218 2009 Constitution of Bolivia, Arts. 30–2.

219 Ibid., Art. 33.

'Pluri-National' state based on the Indigenous principles of *ama qhilla, ama llulla, ama suwa* ('do not be lazy, do not be a liar or a thief'), *suma qamaña* ('live well'), *ñandereko* ('live harmoniously'), *teko kavi* (the 'good life'), *ivi maraei* and *qhapaj ñan* (the 'noble path of life'),[220] in addition to more familiar liberal principles such as 'liberty' and 'equality of opportunity', and socialist principles like 'social justice'.[221]

Without underestimating the significance of these developments, however, the Indigenous-Peruvian legal scholar Roger Merino Acuña warns that these kinds of constitutional protections for Indigenous 'self-determination' remain acutely vulnerable to co-optation by the state and by international capital. Both the Ecuadorian and Bolivian Constitutions, as we have just seen, attempt to balance such rights against much more straightforward understandings of legal subjectivity and economic development. In Ecuador, for example, Merino notes that the constitutional permission for 'prospecting, producing and marketing nonrenewable resources located on [Indigenous] lands', provided the relevant Indigenous communities have been 'consulted', has allowed the state to continue extracting non-renewable resources on the same scale.[222] The key difference is that in Ecuador, unlike in Canada, Australia or the United States, such extraction is justified on the basis of the requirements of a socialist development model, the aim of which is not just to generate profits but, crucially, also to redistribute them in such a way as to lead to a more equal, less impoverished, healthier society. There is no doubt that this represents an enormous improvement for many of Ecuador's citizens. The same cannot be said, however, for many of its Indigenous communities, understood as a discrete group with a specific set of needs. Within the context of the state, in other words, what is good for Ecuadorian society as a whole and what is good for its individual Indigenous communities is, it seems, a zero-sum game. This is particularly evident in the context of an increasingly integrated global order which is fundamentally committed to the supposedly

220 Ibid., Art. 5(1).

221 Ibid., Art. 5(2).

222 Roger Merino Acuña, 'An Alternative to "Alternative Development"?: *Buen Vivir* and Human Development in Andean Countries', 44 *Oxford Development Studies* (2016): 1–16, 2–6. See also Roger Merino Acuña, 'Descolonizando los Derechos de Propiedad. Derechos Indígenas Comunales y el Paradigma de la Propriedad Privada', 47 *Boletín Mexicano de Derecho Comparado* (2014): 935–64; Merino Acuña, 'Law and Politics of Indigenous Self-determination: The Meaning of the Right to Prior Consultation', in Watson (ed.), *Indigenous Peoples as Subjects of International Law*, 120–40; Merino Acuña, 'The Politics of Indigenous Self-Determination: Extractive Industries, State Policies and Territorial Rights in the Peruvian Amazon' (PhD thesis, University of Bath, 2015).

'universal right' to participate in 'representative, accountable, and transparent governance and open economies'.[223] For Rafael Correa, Ecuador's President from 2007 to 2017, the choice could only go one way. As he put it in 2012:

> It is madness to say no to natural resources ... no to oil, no to mining, no to gas, no to hydroelectric power, no to roads ... We cannot lose sight of the fact that the main objective of a country such as Ecuador is to eliminate poverty. And for that we need our natural resources.[224]

Correa, therefore, declared that his government did not 'share the view of the indigenous question as a problem only for the indigenous, to be dealt with through indigenous institutions ... The indigenous problem is an issue for Ecuador as a whole, and all public institutions should contribute to solving it, regardless of whether they are run by indigenous people or not'.[225] For Merino and other Indigenous scholars, however, the idea that an Indigenous 'problem' can only be 'dealt with through indigenous institutions' is something that cannot be compromised without abandoning the entire rationale behind the struggle.

As this dilemma demonstrates, there is quite simply no space for a resolution to this impossible choice within the context of the 'self-governing' state. More specifically, there is no scope for a solution within the context

[223] Clinton, Address to the UN Human Rights Council. Ironically, as Libya has been gripped by chaos bordering on civil war in the wake of the ousting of its dictator, Muammar Qadhafi, the intervention itself is now being blamed for transforming that country into a seriously 'failed state'. See e.g. comments of General David Rodriguez, the top US military commander in the African continent, before the US Senate Armed Services Committee, reported in Richard Lardner, 'The Top American General in Africa says Libya is a Failed State', *US News*, 8 March 2016, at www.usnews.com/news/politics/articles/2016-03-08/us-commander-in-africa-says-libya-is-a-failed-state (accessed 2 March 2017). One paradigmatic illustration concerns the fate of the Yasuni National Park in Ecuador, an area of untouched Amazonian rainforest, designated a UNESCO biosphere reserve in 1898, beneath which lie an estimated 1.67 billion barrels of oil, some 40 per cent of Ecuador's total reserves. This is the territory of the Huaroani people, and is also home to two uncontacted peoples, the Tagaeri and the Taromenane. In 2007, Ecuador's President, Rafael Correa, presented a plan to the international community in which wealthy states were asked to donate $3.6 billion to offset the opportunity cost of reserving the area from oil drilling. However, by 2013 the plan had generated only 4 per cent of that amount, and the decision – extremely controversial – was taken to scrap it. Drilling began in 2016. See e.g. José Llangari, 'Ecuador Begins Drilling for Oil in Pristine Corner of the Amazon', Reuters, 8 September 2016, at www.reuters.com/article/us-ecuador-oil-yasuni/ecuador-begins-drilling-for-oil-in-pristine-corner-of-amazon-idUSKCN11D2SQ (accessed 16 February 2018). My thanks to Luis Eslava for pointing me in this direction.

[224] Rafael Correa, 'Ecuador's Path', 77 *New Left Review* (2012): 89–111.

[225] Correa, 'Ecuador's Path', 109.

of a legal system embedded in a global order that is, in turn, dedicated to reproducing 'self-ruling' or 'self-governing', 'rational' capitalist subjects.[226] What this appalling dilemma – which transforms 'democracy' into a bitter trade-off between race and class, discrimination and poverty, present and future, human and non-human – reveals is that there is something about the state – even a state as deeply committed as Ecuador has been to protecting Indigenous 'rights' and challenging the logic of capital accumulation – that cannot tolerate normative, ontological and epistemological dissent on the level which the realisation of Indigenous forms of self-determination on Indigenous terms would require. To return to Bakhtin's analysis, this clash highlights how difficult it can be, even where the will exists to compromise, to prevent a strategy of 'intentional' hybridisation from collapsing into a situation of 'organic' hybridisation, or straightforward assimilation, as soon as that strategy comes to be articulated in the language of 'rights' which the state is then called upon to balance. In such a context, the 'authoritative' discourse of (Western) law – backed up by both the normative 'pull' of the idea that each individual must enjoy an 'equal opportunity' to accumulate resources, and by the coercive 'push' of the state's monopoly of access to 'law-preserving' violence (as Benjamin called it[227]) – will continue to triumph at the expense of Indigenous world views. Above all, as Escobar points out, meaningful change cannot be brought about by tinkering with the existing machinery, whether normative/legal/institutional or epistemological/ontological. As he puts it: '*[h]ow one thinks about these processes is itself an object of struggle and debate*', such that 'the questions of *where one thinks from, with whom, and for what purpose* become important elements of the investigation; this also means that the investigation is, more than ever, simultaneously theoretical and political'.[228] As Escobar notes, Latin America is at once 'the original space of the emergence of modern/colonial capitalism',[229] and at the same time, the continent which 'most earnestly embraced neo-liberal reforms'. Yet it is also 'the only region in the world where some counter-hegemonic processes of importance might be taking place at the level of the State', and perhaps even moving towards the creation

[226] Luis Eslava, 'The Moving Location of Empire: Indirect Rule, International Law and the Bantu Experiment (1935–1937)', *Leiden Journal of International Law* (forthcoming), 31–2 (manuscript on file with the author).

[227] See Frame, Section 1.2.2, above.

[228] Escobar, 'Latin America at a Crossroads', 2–3. Emphasis in the original.

[229] Aníbal Quijano, *Des/colonialidad del poder: el horizonte alternativo* (Lima, 2008), 3, unpublished manuscript translated by and quoted in Escobar, 'Latin America at a Crossroads', 2.

of 'alternative forms of modernization; or even in the direction of more radical societal transformations towards post-capitalist, post-liberal, and poststatist options'.[230] However, he cautions, the success or failure of these projects will depend on their capacity to 'activate', rather than to assimilate, 'relational ontologies, such as those of indigenous peoples and Afro-descendants'.[231]

3.3 *Indigeneity and the Historiography of Revolution*

The final aspect of the contemporary Indigenous struggle that I would like to call attention to here concerns the insistence of many settler-states that colonialism is over. One example can be found in *Gathering Strength: Canada's Aboriginal Action Plan*, a programme of Indigenous–non-Indigenous reconciliation issued by the Canadian Government in 1997. In this 'action plan', the 'historical' nature of the wrongs suffered by Indigenous peoples is emphasised repeatedly, through references to 'the mistakes which marked our [Canada's] past', for instance, and to the need for Indigenous and non-Indigenous communities to 'work together' on 'healing the past' and 'building the future'.[232] In the Australian context, a similar logic attaches to what has become known as the 'black armband' view of history. As John Howard, then the Australian Prime Minister, argued in 1996:

> The 'black armband' view of our history reflects a belief that most Australian history since 1788 has been little more than a disgraceful story of imperialism, exploitation, racism, sexism and other forms of discrimination. I take a different view. I believe that the balance sheet of our history is one of heroic achievement and that we have achieved much more as a nation of which we can be proud than of which we should be ashamed ... We need to acknowledge as a nation the realities of what European settlement has meant for the first Australians, the Aboriginals and Torres Strait Islanders, and in particular the assault on their traditions and the physical abuse they endured. But in understanding these realities our priority should not be to apportion blame and guilt for historic wrongs but to commit to a practical program of action that will remove the enduring legacies of disadvantage.[233]

Though somewhat softer in its approach, the 'apology' offered to 'Australia's Indigenous peoples' in 2008 by the Kevin Rudd administration

[230] Escobar, 'Latin America at a Crossroads', 1–3.

[231] Ibid., 4.

[232] *Gathering Strength: Canada's Aboriginal Action Plan – A Progress Report* (Ottawa: Canadian Ministry of Indian Affairs and Northern Development, 2000), 4.

[233] John Howard, *Sir Robert Menzies Lecture*, Melbourne, 18 November 1996, at http://pmtranscripts.pmc.gov.au/release/transcript-10171 (accessed 4 June 2018).

also insisted that it was necessary 'to turn a new page in Australia's history by righting the wrongs of the past and so moving forward with confidence to the future'.[234]

These statements point towards a set of underlying assumptions about the nature of historical time, as viewed from the perspective of the self-governing state.[235] I suggested in the Frame that the time of law, international law and the sovereign state, 'progresses' along in a conveniently linear fashion.[236] The ideological nature of this linear approach to history is manifest, in the context of the Indigenous struggle, in at least three different ways. Most obviously, the persistent narration of Indigenous or Aboriginal ways of being and knowing as belonging to a past that is long gone and as continuing to exist exclusively in 'traditional' practices continues to position these peoples as somehow primitive or backward, just as they were positioned prior to the mid-twentieth century, if not earlier.[237] Secondly, as Coulthard points out, the strategy of casting the harm done to Indigenous peoples and societies by the appropriation and colonisation of their lands and institutions as belonging to a past that must be left behind in the interests of everyone makes it possible to construct those who refuse to 'forgive and forget' as 'unhealthy, irrational, retrograde, and, … prone to producing increased social instability and political violence'.[238] This tendency, he points out, underlies the routine dismissal of the invocation of Indigenous ways of being and knowing as 'romanticised'; in this context, a euphemism for 'anachronistic'.[239] By way of illustration, Couthard cites a newspaper article from January 2013 in which a Canadian newspaper columnist, Jeffrey Simpson, characterised the Indigenous 'Idle No More' movement's demands as being 'of the usual dreamy, flamboyant variety, a mixture of anti-capitalism and anti-colonialism, blended with the mythology (blasted by the reality of what one actually sees on too many reserves) about environmental protection and its aboriginals' sacred link to their lands'. The columnist continued:

> To this is then added a desire to protect 'traditional' ways, which in some cases means hunting, fishing and trapping, noble ventures that can lead

[234] Kevin Rudd, *Apology to Australia's Indigenous Peoples*, 13 February 2008 at www.australia.gov.au/about-australia/our-country/our-people/apology-to-australias-indigenous-peoples (accessed 4 June 2018).

[235] See Carol J. Greenhouse, *A Moment's Notice: Time Politics Across Cultures* (Ithaca, NY: Cornell University Press, 1996).

[236] Frame, Section 1.2.2.

[237] See Frame, Section 3.1.

[238] Coulthard, *Red Skin, White Masks*, 108.

[239] Ibid., 159–79.

> economically to something only slightly better than subsistence. Without a wage economy beyond these 'traditional' ways, the path lies clear to dependence on money from somewhere else, namely government, which, in turn, leads to the lassitude and pathologies that plague too many aboriginal communities.
>
> Of course, there are some communities that offer the antithesis of dependency. They benefit from participating directly in the exploitation of natural resources near their communities, which should be the driving thrust of all public policy.
>
> These communities have decided collectively to integrate to varying degrees with the majority cultures, to form business arrangements (where possible) in a vital attempt to create own-source revenues that will dilute or end the spirals of dependency.
>
> But too many communities remain within the dream palace, hungering for a return to a more separate existence, even if the lands on which they sit are – and likely always will be – of marginal economic value ...
>
> To imagine that isolated communities of a thousand or so people can be vibrant and self-sustaining, capable of discharging the panoply of responsibilities of 'sovereignty,' is to live within the dream palace of memory.[240]

A third way in which the linear temporality of statehood as a supposedly emancipatory alternative to colonialism displays its ideological qualities concerns the use of the law to make the state's 'progressive' linear temporality increasingly non-negotiable by strengthening the interpellative 'pull' of legal subjectivity. In the Australian context, perhaps most glaringly, this can be seen in the way in which 'native title' claims (as mentioned above) have been conditioned on the capacity of Indigenous claimants to demonstrate an 'unbroken' connection to the land in question, in the form of a demonstrably continuous observance of the 'traditional laws'[241] from whence their claim to it is understood to derive. As Kathleen Birrell, among others, has pointed out, Australian law's insistence on the performance of 'authentic' Indigeneity seems entirely blind to the 'emphatic absurdity of such a requirement' in a country 'so manifestly affected by colonisation' and colonialism's projects, from forcible resettlement to the abduction of Indigenous children to the rendering unliveable of Indigenous lands by mining and other state-sanctioned

[240] Jeffrey Simpson, 'Too Many First Nations People Live in a Dream Palace', *The Globe and Mail*, 5 January 2013, available at www.theglobeandmail.com/opinion/too-many-first-nations-people-live-in-a-dream-palace/article6929035/ (accessed 28 April 2017).

[241] *Native Title Act* (1993), Sec. 223.

extractive industries.[242] Or as the anthropologist Elizabeth Povinelli has put it:

> No indigenous subject can inhabit the temporal or spatial location to which indigenous identity refers – the geographical and social space and time of authentic Ab-originality. And no indigenous subject can derive her or his being outside a relation to other social identities and values currently proliferating in the nation-state. The category of indigeneity came to being in relation to the imperial state and the social identities residing in it, and it continues to draw its discursive value in relation to the state (and other states) and to other emergent national subjects (and other transnational subjects). To be indigenous, therefore, requires passing through, and in the passage being scarred by the geography of the state and topography of other social identities. Producing a present-tense indigenousness in which some failure is not a qualifying condition is discursively and materially impossible. These scars are what Aborigines are, what they have.[243]

If settler-colonialism is predicated on securing, into the future, that control over 'territory' which was so violently established in the past, these critics suggest, it cannot be consigned to the past without conceding to the state's emancipatory and universalist self-image. 'The colonizers come to stay', as the anthropologist Patrick Wolfe has argued, famously. '[I]nvasion is a structure not an event.'[244]

The challenge Indigenous scholars, activists and their collaborators have taken up, then, is to find ways of resisting the linear temporality which legal subjectivity, in its individual (citizen) and collective (state) manifestations, perpetuates – and of doing so in a manner predicated not on forgetting the past but on reclaiming it in a critical, counter-linear way. One such strategy (as discussed above) consists in Audra Simpson's deployment of 'refusal' as an explicit rejection of recognition aimed at 'producing and maintaining alternative structures of thought, politics and traditions away from and in critical relationship to states'.[245] As Simpson insists,

> the implicit demand to forget, through the operation of 'consent' and 'citizenship', is challenged by the counter that Indigenous people represent simply by (a) living and (b) knowing this. In living and knowing themselves as such, they pose a demand upon the newness of the present, as

[242] Kathleen Birrell, *Indigeneity: Before and Beyond the Law* (Abingdon: Routledge, 2016), 26.

[243] Elizabeth Povinelli, *The Cunning of Recognition: Indigenous Alterities and the Making of Australian Multiculturalism* (Durham, NC, London: Duke University Press, 2002), 49.

[244] Patrick Wolfe, *Settler Colonialism and the Transformation of Anthropology: The Politics and Poetics of an Ethnographic Event* (London, New York: Cassell, 1999), 2.

[245] Audra Simpson, 'The Ruse of Consent and the Anatomy of "Refusal": Cases from Indigenous North America and Australia', 20 *Postcolonial Studies* (2017): 1–16 at 2.

> well as a knotty reminder of something else. That 'something else' is the ongoing work of dispossession, and its handmaiden of failed assimilation. Indigenous peoples are reminders, sometimes indecipherable announcements of other orders, other authorities, and an earlier time that has not fully passed. 'Settler time' is revealed as the fiction of the presumed neutrality of time itself, demonstrating the dominance of the present by some over others, and the unequal power to define what matters, who matters, what pasts are alive and when they die.[246]

In a parallel way, Coulthard has also turned the accusations levelled by Jeffrey Simpson and others on their head. As Coulthard argues, 'what gets implicitly represented by the state as ... Indigenous peoples' seemingly pathological inability to get over harms inflicted in the past ... is actually a sign of our *critical consciousness*, of our sense of justice and injustice, and of our awareness of and unwillingness to *reconcile* ourselves with a structural and symbolic violence that is still very much present in our lives'.[247] In his view, this 'critical consciousness' is key to unlocking the revolutionary energy necessary to break free from what Frantz Fanon, in the context of French colonialism, described as a 'double process' at work in the psychology of the colonial subject. This process, Fanon argued, was 'primarily economic', stemming from impoverishment, exclusion and other signs of material inequality; yet it was also psychological, resulting from the 'internalisation' by the colonial subject of the racism used by the colonial administration to justify her conditions of blatant material inequality.[248] In order to overcome this 'inferiority complex', as Fanon termed it, Coulthard argues that the past is an essential critical resource. On the one hand, only by taking stock of centuries of oppression can Indigenous peoples generate a collective anger strong enough to be deployed, as a real force for change, against the state and the capitalist mode of production. On the other hand, Coulthard argues (here parting company with Fanon),[249] fostering, recovering and regenerating the traditions of Indigenous peoples is the most effective way of ensuring that this anger is used constructively to generate alternatives to the state. Establishing some kind of critical alternative to the assumption that colonialism is 'over' is, Coulthard writes, central to the '*resurgent* approach to Indigenous decolonization that builds on the value and insights of our past in our efforts to

[246] Ibid., 5.

[247] Coulthard, *Red Skin, White Masks*, 126. Emphasis in the original.

[248] Frantz Fanon [1952], *Black Skin, White Masks*, trans. Charles Lam Markmann (London: Pluto Press, 1986), 4.

[249] Coulthard, *Red Skin, White Masks*, 148.

secure a noncolonial present and future'.[250] Only this can offer Indigenous peoples in 'Canada' and elsewhere a form of 'decolonial praxis' with which individuals and collectives can 'subvert the interplay between structure and subjectivity that sustain colonial relations over time'.[251]

It is at this point that another affinity might catch the eye – a form of counter-hegemonic methodological *correspondance*, as it were, between the thinking of the Indigenous scholars, activists and their fellow travellers examined here, on the one hand, and the work of Walter Benjamin, examined in the Frame on the other. In particular, Benjamin's critique of the teleology of progress,[252] is, very much like Coulthard's, a counter-attack on the idea that social conflict can only be resolved if the 'downtrodden' can be persuaded to forget the 'mistakes' of the past. In 'cast[ing] the working class in the role of a redeemer of *future* generations', Benjamin (as we saw at the very beginning) argued in 1940 that mainstream social democracy had cut 'the sinews of its greatest strength' – namely 'its hatred and its spirit of sacrifice', which was better 'nourished' by the image of enslaved ancestors' than 'by the ideal of liberated grandchildren'.[253]

Benjamin was, of course, a European man focused on a European problem, with a training in European philosophy, history and political economy.[254] Let me underline, then, that in noting this affinity I do not intend to suggest that the solution to the problem of how to realise Indigenous self-determination on Indigenous terms is to be found anywhere other than in Indigenous traditions of thought and practice themselves. Nor do I want to smuggle the assumed universality of European ideas and categories into the language of critique. Instead, my intention is to take seriously the idea that – as Black, Neidjie, Blake and others point out – the state's efforts to suppress Indigenous ways of being and knowing, and its disregard for the lawfulness of Indigenous law, are problems

250 Ibid., 149. Emphasis in the original.

251 Ibid., 140.

252 Frame, Section 1.2.2.

253 Walter Benjamin, 'On the Concept of History' [1940], in *Walter Benjamin: Selected Writings*, Vol. 4: 1938–1940, eds. Howard Eiland and Michael W. Jennings, trans. Harry John (Cambridge, MA: Harvard University Press, 2003), 389–400, at 394. Emphasis in the original.

254 A huge amount of work has been done on the relationship between race and class. For one very important contribution, see e.g. Cedric Robinson, *Black Marxism: The Making of the Black Radical Tradition* (Chapel Hill, NC, London: University of North Carolina Press, 1983). In the international law context, see e.g. Robert Knox, 'Valuing Race? Stretched Marxism and the Logic of Imperialism', 4 *London Review of International Law* (2016): 81–126.

for the planet as a whole, and not only for Indigenous peoples themselves. Against that backdrop, the objective of linking back to Benjamin at this point is to try to bring into being a set of conditions under which a connection might be made between certain aspects of this struggle against the state and state law, and certain aspects of other struggles against the process of international legal reproduction. If such connections can be made, it is not impossible that certain trans-temporal and trans-spatial solidarities will arise.

One such connection concerns the possibility that the radical demand for Indigenous self-determination on Indigenous terms might be read as an effort to construct (or reconstruct) a truly revolutionary temporality of precisely the kind that Benjamin was calling for with his unapologetically romanticised Marxist-messianic historiography. Watson, for example, arguably makes just this kind of intervention when she suggests that '[t]he genocide that came with the invasion of "Australia" might have been avoided if [Captain James] Cook and all who followed had entered into the laws and ceremonies of the land'.[255] Importantly, the temporality Watson employs to arrive at this point is not the 'homogeneous, empty' temporality of capitalist/historicist 'progress', as Benjamin described it,[256] a temporality which is propelled along (I have argued) by the coercive 'push' and normative 'pull' of international law in a relentless forwards march which is oblivious to the (linear) trail of trampled victims it leaves in its wake. Watson's temporality, by contrast, invokes an entirely different, avowedly non-linear relationship between yesterday, today and tomorrow. For instance, she describes what happened when Cook 'first stepped ashore in 1770' near what is now Sydney: 'Surrounded by Cook's crew, the Eora People were murdered by the blast, from bombs secretly laid, so that before the Eora were able to initiate a welcoming ceremony the law was violated, as was the possibility of peace.'[257] Watson's conclusion is not that the Eora and other Aboriginal peoples should accept the Australian Government's apology and 'move on'. Instead, she insists, 'for "proper" dialogue to begin, we need to begin again'. Cook 'needs to walk back in time, holding the flag in his hand, row back to his ship, and wait there, wait there for the old people to sing him a welcoming to ruwe [country].

[255] Watson, *Raw Law*, 109. Though 'Australia' was first 'discovered' by the Dutch in around 1606, the British 'explorer', James Cook, was the first European to set foot on the eastern coast, in what is now New South Wales, on 19 April 1770.

[256] Frame, Section 1.2.2.

[257] Ibid., 109.

Then he needs to sit down and wait for the smoking and the cleansing of his spirit. Then the teaching could begin.'[258]

In Watson's argument, to return to Benjamin's imagery, the 'sinews' connecting Cook's arrival with the ongoing experience of displacement and oppression by Aboriginal communities in 'Australia' today have not been 'cut', as in the state's teleological account of 'moving on'. Or, perhaps more accurately, Watson might be understood as setting out to reconstitute those 'sinews' herself for precisely the kind of revolutionary purpose Benjamin had in mind – that is, in order to 'blast' the moment of Cook's arrival 'out of the continuum of history', and in doing so to 'charge' Australia's colonial past with revolutionary 'now-time'.[259] The 'material' Watson uses to re-attach past to present also becomes crucially important here. Rejecting efforts (like 'native title') to 'reconcile' Aboriginal and Western law, this material is what she calls 'raw law', that is, the law of Aboriginal peoples and Torres Straight Islanders in what is now Australia. Her method is to take this 'raw' material, embodied in concepts like *ruwe* (referring to a particular relationship between law and land) and *muldarbi* (the name of 'an ancestor spirit who failed to uphold the best interests of the collective in relation to the natural world'), and then to use it 'to describe the phenomenon of colonialism and the impact it has had upon Indigenous Peoples' lives, laws and territories, worldwide'.[260] However, rather than attempting to merge these concepts with the legal terminology employed by the Australian state and by international law, she simply sets one against the other. As Watson explains this concept of 'raw law':

> Our First Nations ancestors were once naked. I see a connection in that with our sung laws and the land, all of which are also naked or 'raw', undressed from the baggage of colonialism. From my Tanganekald and Meintangk standpoint, what I know as law, what I have named 'Raw Law', is unlike the colonial legal system imposed upon us, for it was not imposed, but rather lived. It is a law way, which emanates from the ruwe and connects the collective or mob of First Nations Peoples. Knowing law through living, it is different from colonial manifestations of law. The First Nations' view of law now has little place in which to live and living law as a way of life is no longer a possibility or an experience known to the greater part of humanity. The greater part of humanity has come to know 'law' as a complex maze of rules and regulations while the body of Raw Law is being buried beneath muldarbi layers of colonialism.[261]

[258] Ibid., 160.
[259] Benjamin, 'On the Concept of History', 395.
[260] Watson, *Raw Law*, 1.
[261] Ibid., 12.

If we look at Watson's intervention by setting her argument, in turn, against the various items, or historical debris, from the process of international legal reproduction that are already sitting in the shadow-box, it might be argued that the product of Watson's counter-history is precisely critical constellations connecting the 'now' of ongoing Aboriginal oppression with the 'then' of first contact, using 'raw law' to 'charge' the still-colonised present with immediate revolutionary potential.

4 Conclusion

As noted at the start, my hope is that this final chapter will function as something along the lines of a glass lid for this shadow-box, otherwise composed of a stand and a frame, with six items assembled together inside it (see Figure 11). The task of getting across the gap that lies between the upper surface of Item 6 and the lid itself has involved an enormous leap across a tumultuous and incredibly destructive period in human history – though not a particularly long one when seen in relation to some communities' 60,000 years of existence on the planet. In the course of making that leap, many places, many experiences and many processes have necessarily been overpassed or left behind. The purpose of this lid, however, was not to offer a blow-by-blow account of the international legal history of the twentieth and early twenty-first century – an impossible task, in any case. It was, instead, to show that, while the eight decades that stand between ourselves and late 1938 (where Item 6 left off) undeniably do constitute a barrier between 'then' and 'now', that barrier is, up to a point, transparent. What I mean by this is not that we can recover the past in any 'accurate' way which might allow us (to return to Ranke) to 'show, essentially, how things happened'.[262] Instead, this transparency arises from the fact that we, the 'present generation', are pushed and pulled around by many of the same forces which pushed and pulled those who came before us. As this book has shown, when one considers the increasingly similar set of legal and institutional structures we inhabit, and the manner in which they became so similar, this is hardly surprising. This transparency, then, our capacity to communicate with the past, is not only a question of compiling an ever more

[262] Leopold von Ranke [1824], 'Preface to the First Edition', in George Iggers (ed.), *Histories of the Latin and German Nations*, trans. Wilma Iggers (Indianapolis, IN: Bobbs-Merill, 1973), 136, 138. See also Wilhelm von Humboldt [1822], 'On the Historian's Task', trans. Louis O. Mink, 6 *History and Theory* (1967): 57–71, 57.

detailed 'context' with the aim of 'seeing' the past 'as it really was'. It is also, and perhaps even more importantly, a question of solidarity – of shared suffering and shared revolutionary instinct. From the 'collateral damage' visited upon Iraqi, Libyan, Syrian and Yemeni families since 2003, to the political deadlock endured and protested by Kosovan and Bosnian voters since 1992, to the desperation of Oromo communities caught between Abyssinian and Italian imperialism in the late 1930s, to the humiliations which inspired the 'Boxers' with mystical anger in the final decades of the Chinese Empire, to the radical impoverishment of present-day communities all over the world – Indigenous and non-Indigenous, European and non-European – who are failing, and who will continue to fail, to scrape out a living from the few cracks that remain in the architecture of global capital accumulation – there is a certain angle from which all of these struggles can be seen together. If we look at the shadow-box which contains them from this angle and screw up our eyes (metaphorically speaking), it seems to me that a pattern emerges.

If this pattern is, indeed, visible and tangible, and not a figment of my imagination, then it carries us back to some of the historiographical and distributional questions I began with in the Frame, concerning the relationship between 'necessity' and 'contingency'.[263] If nothing else, the details of all of these histories prove that each 'generation', and each struggle within each generation, brings into being a very specific set of critical responses to a very specific constellation of oppressive structures. Contingent as these struggles and responses may be, however, I have suggested that there are certain affinities among them which are, in turn, linked to a logic of conditionality that runs right across the history of the emergence and consolidation of the state system, predicating the constitution of international legal subjectivity on the reproduction of individual legal subjectivity. But these affinities are visible only if we move outside the categories of 'free' and 'equal' subjectivity that (Western) law and international law take for granted. Certainly, that endeavour is becoming increasingly difficult as deviant forms of thinking and being continue to be disciplined and suppressed in the name of 'freedom' and 'equality'. It is, however, necessary if we are to register the truly cosmic extent of the destruction which the process of reproducing and enforcing these categories has wrought, and continues to inflict, both on human societies and on the non-human world.

[263] Susan Marks, 'False Contingency', 62 *Current Legal Problems* (2009): 1–21. See above, Frame, Section 1.

If Lorde's admonishment, to her colleagues at the 1979 Second Sex Conference in New York, that it is necessary to grasp the 'interdependence of mutual (nondominant) differences', and in doing so 'descend into the chaos of knowledge and return with true visions of our future', resonates with Benjamin's exhortation, to the 'present generation', that we must blast into tiny pieces the progress narratives which legitimise the existing *status quo*, and in doing so crystallise the 'constellation into which [her] own era has entered, along with a very specific earlier one';[264] and if these declarations resonate, in turn, with Borrows' account of his jurisprudence as 'embedded ... deeply in the world of Anishinabek clan and kin', which 'both significantly predates' him and speaks to the 'great-great-great grandchildren' of his future,[265] and also with the prayer of the aristocratic leaders of the anti-Italian forces in occupied Ethiopia that their 'Creator, who delivered Jonah from the belly of the whale',[266] would also punish Italy for its 'transgression of the Covenant of the League of Nations' and deliver 'equitable justice' for Ethiopia,[267] and beyond, then we are left, not with a conclusion, but with a question. What do such *correspondances* have to tell us about the cross-temporal and cross-spatial relationships that might exist between these and other very different, very distant struggles, and what might such relationships offer their current and future protagonists in terms of conceptual resources and material alternatives? With this question, I can only lower the lid of the shadow-box, in the hope that readers will lift it straight back up again.

'Melbourne', 22 'February' '2018'

[264] Benjamin, 'On the Concept of History', 397, 390.

[265] Borrows, *Drawing Out Law*, ix–xii.

[266] In 'Communication from the Permanent Ethiopian Delegate Accredited to the League of Nations to the Secretary-General', London, 28 December 1938, *LNOJ* (January 1939): 8–22 at 10. See Layer 6, Section 2.2.

[267] In 'Communication from the Permanent Ethiopian Delegate', 20.

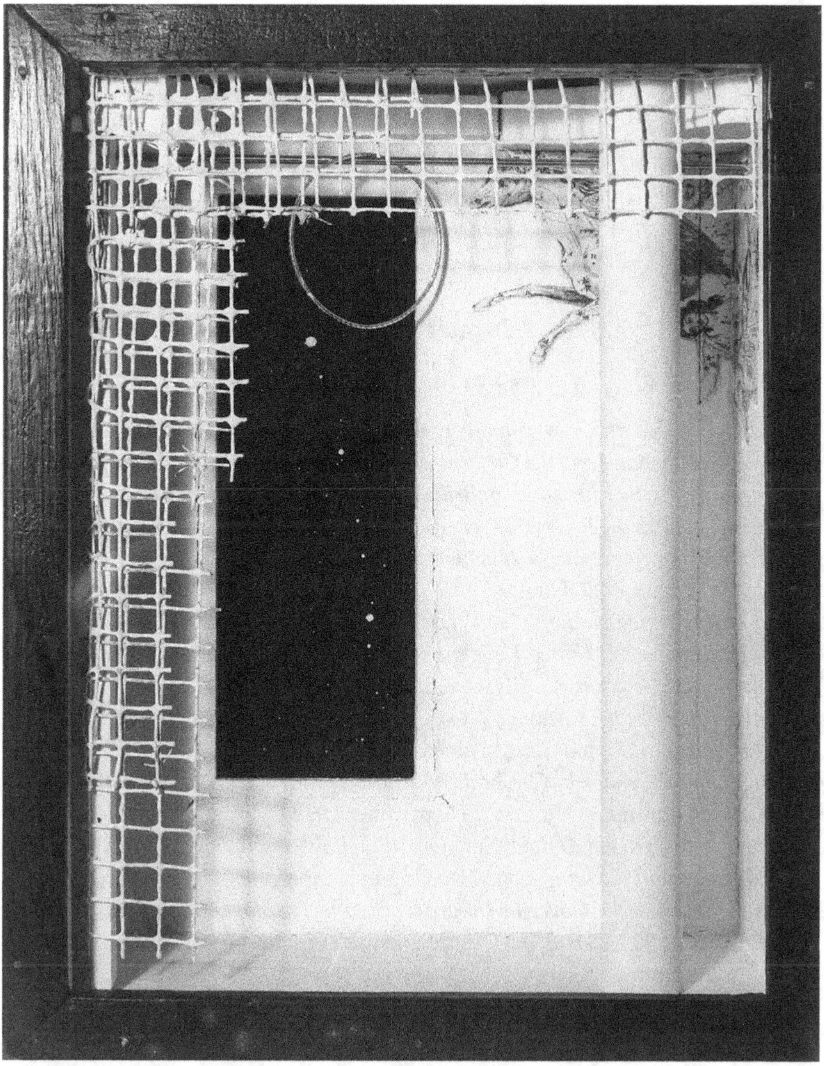

Figure 11 Joseph Cornell, *Midnight Carousel: Winter Night Sky* (1954), assemblage, mixed media, 35.56 x 27.94 x 16.1 cm. © The Joseph and Robert Cornell Memorial Foundation. VAGA/Licenced by Viscopy, 2018. Photographed by Peter A. Juley & Son © Peter A. Juley & Son Collection, courtesy of the Smithsonian American Art Museum and the Harvard Arts Museum/Fogg Museum.

SOURCES[1]

Primary Sources

a) Treaties and International Agreements

Agreement between the Government of the United Kingdom of Great Britain and Northern Ireland and the Government of Ethiopia relating to certain matters connected with the withdrawal of British Military Administration from the territories designated as the Reserved Area and the Ogaden, London, 29 November 1954.

Statute of the International Court of Justice, San Francisco, 24 October 1945, annexed to UN Charter ('ICJ Statute').

Charter of the United Nations, San Francisco, 26 June 1945 ('UN Charter').

Agreement between the United Kingdom and the Ethiopian Empire for the Regulation of Mutual Relations, Addis Ababa, 19 December 1944.

Agreement between His Majesty's Government in the United Kingdom and the Emperor of Ethiopia, Addis Ababa, 31 January 1942.

Agreement for the Cession by Czechoslovakia to Germany of Sudeten German Territory, with Declarations, Munich, 29 September 1938 ('Munich Agreement').

Agreement between the United Kingdom and Italy, consisting of a Protocol with Annexes and Exchanges of Notes, Rome, 16 April 1938 ('Easter Accords').

Agreement between the Government of Liberia and Firestone Plantations Company, Freetown, 20 March 1935 ('Supplementary Plantations Agreement').

[1] In order to reflect the way in which the argument in this book has been constructed more accurately, this bibliography has been organised on the basis of the different 'sources' of international law, as classified in the Statute of the International Court of Justice (ICJ), Art. 38(1):

1. The Court, whose function is to decide in accordance with international law such disputes as are submitted to it, shall apply:
   a. International conventions, whether general or particular, establishing rules expressly recognized by the contesting states;
   b. International custom, as evidence of a general practice accepted as law;
   c. The general principles of law recognized by civilized nations;
   d. ... Judicial decisions and the teachings of the most highly qualified publicists of the various nations, as subsidiary means for the determination of rules of law.

I have taken some liberties when it comes to the question of what to include where, which likewise reflect the central point of the book. See further Rose Parfitt, 'The Spectre of Sources', 25 *EJIL* (2014): 297–306.

Agreement between the Government of Liberia and the Finance Corporation of America, Freetown, 16 March 1935.

Treaty between France and Italy regarding the Settlement of their Interests in Africa, Rome, 7 January 1935 ('Mussolini-Laval Accords').

Inter-American Convention on the Rights and Duties of States, Montevideo, 26 December 1933 ('Montevideo Convention').

Treaty between Ethiopia, France, the United Kingdom and Italy concerning the Importation of Arms, Paris, 21 August 1930.

Treaty of Alliance between His Majesty in respect of the United Kingdom and His Majesty the King of Iraq, Baghdad, 30 June 1930 ('1930 Iraqi-Anglo Treaty').

Convention Concerning Forced or Compulsory Labour, Geneva, 28 June 1930 ('Forced Labour Convention').

Treaty between the United States, Germany, Belgium, France, Britain, Italy, Japan, Poland and Czechoslovakia providing for the Renunciation of War as an Instrument of National Policy, Paris, 27 August 1928 ('Kellogg-Briand Pact'/'Pact of Paris').

Convention between Abyssinia and Italy for the Construction of a Motor Road from Assab to Dessieh and the Concession of an Abyssinian Free Zone at Assab, Addis Ababa, 2 August 1928.

Treaty of Friendship, Conciliation and Arbitration between Italy and Ethiopia, Addis Ababa, 2 August 1928.

International Convention with Object of Securing the Abolition of Slavery and the Slave Trade, Geneva, 25 September 1926 ('Slavery Convention').

Exchange of Notes between the United Kingdom and Italy, Respecting Certain British and Italian Interests in Abyssinia, Rome, 14 and 20 December 1925, in 50 *League of Nations Treaty Series* (1926) ('Anglo-Italian Exchange of Notes').

Treaty of Mutual Guarantee between Germany, Belgium, France, Great Britain and Italy, Locarno, 16 October 1925.

Treaty of Peace between the British Empire, France, Italy, Japan, Greece, Roumania and the Serb-Croat-Slovene State and Turkey, Lausanne ('Treaty of Lausanne'), 24 July 1923.

Treaty of Alliance between Great Britain and Irak, Baghdad, 10 October 1922 ('1922 Iraqi-Anglo Treaty').

French Mandate for Syria and the Lebanon, Geneva, 12 August 1922.

British Mandate for Palestine, Geneva, 24 July 1922.

Anglo-Soviet Trade Agreement, 16 March 1921.

Treaty of Peace between the Allied and Associated Powers with Turkey, Sèvres, 10 August 1920.

Treaty of Peace between the Principal Allied and Associated Powers and Hungary, Trianon, 4 June 1920 ('Treaty of Trianon').

Treaty between the Principle Allied and Associated Powers and Roumania, Paris, 9 December 1919 ('Treaty of Paris').

Treaty of Peace between the Allied and Associated Powers and Bulgaria, and Protocol and Declaration, Neuilly-sur-Seine, 27 November 1919 ('Treaty of Neuilly').

Convention Revising the General Act of Berlin, February 26, 1885, and the General Act and Declaration of Brussels, 2 July 1890, Saint-Germain-en-Laye, 10 September 1919.

Convention for the Control of the Trade in Arms and Ammunition, and Protocol, Saint-Germain-en-Laye, 10 September 1919.

Treaty between the Principal Allied and Associated Powers and Czecho-Slovakia, Saint-Germain-en-Laye, 10 September 1919.

Treaty of Peace between the Allied and Associated Powers and Austria with Protocol, Declaration and Special Declaration, Saint-Germain-en-Laye, 10 September 1919.

Treaty between the Principal Allied and Associated Powers (the British Empire, Italy, Japan and the United States) and Poland, Versailles, 28 June 1919 ('Polish Minorities Treaty').

Covenant of the League of Nations, annexed to *Treaty of Peace between the British Empire, France, Italy, Japan and the United States (the Principal Allied and Associated Powers), and Belgium, Bolivia, Brazil, China, Cuba, Czechoslovakia, Ecuador, Greece, Guatemala, Haiti, the Hedjaz, Honduras, Liberia, Nicaragua, Panama, Peru, Poland, Portugal, Roumania, the Serb-Croat-Slovene State, Siam, and Uruguay, and Germany*, Versailles, 28 June 1919 ('Covenant').

Treaty of Peace between the British Empire, France, Italy, Japan and the United States (the Principal Allied and Associated Powers), and Belgium, Bolivia, Brazil, China, Cuba, Czechoslovakia, Ecuador, Greece, Guatemala, Haiti, the Hedjaz, Honduras, Liberia, Nicaragua, Panama, Peru, Poland, Portugal, Roumania, the Serb-Croat-Slovene State, Siam, and Uruguay, and Germany, Versailles, 28 June 1919 ('Treaty of Versailles').

Treaty of Peace between Russia and Germany, Austria-Hungary, Bulgaria and Turkey, Brest-Litovsk, 3 March 1918 ('Treaty of Brest-Litovsk').

Agreement between Great Britain, France, Russia and Italy providing for Italian Naval and Military Co-operation with the Allied Powers in the European War, and Making Certain Territorial and Other Arrangements, London, 26 April 1915 ('Treaty of London').

Treaty of Commerce between the United States and the Ethiopian Empire, Addis Ababa, 27 June 1914.

Treaty of Friendship and Commerce between Ethiopia and France, Addis Ababa, 10 January 1908 ('Klobukowski Treaty').

Agreement between the United Kingdom, France, and Italy respecting Abyssinia, London, 13 December 1906 ('Tripartite Agreement').

Agreement between the United Kingdom, France and Italy Respecting the Importation of Arms and Ammunition into Abyssinia, London, 13 December 1906, 001/1907: Cd. 3298 ('Tripartite Agreement').

Treaty between the Austro-Hungarian Empire and the Ethiopian Empire, Addis Ababa, 21 March 1905.

Treaty to Regulate Commercial Relations between the United States of America and the Ethiopian Empire, Addis Ababa, 27 December 1904.

Treaty between Great Britain and Ethiopia, and between Great Britain, Italy and Ethiopia, relative to the Frontiers of the Soudan [sic], Ethiopia, and Eritrea, Addis Ababa, 15 May 1902.

Peace Agreement between Austria-Hungary, Britain, France, Germany, Italy, Japan, Russia and the United States and China, Peking, 7 September 1901 ('Boxer Protocol').

Treaty between Italy and Ethiopia, for the Delimitation of the Frontier between Eritrea and Ethiopia, Addis Ababa, 10 July 1900.

Treaty between Great Britain and Ethiopia (Frontiers of British Protectorate on Somali Coast), Addis Ababa, 14 May 1897.

Treaty of Peace between the Kingdom of Italy and the Ethiopian Empire, Addis Ababa, 26 October 1896 ('Treaty of Addis Ababa').

Protocol between Great Britain and Italy defining their respective Spheres of Influence in Eastern Africa, Rome, 5 May 1894.

Protocol between Great Britain and Italy for the Demarcation of their respective Spheres of Influence in East Africa, from Ras Kasar to the Blue Nile, Rome, 15 April 1891.

Protocol between the British and Italian Governments for the Demarcation of their respective Spheres of Influence in Eastern Africa, from the River Juba to the Blue Nile, Rome, 24 March 1891.

Convention Relative to the Slave Trade and Importation into Africa of Firearms, Ammunition, and Spiritous Liquors, between the United States, the German Empire, Austria-Hungary, Belgium, Denmark, Spain, Great Britain, Congo Free State, France, Italy, Netherlands, Luxembourg, Persia, Portugal, Russia, Sweden and Norway, the Ottoman Empire, Zanzibar, Brussels, 2 July 1890 ('Brussels Act').

Convention Additional to the Treaty of Friendship and Commerce signed at the Camp of Ucciali, Naples, 1 October 1889.

Treaty of Perpetual Peace and Friendship between Ethiopia and Italy, Wich'alle, 29 September 1889 ('Treaty of Wich'alle').

Treaty of Friendship and Commerce between Italy and the Sultan of Aussa (Danakils), Adelé Gubó, 9 December 1888.

Convention between the Sultan of Aussa (Danakils) and Italy for the Opening of the Assab-Aussa-Shewa Road, 7 July 1887.

Treaty of Friendship, Commerce and Navigation between the United Kingdom of Great Britain and Ireland and Honduras, and Protocol, Guatemala, 21 January 1887.

Treaty of Peace, Friendship and Commerce between the Republic of France and the Chinese Empire, Tientsin, 13 April 1885.

General Act of the Conference of Berlin Concerning the Congo, between Austria-Hungary, Belgium, Denmark, France, the German Empire, Great Britain, Italy, Netherlands, Ottoman Empire, Portugal, the Russian Empire, Spain, Sweden and Norway, the United States, Berlin, 26 February 1885 ('Berlin Act').

Treaty of Friendship, Commerce and Navigation between the United Kingdom of Great Britain and Ireland and Paraguay, Buenos Aires, 16 October 1884.

Treaty between Great Britain and Abyssinia for the Suppression of the Slave Trade, Adwa, 3 June 1884.

Treaty of Peace, Friendship and Commerce between France and the Sultan of Gobad, Obock, 9 April 1884.

Treaty of Commerce and Navigation between Her Majesty and the King of Italy, Rome, 15 June 1883.

Treaty between the Italian Government and the Sultan of Assab, Mohamed Hanfari, Chief of the Danakils, Kadeli Gubo, 15 March 1883.

Treaty of Friendship and Commerce between Shewa and Italy, Ancober, 21 May 1883.

Convention between Danakil Chiefs and Rubattino Company for the Cession of the Island of Sennabor and the Continental Region between Ras Darmab and Ras Lumah, Assab, 15 May 1880.

Convention between Berehan Dini, Sultan of Raheita, and the Rubattino Company for the Cession of the Islands of Ommel-Buchar, Ras-er-Raml, and the Darmachie Group, Raheita, 30 December 1879.

Final Act of the Congress of Berlin Between Great Britain, Austria-Hungary, France, Germany, Italy, Russia and Turkey, Berlin, 13 July 1878 ('Treaty of Berlin').

Treaty of Peace between the United States and Representatives of the Different Bands of the Sioux Nation, Fort Laramie, 29 April 1868 ('Fort Laramie Treaty').

Treaty of Friendship, Commerce and Navigation between the United Kingdom of Great Britain and Ireland and Colombia, London, 16 February 1866.

Treaty of Amity, Commerce, and Navigation; Extradition between the United States of America and the Republic of Hayti, Port-au-Prince, 3 November 1864.

Treaty of Friendship, Commerce and Navigation between the United Kingdom of Great Britain and Ireland and El Salvador, Guatemala, 24 October 1862.

Treaty of Commerce and Navigation between the United States of America and the Republic of Liberia, London, 21 October 1862.

Treaty between Her Majesty the Queen of the United Kingdom of Great Britain and Ireland, and His Majesty the Emperor of China, Tientsin [Tianjin], 26 June 1858 ('Treaty of Tiensin').

Treaty between the United States of America and the Chinese Empire, Tientsin [Tianjin], 18 June 1858.

Treaty between His Majesty the Emperor and Autocrat of All the Russias, and His Majesty the Emperor of China, Tientsin [Tianjin], 13 June 1858.

Treaty of Friendship, Commerce and Navigation between the United Kingdom of Great Britain and Ireland and Peru, London, 10 April 1850.

Treaty of Friendship, Commerce and Navigation between the United Kingdom of Great Britain and Ireland and Costa Rica, San José, 27 November 1849.

Treaty of Friendship and Commerce between Great Britain and Abyssinia, Ennowga, 2 November 1849.

Treaty of Friendship and Commerce between the United Kingdom of Great Britain and Ireland and Liberia, London, 21 November 1848.

Treaty between Her Majesty and the Emperor of China, Nanking, 29 August 1842.

Treaty of Amity and Commerce between Great Britain and Shewa, Angollah, 15 November 1841.

Declaration of the Eight Powers on the Abolition of the Slave Trade, 8 February 1815, annexed to *General Treaty between Great Britain, Austria, France, Portugal, Prussia, Russia, Spain and Sweden*, Vienna, 9 June 1815 ('Final Act of the Congress of Vienna').

Treaty between the Dutch Republic and the Kingdom of Spain, 30 January 1648, Münster, 15 May 1648.

Treaty between the Holy Roman Empire of the German Nation and Sweden and their Respective Allies, Münster, 24 October 1648 ('Treaty of Münster'/'Peace of Westphalia').

Treaty between the Holy Roman Empire of the German Nation, France and the respective allies, Osnabrück, 24 October 1648 ('Treaty of Osnabrück'/'Peace of Westphalia').

b) 'State Practice' and 'Opinio Juris'

i Official Speeches, Statements and Correspondence

Allied and Associated Powers, 'Reply to the Comments of the German Delegation on the Conditions of Peace,' 16 June 1919 in 6 *International Conciliation* (1919): 1341–424.

Archer, G. F., 'Submission of the Government of Sudan' (Anti-Slavery Conference, 31 January 1926), Dossier 1/49465x/46781, Box R.76 (LONA).

Baldwin, Stanley, Statement to Parliament, 10 December 1935 in Heald (ed.), *Documents on International Affairs* 350.

Balfour, Arthur, Telegram to Claud Russell, 6 June 1922, FO 371/7148: Political (Abyssinia) 1922, A. 3428/486/1, UKNA.

Ban Ki-moon, *A Vital and Enduring Commitment: Implementing the Responsibility to Protect*, Report of the UN Secretary-General, GA/SC Res. A/69/981-S /2015/500, 13 July 2015.

Fulfilling our Collective Responsibility: International Assistance and the Responsibility to Protect, Report of the UN Secretary-General, A/68/947-S/2014/449, 11 July 2014.

Responsibility to Protect: State Responsibility and Prevention, Report of the UN Secretary-General, A/67/929-S/2013/399, 9 July 2013.

Barton, Sidney, Telegram to Samuel Hoare, Addis Ababa, 13 August 1935, in Medlicott, Dakin and Lambert (eds.), *Documents*, Vol. 14, 478–9.

Beauchamp (Earl), 'Slavery in Abyssinia', Statement to the House of Lords, HL Deb, 30 July 1923, Hansard, Vol. 54, Col. 1461.

Beneš, Edvard, Statement by the President of the League Assembly, 11 October 1935 in Heald (ed.), *Documents on International Affairs*, 191.

Blair, Tony, Speech to the House of Commons, 19 March 2003, *The Guardian*, at www.theguardian.com/politics/2003/mar/18/foreignpolicy.iraq1 (accessed 17 February 2018).

Blake, Philip, Statement to the Mackenzie Valley Pipeline Inquiry ('Berger Inquiry')', in Mel Watkins (ed.), *Dene Nation: The Colony Within* (University of Toronto Press, 1977), 5–9.

Clemenceau, Georges, 'Letter Addressed to M. Paderewski by the [Paris Peace] Conference', 24 June 1919, in *La Documentation international: La Paix de Versailles*, Vol. X: (Commission de nouveaux Etats et des Minorités, 1932), 162.

Clinton, Hillary, Address to the UN Human Rights Council, New York, 3 March 2011, at UN Mission at Geneva, https://geneva.usmission.gov/2011/02/28/sec-clinton-hrc-geneva-2011/ (accessed 22 May 2018)

Dodds, J. H., Memorandum, 24 January 1922, A 486/486/1, FO 371/7141 Political (Abyssinia) 1922 (UKNA).

Drummond, Eric, Telegram to Samuel Hoare, Rome, 17 August 1935, in Medlicott, Dakin and Lambert (eds.), *Documents*, Vol. 14, 501–3.

Eden, Anthony and Pierre Laval, 'Letter from the Representatives of the United Kingdom (Anthony Eden) and France (Pierre Laval) to the Secretary-General communicating the Suggestions for an Agreed Settlement of the Conflict,' Geneva, 13 December 1935, *LNOJ* (January 1936): 39–40.

Eden, Anthony, Statement to Parliament, 10 December 1935 in Heald (ed.), *Documents on International Affairs*, Vol. 2, 351.

Eden, Anthony, Statement to the House of Commons, 3 September 1935, in Heald (ed.), *Documents on International Affairs, 1935*, Vol. 2, 35.

Ethiopian Government, Reply of the Abyssinian Government to the Suggestions and Communications of the Committee of Five, 23 September 1935, *LNOJ* (November 1935): 1626.

Dispute between Ethiopia and Italy: Request of the Ethiopian Government, 6 September 1935, *LNOJ* 16 (November 1935): 1144–5.

Dispute between Ethiopia and Italy: Request by the Ethiopian Government, 3 August 1935, *LNOJ* (August 1935): 967–8.

Letter from the Ethiopian Government to the Secretary-General, 29 March 1935, *LNOJ* (May 1935): 576.

'Letter from the Ethiopian Government to the Secretary-General, 17 March 1935', *LNOJ* (May 1935): 572.

Request by the Abyssinian Government under Article 11, Paragraph 2, of the Covenant of the League of Nations: Inclusion of this Item in the Agenda of the Session of 17 January 1935 *LNOJ* (February 1935).

Demande d'admission à la Société des Nations présentée par l'Empire d'Ethiopie, Geneva, 6 September 1923, A.55.1923.VI, bound in *Société des Nations, Assemblée 4* (1923), Docs. 41–144, LONA.

Request for Admission to the League of Nations from Abyssinia, 6 September 1923, in Société des Nations, Assemblée 4 (1923), Documents 41–144, A.55.1923.VI, Appendix III (LONA).

German Delegation to the Paris Peace Conference, Comments on the Conditions of Peace 6 *International Conciliation* 143 (1919), 1201–338.

Griaule, Marcel, 'Comments by M. Marcel Griaule on Some of the Questions Dealt with in the Italian Government's Memorandum on the Situation in Ethiopia,' 14 September 1935 in *LNOJ* (November 1935): 1588–95.

Haile Selassie, Telegram from His Majesty the Emperor of Ethiopia to the President of the Council, 28 September 1935, *LNOJ* (November 1935): 1603.

Telegram from His Majesty the Emperor of Ethiopia to the Secretary-General, 25 September 1935, *LNOJ* (November 1935): 1602.

Hoare, Samuel, Speech to the House of Commons, Hansard, HC, col. 516–18, 11 July 1935.

Speech at the League Assembly, 11 September 1935, in Medlicott, Dakin and Lambert (eds.), *Documents*, Vol. 14, 784–90.

Speech to the Sixteenth Assembly of the League of Nations, 11 September 1935, in Medlicott, Dakin and Lambert (eds.), *Documents*, Vol. 14, 784–90.

Speech to the Sixteenth Assembly of the League of Nations, 11 September 1935, in Heald (ed.), *Documents*, 100–5.

Statement to Parliament, 19 December 1935, in Heald (ed.), *Documents on International Affairs*, 386.

Statement to the Coordination Committee, 2 November 1935, in Heald (ed.), *Documents on International Affairs*, 336.

Howard, John, Sir Robert Menzies Lecture, Melbourne, 18 November 1996, at http://pmtranscripts.pmc.gov.au/release/transcript-10171 (accessed 4 June 2018).

Husayn, Sharif of Mecca correspondence with Sir Henry McMahon, British High Commissioner at Cairo, 14 July–10 March 1916 in *World War One Document Archive* (Brigham Young University Library), at https://wwi.lib.byu.edu/index.php/Letters_between_Hussein_Ibn_Ali_and_Sir_Henry_Mcmahon (accessed 22 May 2018).

Italian Government, 'Letter from the Italian Government to the Secretary-General of the League of Nations, 7 August 1926', *LNOJ* (November 1926): 1525.

Italian Government, 'Telegram from the Italian Government to the Secretary-General, 22 March 1935', *LNOJ* (November 1935): 573.

Italian Minister at Addis Ababa, 'Letter to His Highness Tafari Makonnen, Heir to the Throne of Abyssinia', 9 June 1926, *LNOJ* (November 1926): 1520.

Italian Representative at Geneva, 'Letter to the Secretary-General, Transmitting Other Books Concerning Ethiopia', 16 September 1935, *LNOJ* (November 1935): 1586.

Laval, Pierre, Statement to the Committee of Eighteen, 12 December 1935 in Heald (ed.), *Documents*, 362.

Statement to the Coordination Committee 2 November 1935 in Heald (ed.), *Documents on International Affairs*, 337.

Lenin, Vladimir Ilich, 'Declaration of Rights of the Working and Exploited People', 4 January 1918, approved 12 January 1918 by the Third All-Russia Congress of Soviets, at www.marxists.org/archive/lenin/works/1918/jan/03.htm (accessed 22 May 2018).

'Report on Peace', delivered to the Second All-Russia Congress of Soviets of Workers' and Soldiers' Deputies, 8 November 1917, at www.marxists.org/archive/lenin/works/1917/oct/25-26/26b.htm (accessed 22 May 2018).

Lindsay, Ronald, British Ambassador to the United States the US Secretary of State, Washington, 17 January 1935, in *Foreign Relations of the United States Diplomatic Papers, 1935, General, The Near East and Africa*, Vol. I, available at https://history.state.gov/historicaldocuments/frus1935v01/d806 (accessed 22 May 2018).

Litvinov, Maxim, People's Commissar for Foreign Affairs for the USSR, correspondence with Franklin D. Roosevelt, President of the United States, 16 November 1933, at US National Security Archives Online, at http://nsarchive.gwu.edu/coldwar/documents/episode-1/fdr-ml.htm (accessed 22 May 2018).

McCain, John, Speeches presented on 8 February 2003, 39th Munich Conference on Security Policy, Bayerischer Hotel, Munich, Germany, 7–9 February 2003, at The Acronym Institute for Disarmament Diplomacy, www.acronym.org.uk/old/archive/docs/0302/doc12.htm#07 (accessed 22 May 2018).

Menelik II, Letter to President Carnot (France), 30 October 1890, in Rubenson, *The Survival*, 392.

Letter to the Heads of State of Britain, France, Germany, Italy and Russia, 10 April 1891, in Brownlie and Burns, *African Boundaries: A Legal and Diplomatic Encyclopaedia*, 777–8.

Letter to the Government of Italy, 4 December 1906 in *Ministero degli affari esteri, Trattati, convenzioni, accordi, protocolli ed altri documenti, relative all'Africa (1825–1906)*, Vol. 2 (Rome: Italia Direzione Centrale degli Affari Coloniali, 1906), 1257.

Miliband, David, 'Political Developments in Kosovo', Written ministerial statement by the Secretary of State for Foreign and Commonwealth Affairs, 28 February 2008.

Molle, Joseph van (Belgium), 'Letter addressed to M. Jèze, posted on September 10th, 1935, and received at Geneva on September 12th, 1935', *LNOJ* (November 1935): 1587.

Organisation of African Unity Heads of State and Government, 'Cairo Declaration on Boundaries'. Cairo, July 1964, AHG/Res.16(1) 1964.

Paderewski, Ignacy Jan, Memorandum, 25 June 1919 in *La Documentation international: La Paix de Versailles, Vol. X: Commission de nouveaux Etats et des Minorités* (Paris: Editions internationals, 1932), 129–30.

Pignatti, Morano, Commissione Conciliazione – Quinto [A]rbitro, telegram from Ambassador Pignatti, Paris, 6 August 1935, Gabinetto 249, Busta 566 (MAE Archives).

Politis, Nikolaos, Telegram to Dr. Zervos, intercepted by Ambassador Vinci, in Guido Vinci, 'Telegramma Ministro Politis al Dr. Zervos,' Addis Ababa, 13 August 1935, in Gabinetto 249, Busta 566 (MAE Archives).

Qianlong, Emperor of China, Imperial Mandate to King George III of Britain, in E. Backhouse and J. O. P. Bland, *Annals and Memoirs of the Court of Peking* (Boston, MA, New York: Houghton Mifflin, 1914), 322–34.

Rappard, William, Letter to Captain Tracy Philipps, 11 April 1923 in *La question de l'esclavage*, File 1/27748/23252, Box R.62, LONA.

Rice, Condoleezza, 'US Recognises Kosovo as Independent State', *Statement by Secretary of State*, 18 February 2008, at https://2001-2009.state.gov/secretary/rm/2008/02/100973.htm (accessed 5 June 2018).

Roosevelt, Franklin D., Appeal to the American People, 29 February 1936, in Heald (ed.), *Documents on International Affairs*, 293–4.

Rudd, Kevin, 'Apology to Australia's Indigenous Peoples', 13 February 2008, at www.australia.gov.au/about-australia/our-country/our-people/apology-to-australias-indigenous-peoples (accessed 4 June 2018).

Russell, Claud, to the Marquis Curzon of Kedleston, 16 March 1922, A1799/486/1, in FO 371/7141: Political (Abyssinia) 1922, UKNA.

Russell, Claud, Telegram to the Marquis Curzon of Kedleston, 16 March 1922, A1799/486/1, FO 371/7141 Political (Abyssinia) 1922, UKNA.

Sperling, Roland, 'Slavery in Abyssinia: Origin of Present Agitation', 23 May 1922, A. 3326/486/1, in FO 371/7148: Political (Abyssinia) 1922, UKNA.

Memorandum, 10 February 1922, A1475/486/1, in FO 371/7147: Political (Abyssinia) 1922, UKNA.

Memorandum, 3 March 1922, A 1475/136; Harris to Curzon, 28 Aug 1923; Sperling to Harris, 4 September 1923, all in FO 371/8406: Political (Abyssinia) 1923, UKNA.

Tafari Mackonen, 'Protest sent by His Imperial and Royal Highness Tafari Mackonen, Regent and Heir to the Throne of Abyssinia, to the States Members of the League of Nations,' 19 June 1926, *LNOJ* (November 1926).

Täklä-Hawaryat Täklä-Maryam, 'Aide-mémoire left with Mr Eden by the Abyssinian Minister in Paris,' 15 August 1935, enclosed in Clerk to Hoare, 16 August 1935, in Medlicott, Dakin and Lambert (eds.), *Documents*, Vol. 14, pp. 492–4.

'Communication from the Permanent Ethiopian Delegate Accredited to the League of Nations to the Secretary-General', London, 28 December 1938, *LNOJ* (January 1939): 8–22.

'Preliminary Observations of the Ethiopian Delegation on the Italian Government's Memorandum', 14 September 1935, *LNOJ* (November 1935).

Communication from the Permanent Ethiopian Delegate Accredited to the League of Nations to the Secretary-General', London, 28 December 1938' *LNOJ* (January 1939): 8–22.

Letter from the Representative of Ethiopia to the Secretary-General, 12 August 1935, *LNOJ* (November 1935): 1602.

Letter from the Representative of Ethiopia to the Secretary-General, 10 September 1935, *LNOJ* (November 1935): 1602.

United Kingdom Delegation at Geneva, Letter to the Secretary-General, Geneva, 26 September 1936, *LNOJ* (December 1936), 1408.

United States Government, Statement in Regard to Support Requested by the American Group, 18 March 1913 in MacMurray, John V. A. (ed.), *Treaties and Agreements with China, 1894–1919*, Vol. II (New York: Oxford University Press, 1921), 1025.

Vansittart, Robert (Sir), Memorandum enclosed in Vansittart, letter to G. Clerk, 16 December 1935', in Medlicott, Dakin and Lambert (eds.), *Documents on British Foreign Policy, 1919–1939*, Second Series, Vol. 15, pp. 784–90.

Vasconcelos, Augusto de (Chairman), Statement to the Coordination Committee, 2 November 1935 in Heald (ed.), *Documents on International Affairs*, p. 341.

Vinci, Guido, 'Incidente di Ualual: Politis e Commissione Arbitrato' (telegram), Addis Ababa, 26 April 1935 in Gabinetto 249, Busta 566 (MAE Archives).

'Telegramma Ministro Politis al Dr. Zervos', telegram intercepted and transmitted by Ambassador Vinci, Addis Ababa, 13 August 1935 (Gab. 249, Busta 566, MAE Archives).

Walton, Lester A., US Minister in Liberia to the Secretary of State, Monrovia, 19 December 1936, 882.01/76, in *Foreign Relations of the United States Diplomatic Papers, 1935, General, The Near East and Africa*, Vol. 1, available at https://history.state.gov/historicaldocuments/frus1936v03/d500 (accessed 22 May 2018).

Wilson, Woodrow, 'The Fourteen Points', Address to Congress, 8 January 1918, available at http://avalon.law.yale.edu/20th_century/wilson14.asp (accessed 11 August 2016).

Zeeland, Paul van, Statement to the Coordination Committee, 2 November 1935 in Heald (ed.), *Documents on International Affairs*, 338.

ii Constitutions, Declarations of Independence and Municipal Laws

Australia, *Native Title Act* No. 100 (1993).

Bolivia, *Constitución Política del Estado de Bolivia*, Sucre, 7 February 2009.

Bosnia and Herzegovina, *Constitution of Bosnia and Herzegovina*, General Framework Agreement for Peace in Bosnia and Herzegovina ('Dayton Accords'), Dayton, 14 December 1995, Annex 4, 59–80.

China, *Provisional Constitution of the Republic of China*, 10 March 1912.

Colombia, *Constitución de la República de Colombia*, Bogotá, 20 July 1991.

Ecuador, *Constitución de la República del Ecuador*, Quito, 28 September 2008.

Ethiopia, *Constitution of the Empire of Ethiopia*, Addis Ababa, 16 July 1931.

Ethiopia, *Constitution of the Federal Democratic Republic of Ethiopia*, Addis Ababa, 8 December 1994.

France, *Constitution of the French National Assembly*, Paris, 3 September 1791.

France, *La Déclaration des droits de l'Homme et du citoyen*, Assemblée nationale constituante, 26 August 1789, Arts. 1–4.

Germany, *Law for the Prevention of Genetically Diseased Offspring*, 14 July 1933.

Iraq, *Organic Law of 'Iraq*, 10 July 1924, annexed to Letter from the British Government to the Secretary-General of the League, 5 August 1924, in *LNOJ* (November 1924): 1759.

Japan, *Constitution of the Empire of Japan*, Tokyo, 29 November 1890.

Kosovo, *Declaration of Independence of Kosovo*, 17 February 2008.

Liberia, *Constitution of the Commonwealth of Liberia*, Freetown, 26 July 1847.

United States, *American Declaration of Independence*, Philadelphia, 4 July 1776.

United States, *Constitution of the United States of America*, Washington DC, 17 September 1787.

USSR, *Constitution of the Union of Soviet Socialist Republics*, Moscow, 31 January 1924.

iii Official Proposals, Resolutions, Declarations and Reports

Ahtisaari, Martti, 'Report of the Special Envoy of the Secretary-General on Kosovo's Future Status', UN Security Council, S/2007/168, 26 March 2007 ('Ahtisaari Plan').

Anan, Kofi, *Larger Freedom: Towards Development, Security and Human Rights for All*, Report of the UN Secretary-General, A/59/2005, 21 March 2005.

Anti-Slavery and Aborigines Protection Society ('Anti-Slavery Society'), *Slavery and the League of Nations: The Appeal of the Anti-Slavery and Aborigines Protection Society*, 9 August 1923. FO 371/8406: Political (Abyssinia) 1923, A. 3428/486/1 (UKNA)

Assemblée nationale constituante, *La Déclaration des droits de l'Homme et du citoyen*, 26 August 1789, Arts. 1–4.

Boutros-Ghali, Boutros, *An Agenda for Peace: Preventive Diplomacy, Peacemaking, and Peacekeeping*, Report of the UN Secretary-General, A/47/277, 17 June 1992.

British Delegation to the Paris Peace Conference, *Draft Convention Regarding Mandates*, 24 January 1919 in Miller, *The Drafting of the Covenant*, pp. 106–08 ('Cecil Plan').

Canadian Ministry of Indian Affairs and Northern Development, *Gathering Strength: Canada's Aboriginal Action Plan – A Progress Report* (Ottawa: Canadian Ministry of Indian Affairs and Northern Development, 2000).

Central Land Council, 'What is Native Title?', at www.clc.org.au/articles/info/what-is-the-native-title/ (accessed 2 May 2017).

Centre for Biological Diversity, 'The Extinction Crisis', at www.biologicaldiversity.org/programs/biodiversity/elements_of_biodiversity/extinction_crisis/ (accessed 6 October 2017).

European Community (EC) Foreign Ministers, 'Declaration on the Guidelines on the Recognition of New States in Eastern Europe and in the Soviet Union', 16 December 1991 in 61 *British Yearbook of International Law* (1991): 559.

French and British Governments, 'Revised Draft prepared by United Kingdom Delegation as Amended after Discussion with French Delegation, 16 August 1935,' enclosed in Clerk to Hoare, Paris, 16 August 1935, in Medlicott, Dakin and Lambert (eds.), *Documents*, Vol. 14, 496–7 ('Paris Proposals').

Outline of an Agreed Settlement of the Italo-Ethiopian Conflict, Paris, 10 December 1935, in *LNOJ* (January 1936): 40–1 ('Hoare-Laval Pact').

French Government, Renseignements communiqués par le government française, in *Société des Nations: La question de l'esclavage*, 10 August 1923, A.18.1923. VI, 2–11, in dossier 'League of Nations: Documents on Slavery' (no dossier number), Box R.64, 8–11, LONA.

International Monetary Fund, 'The Role of the IMF in Governance Issues: Guidance Note', Approved by the IMF Executive Board, 25 July 1997.

Irish Rule of Law International, 'Our Projects in Ethiopia', at http://irishruleoflaw.ie/our-projects/ethiopia/ (accessed 15 February 2018).

Italian Government, 'Situation in Ethiopia. Memorandum by the Italian Government, and Documents Relating Thereto', 4 September 1935, in *LNOJ* (November 1935) ('Italian Memorandum').

Royal Decree placing Abyssinia under Italian Sovereignty, 9 May 1936, in Heald (ed.), *Documents on International Affairs*, 472–3.

Latrobe, H. B. (President), 'Memorial of the American Colonization Society praying An Appropriation for the Purpose of Making Explorations and Surveys on the Western Coast of Africa, and from Liberia into the Interior of that Continent, with a View to Building Up American Trade and Commerce Therewith', 12 February 1879, Senate of the United States, 45th Congress, 3rd Session, Mis. Doc. 65: 1–3 at 1.

League of Nations, 'Annex 5: Abyssinia's Application for Admission to the League', Report of the Second Sub-Committee, Annex 5, Revised Text, adopted by Sixth Committee 20 September 1923, Minutes of the Sixth Committee (Political Questions), Meetings of the Committees, Records of the Fourth Assembly, *LNOJ* Sp. Supp. No. 19 in *League of Nations, Assembly 4 1923, Committees 4–6*, 34–5 (LONA).

'Report of the International Commission of Enquiry into the Existence of Slavery and Forced Labour in the Republic of Liberia', Monrovia, 8 Sep. 1930. Washington: US Department of State, 1931 ('Liberia Commission Report').

'Question of the Consequences arising out of the Existing Situation in Ethiopia', Fifth Meeting of the Council (Public), 23 May 1938, *LNOJ* (May–June 1938).

Report of the League of Nations Council Committee ('Committee of Six'), *LNOJ* (November 1935): 1225.

'Resolution of the League Assembly, 11 March 1932', in 'Letter from the Secretary-General to the United States Minister at Berne', Fourth Plenary Meeting of the Assembly, 11 March 1932, *LNOJ*, Sp. Supp. No. 101 (1932), 90 (resolution adopting the 'Stimpson Doctrine').

'Report of the League of Nations Council Committee', 7 October 1935, in 30 *AJIL*, Sp. Supp. (1936): 37–40.

'Dispute between Ethiopia and Italy: Report of the Council of the League of Nations under Article 15, paragraph 4 of the Covenant, 7 October 1935', in *LNOJ* (November 1935): 1605–32 ('Report of the Council').

'Abyssinia's Request for Admission', Fourth Meeting, 19 September 1923, Records of the Fourth Assembly, Meetings of the Committees, Minutes of the Sixth Committee (Political Questions), in *LNOJ*, Sp. Supp. No. 19 (1923): 12–16.

'Abyssinia's Request for Admission', Fifth Meeting, 20 September 1923, Records of the Fourth Assembly, Meetings of the Committees, Minutes of the Sixth Committee (Political Questions), in *LNOJ*, Sp. Supp. No. 19 (1923): 17–21.

'Slavery in Africa', Motion Proposed by Sir Arthur Steel-Maitland, Delegate for New Zealand, 7 September 1922, Third Assembly of the League of Nations, in File 1/23252/23252, Box R61, LONA.

Ligue Suisse pour la Défense des Indigènes, '*L'Esclavage en Abyssinie, Rapport rédigé à la demande de la Ligue Suisse pour la Défense des Indigènes*' (Geneva, 1923), in Société des Nations, Assemblée 4 (1923), Documents 41–144, League of Nations Archives, Geneva (LONA).

Lugard, Frederick, 'Memorandum on Slavery and Systems of Restrictive Liberty for the Temporary Slavery Commission', 4 December 1922, in *League of Nations, Assembly 4 1923, Committees 4–6, LONA*, 104 ('Lugard Memorandum').

Maffey, John (Chairman), 'Report of the Inter-Departmental Committee on British Interests in Ethiopia', 18 June 1935, in Medlicott, Dakin and Lambert (eds.), *Documents*, Vol. 14, 743–77 ('Maffey Report').

Martínez, Miguel Alfonso, *Study on Treaties, Agreements and Other Constructive Arrangements between States and Indigenous Populations*, July 1997, Final Report by the United Nations Special Rapporteur on Indigenous Peoples. New York: United Nations, 1997.

National Constitutional Convention, *Uluru Statement from the Heart*, 26 May 2017, at www.referendumcouncil.org.au/sites/default/files/2017-05/Uluru_Statement_From_The_Heart_0.PDF (accessed 7 August 2018).

'People's Republic of China, 'China and the International Monetary Fund (IMF)', Permanent Mission of the People's Republic of China to the United Nations Office at Geneva, 19 April 2004.

Permanent Mission of the People's Republic of China to the United Nations Office at Geneva, 'China and the International Monetary Fund (IMF)', 19 April 2004.

Rappard, William E., Note from William E. Rappard, Director of the Mandates Section to the Secretary-General forwarding a Memorandum from Lord Lugard on Slavery in Abyssinia, 4 December 1922, Dossier 1/24628/23252, Box R.61, LONA.

United Nations, European Union, United States and Russian Federation ('the Quartet'), *A Performance-Based Roadmap to a Permanent Two-State Solution to the Israeli-Palestinian Conflict*, 30 April 2003 ('Roadmap to Peace').

United Nations General Assembly, 'Draft Declaration on Rights and Duties of States', annexed to GA Res. 375 (IV), 6 December 1949.

'Declaration by the General Assembly on the Rights of Indigenous Peoples', Annexed to GA61/295, 13 September 2007 ('UNDRIP').

'Declaration on the Granting of Independence to Colonial Countries and Peoples', GA Res. 1514 (XV), 14 December 1960 ('Colonial Declaration').

GA Res. 1941 (XV), 15 December 1960 ('Principles which should guide members in determining whether or not an obligation exists to transmit the information called for under Article 73e of the Charter').

GA Res. 60/1, 24 October 2005 ('World Summit Outcome 2005').

United Nations Permanent Forum on Indigenous Issues, 'Indigenous Peoples, Indigenous Voices', at www.un.org/esa/socdev/unpfii/documents/5session_factsheet1.pdf (accessed 24 April 2017).

United Nations Security Council, SC Res. 1973, 26 February 2011 ('Situation in Libya').

SC Res. 1244, 10 June 1999 ('Situation in Kosovo').

United Nations, 'Implementing "Standards Before Status" Policy Core Political Project for UN Kosovo Mission, Security Council Told', UN Press Release SC/7999, 6 February 2004.

United States Bureau of Economic and Business Affairs, *Investment Climate Statements*, 2017.

United States, United Kingdom, European Union and Russia, *General Framework for Peace in Bosnia and Herzegovina*, Dayton, 21 November 1995 ('Dayton Accords').

World Bank, *Indigenous Knowledge for Development: A Framework for Action*, Washington, DC: World Bank Group, 1998.

'Effective Implementation: Key to Development Impact', World Bank Portfolio Management Task Force, 22 September 1992 (Washington, DC: World Bank Group, 1992) ('Wapenhans Report').

'The World Bank in Ethiopia' (updated 30 October 2017), at www.worldbank.org/en/country/ethiopia/overview (accessed 15 February 2018).

'Worldwide Governance Indicators' (WGI) Project, at http://info.worldbank.org/governance/wgi/#doc (accessed 26 December 2017).

iv Memoirs, Books, Editorials, Private Correspondence and other Interventions by State Officials

Acheson, Dean (ed.), *United States Relations with China, with Special Reference to the Period 1944–1949* (Washington, DC: US Department of State, 1949).

Buxton, Noel Edward (Lord), *The Times*, 9 April 1932, quoted in Italian Memorandum.

Ciano, Galeazzo, *L'Europa verso la catástrofe* (Milan: Mondadori, 1948).

Correa, Rafael, 'Ecuador's Path', 77 *New Left Review* (2012): 89–111.

Darley, Henry, *Slaves and Ivory* (London: Mellifont Press, 1925).

Darley, Major Henry, 'Abyssinia of To-Day', 22 *Outward Bound* (1922): 689–96, in FO371/8406: Political (Abyssinia) 1923 (UKNA).

Deng, Francis M., 'From "Sovereignty as Responsibility" to the "Responsibility to Protect"', 2 *Global Responsibility to Protect* (2010): 353–70.

Deng, Francis M. et al., *Sovereignty as Responsibility: Conflict Management in Africa* (Washington, DC: Brookings Institution, 1996).

Gäbra-Heywät Baykädañ, '*Até Menilek-na Ityopya*' ('Emperor Menilek and Ethiopia') (Berhan Yehun, Asmara, 1912).

Gäbra-Heywät Baykädañ, *Mangest-na YäHezb Astädadär* ('Government and Public Administration') (Addis Ababa, 1952 EC).

Gabrahiwot Baykadagn, *State and Economy in Early Twentieth Century Ethiopia*. Tenkir Bonger (trans.) (London: Karnak House, 1999).

Gleichen, Edward (Count), *With the Mission to Menelik, 1897* (London: Edward Arnold, 1898).

Haile Selassie I, *My Life and Ethiopia's Progress*, Vol. 2, Harold G. Marcus, Ezekiel Gebissa and Tibebe Eshete (eds.) Edward Ullendorff (trans.) (Chicago, IL: Research Associates School Times, 1999).

Harris, William Cornwallis, *The Highlands of Æthiopia, Described, During Eighteen Months' Residence of a British Embassy at the Christian Court of Shewa* (London: Gilbert & Rivington, 1844).

Kenyatta, J. M., 'Hands off Abyssinia!' 17 *Labour Monthly* (September 1935): 532–45.

Lenin, V. I., 'Big Achievement of the Chinese Republic', Hanna George (trans.) 68 *Pravda*, 22 March 1913, *Marxists' Internet Archive*, available at www.marxists.org/archive/lenin/works/1913/mar/22.htm (accessed 22 May 2018).

Lugard, Frederick J. D., *The Dual Mandate in British Tropical Africa* (Edinburgh, London: W. Blackwood and Sons, 1922).

'Slavery in Abyssinia – Views of Sir Fredrick Lugard', *Westminster Gazette*, 5 May 1922.

Mao Tse-Tung [1939], 'The Chinese Revolution and the Chinese Communist Party' in *Selected Works of Mao Tse-Tung*, Vol. 2 (Peking: Foreign Languages Press, 1967).

Miller, David Hunter, *The Drafting of the Covenant*, Vols. I & II (New York: G. P. Putnam & Sons, 1928).

Nkrumah, Kwame, *Neocolonialism: The Last Stage of Imperialism* (New York: International Publishers, 1966).

Owen, David, *Balkan Odyssey* (San Diego, CA: Harvest Books, 1995).

Phelan, E. J., 'The Sovereignty of the Irish Free State', 1 *The Review of Nations* (1927): 39–45.

Philipps, Captain J. E. T., Letter to the Editor, *The Times*, 10 April 1923, in *La question de l'esclavage*, File 1/27748/23252, Box R.62, LONA.

Plowden, Walter Chichele, *Travels in Abyssinia and the Galla Country: An Account of a Mission to Ras Ali in 1848* (London: Longmans Green & Co., 1868).

Rivoyre, Denis de, 'L'Abyssinie pittoresque et commerciale', 7 *Annales de l'Extreme Orient et de l'Afrique* (1885): 97–111.

Shihata, Ibrahim, 'Preface: Good Governance and the Role of Law in Economic Development', in Ann Seidman, Robert B. Seidman and Thomas W. Walde (eds.), *Making Development Work: Legislative Reform for Institutional Transformation and Good Governance* (The Hague etc.: Kluwer Law International, 1999), xvi–xvii.

Skinner, Robert P, *Abyssinia of To-Day: An Account of the First Mission Sent by the American Government to the Court of the King of Kings (1903–1904)* (New York: Longmans, Green & Co., 1906).

Smuts, Jan C., *The League of Nations: A Practical Suggestion* (London, Toronto, New York: Hodder & Stoughton, 1918).

Spencer, John H., 'The Italian-Ethiopian Dispute and the League of Nations', 31 *AJIL* (1937): 614–41.

Stiglitz, Joseph E., *More Instruments and Broader Goals: Moving Towards the Post-Washington Consensus*, World Institute for Development Economics Research Annual Lecture, January 1998 (Helsinki: UNU/WIDER, 1998).

v Other Legal Systems Recognised as Such by States in this Book (Selected)

Fetha Nagast [c. 1240], English translation: Peter Strauss (ed.), *The Fetha Nagast: The Law of the Kings* (Durham, NC: Carolina Academic Press, 2009).

c) *'General Principles of Law Recognised by Civilised Nations'*

N/A.[2]

d) *'Subsidiary Means for the Determination of Rules of Law'*

i 'Teachings of the Most Highly Qualified Publicists of the Various Nations' (selected)

Alfred, Taiaiake, *Wasáse: Indigenous Pathways of Action and Freedom* (Peterborough, Ontario: Broadview Press, 2005).

Peace, Power, Righteousness: An Indigenous Manifesto (Don Mills, Ontario, New York: Oxford University Press, 1999).

Heeding the Voices of Our Ancestors: Kahnawake Mohawk Politics and the Rise of Native Nationalism (Don Mills, Ontario: Oxford University Press, 1995).

Anzilotti, Dionisio, *Cours de droit international*, 3rd edn Gilbert Gidel (trans.) (Paris: Recueil Sirey, 1919).

[2] In addition to the controversy over the ICJ's continued use, in its Statute, of the adjective 'civilised', the question of what principles 'general principles of law' might mean is hotly disputed. I have not relied on any 'general principles' to make this book's argument. However, a brief examination of the role of this 'source' in the doctrine of international law can help to underscore the central point of that argument. For example, the principle of 'estoppel', applied over the years by several international courts, is one of the most widely accepted and least controversial 'general principles of law'. As the Permanent Court of International Justice defined it in one of its *Factory at Chorsów Case(s)*: 'It is ... a principle generally accepted in the jurisprudence of international arbitration, as well as by municipal Courts, that one party cannot avail himself of the fact that the other has not fulfilled some obligation or has not had recourse to some means of redress, if the former party has by some illegal act prevented the latter from fulfilling the obligation in question, or from having recourse to the tribunal which would have been open to him' (*Factory at Chorsów, Germany* v. *Poland*, PCIJ Series A, No. 9, 26 July 1927, para. 84). How is it possible that estopple could have been accepted as a 'general principle of law' in a context in which the vast majority of the world's communities and individuals had been systematically 'prevented' from fulfilling legal 'obligations' by acts that were 'illegal' under non-Western legal systems, and in which other individuals and communities (that is, legal subjects both individual and international) then proceeded to 'avail' themselves of that situation in diverse ways? Attending to the process (or principle?) of international legal reproduction supplies an answer. Specifically, it draws attention to the fact that these individuals and communities were not 'parties' for the purpose of (Western/international) 'law' precisely because they had failed to fulfil (been prevented from fulfilling) 'obligations' (such as protecting foreign property rights).

Black, C. F., *The Land is the Source of the Law: A Dialogic Encounter with Indigenous Jurisprudence* (London, New York: Routledge, 2011).

Borrows, John, (Kegedonce), John, *Drawing Out Law: A Spirit's Guide* (Toronto, Buffalo, London: University of Toronto Press, 2010).

Freedom and Indigenous Constitutionalism (University of Toronto Press, 2016).

Brownlie, Ian, with the assistance of Ian R. Burns, *African Boundaries: A Legal and Diplomatic Encyclopaedia* (Berkeley and Los Angeles, CA: University of California Press, 1979).

Cassese, Antonio, *International Law* (2nd edn Oxford University Press, 2005).

Self-determination of Peoples: A Legal Reappraisal (Cambridge University Press, 1995).

Coulthard, Glen, *Red Skins, White Masks* (Minneapolis, MN: University of Minnesota Press, 2014).

Cusicanqui, Silvia Rivera, '*Oprimidos pero no vencidos*': *Luchas del Campesino Aymara y Qhechwa, 1900–1980* (La Paz: La Mirada Salvaje, 1984).

Digges, Dudley [1648], *The Unlawfulness of Subjects Taking up Arms Against their Soveraigne* (London: Peter Parker, 1679).

Du Bois, W. E. B., 'Inter-Racial Implications of the Ethiopian Crisis: A Negro View', *Foreign Affairs* (October 1932): 82–92.

'Liberia, the League and the United States', 11 *Foreign Affairs* (1933): 682–95.

Fiore, Pasquale, in*ternational Law Codified and Its Legal Sanction or the Legal Organization of the Society of States* (New York: Baker, Voorhis and Company, 1918).

Grotius, Hugo [1738], 'The Rights of War and Peace', In Hugo Grotius, *Three Books. Wherein are Explained, the Law of Nature and Nations, and the Principal Points Relating to Government* (Indianapolis, IN: Liberty Fund, 2005).

Hall, William E. A., *Treatise on International Law* (4th edn Oxford: Clarendon Press, 1895).

Hegel, Georg W. F., [1820], *Elements of the Philosophy of Right*, Allan W. Wood (ed.) and H. B. Nisbet (trans.) (Cambridge University Press, 1991).

[1827–28], *Hegel's Philosophy of Subjective Spirit*, Vol. 2. M. J. Petry (ed. and trans.) (Dordrecht, Boston, MA: D. Reidel Publishing Company, 1979).

[1807], *The Phenomenology of Spirit*, A.V. Miller (trans.) (Oxford, New York: Oxford University Press, 1977).

[1837], *Lectures on the Philosophy of World History*, H. B. Nisbet (trans.) (New York: Cambridge University Press, 1975).

[1817], *The Philosophy of Mind*, William Wallace and A. V. Miller (trans.) (Oxford University Press, 1971).

Hewitt, Jeffrey, 'Decolonizing and Indigenizing: Some Considerations for Law Schools', 33 *Windsor Yearbook of Access to Justice* (2016): 65–84.

'How Indigenous Art is Challenging Colonial Law', *Cigionline*, 27 September 2017.

Hobbes, Thomas [1640], *The Elements of Law, Natural and Politic*. J. C. A. Gaskin (ed.) (Oxford University Press, 2008).

[1651], *Leviathan, or the Matter, Forme and Power of a Common-Wealth Ecclesiastical and Civil* (London: J. M. Dent & Sons, 1914).

Jellinek, Georg, *Allgemeine Staatslehere* (3rd edn Berlin: Verlag von O. Häring, 1914).

Kelsen, Hans, 'The Pure Theory of Law and Analytical Jurisprudence', 55 *Harvard Law Review* (1941–42): 44–70.

Korovin, Evgeny A., *International Law of the Transitional Period* [Международное право переходного времени] (Moscow: Gosudarstvennoe Izdatel'stvo, 1924).

Lauterpacht, Hersch, *Recognition in International Law* (Cambridge University Press, 1947).

Lawrence, Thomas J., *The Principles of International Law* (London, New York: MacMillan, 1895).

Liszt, Franz von, *Le droit international: exposé systematique*, Gilbert Gidel and Leon Alcindor (trans.) (Paris: Pedone, 1927).

Locke, John [1689], 'Of Civil Government', in Ian Shapiro (ed.), *John Locke: Two Treatises of Government and a Letter Concerning Toleration* (New Haven, CT, London: Yale University Press, 2003), 247–484.

Lorimer, James, *The Institutes of International Law: A Treatise of the Principles of Jurisprudence as Determined by Nature* (Edinburgh: T & T Clark, 1872).

Machiavelli, Niccolò, *I discorsi di Nicolo Machiavelli*, Bk II (Palermo: Antonielli; London: J. Wolfe, 1584).

Martínez, Miguel Alfonso, *Study on Treaties, Agreements and Other Constructive Arrangements between States and Indigenous Populations*, Final Report from the Special Rapporteur, UNESCO Commission on Human Rights, E/CN.4/Sub.2/1999/20, 22 June 1999.

McMillan, Mark, 'Koowarta and the Rival Indigenous International: Our Place as Indigenous Peoples in the International', 23 *Griffith Law Review* (2014): 110–26.

McNair, Arnold. *Legal Effects of War* (Cambridge University Press, 1944).

Merino Acuña, Roger, 'Law and Politics of Indigenous Self-Determination: The Meaning of the Right to Prior Consultation', in Irene Watson (ed.), *Indigenous Peoples as Subjects of International Law* (Abingdon: Routledge, 2017), 120–40.

Roger, 'An Alternative to "Alternative Development"?: Buen Vivir and Human Development in Andean Countries', 44 *Oxford Development Studies* (2016): 1–16.

'The Politics of Indigenous Self-Determination: Extractive Industries, State Policies and Territorial Rights in the Peruvian Amazon' (PhD thesis, University of Bath, 2015).

'Descolonizando los Derechos de Propiedad. Derechos Indígenas Comunales y el Paradigma de la Propriedad Privada', 47 *Boletín Mexicano de Derecho Comparado* (2014): 935–64

Napoleon, Val, 'Aboriginal Self-Determination: Individual Self and Collective Selves', 29 *Atlantis* (2015): 31–46.

Neidjie, Bill, *Story About Feeling* (Broome: Magabala Books, 1989).

Oppenheim, Lassa, *International Law: A Treatise*, Vol. 1 (London, New York and Bombay: Longmans, Green & Co., 1905).

The League of Nations and its Problems: Three Lectures (London and Bombay: Longmans, Green & Co., 1919.

Pashukanis, Evgeny [1924], *The General Theory of Law and Marxism*. Barbara Einhorn (trans.) (New Brunswick, London: Transaction Publishers, 2002).

[1925] 'International Law', in Piers Beirne and Robert Sharlet (eds.), Peter B. Maggs (trans.), *Pashukanis: Selected Writings on Marxism and Law* (London: Academic Press, 1980), 168–83.

Pashukanis: Selected Writings on Marxism and Law, in Piers Beirne and Robert Sharlet (eds.) and Peter B. Maggs (trans.) (London: Academic Press, 1980).

Rousseau, Jean-Jacques [1762], *The Social Contract* (Harmondsworth: Penguin, 1968).

Schmitt, Carl [1950], *The Nomos of the Earth* (New York: Telos Press, 2003).

'Die siebente Wandlung des Genfer Völkerbundes', in Carl Schmitt. *Positionen und Begriffe in Kampf mit Weimar-Genf-Versailles 1923–39* (2nd edn Duncker & Humblot: Berlin, 1988), 2010–13.

Schwarzenberger, Georg, *The League of Nations and World Order: A Treatise on the Principle of Universality in the Theory and Practice of the League* (London: Constable and Co., 1936).

'The Standard of Civilisation in International Law', 8 *Current Legal Problems* (1955): 212–34.

Simpson, Audra, 'The Ruse of Consent and the Anatomy of "Refusal": Cases from Indigenous North America and Australia', 20 *Postcolonial Studies* (2017): 1–16.

Mohawk Interruptus: Political Life Across the Borders of Settler States (Durham, NC: Duke University Press, 2014).

Smith, Adam [1776], *An Inquiry into the Nature and Causes of the Wealth of Nations* (London, J. M. Dent & Son; New York: E. P. Dutton & Co., 1910).

Lectures on Justice, Police, Revenue and Arms, Edwin Cannan (ed.), (Oxford: Clarendon Press, 1896).

Suàrez, Francisco, 'On Laws and God the Lawgiver', in *Selections from Three Works*, Vol. 2, G. Williams (trans.) (Oxford University Press, 1965), 3–754.

Trask, Haunani-Kay, *From a Native Daughter: Colonialism and Sovereignty in Hawaii* (Monroe, ME: Common Courage Press, 1993).

Vitoria, Francisco de [1532], *De Indis et de Iure Belli Reflectiones*. John Pawley Bate (trans.) (Washington, DC: Carnegie Institution of Washington, 1917).

Watson, Irene, *Aboriginal Peoples, Colonialism and International Law: Raw Law* (Abingdon: Routledge, 2015).

Westlake, John, *Chapters on the Principles of International Law* (Cambridge University Press, 1894).

The Collected Papers of John Westlake on International Law, ed. Lassa Oppenheim (Cambridge University Press, 1914).

Wright, 'The End of Extraterritoriality in China', 37 *AJIL* (1943): 286–9.

'The British Courts and Ethiopian Recognition', 31 *AJIL* (1937): 683–8.

'The Test of Aggression in the Italo-Ethiopian War', 30 *AJIL* (1936): 45–56.

Quincy, 'Sovereignty of the Mandates', 17 *AJIL* (1923): 691–703.

Mandates under the League of Nations (University of Chicago Press, 1930).

ii Judicial Decisions

Australian High Court, *Mabo and Ors* v. *Queensland (No. 2)* (1992) 175 CLR 1.

Australian High Court, *Members of the Yorta Yorta Aboriginal Community* v. *Victoria* (2002) 214 CLR 422.

Corte Constitucional de Colombia, *Sentencia T-129/11.*

Cour d'appel de Paris (France), *Haïlé Selassié* v. *Etat italien*, GP.1939.I.640.

Federal Court of Australia, *Members of the Yorta Yorta Aboriginal Community* v. *Victoria & Ors* (1998) FCA 1606, 18 December 1998.

High Court of Justice (England and Wales), *Bank of Ethiopia* v. *National Bank of Egypt and Liguori*, Chancery Division, 11 May 1937.

High Court of Justice (England and Wales), *Haile Selassie* v. *Cable and Wireless Ltd (No. 2)*, Chancery Division, 6 December 1938.

High Court of Justice (England and Wales), *Haile Selassie* v. *Cable and Wireless Ltd*, Chancery Division (Bennett J.), 23 March 1937.

High Court of Justice (England and Wales), *Haile Selassie* v. *Cable and Wireless Ltd*, Chancery Division, Court of Appeal 30 June 1937.

High Court of the Admiralty, *Le Louis Case* [1817] 12 Dods 210, 165 ER 1464, 15 December 1817.

International Court of Justice, *Case Concerning the Frontier Dispute (Burkina Faso* v. *Republic of Mali)*, 22 December 1986, ICJ Rep. 1986.

International Court of Justice, *International Status of South-West Africa*, Advisory Opinion, 11 July 1950.

Italo-Ethiopian Commission of Conciliation and Arbitration, *Award of the Commission*, 3 September 1935 ('Walwal Arbitration').

Permanent Court of Arbitration, *Island of Palmas Case*, *Netherlands* v. *USA*, 2 U.N. Rep. Intl. Arb. Awards 829, 4 April 1928.

Permanent Court of International Justice, *Acquisition of Polish Nationality*, Advisory Opinion, PCIJ Series B, No. 7, 15 September 1923.

Permanent Court of International Justice, *Factory at Chorsów*, *Germany* v. *Poland*, Series A, No. 9, 26 July 1927.

Permanent Court of International Justice, *Questions relating to Settlers of German Origin in Poland*, *Germany* v. *Poland*, Advisory opinion, PCIJ Series B, No. 6, 10 September 1923 ('German Settlers in Poland Case').

Permanent Court of International Justice, *The Case of the SS Lotus* (*France* v. *Turkey*), Judgment, PCIJ Rep Series A No. 10, 1927 ('Lotus Case').

Supreme Court of Canada, *Reference re: Secession of Quebec*, 2 S.C.R. 297.

Tribunal civil de la Seine, Paris (France), *Haïlé Selassié* v. *Gouvernement italien*, GP.1937.II.924.

Secondary Sources

Abdussamad H. Ahmad and Richard Pankhurst (eds.), *Adwa: Victory Centenary Conference, 26 Feb.–2 March 1996* (Addis Ababa: Institute of Ethiopian Studies, Addis Ababa University, 1998).

Abir, Mordechai, *Ethiopia: The Era of the Princes: The Challenge of Islam and Re-Unification of the Christian Empire, 1769–1855* (New York: Praeger, 1968).

Abraha Weldu, '*Mahebär*: Dynamics of a Social Self-Help Association', 9 *African Journal of History and Culture* (2017): 27–33.

Addis Hiwet, *From Autocracy to Revolution* (London: Review of African Political Economy, Occasional Publication No. 1, 1975).

Ahmad, Feroz, 'Ottoman Perceptions of the Capitulations 1800–1914', 11 *Journal of Islamic Studies* (2000): 1–20.

Ahmed Hassan Omer, 'The Italian Impact on Ethnic Relations: A Case Study of a Regional Policy in Northern Shoa (Ethiopia), 1936–1941', 16 *Annales d'Ethiopie* (2000): 147–59.

Alemayehu Haile, *History of the Oromo to the Sixteenth Century* (2nd edn Finfinne: Oromia Culture and Tourism Board, 2006).

Alexandrowicz, C. H., 'The Theory of Recognition in Fieri', 34 *British Yearbook of International Law* (1958): 176–98.

Allain, Jean, 'Slavery and the League of Nations: Ethiopia as a Civilised Nation', 8 *JHIL* (2006): 213–44.

Allen, Graham, *Intertextuality* (London: Routledge, 2000).

Althusser, Louis, 'Idéologie et appareils idéologiques d'État. (Notes pour une recherche)', 151 *La Pensée* (June 1970). English translation: 'Ideology and Ideological State Apparatus (Notes towards an Investigation)', Ben Brewster (trans.) in Louis Althusser (ed.), *Essays on Ideology* (London: Verso, 1984).

Ancel, Stéphane, '"Mahbärs" et "Sänbäte"': Associations Religieuses en Éthiopie', 8 *Aethiopica* (2005): 95–111.

Anghie, Antony, '"The Heart of my Home": Colonialism, Environmental Damage and the Nauru Case', 34 *HIJL* (1993): 445–506.

Imperialism, Sovereignty and the Making of International Law (Cambridge University Press, 2004).

Anker, Kirsten, *Declarations of Interdependence: A Legal Pluralist Approach to Indigenous Rights* (Burlington, VT: Ashgate, 2014).

Anon, 'Dozens Killed in Ethnic Clashes in Ethiopia's Oromia', Al Jazeera News, 19 December 2017.

'Obama Praises Ethiopia over Fight Against al-Shabab', BBC News, 27 July 2015.

'China Expresses Concerns over Kosovo', *China Daily*, 19 February 2008.

'Russia Rejects New Kosovo Draft', BBC News, 1 June 2007.

'Haile Selassie Moves in Paris to Sue Italy on $1,500,500 in Ethiopian Railway Stock', *New York Times*, 10 June 1937, 7.

'Abyssinia To-Day – 1: The Home of Slavery', *Westminster Gazette*, 18 January 1922. Filed in FO 371/7141 Political (Abyssinia) 1922 (UKNA).

'Abyssinia To-Day – 2: Impossibility of Trade', *Westminster Gazette*, 19 January 1922 in FO 371/7141 Political (Abyssinia) 1922 (UKNA).

'Abyssinia To-Day – 3', *Westminster Gazette*, 20 January 1922 in FO 371/7141 Political (Abyssinia) 1922 (UKNA).

Anstey, Roger, *The Atlantic Slave Trade and British Abolition, 1760–1810* (London: Macmillan, 1975).

Applebaum, Anne, *Gulag: A History* (New York: Broadway Books, 2003).

Arendt, Hannah, [1958] *The Origins of Totalitarianism* (New York: Harcourt Books, 1994).

Men in Dark Times (New York: Harcourt, Brace & World, 1968).

Arvidsson, Matilda, 'The Subject in International Law: The Administrator of the Coalition Provisional Authority of Occupied Iraq and its Laws' (PhD thesis, University of Lund, 2016).

Askew, William C., 'The Secret Agreement between France and Italy on Ethiopia, January 1935', 25 *Journal of Modern History* (1935): 47–8.

Ayalew, Daniel, Ali Stefan Dercon and Madhur Gautam, 'Property Rights in a Very Poor Country: Tenure Insecurity and Investment in Ethiopia', *World Bank Policy Research Working Paper 4363* (Washington, DC: World Bank, 2007).

Baars, Grietje, *Law, Capital and the Corporation* (Leiden: Brill, forthcoming, 2018).

Bacca, Paulo Illich, 'Indigenizing International Law from an Inverse Legal Anthropology', *Naked Punch* (13 May 2017).

'Indigenous Peoples and the Legacies of Colonialism in International Criminal Law: The Challenging Crime of Genocide', *Critical Legal Thinking* (7 October 2015).

Baer, George W., *Test Case: Italy, Ethiopia and the League of Nations* (Stanford, CA: Hoover Institution Press, 1976).

'Haile Selassie's Protectorate Appeal to King Edward VIII', 9 *Cahiers d'Études Africaines* (1969): 306–12.

Bahru Zewde, *Pioneers of Change in Ethiopia: The Reformist Intellectuals of the Early Twentieth Century* (Oxford, Athens, OH, Addis Ababa: James Currey, Ohio University Press, Addis Ababa University, 2002).

'Concessions and Concession-Hunters in Post-Adwa Ethiopia: The Case of Arnold Holz', 45 *Africa: Rivista trimestrale di studi e documentazione dell'Istituto italiano perl'Africa e l'Oriente* (1990): 365–83.

A History of Modern Ethiopia, 1855-1991 (2nd edn Oxford, Athens, OH, Addis Ababa: James Currey, Ohio University Press, Addis Ababa University Press, 2002).

Bakhtin, Mikhail, 'Response to a Question from the *Novy Mir* Editorial Staff', in *Speech Genres and Other Late Essays*, Vern W. McGee (trans.) (Austin, TX: University of Texas Press, 1986).

Speech Genres and Other Late Essays, Vern W. McGee (trans.) (Austin, TX: University of Texas Press, 1986).

Problems of Dostoevsky's Poetics, Caryl Emerson (ed. and trans.) (Minneapolis, MN: University of Minnesota Press, 1984).

'Discourse and the Novel', in Michael Holquist (ed.), *The Dialogic Imagination: Four Essays by M. M. Bakhtin*, Caryl Emerson and Michael Holquist (trans.) (Austin, TX: University of Texas Press, 1981).

Balibar, Étienne, 'Subjection and Subjectivation', in Joan Copjec (ed.), *Supposing the Subject* (London: Verso, 1994), 1–16.

Banning, Tim, 'The "Bonn Powers" of the High Representative in Bosnia Herzegovina: Tracing a Legal Figment', 6 *Goettingen Journal of International Law* (2014): 259–302.

Barr, Olivia, *A Jurisprudence of Movement: Common Law, Walking, Unsettling Place* (Abingdon: Routledge, 2016).

Barten, Ulrike, *Minorities, Minority Rights and Internal Self-Determination* (Cham etc.: Springer, 2015).

Baskin, Jeremy, 'Paradigm Dressed as Epoch: The Ideology of the Anthropocene', 24 *Environmental Values* (2015): 9–29.

Battaglia, Roberto, *La prima guerra d'Africa* (Turin: Einaudi, 1958).

Baty, Thomas, *The Canons of International Law* (London: Murray, 1930).

Baucom, Ian, *Specters of the Atlantic: Finance Capital, Slavery, and the Philosophy of History* (Durham, NC: Duke University Press, 2005).

Baudelaire, Charles [1857], 'Correspondances', in *Les Fleurs du Mal*, Richard Howards (trans.) (Boston, MA: David R. Godine, 1982).

Baum, James E., *Savage Abyssinia* (London: Cassell, 1928).

Baxter, P. T. W., 'Ethiopia's Unacknowledged Problem: The Oromo', 77 *African Affairs* (1978): 283–96.

Baxter, P. T. W., Jan Hultin, and Alessandro Triulzi (eds.), *Being and Becoming an Oromo: Historical and Anthological Enquiries* (London: Africa Book Centre, 1996).

Beard, Jennifer, *The Political Economy of Desire: International Law, Development and the Nation State* (Abingdon, New York: Routledge-Cavendish, 2007).

Becker Lorca, Arnulf, 'Petitioning the International: A "Pre-History" of Self-Determination,' 25 *EJIL* (2014): 497–523.

Mestizo International Law: A Global Intellectual History, 1842–1933 (Cambridge University Press, 2014).

Beckingham, Charles F. and G. W. B. Huntingford (eds. and trans.), *Some Records of Ethiopia, 1593–1646: Being Extracts from 'The History of High Ethiopia or Abassia' by Manoel de Almeida Together with Bahrey's 'History of the Galla'* (London: Hakluyt Society, 1954).
Behrman, Cynthia F., 'The After-Life of General Gordon', 3 *Albion: A Quarterly Journal Concerned with British Studies* (1971): 47–61.
Beirne, Piers and Robert Sharlet, 'Editors' Introduction', in Beirne and Sharlet (eds.), *Pashukanis: Selected Writings on Marxism and Law*, Peter B. Maggs (trans.) (London: Academic Press, 1980), 1–36.
Belloc, Hilaire, *The Crisis of Our Civilization* (London etc.: Cassell, 1937).
Benjamin, Walter, 'On Some Motifs in Baudelaire', in Howard Eiland and Michael W. Jennings (eds.), *Walter Benjamin: Selected Writings*, Vol. 4: 1938–1940 (Cambridge, MA: Belknap Press, 2006), 313–55.
[1940], 'On the Concept of History', in *Walter Benjamin: Selected Writings*, Vol. 4: 1938–1940, Howard Eiland and Michael W. Jennings (eds.) and Harry John (trans.) (Cambridge, MA: Harvard University Press, 2003), 389–400.
'Critique of Violence' [1921], in *Walter Benjamin: Selected Writings*, Vol. 1: 1913–1926, Marcus Bullock and Michael W. Jennings (eds.), Edmund Jephcott (trans.) (Cambridge, MA: Harvard University Press, 2003), 236–52.
The Arcades Project, Rolf Tiedemann (ed.) and Howard Eiland and Kevin McLaughlin (trans.) (Cambridge, MA: Harvard University Press, 1999).
Benton, Lauren, *A Search for Sovereignty: Law and Geography in European Empires, 1400–1900* (Cambridge University Press, 2010).
Berman, Nathaniel, *Passion and Ambivalence: Colonialism, Nationalism and International Law* (Leiden: Martinus Nijhoff, 2012).
'In the Wake of Empire', 14 *American University International Law Review* (1999): 1521–69.
'The International Law of Nationalism: Group Identity and Legal History', in David Wippman (ed.), *International Law and Ethnic Conflict* (Ithaca, NY: Cornell University Press, 1998), 25–57.
Bhabha, Homi K., *The Location of Culture* (London, New York: Routledge, 1994).
Bhandar, Brenna, *Colonial Lives of Property: Law, Land and Racial Regimes of Ownership* (Durham, NC: Duke University Press, 2018).
'Property, Law, and Race: Modes of Abstraction', 4 *UC Irvine Law Review* (2014): 203–18.
'Plasticity and Post-Colonial Recognition: "Owning, Knowing and Being"', 22 *Law and Critique* (2011): 227–47.
Birhanu Teferra, 'European Press Reactions to Adwa', in Abdussamad and Pankhurst (eds.), *Adwa: Victory Centenary Conference*, 441–77.
Birrell, Kathleen, *Indigeneity: Before and Beyond the Law* (Abingdon: Routledge, 2016).
Blake, William, *Illustrations of the Book of Job* (London: n.p., 1825).

Blank, Yishai, 'Localism in the New Global Legal Order', 47 *HIJL* (2006): 263–81.

Bodenstein, Thilo, Jörg Faust and Mark Furness (eds.), 'Special Issue: European Union Development Policy: Collective Action in Times of Global Transformation and Domestic Crisis', 35 (issue 4) *Development Policy Review* (July 2017): 439–597.

Bodian, Miriam, '"Liberty of Conscience" and the Jews in the Dutch Republic', 6 *Studies in Christian-Jewish Relations* (2011).

Bodin, Jean [1576], *Six Books of the Commonwealth*, M. J. Tooley (ed. and trans.) (Oxford: Blackwell, 1955).

Bogdandy, Armin von and Sergio Dellavalle, 'George Wilhelm Friedrich Hegel (1770–1831)', in Bardo Fassbender and Anne Peters (eds.), *The Oxford Handbook of the History of International Law* (Oxford University Press, 2012), 1127–31.

Boghardt, Thomas, *The Zimmermann Telegram: Intelligence, Diplomacy, and America's Entry into World War I* (Annapolis, ND: Naval Institute Press, 2012).

Boogert, Maurits H. van den, *The Capitulations and the Ottoman Legal System: Qadis, Consuls, and Beraths in the 18th Century* (Leiden, Boston, MA: Brill, 2005).

Bookchin, Murray, *The Third Revolution: Popular Movements in the Revolutionary Era*. Vol. 3 (London, New York: Continuum, 2014).

Bottici, Chiara, *Men and States: Rethinking the Domestic Analogy in a Global Age*, Karen Whittle (trans.) (Basingstoke: Palgrave Macmillan, 2009).

Bowring, Bill, *The Degradation of the International Legal Order: The Rehabilitation of Law and the Possibility of Politics* (Abingdon: Routledge-Cavendish, 2008).

Brabazon, Honor, 'Introduction: Understanding Neoliberal Legality', in Honor Brabazon (ed.), *Neoliberal Legality: Understanding the Role of Law in the Neoliberal Project* (New York: Routledge, 2016), 1–21.

'*The Master's Tools': The Possibilities and Perils of Law-Based Resistance to Neoliberalism* (manuscript under review).

Braudel, Fernand, 'Histoire et Sciences sociales. La longue durée', 13 *Annales. Histoire, Sciences Sociales* (1958): 725–53.

Brennan, Timothy, 'Hegel, Empire, and Anti-Colonial Thought', in Graham Huggan (ed.), *The Oxford Handbook of Postcolonial Studies* (Oxford University Press, 2013), 142–61.

Brenner, Neil, *New State Spaces: Urban Governance and the Rescaling of Statehood* (Oxford University Press, 2004).

Brett, Annabel S., *Liberty, Rights and Nature: Individual Rights in Later Scholastic Thought* (Cambridge University Press, 1997).

Brooks, Miguel F. (ed. and trans.), *A Modern Translation of the Kebra Nagast: The Glory of Kings* (Lawrenceville, NJ: Red Sea Press, 1996).

Buck-Morss, Susan, *Hegel, Haiti and Universal History* (University of Pittsburgh Press, 2009).

'Hegel and Haiti', 26 *Critical Inquiry* (2000): 821–65.

Bugajski, Janusz, R. Bruce Hitchner and Paul Williams, *Achieving a Final Status Settlement for Kosovo* (Washington, DC: Center for Strategic and International Studies, 2003).

Bullock, Marcus and Michael W. Jennings (eds.), *Walter Benjamin: Selected Writings*, Vol. 1: 1913–1926, Edmund Jephcott (trans.) (Cambridge, MA: Harvard University Press, 2003).

Burkman, Thomas W., *Japan and the League of Nations: Empire and World Order, 1914–1938* (Honolulu, HI: University of Hawai'i Press, 2008).

Buzinkai, Donald I., 'The Bolsheviks, the League of Nations and the Paris Peace Conference, 1919', 19 *Soviet Studies* (1967): 257–63.

Campbell, Ian, *The Addis Ababa Massacre: Italy's National Shame* (London: Hurst, 2017).

Capriccioso, Rob, 'A Sorry Saga: Obama signs Native American Apology Resolution; Fails to Draw Attention to it', *Indian Country Today*, 13 January 2010.

Ceric, Irina, 'The Sovereign Charter: Security, Territory and the Boundaries of Constitutional Rights', 44 *Ottawa Law Review* (2013): 353–40.

Ch'ên, Jerome, 'The Nature and Characteristics of the Boxer Movement–A Morphological Study', 23 *Bulletin of the School of Oriental and African Studies, University of London* (1960): 287–308.

Chalk, Frank, 'Du Bois and Garvey Confront Liberia: Two Incidents from the Coolridge Years', 1 *Canadian Journal of African Studies / Revue Canadienne des Études Africaines* (1967): 135–42.

Chandler, David, *International Statebuilding: The Rise of Post-Liberal Governance* (Hoboken, NJ: Taylor & Francis, 2010).

Peacebuilding: The Twenty Years' Crisis, 1997–2017 (New York: Springer, 2017).

Chandra, Rajshree, *The Cunning of Rights: Law, Life, Biocultures* (Oxford University Press, 2016).

Chang, Ha-Joon, *Kicking Away the Ladder: Development Strategy in Historical Perspective* (London: Anthem Press, 2005).

Charlesworth, Hilary and Christine Chinkin, *The Boundaries of International Law: A Feminist Analysis* (Manchester University Press, 2000).

Chaudron, Gerald, *New Zealand in the League of Nations: The Beginnings of an Independent Foreign Policy, 1919–1939* (Jefferson, NC: McFarland, 2011).

Chimni, B. S., *International Law and World Order: A Critique of Contemporary Approaches* (2nd edn Cambridge University Press, 2017).

Christenson, Gordon A., 'Liberty of the Exercise of Religion in the Peace of Westphalia', 21 *Transnational Law & Contemporary Problems* (2013): 721–61.

Clarke III, J. Calvitt, 'Seeking a Model for Modernization: Ethiopia's Japanizers', 10 *Selected Annual Proceedings of the Florida Conference of Historians* (2004): 35–51.

Clayton, Lawrence, 'Bartolomé de las Casas and the African Slave Trade', 7 *History Compass* (2009): 1526–41.

Company Histories, 'Cable and Wireless Ltd', at www.company-histories.com/Cable-and-Wireless-plc-Company-History.html (accessed 22 May 2018).

Contarini, Gasparo [1543], *Casparis De republica Venetorum libri quinque* (Lugd. Batavorum. Ex officina Elseviriana, 1628).

Cornell, Drucilla and Nyoko Muvangua, *uBuntu and the Law* (New York: Fordham University Press, 2012).

Cox, Michael, 'Northern Ireland: The War that Came in from the Cold', 9 *Irish Studies in International Affairs* (1998): 73–84.

Craven, Matthew, 'Between Law and History: The Berlin Conference of 1884–1885 and the Logic of Free Trade', 3 *London Review of International Law* (2015): 31–59.

'What Happened to Unequal Treaties? The Continuities of Informal Empire', 74 *Nordic Journal of International Law* (2005): 335–82.

Craven, Matthew and Rose Parfitt, 'The Subjects of the International Legal Order' in Malcolm D. Evans (ed.), *International Law* (5th edn Oxford University Press, 2018), 177–226.

Crawford, James, *The Creation of States in International Law* (2nd edn Oxford University Press, 2007).

Cronon, E. David, *Black Moses* (Madison, WI: University of Wisconsin Press, 1955).

Croxton, Derek, 'The Peace of Westphalia of 1648 and the Origins of Sovereignty', 21 *The International History Review* (1999): 569–91.

Crutzon, Paul J., 'Geology of Mankind', 23 *Nature* (2002): 23.

Curle, Alex ('Sandy') T., 'They Hold a Secret of International Importance[:] They will Not Disclose It', unpublished memoirs, I. Courtesy of Christian Curle. Notes on file with the author.

Curle, Christian (ed.), *Letters from the Horn of Africa, 1923–1942: Sandy Curle, Soldier and Diplomat Extraordinary* (Barnsley: Pen & Sword Military, 2008).

Curthoys, Ann, Ann Genovese and Alexander Reilly, *Rights and Redemption: History, Law and Indigenous Peoples* (Sydney: UNSW Press, 2008).

Cypher, James M. and Dietz, James L., *The Process of Economic Development* (3rd edn London, New York: Routledge, 2009).

Davis, David Brion, *The Problem of Slavery in Western Culture* (New York: Cornell University Press, 1966).

Davis, F. James, *Who is Black? One Nation's Definition* (University Park, PA: Pennsylvania State University Press, 1991).

Davis, Norman [1972], *White Eagle, Red Star: The Polish-Soviet War 1919–1920 and the 'Miracle on the Vistula'* (London: Pimlico Press, 2003).

Dawisha, Adeed, *Iraq: A Political History* (Princeton University Press, 2004).

Degras, Jane (ed.), *The Communist International, 1919–1943: Documents, Vol. 1* (Oxford University Press, 1956).

Dehm, Julia, 'Carbon Colonialism or Climate Justice? Interrogating the International Climate Regime from a TWAIL Perspective', 33 *Windsor Yearbook on Access to Justice* (2017): 129–61.

Donham, Donald D. and Wendy James (eds.), *The Southern Marches of Imperial Ethiopia: Essays in History and Social Anthropology* (Oxford, Athens, OH, and Addis Ababa: James Currey, Ohio University Press and Addis Ababa University Press, 2002).

Donnelly, Jack, 'Human Rights: A New Standard of Civilization?', 74 *International Affairs* (1998): 1–23.

Doyle, Don H., 'Slavery or Independence: The Confederate Dilemma in Europe', in Cornelis A. van. Minnen and Manfred Berg (eds.), *The U.S. South and Europe: Transatlantic Relations in the Nineteenth and Twentieth Centuries* (Lexington, KT: University Press of Kentucky, 2013, 105–24.

Drescher, Seymour and Paul Finkelman, 'Slavery', in Bardo Fassbender and Anne Peters (eds.), *The Oxford Handbook of the History of International Law* (Oxford University Press, 2012, 890–916.

Drew, Catriona, 'The Meaning of Self-Determination: "The Stealing of the Sahara" Redux?' in Karin Arts and Pedro Pinto Leite (eds.), *International Law and the Question of Western Sahara* (Leiden: International Platform for Jurists of East Timor, 2007), 87–105.

'The East Timor Story: International Law on Trial', 12 *EJIL* (2001): 651–84.

Duchhardt, Heinz, 'Das "Westfälische System": Realität und Mythos', in Hillard von Thiessen and Christian Windler (eds.), *Akteure der Aussenbeziehungen: Netzwerke und Interkulturalität im historischen Wandel* (Cologne: Böhlau Verlag, 2010, 393–401.

Eagleton, Terry, *The English Novel* (Oxford: Blackwell, 2005).

Edelman, Bernard, *Le droit saisi par la photographie: Éléments pour une théorie marxiste du droit* (Paris: Éditions François Maspero, 1973). English translation: *Ownership of the Image: Elements of Marxist Theory of Law*, Elizabeth Kingdom (trans.) (London: Routledge & Kegan Paul, 1979).

Eiland, Howard and Michael W. Jennings (eds.), *Walter Benjamin: Selected Writings*, Vol. 4: 1938–1940 (Cambridge, MA: Belknap Press, 2006).

Elden, Stuart, *The Birth of Territory* (Chicago, IL, London: University of Chicago Press, 2013).

'Missing the Point: Globalization, Deterritorialization and the Space of the World', 30 *Transactions of the Institute of British Geographers* (2005): 8–19.

Engels, Frederick [1877], 'Anti-Dühring. Herr Eugen Dühring's Revolution in Science', Emile Burns (trans.), in *Marx and Engels: Collected Works*, Vol. 25 (Lawrence & Wishart Electronic Book, 2010), 5–311.

Epstein, Helen, 'Cruel Ethiopia', *The New York Review of Books*, 13 May 2010, at www.nybooks.com/articles/2010/05/13/cruel-ethiopia/ (accessed 5 June 2018).

Escobar, Arturo, 'Latin America at a Crossroads: Alternative Modernizations, Post-Liberalism, or Post-Development?', 24 *Cultural Studies* (2010): 1–65.

Eslava, Luis, 'The Moving Location of Empire: Indirect Rule, International Law and the *Bantu Educational Kinema Experiment*', 31 *Leiden Journal of International Law* (2018): 539–67.

'The Materiality of International Law: Violence, History and Joe Sacco's The Great War', 5 *London Review of International Law* (2017): 49–86.

Local Space, Global Life: The Everyday Life of International Law and Development (Cambridge University Press, 2015).

Eslava, Luis, Usha Natarajan and Rose Parfitt, '(Post)Revolutionary Interlinkages: Labour, Environment and Accumulation', 4 *Transnational Legal Theory* (2013): 108–25.

Esmeir, Samera, *Juridical Humanity: A Colonial History* (Stanford University Press, 2010).

Esslemont, Tom, 'As Syrian Deaths Mount, World's "Responsibility to Protect" Takes a Hit', *Reuters*, 25 October 2016.

Evans, Julie, Ann Genovese, Alexander Reilly and Patrick Wolfe (eds.), *Sovereignty: Frontiers of Possibility* (Honolulu, HI: University of Hawai'i Press, 2012).

Ezekiel Gebissa, 'The Italian Invasion, the Ethiopian Empire, and Oromo Nationalism: The Significance of the Western Oromo Confederation of 1936', 9 *Northeast African Studies* (2002): 75–96.

Fairbank, John King (ed.), *The Chinese World Order: Traditional China's Foreign Relations* (Cambridge, MA: Harvard University Press, 1968).

Fakhri, Michael, *Sugar and the Making of International Trade Law* (Cambridge University Press, 2014).

Fanon, Frantz [1952], *Black Skin, White Masks*, Charles Lam Markmann (trans.) (London: Pluto Press, 1986).

Peau Noire, Masques Blanc (Paris: Editions de Seuil, France, 1952).

The Wretched of the Earth (New York: Grove Press, 1963).

Federici, Silvia, *Caliban and the Witch: Women, the Body and Primitive Accumulation* (New York: Autonomedia, 2004).

Felice, Renzo De, *Mussolini il duce. Lo stato totalitario, 1936–1940* (Turin: Einaudi tascabili, 1996).

Fine, Ben, 'Neither the Washington nor the Post-Washington Consensus: An Introduction', in Ben Fine, Costas Lapavitsas and Jonathan Pincus (eds.), *Development Policy in the 21st Century: Beyond the Post-Washington Consensus* (London: Routledge, 2001), 1–27.

Fink, Carole, *Defending the Rights of Others: The Great Powers, the Jews, and International Minority Protection, 1878–1938* (Cambridge University Press, 2004).

Fisch, Jörg, *The Right of Self-Determination of Peoples* (Cambridge University Press, 2015).

Flemmen, Anne Britt, 'Religious *Mahbär* in Ethiopia: Ritual Elements, Dynamics, and Challenges', 46 *Journal of Religion in Africa* (2016): 3–31.

Foucault, Michel, 'Nietzsche, Genealogy, History', in Paul Rainbow (ed.), *The Foucault Reader* (New York: Pantheon, 1984), 76–100.

[1969], *The Archaeology of Knowledge*, A. M. Smith (trans.) (New York: Routledge, 2002).

[1975], *Discipline and Punish: The Birth of the Prison*, Alan Sheridan (trans.) (New York: Vintage Books, 1997).

[1978], 'On Power', in Lawrence Kritzman (ed.), *Michel Foucault: Politics, Philosophy, Culture: Interviews and Other Writings, 1977–1984* (New York: Routledge, 1988).

Franck, Thomas M., 'The Emerging Right to Democratic Governance', 86 *American Journal of International Law* (1992): 46–91.

Frank, Andre Gunder, *The Development of Underdevelopment* (Boston, MA: New England Free Press, 1966).

Friedlander, Henry, *The Origins of Nazi Genocide: From Euthanasia to the Final Solution* (Chapel Hill, NC: University of North Carolina Press, 1995).

Friedlander, Lilian M., 'The Admission of States to the League of Nations', 9 *British Yearbook of International Law* (1928): 84–100.

Fukuyama, Francis. *The End of History and the Last Man* (New York: Free Press, 1992).

Gaja, Giorgio, 'General Principles of Law', in *The Max Planck Encyclopedia of Public International Law* (2nd edn Oxford University Press, 2013).

Gallagher, John and Ronald Robinson, 'The Imperialism of Free Trade', 6 *The Economic History Review* (1953): 1–15.

Garretson, Peter P., 'Vicious Cycles: Ivory, Slaves, and Arms on the New Maji Frontier', in Donham and James (eds.), *The Southern Marches*, 196–218.

Gashahun Lemessa Fura, 'Transnational Land Acquisitions in Sub-Saharan Africa: Competing Claims and the Role of (International) Law' (PhD thesis, Melbourne Law School, 2017).

Gates, Henry Louis, 'Editor's Introduction: Writing "Race" and the Difference it Makes', 12 *Critical Inquiry* (1985): 1–10.

Gathii, James T., 'Good Governance as a Counterinsurgency Agenda to Oppositional and Transformative Social Projects in International Law', 5 *Buffalo Human Rights Law Review* (1999): 107–74.

Gebre-Wold-Ingida Worq, 'Ethiopia's Traditional System of Land Tenure and Taxation', 5 *Ethiopian Observer* (1962): 302–39.

Gong, Gerrit W., *The Standard of 'Civilization' in International Society* (Oxford: Clarendon Press, 1984).

Gordon, Robert W., 'Critical Legal Histories', 36 *Stanford Law Review* (1984): 57–125.

'Forward: The Arrival of Critical Historicism', 49 *Stanford Law Review* (1997): 1023–9.

Gordon, Ruth, 'Saving Failed States: Sometimes a Neocolonialist Notion', 12 *American University Journal of International Law and Policy* (1997): 903–74.

Gouges, Olympe de, *Déclaration des droits de la femme et de la citoyenne*, 5 September 1791.

Gover, Kirsty, *Tribal Constitutionalism: States, Tribes, and the Governance of Membership* (Oxford University Press, 2010).

Grant, Thomas D., 'Defining Statehood: The Montevideo Convention and its Discontents', 37 *Columbia Journal of Transnational Law* (1998): 403–57.

Greenhouse, Carol J., *A Moment's Notice: Time Politics Across Cultures* (Ithaca, NY: Cornell University Press, 1996).

Griaule, Marcel, 'Labour in Abyssinia', 23 *International Labour Review* (1931): 181–202.

Grigorescu, Alexandru, 'Mapping the UN – League of Nations Analogy: Are There Still Lessons to be Learned from the League?', 11 *Global Governance* (2005): 25–42.

Grip, Lina and John Hart, 'The Use of Chemical Weapons in the 1935–36 Italo-Ethiopian War', *SIPRI Arms Control and Non-Proliferation Programme*, October 2009, at www.sipri.org/sites/default/files/Italo-Ethiopian-war.pdf (accessed 5 December 2017).

Güçlü, Yücel, 'Turkey's Entrance into the League of Nations', 38 *Middle Eastern Studies* (2003): 186–206.

Guldi, Jo and David Armitage, *The History Manifesto* (Cambridge University Press, 2014).

Gunneflo, Markus, *Targeted Killing: A Legal and Political History* (Cambridge University Press, 2016).

Gutteridge, H. C., 'The Meaning of the Scope of Article 39(1) of the Statute of the International Court of Justice', 38 *Transactions for the Year* (1952): 12534.

H. L. 'The U.S.S.R. and the League of Nations', 11 *Bulletin of International News* (1934): 3–12.

Hailegabriel G. Feyissa, 'European Extraterritoriality in Semicolonial Ethiopia', 17 *Melbourne Journal of International Law* (2016): 1–28.

Hale, Robert, 'Coercion and Distribution in a Supposedly Non-Coercive State', 38 *Political Science Quarterly* (1923): 470–94.

Hall, Stuart, 'Race, the Floating Signifier', Talk at Goldsmiths College, London, directed by Sut Jhally, Media Education Foundation, 1997.

Hallward, Peter, 'Operation Zero in Haiti', 27 *New Left Review* (2004): 23–47.

Hanieh, Adam, *Lineages of Revolt: Issues of Contemporary Capitalism in the Middle East* (Chicago, IL: Haymarket Books, 2013), 431.

Haraway, Donna J., 'Staying with the Trouble: Anthropocene, Capitalocene, Chthulucene', in Jason W. Moore (ed.), *Anthropocene or Capitalocene? Nature, History, and the Crisis of Capitalism* (Oakland, CA: PM Press, 2016), 32–76.

Haraway, Donna, 'Situated Knowledges: The Science Question in Feminism and the Privilege of Partial Perspective', 14 *Feminist Studies* (1988): 575–99.

Hardie, Frank, *The Abyssinian Crisis* (London: Batsford, 1974).

Harper, Douglas, 'Mulatto', *Online Etymology Dictionary* (2014).

Harris, John, 'Slavery in Abyssinia – How the League Could Help – a Modern Gordon Needed – Weakness of 1906 Agreement', *Westminster Gazette*, 28 April 1922.

Harris, Joseph E., *African-American Reactions to War in Ethiopia, 1936–1941* (Baton Rouge, LA: Louisiana State University Press, 1994).

Harris, Mark, *Human Rights, the Rule of Law and Exploitation in the Postcolony: Blood Minerals* (Abingdon: Routledge, forthcoming, 2019).

Hayek, Friedrich A. [1944], *The Road to Serfdom* (University of Chicago Press, 1994).

Heald, Stephen and John W. Wheeler-Bennett, *Documents on International Affairs, 1935*, Vol. 1 (Oxford University Press, 1936).

Heald, Stephen (ed.), *Documents on International Affairs, 1935*, Vol. 2 (Oxford University Press, 1937).

Heathcote, Gina, *The Law on the Use of Force: A Feminist Analysis* (London: Routledge Cavendish, 2011).

Helman Gerald B. and Steven R. Ratner, 'Saving Failed States', 89 *Foreign Policy* (1993): 3–20.

Henze, Paul B., *Layers of Time: A History of Ethiopia* (New York: C. Hurst & Co., 2000).

Hess, Robert L., 'Italy and Africa: Colonial Ambitions in the First World War', 4 *Journal of African History* (1963): 105–26.

Hillgruber, Christian, 'The Admission of New States into the International Community', 9 *EJIL* (1998): 491–509.

Hoben, Allan, 'Family, Land and Class in Northwest Europe and Northern Highland Ethiopia', in Harold Marcus (ed.), *Proceedings of the First United States Conference of Ethiopian Studies* (East Lansing, MI: Michigan State University Press, 1975).

Land Tenure among the Amhara of Ethiopia: The Dynamics of Cognatic Descent (University of Chicago Press, 1973).

Hobsbawm, Eric, *On History* (London: Hachette, 2011).

Holland, Thomas Erskine, *Studies in International Law* (Oxford: Clarendon Press, 1898).

Homsy, Basile. *Les capitulations & la protection des chrétiens au Proche-Orient aux XVIe, XVIIe et XVIIIe siècles* (Harissa: L'Imprimerie Saint Paul, 1956).

Horowitz, Richard S., 'International Law and State Transformation in China, Siam, and the Ottoman Empire during the Nineteenth Century', 15 *Journal of World History* (2004): 445–86.

Hudson, Manly O., 'Afghanistan, Ecuador and the Soviet Union in the League of Nations', 29 *AJIL* (1935): 112–16.

Human Rights Watch, *Ethiopia: Country Report* 2016.

Humboldt, Wilhelm von [1822], 'On the Historian's Task', Louis O. Mink (trans.), 6 *History and Theory* (1967): 57–71.

Iadarola, Antoinette, 'Ethiopia's Admission into the League of Nations: An Assessment of Motives', 8 *International Journal of African Historical Studies* (1975): 601–22.

Ifversen, Jan, 'The Crisis of European Civilization: An Inter-War Diagnosis', in Mehdi Mozaffari (ed.), *Globalization and Civilizations* (London, New York: Routledge, 2002), 151–77.

Ince, Onur Ulas, *Colonial Capitalism and the Dilemmas of Liberalism* (Oxford University Press, 2018).

Jackson, Robert H., *Quasi-states: Sovereignty, International Relations and the Third World* (Cambridge University Press, 1990).

Jackson, Robert H. and Carl G. Rosberg, 'Why Africa's Weak States Persist: The Empirical and the Juridical in Statehood', 35 *World Politics* (1982): 1–24.

Jalata, Asafa, 'The Struggle for Knowledge: The Case of Emergent Oromo Studies', 39 *African Studies Review* (1996): 95–123.

James, C. L. R., 'Abyssinia Betrayed by the League of Nations', *The Crisis*, June 1937: 166–8.

'I.L.P. Abyssinian Policy', *Controversy*, October 1935.

'Intervening in Abyssinia', *The New Leader*, 4 October 1935.

James, Wendy, 'Lifelines: Exchange Marriage among the Gumuz', Donham and James (eds.), *The Southern Marches*: 119–47.

Johnston, Harry H., *The Backward Peoples and Our Relations with Them* (London, New York: Oxford University Press, 1920).

Johnston, Harry, Letter to the Editor, in 'Abyssinian Slaves – Prof. Murray on League Action – Import of Arms', *Westminster Gazette*, 2 May 1922 in FO 371/7141 Political (Abyssinia) 1922 (UKNA).

Jones, A. M. H. and Elizabeth Monroe, *A History of Abyssinia* (Oxford: Clarendon Press, 1935).

Joyce, Richard, 'International Law and the Cold War – Reflections on the Concept of History', in Matthew Craven, Sundhya Pahuja and Gerry Simpson (eds.), *International Law and the Cold War* (Cambridge University Press, forthcoming).

'Westphalia: Event, Memory, Myth', in Fleur Johns, Richard Joyce and Sundhya Pahuja (eds.), *Events: The Force of International Law* (Abingdon: Routledge, 2011), 55–68.

Kendall, Sara, 'Cartographies of the Present: "Contingent Sovereignty" and Territorial Integrity', in Martin Kuijer and Wouter Werner (eds.), 47 *Netherlands Yearbook of International Law* (2016): 83–105 at 100.

Kennedy, David, 'The International Human Rights Movement: Part of the Problem?' 15 *Harvard Human Rights Journal* (2002): 101–26.

'International Law and the Nineteenth Century: History of an Illusion', 65 *Nordic Journal of International Law* (1996): 385–420.

'Theses About International Law Discourse', 23 *Germany Yearbook of International Law* (1980): 353–91.

Kevles, Daniel J., *In the Name of Eugenics: Genetics and the Uses of Human History* (Cambridge, MA and London: Harvard University Press, 1995).

Khoday, Kishan, Vanessa Lamb, Tyler McCreary, Karin Mickelson, Usha Natarajan and Ileana Porras (eds.), 'International Legal Theory Symposium: Locating Nature', 27 *Leiden Journal of International Law* (2014) (issue 3): 571–660.

Kittsteiner, H.D., Jonathan Monroe and Irving Wohlfarth, 'Walter Benjamin's Historicism', 39 *New German Critique* (1986): 179–215.

Klabbers, Jan, *International Law* (2nd edn Cambridge University Press, 2017).

Klimchuk, Dennis, 'Hobbes on Equity', in David Dyzenhaus and Thomas Poole (eds.), *Hobbes and the Law* (Cambridge University Press, 2012), 165–85.

Kohn, Eduardo, *How Forests Think: Toward an Anthropology Beyond the Human* (Berkeley, CA: University of California Press, 2013), 69.

Knop, Karen, 'Lorimer's Private Citizens of the World', 27 *EJIL* (2016): 447–75.

'Re/Statements: Feminism and State Sovereignty in International Law', 3 *Transnational Law & Contemporary Problems* (1993): 293–344.

Knox, Robert, 'Marxist Approaches to International Law', in Florian Hoffmann and Anne Orford (eds.), *The Oxford Handbook of the Theory of International Law* (Oxford University Press, 2016), 306–26.

'Valuing Race? Stretched Marxism and the Logic of Imperialism', 4 *London Review of International Law* (2016): 81–126.

'Marxism, International Law and Political Strategies', 22 *Leiden Journal of International Law* (2009): 413–36.

Koopman, Colin, *Genealogy as Critique: Foucault and the Problems of Modernity* (Bloomington and Indianapolis, IN: Indiana University Press, 2013).

Koskenniemi, Martti, 'Race, Hierarchy and International Law: Lorimer's Legal Science', 27 *EJIL* (2016): 415–29.

'International Law and the Emergence of Mercantile Capitalism: Grotius to Smith', in Pierre-Marie Dupuy and Vincent Chetail (eds.), *The Roots of International Law/Les fondements du droit international* (Leiden: Brill, 2013), 1–37.

'Empire and International Law: The Real Spanish Contribution', 61 *University of Toronto Law Journal* (2011): 1–36.

From Apology to Utopia: The Structure of International Legal Argument (Cambridge University Press, 2005).

The Gentle Civilizer of Nations: The Rise and Fall of International Law, 1870–1960 (Cambridge University Press, 2001).

Kraaij, Fred P. M. van der, *The Open Door Policy of Liberia: An Economic History of Modern Liberia* (Bremen: Im Selbstverlag des Museums, 1983).

Kreijen, Gerard, 'The Transformation of Sovereignty and African Independence', in Gerard Kreijen, Marcel Brus, Jorris Duursma, Elizabeth De Vos and John Dugard (eds.), *State, Sovereignty and International Governance* (Oxford University Press, 2002), 45–107.

Krever, Tor, 'Law, Development, and Political Closure under Neoliberalism', in Honor Brabazon (ed.), *Neoliberal Legality: Understanding the Role of Law in the Neoliberal Project* (New York: Routledge, 2016), 22–42.

Kumar, Vidya, 'International Law, Kelsen and the Aberrant Revolution: Excavating the Politics and Practices of Revolutionary Legality in Rhodesia and Beyond', in Nikolas M. Rajkovic, Tanje E. Aalberts and Tomas Gammeltoft-Hansen (eds.), *The Power of Legality: Practices of International Law and their Politics* (Cambridge University Press, 2016), 157–87.

Kurland, Philip B. and Ralph Lerner (eds.), *The Founders' Constitution*, Vol. 1 (University of Chicago Press, 1987).

Lamont, Thomas W., 'The Final Reparations Settlement', 8 *Foreign Affairs* (1930): 338.

Lane, Melissa, 'Doing our Own Thinking for Ourselves: On Quentin Skinner's Genealogical Turn', 73 *Journal of the History of Ideas* (2012): 71–82.

Lardner, Richard, 'The Top American General in Africa says Libya is a Failed State', *US News*, 8 March 2016.

Léger, Jacques Nicolas, *Haiti: Her History and Her Detractors* (New York, Washington, DC: The Neale Publishing Company, 1907).

Lendvai, Paul, *One Day That Shook the Communist World: The 1956 Hungarian Uprising and Its Legacy* (Princeton University Press, 2008).

Lesaffer, Randall, 'International Law and its History: The Story of an Unrequited Love', in Matthew Craven, Malgosia Fitzmaurice and Maria Vogiatzi (eds.), *Time, History and International Law* (The Hague: Martinus Nijhoff, 2007), 27–41.

Lévinas, Emmanuel, 'La Trace de L'Autre', 25 *Tijdschrift voor Filosophie* (1963): 603–23. English translation: 'The Trace of the Other', Alphonso Lingis (trans.) in Mark Taylor (ed.), *Deconstruction in Context* (University of Chicago Press, 1986), 345–59.

Liano, Alejandro, *Éthiopie: Empire des Nègres blancs* (Paris: Éditions Pierre Roger, 1929).

Liddell, Henry George and Robert Scott, *A Greek-English Lexicon* (Oxford: Clarendon Press, 1940).

Lightfoot, Kent G., Lee M. Panich, Tsim D. Schneider and Sara L. Gonzalez, 'European Colonialism and the Anthropocene: A View from the Pacific Coast of North America', 4 *Anthropocene* (2013): 101–15.

Lino, Dylan, 'Thinking Outside the Constitution on Indigenous Constitutional Recognition: Entrenching the Racial Discrimination Act', 91 *Australian Law Journal* (2017): 381–5.

Liu, Lydia H., *The Clash of Empires: The Invention of China in Modern World Making* (Cambridge, MA: Harvard University Press, 2004).

Llangari, José, 'Ecuador Begins Drilling for Oil in Pristine Corner of the Amazon,' *Reuters*, 8 September 2016.

London International Model United Nations (LIMUN), 'League of Nations' Materials, LIMUN 17th Session, 2016, at http://limun.org.uk/FCKfiles/File/2016_LoN_Guides.pdf.

Long, Edward [1774], *The History of Jamaica: Reflections on its Situation, Settlements, Inhabitants, Climate, Products, Commerce, Laws and Government* (Montreal: McGill-Queens University Press, 2003).

Lopez, Roberto Sabatino, *The Commercial Revolution of the Middle Ages* (Cambridge, New York: Cambridge University Press, 1976).

Lorde, Audre, *Sister Outsider: Essays and Speeches* (Berkeley, CA: Crossing Press, 2007).

Löwy, Michael, *Fire Alarm: Reading Walter Benjamin's 'On the Concept of History'*, Chris Turner (trans.) (London: Verso, 2005).

Lucien-Brun, Jean, *Le Problème des minorités devant le droit international* (Lyon: Imprimerie Express, 1923).

Lustig, Doreen, 'The Loss of Slavery as a Humanitarian Cause? The League of Nations and the Case of Firestone in Liberia', available at http://weblaw.haifa.ac.il/en/Events/IntlLaborLaw/Documents/Doreen.pdf (accessed 11 September 2017).

MacMillan, Margaret, *Peacemakers: Six Months that Changed the World* (London: John Murray, 2001).

Mahteme Sellassie Wolde Maskel, *Zikre Neger* (Addis Ababa: Netsanet Press, 1942).

Maillard, Kevin Noble, 'The Pocahontas Exception: American Indians and Exceptionalism in Virginia's Racial Integrity Act of 1924', *BePress* Legal Series Working Paper 1187, 2006.

Malabou, Catherine, *Plasticity at the Dusk of Writing: Dialectic, Destruction, Deconstruction*, Carolyn Shread (trans.) (New York: Columbia University Press, 2010).

Malanczuk, Peter (ed.), *Akehurst's Modern Introduction to International Law* (7th edn London, New York: Routledge, 1997).

Mälksoo, Lauri, *Russian Approaches to International Law* (Oxford University Press, 2015).

Maloney, Pat, 'Hobbes, Savagery, and International Anarchy', 105 *American Political Science Review* (2011): 189–204.

Mansell, Wade and Karen Openshaw, *International Law: A Critical Introduction* (Oxford and Portland, OR: Hart, 2013).

Maragh, G. G. (Leonard P. Howell) [1935], *The Promised Key* (Kingston, Jamaica: Headstart Printing & Publishing, 2003).

Marcus, Harold G., '*Racist Discourse about Ethiopia and Ethiopians Before and After the Battle*', in Abdussamad H. Ahmad and Richard Pankhurst (eds.), *Adwa: Victory Centenary Conference, 26 February–2 March 1996* (Addis Ababa University Press, 1998): 391–402.

[1975], *The Life and Times of Menelik II of Ethiopia, 1844–1913* (Lawrenceville, NJ: Red Sea Press, 1995).

[1987], *Haile Selassie I: The Formative Years, 1892–1936* (Lawrenceville, NJ: Red Sea Press, 1995).

'The Embargo on Arms Sales to Ethiopia, 1916–1930', 16 *The International Journal of African Historical Studies* (1983): 263–379.

The Politics of Empire: Ethiopia, Great Britain, and the United States, 1941–1974 (Berkeley, CA: University of California Press, 1983).

'The Black Men Who Turned White: European Attitudes Towards Ethiopians, 1850–1900', 39 *Archiv Orientální* (1971): 155–265.

Marek, Rkystyna, *Identity and Continuity of States in Public International Law* (2nd edn Geneva: Libr. Droz, 1968).

Markakis, John, *Ethiopia: The Last Two Frontiers* (Martlesham: Boydell & Brewer, 2011).

Markell, Patchen, *Bound by Recognition* (Princeton University Press, 2003).

Marks, Susan, *The Riddle of All Constitutions: International Law, Democracy and the Critique of Ideology* (Oxford University Press, 2000).

'Big Brother is Bleeping You – With the Message that Ideology Doesn't Matter', 12 *EJIL* (2001): 109–23.

'False Contingency', 62 *Current Legal Problems* (2009): 1–21.

Martell, James, *The Misinterpellated Subject* (Durham, NC: Duke University Press, 2017).

Marx, Karl, *Capital: A Critique of Political Economy*, Vol. 1, Ben Fowkes (trans.) (Harmondsworth: Penguin, 1978).

[1849], *Wage Labour and Capital*, Frederick Engels (trans.), available at www.marxists.org/archive/marx/works/1847/wage-labour/.

[1844], 'On the Jewish Question', in *Collected Works of Karl Marx & Friedrich Engels*, Vol. 3: March 1834–August 1844 (Lawrence & Wishart Electronic Book, 2010), 146–74.

Masri, Mazen, *The Dynamics of Exclusionary Constitutionalism: Israel as a Jewish and Democratic State* (Oxford: Hart Publishing, 2017).

Mauri, Arnaldo, 'The Short Life of the Bank of Ethiopia', 6 *Œconomica* (2010): 104–16.

Mazower, Mark, *Governing the World: The History of an Idea* (London: Allen Lane 2012).

No Enchanted Palace: The End of Empire and the Ideological Origins of the United Nations (Princeton, NJ, Oxford: Princeton University Press, 2009).

McClellan, Charles W., 'Coffee in Centre-Periphery Relations: Gedeo in the Early Twentieth Century', in Donham and James (eds.), *The Southern Marches*: 175–95.

McGlynn, Frank and Seymour Drescher (eds.), *The Meaning of Freedom: Economics, Politics, and Culture After Slavery* (University of Pittsburgh Press, 1992).

McIlwraith, Malcolm, 'The Declaration of a Protectorate in Egypt and its Legal Effects', 17 *Journal of Social and Comparative Legislation* (1917): 238–59.

McVeigh, Shaun and Shaunnagh Dorsett, 'Conduct of Laws: Native Title, Responsibility, and some Limits of Jurisdictional Thinking', 36 *Melbourne University Law Review* (2012): 470–93.

Medlicott, W. N., Douglas Dakin and M. E. Lambert (eds.), *Documents on British Foreign Policy, 1919–1939*, Second Series, Vol. 14 (London: HMSO, 1976).

Documents on British Foreign Policy, 1919–1939, Second Series, Vol. 15, 784–90.

Meek, Ronald L., *Social Science and the Ignoble Savage* (Cambridge University Press, 1976).

Mekuria, Bulcha, 'Conquest and Forced Migration: An Assessment of the Oromo Experience', in Seyoum H. Hameso and Mohammed Hassen (eds.), *Arrested Development in Ethiopia: Essays on Underdevelopment, Democracy, and Self-Determination* (Lawrenceville, NJ: Red Sea Press, 2006), 38–82.

Miers, Suzanne, *Slavery in the Twentieth Century: The Evolution of a Global Problem* (Lanham, MD: Altamira, 2003).

Miéville, China, *Between Equal Rights: A Marxist Theory of International Law* (Leiden, Boston: Brill, 2005).

Mitchener, Patsy, Interview conducted at Raleigh, North Carolina, 24 July 1937. Federal Writers' Project of the Works Progress Administration for the State of North Carolina, *Slave Narratives: A Folk History of Slavery in the United States from Interviews with Former Slaves*, Vol. II, Part 2 (Washington, DC: Library of Congress, 1941), 116–23.

Mockler, Anthony, *Haile Selassie's War* (New York: Olive Branch Press, 2003).

Moffat, Ian C. D., *The Allied Intervention in Russia, 1918–1920: The Diplomacy of Chaos* (Basingstoke, New York: Palgrave Macmillan, 2015).

Moffitt, John F. and Sebastían Santiago, *'O Brave New People': The European Invention of the American Indian* (Albuquerque, NM: University of New Mexico Press, 1996).

Mohammed, Hassen, *The Oromo and the Christian Kingdom of Ethiopia: 1300–1700* (Woodbridge: Boydell & Brewer, 2015).

'Revisiting Abba Bahrey's "The News of the Galla"', 34 *International Journal of African Historical Studies* (2012): 273–94.

The Oromo of Ethiopia: A History, 1570–1860 (Cambridge University Press, 1990).

Mohammed, Seid A., 'A Social Institution of Slavery and Slave Trade in Ethiopia: Revisited', 7 *African Journal of History and Culture* (2015): 85–90.

Monroy, Cabra and Marco Gerardo, *Derecho Internacional Público* (6th edn Bogotá: Temis, 2011).

Mont Pelerin Society, 'Statement of Aims', The Mont Pelerin Society, at www.montpelerin.org/statement-of-aims/ (accessed 22 May 2018).

Moore, Jason W., *Capitalism in the Web of Life* (New York: Verso, 2015).

Moreton-Robinson, Aileen, *The White Possessive: Property, Power, and Indigenous Sovereignty* (Minnesota, MN: University of Minneapolis Press, 2015).

Motta, Giuseppe, *Less Than Nations: Central-Eastern European Minorities after WW1*, Vol. 1 (Newcastle-upon-Tyne: Cambridge Scholars Publishing, 2013).

Mummé, Claire, 'Property in Labour and the Limits of Contract', in Ugo Mattei and John Haskell (eds.), *Research Handbook on Political Economy and Law* (Cheltenham, Northampton, MA: Edward Elgar, 2015), 400–21.

Murphy-Bates, Sebastian, 'Anne Marie Waters of Sharia Watch UK and Pegida UK to address Barking and Dagenham Ukip', *Barking and Dagenham Post*, 17 March 2017.

Mutua, Makau wa, 'Why Redraw the Map of Africa? A Moral and Legal Inquiry', 16 *Michigan Journal of International Law* (1994–95): 1113–76.

N'Dimina-Mougala, Antoine-Denis, 'Les manifestations de la guerre froide en Afrique centrale (1961–1989)', 233 *Guerres Mondiales et Conflits Contemporains* (2009): 53–65

Nadasdy, Paul, '"Property" and Aboriginal Land Claims in the Canadian Subarctic: Some Theoretical Considerations', 104 *American Anthropologist* (2002): 247–61.

Nakashima, Douglas, Lyndel Prott and Peter Bridgewater, 'Tapping into the World's Wisdom', 125 *UNESCO Sources* (2000): 11–12.

Natarajan, Usha, 'Creating and Recreating Iraq: Legacies of the Mandate System in Contemporary Understandings of Third World Sovereignty', 24 *Leiden Journal of International Law* (2011): 799–822.

Natarajan, Usha and Kishan Khoday, 'Locating Nature: Making and Unmaking International Law', 27 *Leiden Journal of International Law* (2014): 573–93.

Newton, Scott, *Law and the Making of the Soviet World: The Red Demiurge* (Abingdon: Routledge, 2015).

Nicholson, Matthew, 'Walter Benjamin and the Re-Imageination of International Law', 27 *Law and Critique* (2016): 103–29.

Nietzsche, Friedrich, *On the Genealogy of Morality*, Keith Ansell-Pearson (ed.) and Carol Diethe (trans.) (Cambridge University Press, 2006).

Nijman, J. E., *The Concept of International Personality: An Inquiry into the History and Theory of International Law* (The Hague: TMC Asser Press, 2004).

Nitti, Francesco Saverio, *La Decadenza dell'Europa: Le Vie dell Ricostruzione* (Florence: R Bemporad & Figlio, 1922).

Norden, Hermann, *Africa's Last Empire: Through Abyssinia to Lake Tana and the Country of the Falasha* (London: H. F. & G. Witherby, 1930).

Nussbaum, Arthur, *A Concise History of the Law of Nations* (New York: Macmillan, 1950).

Nuzzo, Luigi, 'The Birth of an Imperial Location: Comparative Perspectives on Western Colonialism in China', 31 *Leiden Journal of International Law* (2018): 569–96.

Oakland Institute, *Understanding Land Investment Deals in Africa: Ethiopia* (The Oakland Institute, 2011).

Obregón, Liliana, 'Empire, Racial Capitalism and International Law: The Case of Manumitted Haiti and the Recognition Debt', 31 *Leiden Journal of International Law* (2018): 597–615.

'Between Civilization and Barbarism: Creole Interventions in International Law', 27 *Third World Quarterly* (2006): 815–32.

'Spanish Colonial Critiques of African Enslavement', 8 *Beyond Law* (2002): 41–66.

Oklopcic, Zoran, *Beyond the People: Social Imaginary and Constituent Imagination* (Oxford University Press, 2018).

Olsthoorn, Johan, 'Hobbes's Account of Distributive Justice as Equity', 21 *British Journal for the History of Philosophy* (2013): 13–33.

Ong, Aihwa, *Fungible Life: Experiment in the Asian City of Life* (Durham, NC: Duke University Press, 2016).

Ong, Aihwa and Nancy N. Chen (eds.), *Asian Biopolitic: Ethics and Communities of Fate* (Durham, NC: Duke University Press, 2010).

Onuf, Nicholas and Peter Onuf, *Nations, Markets and War: Modern History and the American Civil War* (Charlottesville, VA: University of Virginia Press, 2006).

Onuma, Yasuaki, 'When was the Law of International Society Born? An Inquiry into the History of International Law from an Intercivilisational Perspective', 2 *JHIL* (2000): 1–66.

Orford, Anne, 'Surplus Population and the History of International Law', Kent Law School, Centre for Critical International Law Annual Lecture, 30 November 2017.

'On International Legal Method', 1 *London Review of International Law* (2013): 166–97.

'Constituting Order', in James Crawford and Martti Koskenniemi (eds.), *The Cambridge Companion to International Law* (Cambridge University Press, 2012), 271–89.

'What Kind of Law is This?' *LRB Blog*. 29 March 2011.

International Authority and the Responsibility to Protect (Cambridge University Press, 2011).

Reading Humanitarian Intervention: Human Rights and the Use of Force in International Law (Cambridge University Press, 2003).

'Muscular Humanitarianism: Reading the Narratives of the New Interventionism', *EJIL* 10 (1999): 679–711.

'Locating the International: Military and Monetary Interventions after the Cold War', 38 *HIJL* (1997): 443–85.

Orlowska, Izabela, 'Re-imagining Empire: The Coronation of Yohannis IV as an Expression of Historical Memory', in Witold Witakowski and Laura Lykowska (eds.), *Wälättä Yohanna: Ethiopian Studies in Honour of Joanna Mantel-Niecko on the Occasion of the 50th Year of Her Work at the Institute of Oriental Studies* (Warsaw University Oriental Institute, 2006), 173–80.

'Re-imagining Empire: Ethiopian Political Culture under Yohannis IV, 1872–89' (PhD thesis, SOAS, University of London, 2006).

Oromo Liberation Front. 'Finfinne ("Addis Ababa") is an Oromo Land', 6 May 2017, at http://oromoliberationfront.org/english/finfinne-addis-ababa-is-an-oromo-land/ (accessed 24 October 2017).

Otto, Dianne (ed.), *Queering International Law: Possibilities, Alliances, Complicities, Risks* (New York: Routledge, 2017).

Özsu, Umut, 'From the "Semi-Civilized State" to the "Emerging Market": Remarks on the International Legal History of the Semi-Periphery', in Ugo Mattei and John Haskell (eds.), *Research Handbook on Political Economy and Law* (Cheltenham, Northampton, MA: Edward Elgar, 2015), 246–59.

'The Ottoman Empire, the Origins of Extraterritoriality, and International Legal Theory', in Florian Hoffmann and Anne Orford (eds.), *The Oxford Handbook of the Theory of International Law* (Oxford University Press, 2016), 123–37.

Padmore, George, 'Abyssinia Betrayed by the League of Nations', *The Crisis* (June 1937): 166–8.

'Ethiopia Thrown to the Wolves', *The Crisis* (July 1935): 48.

Pahuja, Sundhya, 'Public Debt, The Peace of Utrecht, and the Rivalry between Company and State', in Alfred Soons (ed.), *The 1713 Peace of Utrecht and its Enduring Effects* (Leiden: Brill, forthcoming).

'Laws of Encounter: A Jurisdictional Account of International Law', 1 *London Review of International Law* (2013): 63–98.

Decolonising International Law: Development, Economic Growth and the Politics of Universality (Cambridge University Press, 2011).

Painter, Genevieve Renard, 'A Letter from the Haudenosaunee Confederacy to King George V: Writing and Reading Jurisdictions in International Legal History', 5 *London Review of International Law* (2017): 7–48.

'Law as Minor Jurisprudence: Is it a Mistake?', 21 *Law, Text, Culture* (2017): 276–300.

Pal, Maïa, *Jurisdictional Accumulation: An Early Modern History of Law, Empires and Capital* (Cambridge University Press, forthcoming).

Pankhurst, Richard, 'Ethiopia and the Great Transformation', 7 *Aethiopica* (2004): 84–113.

'Post-World War II Ethiopia: British Military Policy and Action for the Dismantling and Acquisition of Italian Factories and other Assets, 1941–2', 29 *Journal of Ethiopian Studies* (1996): 35–77.

'Ras Alula, Dogali and the Beginnings of Italian Colonialism on the Horn of Africa', in Taddesse Beyane et al. (eds.), *The Centenary of Dogali: Proceedings of the International Symposium, Addis Ababa-Asmara, January 24–25, 1987* (Addis Ababa: Institute of Ethiopian Studies, Addis Ababa University, 1988), 123–6.

An Introduction to the Economic History of Ethiopia, Vol. 1: From Early Times to 1800 (Addis Ababa: Haile Selassie I University Press, 1961).

Pankhurst, Richard and Estelle Sylvia Pankhurst, *Sylvia Pankhurst, Artist and Crusader: An Intimate Portrait* (London: Paddington Press distributed by Grosset & Dunlap, 1979).

Parfitt, Rose, 'Fascism, Imperialism and International Law: An Arch Met a Motorway and the Rest is History ...' 31 *Leiden Journal of International Law* (2018): 509–38.

'Is Fascism Making a Comeback?' StateOfNatureBlog.com. 3 December 2017.

'The Anti-Neutral Suit: International Legal Futurists, 1914–2017', 5 *London Review of International Law* (2017): 87–123.

'Theorizing Recognition and International Personality', in Florian Hoffmann and Anne Orford (eds.), *The Oxford Handbook of the Theory of International Law* (Oxford University Press, 2016), 583–99.

'The Spectre of Sources', 25 *EJIL* (2014): 297–306.

Pasternak, Shiri, *Grounded Authority: The Algonquins of Barriere Lake Against the State* (Minneapolis, MN: University of Minnesota Press, 2017).

Patenaude, Bertrand M., *Stalin's Nemesis: The Exile and Murder of Leon Trotsky* (London: Faber & Faber, 2009).

Patterson, Orlando, *Slavery and Social Death: A Comparative Study* (Cambridge, MA: Harvard University Press, 1985).

Pausewang, Siegfried, 'Local Democracy and Central Control', in Abebe Zegeye and Siegfried Pausewang (eds.), *Ethiopia in Change: Peasantry, Nationalism and Democracy* (London, New York: British Academic Press, 1994), 209–30.

Pedersen, Susan, 'Back to the League of Nations', 112 *American Historical Review* (2007): 1091–117.

'Getting out of Iraq – in 1932: The League of Nations and the Road to Normative Statehood', 115 *The American Historical Review* (2010): 975–1000.

'The Meaning of the Mandates System: An Argument', 32 *Geschichte und Gesellschaft* (2006): 560–82.

The Guardians: The League of Nations and the Crisis of Empire (Oxford University Press, 2015).

Peevers, Charlotte, *The Politics of Justifying Force: The Suez Crisis, the Iraq War, and International Law* (Oxford University Press, 2014).

Percox, David, *Britain, Kenya and the Cold War: Imperial Defence, Colonial Security and Decolonisation* (London: I. B. Tauris, 2004).

Perham, Margery, *The Government of Ethiopia* (2nd edn Evanston, IL: Northwestern University Press, 1969).

Perrone, Nicolás M., 'The Emerging Global Right to Investment: Understanding the Reasoning behind Foreign Investor Rights', 8 *Journal of International Dispute Settlement* (2017): 673–94.

Pommereau, Isabelle de, 'Germany Finishes Paying WWI Reparations, Ending Century of "Guilt"', *Christian Science Monitor*, 4 October 2010.

Potter, Pitman B., 'The Wal Wal Arbitration', 30 *AJIL* (1936): 27–44.

Povinelli, Elizabeth, *The Cunning of Recognition: Indigenous Alterities and the Making of Australian Multiculturalism* (Durham, NC, London: Duke University Press, 2002).

Prince, Charles, 'The USSR and International Organizations', 36 *AJIL* (1942): 427–8.

Proctor, Robert N., *Racial Hygiene: Medicine under the Nazis* (Cambridge, MA: Harvard University Press, 1990).

Quijano, Aníbal, *Des/colonialidad del poder: el horizonte alternativo* (Lima, 2008), unpublished manuscript.

Rajagopal, Balakrishnan, 'International Law and the Development Encounter: Violence and Resistance at the Margins', 93 *American Society of International Law Proceedings* (1999): 16–27.

International Law from Below: Development, Social Movements, and Third World Resistance (New York: Cambridge University Press, 2003).

Rajah, Jothie, '"Rule of Law" as Transnational Legal Order', in Terence C. Halliday and Gregory Shaffer (eds.), *Transnational Legal Orders* (Cambridge University Press, 2015), 340–73.

Rancière, Jacques, 'Who Is the Subject of the Rights of Man?', 103 *South Atlantic Quarterly* (2004): 297–310.

Randazzo, Antonella, *L'Africa del Duce: I crimini fascisti in Africa* (Varese: Arterigere Editore, 2008).

Ranke, Leopold von [1824], 'Preface to the First Edition', in George Iggers (ed.), *Histories of the Latin and German Nations*, Wilma Iggers (trans.) (Indianapolis, IN: Bobbs-Merill, 1973).

Über die Epochen der neueren Geschichte (Darmstadt: Wissenschaftliche Buchgesellschaft, 1965).

Rasulov, Akbar, 'The Nameless Rapture of the Struggle: Towards a Marxist Class-Theoretic Approach to International Law', 19 *Finnish Yearbook of International Law* (2008): 243–94.

Retallack, James N. (ed.), *Imperial Germany, 1871–1918* (Oxford University Press, 2008).

Rigney, Sophie, 'The Hopes and Discontents of Indigenous-Settler Reconciliation', 11 *International Journal of Transnational Justice* (2017): 359–68.

Ritter, David, 'The "Rejection of Terra Nullius" in *Mabo*: A Critical Analysis', 18 *Sydney Law Review* (1996): 5–33.

The Native Title Market (Perth: UWA Publishing, 2009).

Rittich, Kerry, 'Occupied Iraq: Imperial Convergences?', 31 *Leiden Journal of International Law* (2018): 479–508.

'The Future of Law and Development: Second Generation Reforms and the Incorporation of the Social', 26 *Michigan Journal of International Law* (2004): 199–243.

Robertson, James C., 'The British General Election of 1935', 9 *Journal of Contemporary History* (1974): 149–64.

'The Hoare-Laval Plan', 10 *Journal of Contemporary History* (1975): 433–64.

Robinson, Cedric, 'DuBois and Black Sovereignty: The Case of Liberia', 32 *Race and Class* (1990): 39–50.

Black Marxism: The Making of the Black Radical Tradition (Chapel Hill, NC, London: University of North Carolina Press, 1983).

Robinson, William I., 'Promoting Polyarchy in Latin America: The Oxymoron of "Market Democracy"', in Eric Hershberg and Fred Rosen (eds.), *Latin America and Neoliberalism* (New York: The New Press, 2006: 96–119.

Rocco, Giuseppe, *L'Europa verso la seconda guerra mondiale* (Milan: Greco & Greco Editore, 1997).

Rodogno, Davide, 'European Legal Doctrines on Intervention and the Status of the Ottoman Empire within the "Family of Nations" Throughout the Nineteenth Century', 18 *JHIL* (2016): 5–41.

Against Massacre: Humanitarian Interventions in the Ottoman Empire, 1815–1914 (Princeton University Press, 2012).

Rowse, Tim, 'Cook, Cecil Evelyn Aufrere (Mick) (1897–1985)', *Australian Dictionary of Biography*, Vol. 17 (Melbourne University Press, 2007).

Rubenson, Sven R., *The Survival of Ethiopian Independence* (London: Heinemann Educational Books Ltd, 1976).

Ruskola, Teemu, 'Raping Like a State', 57 *UCLA Law Review* (2010): 1477–536.

Said, Edward [1978], *Orientalism* (London: Penguin, 2003).

Salacuse, Jeswald W., 'From Developing Countries to Emerging Markets: A Changing Role for Law in the Third World', 33 *The International Lawyer* (1999): 875–90.

Samson, Jane, *Race and Empire* (London, New York: Routledge: 2004).

Sand, Peter H., 'Roman Origins of the Ethiopian "Law of Kings" (*Fetha Nagast*)', in Peter Strauss (ed.), *The Fetha Nagast: The Law of the Kings* (Durham, NC: Carolina Academic Press, 2009), xxxix–l.

Santos, Alvaro, 'The World Bank's Uses of the "Rule of Law" Promise in Economic Development', in David M. Trubek and Alvaro Santos (eds.), *The New Law and Economic Development: A Critical Appraisal* (Cambridge University Press, 2006), 253–300.

Sayer, Francis Bowes, 'The Passing of Extraterritoriality in Siam', 22 *AJIL* (1928): 70–88.

Sbacchi, Alberto, *Legacy of Bitterness: Ethiopia and Fascist Italy, 1935–1941* (Lawrenceville, NJ: The Red Sea Press, 1997).

Schaefer, Charles, 'Maĥbär', in Siegbert Uhlig (ed.), *Encyclopaedia Aethiopica*, Vol. 3, He – N, (Wiesbaden: Harrossowitz Verlag, 2007), 649–50.

'The Politics of Banking: The Bank of Abyssinia, 1905–31', 25 *The International Journals of African Historical Studies* (1992): 361–89.

Schmidt, Elizabeth, *Foreign Intervention in Africa: From the Cold War to the War on Terror* (Cambridge University Press, 2013).

Scholler, Heinrich, *The Special Court of Ethiopia, 1920–1935* (Stuttgart: Äthiopistiche Forschungen, 1985).

Schröder, Meinhard, 'Der Westfälische Friede – eine Epochengrenze in der Völkerrechtsentwicklung?', in Meinhard Schröder (ed.), *350 Jahre Westfälischer Friede: Verfassungsgeschichte Staatskirchenrecht, Völkerrechtsgeschichte* (Berlin: Duncker & Humblot, 1999), 119–37.

Scott, George, *The Rise and Fall of the League of Nations* (London: Hutchinson, 1973).

Scott, William R., *The Sons of Sheba's Race: African-Americans and the Italo-Ethiopian War 1935–41* (Bloomington, IN: Indiana University Press, 1993).

Seyoum H. Hameso, 'Notes on the Ethiopian Empire: Myth and History', in Seyoum H. Hameso, Trevor Trueman and Temesgen Mutela Erena (eds.), *Ethiopia: Conquest and the Quest for Freedom and Democracy* (London: TSC Publications, 1997), 17–18.

Shaer, Matthew, 'The Sordid History of Mount Rushmore', *Smithsonian Magazine* (October 2016).

Shahabuddin, Mohammad, *Ethnicity and International Law: Histories, Politics and Practices* (Cambridge University Press, 2016).

Sherman, Charles Phineas, *Roman Law in the Modern World*, Vol. 1 (Boston, MA: The Boston Book Co., 1917).

Shiferaw Bekele, 'Reflections on the Power Elite of the Wärä Mäsfenate', 15 *Annales d'Etiopie* (1990): 157–79.

'The Ethiopian Railway and British Finance Capital, 1896–1902', 46 *Africa: Rivista trimestrale di studi e documentazione dell'Istituto italiano perl'Africa e l'Oriente* (1991): 351–74.

Shilliam, Robbie, 'Intervention and Colonial-Modernity: Decolonising the Italy/Ethiopia Conflict Through Psalms 68:31', 39 *Review of International Studies* (2013): 1131–47.

'What about Marcus Garvey? Race and the Transformation of Sovereignty Debate', 32 *Review of International Studies* (2006): 379–400.

Shillington, Kevin (ed.), *Encyclopaedia of African History*, Vol. 1 (New York: Fitzroy Dearborn, 2005).

Shirreff, David, *Bare Feet and Bandoliers: Wingate, Sandford, the Patriots and the Part they Played in the Liberation of Ethiopia* (London, New York: Radcliffe Press, 1995).

Shklovskii, Viktor, 'Fransua Rable i kniga M. Bakhina,' in *Tetiva: O neskhodstve skhodnogo* (Moscow: Sovietskii pisatel, 1970), 257–96.

Shklovsky, Viktor [1917], 'Art as Technique', in Lee T. Lemon and Marian J. Reis (eds. and trans.), *Russian Formalist Criticism: Four Essays* (Lincoln, NE: University of Nebraska Press, 1965), 3–24.

Sicilianos, Linos-Alexander and Thomas Skouteris (eds.), 'Special issue: The European Tradition in International Law: Nikolaos Politis', 23 *EJIL* (2012) (issue 1): 215–73.

Sihab ad-Din Ahmad ibn 'Abd-al-Qadir [c. 1537], *Futuh al-habaša (The Conquest of Abyssinia)*, Paul Sternhouse (trans.) (Hollywood, CA: Tsehai Publishers, 2005).

Simms, Brendan and D. J. B. Trim (eds.), *Humanitarian Intervention: A History* (Cambridge University Press, 2011).

Simpson, Gerry, 'Something to do with States', in Florian Hoffmann and Anne Orford (eds.), *The Oxford Handbook of the Theory of International Law* (Oxford University Press, 2016), 564–83.

Great Powers and Outlaw States: Unequal Sovereigns in the International Legal Order (Cambridge University Press, 2004).

Simpson, Jeffrey, 'Too Many First Nations People Live in a Dream Palace', *The Globe and Mail*, 5 January 2013.

Skinner, Quentin, *Liberty before Liberalism* (Cambridge University Press, 1998).

Visions of Politics. Vol. I: Regarding Method (Cambridge University Press, 2002).

Visions of Politics. Vol. II: Renaissance Virtues (Cambridge University Press, 2002).

Smith, Nicholas D., 'Aristotle's Concept of Natural Slavery', 37 *Phoenix* (1984): 110–14.

Snyder, Anthony and Sherri West (eds.), *Readings in Global History*, Vol. 2 (2nd edn Dubuque, IA: Kendall-Hunt, 1997).

Spears, Ian S., 'The Ethiopian Crisis and the Emergence of Ethiopia in a Changing State System', in G. Bruce Strange (ed.), *Collision of Empires: Italy's Invasion of Ethiopia and its International Impact* (Farnham: Ashgate, 2013), 34–51.

Speidel, William M., 'The Administrative and Fiscal Reforms of Liu Ming-ch'uan in Taiwan, 1884–1892: The Foundation of Self-Strengthening', 35 *The Journal of Asian Studies* (1976): 441–59.

Spivak, Gayatri Chakravorty, 'Can the Subaltern Speak?', in Cary Nelson and Lawrence Grossberg (eds.), *Marxism and the Interpretation of Culture* (Urbana, IL, Chicago, IL: University of Illinois Press, 1988), 271–313.

Stapelbroek, Koen, 'Trade, Chartered Companies, and Mercantile Associations', in Bardo Fassbender and Anne Peters (eds.), *The Oxford Handbook of the History of International Law* (Oxford University Press, 2012), 338–58.

Steffen, Will, Wendy Broadgate, Lisa Deutsch, Owen Gaffney and Cornelia Ludwig, 'The Trajectory of the Anthropocene: The Great Acceleration', 2 *Anthropocene Review* (2015): 81–98.

Steffen, Will Regina Angelina Sanderson, Peter D. Tyson, Jill Jäger, Pamela A. Matson, Berrien Moore III, Frank Oldfield, Katherine Richardson, Hans-Joachim Schellnhuber, Billie L. Turner and Robert J. Wasson, *Global Change and the Earth System: A Planet Under Pressure* (Berlin, Heidelberg, New York: Springer-Verlag, 2004).

Stern, W. B., 'The Treaty Background of the Italo-Ethiopian Dispute', 30 *AJIL* (1936): 189–203.

Stewart, John Hall (ed.), *A Documentary Survey of the French Revolution* (New York: Macmillan, 1951).

Stokes, Jamie, Anthony Gorman and Andrew Newman (eds.), *Encyclopaedia of the Peoples of Africa and the Middle East* (New York: Facts on File, 2008).

Storr, Cait, *Nauru: International Status, Imperial Form and the Histories of International Law* (PhD thesis, Melbourne Law School, 2017).

Straight, William, 'China's Loan Negotiations', 3 *Journal of Race Development* (1913): 369–411.

Strang, G. Bruce, 'Imperial Dreams: The Mussolini-Laval Accords of January 1935', 44 *The History Review* (2001): 799–809.

Sundiata, Ibrahim, *Brothers and Strangers: Black Zion, Black Slavery, 1914–1940* (Durham, NC, London: Duke University Press, 2003).

Sutter, Laurent de (ed.), *Althusser and Law* (Abingdon: Routledge, 2013).

Taddesse Beyane, Taddesse Tamrat and Richard Pankhurst (eds.), *The Centenary of Dogali: Proceedings of the International Symposium, Addis Ababa-Asmara, 24–25 January 1987* (Addis Ababa: Institute of Ethiopian Studies, Addis Ababa University, 1988).

Talmon, Stefan, *Recognition of Governments in International Law: With Particular Reference to Governments in Exile* (Oxford: Clarendon Press, 1998).

Tanner, Harold M., *China: A History. Vol. II: From the Great Qing Empire through The People's Republic of China, 1644–2009* (Cambridge, MA: Hackett, 2010).

Tasema Ta'a, 'Religious Beliefs among the Oromo: Waaqeffannaa, Christianity and Islam in the Context of Ethnic Identity, Citizenship and Integration', 8 *Ethiopian Journal of the Social Sciences and Humanities* (2012): 87–111.

Taylor, A. J. P., *The Origins of the Second World War* (London: Hamish Hamilton, 1961).

Telders, B. M., 'La reconnaissance de l'empire italien et le droit international', 9 *Nordisk Tidsskrift for International Ret* (1938): 3–13.

Teller, Matthew, 'Why Do So Many Nations Want a Piece of Antarctica?', *BBC News*, 20 June 2014.

Tekalign Woldemariam, 'The Slave Trade in the Economy of Jimma', in Taddese Beyene (ed.), *Proceedings of the Eighth International Conference of Ethiopian Studies, 1984*, Vol. I (Addis Ababa: Institute of Ethiopian Studies, 1989), 309–16.

Teschke, Benno, *The Myth of 1648: Class, Geopolitics, and the Making of Modern International Relations* (London, New York: Verso, 2003).

Teshale Tibebu, *The Making of Modern Ethiopia, 1896–1974* (Lawrenceville, NJ: Red Sea Press Inc., 1995).

Thompson, Christopher, 'Africa's Secret Prisons', *New Statesman*, 21 May 2007.

Thompson, John M. *Russia, Bolshevism, and the Versailles Peace* (Princeton University Press, 1966).

Thompson, Niobe and Tom Radford, *To the Last Drop*, 'Witness' Documentary (Doha: Al Jazeera, 2012).

Tierney, Stephen and Neil Walker (eds.), 'Symposium: The European Tradition in International Law: James Lorimer', 27 *EJIL* (2016): 409–92.

Tomlins, Christopher, 'After Critical Legal History: Scope, Scale, Structure', 8 *Annual Review of Law and Social Science* (2012): 31–68.

Tomlins, Christopher and John Comaroff, 'Afterword, "Law As . . .": Theory and Practice in Legal History', 1 *UC Irvine Law Review* (2011): 1039–79.

Tsegaye R. Ararssa. 'The Official Narrative and the Federation to Come', *Addis Standard*, 20 September 2017, at http://addisstandard.com/commentary-ethiopias-experiment-federalism-eyeing-federalism-come/ (accessed 5 June 2015).

'Ethiopia's Experiment with Federalism: Why it's not South Africa's Apartheid?' (Part I), *Addis Standard*, 29 September 2015, at http://addisstandard.com/ethiopias-experiment-with-federalism-why-its-not-south-africas-apartheid-part-i/ (accessed 5 June 2015).

'Did Menelik II Really Say he is Caucasian? A Call for Caution – Lest We Rewrite History in The Name of Contextual Interpretation', *Addis Standard*, 7 June 2016, at http://addisstandard.com/opinion-menelik-ii-really-say-caucasian/ (accessed 18 October 2017).

'Presenting Absence: The Figure of the Oromo in the Constitutions of Ethiopia' (PhD thesis, Melbourne Law School, in progress).

Tuori, Kaius, *Lawyers and Savages: Ancient History and Legal Realism in the Making of Legal Anthropology* (Hoboken, NJ: Taylor & Francis, 2014).

Twitchett, Denis and John K. Fairbank (eds.), *The Cambridge History of China*, Vol. 12, Pt. 1. (Cambridge University Press, 1983).

Tzouvala, Konstantina, 'Letters of Blood and Fire: A Socio-Economic History of International Law' (PhD thesis, Durham University, 2016).

Tzouvala, Ntina, 'Food for the Global Market: The Neoliberal Reconstruction of Agriculture in Occupied Iraq and the Role of International Law', 17 *Global Jurist* (2016): 1–27.

Ullendorff, Edward, *Ethiopia and the Bible* (Oxford University Press, 1968).

The Ethiopians: An Introduction to Country and People (2nd edn London: Oxford University Press, 1975).

Valéry, Paul, 'La Crise de l'esprit' (1919), available at https://biblio.wiki/wiki/La_Crise_de_l'esprit (accessed 22 May 2018).

Vestal, Theodore M., 'Reflections on the Battle of Adwa and its Significance Today', in Paulos Milkias and Getachew Metaferia (eds.), *The Battle of Adwa: Reflections on Ethiopia's Historic Victory Against European Colonialism* (New York: Algora Publishing, 2005), 21–36.

Vivian, Herbert, *Abyssinia: Through the Lion-Land to the Court of the Lion of Judah* (London: C. Arthur Pearson Ltd, 1901).

Vološinov, Valentin Nikolaevich, *Marxism and the Philosophy of Language*, Ladislav Matejka and I. R. Titunik (trans.) (Cambridge, MA: Harvard University Press, 1986).

Wallace, Michelle, *Invisibility Blues: From Pop to Theory* (London, New York: Verso, 1990).

Wang, Dong, *China's Unequal Treaties: Narrating National History* (New York: Lexington Books, 2005).

Wang, Edward Q., 'History, Space, and Ethnicity: The Chinese Worldview', 10 *Journal of World History* (1999): 285–305.

Warbrick, Colin, 'States and Recognition in International Law', in Malcolm D. Evans, *International Law* (2nd edn Oxford University Press, 2006), 217–75.

Watson, Geoffrey R., *The Oslo Accords: International Law and the Israeli-Palestinian Peace Agreements* (Oxford University Press, 2000).

Wells, H. G., *The Shape of Things to Come* (New York: Macmillan, 1936).

Wesley, Charles H., 'The Significance of the Italo-Abyssinian Question', *Opportunity* (May 1935): 148–51.

'The Struggle for the Recognition of Haiti and Liberia as Independent Republics', 2 *The Journal of Negro History* (1917): 369–83.

Westad, Odd Arne, *The Global Cold War: Third World Interventions and the Making of our Times* (Cambridge University Press, 2006).

Wheatley, Natasha, 'Spectral Legal Personality in Interwar International Law: On New Ways of Not Being a State', 35 *Law and History Review* (2017): 753–87.

Wheatley, Natasha, *The Temporal Life of States: Sovereignty, Legal Knowledge, and the Archive of Empire in Central Europe* (under review).

Wheaton, Henry, *Elements of International Law* (2nd edn London: Sampson Low, 1863).

White, Hayden, *The Practical Past* (Evanston, IL: Northwestern University Press, 2014).

Whiteway, R. S. [1902], *The Portuguese Expedition to Abyssinia in 1541–1543* (Nendeln, Liechtenstein: Kraus Reprint Limited, 1967).

Wilde, Ralph, *International Territorial Administration: How Trusteeship and the Civilizing Mission Never Went Away* (Oxford University Press, 2008).

Williams, Paul R., 'Earned Sovereignty: The Road to Resolving the Conflict over Kosovo's Final Status', 31 *Denver Journal of International Law and Policy* (2003): 387–425.

Williams, Paul R. and Francesca Jannotti Pecci, 'Earned Sovereignty: Bridging the Gap Between Sovereignty and Self-Determination', 40 *Stanford Journal of International Law* (2004): 347–86.

Williams, Paul R., Abigail J. Avoryie and Carlie J. Armstrong, 'Earned Sovereignty Revisited: Creating a Strategic Framework for Managing Self-Determination Based Conflicts', 21 *ISLA Journal of International and Comparative Law* (2015): 1–26.

Williamson, John, *Latin American Adjustment: How Much Has Happened?* (Washington, DC: Institute for International Economics, 1990), 7–41.

Wilson, Theodore Branter, *The Black Codes of the South* (Tuscaloosa, AL: University of Alabama Press, 1965).

Wolfe, Patrick, *Settler Colonialism and the Transformation of Anthropology: The Politics and Poetics of an Ethnographic Event* (London, New York: Cassell, 1999).

Woolbert, Robert Gale, 'Feudal Ethiopia and Her Army', 14 *Foreign Affairs* (1935): 71–81.

Wright, David Curtis, *The History of China* (2nd edn Santa Barbara, CA: Greenwood, 2011).

Yellin, Eric S., *Racism in the Nation's Service: Government Workers and the Colour Line in Woodrow Wilson's America* (Chapel Hill, NC: University of North Carolina Press, 2013).

Yirga Gelaw Woldeyes, 'Reflections on Ethiopia's Stolen Treasures on Display in a London Museum,' The Conversation, 5 Jun. 2018, at https://theconversation.com/reflections-on-ethiopias-stolen-treasures-on-display-in-a-london-museum-97346 (accessed 3 Aug. 2018).

Young, Robert J. C., *White Mythologies: Writing History and the West* (2nd edn London, New York: Routledge, 2004).

Colonial Desire: Hybridity in Theory, Culture and Race (New York, London: Routledge, 1985).

Zewde Gebre-Sellassie, *Yohannes IV of Ethiopia: A Political Biography* (Oxford: Clarendon Press, 1975).

Zewde Retta, *Tafari Makonnen: The Long Journey to Civilisation and during Menelik, Iyassu and Zewditu 1884–1922* (Addis Ababa: Central Publishing, 1998).

Zheng, Yangwen, Hong Liu and Michael Szonyi (eds.), *The Cold War in Asia: The Battle for Hearts and Minds* (Leiden, Boston, MA: Brill, 2010).

Ziegler, Karl-Heinz, 'Die Bedeutung des Westfälischen Friedens von 1648 für das europäische Völkerrecht', 37 *Archiv des Völkerrechts* (1999): 129–51.

Zuber, Terence, *Inventing the Schlieffen Plan: German War Planning, 1871–1914* (Oxford University Press, 2002).

INDEX

CAMBRIDGE STUDIES IN INTERNATIONAL AND COMPARATIVE LAW

Books in the Series

137 *The Process of International Legal Reproduction: Inequality, Historiography, Resistance*
Rose Parfitt

136 *State Responsibility for Breaches of Investment Contracts*
Jean Ho

135 *Coalitions of the Willing and International Law*
Alejandro Rodiles

134 *Self-Determination in Disputed Colonial Territories*
Jamie Trinidad

133 *International Law as a Belief System*
Jean d'Aspremont

132 *Legal Consequences of Peremptory Norms in International Law*
Daniel Costelloe

131 *Third-Party Countermeasures in International Law*
Martin Dawidowicz

130 *Justification and Excuse in International Law: Concept and Theory of General Defences*
Federica Paddeu

129 *Exclusion from Public Space: A Comparative Constitutional Analysis*
Daniel Moeckli

128 *Provisional Measures before International Courts and Tribunals*
Cameron A. Miles

127 *Humanity at Sea: Maritime Migration and the Foundations of International Law*
Itamar Mann

126 *Beyond Human Rights: The Legal Status of the Individual in International Law*
Anne Peters

125 *The Doctrine of Odious Debt in International Law: A Restatement*
Jeff King

124 *Static and Evolutive Treaty Interpretation: A Functional Reconstruction*
Christian Djeffal

123 *Civil Liability in Europe for Terrorism-Related Risk*
Lucas Bergkamp, Michael Faure, Monika Hinteregger and Niels Philipsen

122 *Proportionality and Deference in Investor-State Arbitration: Balancing Investment Protection and Regulatory Autonomy*
Caroline Henckels

121 *International Law and Governance of Natural Resources in Conflict and Post-Conflict Situations*
Daniëlla Dam-de Jong

120 *Proof of Causation in Tort Law*
Sandy Steel

119 *The Formation and Identification of Rules of Customary International Law in International Investment Law*
Patrick Dumberry

118 *Religious Hatred and International Law: The Prohibition of Incitement to Violence or Discrimination*
Jeroen Temperman

117 *Taking Economic, Social and Cultural Rights Seriously in International Criminal Law*
Evelyne Schmid

116 *Climate Change Litigation: Regulatory Pathways to Cleaner Energy*
Jacqueline Peel and Hari M. Osofsky

115 *Mestizo International Law: A Global Intellectual History 1842–1933*
Arnulf Becker Lorca

114 *Sugar and the Making of International Trade Law*
Michael Fakhri

113 *Strategically Created Treaty Conflicts and the Politics of International Law*
Surabhi Ranganathan

112 *Investment Treaty Arbitration As Public International Law: Procedural Aspects and Implications*
Eric De Brabandere

111 *The New Entrants Problem in International Fisheries Law*
Andrew Serdy

110 *Substantive Protection under Investment Treaties: A Legal and Economic Analysis*
Jonathan Bonnitcha

109 *Popular Governance of Post-Conflict Reconstruction: The Role of International Law*
Matthew Saul

108 *Evolution of International Environmental Regimes: The Case of Climate Change*
Simone Schiele

107 *Judges, Law and War: The Judicial Development of International Humanitarian Law*
Shane Darcy

106 *Religious Offence and Human Rights: The Implications of Defamation of Religions*
Lorenz Langer

105 *Forum Shopping in International Adjudication: The Role of Preliminary Objections*
Luiz Eduardo Salles

104 *Domestic Politics and International Human Rights Tribunals: The Problem of Compliance*
Courtney Hillebrecht

103 *International Law and the Arctic*
Michael Byers

102 *Cooperation in the Law of Transboundary Water Resources*
Christina Leb

101 *Underwater Cultural Heritage and International Law*
Sarah Dromgoole

100 *State Responsibility: The General Part*
James Crawford

99 *The Origins of International Investment Law: Empire, Environment and the Safeguarding of Capital*
Kate Miles

98 *The Crime of Aggression under the Rome Statute of the International Criminal Court*
Carrie McDougall

97 *'Crimes against Peace' and International Law*
Kirsten Sellars

96 *Non-Legality in International Law: Unruly Law*
Fleur Johns

95 *Armed Conflict and Displacement: The Protection of Refugees and Displaced Persons under International Humanitarian Law*
Mélanie Jacques

94 *Foreign Investment and the Environment in International Law*
Jorge E. Viñuales

93 *The Human Rights Treaty Obligations of Peacekeepers*
Kjetil Mujezinović Larsen

92 *Cyber Warfare and the Laws of War*
Heather Harrison Dinniss

91 *The Right to Reparation in International Law for Victims of Armed Conflict*
Christine Evans

90 *Global Public Interest in International Investment Law*
Andreas Kulick

89 *State Immunity in International Law*
Xiaodong Yang

88 *Reparations and Victim Support in the International Criminal Court*
Conor McCarthy

87 *Reducing Genocide to Law: Definition, Meaning, and the Ultimate Crime*
Payam Akhavan

86 *Decolonising International Law: Development, Economic Growth and the Politics of Universality*
Sundhya Pahuja

85 *Complicity and the Law of State Responsibility*
Helmut Philipp Aust

84 *State Control over Private Military and Security Companies in Armed Conflict*
Hannah Tonkin

83 *'Fair and Equitable Treatment' in International Investment Law*
Roland Kläger

82 *The UN and Human Rights: Who Guards the Guardians?*
Guglielmo Verdirame

81 *Sovereign Defaults before International Courts and Tribunals*
Michael Waibel

80 *Making the Law of the Sea: A Study in the Development of International Law*
James Harrison

79 *Science and the Precautionary Principle in International Courts and Tribunals: Expert Evidence, Burden of Proof and Finality*
Caroline E. Foster

78 *Transition from Illegal Regimes in International Law*
Yaël Ronen

77 *Access to Asylum: International Refugee Law and the Globalisation of Migration Control*
Thomas Gammeltoft-Hansen

76 *Trading Fish, Saving Fish: The Interaction between Regimes in International Law*
Margaret A. Young

75 *The Individual in the International Legal System: Continuity and Change in International Law*
Kate Parlett

74 *'Armed Attack' and Article 51 of the UN Charter: Evolutions in Customary Law and Practice*
Tom Ruys

73 *Theatre of the Rule of Law: Transnational Legal Intervention in Theory and Practice*
Stephen Humphreys

72 *Science and Risk Regulation in International Law*
Jacqueline Peel

71 *The Participation of States in International Organisations: The Role of Human Rights and Democracy*
Alison Duxbury

70 *Legal Personality in International Law*
Roland Portmann

69 *Vicarious Liability in Tort: A Comparative Perspective*
Paula Giliker

68 *The Public International Law Theory of Hans Kelsen: Believing in Universal Law*
Jochen von Bernstorff

67 *Legitimacy and Legality in International Law: An Interactional Account*
Jutta Brunnée and Stephen J. Toope

66 *The Concept of Non-International Armed Conflict in International Humanitarian Law*
Anthony Cullen

65 *The Principle of Legality in International and Comparative Criminal Law*
Kenneth S. Gallant

64 *The Challenge of Child Labour in International Law*
Franziska Humbert

63 *Shipping Interdiction and the Law of the Sea*
Douglas Guilfoyle

62 *International Courts and Environmental Protection*
Tim Stephens

61 *Legal Principles in WTO Disputes*
Andrew D. Mitchell

60 *War Crimes in Internal Armed Conflicts*
Eve La Haye

59 *Humanitarian Occupation*
Gregory H. Fox

58 *The International Law of Environmental Impact Assessment: Process, Substance and Integration*
Neil Craik

57 *The Law and Practice of International Territorial Administration: Versailles to Iraq and Beyond*
Carsten Stahn

56 *United Nations Sanctions and the Rule of Law*
Jeremy Matam Farrall

55 *National Law in WTO Law: Effectiveness and Good Governance in the World Trading System*
Sharif Bhuiyan

54 *Cultural Products and the World Trade Organization*
Tania Voon

53 *The Threat of Force in International Law*
Nikolas Stürchler

52 *Indigenous Rights and United Nations Standards: Self-Determination, Culture and Land*
Alexandra Xanthaki

51 *International Refugee Law and Socio-Economic Rights: Refuge from Deprivation*
Michelle Foster

50 *The Protection of Cultural Property in Armed Conflict*
Roger O'Keefe

49 *Interpretation and Revision of International Boundary Decisions*
Kaiyan Homi Kaikobad

48 *Multinationals and Corporate Social Responsibility: Limitations and Opportunities in International Law*
Jennifer A. Zerk

47 *Judiciaries within Europe: A Comparative Review*
John Bell

46 *Law in Times of Crisis: Emergency Powers in Theory and Practice*
Oren Gross and Fionnuala Ní Aoláin

45 *Vessel-Source Marine Pollution: The Law and Politics of International Regulation*
Alan Khee-Jin Tan

44 *Enforcing Obligations Erga Omnes in International Law*
Christian J. Tams

43 *Non-Governmental Organisations in International Law*
Anna-Karin Lindblom

42 *Democracy, Minorities and International Law*
Steven Wheatley

41 *Prosecuting International Crimes: Selectivity and the International Criminal Law Regime*
Robert Cryer

40 *Compensation for Personal Injury in English, German and Italian Law: A Comparative Outline*
Basil Markesinis, Michael Coester, Guido Alpa and Augustus Ullstein

39 *Dispute Settlement in the UN Convention on the Law of the Sea*
Natalie Klein

38 *The International Protection of Internally Displaced Persons*
Catherine Phuong

37 *Imperialism, Sovereignty and the Making of International Law*
Antony Anghie

35 *Necessity, Proportionality and the Use of Force by States*
Judith Gardam

34 *International Legal Argument in the Permanent Court of International Justice: The Rise of the International Judiciary*
Ole Spiermann

32 *Great Powers and Outlaw States: Unequal Sovereigns in the International Legal Order*
Gerry Simpson

31 *Local Remedies in International Law (second edition)*
Chittharanjan Felix Amerasinghe

30 *Reading Humanitarian Intervention: Human Rights and the Use of Force in International Law*
Anne Orford

29 *Conflict of Norms in Public International Law: How WTO Law Relates to Other Rules of International Law*
Joost Pauwelyn

27 *Transboundary Damage in International Law*
Hanqin Xue

25 *European Criminal Procedures*
Edited by Mireille Delmas-Marty and J. R. Spencer

24 *Accountability of Armed Opposition Groups in International Law*
Liesbeth Zegveld

23 *Sharing Transboundary Resources: International Law and Optimal Resource Use*
Eyal Benvenisti

22 *International Human Rights and Humanitarian Law*
René Provost

21 *Remedies against International Organisations*
Karel Wellens

20 *Diversity and Self-Determination in International Law*
Karen Knop

19 *The Law of Internal Armed Conflict*
Lindsay Moir

18 *International Commercial Arbitration and African States: Practice, Participation and Institutional Development*
Amazu A. Asouzu

17 *The Enforceability of Promises in European Contract Law*
James Gordley

16 *International Law in Antiquity*
David J. Bederman

15 *Money Laundering: A New International Law Enforcement Model*
Guy Stessens

14 *Good Faith in European Contract Law*
Reinhard Zimmermann and Simon Whittaker

13 *On Civil Procedure*
J. A. Jolowicz

12 *Trusts: A Comparative Study*
Maurizio Lupoi and Simon Dix

11 *The Right to Property in Commonwealth Constitutions*
Tom Allen

10 *International Organizations before National Courts*
August Reinisch

9 *The Changing International Law of High Seas Fisheries*
Francisco Orrego Vicuña

8 *Trade and the Environment: A Comparative Study of EC and US Law*
Damien Geradin

7 *Unjust Enrichment: A Study of Private Law and Public Values*
Hanoch Dagan

6 *Religious Liberty and International Law in Europe*
Malcolm D. Evans

5 *Ethics and Authority in International Law*
Alfred P. Rubin

4 *Sovereignty over Natural Resources: Balancing Rights and Duties*
Nico Schrijver

3 *The Polar Regions and the Development of International Law*
Donald R. Rothwell

2 *Fragmentation and the International Relations of Micro-States: Self-Determination and Statehood*
Jorri C. Duursma

1 *Principles of the Institutional Law of International Organizations*
C. F. Amerasinghe

For EU product safety concerns, contact us at Calle de José Abascal, 56–1°, 28003 Madrid, Spain or eugpsr@cambridge.org.

www.ingramcontent.com/pod-product-compliance
Lightning Source LLC
LaVergne TN
LVHW052211200926
848481LV00001B/79